GOD AS LOVE

GOD AS LOVE

The Concept and Spiritual Aspects of Agapē *in Modern Russian Religious Thought*

Johannes Miroslav Oravecz

William B. Eerdmans Publishing Company
Grand Rapids, Michigan / Cambridge, U.K.

Published 2014 by
Wm. B. Eerdmans Publishing Co.
2140 Oak Industrial Drive N.E., Grand Rapids, Michigan 49505 /
P.O. Box 163, Cambridge CB3 9PU U.K.

Printed in the United States of America

20 19 18 17 16 15 14 7 6 5 4 3 2 1

Library of Congress Cataloging-in-Publication Data

Oravecz, Johannes Miroslav, 1970-
God as love: the concept and spiritual aspects of agape in
modern Russian religious thought / Johannes Miroslav Oravecz.
pages cm
Includes bibliographical references and index.
ISBN 978-0-8028-6893-0 (pbk.: alk. paper)
1. God (Christianity) — Love. 2. Agape. 3. Love — Religious aspects —
Christianity. 4. Theology, Doctrinal — Russia — History — 19th century.
5. Theology, Doctrinal — Russia — History — 20th century. I. Title.

BV4639.O73 2013
231′.6 — dc23

2013031773

www.eerdmans.com

To my family and friends
in whose humanity I have
come to know divine love —
a gift of the Church to the world

Contents

Foreword

When I first met Father Johannes Oravecz, he was already at work on his doctoral dissertation on the theme of divine love in modern Russian religious thought. He was doing his degree in Rome under the guidance of Father Lubomir Žak, a distinguished scholar of Russian theology and religious philosophy who is now Vice-Dean of Theology at the Pontifical Lateran University. Father Johannes visited North America occasionally, and on one of his trips he looked me up and invited my comments on his doctoral project.

When I examined his outline, I was startled. The author planned to present the thought of no fewer than twenty-five Russian Orthodox thinkers, not counting a few more who would figure in the background story. Since overextended boundaries are one of the commonest faults of dissertation projects, I suggested to Father Johannes, as politely as I could, that he might want to restrict his study to a smaller number of figures and deal with the others at a later time. He was, after all, still at the beginning of his academic career. But Father Johannes did not take my advice. He pressed on with his original plan, and it is good that he did so. This important book is the product of his perseverance.What is impressive about this work goes beyond the fact that the author canvasses so many different thinkers with such competence and confidence. Right from the start, the reader will see that this book is not a compendium or catalogue. It is a rigorously focused essay featuring a single commanding theme: the interpretation of divine love in modern Russian Orthodox thought. The multiplicity of the sources which the author canvasses is essential to his thesis, since only by showing how widely disseminated the theme of divine love was in modern Russian Orthodox thought can he prove that this theme was not the idiosyncratic focus of a few unrepresentative individuals but a significant aspect of the modern Russian Orthodox intellectual tradition as a whole.

Father Johannes is the first scholar to publish such a comprehensive study of this theme. While Father Michael Meerson must be regarded as the pioneer of the subject in the scholarly literature, his important monograph on the impact of Christian love-mysticism on Russian religious thought has a more restricted focus than the present volume.[1] Father Johannes is thus quite right to observe: "Astonishingly, up till now no one has undertaken the task of tracing and systematically investigating the concepts of *love* and *agapē* in modern Russian religious thought, revealing its *unifying, divinizing,* and *humanizing,* as well as its *kenotic* aspects, and its fundamental element as rooted in 1 John 4:8, 16: *God is love*" (p. 7).

It is worth pausing over this observation, for it is indeed astonishing that the theme of divine love has not received more attention than it has in treatments of modern Russian Orthodox thought. Why is this so? Divine love seems so axiomatic for the Christian religion. The closest thing to an explicit characterization of the transcendent God in the New Testament is the affirmation just quoted from 1 John: "God is love." The two commandments that Jesus identified as the greatest are both about love: "Love the Lord your God with all your heart and with all your soul and with all your mind," and "Love your neighbor as yourself" (Matt. 22:38-39). So why have these verities not received the sustained focus that Father Johannes has now brought to them? While it is true that modern Russian religious thought has only recently begun to receive the attention it deserves after the long Soviet night, we do now have a growing body of scholarship on any number of themes in Russian Orthodox thought, some of them rather specialized, such as the distinction between the essence and energies of God, apophaticism, the veneration of the name of God, the metaphysics of All-Unity, the concept of Sophia, and the concept of tradition, to name a few. Yet the idea of divine love seems to have escaped scholarly attention for the most part. Is it because the concept seems too familiar, too ordinary? Do we secretly want Russian Orthodox thinkers to sound more exotic than they might sound if it turned out that the main thing they have to say, or one of the main things they have to say, is that God is love?

More is at stake here, however, than the shortcomings of contempo-

1. Michael Aksionov Meerson, *The Trinity of Love in Modern Russian Theology: The Love Paradigm and the Retrieval of Western Medieval Love Mysticism in Modern Russian Trinitarian Thought (from Solovyov to Bulgakov)* (Quincy, IL: Franciscan Press, 1998).

rary scholarship. By showing that the centrality of divine love in the Christian faith was something that had to be *rediscovered* in Russian Orthodox theology, Father Johannes calls our attention to two other important facts. The first is the extraordinary capacity of Christian theologians, not to speak of other Christian leaders, to *miss the point* that the Christian faith is first and foremost a set of affirmations about divine love. In Orthodoxy, as in all other long-established Christian denominations, the love-letter at the heart of the Christian gospel is constantly in danger of being reduced to the dimensions of a scrap of paper in a bottle floating haphazardly on a sea of inherited traditions, ritual practices, church politics, ethnic loyalties, loveless moralism, scholastic abstractions, and worldly distractions. Divine love — God's "heartbeat," as Father Johannes calls it (pp. 107, 474) — is so drowned out by the noisy processes of organized religion and its adjuncts that hearing it can be as difficult as detecting the echo of the Big Bang. Father Johannes adduces a stunning example of the problem: the dogmatic theology of Metropolitan Makarii (Mikhail) Bulgakov, the largest, most architectonic, and most influential synthesis of dogmatic theology in nineteenth-century Russian Orthodoxy, in which there is "not a single chapter or article devoted to the theological virtue of love" (p. 104). A less charitable critic than Father Johannes might be tempted to respond to a case such as this by assuming the mantle of a Christian Zarathustra and exclaiming, "Is it really possible? This old bishop has not yet heard the news that *God is love!*" Father Johannes takes a gentler approach based on sound scholarship, rational discourse, pastoral concern, and Christian patience. But he is no less insistent about the essential point: God is love.

A second fact that Father Johannes's study illustrates is the healthfulness of modern intellectual culture for Christian theology and religious thought generally. The remarkable achievements of Russian religious thought were not home-grown products of the Orthodox tradition operating independently and sealed off from the rest of the world. They sprang from the interaction between indigenous Orthodox tradition and modern Western, or global, civilization. While the religious thinkers who figure in this book include at least a couple of religious geniuses — Solov'ev and Florenskii appear to fit the description — genius was not the engine of modern Russian religious thought. It was the protocols of modern critical and scientific inquiry along with the enhanced appreciation for human subjectivity characteristic of modern civilization that empowered Russian Orthodox thinkers, clerical and lay, to express their faith in a new key, to see it with a new clarity, to reorder priorities. Spiritual inspiration *and* rationality, faith *and* critical intelligence, love for divine things *and* love for human things — these were the linkages that drove modern Russian theology and religious philosophy. Father Johannes's book makes it clear that nineteenth- and twentieth-century Russian religious thought was as much about the humanization of the divine as it was about the divinization of the human.

A new appreciation for other religious traditions, in the first instance the Western Christian confessions, is another contribution of modern Russian religious thought to Orthodoxy. While a strong sense of Orthodox distinctiveness continues to make many contemporary Orthodox leaders wary of ecumenism, the thinkers Father Johannes surveys include several enthusiastic ecumenists. Their vision remains relevant, if not for the present, then for the future of Orthodox Christianity. In any case, all modern Russian Orthodox thinkers, whatever their views on ecumenism, were and still are in debt to Western Christian scholarship and practice. The relationship is also reciprocal, for an ever-growing number of Western Christians readily acknowledge the inspiration they have derived from their encounters with the Orthodox tradition. Father Johannes embodies this relationship. Using skills and insights acquired in Rome to analyze modern Russian religious thought, he is also clearly inspired by the Russians whose story he tells. His work bears witness to the truth of Gregory of Nyssa's observation (see pp. 264-92) that, in matters of consequence for Christian faith, "Knowledge becomes love."

Paul Valliere
Butler University

Abbreviations

AGB	Bulgakov, S. N., *Agnets Bozhii* (Moskva: Obshchedostupnyi Pravoslavnyi Universtitet osnovannyi Prot. A. Menem, 2000).
AKSS I-II	Mitropolit Antonii (Khrapovitskii), *Sobranie sochinenii v dvukh tomakh,* vols. 1-2 (Moskva: Izd. Dar", 2007).
CHK	Ivanov, V., *L'uomo,* a bilingual edition, ed. M. T. Mayer (Milano: Aquilegia Edizioni, 1999).
ChSD	*Choix de sermons et discours de S. Ém. Mgr. Philarète,* trans. A. Sarpinet, vol. 1 (Paris 1866).
CWF I-XIII	*Collected Works of Georges Florovsky* (Belmont, MA: Nordland, 1972).
DOB	Frank, S. L., *Dukhovnye osnovy obshchestva* (Moskva: Izd. "Respublika," 1992).
FOD	Fedorov, N. F., *Filosofiia obshchego dela* (Moskva: AST, 2003).
FSD	Berdiaev, N. A., *Filosofiia svobodnogo dukha* (Moskva: Izd. "Respublika," 1994).
FSV	Berdaiev, N. A., *Filosofiia svobody* (Moskva: Izd. "Act," 2005).
HRE	Schmemann, A., *The Historical Road of Eastern Orthodoxy* (New York: Holt, Rinehart & Winston, 1963).
IB	Taarev, M. M., *Iskusheniia Bogocheloveka kak edinyi iskupitel'nyi podvig vsei zemnoi zhizni Khrista, v sviazi s istorieiu dokhristianskikh religii i khristianskoi Tserkvi* (Moskva: Izd. Obshchestva Liub. dukh. Prosveshcheniia, 1892).
ILG	Lossky, V., *In the Image and Likeness of God* (Crestwood, NY: St. Vladimir's Seminary Press, 2001).
IPP	Schmemann, A., *Istoricheskii put' Pravoslviia* (New York: Izd. Imeni Chekhova, 1954).
ITPV	Sviatitel Filaret (Drozdov), *Izbrannye trudy, pis'ma, vospominania* (Moskva: Pravoslavnyi Sviato-Tixonovskii Bogoslovskii Institut, 2003).
ITsB	Svetlov, P. I., *Ideia Tsarstva Bozhiia v ee znachenii dlia khristianskago mirosozertsaniia* (Sviato-Troitskaia Sergieva Lavra, 1905).

ITvB	Svetlov, P. I., *Ideia Tsarstva Bozhiia v eia znachenii dlia khristianskago mirosozertsaniia* (Sviato-Troitskaia Sergieva Lavra 1905).
KAB	Svetlov, P. I., *Kurs apologeticheskago bogosloviia* (Kiev: Tipografiia S. V. Kul'zhenko, 1912).
KHT	Florovskii, G., *Khristianstvo i tsivilizatsiia* (Sankt-Peterburg: Izd. Russkoi Khristianskoi gumanitarnoi akademii, 2005).
KRK	*Krushenie kumirov* in *S. L. Frank: Sochineniia* (Moskva: Izd. "Pravda," 1990).
LB	Beliaev, A., *Liubov' Bozhestvennaia: Opyt raskrytiia glavneishikh khristianskikh dogmatov iz nachala liubvi Bozhestvennoi* (Sankt-Peterburg: "Nevskaia zhemchuzhina," 2006).
LVI	Bulgakov, S. N., *Lestvitsa Iakovlia: Ob angelakh* in *Malaia Trilogiia* (Moskva: Obshchedostupnyi Pravoslavnyi Universtitet osnovannyi Prot. A. Menem, 2008).
MSA	Evdokimov, P., *Il matrimonio, sacramento dell'amore* (Bose-Magnano: Qiqajon, 2008).
MTE	Lossky, V., *The Mystical Theology of the Eastern Church* (Crestwood, NY: St. Vladimir's Seminary Press, 1976).
NIE	*Fr. Nitsshe i etika "liubvi k dal'nemu,"* in *Semen Frank: Sochineniia* (Kharvest, Minsk, Moskva: Ast, 2000).
NPO	Frank, S. L., *Nepostizhimoe,* in *S. L. Frank: Sochineniia* (Moskva: Izd. "Pravda," 1990).
ODPZ	Arkhimandrit Feodor (A. M. Bukharev), *O dukhovnykh potrebnostiakh zhizni* (Moskva: Izdatel'stvo Stolica, 1991).
OPDB	Malevanskii, S., *Opyt pravoslavnogo dogmaticheskogo bogosloviia: S istoricheskim izlozheniem dogmatov,* vols. 1-4 (Kiev: Tipografia G. T. Korcsak-Novickogo, 1884).
OPOS	Arkhimandrit Feodor (A. M. Bukharev), *O Pravoslavii v otnosheniik sovremennosti: V raznykh stat'iakh Arkhimadrita Feodora* (Sankt-Peterburg: Tipografiia Torgovago Doma S. Strugovshchikova, 1860).
OS	Stragorodskii, S., *Pravoslavnoe uchenie o spasenii: Opyt raskrytiia nravstvenno-subektivnoi storony spaseniia na osnovanii Sv. Pisaniia i tvorenii sviato-otecheskikh.*
PBvP	Sviatitel Filaret Moskovskii, *Prizovite Boga v pomoshch: Sbornik pisem* (Moskva: Izd. Sretenskogo monastyria, 2006).
PDBG	Gumilevskii, F., *Pravoslavnoe dogmaticheskoe bogoslovie,* vols. 1-2 (Sankt-Peterburg: Tuzov, 1882).
PDBM	Malinovskii, N. P., *Pravoslavnoe dogmaticheskoe bogoslovie,* vols. 1-4 (Sergiev Posad: Tip. Sergievoi Lavry, 1909-10).
PDBo	Bulgakov, M., *Pravoslavno-dogmaticheskoe bogoslovie,* vols. 1-2 (Sankt-Peterburg: Tipografia Koroleva, 1856-57).
PGT	Florensky, P., *The Pillar and Ground of the Truth: An Essay in Orthodox Theodicy in Twelve Letters,* trans. B. Jakim (Princeton and Oxford: Princeton University Press, 2004).
PKhK	Filaret of Moscow, *Prostrannyi khristianskii katikhizis Pravoslavnyia*

	Katholicheskiia Vostochnyia Tserkvi (Moskva: Sinodal'naia Tipografiia, 1852).
PPR	Karsavin, L. P., *Put' Pravoslavia* (Moskva: Izd. Folio, 2003).
PSSK	*Polnoe sobranie sochinenii Alekseia Stepanovicha Khomiakova,* vols. 1-8 (Moskva: Universitetskaia tipografiia, 1900).
RIV	Ivanov, V. I., *Rodnoe i vselenskoe* (Moskva: Izd. "Respublika," 1994).
RMIU	Filaret Drozdov, *Rozgovory mezhdu ispytuiushchim i uverenym o pravoslavii Vostochnoi Katholicheskoi Tserkvi* (Moskva: Sinodal'naia Tipografiia, 1841).
RRR	Zernov, N., *The Russian Religious Renaissance of the Twentieth Century* (London: Darton, Longman & Todd, 1963).
RTCh	Zernov, N., *The Russians and Their Church* (Crestwood, NY: St. Vladimir's Seminary Press, 1978).
SaO	Schmemann, A., *Sacraments and Orthodoxy* (London: Herder & Herder, 1965).
SDA	Evdokimov, P., *Le Sacrement de l'Amour: Le mystère conjugal à la lumière de la tradition orthodoxe* (Paris: L'ÉPI, 1962).
SMZ	Frank, S., *Smysl zhizni* (Bruxelles: Izd. "Zhin's Bogom," Foyer Oriental Chrétien, 1992).
SPFR	Piovesana, G., *Storia del pensiero filosofico russo (988-1988)* (Torino: Cinisello Balsamo, Edizioni Paoline, 1992).
SUI	Florenskii, P., *Stolp i utverzhdenie istiny: Opyt Pravoslavnoi teoditsei* (Moskva: Izd. "ACT," 2002).
STO	Evdokimov, P., *L'Esprit Saint dans la Tradition Orthodoxe* (Paris: Cerf, 1969).
STV	Berdiaev, N. A., *Smysl tvorchestva* (Moskva: Izd. Khranitel'/Ast, 2007).
SVN	Bulgakov, S. N., *Svet nevechernii* (Sankt-Peterburg: Izd. Olega Abyshko, 2008).
SVT	Frank, S. L., *Svet vo t'me* (Moskva: "Faktorial," 1998).
TDS	Afanes'ev, N. N., *Tserkov' Dukah Sviatogo* (Kiev: Tsentr Pravoslavnoi knigi, 2005).
TPh	Bulgakov, S. N., *Die Tragödie der Philosophie* (Darmstadt: Otto Reichl Verlag, 1927).
TsOd	*Tserkov' odna* in *Polnoe sobranie sochinenii Alekseia Stepanovicha Khomiakova,* vol. 2 (Moskva: Universitetskaia tipografiia, 1900).
UTE	Bulgakov, S. N., *Uteshitel'* (Moskva: Obshchedostupnyi Pravoslavnyi Universtitet osnovannyi Prot. A. Menem, 2003).
VLB	Shmeman, A., *Vvedenie v liturgicheskoe bogoslovie* (Paris: YMCA Press, 1961).
VOG	Lossky, V., *The Vision of God* (New York: Athens Printing Company, 1973).
VvPB	Makarii (Bulgakov), *Vvedenie v pravoslavnoe bogoslovie* (Sankt-Peterburg: Tipografiia Departamenta Udelov, 1852).
VZVB	Arkhiepiskop Sergii, *Vechnaia zhizn' kak vysshee blago* (Moskva: Pechatnia A. I. Snegirevoi, 1917).

WoRT	Florovsky, G., *Ways of Russian Theology 1-2*, vol. 5 (Belmont, MA: Nordland, 1979).
ZhMP	*Zhurnal moskovskogo Patriarkhata.*
ZKhK	Svetlov, P. I., *Znachenie Khresta v dele Khristovom: Opyt iziasneniia dogmata iskupleniia* (Kiev: Tip. C. V. Kul'zhenko, 1907).

Introduction

Ὁ θεὸς ἀγάπη ἐστίν
Бог есть любовь
1 John 4:8, 16

Sapevo che ci fossi
ma non credevo
[che] tanto.[1]

1. Personal Encounter with God

The proclamation of the *Good News* is a visible and audible manifestation of a prior interior experience: that of an intimate, personal encounter with the *living* and *loving* God that spurs *a believer* to paint his creed with hasty movements on a hidden wall of a forgotten church on the outskirts of a great city. Depths call upon depths, and love answers to Love. There is one sole matching response: "I love; therefore, I believe — I believe; therefore, I love." One can ask, "Which love?" since there are so many kinds. Which love quenches our thirst so that we do not need to fetch more water from strange wells with murky waters at the roadside? The *living water* promised by God's *Word* and *Loving Compassion,* Jesus Christ, is that divine relationship that not only promises but also *is* our fulfillment, and not only of our needs and restless desires, but of our essential, *existential,* personal realiza-

1. *I knew that you existed but did not believe it was so real.* Graffiti on the side wall of a church near the catacombs of St. Calistus and St. Sebastian on the outskirts of Rome.

tion. God *is* our life. And, since God *is* love, God *is* our love. These are the foundations of our faith, of our joyful faith. For that is how we can recognize the truthfulness and authenticity of our invitation (vocation) to Christ's discipleship: by the joy of salvation. In the torn history of humankind's religious struggles for the possession of "*the* only True God," the human being (i.e., us) so often forgets to ask: Is it about a relational, caring, *loving* God? The visible *image of the invisible God* (cf. Col. 1:15), Jesus Christ, in words and works, always presented his Father *as* a *loving God,* whose love endures to the humanly incomprehensible self-sacrifice on the cross of Golgotha — and beyond. This *beyond* on earth is the *ecclesia* (those called out together to worship God) guided by God's Holy Spirit, which is another personification of Love. The other *beyond* is the fulfilled promise of redemption, God's divine, eternal plan of love to save the fallen human being and the world.

2. A Choice Guided by Initial Epistemology

So which love truly quenches our existential thirst? There is only one — the one that an aged bishop of Hippo, St. Augustine, describes as closer to himself than he himself ever could be: the divine love in and of the Trinity, the love that the early Church very soon designated as ἀγάπη. . . . The retrospective reflection on such love, *agapē,* opened up the road to new faith-solutions for a large number of Russian religious thinkers, theologians, and philosophers of modern times. They possessed diverse personalities; some had common life-stories, others less so, but a typical unifying aspect to all of them was a social involvement that completes the other indispensable, humanizing dimension of the *divine love:* it not only responds, but also spreads out and finds new responses in and through its multiplication. Horizontal and vertical, God-human and human-human, as there is nothing outside of God, so we relate to each other in God, in the Trinity. There is only one *love* and *one God* infinitely revealed, which also applies to the (universal) Church and its theologies. How to safeguard the *message,* to transmit it, share it, so that it is not only appealing and comprehensive but above all *comprehensible* for our age? This was the major preoccupation of modern Russian religious thinkers, and this makes their strains and struggles so near and dear to us in the twenty-first century. Many initially left their church and then returned, for they were *invited* and they *responded.* They were called to find that lost divine language of communication between God and his image, the human being, humankind — that *language of heaven* which V. Solov'ev calls *love.* And since we already are participants in the kingdom of heaven, as it is among us, it is also up to us to cooperate with God's divine grace and wisdom to find and relearn heaven's silent yet ever-creative language: *agapē.*

3. Ardent Research for a New Approach

The social and ecclesial controversies and overall complexity of the last two centuries in Russia, primarily caused by the reforms of Tsar Peter I, created the urgent need and ardent desire for a new (yet ever-valid) view and approach to the Divine, to God, and his visible communion-representation on earth, the Church, as well as the Church's direct social involvement. This brought forth enriching novelties but also set off supplementary divisions and, at times, painful splits into groups, such as the Slavophils and Westernizers, who represented the offspring of Russia's intellectuals, as well as later the multitude of interactions between them and their forthcoming philosophical and theological schools or tendencies. Perhaps it is more astonishing that in the midst of this turmoil the sparkling idea of understanding God *as* love found its way to the hearts, souls, and minds, and that as a result many of these young intellectual "rebels" found their way back to Christian faith and the Church, revitalizing it in an unprecedented mode. Through them the theme of love became a leitmotiv of intellectual spiritual research in the nineteenth and twentieth centuries, in Russia and in exile, in philosophy, theology, theosophy, and even some of the countless esoteric groupings. The decisive difference was that while the latter were looking for some kind of satisfactory spiritual experience or (secret) gnosis, the former were driven by an existential quest; being highly intellectual, extremely well educated, and gifted in intuition and insight, they were disillusioned — in the proper sense of the word — by the empty promises of Marxism, yet heartened by German Idealism, Schelling's Christian(izing) philosophy, and an emerging new concept of Christianity, that in fact was the initial one but in a new interpretational key of *love.* Thus our topic is indeed a carefully chosen one — being not only *at* the epicenter but in fact being *the* epicenter of Christianity. The intuition was simply in the air:

"The theme of love burst with volcanic energy into Russian literature, journalism, literary criticism, philosophy, and theology. . . . Over the span of just a few decades, more was written on love in Russia than had been written over the preceding several centuries."[2] We encountered this notion repeatedly during our research, and we fully agree with it. The above-mentioned flowering resulted in what we know as the *Silver Age*, the flourishing religious and intellectual creativity exhibited by Russian theologians and thinkers even during and after the dramatic events of the 1917 revolution and the following era of tragic Christian persecution, as well as in exile abroad. Our authors were children of their times (as indicated by their social, political, and ecclesial contexts) and one must bear this in mind or run the risk of jumping to premature conclusions.[3] In this quest for the *divine love*, a number of them laid down their lives, or, as the Russian language puts it, their souls *(dushi)* for their faith. As we know, *Greater love has no one than this, that someone lays down his life for his friends* (John 15:13). Shaped by their personal spiritual and mystical experiences and suffering, especially those who died in the gulags or in exile, they left us a precious testimony of true *orthodoxy* in faith, hope, and love, namely that of imitating Jesus' *kenotic* self-sacrifice out of love for God and one's fellow human beings. It also needs to be mentioned that a number of them worked on restoring and proving the conceptual sanctity and true divine dignity of matrimonial love, on its own. May their struggle and achievements promote the common ecumenical understanding of our *one* Christian vocation, like Mary the Mother of God: to magnify the Lord.

4. The Ecumenical Dimension of the *Love-Theme*

The magnitude of the *agapic-theme* on Divine Love is well reflected in the fact that Pope Benedict XVI's very first encyclical was dedicated to *Deus Caritas Est*, with an exposition of relations between *agapē* and *erōs*, a first in the history of pontifical encyclicals, and also his third encyclical *Caritas in Veritate*, which carries the honor of being his first *social* encyclical. Pope Benedict XVI made the theme of divine love, also applied in charitable and fraternal love, the center of his theology and ecclesial teaching.[4] Similarly, the late Pope St. John Paul II dedicated a re-collection of his 129 lectures

2. *Russkii Eros ili filosofiia liubvi v Rossii (Russian Eros, or the Philosophy of Love in Russia)*, ed. V. P. Shestakov (Moscow: Progress, 1991), pp. 6-7.

3. As to the question of the orthodoxy of their teaching, for instance.

4. Of particular interest to us is his address given to the participants at the meeting promoted by the pontifical council "Cor Unum" in the *Sala Clementina* on Monday, January 23, 2006.

from the Wednesday audiences (1979-84). This was his first major teaching in *The Theology of the Body: Human Love and Divine Plan.*[5] The fourth chapter of his *Novo Millennio Ineunte* presents God as love *(Witnesses to Love),* next to the centrality of Jesus Christ's person in the third chapter, in the very core of this apostolic letter at the conclusion of the millennium addressed to bishops, clergy, and lay faithful. There are some who understand the *Deus Caritas Est* to be a culmination of Pope John Paul's pastorally sensitive theology. It needs to be recalled that both pontiffs are considered among the greatest promoters of the ecumenical dialogue with the East in modern times and unremittingly worked on furthering mutual fraternal understanding and *rapprochement.*[6] Pope Francis I shows an equally great concern for ecumenical dialogue as well as for the charitable expression of faith in our everyday lives.

This effort for a clear Christian concept of love, *agapē,* that reflects precisely "God *as* Love" in our modern world, is a unifying liaison between East and West, and the Catholic, Orthodox, and Protestant tradition(s). This concept is rooted in the Johannite love-messages and St. Paul's *kenotic* hymn in Philippians 2:5-11, but there are numerous other important *springs of living waters* in the Gospels that will quench our intellectual thirsting for a more profound understanding of God and his true entity.

At the base of modern Russian theology and Christian philosophy, which we also wish to illuminate, lies a profound *divinizing* hope for the human family and the world — that God has not abandoned either of them.

5. Also appeared under the title: *Man and Woman He Created Them: A Theology of the Body.*

6. Since Pope St. John XXIII and the epochal encounter of Pope Paul VI and Patriarch Athenagoras, as well as the promulgation of the decree on ecumenism *Unitatis Redintegratio* on November 21, 1964, ecumenism has been of fundamental interest for the Catholic Church.

Methodological Considerations

1. The Scope of This Work

The scope of this work is to individuate, contextualize, and emphasize the concept and spiritual aspects that best represent "God *as* Love," i.e., understanding the value and role of *agapē* as *divine love* in Russian religious thought of the last two centuries. In order to achieve this, an interdisciplinary approach was indispensable, as it was proper also to the representatives of Russian religious thought in the nineteenth and twentieth centuries. Thinkers of this period rarely constrained themselves to any late-scholastic frame of mind in a strict division of theology from philosophy, and they frequently included literature and modern sciences as well. Our choice of authors follows the significance of their contributions (those known and recognized, and those not yet) to the advancement of religious thought in Russia and abroad. This also elucidates the quantity of thinkers that we addressed in our work — in the case of some, certainly not exhaustively — focusing on their substantial, original, and most revelatory ideas in, and in connection to, the subject of divine love.

2. The Scientific Contribution of This Work

As indicated previously, our aim is to identify and underscore the centrality of *love, agapē* in modern Russian religious thought, in particular, in its metaphysics and philosophy, but even more so in its theology. The following chapters follow a chronological and notional pattern of diverse schools of thought that, in their complexity, have not been defined so far, as the tendency was and often still is to generalize and group all of them simply under the umbrella of *Russian religious thought.* Yet such unspecified representation cannot withstand serious scientific criticism.

A great number of authors and their works addressed here (especially with regard to academic and moralistic theology, but also to personalities such as L. P. Karsavin, for instance), are meagerly known or entirely unknown in the West. Their works have not been translated into western languages, and their thoughts have thus far not been, or have rarely been divulged in the western world. To some extent, we hope to fill this vacuum, and to open new horizons for further research into the vastness of available (and partially unpublished) material.

Astonishingly, up till now no one has undertaken the specific task of tracing and systematically investigating the concepts of *love* and *agapē* in modern Russian religious thought, revealing its *unifying, divinizing,* and *humanizing,* as well as its *kenotic* aspects, and its fundamental element as rooted in 1 John 4:8, 16: *God is love.* This, in particular, we wish to portray in its profoundly anthropological aspect, so proper to modern Orthodox theology, but also in its principle, which is in the depth of all Christian teaching: "God *as* Love."

Last but not least, and in the hope of further research in this field, we wish to elucidate the mutual inspiration and influences of East and West, mirroring the wealth of western traditions, opening the riches of eastern traditions, and above all, raising an awareness for the need of communication and a common language rooted in mutual respect and appreciation, because the results of these magnificent works and life-stories are ecclesial, social, and cultural divergences that create opportunities to grow in wisdom and the love of God and for our fellow human beings. We are invited to take inspiration from the example of the Holy Trinity: three distinct Persons, yet one God, in the unity of love.

This work is intended to give glory to God and to grant insight and stimulus for further mutual appreciation and an ever-growing respect for the beloved children of God, who we *all* are, and who bear witness to the world: *See what kind of love the Father has given to us, that we should be called children of God; and so we are. . . . Beloved, we are God's children now, and what we will be has not yet appeared; but we know that when He appears we shall be like Him, because we shall see Him as He is* (1 John 3:1-2).

3. Method and Limitations

First and foremost, we directly analyze the texts of our authors, always focusing on their original language, searching for concepts of *agapē* and/or *love,* the synthesis of the principal works, and if possible, the chronological progress, in order that the particular changes or the evolution of ideas may be revealed. We pay particular attention to their personal and overall contextualization as well as their spiritual and human development. With some authors, we forcefully had to limit ourselves to a selection of their works, since some were so prodigiously productive (e.g., V. Solov'ev, N. Berdiaev, S. N. Bulgakov, A. Schmemann, etc.) that it would have multiplied the sum of this work, oversizing it into various volumes. This, too, is the sole reason that we consistently omitted the works of the giants of modern Russian spiritual literature, such as F. Dostoevsky, L. Tolstoy, and others. After proper analysis and reflection, we synthesized the acquired insights and aimed at rendering them in a comprehensible and accessible language, which, of course, is dependent on the subject being treated. We dedicated a substantial size to the first chapter in order to provide a solid overall introduction for the western reader into the epoch and its context of nineteenth- to twentieth-century Russia, but also to provide a general orientation and clarification of basic concepts of the Russian realm and socioecclesial happenings of the epoch.

3.1. The Kind and Number of Authors Addressed

The unusually great number of authors addressed here is the result of long, careful reflection and research. In order to cover the novelty of two centuries of modern Russian religious thought, its representatives, and its universal significance, we needed to consider the most prominent and originally creative minds of this period. Their time — then the following epoch of the so-called *Silver Age,* and the later decades, in Russia as well as in exile — was preceded by the time of academic theology and its manuals of dogmatic theology, which was an equally important and dominant era in Russian theology. Yet the truly exhilarating period began with the *Slavophil* and *Westernizer* groups, both of which, directly or indirectly, derived from the Russian *intelligentsia,* or at least were formed from intellectuals in tsarist Russia. The large number of young intellectuals and their variety of notions and currents reflect well the intellectual capacity of this country, as being capable of dialogue with East and West, but at times also present difficulties in distinguishing between the various streams of thought.

3.2. Translations

All translations are our own (if not indicated otherwise), especially in the initial and core chapters (i.e., II, III, IV, V, VI, but also some authors from VII and VIII); in the majority of cases, there are no existing translations into western languages. If other translations were available, we constantly confronted our work with those. Vice versa, where works were written in French, English, or other western languages (as in the case of N. Berdiaev, P. Evdokimov, and A. Schmemann, for example), we compared these with available Russian editions (some of which were prepared by the authors themselves). Original quotes and terms are indicated between quotation marks, and repeated or repetitive concepts and terms in italics, in order to distinguish them from the rest of the commentary. We placed in parentheses or brackets some of the original Russian terms or expressions transliterated, especially in cases where they represent a novelty, neologism, multiple meanings, or even a nonconclusive meaning.

Here, we need to mention also that our preference was for renderings closer to the conceptual rather than an aesthetic meaning of the original Russian, except perhaps in the few rare and indicated cases of poetry (e.g., V. Solov'ev, L. Karsavin, and in particular, V. Ivanov).

3.3. Transliteration and Notes

For transliteration, we applied the norms indicated by the U.S. Library of Congress, also omitting the prerevolutionary signs that were abolished with the language reform after 1918. In order to safeguard consistency in the transliteration of Russian personal names, we followed the same rule, nevertheless maintaining the transliterations of different western editors in their editions; we did not take the liberty of interfering with their choices. Therefore, the reader will encounter at least two forms of transcription: one according to the above-indicated standard and the other according to westernized renderings of proper names. For the notes, some are rather substantial in order to safeguard the textual flow of the main text-corpus, and for annotations we used the North American standard scientific MLA style.

3.4. The Question of Gender

The Russian *chelovek,* commonly translated into English and western languages as *man,* in Russian is understood to include both genders (as opposed to *muzhshchina,* which means exclusively *man,* and *zhenshchina,* which means exclusively *woman*). We have tried to remain sensitive to the question of gender and translated *chelovek* with *human being* instead of *man* and used *human beings, humankind,* or *humanity* for plural, where possible, and where it did not corrupt the original text. Exceptions were made for quotations from previously translated works (prevalently in English), where again we did not take the liberty of altering the original text.

I. The Development and Principal Characteristics of Russian Religious Thought in the Nineteenth and Twentieth Centuries

1. Encounter with Modernity under the Censorship of the Tsar

1.1. Towards a Modern Russia

The development of religious thought and theology during the nineteenth and early twentieth centuries in Russia was a unique sociopolitical as well as religious occurrence, yet of universal importance and impact.[1] According to N. Gorodetzky, "It was then that Russians began to meditate upon their national task, upon their place in the European family, and upon the historical and spiritual destiny of Russia. It was during this period that Russia was exhorted to become 'the most Christian of all human societies.'"[2] Russian historian N. Zernov goes as far as to proclaim the nineteenth century as the most optimistic in universal history.[3] This era of new ideas was the origin of unprecedented changes triggered at the end of the seventeenth century by

1. "The Russian culture of the nineteenth and the beginning of the twentieth century has a world-wide significance. Such significance may be said to attach to a nation's culture when the values developed in it hold for humanity as a whole. . . . Russian culture in the form it had before the Bolshevik revolution undoubtedly also has a universal significance." N. O. Lossky, *History of Russian Philosophy* (New York: International Universities Press, 1951), p. 9.

2. N. Gorodetzky, *The Humiliated Christ in Modern Russian Thought* (London and New York: SPCK, 1938), p. x. She also gives in the first chapter of her book an introduction into the spiritual realm of the nineteenth century in Russia, and among others to its "ten-year-rhythm," where each new decade brought along "a change in the governing ideas." Cf. Lossky, *History of Russian Philosophy*, pp. 1-26.

3. N. Zernov, *The Russians and Their Church* (Crestwood, NY: St. Vladimir's Seminary Press, 1978), p. 3.

Tsar Peter I (1682-1725),[4] and later promoted and expanded by Catherine II (1762-1796), when it also reached its "peak of self-confident enlightenment."[5] By "cutting a window into Europe,"[6] Peter I ended the country's isolation from the West[7] and, with his wide-ranging reforms, gave rise to new streams and approaches in spiritual thought, a complex notion and history that would eventually result in the crystallization of the existing, as well as the forming of new, philosophical and theological terms and concepts. Nonetheless, a precise distinction between religious philosophy and theology in Russia of the era remains somewhat elusive.[8]

1.2. Peter I and the Russian Empire of His Time

There are opinions that Russia was "on its way to Europe" anyway and was opening to western influence long before the reforms of Peter the Great.[9]

4. Commonly known as "Peter the Great."

5. N. Zernov, *The Russian Religious Renaissance of the Twentieth Century* (London: Darton, Longman & Todd, 1963), p. 10. (RRR)

6. Lossky, *History of Russian Philosophy,* p. 10. The expression, however, was coined by the nation's poet Alexandr S. Pushkin.

7. Cf. G. Piovesana, *Storia del pensiero filosofico russo (988-1988),* Cinisello Balsamo (Torino: Edizioni Paoline, 1992), p. 42. (SPFR)

8. Cf. G. Cioffari, "Breve storia della teologia russa," *Quaderni di O Odigos,* Anno VI–N. 4 (Ottobre-Dicembre, Bari, 1987): 23. Thus one studying the subject and its time will face the concepts of *religious thought, religious philosophy,* or *the Russian idea,* struggling to identify, especially in the first part of the nineteenth century, the notion of *theology,* in terms of modern western concepts. Thanks also to recent progress in understanding the historical development of theology, its hermeneutics, and its *Sitz im Leben,* broader boundaries than usually set by our western categories have been allowed for the term *theology* in modern Russian religious thought. In his article, Paul Valliere makes the following astute observation, addressing also the historicity of its development: "Russian religious thought, is a historical phenomenon" and is also being called "Russian religious philosophy." Cf. Paul Valliere, "Russian Religious Thought and the Future of Orthodox Theology," *St. Vladimir's Theological Quarterly* 45, no. 3 (2001): 227-41. Conversely, in his book *The Russian Idea,* N. Berdiaev stresses that when he discusses *religious philosophy,* it is definitely meant to be *religious philosophy* and not *theology,* especially contrasting the Western differentiation in categories. "In the West thought and learning are very much differentiated; everything is distributed according to categories." Cf. N. Berdiaev, *The Russian Idea* (Hudson, NY: Lindisfarne Books, 1992), pp. 172-73.

9. Cf. G. Stökl, *Russische Geschichte* (Stuttgart: Kröner, 1973), p. 331. As a religious opposition to this opening towards Western customs could be seen the *Raskol' (Schism),* which reaches back even before the reforms of Peter the Great and formed the so-called *Old Be-*

Certainly, Peter's reforms were not well received by all. Reactions were mixed, even though these opinions could not always be expressed aloud. G. Florovskii compares Peter's reforms to a revolution[10] in the history of Russia, in particular, in Russia's historical consciousness, and Zernov makes a daring historical comparison to the Tartar invasions of the Kievan Rus of the thirteenth century.[11] One way or the other, Peter's regency made history, and as much as his reforms may have appeared timebound at first, they had a deep and long-lasting impact on the Russian Empire, church, and society. Some historians claim that the changes initiated by Peter I were the only possible way Russia could have moved forward, leaving no option for a volte-face,[12] by which is meant above all the socioeconomical and cultural development of the country; in fact, nothing remained untouched by Peter's reforms.[13] A. Rexheuser, in his article on Orthodox piety and western education, notes Russia's remarkable adaptability in catching up from its "backwardness." First, at the end of the eighteenth and beginning of the nineteenth centuries, Russian (mainly religious) culture and education stood in "opposition to the West," due to the perception that its Western European counterpart had already ceased to be Christian at its core. Yet after the "forced opening of the country to the West through Peter I," Russian culture,

---

lievers. The latter's vision was based on a utopia of a "sacred kingdom" and had also a cosmological and eschatological dimension. It is important to note that there was an imminent fear before the "infection of the Church by the secular spirit" that would rob its "purity." Yet, as Zenkovskii rightly points out, the process set off by the *Raskol'* came into full light only in the eighteenth century, the "century of secularization." Cf. V. V. Zenkovsky, *A History of Russian Philosophy,* vol. 1 (London: Routledge & Kegan Paul, 1953), pp. 40-43.

10. Cf. G. Florovsky, *Ways of Russian Theology I,* vol. 5 (Belmont, MA: Nordland, 1979), p. 114 (WoRT I-II).

11. "The consequences of the reforms of Peter the Great can only be compared with those of the Tartar invasions. Both movements marked a turning point in the history of the nations. In the thirteenth century, the Tartar invasions cut off Russia from the rest of Europe and turned its face towards Asia; in the eighteenth century, Peter the Great's reforms brought Russia again into the society of the European nations and opened a gulf between the Eastern and Western elements of its civilization. In both cases there was a change in mentality, in political and social order, even in language." N. Zernov, *Moscow the Third Rome* (London: SPCK, 1937), p. 77.

12. Cf. Stökl, *Russische Geschichte,* p. 389.

13. These all-embracing reforms, considered by the conservative and religious spheres as misguided, have ever since caused divisions in Russia's multifaceted society. Ultimately Peter's reforms resulted in concretizing the disputes on Russian's national identity and its destiny between the *Slavophils* and the *Westernizers* in the mid-nineteenth century. We shall dedicate more attention to this argument and these two groups in a separate treatise.

especially literature, went through a rapid development of its own. Thus, eventually the great discrepancies between Russia and Europe of the seventeenth and eighteenth centuries were relieved by an impressive adjustment in the nineteenth and subsequent century.[14]

1.2.1. The Modes and Models of Changes

In preparation for his future role and reforms, Peter I had spent numerous years in Europe acquiring a variety of experiences, including the learning of manual labor and craftsmanship. Thus upon his return to Russia in 1699 he started with full attention to direct Russia's path westward,[15] away from the customs and structures of the "Muscovit Rus," which he detested for its intrigues and bloody revolts, personally experienced in the Kremlin during his childhood.[16] Not everything, though, can be changed at will, for these large

14. Cf. A. Rexheuser, "Orthodoxe Frömmigkeit und westliche Bildung in Russland Ende des 18. anfang des 19. Jahrhunderts," in *Tausend Jahre Christentum in Russland,* ed. K. Ch. Felmy, G. F. Kretschmar von Lilienfeld, and C.-J. Roepke (Göttingen: Vandenhoeck & Ruprecht, 1988), p. 915.

15. This was even truer of the Russian Orthodox Church of the epoch, which "living in isolation from the West," represented a haven for the faithful of the Russian Empire up till then. Belonging to the most secluded part of the European Christian community with no contact with western Christendom over centuries, the clergy and faithful equally had little notion of the realm beyond their own church. Contradictions reigned and were caused partially by the lack of contact with the external world, but even more so for the ruling omnipresence of the Empire. Cf. RRR, p. 250. Also: "The centuries of the Tartar domination and then the isolationism of the Moscow state prevented the Russian people from becoming acquainted with Western-European philosophy. Not until Peter the Great had 'cut a window into Europe' was Russian society introduced to the western culture on a wide scale. The western influence at once affected the attitude toward the Church." Lossky, *History of Russian Philosophy,* p. 10.

16. "Tsar Peter (1682-1725) was happy that Great Russia, not only industrially, militarily, culturally, but also theologically, was turning Westward away from Byzantine influences. Early in childhood, having witnessed the bloody revolutions in the Kremlin, Peter developed a hatred for Moscow and all of its ancient traditions. He was pragmatic and technical by character and schooling. After spending much time in Europe, he returned to Russia in 1699 to begin in earnest a complete westernization of all Russia. The autocratic, absolute monarchy, modeled on Sweden, replaced the ancient familiar dialogue between Tsar and Patriarch. The Church for Peter was a mere instrument in service to the State." G. A. Maloney, *A History of Orthodox Theology since 1453* (Belmont, MA: Nordland, 1976), p. 40. As for the church and society, this meant confrontations with entirely new realms, such as modernity, and challenges arising from Russia's backwardness to the progressive Europe of its time — which was a shameful abomination in Peter I's eyes.

and extensive reforms did not fundamentally alter the uniquely Russian spirit. The emperor's excesses in his effort of (forced) westernization would go from requiring European clothing, manners, and customs, to forbidding men to grow or wear a beard. This may seem ridiculous, yet in the Russia of the epoch this was considered offensive and even outrageous. Peter I was not blatantly anti-religious, although he would not shrink from ridiculing the church and its ancient traditions since he disregarded tradition and anything that may have transmitted the slightest sensation of *backwardness*. This behavior, which appeared scandalous to some, was viewed as progressive and future-oriented by others.[17] The majority of the nobility, for example, but even some of the clergy, soon became acquainted with and conformed to western culture and education. They had to face a strong inner conflict regarding their own tradition, culture, and background, as well as the questions necessarily arising from their cognitive dissonance.[18] One of the secrets of Russian culture was and remains both its Christian and nonwestern origin, thus a character that often creates difficulties in understanding the Russian spirit.[19] Individuals or groups who did not meet the terms or fell short in terms of the imperial guidelines, such as in teaching, publishing, and public activities, had to face censorship, surveillance, and, not in rare cases, a complete ban or exile. Despite all the negative effects the Petrine reforms may have had on the church and society, one must remem-

17. Zernov pulls a valuable and elucidating quintessence from a comparison of the Petrine reforms anew to the Tartar invasion that directly relates to our point here, in particular, with the impact on the Russian church: "There was, however, one fundamental difference between these two revolutions. The Tartar yoke affected equally all classes of Russian society, while the reforms of the eighteenth century touched only its upper strata and left the nation divided between two cultures, each with its own dress and its own language. Peter the Great inaugurated a systematic process of westernization which thrust European dress, European bureaucracy, and European thought upon the nation, yet behind the new façade there still lived the Russian soul with its old traditions and ideals. The old Russia was not destroyed, but lay hidden under the outer shell of foreign culture. During the first hundred years, after Peter the Great, the borrowed customs and ideas existed side by side with the native, and no organic fusion seemed possible. But in the first part of the nineteenth century there came to birth the new Russian culture which, though deeply rooted in the national soil, was yet an offshoot of Western civilization. Russia since the nineteenth century has had two spiritual backgrounds, and the synthesis of the two has created Russia's modern art, and also her literary language, one of the greatest achievements of the nation." Zernov, *Moscow the Third Rome*, p. 77.

18. Cf. W. Goerdt, *Russische Philosophie: Zugänge und Durchblicke* (Freiburg/München: Alber, 1984), p. 262.

19. Cf. Zernov, *The Russians and Their Church*, p. 4.

ber that Peter's primary scope and interest was in Russia's industrialization, through which he hoped to raise the country to the western standards and achievements of the time.[20]

1.2.2. State and Church Relations under Peter I

The state-church bond changed from a partnership-like relationship between tsar and patriarch to a ruler-subject one, the state requesting absolute obedience from the church, which inevitably had a profound impact on the bilateral relations as well as on the country's spiritual life.[21] The extent of the state's interference in church affairs was in the hands of a person and institution appointed by the tsar himself: the "procurator." The procurator for religious affairs "was accountable only directly to the emperor, which meant he enjoyed an almost limitless influence and authority over his subjects." Florovskii describes these stipulations unambiguously as typical of a "police state" that "inescapably turns against the church,"[22] where schools, seminaries, and universities were reformed according to the Emperor's wishes and visions. Spying on scholars, theologians, professors, and clergy as well as direct censorship became a matter of daily routine.[23]

20. To one's astonishment the *westernization* of Russia would eventually be completed by the last rulers of the country: the Communists. They alternated even the name of "Russia" into "Union of Soviet Socialist Republics. . . . Thus the Communist revolution seemed to be a final stage in the westernization of Russia, the culmination of the process begun by Peter the Great, a renunciation of Russia's Messianic dreams, and of the belief in Moscow as the third Rome." This is an idea that would develop gradually but consistently in Russia primarily during the nineteenth century and vanish definitely with the Bolshevik revolution. Cf. Zernov, *Moscow the Third Rome,* p. 80.

21. "The autocratic, absolute monarchy, modeled on Sweden, replaced the ancient familiar dialogue between Tsar and Patriarch. The Church for Peter was a mere instrument of service to the State." Maloney, *A History of Orthodox Theology since 1453,* p. 40. Also: "The great and genuine Russian schism began with Peter. The schism occurred between church and state, not between the government and the people (as the Slavophils believed). A certain polarization took place in Russia's spiritual life — the Russian spirit stretched and strained to the utmost. Peter's reform signified a displacement or even a rupture in Russia's spiritual depths. . . . The state not only demanded obedience from the church as well as its subordination, but also to absorb and include the church within itself. . . . The church did not retain and was not permitted to retain any independent or autonomous sphere of activity, for the state regarded all matters as its own." WoRT I, p. 115.

22. WoRT I, p. 115.

23. "During the period of the St. Petersburg Empire a heavy censorship was imposed upon them. The study of modern Church history was particularly discouraged as well as any

1.2.3. The Church's Loss of Freedom

To implement his church reforms — or more precisely *reformation* — Peter took the willing services of a well-educated convert to Orthodoxy: Feofan Prokopovich (1681-1736).[24] Feofan was educated in Europe and was well versed in Catholic as well as Protestant theology; however, he turned his back entirely on the former, and, after his return from Europe, his full interest was focused on Protestantism as a model with which he intended to reform the Orthodox Church.[25] It was he who composed, with a few corrections from Peter, the *Duchovnyi reglament (Spiritual Regulations)*, an infamous document that was supposed to bring about the reformation of the Russian Orthodox Church and its subordination to the state.[26] It is a complex yet unrefined text conveying an impression of "precipitated and provisional" reforms, as so many of Peter's reforms would.[27] Thanks to *Duchovnyi reglament* Peter definitely got rid of the state-church double-regency, the so-called *Diarchie*, which he deeply detested, and which had characterized Russia up to his regency. Thus, contemporarily with "enlightenment" and absolutism having established themselves in the country, the peaceful *harmony* of state and church, tsar and patriarch, ceased to exist for good.[28] Whether there ever existed such *harmony*, and to what extent it was

---

subjects which dealt with the Christian attitude to the problems of contemporary life. The Imperial Government was unwilling to reveal to the wider world the state of captivity in which the Russian Church had been kept since the time of Peter the Great, and that Christians should be inarticulate suited this policy." Zernov, *The Russians and Their Church*, pp. 4-5.

24. "It seems that Feofan sincerely believed only in Peter, as the Reformer and as a hero," and thus became the tsar's closest collaborator. WoRT I, p. 122.

25. There were others, like Platon Levshin, the rector of the Moscow Academy (1761), who held the opinion that the Latin theology coming from other countries and being implanted in Russia could never become a "living theology." Cf. Maloney, *A History of Orthodox Theology since 1453*, pp. 46-47.

26. Florovskii writes: "A morbid passion to break with the past can be detected in the book — not just a desire to cast off from old moorings, but to destroy the old moorings being left behind, so that no one could ever consider returning." WoRT I, p. 117.

27. Cf. H-J. Härtel, "Feofan Prokopovič," in *Tausend Jahre Christentum in Russland*, p. 370. Härtel, in his article, highlights the fact that Prokopovich's theological lectures served as a "compendium of dogmatics" on which generations of theologians have been trained, and that his somewhat hastily elaborated system has notable lacunae.

28. Peter sought the advice of Leibniz and Wolff on how to introduce enlightenment into Russia, who in answer to the emperor's request dispatched their disciples to spread the ideas of Descartes, yet in such a way that they would not clash with Christian ideas. Wolff was also convinced that education should serve strictly the good of the state, and it was he

true, we need not discuss in detail here. It will suffice to say that the edict effectively changed the church's status into a mere instrument of the state, a *status quo* that would become practically irreversible henceforth, a situation that Florovskii defined as "a certain caesaropapism"[29] of the tsar that bound both powers in his person. A further step in the Petrine reformation was the introduction of the *Holy Governing Synod* that entirely replaced the members of the Muscovite Patriarchate and stripped them of power, thus completing the tsar's acquisition of unlimited control over the church.

The Synod was presided over by an *over-procurator* who was installed personally by the tsar. It functioned "as an imperial council 'with authority granted by His Tsarist Majesty' or 'by decree of His Imperial Highness.'"[30] That these imposed "regulations" were never freely accepted by the church leaders is self-revelatory; also, their decisions had no weight until approved by the over-procurator and could still be revoked at will by the tsar. Florovskii compares Peter's epoch and his reforms to the "Babylonian captivity," in which the Russian church had been enslaved by the state, the priests of its time a mere "frightened class" that "was driven into the lower social strata"[31] with all its conceivable consequences. The massive impositions and intrusions into the church's sovereignty — and that of the individual faithful — resulted in systematic restrictions and an all-encompassing state control that remained in force with some variations until the end of the imperial era in Russia. In fact, it progresses with renewed severity in the Bolshevik and Communist regimes. No one with even the slightest opposition, including members of the Russian Intelligentsia, was exempt from the censorship that would increase or decrease in harshness according to the ruling emperor.

---

who introduced education in Latin. The former idea pleased Peter very much and since Wolff was favored also by Feofan Prokopovich, the tsar discarded any accusations regarding Wolff's "atheism," no matter how preoccupying they were. Cf. SPFR, pp. 43-44. Also cf. F. Jockwig, "Die Situation der russischen Orthodoxen Kirche am Ende des 19. Jahrhunderts," in *Tausend Jahre Christentum in Russland*, p. 401.

29. WoRT I, p. 121.

30. WoRT I, p. 121.

31. "Subsequently Russian ecclesiastical consciousness languished in the double imprisonment of administrative decree and inner fear." WoRT I, p. 121.

1.3. Nicolas I's Severe Censorship and the Russian Intelligentsia

Nicolas I (1825-1855) followed Peter's policy of rigid state control, as he was firmly convinced that a renewal of the empire was impossible without the active assistance of the church. Therefore under Nicolas, all members of the Holy Synod lost the last shred of autonomy to make free decisions, and the church found itself under an extreme and unprecedented censorship,[32] resulting in the "thirties of dreamy inactivity" inflicted upon a "romantic and utopistic generation."[33] Nicolas I chose Count N. A. Protasov (1798-1855) to oversee the Holy Synod. Protasov fostered a return to Orthodoxy and tried to eradicate any Protestant trends from Russian theology, encouraging instead a return to the Church Fathers. As a result, after a long period of strict censorship, finally some original contributions started to see the light of day, especially in theology; and these works began little by little to yield fruit. Here is collocated also an important creative epoch described by P. Annenkov as the "Remarkable Decade," created by the Russian intellectuals commonly known as the *Intelligentsia.*[34]

1.4. New Hopes of the Happy Sixties

Some relief in censorship (but not so much in the state-church relationship) came with the so-called "happy sixties" of the nineteenth century, during the reign of Alexander II (1855-1881). Known as a reformer and softer than his fa-

32. Cf. Jockwig, "Die Situation der russischen Orthodoxen Kirche," pp. 403-4.

33. Gorodetzky, *The Humiliated Christ,* p. 1. Some cast a similar parallel to Alexander I (1801-1825) who grew up and got used to lying in an "atmosphere of dreams and expectations, in a peculiar intellectual mimicry, in aspirations and dreams for 'the ideal.'" Later, the influences of "sentimental humanism" became the undercurrent of his spiritual views and decisions. Cf. WoRT I, p. 164.

34. "'A Remarkable Decade' is a description [by Annenkov] of the life of some among the early members — the original founders — of the Russian intelligentsia, between 1838 and 1848, when they were all young men, some still at the university, some just emerged from it. The subject is of more than literary or psychological interest because these early Russian intellectuals created something which was destined ultimately to have world-wide social and political consequences. The largest single effect of the movement, I think it would be fair to say, was the Russian Revolution itself. These *révoltés* early Russian intellectuals set the moral tone for the kind of talk and action which continued throughout the nineteenth and early twentieth centuries, until the final climax in 1917." I. Berlin, *Russian Thinkers* (London: Penguin Books, 1994), pp. 114-15.

ther Nikolas I, Alexander's regency had the greatest transforming impact on the Russian realm since Peter the Great. He introduced some of the overdue educational reforms, abolished serfdom, and loosened censorship, thanks to which all sorts of publications, especially newspapers and magazines, prospered greatly. What followed was a wealth of free and freely expressed ideas in articles and books published by the Intelligentsia. They addressed issues such as how and why society should evolve and that the church should move away from extreme conservatism. These strong voices were gaining intensity, and more newspapers were founded to disseminate these ideas. One of the church newspapers, for instance, the *Pravoslavnoe Obozrenie (Orthodox Review)* was well known to Russian clerics.[35] Still, expectations varied: for some, Alexander's reforms did not go far enough; for others, they incorporated dangerous signs of liberalism. Unfortunately, these hope-filled and progressive times did not withstand the changing policy of the following two emperors.

1.5. The Patriarchal Order *and the End of Tsardom*

The new tsar Alexander III (1881-1894), with his faithful advisor and former teacher, K. P. Pobedonostsev (1827-1907), maintained an explicit dislike for the sixties and its reforms. Nevertheless, Alexander III felt a constraint to fulfill his father's will (i.e., Alexander II) to grant Russia a constitution. Pobedonostsev discouraged him from such concessions, claiming that what Russia really needed was a strong autocrat of a *Muscovite* type and not a constitution, convincing Alexander III eventually to abandon his former intention. Due to his rootedness in *Slavophilism,*[36] ignoring completely any factual enrichment of Russia by the West in the past, Pobedonostsev turned entirely against any western influence. As a Slavophil, his vision was a Russian nation built upon the state and church. The *Patriarchal Order,* which was a fundamental Slavophil ideal that fulfilled the role of an *extended family* in its conception, took concrete shape precisely in the state. Pobedonostsev had little regard for the sovereignty of the nation as such and even less for democracy, which in his view led the nation into disorder. Given his attitude and ideas, his tactics and methods could not be much different: namely that

35. I. Smolitsch, *Geschichte der Russischen Kirche 1700-1917,* vol. 1 (Leiden: Brill, 1964), p. 300.

36. The unique role of Slavophilism and Westernism will be discussed in the following section.

of "blind obedience and submission to the autocrat," the tsar. The "firm faith and fervor of individuals" would preserve the unity of the nation and trust in the state. This scheme remained determinative until the end of the nineteenth century, and the ideology of it was expressed in the famous maxim formulated by Pobedonostsev: "One tsar, one nation, one faith." Censorship was compliant to the need of this axiom as never before, and the autocrat's power over the church surpassed even that of the Byzantine emperors.[37]

This situation produced apathy and discouragement in the church as well as in the circle of the intellectuals, which again suited well the primary intentions of the state to keep the church fully under control. The following and final tsar, Nicolas II (1894-1917), was an indecisive emperor, keen on maintaining the existing order. Although he possessed some personal charm, he was incapable of governing and was void of a vision for the nation. He lost first the empire, then his and his family's lives through the Bolsheviks, who not only overthrew and abolished the Romanov aristocracy but brought to a definitive end the tsardom in Russia.[38]

1.6. The Intellectuals' Desertion of the Church

As a matter of fact, not the entire Orthodox Church was opposed, or perhaps not vehemently enough, to state censorship. It originated from the concept and in the understanding of *fidelity* to the Emperor, who was regarded to be

37. Cf. Jockwig, "Die Situation der russischen Orthodoxen Kirche," pp. 404-8. A somewhat different vision and approach regarding the inner situation of the church is offered by Zernov in his analysis of the time: "The life of the Russian Church in the nineteenth century was full of strange contradictions. Externally it was lamentably crippled by the deadly grip of the Empire, which imposed an artificial immobility upon Christian thought and action. But inwardly it was free and experienced an outpouring of the Holy Spirit greater than ever in its history. Officially, the Church was identified with the policy of Chauvinism pursued in imitation of Germany by the St. Petersburg bureaucracy, but the missionaries of the same Church taught the newly converted to love their own language and culture." Zernov, *The Russians and Their Church,* p. 139.

38. Regarding the state-church relationship and the end of tsardom, the following acute observation is noteworthy: "Of the two partners, the one who lost more was not the Church, but the Empire, for, by denying Christians freedom of speech and action, the rulers of Russia deprived themselves of the benefit of friendly but independent criticism. They became morally isolated from the best elements of the nation, and they created around themselves that vacuum which caused the inglorious collapse of the whole State edifice in 1917." Zernov, *The Russians and Their Church,* p. 130.

on the throne due to the *Divine Will.* Such loyalty was among the main reasons why so many of the Intelligentsia turned their backs on the church and the Orthodox faith: "On the other side the fidelity of the Church to the Emperors represented a setback for freedom, self-government or local initiatives resulting in 'mass desertion' of the upper classes who have had the experience of western culture and education and began to look upon the Church as an institution suitable only for the lower, uneducated classes of society."[39] A regional council of the Orthodox Church in 1917 was supposed to introduce major adjustments, but the terms of discussion again were overtaken by the Provisional Government and the Bolsheviks successively. "The mass desertion of the upper classes" described by Zernov started slowly but grew steadily. This desertion included Christians of traditional as well as more progressive thinking and resulted in the formation of the two major schools or notions of thought and trend, the so-called *Slavophils* and the *Westernizers.*[40]

2. The Debate between the *Slavophils* and the *Westernizers*

2.1. The Spiritual and Intellectual Realm of Twentieth-Century Russia

Zernov, in yet another of his standard works, *The Russian Religious Renaissance of the Twentieth Century,* gives us a pointed summary of the ecclesial and social development in the second part of the nineteenth century that finally led to the separation of the *Intelligentsia* from what he designates as "the rest of the population." The real or apparent *oneness* of the nation suffered a further and — today, we can say — unique split, which estranged the major part of the educated layers of Russian society such as the *dvorianstvo*[41]

39. Cf. Zernov, *The Russians and Their Church,* pp. 139-40.

40. Cf. Gorodetzky, *The Humiliated Christ,* p. xi. In this context, Gorodetzky is referring primarily to the lack of freedom of religious expression in the literature of nineteenth-century Russia through political and religious censorship. Her central question, however, is how explicit or implicit was the person of Jesus Christ in the works of Russian writers of the era. Pertaining to this topic is also the following observation: "Die russische Intelligenz, die sich aus adeligen und wohlhabenden Bürgern zusammensetzte, war in der zweiten Hälfte des 19. Jh. nicht länger mehr gewillt, die Vergewaltigungen der Zensurbehörde zu ertragen. Schon die Erleichterungen, die Alexander gewährte, ließe Literatur und Journalismus in wenigen Jahren zu Großmächten aufsteigen." Jockwig, "Die Situation der russischen Orthodoxen Kirche," p. 404.

41. The "*dvorianstvo*" were the *courtiers,* the serving nobility, created on purpose by Pe-

from the church and the lower, noneducated general masses. This group perceived that their own and the nation's spiritual as well as intellectual needs were no longer satisfied in the Orthodox Church's mere traditionalism and dogmatism. Out of the *Intelligentsia,*[42] which in the 1830s was still considered *religious,* surfaced a group later known as the "*Westernizers.*"[43] These

---

ter I to counterbalance and gradually take over the power from "the old feudal nobility and to provide an educated upper class loyal to the crown." Cf. A. Pyman, *A History of Russian Symbolism* (Cambridge: Cambridge University Press, 1994), p. 93. It was from this privileged group, the *dvorniky,* from which the majority of Russian intellectuals initially derived.

42. The *Intelligentsia* was an unparalleled *phenomenon* of Russian society unknown to other nations. They could not be classified, as insinuated above, by affiliation to a single political party, social class, or distinct intellectual stream; what universally characterized them were the common goals, which, nevertheless, were to be achieved with rather diverse methods. The term *Intelligentsia* itself became commonly used in the 1860s (under Alexander II) and derives from Latin, the lingua franca of the Russian seminaries. Many of the *Intelligenty* came in fact from the seminaries and till the 70s the clergy was predominant in the movement when the number of laypersons started gradually to increase. It was equally in the 70s that the Intelligentsia became aware of its role and influence in and on the society. Cf. SPFR, pp. 187-90.

Anew, Zernov provides valuable insight into the "three headings" under which he summarized their affinities and principles: "that the injustice from which the peasants suffered was a national sin and that the privileged minority was morally responsible for it; that autocracy was an evil which caused economic backwardness and social inequality and ought therefore to be ended; and that the radical political and philosophical theories of the West if applied to Russia were bound to produce immediate improvements in all spheres of life." There was a certain "religious fervor," an understanding of "sacred cause," among those who shared these ideals as they searched for a fitting and lasting solution. Most of them, being Russians, had a Christian education and background that soon yielded to the more compelling and aggressive ideas of materialism and Marxism. Cf. N. Zernov, *Eastern Christendom: A Study of the Origin and Development of the Eastern Orthodox Church* (New York: G. P. Putnam's Sons, 1961), pp. 197-98. Nevertheless, generalizations should be avoided, or else one could easily negate any genuine spiritual striving among the *Intelligenty,* which certainly would be a one-sided view.

43. A clear distinction of terms in this case is at times hampered by their interference: the *Intelligentsia* originated predominantly from the westernized upper classes *(dvorianstvo),* a creation of Peter I and his ongoing reforms in the eighteenth century. The *Westernizers* were an offspring of the Russian Intelligentsia, which stands also for the early *Slavophils.* The composition of the Westernizers started changing when Nicolas I began recruiting for his bureaucracy from other classes at Russia's universities, which, formerly reserved to the gentry, became available "to the sons of the rural clergy, the small state officials and even to liberated serfs. These new comers became the majority in the second half of the century" and shared the discontent of the landed gentry, however, without any sentiment of gratitude towards the state. Despite this the Intelligentsia "never absorbed all the westernized Russians." Cf. RRR, pp. 15-21. The Slavophils on their end eventually distanced them-

members of the *westernized* Intelligentsia came to know and respect European culture, literature, and philosophy during their trips abroad or their extended study-stays as students, mostly sponsored by the Russian tsarist government. They not only kindled an unveiled affection for western culture and society, but considered the West to be the sole possible model for Russia's future development; yet, the beginnings of this social-class division were present already before the Petrine reforms:[44]

> The original remarkable cultural oneness of the nation was challenged, however, by the schism in the Russian church in the seventeenth century, which prepared the ground for the cultural revolution inaugurated by Peter the Great in the next century. The result was that the westernized upper classes became cut off from the rest of the population.
>
> The tragic consequences of these two splits became fully apparent in the second part of the nineteenth century when a numerically small but politically aggressive group of westernized Russians, known as the Intelligentsia, started an energetic campaign aimed at the further undermining of the religious unity of the Russian people. The weapons used were the preaching of socialism based on materialism and atheism.[45]

Zernov may have gone a bit too far by claiming that among the explicit goals of all "westernized Russians" was the undermining of the "religious unity" of the Russian people, but the rest of his observations are astute. He himself lived in Russia during a time of deep-rooted changes at the beginning of the twentieth century and in his early twenties was forced into

---

selves from the Intelligentsia and the Westernizers as well because of the latter group's preferences for "western-type-solutions" to Russia's national and social problems and a general tendency for Europeanization. Nevertheless, the Slavophils too were influenced by the ideas of the Intelligentsia and of the Westernizers. The truth is that none of the aforementioned groups were homogeneous, but the Slavophils could be considered as a more compact and easily distinguishable entity than the Westernizers.

44. "Just as educational institutions in Poland and Lithuania served as centers for opposition to autocracy and Russian Orthodoxy, so did the educational institutions created in the Great Russian territorial core of the empire. Beginning in the 1840s, when graduate students trained at Russian government expense in German and French universities returned to Russia to become professors in Russian universities, their heads and notebooks filled with the ideas of Western thinkers, Russian universities became vehicles that transformed the lives of many teachers and students." *Religious and Secular Forces in Late Tsarist Russia,* ed. Charles E. Timberlake (Seattle and London: University of Washington Press, 1992), p. 4.

45. RRR, p. vii.

exile by the Bolsheviks along with his family.[46] Materialism and atheism, on the other hand, played a significant role, and therefore should be considered more the result of a development, even though an erroneous one, than a goal in itself. The key notions to keep in mind are "disappointment in" and "disillusion[ment] with" the ruling unjust social order,[47] especially with regard to the lower and disadvantaged classes, and the church of the time that officially supported the tsarist government.[48] Analyzed from this perspective *westernism,* as a social phenomenon, could be considered a *catalyst* in a process that was already penetrating all layers of society,[49] and which eventually, and ironically, turned against the institution that created

46. An inspiring and moving description of this significant Russian historian's life, the Russian emigration after 1921, his relationship with his wife as well as his work can be found in: N. Zernov, *Sunset Years: A Russian Pilgrim in the West* (London: The Fellowship of St. Alban and St. Sergius, 1983).

47. In addition there was the "heritage" of Nicolas I (1825-1855), which imposed the rigidity of militaristic and bureaucratic order that lasted over thirty years and that not even the belated liberal reforms of Alexander II in 1861 could fully dispel.

48. The main criticism of the Orthodox Church (at least from some of the radicals among them) was that it refused to engage in fighting the autocracy with revolutionary means (in which *an armed fight* was understood literally). After discovering and embracing positivism and nihilism, faith and the Orthodox Church for many became outdated, similarly to developments in Western societies, and though the Intelligentsia was *passionate* to ameliorate the shameful situation of the peasantry, it would preferably do so by turning away from faith and tradition to modern, primarily Western, means and manners. The majority of the simple Russian folk, however, neither understood nor accepted the members of the Intelligentsia. For the Slavophils, on the contrary, *khrestianin* (peasant) was not only the same sound but also the same connotation as *Christian,* which meant their whole approach had a religious undercurrent. Cf. Zernov, *Eastern Christendom,* pp. 3-26.

49. It was above all in the spiritual and intellectual realm that the Slavophils and the Westernizers (despite of, or maybe precisely because of, their diversity of approaches) exercised an enriching influence on each other. The difference in their approaches was that while the Westernizers embraced western philosophy, tradition, and the ideas of the Enlightenment as *the* solution for the social and political problems of Russia, the Slavophils opposed them, above all in one point: that this could not be done by ignoring or denying the Christian-Orthodox Faith and tradition of Russia. However, the presence of Western ideas in Russian universities and among the educated classes was already notable and was gaining further terrain. J. Kornblatt and R. Gustafson attribute precisely to this *fruitful tension* the appearance of *modern Russian religious thought* as such: "Modern Russian religious thought springs from the tradition of the Slavophil thinkers of the nineteenth century, not untouched, however, by 'Western' ideas, for the Slavophiles would have had few critical or historical genres with which to enter the philosophical arena were it not for the German Idealists." "Introduction," in *Russian Religious Thought,* ed. J. D. Kornblatt and R. F. Gustafson (Madison: University of Wisconsin Press, 1996), p. 7.

it: tsarism.[50] The members of the Intelligentsia often differed in origin, background, and political orientation, yet the majority of them must be credited for having "always felt so passionately and warmly their 'responsibility' for the destiny not only of Russia but of the *whole world*."[51]

2.2. *In Search of a New Worldview*

Zenkovskii speaks in this circumstance of a "break with the ecclesiastical world-view"[52] resulting in the need of a "new ideology" that finally culminated in the nineteenth century.[53] It was not simply a *turn against* the church that would justly describe the motivation of the Intelligentsia, but much more a *breaking away* for reasons described above, out of an urgent call for *new ideals.* Thus, in a new context, a new way of life[54] seemed to be a coherent and even an inevitable element of transition. They were greatly inspired

50. It was a time of growing complexity in political orientation and interests, a time also known as "the period of reaction" that would not shrink back from militant actions such as the assassination of Tsar Alexander II on March 13, 1881 in Petersburg that, in the end, did not deliver the results the perpetrators hoped for. This was the (extreme) *left wing* of the Intelligentsia, which believed that progress and a just social order would come automatically once the old structures were destroyed. That their expectations remained unfulfilled is partially due to the lack of pragmatic and realistic understanding on how society and political life should function. This elucidates the reasons that a promising and needed creative sociopolitical tension could end up in the shameful disaster of the Bolshevik and, successively, Communist rule. Only the visionary spirit of a V. S. Solov'ev, F. M. Dostoevsky, or an eccentric V. S. Pechorin could foresee and predict the dangers and suffering that would result from such a totalitarian realm introduced by the material civilization, or a civilization of materialism, which had lost or abandoned its spiritual foundation. As an *oddness,* we shall mention Pechorin's belief that Russia and the United States would "inaugurate a new cycle of history." Cf. Berdiaev, *The Russian Idea,* pp. 55-89.

51. Zenkovsky, *A History of Russian Philosophy I,* p. 169.

52. This started in the second half of the seventeenth century and reached its height in the eighteenth century.

53. A "return to the ecclesial worldview" will begin with the work and influential writing of Nikolai Vasilievich Gogol' (1809-1852). Cf. Zenkovsky, *A History of Russian Philosophy I,* pp. 171-79.

54. Still introduced by Peter the Great; not welcomed by many, especially the lower social classes, peasants, and the majority of folk, despised as "arrogant secularism." Also: "The conflict between the new political realism and the spiritual traditions of the past came to a head only during the Russian intellectual and spiritual renaissance in the nineteenth century." J. Meyendorff, *The Orthodox Church* (Crestwood, NY: St. Vladimir's Seminary Press, 1981), p. 141.

by Romanticism and even more with German Idealism; therefore eventually a *moralistic humanism* enriched by Schiller's idea of the *Schöne Seele* filled the breach and remained for a long time the dominant Russian ideology.[55] According to J. Meyendorff, each year in the 1850s and 60s "a new class of students graduated, or left, the universities to swell the ranks of the *Intelligentsia,* a member of which was called an *Intelligent.* Bound by the common experience of alienation from society through education this new group formed a brotherhood devoted to serving the people, the *narod.*"[56] The *narod (nation)* was at times an idealized image of a united Russian nation with which the Intelligentsia identified itself and whose improved, dignified life it considered as its utmost mission. Indeed, it was a question of a national identity, and even more: of Russia's *national task.*

2.3. Intelligenty *with Deep Christian Roots*

Among the leading and most popular personalities of the Intelligentsia were often Orthodox Christians from priestly families such as Nikolai Chernishevskii (1828-1889), Nikolai Dobroliubov (1836-1861), and Sergei Bulgakov (1871-1944), all of whom initially abandoned the church, considering it as "obsolete," which, however, may have not been the case for their individual faith.[57] Bulgakov, for instance, after his experience and profound disenchantment with Marxism, which had fully entered the "pool of ideas" in the 1880s,[58] returned to the church as a convinced Christian and later even became a priest. A similar intellectual and faith journey (except for the priesthood, perhaps) was the experience of some other significant personalities, brilliant thinkers, authors, and philosophers of the Intelligentsia. Among them was Feodor Dostoevsky (1821-1881) or Vladimir Solov'ev (1853-1900), who was briefly attracted by positivism and materialism and re-

55. Cf. Zenkovsky, *A History of Russian Philosophy I,* p. 171.

56. Meyendorff, *The Orthodox Church,* p. 122.

57. Others may disagree on this point.

58. "As schools and students became more numerous in the 1870's and 1880's, tsarist officials could not completely stop the flow of secular and revolutionary ideas from the cities into the villages. In the 1880's, Marxism entered the pool of ideas being disseminated inside educational institutions and among former students living in university towns. Disappointed that their assassination of Alexander II in 1881 failed to produce the changes they desired, many of the young *Intelligenty* abandoned, or adapted, their populist notions in order to embrace Marxism." Meyendorff, *The Orthodox Church,* p. 20.

nounced his Christian faith just to return to it soon.[59] Other converts from Marxism to Christianity that need to be mentioned were Piotr Struve (1870-1944), Nikolai Berdiaev (1874-1948), and Simeon Frank (1877-1950). Their faith conversion, together with Bulgakov, and revisions of their previous negative attitude toward Christianity and the faith, recognized also the fundamental role of the Orthodox Church, which brought along a definitive watershed in the development of the Intelligentsia. This applies especially to the intellectual core, i.e., the heart of the movement whose return to faith also steered other *Intelligenty*'s attention back from purely economic and social issues to religion, culture, and art. Henceforth, the problems and challenges of the nation were to be resolved through solutions based on Christianity and the Christian faith.[60] It was they who first gained the awareness that if there was to be cultural, political, and social progress in the future of Russia, the wounds inflicted on the nation by the forced Petrine reforms needed healing and reconciliation. Unfortunately, this promising and gradual notion of reconciliation came to an abrupt halt, and was even reversed, once the Bolsheviks and successively the Communists came to power in the twentieth century.

The *Slavophil* group, defined by some also as the *Nationalists,* was at its start a casual association of Russian thinkers. As the name implies, they were Russian intellectuals with a special affinity and love for the Slav — above all Russian — tradition(s) and customs, with "a religious conception of the world rather than a nationalistic current of thought."[61] This title initially referred to six *Slavophils:* Konstantin Aksakov, Aleksei Khomiakov, Ivan Kireevskii, his brother Peter Kireevskii, Aleksander Koshelev, and Iuri Samarin. Although some of them met earlier, nonetheless, an articulate Slavophil group — by far not always unanimous — was formed first during the 1840s, a *decade* commonly known as the *marvelous* or *remarkable.*[62] The

59. There was a severe critique of the revolutionary Intelligentsia published in 1909 by seven *Intelligenty* who had abandoned Marxism for its "fanatically upholding materialism and atheism." They drew a comparison between a "classical Russian intellectual," and "a militant monk of the nihilist religion of worldly well-being." Cf. S. Pushkarev, *The Emergence of Modern Russia, 1801-1917* (New York: Holt, Rinehart & Winston, 1963), p. 298.

60. More on this: cf. Zernov, *Eastern Christendom,* pp. 202-6, and RRR, pp. 131-65.

61. Gorodetzky, *The Humiliated Christ,* p. 7. The national and nationalistic notions were certainly known to the Slavophils.

62. For a concise introduction to Slavophilism, see *On Spiritual Unity: A Slavophile Reader,* trans. and ed. B. Jakim and R. Bird (New York: Lindisfarne Books, 1998), pp. 7-25. Further, the anthology *Slavianofil'stvo: Pro et Contra* (Sankt-Peterburg: Sankt-Peterburgskogo universiteta, 2009).

first three of them, Aksakov, Khomiakov, and Ivan Kireevskii, as well as Samarin, are known as the *Senior Slavophils.* In their spirituality they were very close to one another, the Khomiakovs and Kireevskiis even related, and with their brilliance constantly influenced each other. Yet they all maintained their uniqueness of thought and style and, therefore, must be considered individually. And if the members of the Intelligentsia in the later decades were called and defined in general as *Westernizers,* the denomination *Slavophils* also contained a broader spectrum of nationalist streams and interests. Let us simply mention some of the major ones: the religious nationalists, the conservatives, the assertive nationalists, or the Pan-Slav nationalists, also known as *Panslavists.*[63] The main representatives of the *Slavophil* movement (i.e., the senior Khomiakov, Kireevskii, and their disciples) would probably have preferred the designation "Orthodox-Russian orientation" to any of the later labels.[64]

Most of the Westernizers considered the Slavophils backward-tendentious, which was not that farfetched if we consider that some extremists among them still kindled dreams of restoring the *Muscovite Order.* This would explain the "Nationalists" byname, even though the early Slavophils were rather romantic conservatives with a vision inspired by the Russian past, its religious heritage, and with a notable appreciation for art and culture.[65] Accordingly, the Slavophils played an important role in establishing and reviving Russian poetry, prose, and literature in general.

2.4. Russia's Mission *and Chaadaev's Provocation*

Although the Slavophils were conservatives, or perceived as such,[66] they often shared the same goals with the Westernizers. The means and methods

63. This latter stage is considered by some as a "degradation" of Slavophilism occurring in the 1870s-1880s and creating the ideological support of new Russian nationalism, which, although under a different guise, persists to the present time. The Westernizers' ideological "message" continues in its impact primarily on the history of Russian thought. Cf. SPFR, p. 109.

64. Cf. *On Spiritual Unity: A Slavophile Reader,* p. 7. Note: The listing of names of both groups is indicative and by all means not comprehensive.

65. Cf. P. Valliere, *Modern Russian Theology: Bukharev, Soloviev, Bulgakov; Orthodox Theology in a New Key* (Grand Rapids: Eerdmans, 2000), p. 85.

66. They were brought up educated in western culture in the same manner as their peers, were fluent in European languages, with travels and study permanencies abroad, yet were convinced of the Russian originality. In their view, their nation had to share with the

by which to achieve such goals were the primary cause of their disagreement; nevertheless, both groups strove for social and political reforms, which initially were inspired by Christian ideals.[67] Furthermore, they wanted to see Russia's tradition and past implemented in the present, namely as proper national values and as part of the nation's identity. But would that suffice in the future for an independent development from the West? And there was the conditioning retrospective view: Did Russia indeed owe its cultural identity solely to the West, or in the same measure to its own past and tradition, or possibly to its opposition to western influence? Or was it a result of the interaction between the two, East and West? This vital query about identity and self-definition, in the views of many Slavophils, foreshadowed a question of equal urgency, namely: What is the mission of Russia in the world and for the world? The matter crystallized in the early 1840s and became one of the main topics henceforth in the dialogue between the two exponent groups.[68] However, the initial collegial manner of conversation and common reflection took a sudden change in tone and reciprocal aloofness after the publication of Piotr Chaadaev's[69] fa-

---

West in the same measure as it was receiving or learning from it. They led heated debates and ideological disputes with the Westernizers during the *Remarkable Decade.* However, they soon became suspicious to the government, which first limited and later even prohibited the spreading of their ideas. Cf. Zernov, *Eastern Christendom,* pp. 184-86.

67. "The question of peasantry was central for both the Slavophils and the Westernizers, the former trying to give a definition of the national and religious character of Russia, the latter concerned with the political situation of their country; both were eager to see the emancipation of the peasants." Gorodetzky, *The Humiliated Christ,* p. 2.

68. Into the mid-1840s Florovskii collocates the period when the debates between the two groups "sharpened into a division or split." Cf. WoRT II, pp. 12-13. An excellent rendering of the time's spirit and feeling is provided by Berdiaev: "In the debating circles of the forties Slavophils and Westernizers could still carry on their disputes in the same salons. Khomiakov, a passionate disputant and powerful dialectician, engaged in battle with Herzen. Herzen said of Khomiakov that he was like a mediaeval knight on guard before the Blessed Virgin; he slept weapon in hand. They carried on their disputes the whole night through. Turgenev remembers that when a controversy was raging at its height and someone proposed they should have something to eat, Belinsky shouted out: 'We have not yet decided the question of the existence of God and you want to eat!' The forties were a period of intense intellectual life. There were many gifted people among the Russians at that time. Speaking of the Westernizers and Slavophils of those times Herzen said: 'We had one love, but it was not the same love.' He called them a two-faced Janus, and both sides loved freedom, and both sides loved Russia. The Slavophils loved her as a mother, the Westernizers as a child. The children and grandchildren of the Slavophils and the Westernizers have now already grown so far apart that they would not be able to dispute in the same salons." Berdiaev, *The Russian Idea,* p. 56.

69. Piotr I. Chaadaev (1794-1856) was one of the foremost representatives of the Rus-

mous *First Philosophical Letter* in 1836.[70] In this letter, Chaadaev questioned any Russian originality in the sphere of philosophy (and beyond) on which one could base a proper philosophical system in his country. Further, by denying a proper, original culture and history to Russia, he understandably stirred up negative feelings and indignation:

> It is one of the most deplorable traits of our strange civilization that we are still discovering truths that are commonplace even among peoples much less advanced than we. This is because we have never moved in concert with the other peoples. We are not a part of any of the great families of the human race; we are neither of the West nor of the East, and we have not the traditions of either. . . . We stand, as it were, outside of time, the universal education of mankind has not touched us. . . . We have nothing that is ours on which to base our thinking. . . . We are, as it were, strangers to ourselves . . . a culture based wholly on borrowing and imitation.[71]

A good provocation, however, provides impetus for reflection, and the type of reaction given upon it is often an accurate barometer of the provocation's effectiveness. Thus most of the notable Russian thinkers of the time either related to Chaadaev's thought, or at least wrote about him, especially after the publication of his famous and never-concluded *Apologie d'un fou (The Apology of a Madman)* in 1837.[72] In it Chaadaev apologized for his pos-

---

sian Intelligentsia who possessed a profound conviction for the historical nature of Christianity. Chaadaev was considered to be the first Russian philosopher of history and an awakener of the independent original Russian thought. He had a pessimistic view on Russia's past and present, which he expressed with "deepest pain," but also an "optimistic faith and hope with regard to its future." These ideas of Chaadaev were revealed to the public in 1829 in his famous philosophical letter, which drew harsh consequences. After being declared *mad* by the government of Nicolas I, he had to be visited weekly by a doctor and was forbidden to write or publish. Cf. Berdiaev, *The Russian Idea,* pp. 51-54. It is important to note that Chaadaev was strongly influenced by Schelling, whom he knew in person. According to Berdiaev, Chaadaev along with V. Pechorin "represented the religious aspect of the Westernizing movement." Berdiaev, *The Russian Idea,* p. 55.

70. Written in a *climate permeated by romantic nationalism,* it circulated at first as a manuscript. Later it was published in the journal *Telescope* by Nikolai Nadezhdin, apparently at the behest of Chaadaev himself.

71. P. I. Chaadaev, *Sochinenia i pis'ma II* (Moskva 1914), pp. 6-8.

72. Berdiaev qualified it as "a notable production." Cf. Berdiaev, *The Russian Idea,* pp. 52-53.

sible exaggerations,[73] defines a universal mission of Russia for humankind, exalts the Orthodox Church as *so humble and sometimes so heroic,* and exposes his love for the *fatherland.* Yet he also makes it clear that the "love of truth" stands above the fatherland's beauty and that the path to Heaven leads not through one's homeland but through *the truth.*[74] Chaadaev not only verbalized and summarized the nature of the dilemma and its challenges, but, voluntarily or not, awakened an awareness of Russia's historicity, its unique past, present, and consequently future.[75] A proper and pragmatic Slavophil response took its time and eventually arrived in 1856 from I. Kireevskii, who proposed a *new principle in philosophy.* It suggested integrating the philosophy of Schelling and Hegel and paving the way towards a genuine Russian culture. Eventually it would be the Slavophil movement that produced a proper school of *Modern Russian Theology* along with a more conservative, strictly patristic approach to theology, the so-called *Neopatristic school.*

2.5. Europe or Asia

The state of the political and religious spheres in Russia at the end of the nineteenth century was complex, at times even confused, due partly to what W. Goerdt describes as a "fluent passage" between the terms of *Slavophil* and *Westernizer.* The big topic of "Russia and Europe" raised two questions simultaneously, both of which are expressed plainly by the difference between the conjunctions "and" and "or." Both questions were legitimate, i.e., "Russia *and* Europe" as well as "Russia *or* Europe." Yet there was a certain radicalism about the *either-or* in the relationship between Europe and Russia. Besides, there was a seemingly endless combination of *Westernizer* and *Slavophil elements* in the views of each thinker involved.[76] In other words, the above

73. Chaadaev felt also misunderstood and misinterpreted. Further in his later works he concedes a development of his own views.

74. Cf. Zenkovsky, *A History of Russian Philosophy I,* pp. 164-69.

75. At the same time he had "brutally" exposed the problematic nature of the relationship between East and West, of the contrast between a "progressive" Europe and an "antiquated and reactionary" Russia. The other idea that preoccupied him was the insertion of Russia into the universal history of mankind. He was convinced that only "a union" with the West and the Western Church would save Russia. Cf. SPFR, p. 105.

76. There definitely was a religious aspect in the Westernizing movement too, and it "preceded the actual rise of Westernizing and Slavophil currents of thought. But there were Slavonic elements also in these religious Westernizers." For more on the debate between the Slavophils and the Westernizers, see Berdiaev, *The Russian Idea,* pp. 55-89.

terms were excessively fluid at the end of the nineteenth century.[77] The Slavophils did not despise western culture for its own sake but were repulsed by its negative and distorting influence on the genuine Russian tradition, an influence that seemed to rob, or at least deny, the nation's (religious) identity. That meant first of all Russia's past, and thus its future, which would reveal itself in the *present.* Hence, the need for action and clear concepts was more urgent than ever, and the nineteenth-century revival of the Russian intellectual mind brought forth an exceptional spiritual richness in literature, philosophy, and theology, undoubtedly becoming part of the "*narod*'s great mission" and its message to humankind.[78] There was a rapprochement between the two groups at the beginning of the twentieth century, a reconciliation initiated by the Slavophils; but it was unfortunately interrupted by the Bolshevik Revolution of October 1917.[79]

3. The Rise of Distinct Theological Schools

3.1. First Notions and Ideas

Modern Russian religious thought remains a phenomenon that contains a great diversity of spiritual and intellectual *streams.*[80] Therefore, it may be

77. Cf. Goerdt, *Russische Philosophie,* p. 264.

78. "The discussions of the problem of Russia took a more definite character after the publication of the *Philosophical Letters.* . . . The position of the Slavophils and the Westernizers was henceforward clear. They continued their discussions but remained friends until 1845, when those who wanted to follow Western ways were accused by the poet N. M. Yazykov (1803-1846) of treason. This was the date of formal break." Gorodetzky, *The Humiliated Christ,* p. 5.

79. Cf. Zernov, *Moscow the Third Rome,* pp. 87-88.

80. As an example, apart from the *Raskol'niky,* the so-called "Old Believers," who were residing in the country, Western Catholicism and Protestantism, German and French philosophy, pietism and medieval mysticism, and also Masonry and sectarianism were widely present in the Russian mind and society. Their influence, toleration, and even fashion varied — as among the ruling, so in the subdued classes of the society. Masonry and western pietism, greatly promoted by Catherine II, for example, influenced the religious life of the Russian Intelligentsia at its beginnings. Cf. Maloney, *A History of Orthodox Theology since 1453,* p. 48.

We agree with Maloney that there was an intense search for interior spiritual values, which were forcibly replaced by a "pragmatic utilitarianism [of Peter's and, even more so, Catherine's reforms] that infected the money class of Russia." Cf. Maloney, *A History of Orthodox Theology since 1453,* p. 48. However, we need to add that this may not have been the

more sensitive and correct to discuss *theological tendencies* or *streams* instead of schools, except, of course, in cases where these *tendencies* and *streams* evolved into proper *theological schools* based on similarities in structure, applied methodology, and diverse literary activities.[81]

Russian theology and theological culture had a notable influence on other Orthodox countries, directly or indirectly shaping their cultures and theologies: Greece, Bulgaria, and Serbia, for instance, were among them.[82] It is difficult to mention a *single* and *genuine* Russian Orthodox theology during the nineteenth and twentieth centuries in Russia. Some scholars prefer to speak simply of "Russian theology," omitting the adjective "orthodox."[83]

sole reason since there was significant social change in the society due also to education and travel. This necessarily changed the intellectual approach to the questions of belief and practice similar to eleventh- and twelfth-century Europe where, with the growing urbanization of the population, changed living conditions and vivid interactions among the citizens, first universities sprang into being and *dialectics* as the method of instruction gradually replaced the ancient monastic theology. Here, *dialectics* was certainly not a countercurrent to spirituality, as it is oftentimes understood, but a complementary, even catechetical, method to approach faith with reason and respond to the new challenges of faith (in both meanings of the expression). St. Anselm's famous and genuine search for faith formed by reason, i.e., *fides quaerens intellectum (faith yearns to comprehend)* would apply equally to the genuine search of many *Intelligenty* for a deeper understanding of God, faith, and worship.

81. Research, translating, editing, and publication, for instance, are considered indispensable features of a school of higher education, especially a university.

82. The influence was real in the western world, especially what C. Yanaras calls the "Theology of the Russian Diaspora." In this context, he compares the "vehement westernization of the ecclesial thinking and theology" that occurred between the fifteenth and nineteenth centuries in Greece with that of Russia and states that this "westernization distorted and deformed" the identity of the Orthodox. This applies less to what he calls the "recognized formulations of Church theology" but rather to the entire *way of life*, which became *individualistic* and *rationalistic*. He ascribes the merit of clarification of this "Orthodox identity" in the historical path of the Russian church first to the *opposition* (Slavophils), before the Revolution, and to the Russian theologians of the Diaspora in subsequent times. Cf. C. Yanaras, "Der Beitrag der russischen Orthodoxie zur Klärung der orthodoxen Identität," in *Tausend Jahre Christentum in Russland*, pp. 955-57. Also: "Russia was generous towards the less fortunate nations and Slav brethren" of eastern lands as early as from the seventeenth century. Its help ranged from alms collecting and giving generous gifts to military involvement against the Turks in the Balkans early in 1877 as a response to the Turkish violence against Orthodox Christians in the region. For more on this, see Zernov, *Moscow the Third Rome*, pp. 54-60.

83. Cf. "Introduction," in Cioffari, "Breve storia della teologia russa." Similarly, "eastern theology," an expression fondly used in some eastern ecclesial movements, can be misleading or not comprehensive to say the least for its exclusiveness towards exiled Orthodox theologians or those otherwise living abroad. Cf. B. Schultze, "Probleme der orthodoxen

This is due not only to the massive western influence on Russian education, universities, and seminaries, but also to the originality with which some authors consciously integrated ideas and drew inspiration for their works from western theology and mysticism.[84] Furthermore, the "absence of clarity in the relationship between theology and philosophy, knowledge and faith" needs to be mentioned.[85] This lack of clarity was due, on the one hand, to the role that schools of higher education — theological as well as secular — played in teaching philosophy.[86] On the other hand, the lack of a clear division of subjects was due to what Goerdt remarks on as "a lack in urgent need for the clarification of this matter" due to the patristic and byzantine concept that saw the "true Logos, true reason" and *philosophy* "definitively revealed in Christianity."[87]

3.2. The Need for Higher Education

The first universities of the empire, which were secular in nature, were founded in 1755 in Moscow,[88] in 1804 in Kazan, in 1805 in Kharkov (converted from a Collegium), and in 1829 in St. Petersburg. These universities sprang into being partially as a result of Peter I's absolutistic, enlightened spirit that lived on in Elizabeth II and the liberal Alexander I, but also due to the undeniable need for institutes of higher education of western standard. Zenkovskii's thorough study of the history of philosophy reveals that the University of Kharkov in the eighteenth century "differed little" from a proper Theological Academy and that there were forty-four theological seminaries in Russia at the time. Even the University of Moscow was dependent on Theological Academies "for its Russian professors," Kiev not

Theologie," in *Handbuch der Ostkirchenkunde,* ed. E. v. Ivánka, J. Tyciak, and P. Wiertz (Düsseldorf: Patmos Verlag, 1971), p. 97.

84. Especially medieval love mysticism and mystical theology.

85. Goerdt, *Russische Philosophie,* pp. 45-48.

86. Cf. Zenkovsky, *A History of Russian Philosophy I,* pp. 103-7.

87. Cf. Goerdt, *Russische Philosophie,* pp. 45-48. At the same time, Peter I's reforms intended to free Russia from Byzantine influence and deepen the *theological break from Byzantium.* For this purpose, the tsar in person appointed Stefan Iavorskii (1658-1722), a theologian, as an administrator to the vacant Kievan patriarchal throne in 1700. Peter I's choice, however, turned out to be poor when Iavorskii's book, *Kamen' very (The Rock of Faith),* took aim to criticize the Protestants living in the country. Cf. Maloney, *A History of Orthodox Theology since 1453,* pp. 40-45.

88. The first secular institution of higher learning.

being an exception. As a result, theology and professors of theology had a notable impact on philosophy and gave it a direction that was related more to *ecclesial functions.* This was the case until philosophy took off and started its own independent development. Professor F. A. Golubinskii (1797-1854) was the first true representative of philosophy, with his fundamental idea of the *Infinite Being,* in his epistemological realism, and with a genuine attempt at an independent philosophical system.[89] The reciprocal influence of theology and philosophy was notable, which is why *religious thought* seems to be more adequate for Russia, and explains in part the metaphysical and highly speculative tendencies of Russian theology, especially in exile and the Diaspora.[90]

3.3. *The First Attempt of a Proper Russian Systematic Theology*

The development of theology and theological culture in Russia was, apart from its proper monastic spirituality, molded by two distinct, major influences. One was Catholicism, from Latin manuals brought along and taught by Jesuits in the seventeenth century. The other was Protestantism, which was strongly supported by Peter I who tried to replicate the Swedish model of governance, including religion. In this, the aforementioned Feofan Prokopovich, who abandoned his previous Roman Catholic source of inspiration and preferred implementing Protestant theology, was of utmost help to the tsar, especially after the fiasco with Stefan Iavorskii who turned out to be much more Orthodox than philo-Protestant. Prokopovich's theological thought never reached the maturity of a complete system, and his theological works were collected and published first posthumously by his followers,[91] his theological lectures serving as a basis for a compendium of dogmatic theology. Its influence lasted over one hundred years and formed generations of theology students in Kiev and in the Alexandr-Nevskii priestly seminary in Petersburg.[92] Without hesitancy we can speak of an existing *theological stream* or *effort* to establish an original systematic theology (even though modeled on Protestant authors) during the Petrine reforms.

89. Cf. Zenkovsky, *A History of Russian Philosophy I,* pp. 103-5, 300-304.
90. Father S. Bulgakov, for instance, was well known for his *speculative theology.*
91. Maloney, *A History of Orthodox Theology since 1453,* p. 43.
92. Cf. Härtel, "Feofan Prokopovič," pp. 367-75.

3.4. *Pietism, Russian Language,* Dobrotoliubie, *and the Return to the Sources*

Theologia Christiana super fundamentum Verbi Dei exstructa ad praxim pietatis et promotionem fidei Iesu Christi unice directa is the title of the main dogmatic work of Platon Levshin (1737-1812),[93] a key theologian of his time. Levshin provides an exemplary illustration of the Latin, or "Latinized," nature of the seminaries and theological institutions. Latin was the *lingua franca* of the seminaries and the language of study to such an extent that seminarians were fluent in Latin but struggled to write in Russian.[94] The core of the problem was, in Florovskii's view, not simply the foreign language in the education of the clergy and theologians but rather the foreign, imported, and definitely scholastic concepts — a theology of and from a different culture "transplanted into Russia." For this very reason, it could not become a "lively and living theology which could be found only in Scripture," and so it was diametrically opposed to Levshin's primary intention to bring "theology in contact with life."[95] The title of Levshin's work reveals its dedication to the "practice of piety and promotion of faith in Jesus Christ" and his practical sense for catechesis and the spiritual needs of the faithful as opposed to proper theological treatises. The first part of the title demonstrates an awareness of the Holy Scripture, which was raised through the efforts of the Protestant *Bible Society* at that time, which was already assiduously working on the new publication and spreading the Bible in Russia. Levshin possessed the courage and determination to "write his treatises in Russian instead of Latin or Slavonic," a fact that S. Bolshakoff connects with the rise of the Russian church after the eighteenth century, which "makes a painful reading."[96] His theology is not just directed at piety but is inspired by pietism and is considered pietistic.[97] Yet his greatest merits, according to

93. Levshin, considered by many to be the most important contributor to ecclesial education in the eighteenth century, became in 1761 the rector of the renowned and most important theological academy of the time, the Moscow Academy. In 1775, he was appointed Metropolitan of Moscow.

94. Cf. Maloney, *A History of Orthodox Theology since 1453*, p. 47.

95. Cf. WoRT I, p. 144.

96. Cf. S. Bolshakoff, *Russian Nonconformity* (Philadelphia: Westminster, 1950), p. 154. "Levshin was the first prelate who dared to write his treatises in Russian instead of Latin or Slavonic; and his work *Pravoslavnoe uchenie ili sokrashchennoe khristianskoe bogoslovie (The Orthodox Doctrine or Brief Christian Theology),* which appeared in 1765, was translated into eight languages, including English." Bolshakoff, *Russian Nonconformity,* p. 155.

97. Airing Florovskii's indignant voice about *western pietism:* "The Russian soul

Florovskii who puts Levshin's "*theology*" in quotation marks, are his catechisms and conversations *(Elementary Instruction in Christian Law)*, which he considers "a turning point in the history of [Russian] theology." His *Pravoslavnoe uchenie ili sokrashchennoe khristianskoe bogoslovie* (*Orthodox Teaching or a Brief Christian Theology* [1765]) "marks the first attempt at a theological system in Russia."[98]

3.5. *The Role of Monastic Spirituality*

Two contemporaries of Levshin must be mentioned briefly in the context of pietism, and they were St. Tikhon of Zadonsk (1724-1783) and Paisii Velichkovskii (1722-1794). St. Tikhon, whose person "stands out in bold relief against the background of the eighteenth century,"[99] taught theology and philosophy at the Latin school of Novgorod and Tver' and became a bishop in Voronezh for four years, after which he settled in a monastery for the rest of his life. He was well versed in the Scriptures and the readings of the (primarily) Greek Fathers and some western thinkers.[100] Tikhon was known for ample works with a tendency towards a "social doctrine of mercy,"[101] and his objective was to implement personal experience in his theological writings.[102] These facets clearly indicate the presence of a monastic spirituality incorporated especially into Levshin's later thought.

The revival of the ancient *hesychastic* tradition of *Starchestvo* in Russian monasticism at the beginning of the nineteenth century is the merit of Starets Paisii. He became well versed in the *hesychastic spirituality* on Mount Athos where he lived as a monk for a number of years. This spiritual *movement* was a legacy of the earliest Byzantine monastic spirituality, according

passed through the ordeal or seduction of pietism at the outset of the nineteenth century — the apogee of Russia's westernism. Catherine's reign seems absolutely primitive in comparison to the triumphant face of the Alexandrine era, when the soul completely gave itself over to Europe. In any event, such a development occurred no earlier than the appearance of *Letters of a Russian Traveler* (1791-1792)." WoRT I, pp. 162-63.

98. WoRT I, p. 144.

99. WoRT I, p. 157.

100. He was well acquainted with St. Augustine as well.

101. Cf. Maloney, *A History of Orthodox Theology since 1453*, pp. 49-50.

102. It is important to note that St. Tikhon was a mystic and it is interesting that "his mysticism sometimes came close to that of the West," i.e., contemplating the passion of Christ. Yet the rest of his visions and experiences were full of the light and radiance of Tabor or Heaven. Cf. Zenkovsky, *A History of Russian Philosophy I*, pp. 50-52.

to which a *spiritual father* or *mother*, who could be either a priest, monk, or a nun (yet definitely was a wise and virtuous person), carries out the role of a spiritual guide, counselor, and judicious advisor even for everyday matters.[103] These persons frequently functioned as "prophets" and were regarded as such. The other notable merits of Paisii were his creative literary activity and his foresight in "founding a group of writers and translators" with whom he cooperated. The effort of this group made a contribution of some significant works for Russian theology and the spiritual life. Among these was the Slavonic-Russian edition of *Philocalia, Dobrotol'ubie (Love of the Good),*[104] which reintroduced the *Jesus Prayer* and gave rise to a more personal prayer and spirituality. According to Maloney, this "introduced a spirituality of traditional personalism that would initiate in Russia a more *patristic theology.*"[105]

The significance of St. Tikhon's and Paisii's works came to light in the inflexible regime of Nicolas I and elicited an awakening to an awareness of the genuinely Orthodox-Eastern spirituality, definitely closer to the Russian soul than the pietistic mystical movement introduced previously during the Alexandrine epoch.[106] And if the work of the elder Paisii was more as a translator, not even as a writer or an original thinker, his contribution suggested a return to "the living sources of patristic theology and thinking about God" and a revival of the monasticism of a Byzantine type, i.e., "the return of the Russian spirit to the Byzantine fathers."[107] St. Tikhon, on the contrary, was an important writer, less of dogmatic theology than of a "mystical ethics or ascetics." Most importantly, his work "marks the first attempt at a *living theology;* the first at-

103. In the later Russian tradition, this role could be fulfilled also by a layperson. The center of the movement was in *Optina Pustin,* in Central Russia where Paisii's disciple, Leonid, introduced it and the legendary St. Seraphim of Sarov (1750-1833) brought about its lasting fame and recognition. The latter's success was also due to its wise balance between contemplation and the service of one's neighbor. Optina Pustin became in and after the time of St. Seraphim through the monks and the *Startsi* one of *the* spiritual centers of Russia. The role, the spirituality, and the radius of their work would undoubtedly merit a separate chapter. The significance for us is the charitable and anthropologic character of their spirituality and its influence on Russian religious consciousness and theology.

104. Translated by Paisii himself.

105. Cf. Maloney, *A History of Orthodox Theology since 1453,* pp. 49-50. Florovskii speaks in this context of the church's reply "to the shallowness of an Enlightened Age with a renewed spiritual concentration." WoRT I, p. 156.

106. Understood as Alexander I (1801-1825).

107. WoRT I, p. 160.

tempt at a theology based on experience, in contrast and as a counterweight to scholastic erudition."[108]

3.6. *An Absolute Novelty:* Lay Theologians and Modern Theology

There is an entire *panopticum* of theological personalities and religious thinkers who contributed in some way to the development of theology and theological streams that we forcibly will have to omit in our brief introduction to this complex epoch. Apart from their multitude, the challenge of the task consists in the difficulty of making evident these new theological approaches without extensively contextualizing them.

One of the unique occurrences of nineteenth- and twentieth-century Russia in search of a *proper theological identity* was the emergence of "lay theologians," introduced by the revival of the so-called "nonpossessor" tradition.[109] With their surfacing came also the "birth of the first true Russian theology," which was attributed to the person of the *elder Slavophil,* Alexander S. Khomiakov.[110] Khomiakov, a temperamental and gladly polemical, wealthy nobleman and officer of the Royal Cavalry, became, paradoxically, the *first*

108. WoRT I, p. 159. Also: "St. Tikhon combined an intense concentration of the spirit with an exceptional capacity for tenderness and love. He spoke of love of thy neighbor, of social justice and charity no less resolutely than did St. John Chrysostom. St. Tikhon was an important writer. Grace and plasticity of images adorn his books." Ibid.

109. The story of the revival goes back to a time span between the sixteenth and eighteenth centuries and consisted in three streams: two were of the so-called "Possessor," the two sections of the "Josephian party" (those who rejected westernization of the country yet supported the Government and Orthodox tsardom, and those of the so-called "Old Believers" who radically refused any compromising with the government, including in the matters of the imposed over-procurator, liturgical reform, and the official and established Church); the third stream was the "nonpossessor" type, which we could call the "pacific" stream, as it rejected the use of force. According to Zernov, the last one was the least known abroad yet it brought forth the most brilliant minds and greatest saints, such as St. Tikhon of Zadonsk. This illustrates once more the epoch's complexity. Cf. Zernov, *Moscow the Third Rome,* pp. 83-87. A further cause for the appearance of "lay theologians" could be that the theological schools in Russia were externally isolated from everyday life, thus considered by some as uninvolved and life-distant. Cf. Zenkovsky, *A History of Russian Philosophy,* pp. 532-33.

110. It is one of the paradoxes of Russian religious history that a layman, a retired officer of the Royal Guard, Alexis Khomiakov (1804-1860), was the first to formulate in terms of modern thought the experience of his mother church. Cf. Zernov, *Moscow the Third Rome,* p. 86.

Russian lay theologian.[111] The idea of "sobornost'," a fundamental concept of "ecclesial collegiality" and "universality" in ecclesiology,[112] made him well known in the theological world and gained him the fame of an *initiator* of modern theology.[113] Valliere places Archimandrite Feodor, to the world known as Aleksandr Matveevich Bukharev (1824-1871), in the rank of "Russian Orthodoxy's first modern theologian" out of an interesting and compelling need, then and now: he was ". . . the first Russian theologian who recognized modernity as a theological problem and placed the problem at the center of his work." Subsequently, Valliere clarifies that "Bukharev was not the first Russian Orthodox thinker of the modern age" but lists Chaadaev, Odoevsky, Khomiakov, Kireevskii, and "other lay aristocrats," as such. Nevertheless, Valliere poses a valid argument that Bukharev "represents the *starting point* of the Russian school better than the lay philosophers because he was a church theologian" educated in Orthodox theological schools and "spent most of his career in ecclesiastical institutions" with little or no influence from European culture; therefore, he was, so to speak, "completely homegrown."[114]

3.6.1. The Heart of Communion

As for Khomiakov, between the 1850s and the 1860s, his rendering of the term *sobornost'* became *the* designation of what sort the true church's character should be: *a communion of love* based on the model of a primitive Jerusalemite church as described in Acts 2:42.[115] It meant that all, from the laity up to the

111. Cf. Bolshakoff, *Russian Nonconformity,* p. 155. This is a generic view of many historians, whereas I. Kireevskii is considered to be the philosopher of the Slavophils.

112. Translated and interpreted also as *synodal conciliarity, ecclesial collegiality, community,* but equally includes *universality, integrality,* and *catholicity* — from the Russian term *sobor (cathedral, council, synod),* and it refers to the hierarchical relationships in the church that are meant to be based precisely on a *conciliar spirit,* or a communion that reflects *universal ecclesial collegiality.* Cioffari renders it with *free consensus* or *free unanimity (l'unanimità libera).* Cf. Cioffari, "Breve storia della teologia russa," p. 26.

113. Cf. SPFR, p. 110.

114. "Feodor was also a church theologian in the substantive sense of the word, taking Orthodox dogma as the framework for his thought. He did not think *about* Orthodox dogma but by *means of it.* He would not have known how to proceed in any other way. The lay philosophers, by contrast, came to the Orthodox dogmatic tradition, if at all, from an intellectual starting point outside of it." Cf. Valliere, *Modern Russian Theology,* pp. 8-9.

115. With this elaborate yet straightforward concept, Khomiakov proposed the "Orthodox model of Church" relationship also as a counterpart to the perceived Roman Catholic authoritarianism and Protestant individualism. Cf. Piovesana, *Storia del pensiero filosofico russo (988-1988),* pp. 109-10.

bishops, were welcome and expected to take part in the process of decision making of the church and thus safeguard its *true, orthodox,* or *catholic* character. Later, many would refer to this gnoseological concept, namely the quest for truth through the communion of love, including some of the most remarkable philosophers of modern times like Solov'ev, and become followers of his ecclesiology.[116] Khomiakov wrote frequently in French and published abroad, as his writings, due to their criticism of *Westernism* and the Petrine reforms, remained subject to church and governmental censure.[117] What certainly united Khomiakov and Kireevskii in religious thought was their common opposition to the West, even though at the beginning there was some appreciation in Kireevskii for Chaadaev's more moderate views than the ones that Cioffari pointedly titled *Better Rome than Byzantium.*[118]

3.7. Diverse Approaches to Theology and Their Schools

Apart from the lay theologians and the original figure of Bukharev, there were other theological streams — and here we can speak of schools — in nineteenth- and twentieth-century Russia and even abroad that we wish to address and highlight the particularities of. The *dogmatic theology* composed in *manuals,* known as *Manualistic* or *Academic theology,*[119] was created primarily by priests and bishops of the Russian Orthodox Church. Among those who wrote a manual of dogmatic theology, the significant ones were Makarii Bulgakov, Sil'vestr Malevanskii, Nikolai Malinovskii, and Filaret Gumilevskii, who was also known as Chernigovskii. An exception embodies Metropolitan Filaret V. Drozdov, also known as Filaret of Moscow, who never wrote a manual of dogmatic theology in a proper sense but composed

116. Cf. Piovesana, *Storia del pensiero filosofico russo (988-1988),* p. 110. Nevertheless, not all were so enthusiastic about Khomiakov's concept of *sobornost'* (among others, P. Florenskii), lacking its rootedness in the Church tradition, especially the councils, and perceived as denying the longstanding tradition of the visible authority of the Orthodox Church. Cf. p. 120. The other idea that moved this philosophic-theological world of the epoch was Kireevskii's brilliant concept of *tsel'nost'* or *tsel'noe znanie,* i.e., *integral knowledge.*

117. This was true for I. Kireevskii as well, except that he published in Russia and thus was more under the magnifying glass of the authorities. One would assume that there was a substantial and cordial consensus between the two *elder Slavophils,* but their correspondence reveals that that is far from true.

118. Cioffari, "Breve storia della teologia russa," p. 23.

119. Even though its representatives may have not defined themselves as such, namely "Manualists."

a *catechism,* and whose other works were extremely influential during and even after his time.

Any later theological and philosophical development in Russian religious thought is unthinkable without the contribution of nineteenth-century *founders of modern religious philosophy,* N. Fedorov and V. Solov'ev, whereas the accent in this case lies definitively on the second author.

We recognize A. Beliaev, M. Tareev, P. Svetlov, Bishop A. Khrapovickii, and Metropolitan S. Stragorodskii as ambassadors of the *moralist school* for their particular attention to issues concerning ethics, customs and morality, and pastoral care (especially in the case of the latter two) in their works.

P. Florenskii, S. Bulgakov, and in most aspects, L. Karsavin, brought the novelty of a profoundly intuitive, personal, but also speculative theology, compliant with the great *ecclesiastic tradition* of Christ's Church and with particular attention to the intra-Trinitarian and anthropologic aspect of God's divine Presence. We consider them among the true heirs of the Slavophil perceptibility for God's loving care for His creation, and specifically, for his closest resemblance, the human being. Their work and intuition would be best defined with the title of *the mystical-wisdom stream of theology.*

Further, we have created a group from exiled philosophers and an artist who pondered upon *love* in their respective fields while working and publishing in the West. They too remained faithful to their Russian intellectual formation and heritage, meanwhile seeing their forced sojourn in the West as an opportunity and even task for exchange and mutual enrichment between East and West.

Finally, we shall analyze the so-called *Neopatristic school* whose members closely followed the Slavophil ideal of a "return to the Fathers," which at times created an unyielding interpretation of patristic methods. Their works had a deep affinity for spiritual concepts yet possess notable disparities between the criticizing but not always historical-critical approach of a G. Florovskii to a refined and sensitive spirituality of an N. Afanas'ev or A. Schmemann, for instance. As for spiritual and pastoral value, here too we found a wealth of important insights in the majority of their works.[120]

120. "The Orthodox faith is expressed, jointly, by its spiritual tradition and the declared dogmas of the Church, by the lives of the saints, and by the doctrines of its teachers (the Fathers of the Church and other theologians). It is both the *lex orandi* and the *lex credendi* of the Church." Meyendorff, *The Orthodox Church,* p. 191. Or as V. Losskii states: "There is [therefore] no Christian mysticism without theology, but, above all, there is no theology without mysticism." V. Lossky, *The Mystical Theology of the Eastern Church* (Crestwood, NY: St. Vladimir's Seminary Press, 1976), p. 9.

The list of authors of the last two schools (as of the others) are not fully exhaustive since our aim and the frame of this research are focused on those theologians who have had a significant contribution to or novel theological concept of the divine and/or human love, searching above all for the concept commonly known to Christianity as *agapē.*

4. V. S. Solov'ev and the Openness to Christian Metaphysics: The Dialogue between Philosophy and Theology

4.1. The Missing Bridge

By the end of the nineteenth century, almost every western spiritual current and philosophical tendency was present and evident in Russia. With the appearance of the universities, enlightenment further consolidated secular ideas in the society. This included Voltairian freethinking in the first half of the eighteenth century and Freemasonry in the second half, along with the French and German mysticism of Saint-Martin, Jacob Boehme, Johann Arndt, and others. Though there is a general concordance attributing the beginning of independent philosophical thought to the elder Slavophils, especially I. Kireevskii, its proper development began when Russian intellectuals' interest awakened, as already mentioned, to German Idealism. Translations into Russian of the works of Kant, Fichte, Schelling, and Hegel were diligently hand-copied by students who came from all over Russia to study at the universities.[121] These thoughts, unsurprisingly, influenced theology and subsequently clashed openly with atheism, materialism, and Marxism, which were the results of enlightenment.[122] To reconcile what was so alien-

121. According to V. F. Odoevskii (1803-1869), Schelling meant as much to humankind of the nineteenth century as Columbus to the fifteenth by his discovery of a long-forgotten part of the world, its *soul,* and Florovskii speaks of a time induced by German Idealism, a time of excited search and intense discussions where "something very important occurred: thought awakened." WoRT II, p. 3. The latter equally points out that the need for "illumination," which was real and longed for, was expected to be of an inner character and not merely *independent speculative thought,* meaning philosophy. The title of the chapter cited, "Creation of a Theological Consciousness," speaks for itself. Cf. p. 5.

122. "Wollte man dieser Frage nachgehen, so würde sich zeigen, dass sich bei Behandlung theologischer Probleme um die Wende vom Mittelalter zur Neuzeit erst der Einfluss von Humanismus und Renaissance bemerkbar macht — wenn auch überwiegend negativ als Reaktion, wie beispielsweise in der Theologie Maximos' des Griechen. Später muss sich die östliche Theologie mit der Aufklärung, dem modernen Atheismus und dem Materi-

ated from religion, religious perception, and faith seemed to be an unattainable achievement. What were the biggest, yet probably never candidly formulated challenges of the theology of the time? There was tension resulting from vast differences in Russia during the epoch: the Intelligentsia, which was skeptical of anything with the slightest hint of *backwardness,*[123] social classes that ranged from utmost poverty and misery of the *gleb* to the outrageous wealth of some of the nobility,[124] and the (apparent) obsoleteness of Christian teaching in its incapability to bring about change and thus social justice for the masses (causing also the extraordinary popularity of Marxism initially). These were just the tip of an iceberg with regard to social tension. In this context we need to see how the inquisitive personality and inexorable genius of a Vladimir Sergeievich Solov'ev (1853-1900) emerges.

4.2. The First Russian World Conception

V. Solov'ev was the very first to create a proper "Christian world conception" and a "system of Christian philosophy" in Russia, and he was followed by what N. O. Losskii calls "a galaxy of philosophers." Losskii also asserts that the philosophical system elaborated by Solov'ev was in "the spirit of Kireevskii's and Khomiakov's ideas."[125] And since Kireevskii is considered to be the pio-

---

alismus auseinandersetzen. Das Studium der orthodoxen Fundamentaltheologie oder Apologetik zeigt sodann, wie in ihr die moderne Philosophie, der Rationalismus, Kant, der Idealismus, Kritizismus und Historizismus im Mittelpunkt der Aufmerksamkeit stehen." B. Schultze, "Probleme der orthodoxen Theologie," in *Handbuch der Ostkirchenkunde,* p. 128.

123. The "backwardness of Russia" was a shameful thorn in the side, especially for the Westernizers, and was to be remedied as soon as possible. Church, faith, and tradition were the first line of criticism with different degrees of skepticism. For the Slavophils like Khomiakov, the *backwardness* was an undeniable fact too, but was supposed to serve as a springboard to (re-)create something authentically Russian for the future and thus become an "advantage."

124. A profound insight about the social injustice can be obtained by visiting the Petersburger palaces and residencies restored (even if not fully refitted after the sackings in 1917 or after WWII).

125. "He [Solov'ev] was followed by a whole galaxy of philosophers in the same line. Religious philosophers include S. N. Trubetskoy, his brother Prince Eugene Trubetskoy, N. Fyodorov, Father Pavel Florensky, Father Sergius Bulgakov, Ern, N. Berdyaev, N. Lossky, L. P. Karsavin, S. L. Frank, J. A. Ilyin, Father Vassili Zenkovsky, Father George Florovsky, V. Vysheslavtsev, N. Arseniev, P. Novgorodtsev, E. Spektorsky. This movement goes on developing and increasing up to the present day." Cf. Lossky, *History of Russian Philosophy,* pp. (10-)14. The contribution of I. Kireevskii was primarily in the *Russian interpretation* of

neer of modern Russian philosophy, and Khomiakov and Bukharev of modern Russian theology, Solov'ev could be designated, in a somewhat simplistic but faithful presentation, as the pioneer of the "dialogue" between philosophy and theology, including his proper decisive contribution.

This is emphasized even by Solov'ev's life, and by his spiritual and intellectual development. Almost all of his education was secular,[126] similarly to Dostoevsky's, whom he knew in person and greatly appreciated. Solov'ev, inspired by a brief attraction to positivism then materialism, gave up his Christian faith only to fully adhere to it afterwards. Like Dostoevsky, Solov'ev's *enigmatic* personality left an "indelible mark" upon Russian culture, philosophy, and theology from late-nineteenth-century Russia till our times.[127] Solov'ev was an extremely gifted philosopher, a typical genius ahead of his time, and also a visionary in both senses of the word. In his very first philosophical work, a brilliant thesis titled *Krizis zapadnoi filozofii: Protiv Pozitivistov (The Crisis of Western Philosophy: Against the Positivists)*,[128] Solov'ev "asserted the need for a synthesis of faith and reason for further progress in creative thinking."[129] The basic idea was that since western philosophy had "reached its limits," there was a need for a distinct, fresh approach, a synthesis of scientific or formal and theological knowledge that is of the Absolute. In order to achieve this synthesis, it was necessary to become aware of the present spiritual wealth of the ancient Orient, and especially of Christianity.[130]

4.3. *Personal Spirituality and Visions*

Solov'ev's visions mirrored his original personality and animated his thinking as well as his writing. He had several visions during his relatively short

---

philosophical thoughts according to their Slavophil ideals. It was also he who clearly stated that there was a need for a proper Russian philosophy and philosophical system, created out of *and* for Russian reality.

126. Initially he studied science and then philosophy, yet concern for education was in his family. His father, Sergei Mikhailovich, was a renowned professor of history at the Moscow University; his mother, Poliksena Vladimirovna, derived from a military family and was a very pious and organized woman.

127. Cf. Zernov, *Eastern Christendom*, pp. 199-200.

128. It was written and defended as a Master's thesis in philosophy in 1874, when he was merely the age of twenty-one. The qualities of Solov'ev were immediately recognized by his examiners, and the following year he was already lecturing at Moscow University.

129. Zernov, *Eastern Christendom*, p. 200.

130. Cf. SPFR, pp. 248-49.

life, but each one was significant. The first vision he experienced at the early age of nine, and he called her "Sophia," "the eternal Friend," and made her the central point of a religious metaphysics that eventually led him to become the founder of *Sophiology.* The second vision occurred during his study abroad in 1875, in the reading room of the British Museum in London while doing research on Gnosticism and mystical philosophy.[131] He worked for weeks focusing on the mystical notion of *Sophia,* the *Divine Wisdom of God,* when the vision of a "beautiful Lady" appeared to him. This vision, more accurately, *Sophia,* after a short inquiry by Solov'ev to "reveal herself more fully," invited him to Egypt, a call that he promptly followed. This experience turned out to be an adventurous journey that almost cost Solov'ev his life in the desert of Thebaid.[132] Yet the Lady kept her promise. In the desert, he had a crucial revelation of the so-ardently-searched-for *Hagia Sophia,* the *Divine Wisdom,* who, even in the Scriptures, is mentioned as a *person* from before the creation of the world standing at God's side (see the *Book of Wisdom*).

It would be difficult to determine what stimulated the one more than the other: his studies and research of mystical elements in philosophy and (medieval mystical) theology, his visions, or the proper metaphysical predisposition and openness to a divine experience that steered the course of his thoughts and work. This simply may be a too-binary and dialectic inference on a question about a uniquely creative and original spirit. The two elements, as well as the qualities of his upbringing, were indispensable parts of his personality, and consequently, his work.[133]

4.4. Russia's Intermediary Role

Although he was of Slavophil heritage, Solov'ev rose above the traditional differences of the two groups, even the East-West dilemma, and his first book is in fact an invitation to "actuate a synthesis between oriental mysticism and

131. Direct proof that libraries are not eventless places after all.

132. Cf. Valliere, *Modern Russian Theology,* pp. 112-13.

133. "Several features of Vladimir's outlook can be traced to his father's influence: political liberalism, Europeanism and a basic though not uncritical, loyalty to church and state. In taste and temperament, however, the son differed markedly from his father. Sergei was methodical, prosaic, a family man and a punctilious churchman. His scholarship was concrete and historical. Vladimir was a visionary, a poet, a lifelong bachelor. His Orthodox faith was oriented to mysticism and prophecy. His mind thrived on theoretical philosophy." The qualities of his father were especially important for the ecumenical perception that Solov'ev developed through his studies and his own reflections. Cf. Valliere, *Modern Russian Theology,* p. 110.

European thought," i.e., a philosophy with an intrinsic religious thought and approach.[134] After his experiences abroad, his visions, and his publications in French, Solov'ev returned to Russia and to academic teaching in 1876-77, meanwhile working on his second book, *Filosovskie nachala tsel'nogo znania (The Philosophical Principles of Integral Knowledge).* In the very same year, he moved to Petersburg, where he began a publicist career. Influenced by the events of the Russian war against the Ottoman empire in the Balkans in 1877,[135] Solov'ev developed, delivered, and later wrote a series of lectures on the solution of the situation. The "actual stand" was a conflict between two evils — of the European principle of the *Godless human individual* on one side, and the Islamic oriental principle of the *inhuman God* on the other. Solov'ev's proposed solution was a country in-between, Russia, the *third force* possessing a higher spiritual and religious principle of *Bogochelovechestvo,*[136] interpreted by Valliere so splendidly as "the humanity of God," instead of the antiquated and somewhat rough *godmanhood.*[137] Titled the *Chtenia o Bogochelovechestve (Lectures on the Humanity of God or Divine-Humanity),* they were delivered in St. Petersburg in 1878-81 and turned out to be an authentic personal triumph for Solov'ev. Tolstoy and Dostoevsky were repeatedly spotted in his audience. The eleventh and twelfth lessons, in particular, became a turning point towards a *philo-occidental* and *universalistic* approach so typical of the 1880s[138] and played a role in his ecumenical sensitivity and openness. Solov'ev repeatedly tried to define the essence of Christianity and the Christian faith, coming to the profoundly evident, although much-too-often disregarded, logical conclusion: this essence is the very person of Jesus Christ. Since Solov'ev fully belonged to a secular intellectual environment, these reflections of his, his personal conversion to Christianity, and his "genuine attempt to assimilate Christian doctrine to contemporary scientific and philosophic ideas," were regarded as a "genuine accomplishment." Thus, Solov'ev was well received by the majority of the Intelligentsia — however, much less so, or not at all, in the ecclesiastical world.[139]

134. SPFR, p. 249.

135. Where he himself intended to participate either as a soldier or as a war correspondent, yet he never was employed on the actual front.

136. Gorodetzky treats Solov'ev as a theologian who relates to Philippians 2:5-11, the kenotic notion in God, and to the aspects of God's humanity in his lectures on *Godmanhood.* Cf. Gorodetzky, *The Humiliated Christ,* pp. 128-39.

137. Cf. Valliere, *Modern Russian Theology,* p. 114.

138. Cf. SPFR, p. 251.

139. Cf. Zenkovsky, *A History of Russian Philosophy II,* p. 532.

From this point on, in trying to *define* Christ, Solov'ev reconnects to a former metaphysical idea worthy of his brilliance, the concept of *vseedinstvo,* which can be rendered with all-oneness, *omni-totality,*[140] *the whole of things*[141] or even the *all-one existent.* Herewith, Solov'ev addresses a metaphysical problem as ancient as humanity itself, namely the relationship of *unity,* or *oneness,* to *multiplicity* (and their mutual relationships). Philosophically, this is an irresolvable rebus up to current times precisely because the answer is not *what* but *who: the Bogochelovek* (God-man), Jesus Christ. In the Incarnation, God reveals himself as *everything* while remaining *unconditionally one.* This is certainly one of Solov'ev's major contributions in theological epistemology. From here, he develops his cosmic Christology and *integral knowledge* with Kireevskii's "new principle in philosophy"[142] incorporated as one of the basic building elements of his "Christian world view."[143]

Significantly, Solov'ev was not only an exceptionally deep and analytic thinker but also a very fruitful one. By April 1880, at the mere age of twenty-seven, he had published four philosophical, metaphysical, and philosophic-theological books, and at St. Petersburg University he defended his thesis, *Kritika otvlechennykh nachal (The Critique of Abstract Principle),* which was

140. Cf. SPFR, pp. 251-52.

141. Cf. Valliere, *Modern Russian Theology,* p. 121.

142. Kornblatt and Gustafson, eds., *Russian Religious Thought,* p. 9.

143. Solov'ev's philosophical system and conclusions are not entirely exempt from criticism. Zenkovsky brings up a summary of unanswered *questions, defects,* and *weak points* that were not addressed by Solov'ev, some due to his relatively young age at his death, others because they came fully to light first in the work of his followers. For example, "methodological dualism is matched with a metaphysical dualism," and his concept of *vseedinstvo* resembles a "modernized pantheism." Or, he places "Christian principles" as a foundation to his philosophical system, yet his "metaphysics of total-unity leads him to monism." The strongest criticism is that he emptied the Christian concept of *Bogochelovechestvo* and "transformed it from a concept bound up with the theme of man and history, of sin and salvation, into a general metaphysical concept, thus emptying it almost completely of its Christian content. . . . He did not succeed in creating a real synthesis." Cf. Zenkovsky, *A History of Russian Philosophy II,* pp. 530-31. Regarding the remark of transforming a Christian concept with its content into a metaphysical *concept,* there are views that this was precisely how and why Solov'ev reached the minds and hearts of many who previously had rejected Christianity entirely. See also pp. 532-33. In more than one way Solov'ev is to be considered the initiator of Russian religious philosophy in the nineteenth century, as well as the most systematic one, since he implied his concept of *vseedinstvo* in all "branches of philosophy." He was capable of making it accessible to modern thought and, consequently, to the following generations of Russian philosophers "like Berdiaev and Lossky" who, because of that, "could express themselves with much more freedom about religious matters." Cf. SPFR, pp. 272-73.

an extraordinary doctoral dissertation. It is more a pragmatic, philosophical methodology, "a critical method for evaluating truth claims and [Solov'ev] applies it to the dominant systems of thought in his day. His conclusion is that all of the systems fall short because they lack a connection with 'positive religion.'"[144] He also elaborated his ideas on gnoseology, aesthetics, and, primarily, ethics, which eventually paved the road to his sociopolitical concept of *free theocracy.*

4.5. *The Idea of Free Theocracy*

One final essential idea requires our attention in association with this work: a properly Solov'evian construction, already concretized in his first work, that of *theosophy.* Evidently the word derives from the conjunction of *theology* and *philosophy* and emphasizes the reciprocal enrichment and challenge of the two subjects, including science as well. Thus it could be avoided that theology slips into a theoretical dogmatism, and philosophy takes off into abstract reasoning, leaving the living human–loving God behind. The *free theocracy* is the social and political realm where such *theosophy* could prevent religion and religiosity from becoming self-contained and grant them a new opportunity to become more *Bogochelovecheskii.*

Finally, a word on his insinuated sense of ecumenism: Solov'ev was not only a "visionary" but also a "prophet."[145] As Gorodetzky remarks, he was more attracted by Rome than by the Protestant world. Nonetheless, this was not Solov'ev's own view of himself since he affirmed his Orthodox past[146] even though he was not blind to the defects of Orthodoxy. Let the historian speak:

> Before his time the Russians either accepted the West as their teacher or stubbornly adhered to their own tradition. Few contemplated the possi-

144. Valliere, *Modern Russian Theology,* p. 115.

145. "Soloviev was a poet, a social reformer, an original theologian, a forerunner of the Ecumenical movement but, like Dostoevsky, he was above all a prophet who foresaw the approaching cataclysm in the history of Russia and Europe." Zernov, *Eastern Christendom,* p. 200. The view, whether in its proper or allegorical sense, that Solov'ev was a "prophet" is not uncommon in the relevant literature.

146. Cf. Gorodetzky, *The Humiliated Christ,* pp. 127-28. She also expresses some doubts about Solov'ev as theologian and, indeed, he is considered mostly as a philosopher. Yet, fairly enough, Gorodetzky admits, and this is the most accurate description: "It is true that Soloviev . . . was so complex a personality that he should be hardly classified in any definite group" (p. 128).

> bility of restoring communion between Rome and the East and if they did, thought in terms of surrender by one side to the dictates of the other. Soloviev saw the church as consisting of three distinct and equally necessary elements personified by the apostles, John, Peter, and Paul. He identified the Gospel according to St. John with the contemplative spirit of the Christian East. Rome represented the Petrine tradition of action and leadership. The intellectual and scholarly interest of the Protestants he linked with St. Paul and with Pauline interpretation of the Gospel message. Soloviev was an optimist, believing in the possibility of Christian reintegration.[147]

According to this view, all Christians were responsible for reconciliation and social justice and carried the responsibility to work toward it. Solov'ev, way ahead of his time, "prayed and worked for the victory of charity in relations between Jews and Christians."[148] Rarely is a prophet understood and appreciated in his proper time and environment, which holds true for Solov'ev (maybe except the last point). And just as Solov'ev's personality was "complex," so were the reactions to his person, work, and visions.[149] What remains as legacy is more than knowledge; it is experienced *Wisdom,* an *Eternal Friend.*

5. The Principal Protagonists of the Religious Idea of the *Silver Age* in Russia

5.1. *Gold or Silver?*

The *Silver Age,*[150] also called the *Russian Cultural Renaissance, Russian Religious Renaissance,*[151] or "a period of theological liberalism,"[152] was a time of

147. Zernov, *Eastern Christendom,* p. 200.

148. Zernov, *Eastern Christendom,* p. 200.

149. Faithful to the vocation of a "prophet," he foresaw his own sudden death on July 31, 1900.

150. Not to be confounded with the so-called *Magnificent* or *Remarkable Decade* (already mentioned by Annenkov) from 1837 till 1848 (cf. Berlin, *Russian Thinkers,* pp. 114-18), nor with *"fin de siècle,"* where we would "discover thinkers like V. S. Solov'ev," who nevertheless contributed to it (cf. Gorodetzky, *The Humiliated Christ,* p. 127), or the *"fin de siècle"* as "Endzeit-Stimmung," which actually preceded it. Cf. R. Weber, *Die Russische Orthodoxie im Aufbruch* (München: Hieronymus, 1993), p. 298.

151. The historian N. Zernov dedicated an entire book to the subject. Cf. RRR.

152. P. Valliere, "Sophiology as the Dialogue of Orthodoxy with Modern Civilization,"

rebirth of Russian culture and intellectualism in the first two decades of the twentieth century. It followed the *Golden Age,* whose beginnings are generally linked to the short-lived *nation's poet,* the "sun of poetry," A. S. Pushkin (1799-1837), and includes some exquisite thinkers and authors, such as F. I. Tiutchev (1803-1873), N. V. Gogol' (1809-1852), V. G. Belinkskii (1811-1848), A. I. Herzen (1812-1870), M. A. Bakunin (1814-1876), F. M. Dostoevsky (1821-1881), I. G. Chernyshevskii (1828-1889), B. N. Chicherin (1828-1903), L. N. Tolstoy (1828-1910), N. F. Fedorov (1829-1903), K. N. Leontev (1831-1891), D. I. Mendeleev (1834-1907), and I. P. Pavlov (1849-1936).[153] The *Golden Age* concludes in the nineteenth century with the highly original mind and life of V. Solov'ev.[154] Again, Solov'ev's ideas will significantly influence the *symbolist* movement of the early twentieth century, orienting it towards an interpretation of love in the mystical traditions of Christianity.[155]

The adjective *silver* does not entirely do justice to its subject since the successive authors and thinkers were by no means less important than their predecessors. "The Silver Age has been the subject of a steadily growing number of excellent literary and art-historical studies. Even its name has been borrowed from the literary sphere."[156] It is true though that the sparkling originality and novelty of the *Golden Age* was to such an extent unique in imagination, daring, and innovation, not to mention an epoch of ongoing enormous social changes, that it fully merits the recognition of the title. Those who formed and shaped the *Silver Age* were greatly inspired by their forerunners; nevertheless, their work is just as lasting and influential for the twentieth and subsequent centuries. Deserving mention here are N. Berdiaev,

---

in *Russian Religious Thought,* p. 10. In his article, P. Valliere describes what he identifies as "a larger, specifically modern phenomenon" that designates well both periods, the *Golden* and *Silver Age,* especially with regard to the Westernizers or *westernizing* thinkers: "liberal Orthodoxy." It refers in the Russian context to those thinkers (in this article, specifically to the "Sophiologists") "who sought a mutually productive synthesis of Orthodox theology and modern thought — a synthesis of dogma and freedom, Christian faith and modern *creativity,* ecclesiastical tradition and contemporary culture." Cf. p. 178.

153. The list is only representative and omits some of the previously mentioned authors.

154. Cf. R. K. Balandin, *Russkie mysliteli* (Moskva 2006), pp. 161-362.

155. Cf. M. A. Meerson, *The Trinity of Love in Modern Russian Theology* (Quincy, IL: Franciscan Press, 1998), pp. 50-52.

156. "In Russia, too, the Silver Age is supposed to have followed the Golden Age of Pushkin and the poets of the early nineteenth century." In the note: "The term 'Silver Age' is most frequently used to describe the literature of the period from roughly 1890 to 1920, and sometimes is extended to art or even the decorative arts (Fabergé, etc.)." C. Evtuhov, *The Cross and the Sickle* (Ithaca and London: Cornell University Press, 1997), pp. 2-3.

S. Bulgakov, P. Florenskii, V. Ivanov, D. Merezhkovskii and his poetess wife Zinaida Gippius, L. Shestov, V. Rozanov, and the "poets of the *Silver Age* such as A. Blok, A. Bielii,[157] further S. Frank, P. Struve, Prince E. Trubetskoi," and L. Karsavin.[158] Many of these thinkers, especially those of the first part of the twentieth century, lived in exile, which did not prevent them in preserving or even further developing their national culture and heritage. According to R. Balandin, "the greatest contribution comes from those who struggled on in the homeland. Though not all of them may have 'come forth' from the nineteenth century, they descend, nonetheless, from the spiritual disclosure of that age."[159] This statement may reflect the feelings and desires of the author in his rather popularizing book. Yet it would be impossible to defend its validity, especially considering the number of expatriated and émigré Russian intellectuals and their work after 1917. An exception was the notion of the prominently present *Symbolism*[160] that marked the first quarter of the twentieth-century Russian culture and its religious thought.

5.2. Russian Symbolism

In Russia, *Symbolism* was an attempt to respond mostly by means of art to the "unanswered questions" raised and left behind at the end of the nineteenth century and the "fin de siècle."[161] These questions wrestled with the *mystery of creation,* unsatisfactorily solved by the Darwinian theory of evolution. Neither could the "dogmatic" truths of positivism placate the intellects, let alone souls. Solov'ev's and (to some extent his rather unusually original, to say the least, elder contemporary Slavophil) N. Fedorov's visions decisively inspired the "younger generations of Russian thinkers and thus gave rise to the remarkable growth of religious thought in early-twentieth-century Russia."[162] "A desire to understand the symbolic lan-

157. Cf. Berdiaev, *The Russian Idea,* pp. 14-15.

158. A more extensive list can be found in Zernov, *Eastern Christendom,* pp. 202-3.

159. R. K. Balandin, *Russkie mysliteli* (Moskva 2006), p. 372.

160. A. Pyman dedicates an entire elaborate work to the epoch and the phenomena of *Russian Symbolism.* Cf. A. Pyman, *A History of Russian Symbolism* (Cambridge: Cambridge University Press, 1994). The other notable movement was the *Novoe religioznoie soznanie (The New Religious Mind* or *Awareness).*

161. Cf. Pyman, *A History of Russian Symbolism,* p. xi. Among the major symbolists we find Merezhkovskii, Ivanov, Bielii, and Blok.

162. *Russian Religious Thought,* p. 9.

guage of Christianity became fashionable and brought some leaders of the Intelligentsia into the Orthodox Church."[163] M. Meerson's description of the time is rather illuminating in order to establish the connection between *symbolism* and *medieval love mysticism:* "The Russian Silver Age discovered medieval love mysticism and reintroduced it in various forms. Symbolist poets stylized the troubadour poetry of the twelfth and thirteenth centuries and proclaimed Dante their patron and mentor."[164] In this context it is necessary to mention one of the intense theological debates and reflections of the Silver Age, that is, the *Imiaslavie,*[165] a concept and action of praising God's divine Name, correctly rendered as *Name-veneration* or *Veneration of the Name.*[166]

5.3. *The Return of the Intellectuals to Faith*

The influence of positivism on the younger generation of the Intelligentsia that, in most cases, resulted in some of the involvement in materialism and Marxism, has already been mentioned. The Silver Age, a *time of art, poetry, and literature,* was remarkable for a reviewing of positions on the part of those who were disillusioned by the utopian promises of Marxism, which proved even more hollow and pitiful in light of their rediscovered Christian

163. Others embraced occultism, theosophy, or simply relied on their proper inspiration. Cf. Zernov, *Eastern Christendom,* p. 202.

164. Further: "Seeking to re-establish a post-Renaissance humanism upon spiritual foundations, they regarded Dante as 'the chief representative' of the Renaissance because Dante was a Christian mystic who incorporated the legacy of classical antiquity into his Christian Trinitarian outlook. Silver Age thinkers came to consider the Western twelfth to fourteenth centuries with their mystical concept of the human being as [a] microcosm, as the very foundation of Renaissance humanism. They perceived, however, this medieval Christian renaissance through the prism of modern anthropocentrism. They highlighted the mystical foundations of medieval culture, but presented the relations between culture and religion in the existentialist terms of modernity. And they valued medieval mysticism as the religious ground for contemporary personalism. Soloviev's Platonist aesthetic and 'religious materialism' provided fertile soil for Russian Symbolists. They embraced his concrete idealism which, in turn, directed their attention to the exemplarism and symbolism of the Western Middle Ages." Meerson, *The Trinity of Love,* p. 50.

165. Khoruzhii places it in the context of what he defines as the "Moscowian school of Christian Neoplatonism." Cf. S. S. Khoruzhii, *Opyty iz russkoi dukhovnoi traditsii* (Moskva: Parad Izd. Dom, 2005), pp. 287-308.

166. Translations indicating "worship" should be avoided since they do not render the correct concept and can lead to misconceptions.

faith.[167] For many, it was a sensible return to the identity and roots of their own families, except that now it occurred through a fully conscientious and intellectual choice. The secularly trained intellectual skills of the *"Bogoiskately" (Seekers of God)*, as they were known in the Intelligentsia, were implemented with renewed vigor, this time not against but on behalf of the Christian faith, church, theology, and philosophy. Surely, it is not sentimental to recall the Gospel parable about the prodigal son in Luke 15:11-32, especially as their conversion was upheld as "some form of return to the 'faith of our fathers.'"[168] Zenkovskii corroborates that after the Russian Intelligentsia "broke away from the church," it underwent repeatedly and in different *waves* the notion of "reviewing its attitude towards the Church." For the majority of them, the church, and faith in general, meant the Russian Orthodox Church, and only in rare instances was it the Catholic Church.[169] The presence of a "historiosophical universalism" (that according to Zenkovskii "involved an inevitable return to religious questions") came into full bloom during the Silver Age thanks to — and, at the same time, in spite of — Chaadaev:[170]

167. In J. Scanlan's view "trenchant critiques of Marxism and of Bolshevik rule" were the *final* and *very specific* contribution of the *Silver Age* representatives precisely for their own experience and involvement with these movements. The same stands specifically for the criticism coming from the "exiled ones" and the outsiders, which stretched into the late twentieth century: "Others, though not so prophetic [as S. Bulgakov], were able to follow and critically analyze the unfolding Soviet experience from the outside (but with an insider's sympathies) in a way not possible for those caught up in it. Together, these early and later Russian critics of Soviet Marxism created a literature that could explain to Russian readers of the glasnost era and beyond just what had gone wrong in their society. For interested Soviet readers, the sophisticated critiques of Marxism offered by the religious philosophers were one of the main attractions of their writings. Much of the case against Marxism as it is formulated in Russia today consists of arguments originally advanced by Bulgakov, Berdiaev, and other representatives of Russian religious idealism." J. Scanlan, "Religious Philosophy in Russian Culture Today," in *Russian Religious Thought*, p. 252.

168. *Russian Religious Thought*, p. 10.

169. Rumors of Solov'ev's conversion to the Catholic Church have been denied by Solov'ev himself, although he never camouflaged his sympathies and appreciation for the Catholic Church.

170. The above-mentioned *reviewing* of the Intelligentsia and its alienation from the church, in a less dramatic and visible way, began already in the eighteenth century after the first enthusiasm for positivism died away. It then resurfaced after Chaadaev's criticism in his early theories on Russian history as well as Russia's role in history (which in his view was excluded from divine Providence and the "mystery of the age"), and once more after the experience of socialism and materialism in the time of *Silver Age.* In a philosophical context Zenkovskii speaks of a "theurgical restlessness" that was a *retained feature* of the "former ec-

> Finally, in Chaadaev the idea of the church took on such a profound and fundamental importance that the meaning of history itself could no longer be revealed apart from it. . . . But, after Chaadaev, other thinkers appeared who defended the primacy of the idea of the church with just as much passion and inspiration, but found the "true" church in Orthodoxy, with which Russia was organically fused, rather than in Catholicism, which was historically alien to it. This made it possible for the religious position of these thinkers to fructify the ideological searching of the Russian Intelligentsia in a creative way. And, in fact, the religious thinkers who associated themselves with the Orthodox Church became the leaders and inspirers of a powerful, creative, and daring movement that sought in the ecclesiastical consciousness an answer to all the complex and tormenting problems of life. This was also the beginning of a very deep and fruitful tendency in Russian philosophy.[171]

This period fostered the flourishing of new philosophical and religious circles that facilitated encounters between "the newly educated clergy" and the "returning intellectuals" — which was an idea of Merezhkovskii.[172] Some of these circles sprang up as a Christian counterbalance to the violence and violent manners that raged in the country after the devastating defeat of the tsarist army by the Japanese in 1905 and the "Sunday of Blood" on January 22, 1905, which ignited the first revolution of the twentieth century.

Among the returning intellectuals was the economist Pietr B. Struve (1870-1944), the leader of a movement called "legal Marxism," which became more popular and established itself in the 1890s. He got deeply involved in Marxism as early as 1888 during his university years in Petersburg, where he got to know Lenin and Plechanov. The Communists were well aware of the need for a strong working class, "the industrial proletariat," in order to achieve an impact on the peasant class in Russia (a goal that had remained up to that point fruitless). Ironically, on the other hand, obtaining the desired strong working class was possible only through the loathed Capitalism.

---

clesiastical consciousness" and of the themes of *universally human character* that were still alive or even strengthened in most members of the Intelligentsia. Cf. Zenkovsky, *A History of Russian Philosophy I,* pp. 171-72.

171. Zenkovsky, *A History of Russian Philosophy I,* pp. 171-72.

172. Cf. *Russian Religious Thought,* p. 10, and also SPFR, p. 315.

In a way, it was in their utmost interest that Capitalism should not cease until the needed force was at hand.[173] Throughout its history, Communism would prove that its ideology was nothing but a utopian dictatorship where the goals legitimated any means to attain them. The conversion of Struve and others (like Bulgakov, Berdiaev, and Frank, which then inspired and encouraged others) was of utmost significance.[174]

5.4. The Publishing of the Epoch

Leading up to this point in history was the appearance of a volume titled *Problemy idealizma (The Problems of Idealism)* in 1903, written by the aforementioned thinkers, as well as the publication in 1907 of a remarkable volume titled *Vekhi (Signposts)*,[175] in which four of the best-known and respected members of the materialist and Marxist-oriented Intelligentsia, philosophers, and economists[176] aired publicly their disillusionment in positivism and their intention of returning to Christianity. *Vekhi* stirred so much furor that it had to be reprinted five times in the first six months of its first publication. Its success, also called the *succès de scandale*,[177] was due to its "frontal attack of the radical Intelligentsia" primarily launched by Struve. The main intellectual contribution of *Vekhi* was in its precise analysis of the "philosophy professed by the Intelligentsia," the exposition of the inconsistency in the Intelligentsia's political program,[178] and the prediction of the "fatal consequences for the Order of proceeding along the chosen path," i.e., warnings against radicalism:

173. Cf. SPFR, p. 307.

174. Zernov links this event with the collapse of the St. Petersburg Empire in 1917: "On the eve of this momentous event four leading Marxists became converts to Christianity and abandoned their former materialistic outlook." RRR, 131.

175. Or *Landmarks:* "All the authors who contributed to this symposium . . . stood out against the materialism of the Russian intelligentsia and atheism 'uncivilized and uncritical, taken for granted from Belinsky onwards.' *Vehki* marked a date in the history of Russian intelligentsia and, long before the events of 1917, it was a spiritual overcoming of the atheistic revolution." Characteristic for the whole *turn of attention* is a preceding statement on the same page: "Instead of economic systems there is now the vision of Providence and Wisdom." Gorodetzky, *The Humiliated Christ*, p. 157.

176. As mentioned previously: P. Struve, S. Bulgakov, N. Berdiaev, and S. Frank.

177. Cf. RRR, p. 112.

178. Especially, the more radical left and extreme left-wing representatives who would turn to means of terrorism.

> Its philosophical criticism of positivism, its repudiation of the fundamental doctrine of the radical Intelligentsia — belief in the revolution, was shouted down by the left-wing press as an unheard-of betrayal of a sacred heritage. The contributors to *Vekhi* were condemned for their assault on the great "saints" Belinsky, Granovsky, Chernyshevsky, and Pisarev; they were denounced as opponents of enlightenment and enemies of progress. The storm produced by this symposium was an indication that its authors hit accurately at their target.[179]

The definitive split in the ranks of the Intelligentsia, and its division line in the same instance, had plainly become the faith in Christ. The new optic of *return to the faith of the Fathers* fundamentally altered the illumination of the matter of dispute. From this point on, for those involved, faith was not just one among the topics, but the very goal and method of approaching and examining their social, philosophical, and metaphysical quest for *Truth.*[180] After long and tense inner struggles, the ex-Marxists concluded that atheism was a false interpretation of reality and only Christianity had the satisfactory "solutions of life's mystery."[181] Their attention would turn towards *symbolism,* and they "advanced Solov'ev's *participational* metaphysics in the field of aesthetics by drawing generously from mystical sources and making extensive use of western medieval mystical and love traditions."[182] Furthermore, the (re-)discovery of medieval love mysticism and its theology was a precious innovation in theology and greatly inspired theologians, philosophers, and aestheticians (e.g., Florenskii, Bulgakov, Karsavin, and Ivanov), and it was formalized in *religious humanism.* Later it spawned a wider interest in the Solov'evian concepts of *Wisdom, Sophia,* and *Sophiology.*

5.5. Revolution and the Ships of Philosophers

This thriving intellectual-spiritual activity was drastically and sadly interrupted by the tragic events of the civil war and the Bolshevik Revolution, and from 1921 was followed by the expulsion of hundreds of scholars and

179. RRR, p. 112.

180. On this point, Berdiaev, for example, would make a notable distinction between *Istina,* a *philosophical, ideal truth,* and *Pravda,* a *moral truth* of the Intelligentsia.

181. Cf. Zernov, *Eastern Christendom,* p. 204.

182. Meerson, *The Trinity of Love,* p. xvii.

philosophers, along with their families, from the country. They were deported on two infamous ships known as the "Philosophers' Ships."[183] Those few remaining behind who would not or could not leave Russia were silenced, or exiled into "labor" camps and/or executed. Well known is the tragic end of Father Pavel Florenskii who was separated from his family, repeatedly interned in a Soviet concentration camp, and eventually executed with 500 inmates in 1937. An analogous fate awaited the philosopher and distinguished medievalist Lev Karsavin, who died from the consequences of hardship in a similar disgraceful camp. Those who made it abroad got organized and created or joined existing diasporas in Eastern Europe or, for the most part, Paris, "founding universities, theological academies and publishing houses." They published their works in exile,[184] and with the passing of time, writing and publishing in foreign languages became predominant. Some of them moved on to the United States where they became actively involved in intellectual-spiritual work, including teaching and publishing, replicating and continuing their previous efforts in Russia and Europe. The claim of some that those who remained in their homeland made the major contribution is disproved by the very fact that anyone reluctant to comply with the Soviet regime was not allowed to produce, let alone to publish spiritual or intellectual material.[185] On the other side the exiles not only carried on their work but also interacted intensively with their surroundings, enriching and being enriched in their turn by western thinkers and schools. Their work was a substantial contribution to ecumenism and mutual rapprochement between the eastern and western churches, as well as theology and philosophy.

183. As a matter of interest, some of the orders of expulsion, like that of S. Bulgakov, were signed personally by Lenin. See also SPFR, pp. 344-52.

184. Cf. *Russian Religious Thought,* p. 10.

185. "Although neither Russian literature nor Russian Orthodoxy was suppressed to the full extent that Russian religious philosophy was during the Soviet era, each was compelled to exist in a conceptual vacuum that deprived it of its proper philosophical grounding and implications." Scanlan, "Religious Philosophy in Russian Culture Today," in *Russian Religious Thought,* p. 252.

6. Russian Philosophy and Theology of Exile (after 1917)

6.1. New Beginnings and Follow-Ups

The punishment of exile was not unknown in tsarist times, the preferred location being the Siberian plains,[186] as the communist regime favored later. Conversely, there was a brief period after the October revolution when the Bolsheviks chose to eliminate undesirables, especially intellectual members of society, by exiling them to the West. By doing so, they involuntarily "awakened the interest and rapprochement" between Russian Orthodoxy and the Christian West.[187] In Russia itself, the last major event of the Orthodox Church, long yearned for and hastily prepared, was the *All-Russian Church Council,* held from August 18 to November 19, 1917, and from January 20 to April 7, 1918, which was preceded by the collapse of the empire in February 1917.[188] The prompt convocation of the Council was achieved by the final and newly appointed procurator of the Synod, Professor A. Kartashev (1875-1960).[189] These were the last attempts of the Russian Orthodox Church to reestablish the Patriarchate[190] and to acquire the independence from the state that it had never recovered since the reign of Peter I. After brief restorations in 1918, 1943, and 1945, the Patriarchate was finally reestablished after the collapse of the Communist regime introduced by the well-known *Perestroika.*

186. A good example of this practice may be found in the tragic end of the *Dekabristi (Decembrists)* leaders of the revolutionary uprising of December 14, 1825, who were, to the shock of the tsar, members of the most aristocratic Russian families. For punishment, Nicolas I exiled them to Siberia along with their families. Cf. Pushkarev, *The Emergence of Modern Russia,* pp. 16, 62.

187. Cf. Zernov, *The Russians and Their Church,* p. 168.

188. Directly, as a result of the First World War, yet detectable even earlier, this was just the climax of a long-lasting social change. Meaningful are the words of N. Berdiaev, analyzing the situation and the Russian "spirit" of the time: "In the year 1917 in the atmosphere of unsuccessful war everything was ripe for revolution. The old regime had rotted away and had no reputable defenders. The holy Russian Empire collapsed, that holy Russian Empire which the Russian Intelligentsia had for centuries repudiated and combated. . . . In accordance with the Russian spiritual turn of mind the revolution could only be totalitarian. All Russian ideology has always been totalitarian, theocratic or socialist. The Russians are maximalists and it is precisely that which looks like a utopia which in Russia is most realistic." Berdiaev, *The Russian Idea,* pp. 261-62.

189. Cf. Zernov, *Eastern Christendom,* p. 206. Kartashev provided the church with every possible assistance needed in this endeavor.

190. Not all were keen on the restoration of the Patriarchate, and soon there were two camps: the *Renovationist* and the *Patriarchal.*

6.2. The Synod in Serbia and Bishop Evlogii in Paris

The majority of exiles were members of the Russian Intelligentsia,[191] most of whom eventually settled in Paris.[192] There were many who first took up residence in the Balkans and Czechoslovakia.[193] Initially, the exiles believed that the Bolshevik regime would be short-lived, and, precisely for this reason, the émigrés started organizing their daily lives in patterns of diasporas, living in *colonies*, with a priest in their midst, sustained by the assembly, and preserving tradition and customs. Soon, however, the need for a proper ecclesial

191. Zernov offers us an apparently exhaustive list of known exiled Intelligentsia members in what he titled "an epilogue to the Zernov Family Chronicle" in his *Sunset Years*. The Zernovs (including his wife Militza) themselves shared the fate of their fellow émigrés, some of whom they knew in person. The first four "spokesmen of the Renaissance" who were forced into emigration were Struve, Bulgakov, Berdiaev, and Frank. He counts the following authors among the representatives of the religious Renaissance in emigration: "Nikolai Arsenev (1888-1977); Fr. Nikolai Afanasev (1893-1960); Bishop Kassian Bezobrazov (1892-1965); Georgy Fedotov (1886-1951); Fr. Georgy Florovsky (1893-1979); Ivan Ilin (1883-1954); Vladimir Ilin (1891-1974); Anton Kartashev (1875-1960); Fr. Kiprian Kern (1899-1965); Nikolai Lossky (1870-1965); Vladimir Lossky (1903-1958); Konstantin Mochulsky (1892-1948); Vladimir Weidlé (1895-1979); Boris Vysheslavtsev (1877-1954); Lev Zander (1893-1964); [and] Fr. Vasily Zenkovsky (1881-1962)." Cf. Zernov, *Sunset Years*, pp. 34-36.

192. As to the exact figures, there are no definite data, but the total number of émigrés and exiled has been estimated at about one and a half to two million, and, contrary to the "myth" that it was just the aristocracy who left Russia (their number estimated at 140,000, i.e., about 10 percent of the total), there were many of those who were simply looking for a better and more secure life. "The post 1917 exiles were very different: this wave of émigrés represented the political, social and intellectual élite of Imperial Russia. In many respects, and at least initially, these post-revolutionary émigrés saw themselves as repeating the previous patterns of political exile. They considered themselves to be the Russian version of the French Revolutionary exiles, who were able to return within a generation." Among the intellectuals, one could find "the entire spectrum of political opinion." Cf. C. Andreyev and I. Savický, *Russia Abroad: Prague and the Russian Diaspora 1918-1938* (New Haven: Yale University Press, 2004), p. xi.

193. There was an open invitation for these Russians, who mostly taught at the universities, by the government and president of Czechoslovakia, T. G. Masaryk. For a more extensive description on Russian émigrés and, especially, their relation to Czechoslovakia, see Andreyev and Savický, *Russia Abroad*. For a specific attention to the situation and life of the Russians in Slovakia: L. Harbul'ová, *Ruská emigrácia a Slovensko* (Prešov, 2001); *Ruská a Ukrajinská emigrácia na východnom Slovensku v rokoch 1919-1945*, ed. L. Harbul'ová, M. Ňachajová, and L. Babotová, Filozofická fakulta Prešovskej University (Prešov, 2006); for the spiritual aspects of the Russian and Ukrainian émigrés in Czechoslovakia, the Czech-Russian bilingual edition of *Duchovní Proudy ruské a ukrajinské emigrace v Československé republice 1919-1939*, ed. L. Běloševská, Slovanský ústav AV ČR (Praha, 1999).

structure became apparent. The drastic and continuous anti-religious measures of the Communists against the church in the homeland exacerbated this need.[194] Therefore, a Synod was held in Sremsky Karlovtsi[195] from November 21 to December 3, 1921 with the participation of Russian Orthodox bishops, priests, and laity. Instead of unity, however, this conference brought disagreement and jurisdictional division.[196] To avoid further escalation, the Moscow Patriarch Tikhon and the Sacred Synod on April 1921 decreed that all Russian Orthodox churches in Europe submit to Archbishop Evlogii Giorgievski until a normalization of ecclesial relations with Russia would become possible.[197] Archbishop Evlogii resided in Paris and stood in opposition to the Karlovtsi Synod in Serbia. The majority of Russian clergy and laity in the West had been faithful to Evlogii anyway, and it was under him that the key theologians and philosophers of the exiled Russian Intelligentsia thrived. Until then, few Russian religious intellectuals had had serious and long-term interaction with western theology, since "Russian theological schools maintained a purely negative attitude towards the Western Confessions; their doctrinal errors were enumerated, and that was the only side of their life which was studied. Orthodox theologians hardly ever met their opponents personally, and they conducted an abstract textbook controversy against an enemy whom no one was expected to see in the flesh." Philosophy, as such, was in a completely different position because of the intense influence of western philosophers and their schools on modern Russian intellectuals and society, as is well documented. Therefore, the perception on both "philosophical" sides, Russians and the West, was rather different in comparison to the ecclesiastic and theological circles in the strict sense of the word.[198] Nevertheless, all Rus-

194. Bouteneff speaks in this context of "uprootedness" as a common denominator for all exiled Russians. P. C. Bouteneff, "Freedom and Faithfulness: An Afterword," in *Tradition Alive,* ed. M. Plekon (Lanham, MD: Sheed & Ward, 2003), p. 257.

195. Serbia in the former Yugoslavia.

196. More to this topic, see D. H. Shubin, *A History of Russian Christianity,* vol. 4, *The Orthodox Church 1894 to 1990* (New York: Algora, 2006), pp. 64-65.

197. In the hope of avoiding further reprisals as well as not to provide the Communists with additional reasons for augmenting their destructive intrusions into the life of the Orthodox Church in Russia, but also because of the political orientation and decrees of the Karlovtsi conference (namely to restore the monarchy under the Romanov dynasty and to support the White Army of Gen. Wrangel), Patriarch Tikhon and the Sacred Synod formally abolished the Karlovtsi administration by a decree on May 5, 1922 and ordered a transfer of the administration of the parishes to Archbishop Evlogii. See Shubin, *A History of Russian Christianity,* p. 65.

198. The westernized Russians, i.e., the nonconverted Intelligentsia of the time, on the

sian intellectuals shared the same fate of the *outcast*, of which some had already received a foretaste in Russia.[199] As a consequence of the exile, nonetheless, N. Berdiaev became one of the best-known and most frequently translated Russian thinkers in the western world.[200]

6.3. The St. Serge Institute in Paris

Archbishop Evlogii "stood for advance[s] in theology along the way traced by Khomiakov and Soloviev," and though he remained under the jurisdiction of Moscow, in politics, he and his followers were "more liberal and democratic," curious and open to a sincere dialogue with the West and western churches.[201] Many initiatives came forth from this group, for example,

---

other hand "had no interest in religion; they usually had only a superficial acquaintance with their own Church, and they had no desire to learn anything about the Christian tradition of the West, believing philosophy, science and economics were the sole channels leading to the discovery of truth." Zernov, *The Russians and their Church,* p. 169.

199. "Die Lage der Philosophie, des verantwortlichen Denkens in Russland war sobald man von philosophischer Absicht und von philosophischer, dieser Absicht entsprechender Form in Russland sprechen kann — *immer* — wenn auch in verschiedenem Grade der Ausprägung — beeinflusst von Bedrückung und Unterdrückung. Ob man nun die Zeit nach der Oktoberrevolution bis zum Zweiten Weltkrieg oder vom Ende des Zweiten Weltkrieges bis heute betrachtet, ob man die Epoche des Petersburger Imperiums durchforscht — die Philosophie als unvoreingenommenes Erkenntnisstreben, als Suche nach Wahrheit ganz schlicht, sowie als Bemühen, gewonnene Erkenntnisse auch praktisch fruchtbar zu machen, stößt auf gewaltige Hindernisse. . . . In der Auseinandersetzung mit den politischen und sozialen, mit den religiösen und ideologischen Zuständen ihrer Zeit wachsen viele russische Denker in der Bereitschaft, jegliches persönliche 'Ungemache' (das ist nur ein kläglicher Euphemismus für eine in allen nur möglichen Abwandlungen oft grausame Wirklichkeit!) auf sich zu nehmen, zu tragischen, ja heroischen Gestalten heran." Goerdt, *Russische Philosophie,* p. 45. Piovesana speaks in the context of the expulsion of "philosophers in exile and the exile of philosophy in the USSR." Cf. SPFR, p. 344.

200. Cf. SPFR, p. 356. Additional reading on the principal Russian exile-philosophers and their work can be found in the book of the same author: *Russia — Europa nel pensiero filosofico russo,* Roma 1995, pp. 171-93. And somewhat more extensive in F. C. Copleston, *Philosophy in Russia: From Herzen to Lenin and Berdiaev* (Notre Dame: University of Notre Dame Press, 1986), pp. 352-400.

201. Cf. Bolshakoff, *Russian Nonconformity,* pp. 167-68. The Karlovtsi Synod, by contrast, was and remained suspicious "in sentiments and outlook" of the western world. Each party chose its own way of dealing with and relating to the West, as well as to the church in the homeland, and the measure of dialogue with the Communists in Russia. Though Evlogii was keen on "advance in theology," the most able theologian among the bishops was Metro-

the *Russian Student Christian Movement* in 1923, which was a loose union of students dispersed in different capitals of Europe, and the *Orthodox Theological Institute,* founded in 1925 and named after the sixteenth-century Russian saint, St. Sergius. *L'Institut Saint-Serge* became the *spiritual center* of the group, and the representative "centre of Orthodox theology in this century."[202] "The late archpriest Sergius Bulgakov[203] and Nicholas Berdyaev were the most remarkable men in the group, and both further developed Solov'ev's daring speculations,"[204] which combined *theological originality* with *respect for tradition.*[205] In addition, Khomiakov's concept of *sobornost',* which helped those stranded abroad to distinguish between the notion of *nationality* and *nationalism,* exercised major influence on theologians and laity and created an "echo" of due interest for its openness to closer collegiality with the Catholics.[206]

A. Nichols enumerates three innovative attributes of St. Serge that are important to highlight for their joint philosophic-theologic significance: First, "a stress on the liturgical and mystical dimension of Orthodoxy." Second, "complete openness to western scholarship." Third, "a very strong speculative bend." The institute "wanted to make an original contribution to Orthodox dogmatics," and it certainly did. Church history, too, was firmly established in its curriculum. In laïcal circles, even prior to the revolution, an interest in the "philosophy of religion" and "philosophical theology" arose,[207]

---

politan Antoni, who happened to belong to the opposite camp, i.e., the Synod of Karlovtsi. Cf. Zernov, *The Russians and Their Church,* pp. 172-73.

202. "The aim of the school was to keep alive the best of the pre-war Russian theological tradition and to build on it: in expectation that one day its leaders would be called back to Russia to help re-create the Russian Church from the ashes. Well into the 1920s it was confidently asserted in the West that the Communist system in the USSR would collapse of its own internal problems within a few years: a prediction correct in substance, but not in time-scale." A. Nichols, *Light from the East: Authors and Themes in Orthodox Theology* (London: Sheed & Ward, 1995), pp. 14-15.

203. Bulgakov became the institute's founding dean and vice-rector and he elaborated and published most of his works here.

204. "The Paris group broke with the synod in 1926 and submitted to the late patriarch Sergius in 1927. It broke with Sergius in 1930, however, on a political issue and submitted to the patriarch of Constantinople, who claims jurisdiction over all the Orthodox in Diaspora — although Russians generally do not admit his claims." Bolshakoff, *Russian Nonconformity,* pp. 167-68. Once again, we can see how delicate and uncertain the (jurisdictional) relationships continued to be.

205. Cf. Nichols, *Light from the East,* p. 15.

206. Cf. SPFR, p. 121.

207. Cf. Nichols, *Light from the East,* p. 16.

which contributed to speculative dogmatics and nurtured the Russian intellect's delight for metaphysics. A fourth, non-insignificant contribution, often taken for granted, was the fact that most of the expatriated Russians now started to write in western languages; thus Russian thought and culture became (more) accessible to Catholics and Protestants in the West.[208] In a compact synthesis Nichols also addresses the cause of the main divergence of the scholastic method at St. Serge that began upon the dogmatic manual of Makarii Bulgakov.[209] Makarii's manual was a fundamental work, which nonetheless by then became, for both the "liberals" as well as the "traditionalists," outdated, "lifeless and often inconsistent." However, there was no consensus on what should replace it. "The traditionalists wanted a new dogmatic theology founded on the Fathers, the liturgy, and the spiritual experience of the Church. The liberals believed that philosophical thought had moved beyond the stage which the Fathers knew, and that a new Orthodox dogmatics must be a fresh synthesis of ancient theology and contemporary concepts."[210] The quintessence of the dispute and division that occurred soon among the Russian Orthodox intellectuals outside of Russia had a long-lasting effect on Orthodox theology and religious thought in general. The main representative of the "liberals" was S. Bulgakov, and that of the "traditionalist current" Georges V. Florovskii, "who has been called the most Orthodox of all contemporary Orthodox."[211] As a matter of curiosity, they both were devout priests yet cut from completely different cloth.

6.4. The Fellowship of St. Alban and the Nouvelle Théologie

The Theological College and Institute St. Serge was closely associated and aided by the YMCA and its press, and, because it was supervised by Russian theologians, it successfully transmitted the views of the Russian church abroad. The Theological College fostered friendly relations with western Christians; for example, the dialogue with the Anglican Church was so promising that it led to the foundation of a joint effort in 1928: *The Fellowship of St. Alban* and *St. Sergius*. Later, "this society became an important and successful, yet unofficial, channel for the relations between

208. Cf. Cioffari, "Breve storia della teologia russa," p. 43.
209. Metropolitan of Moscow in the 1880s and 1890s.
210. Cf. Nichols, *Light from the East,* p. 16.
211. Cf. Nichols, *Light from the East,* p. 16.

Orthodox and western Christians," certainly also due to the participation of theologians such as Bulgakov on the Orthodox and Bishop Core on the Anglican side.[212] Interestingly, it was the importance of the *celebration of the Eucharist* in the worship of the two traditions that proved to be of common interest and successively served as a base for further theological discussions, founded upon mutual respect and appreciation.[213] Thanks to institutes like St. Serge in Paris, Russian exiled and émigré theologians and philosophers could develop, lecture, and publish their academic work, thus contribute significantly to the intellectual enrichment, reconciliation, and ecumenic rapprochement between East and West, as well as make some surprising discoveries:

> The active participation of the Russian Orthodox in all the theological, social and ecumenical activities of western Christians during the last fifty years[214] has been a revelation to both sides. They have realized that in spite of centuries of isolation and hostility, they agree in the fundamentals of the Faith, and that their differences usually represent complementary aspects of their approach to Christian religion. Where Eastern Christians are strong, their western brothers are often defective; but where the latter can show solid achievements, the Orthodox lag behind, and need advice and help. This is equally applicable to the realm of theological thought and to the church's social action. The new books produced by the Russian theologians in exile bear witness to this truth. They have incorporated many results of western scholarship and Christian experience, whilst, on the other hand, they have themselves proved stimulating both to Roman Catholic and to Protestant writers and readers.[215]

It certainly is not an overstatement that, apart from philosophy, the literary and theological influence was the most significant result from the interaction of the Russian Orthodox with the western world. Safeguarding their tradition, these Russian intellectuals in exile dared to traverse the chal-

212. Also: "To their surprise," the Russians discovered through the dialogue with the Anglican Communion that there were greater reciprocal sympathies between them than with any other Western denomination. Cf. Bolshakoff, *Russian Nonconformity,* pp. 174-75.

213. We may just as well recall that the Anglicans played a significant part in the early ecumenical dialogues.

214. Written before 1978.

215. Zernov, *The Russians and Their Church,* p. 175.

lenges of previously unknown territories,[216] specifically, the concept of church, its nature and boundaries, ecumenism as such, and the interpretation of dogmas, all of which had been unquestioned for centuries. It was reassuring to know that they did not find themselves in *hostile territory*, but were welcomed as intellectuals. In France, they encountered parallel efforts such as the movement of the *Nouvelle Théologie*. However, the "scandal of the division between the Christians" in the church of Christ persisted. The spiritual and intellectual effort of Catholics and Protestants was one of those elements that kept many of the Russian scholars torn when pondering the daily reality of the *Una Sancta* of Christ's church, encountering the other Christians face to face, seeing and experiencing their piety. What remained among the Russian religious scholars themselves was a diversity of approaches and methods to the (re-)interpretation of theology. It created two currents and a gap between them: the *Neopatristic school*, which was aimed at a strict *return to the Fathers* in theology and an imitation of their theological methods, versus the *Modern Orthodox Theology*, which intended to respect the patristic heritage and even to build upon it, yet preserving the freedom of going *beyond* the Fathers in a positive speculation and a creative synthesis of the old and the new. This divergence eventually led to a definitive split and caused some to leave St. Serge and France altogether, and to continue their work in entirely new settings, mainly in the United States.

6.5. *God's Unfathomable Paths*

God's Spirit works in many ways and dimensions, which has been once more proven by the tragedy of exile and dispersion of the Russian intellectuals. Forcing them to abandon their beloved country and requiring them to take on this sacrifice brought forth an immense benefit and wealth for the *uni-*

216. Sure enough, not all exiles and émigrés remained entirely faithful to their own Orthodox tradition; others even completely assimilated into their new surroundings: "The approach taken by the authors here represented [Afanasiev, Bulgakov, Berdiaev, Kern, Meyendorff, etc.] is altogether different. They preserved their identity in exile, yet never retreated into a ghetto. Their writing arose out of several qualities that forbade — or rendered utterly unnecessary — a siege mentality: *security* in their faith, *love* for their Church, and the *missionary commitment* to convey the Gospel to their time and place. These people knew who they were, and were utterly secure in their identity as Orthodox Christians. Security of this kind is not the same thing as personal pride." Bouteneff, "Freedom and Faithfulness," p. 257.

versal church of Christ. The tragic event of exile proved the church's *catholicity* in the original meaning of the term, namely her *universality.* Not all of the questions were resolved, and the initial fervor and enthusiasm abandoned some of the intellectuals fairly soon. However, that we today do not decorate each other with titles such as *breakaways, heretics, apostates,* if not worse, has to do with the effort and sacrifice of Christians like these and the ones who received and welcomed them in their new homelands. There is a common task, a vocation for Christians wherever they may be. This call can be realized only by sharing and coexisting consciously: to preserve the *Good News* by spreading it throughout the world around us. Rendered through the words and experiences of a Russian exiled historian, we may say: "The wall of partition which has for so long kept Russian Christians from contact with the rest of Christendom has at last been breached. The church of Christ has been enriched and strengthened thereby, and its members are now better equipped for their common task of bringing back to Christ a world which has deserted its true Master."[217] Unity, however, can only be achieved in and through *the Love* of God and for one's fellow neighbors that has been revealed to us in His Son. This, *in His Spirit,* the Spirit and Substance of Love, is the ultimate subject and goal of all theology.

7. The Beginnings of the *Neopatristic Theology*

7.1. Traditionalists and Liberals

The appearance of what is to be later called the *Neopatristic theology or school* reaches back to pre-Soviet times in Russia and is rooted, on one hand, in the Slavophil movement and its tendencies of the nineteenth century, as seen before, and on the other hand, in the fertile soil of the Russian intellectual presence in the West. The latter can be seen either as a *locus* of research and enrichment by interaction with western theological and philosophical sources and traditions, or as an opposition to them, which ultimately promoted the original idea of *return to the Fathers.* Most probably, the result was a reading of and reaction to both elements. With regard to their proper tradition and with full exposition to a foreign presence and ideas, the *eagerness to share* and the *anxiety to preserve* mixed freely among the ranks of the Russian expatriates. And since their backgrounds, formation, and perspectives

217. Zernov, *The Russians and Their Church,* p. 175.

on the future were not uniform, the appearance of divergence and disagreement in their methods and measures was not a question of *if* but of *when*.

The two aforementioned groups, the *traditionalists* and the *liberals*, with Florovskii and Bulgakov as their main representatives, became the platform for two different interpretations of theology. There seems to be a general consensus about the reasons why Florovskii broke away from St. Serge in Paris: it was his "bitter opposition" to Bulgakov's speculative theology on *Sophiology*, and, as Bouteneff points out, especially "in its expression by Soloviev."[218] On the other hand, "Fr. Florovskii became the spokesman for what he termed the 'new patristic synthesis'; that is, one must return to patristic thought for a point of departure."[219] Initially, they all lectured and cooperated at the Orthodox Theological Institute St. Serge in Paris, which would emerge "as one of the centers of the *Neopatristic Theology* dominating Orthodox thought for the rest of the century." There Bulgakov taught and presided as the Chair of Dogmatics,[220] A. Kartashev taught church history, B. Vysheslavtsev taught moral theology, V. Zenkovskii and V. Il'in taught philosophy, G. Fedotov[221] taught both hagiography and western church history, and Florovskii held the chair of patristics.[222]

7.2. Quarrels about Sophia

The division was caused on a subject that should unite: *Divine Wisdom*. Bulgakov deepened and furthered Solov'ev's reflections on *Sophia*, God's Divine Wisdom, and surprisingly arrived at the concept of two *Sophias:*[223] *Sophia the noncreated*, the one that always existed in God and represents the inner life of the relations in the Trinity, and *Sophia the created*, which is the emanation and the "personification" of the noncreated Sophia in the created

218. Bouteneff, "Freedom and Faithfulness," p. 261.

219. In R. W. Haugh's "Preface" to WoRT II, p. viii.

220. Bulgakov derived from a clerical family and himself became a priest in 1917 after he turned away from Marxism back to Christianity.

221. "[These] . . . promoted liberal democratic values on theological as well as humanistic grounds." Valliere, *Modern Russian Theology*, p. 281.

222. "Florovsky . . . was the exception and often found himself in the minority of issues that divided the faculty." Cf. Valliere, *Modern Russian Theology*, pp. 280-81.

223. Bulgakov elaborated his coherent reflection and study of Sophia into a system and is one of the most original and notable, even though at times disputed, contributors to Orthodox theology.

World. "It is Sophia created who, in the inanimate world, praises and blesses the Lord. She is not conscious as a person might be, but she is able to give an unhypostatic and answering love to God."[224] Nichols's explanation may be closer to our actual theological comprehension:

> Bulgakov identified the Wisdom of God with the divine *ousia,* the being common to the three persons, and he held that the world had eternally pre-existed in this *ousia,* just as, indeed, according to his way of thinking, the missions of the Son and the Spirit in salvation history had been eternally anticipated in God. On the basis of these affirmations, Bulgakov worked out an entire theological system, deposited in a huge corpus of writing, much of it still untranslated from the Russian.[225]

Bulgakov's reflections on the two Sophias are analogous to the (speculative) relationship between divine *theology* and *economy,* i.e., the questions of intra-Trinitarian as well as the Trinity-creation relationship. The final result sheds plain light on Christianity's primeval and anthropological question: Why and how is God in dialogue with the world and creation? This may lead to an audaciously speculative theology, but nevertheless a legitimate one, possessing a perfectly justifiable epistemology — however, not for all Orthodox Russians, especially when we are talking about the late 1920s. It was of little help that Bulgakov claimed even scriptural and patristic sources as a ground of his theological reflections.[226]

This liberal approach to theology was for Florovskii (and, perhaps, even more so for V. Losskii) far removed from the Fathers. Florovskii's inmost conviction was that the methodology was to be found in the realm of

224. Cf. Gorodetzky, *The Humiliated Christ,* pp. 160-61. Also: "Though she is not a person, she is, if we may risk the term, 'personable' or, to use Bulgakov's words, she is not a hypostasis, but she is a *hypostasibility,* being able to assume an indefinite number of persons and hypostases." Cf. *The Humiliated Christ,* pp. 160-61. We shall briefly accentuate the topic of Sophia in the part dedicated to Bulgakov.

225. Nichols, *Light from the East,* p. 16.

226. Again, Gorodetzky enumerates some of the sources: "The Book of Wisdom, Russian iconography, Russian prayers to the Wisdom of God, some passages of St. Irenaeus, St. Athanasius, St. Maxim the Confessor, St. John of Damascus, pseudo Dionysius, Gregory Palamas." Further: "He has been undoubtedly inspired by the great Alexandrians and by the Cappadocian Fathers, behind whom we find Plato . . . Jacob Boehme and the English Platonists." Cf. Gorodetzky, *The Humiliated Christ,* pp. 160, 158. Which makes one wonder why Bulgakov should not be a "patristic theologian," or a theologian faithful to the teachings of the Fathers, for the mere fact that he goes beyond their methodology and available data.

the patristic concept and was *meant to stay* there. The *Neopatristic* approach tried to re-create the thoughts of the Fathers while rendering them more comprehensible to the current time. Above all, theology was meant to be "exercised" based on the thought and methods of the Church Fathers. Florovskii's interest lay mainly in the Cappadocian Fathers, the hesychasts, Maximus the Confessor, and Gregory Palamas. Based on the "vivid controversy" that arose between the two currents of thoughts, Florovskii eventually broke with the schools of Saint Serge just after the Second World War and left for the United States where he lectured at Harvard and then at Princeton, mainly on church history. The split was preprogrammed[227] also because Bulgakov considered some of his own ideas as well as certain disputes with western Christianity, such as the infamous question of *Filioque,* simply a "theologoumenon."[228] Even this explanation did not suffice to pacify troubled minds since Bulgakov *went beyond* the patristic tradition.[229] Eventually,

227. Florovskii bitterly opposed the sophiological theology of Bulgakov and his *speculative theology* in general. Cf. Nichols, *Light from the East,* pp. 16-17.

228. In Greek, an individual theological thesis. A teaching that has no obliging character, is, however, tolerated by the Church Magisterium and is destined to facilitate a better understanding of dogmas and doctrines. Cf. H. Vorgimler, *Neues Theologisches Wörterbuch* (Freiburg 2000), p. 619. Also: "The authors here represented [N. Afanasiev, S. Bulgakov, N. Berdiaev, C. Kern, J. Meyendorff, A. Men, P. Evdokimov, E. Behr-Sigel, M. Skobtsova, A. Kartashev, L. Zander, and A. Schmemann] were no doubt aware of the possible imperfections of their lines of thought. Consequently, they never expressed their ideas as dogmas, but as theologoumena for the consideration of the wider Church." Bouteneff, "Freedom and Faithfulness," p. 258.

229. This is a hardly sustainable claim unless taken out of context and generalized, in view of Bulgakov's refined spiritual and mystical receptivity, which is clearly reflected in his writings. Therefore, it makes one's mind pensive when one reads the following thought from J. Meyendorff and sees his citing of V. Losskii, who is considered to be the second most prominent representative of the Neopatristic school: "The Orthodox faith is expressed, jointly, by its spiritual tradition and the declared dogmas of the Church, by the lives of the saints, and by the doctrines of its teachers (the Fathers of the Church and other theologians. It is both the *lex orandi* and the *lex credendi* of the Church). According to V. Losskii: Eastern tradition has never clearly distinguished between mysticism and theology, between a personal experience of the divine mysteries and the dogmas declared by the Church. . . . The dogma which expresses a revealed truth and appears to us like an unfathomable mystery, must be lived in such a way that, instead of assimilating the mystery to our manner of understanding it, we must, on the contrary, strive to bring about a profound change, an inner transformation of the soul, so that we will be more receptive toward the mystical experience. Far from being opposed to each other, theology and mysticism mutually support and supplement each other. One is impossible without the other. If mysticism is the application by the individual of the content of the common faith to his own experience, theology is the ex-

in 1935 Bulgakov was accused of heresy and condemned by Metropolitan Sergius of Moscow who compared Bulgakov's views to the Gnostic teachings. Bulgakov responded that if any such view was close to his, it would be the "Christian gnosis."

Florovskii was convinced that there was a "break with patristic tradition" in Russia as early as in the sixteenth century during the crisis of Russian Byzantinism. Nonetheless, it resounded more as *unfaithfulness to the tradition,* and, if this was Florovskii's true perception, one can then perhaps more easily understand his urge to revive or return to patristic tradition. However, the criticism on *modern theology* receives a yet more surprising twist when we read the following lines from Florovskii himself:

> Recovery of the patristic style is the primary and fundamental postulate for Russia's theological renaissance. Renaissance does not mean some sort of "restoration" or some repetition of or return to the past. "Following the Fathers" always means moving forwards, not backwards; it means fidelity to the patristic spirit and not just to the patristic letter. One must be steeped in the inspiration of the patristic flame and not simply be a gardener pottering around amongst ancient texts. *Unde ardet, inde lucet!* One can follow in the path of the Fathers only through creativity, not through imitation.[230]

Apparently, among all the divergences between the two schools, the decisive one consisted in the expected or hoped-for outcome in Orthodox theology, in its relating to the surrounding western (and increasingly secularized) world, the other churches, and their theologies. In this sense, Bulgakov went legitimately *beyond the Fathers,* in fact, being creative in their *tradition* and *spirit* and bringing about an Orthodox theology capable and willing to deal with the (metaphysical) challenges of the day — interestingly, just the way Florovskii himself defined it in the above quote.

An illuminating insight is offered to us by Valliere in his outstanding work on modern Russian theology, where he retrieves from history the patristic proclivity for *Apophatic theology.* In his words: "*Apophatic theology* honors the transcendence of God by avoiding positive propositions, stating

---

pression of that which can be experienced by each one for the benefit of all." Meyendorff, *The Orthodox Church,* pp. 191-92, quoting V. Lossky, *The Mystical Theology of the Eastern Church* (Naperville, IL: Allenson, 1957).

230. WoRT II, p. 294.

the truths of revelation by means of negation instead." This tendency was taken up with a renewed vigor by the Neopatristic school from the 1930s and was kept up consistently in formation of contemporary western students of Orthodox theology till our days. Thus, "the apophatic bias established itself among them as well." In result, "negation" that was meant to be *a* method became *the* exclusive *patristic* method beyond its original scope.[231] Valliere quotes Bulgakov against what became the "ban" on positive definitions misinterpreting the Council of Chalcedon. "The Humanity of God, or the incarnation as a positive religious ideal, is a prime example of what Bulgakov means by a *continuation* of Chalcedon."[232] The focal point here is that before any justified negation, even from the Fathers, there was a positive message of Incarnation that reveals, again positively, *the humanity of God,* namely what and who God really is. If this is the case, then it is necessary to move beyond methodologies of the past, which is not the same as disregarding the teachings of the Fathers, in order to gain new insights and ways of communicating to our age the infinite mystery that God is.

7.3. Legitimate Distinctiveness and Divergence

Eventually, as mentioned, Florovskii, Losskii, and a number of other Orthodox scholars from St. Serge moved to the United States where, similar to Paris, they had an unhindered access to Catholic and Protestant sources as well as direct contact with such scholars.[233]

> If some of the positions of Bulgakov, Kartashev, Afanasiev, and Kern are so familiar to some of the people who never read them, it is because they were so thoroughly digested, synthesized, and re-expressed in the persons of their students — Fr. Alexander Schmemann and Fr. John Meyendorff — who in turn never failed to acknowledge the importance and influence of their teachers upon them. And yet, in our time, the

231. That is, describing God by telling what he is *not* by means of attributes.

232. Cf. Valliere, *Modern Russian Theology,* pp. 299-300.

233. Cf. Nichols, *Light from the East,* pp. 18-19. Nichols very attentively also mentions in his "whistle-stop tour of twentieth century Orthodox theology" the millions of Russian Christians who remained in Russia with very scarce intellectual-material support for maintaining and educating their faith. This has abruptly changed after the Revolution and the "advent of Mikhail Gorbachev," yet no significant theological research and theological intellectual work was possible to be conducted until then. Cf. p. 19.

> reemergence of essays . . . in their raw, original form, may well reveal something about Orthodoxy today. Might they make apparent a rift, which if anything, continues to grow ever deeper since the mid-twentieth century, between those who will leap in welcome recognition at this approach to tradition, and those who will see it as suspect, as modernist, liberal, and westernized?[234]

There are scholarly opinions even nowadays that, similarly to Florovskii, perceive the influence of western theology and thought solely (or primarily) as negative, distorting, and intrusive (in the past or present) for Orthodox theology and even its identity.[235] One has to avoid the impression, or the wishful thinking, that there were no noteworthy discrepancies among the expatriated Russian theologians and religious thinkers. There is a strong and well-founded criticism from Valliere, for example, on behalf of Bouteneff's[236] intention to *round off* the significant differences that existed among the Russian Orthodox theologians in the Diaspora. In fact, some of the tensions were present right from the beginning. Therefore general and *generalizing* terms such as "Russian Idea," "Russian school," "Russian thought in the Diaspora," and others are not necessarily helpful as divergence, discords, and even differences in methods can become a legitimate *space* where theology is progressing.[237] To Bouteneff's merit, we have his crucial observation that the underlying theme of the exiled Russian intellectuals' search was "love" for the church, its tradition, the gospel, and liturgical

234. Bouteneff, "Freedom and Faithfulness," p. 259.

235. Just for illustration, a view of a contemporary Greek theologian Ch. Yanaras: "So vollzog sich vom 15. bis ins 19. Jahrhundert sowohl im Bereich des unterworfenen Griechentums als auch in Russland eine heftige und tiefreichende Verwestlichung der kirchlichen Denkweise und Theologie — eine Erscheinung, die während der letzten Jahrzehnte viel studiert und gründlich analysiert worden ist. Diese Verwestlichung verfälschte und verbildete die Identität der Orthodoxen — nicht auf der Ebene der anerkannten Formulierungen der kirchlichen Theologie, sondern auf der Ebene der gesamten *Lebensweise*, die *individualistisch* und *rationalistisch* wurde. . . . Der hinreißende historische Schwung der Slavophilen-Bewegung lief aus in der großen Theologengeneration der nachrevolutionären Zeit, die im westeuropäischen Raum ansässig war und die hervorbrachte, was wir heute als die "Theologie der russischen Diaspora" bezeichnen. Dieser Theologie vor allem ordne ich den Anteil der Russen an der Klärung der orthodoxen Identität im gesamten historischen Weg der russischen Kirche zu." Christos Yanaras: "Der Beitrag der russischen Orthodoxie zur Klärung der orthodoxen Identität," in *Tausend Jahre Christentum in Russland*, pp. 955-57.

236. Cf. Bouteneff, "Freedom and Faithfulness," pp. 257-61.

237. For further insights, we highly recommend P. Valliere's article. Cf. Valliere, "La Teologia Ortodossa e L'Occidente nel XX Secolo," *Seriate* 30-31 (Ottobre 2004): 41-49.

and patristic texts that led them to their conviction of not dealing with a *dead letter but a living spirit.*[238]

7.4. The Freedom of Christian Creativity

Thus, divergence is needed for a creative theology; "unity" as an ecclesial concept does not necessarily mean *uniformity* of theology or of philosophical thought. Ecclesial unity points toward the goal as an eschatological concept and reality, whereas theology is a present means and tool of progress in understanding.[239] This latter reading would match Bulgakov's view; dogmas, doctrines, and their (re-)interpretation are not the same matter. Dogmas and doctrines are the cornerstone of our faith; they are not sealed off from an up-to-date (re-)interpretation, or from implementing an idiom that is comprehensible to contemporary life and society, consequently to the real needs of the church. Besides, the Fathers, although they laid a solid foundation, could not have possibly elaborated all of the topics and aspects of theology.[240] We shall not forget that the church is a communion, a *living* organism, and it is the Spirit that gives life, not the letter.[241] Did not Jesus

238. "Their clear sense of identity, and their love for the Gospel as expressed in its purity through the Orthodox Church, necessitated for these people the struggle to convey that Gospel to the people around them, where they were in space and time. The Christian pluralism of the West — notably Paris and America — did not threaten them in their Orthodoxy. It drove them to engage with Protestants, Anglicans, and Roman Catholics, to seek out Christ wherever he could be found in their respective theologies and spiritualities." Cf. Bouteneff, "Freedom and Faithfulness," p. 258. Interestingly, in the foreword of the same book, J. H. Erickson, the dean of St. Vladimir's Orthodox Theological Seminary where Bouteneff himself lectures as professor, we are offered a possible explanation of the "strict adherence" to tradition, or what they understood by it, which was the loss of tradition and traditional ways of life, a tradition that was taken for granted in Russia and their own communities, when all this abruptly and drastically disappeared through the massive changes in the lives of these expatriated Russians. The means and way of responding was by *securing* tradition and adhering to even the smallest detail. Cf. "Freedom and Faithfulness," pp. vii-viii. May all that started in fear be transformed by an honest and unbiased search for Christ into love, as we can read in 1 John 4:18: "There is no fear in love, but perfect love casts out fear."

239. Cf. Valliere, "La Teologia Ortodossa e L'Occidente nel XX Secolo," pp. 41-49.

240. Florovskii expresses this in an ecclesiological concept by describing the future-oriented task of Orthodoxy: "The path of history has still not been fully traveled; the history of the Church is not yet finished." WoRT II, p. 308.

241. *Not that we are sufficient in ourselves to claim anything as coming from us, but our*

during most of his earthly time have interpretational disputes with the scribes, pharisees, and teachers of the law? The same mistake in dogmatic theology should not be committed just because it gives a false promise of security through the belief of *being on the right side.* This would not render a just service to the significance and treasure that dogmas represent for the church, and consequently for the world too. The *Spirit* who spoke through the prophets[242] has more to teach us on the *Divine Wisdom* of God and thus on God's Being *as Love.* It has been rightly said that Christianity is the living faith of the dead, not the dead faith of the living. Our faith, as well as intellect, yearns to comprehend and embrace God's divine revelation more fully. The dialogue between God and humankind continues.

---

sufficiency is from God, who has made us competent to be ministers of a new covenant, not of the letter but of the Spirit. For the letter kills, but the Spirit gives life (2 Cor. 3:5-6).

242. This Spirit is not a *cliché* or a *set pattern.* It is a Spirit of a positive tension, of building and inspiration — on a horizontal and on a vertical level. Thus, all theological streams, schools, methods can learn from and inspire each so that theology may not miss its final scope. It is edifying to read Schmemann's reflection, with some justified criticism on "academic theology," on the subject of what he calls "theological task": "But it is at this point, perhaps, that we can turn our eyes to those whom we always claim to be our examples and teachers, the Holy Fathers of the Church, and look a little deeper into their understanding of the theological task. Most certainly they were not less intellectual. And yet, there is one decisive difference between them and modern theological scholars. To all of them, that which we call 'practical' and virtually exclude from our academic concerns meant nothing else but the unique and indeed very practical concern of Christianity: the eternal salvation of man." And to the relationship of the church and the world: "I have no doubts about the urgent need for the Church to remember that she exists not for herself but for the world and its salvation." A. Schmemann, *Church, World, Mission* (Crestwood, NY: St. Vladimir's Seminary Press, 1979), pp. 120-21, 148.

II. The Theme of *Love* in the Manuals of the Nineteenth-Century *Academic Theology*

1. Filaret of Moscow: The Theology of the Heart and the Duties of Love

1.1. Biography

Metropolitan Filaret of Moscow (1782-1867) was also known as Filaret Drozdov — Filaret being his monastic name and Vasilii Mikhailovich his baptismal name. Born in the town of Kolomna, he grew up in a very poor family. His father was a poor deacon and church cantor and it was in great part thanks to a notable sacrifice by his mother that the talented Filaret made it to the seminary. At the age of only twenty-one (in 1809) he became a monk and a priest, whereupon he was sent to St. Petersburg as an exceptionally talented young preacher. It was in this imperial city that he learned open-mindedness and the religious tolerance that was emanating from the throne in those years and then so dramatically changed under the reign of Nicholas I. From 1821 until 1864 Filaret was the Metropolitan of Moscow, an ecclesial hierarch of exceptional strength who with his personality and intellectual brilliance left a stamp on the Russian Orthodox Church and society, during as well as after his lifetime. Filaret was canonized by the Russian Orthodox Church on October 13, 1994.[1]

1. A more detailed biography and bibliography on Filaret can be found in N. Zernov, *Eastern Christendom: A Study of the Origin and Development of the Eastern Orthodox Church* (London: GPPS, 1961), pp. 179-80; *Choix de sermons et discours de S. Ém. Mgr Philarète,* trans. A. Sarpinet, vol. 1 (Paris 1866) (ChSD); WoRT, pp. 212-20 (further references to Filaret: cf. WoRT, pp. 221-59); M. Kozlov, "Sviatitel'," in *Filareta Mitropolita Moskovskogo i Kolomenskogo tvoreniia* (Moskva: "Otchii dom," 1994), pp. 3-34; V. Tsurikov, *Philaret, Metropoli-*

Given that he never wrote or composed a dogmatic manual that would comply with the title of this chapter, why should he then be included, let alone placed at the beginning of this quest? The reasons are twofold: First, we are proceeding chronologically with our authors, and Filaret's theology exercised an undeniable impact on later religious authors. Second, for his exceptional erudition and humanness, his extensive literary knowledge, the breadth of issues addressed in his talks, his vast correspondence,[2] and, most of all, his well-structured, scripturally founded, and deeply spiritual sermons collected in *Slova i rechi (Sermons and Speeches)*,[3] which at times, in their density and elaboration, resemble a spoken catechesis.[4] In 1815 his *Razgovory mezhdu ispytuiushchim i uverenym o pravoslavii Vostochnoi Katholicheskoi Tserkvi (Dialogues Between a Skeptic and a Believer on the Orthodoxy of the Eastern Catholic Church)* appeared, a work that reminds us of a Platonic dialogue between a teacher and a disciple. In the *Dialogues*, two involved interlocutors tap their way through to an answer, or assumed solution, in a thoroughly systematic question-answer, nearly dialectical, method. In 1823, Filaret published the *Prostrannyi khristianskii katikhizis Pravoslavnyia Katholicheskiia Vostochnyia Tserkvi (The Comprehensive Christian Catechism of the Orthodox Eastern Catholic Church)*,[5] which for a long time

---

tan of Moscow 1782-1867 (Jordanville, NY: Variable Press, 2003); "Neusynaiushchee oko mysli," in Sviatitel' Filaret Moskovskii, *Prizovite Boga v pomoshch* (Moskva: Izd. Sretenskogo monastyria, 2008), pp. 5-30; H. M. Knechten, *Filaret von Moskau als geistlicher Schriftsteller* (Waltrop: H. Spenner, 2008).

2. For further reference on personal and official letters see *Pis'ma Filareta, mitropolita Moskovskogo i Kolomenskogo k vysochaishim osobam i raznym drugim litsam*, Izd. Savvoiu Arkhiepiskopom Tverskim i Kashinskim (Tver': Tipografia Gubernskogo Pravleniia, 1888); for resolutions see *Polnoe sobranie rezoliutsii Filareta Mitropolita Moskovskogo*, ed. V. S. Markov, vols. 1-3 (Moskva: Dushepoleznoe chtenie, 1903-6); letters regarding different matters (primarily of ecclesial-administrative character): *Mneniia, otzyvy i pis'ma Filareta, Mitropolita Moskovskago i Kolomenskogo po raznym voprosam za 1821-1867 gg.*, ed. L. Brodski (Moskva: Sinodal'naia Tipografiia, 1905).

3. According to Florovskii these contain Filaret's "principal theological legacy," and although Filaret "never constructed a theological system," his sermons possess an "inner wholeness and . . . unity of concept." Cf. WoRT I, p. 112.

4. Filaret acquired his erudition primarily through vast reading. Yet after 1823, due to his numerous tasks and duties, he refrained from writing books because of time constraints. The vigor, richness, and originality of his thought are in fact best rendered in his sermons. He also left behind several volumes of ecclesial-administrative letters; others build a corpus of personal correspondence. Many agree that his wisdom and opinions expressed the true mind of the Russian church, especially under the unyielding times of Nicholas I.

5. The very first issue raised objections because the *Creed* and the *Lord's Prayer* were

was considered *the* standard work in Christian faith education in Russia as well as other Orthodox Slav countries. It was reedited several times, distributed in virtually millions of copies, and used in teaching all levels of society, above all, in schools and educational institutes of the empire.[6] Filaret was considered a *born* theologian, someone who lived and regarded theology as the aim of spiritual progress. Florovskii considered him the "first person in the history of modern Russian theology for whom theology once more became the aim of life."[7] He also regarded Filaret as the "most influential and prominent representative" of the new "theology of the heart" taught in the reformed ecclesiastical schools. The aim of this instruction was "the education of the inner person by imparting a living and well-founded personal conviction in the saving truths of faith."[8] Florovskii saw Filaret's strong reliance upon the Bible as "intimately and deeply bound up with his conception of the Church," a return to the "patristic style and habit in theology."[9]

---

rendered synoptically in Slavonic and Russian, which for the time appeared to be a blasphemous introduction of a vulgar language into theology. Cf. N. Gorodetzky, *The Humiliated Christ in Modern Russian Thought* (London-New York: Society for Promoting Christian Knowledge, 1938), p. 109. Besides, the Holy Scripture figured as the only source of religion; thus it was also criticized for its "protestant flavor," lacking references to the patristic and universal tradition of the church in the first edition. Filaret, giving ear to the objections, corrected the shortcomings in the following edition. The edition of 1839 was approved by the Holy Synod and became the standard catechism of the church, with an immense diffusion even outside of Russia and in different translations (e.g., Greek in 1848). Both issues have been redressed, and all the later editions that we had at our disposal (1852, 1889, 1914, as well as a dateless one from Berlin) proved to be identical in their content.

6. We can gain a considerable insight from a seventy-six-page introduction to Filaret's homilies from a contemporary editor: "Une œuvre fort importante de Mgr Philarète n'a pas peu contribué, du reste, à lui donner dans tout l'Empire une influence profonde: C'est son *Grand Catéchisme*, qui, approuvé par le Très-Saint Synode de Russie, a été aussitôt adopté dans tous les établissements d'éducation, et dès lors, dans toutes les paroisses, jusque dans toutes les familles, de sorte que l'on ne compte plus depuis longtemps, les millions d'exemplaires qui en ont été répandus de Moscou jusqu'au fond de la Sibérie et au-delà du Caucase, et qu'il n'est pas un Russe aujourd'hui âgé de trente ans et plus qui n'ait puisé dans ce livre son instruction morale et religieuse. Donc, des plus humbles degrés de la société russe à ses sommets les plus élevés, il n'est pas un front qui ne s'incline au nom de Mgr. Philarète." Cf. ChSD, p. xiv.

7. Cf. WoRT I, p. 112.

8. WoRT I, p. 220. Florovskii mentions "two divergent tendencies" of the time: the above-mentioned "theology of the heart" and the "neologism," which was a "moral-rationalistic school of Christian interpretation" introduced by I. Fessler in the St. Petersburg Theological Academy. Cf. WoRT I, p. 220.

9. Cf. WoRT I, p. 214. Also: The Scripture was *the Word of God* and always, and above all, *a book of history* (pp. 214-15).

Filaret was "the most conforming bishop of the nineteenth century"[10] and undoubtedly a "central ecclesiastical figure" in the Russian Empire of his era. By many, he was considered "an authority of the Orthodox world" and one of the "best brains of his time."[11] After the publication of his *Catechism*, he renounced the purely scientific and literary genre and promulgated the teaching of the church chiefly through his countless and extensive sermons given at almost every single liturgy in which he presided, so that he most probably covered all the dogmatic, moral, and other "Christian truths" in them.[12] Filaret was a prudent and reserved monk, a priest of great pastoral concern, and a bishop and metropolitan of great authority, a combination that allowed him to lead, support, and remain at the head of the Russian Orthodox Church for three successive reigns, each of them in character extremely different. At the same time, he was an outstanding statesman, who outlived the difficult period of Nicholas I[13] and Protasov, and who daringly opposed confessional chauvinism equally in the church and in society.[14] With these outstanding human and spiritual qualities, he was, not surprisingly, the author of the 1861 historic manifesto in which Tsar Alexander II released the Russian peasants from serfdom.[15]

10. With regard to the restoration of the church's freedom under Alexander II and the suppressing of the all-powerful procurator Pobedonostsev: "Even such an over-cautious prelate as Filaret, the famous Metropolitan of Moscow (1782-1867), who was one of the most conforming bishops of the nineteenth century, never missed an opportunity of expressing his hope that the Church itself would someday recognize the injury to national life caused by the enslavement of Christian opinion." Cf. RTCh, p. 130.

11. Cf. Gorodetzky, *The Humiliated Christ*, p. 108.

12. Cf. ChSD, pp. xiv-xv. Filaret also wrote spiritual poems from an early age, and he led a poetical correspondence with Pushkin. He was a prominent figure in preparing a Russian translation of the Bible and was also the author of various historical and exegetical works.

13. At whose coronation in 1826 Filaret was raised to the dignity of a Metropolitan, which became, in a way, a substitute for the title of Patriarch abolished by Peter I. Cf. ChSD, p. ix.

14. Cf. RRR, p. 51. Filaret's figure and his sociopolitical relevance are well portrayed by the event around the question of Alexander I's succession. Alexander I, who had no children and whose legitimate successor to the throne was his brother Constantine Pavlovich (who officially renounced the succession by word and letter), chose a secretive and peculiar way of appointing his next brother, the next legitimate successor in the row, by a signed and secret manifesto that was to be opened either at Alexander's direct request or in the case of his death. There were only three other persons in knowledge of the existence of this manifesto; two of them were key members of the tsar's cabinet (Arakcheev and Prince A. N. Golitsyn), and the third was Metropolitan Filaret. Cf. S. Pushkarev, *The Emergence of Modern Russia, 1801-1917* (New York: Holt, Rinehart & Winston, 1963), p. 14.

15. Cf. Zernov, *Eastern Christendom*, p. 180.

1.2. Dialogues between a Skeptic and a Believer

In his *Dialogues,* Filaret engaged two interlocutors in a gentle colloquy, in which the first person displays the problem in the form of a question and the second interlocutor provides the answer either directly or guides the partner towards it. *Dialogues* reflect well Filaret's comprehension of the contemporary problems of Orthodoxy and Russian society. The questions originate in a baptized Orthodox faithful who had lost his faith and abandoned the church, but now is on a quest to find "the right church," since he also wants to gain the certainty that he would attain to the *true* church of Christ. The text is a researched and scholarly reasoning that contains numerous scriptural quotations and some references to the Fathers.

One can almost assume that the "believer" (hereafter "*B*") is Filaret himself. His deep pastoral sensitivity and experience, along with a firm guidance of the quest, is easily detectable. For instance, he steers the reasoning of his skeptical partner (hereafter "*S*") to "respect and not to judge" other churches,[16] especially since this does not represent the skeptic's *real* spiritual needs. *B:* "Instead ask yourself: Are you living in an inner intimate faith (a faith of heart)? Or just as well: Is Jesus Christ dwelling within you? . . . Perhaps there are *attitudes* within you that are obstructing the action of your faith and thus also your communion with Jesus Christ?"[17] Filaret's discernment is essential and based on justice and love towards other faith-traditions, which have to be respected even if one does not concur with their faith-interpretation.[18] Instead of judging others, we shall induce the discernment of our true intentions by self-judgment, according to St. Paul's advice to the Corinthians (1 Cor. 11:31). Only when there is a spirit of reflection and pondering present in the soul should one proceed towards an actual choice of the church that represents most *faithfully* the teaching of Christ. One has

16. "Living in peace with others" and "not judging," yet discerning, were topics of utmost importance to Filaret. He refers to them at diverse occasions: for example at the dedication of the basilica of the *Elevation of the Holy Cross* on December 19, 1855. He makes clear his desire for peaceful coexistence, and only then he reprimands the teachings that contradict the Orthodox faith-tradition and the ones misleading the Orthodox faithful. Cf. *Beseda po osviashchenii khrama Vozdvizheniia Khresta Gospodnia v Preobrazhenskom bogadelennom dome* (Moskva: Tipografiia Vedomostei Moskovskoi gorodskoi policii, 1855), p. 5.

17. Cf. Filaret of Moscow, *Razgovory mezhdu ispytuiushchim i uverenym o pravoslavii Vostochnoi Katholicheskoi Tserkvi* (Moskva: Sinodal'naia Tipografiia, 1841), p. 13 (RMIU).

18. That Filaret himself would not condemn the "Latin faith" and did not allow others to do so was well known and would even leave some perplexed. Cf. WoRT I, p. 118.

to be "armed against doubts" that could obstruct his personal growth in faith and love,[19] which grows out of a deep personal relationship with Jesus Christ.

1.2.1. *In the Heart of Faith's Quest*

In the middle of the *Dialogues,* we could say in the heart of the quest, is collocated the principal *love*-related debate, exemplified on the long-disputed procession of the Holy Spirit using St. Augustine's *De Trinitate* 15,27.[20] The reasoning is based on the relationship between *thinking* or *thought (pomyslenie, cogitatio), knowledge (poznanie, cognitionis)* and the third — *will* or *love (volia ili liubov, dilectio),* which has the following Trinitarian transposition:

> "*Knowledge (vedenie ili poznanie)* is the Father;
> *the thought (pomyslenie)* is the Son;
> *the will* or *love (volia ili liubov)* is the Spirit;
> *Will* derives from *knowledge;* therefore the Holy Spirit comes from the Father."[21]

As for the question of *love* being solely an "attribute" of the Holy Spirit, according to St. Augustine, *B* refers very pointedly to the Holy Scripture:

> He [St. Augustine] thinks that the hypostasis of the Holy Spirit in God is what the *will* or *love* in a human being is. Yet in the word of God I find that *love* is an attribute of not one hypostasis, but of God's nature (essence) in general, as John says: *God is love* (1 John 4:16). The love that sometimes is attributed to God the Father, for the Son of God, is called by the apostle Paul the *Son in the love of God* [the] *Father* (Col 1:13).[22]

To discern how much of this reasoning is truly relevant for the dispute of *Filioque* is not our task here. And to state that Filaret used this passage out of his preference for *love* as *illustrative material* or *relationship* could lead to a

19. Cf. RMIU, pp. 14-16.
20. Cf. RMIU, p. 41.
21. Cf. RMIU, p. 44.
22. . . . *Synom v liubve Boga Otsa.* There is some discrepancy in the rendering of the original text in Col. 1:13, which says: "He has delivered us from the domain of darkness and transferred us to the kingdom of his beloved Son." Cf. RMIU, p. 45.

false conclusion. Nonetheless, one frequently encounters the concept of *divine* and *human love* in Filaret's reflections and correspondence; therefore, this hypothesis is not to be discarded. The true revelation of God's *nature,* the manner of his relating to the world, is *by* and *in* love, as his very essence *is love* (1 John 4:8, 16). Thus, plausibly, *B* concludes with a positive, ecumenical wish of eschatological dimensions for a union of fraternal, respectful *love:* "May the Head of [the] Church, Our Lord Jesus Christ, grant us *to reach the unity of faith,* and may He lead all into that *glorious Church,* in which one does not cast suspicion of division on the other."[23]

1.3. A Comprehensive Christian Catechism

The *Catechism* of Filaret is what we would nowadays regard as a conventional *concise* booklet of catechism. Though not considered as the most representative work of his theology, it possesses an original and deeply scriptural foundation. Filaret framed it meaningfully between the epigraph of 2 Timothy 1:13: *Follow the pattern of the sound words that you have heard from me, in the faith and love that are in Christ Jesus,* and the epilogue from Luke 17:10: *So you also, when you have done all that you were commanded, say, "We are unworthy servants; we have only done what was our duty."*[24] The division of the content follows a question/answer pattern of a textbook divided into sections based on the three theological virtues of *faith, hope,* and *love,* and is progressing in the reciprocal relations of *faith–love* and *act–duty.*

1.3.1. The Creed of True Love

Everything stands in relationship to *faith* as the foundation of truth; therefore the first section is dedicated to an epistemological reflection on the Divine, the Ten Commandments, and the twelve parts of the Creed.[25] The following section takes into consideration the "Christian concept of hope, its foundation and means." Subsequently, Filaret addresses the topic of prayer, which leads to the scrutiny of the "Lord's Prayer" in its seven requests and

23. RMIU, pp. 127-28.

24. Filaret of Moscow, *Prostrannyi khristianskii katikhizis Pravoslavnyia Katholicheskiia Vostochnyia Tserkvi* (Moskva: Sinodal'naia Tipografiia, 1852), pp. 3, 104 (PKhK).

25. There is also an excursus at the tenth part on the sacraments, with an exceptionally extensive ecclesiological chapter in part 9 titled "What Is the Church?"

continues with the "nine commandments" of the Beatitudes.[26] Finally, the third part is placed under the standard of *love* and initiates with a retro-liaison to *faith:* "There is a union between faith and love." The primary key to this relationship is not just any kind, but a proper *union.* In the light of this *union* and *interrelatedness,* Filaret reflects upon the Ten Commandments. Yet before even addressing the matter of the covenants, he places *love* in an unmistakable relationship with *faith* and *hope* and demonstrates in the resulting *good deeds* that without faith there is not genuine love of God: "What should be the work and the fruit of true faith in Christians? Love, and the corresponding *good deeds.* For in Christ Jesus neither circumcision nor un-circumcision counts for anything, but only faith working through love (Gal. 5:6-7)."[27] Similarly, he goes on in the next lines:

> Does it suffice for a Christian of one faith *to be without love and good deeds?* No, it does not. For faith without love and good deeds is ineffective[28] and dead and therefore cannot lead to eternal life. "Whoever does not love [his neighbor] abides in death" (1 John 3:14). As well as: "What good is it, my brothers, if someone says he has faith but does not have works?" (James 2:14) Can that faith save him (James 2:25-26)? "Because just as the body is dead without the spirit, so too faith without works is dead." And the same is true vice versa: "Can one, on the other hand, be saved through love and good deeds *without faith?*[29] Indeed, it is impossible that a person who does not have faith in God would truly love Him. . . .[30] The proof of *true love* is that it produces good deeds. To love God means to remain in God and to keep his word (John 14:21, 23).[31]

26. The *ninth* beatitude is *humiliation, persecution, and poverty* and the act of their acceptance due to a Christian virtue that is rooted in the *kenotic action* of self-abasement. It leads to the greatest humiliation out of love, which is *martyrdom:* "Those wishing the Beatitudes *(Blazhenstva)* must be willing to accept with joy humiliation, persecution, poverty and even death for the name of Christ and for the true Orthodox faith. What is the name of this great divine-salvific act *(podvig),* which this commandment requires? It is the feast of *martyrdom.*" Cf. PKhK, p. 125.

27. PKhK, p. 126.

28. . . . *nedeistvuiushchaia* — not occurring, not acting.

29. Cf. PKhK, p. 126.

30. Supported by Heb. 9:6, Gal. 3:10, 5:5, and Eph. 2:8-9, etc. Cf. PKhK, p. 127.

31. *Whoever has my commandments and keeps them, he it is who loves me* (John 14:21). *If anyone loves me, he will keep my word* (John 14:23). *For this is the love of God, that we keep his commandments* (1 John 5:3). *Let us not love in word or talk but in deed and in truth* (1 John 3:18).

What follows is an essential discernment and description between the "two kinds of divine law" or divine precepts: "the *internal, spiritual-natural*" versus the "*external, imposed, or given*" one.[32] The first is sustained by Romans 2:15 and the second by Galatians 3:19.[33] The differentiation then is extended by the division of the *Ten Commandments* "enclosing" two kinds of *love:* the first four regarding our duties to God and the remaining six to our neighbors. The greatest commandment is the one named by Jesus himself in Matthew 22:36-40, a composite of two love-laws from Genesis and Leviticus.[34] Thus commandments are in the first place *duties of love* performed *out of love* towards God and neighbor.[35] It is well worth noting the "order" and *final* purpose of love discussed by Filaret: "We shall love ourselves only for the sake of God, and partially for the sake of our neighbors: we are to love our neighbors for the sake of God: and we are to love God because of His very Self and in a measure superseding everything else. Our self-love is to be sacrifice *in* the love for our neighbors: and our self-love and that for our neighbors is to be brought in sacrifice *in* our love for God."[36]

1.3.2. "Feed Them with Reciprocal Love"

The commandments are founded in faith, which produces good works: for a faith lacking love cannot be a true faith, just as it cannot bring true fruits of active charity. And *love* is the first and, until the *eschaton,* the lasting fruit of true faith surpassing time and space. An excerpt from a condolence-letter to a mother at her child's death provides a good exemplification what Filaret meant by it: "Consolation and peace to you from God! Faith may sweeten for you the past, love the present, hope the future. At last, as past and future will once become a present, so faith and hope will be replaced by eternal love."[37] In his *Catechism,* Filaret sustains his answers by an abundance of scriptural citations as well as some patristic ones, leaving no doubt about the outstand-

32. The latter came as a result of not obeying the inner law planted in the human soul by God.

33. *They show that the work of the law is written on their hearts, while their conscience also bears witness, and their conflicting thoughts accuse or even excuse them . . .* (Rom. 2:15); *Why then the law? It was added because of transgressions . . .* (Gal. 3:19). Cf. PKhK, pp. 128-30.

34. Cf. PKhK, p. 132.

35. Cf. PKhK, pp. 130-31.

36. PKhK, p. 131.

37. Sviatitel Filaret Moskovskii, *Prizovite Boga v pomoshch: Sbornik pisem* (Moskva: Izd. Sretenskogo monastyria, 2006), p. 448 (PBvP).

ing exegetical competence of the author.[38] In a final verse of a different letter, following monastic traditions by quoting Scripture with pastoral sensitivity, Filaret ensures that no zealous soul shall fall into the temptation of "self-righteousness": ". . . when you have done all that you were commanded, just say: 'We are unworthy servants; we have only done what our duty was' (Luke 17:10)."[39] Similarly in the case of an *igumena* (abbess) who received too much attention and was in danger of self-complacency, with the watchful pastor's eye of a spiritual father and monk, bishop Filaret directs this advice: "If they love you, bless God for those who have loved you and that He gives you the delight to apperceive it. Only beware of thinking that you deserve it. It is God's love that *loves* in the children of God. . . . That's why nobody can ever claim: 'If they love me, it is just evident that I am worthy of it.' — Not so. Rather it is by the grace of God that good souls love you. Feed them with goodness and reciprocal love, serve them with love. . . ."[40]

1.4. Letters and Sermons

Filaret's letters and even more so his sermons are overflowing with Christ's "kenotic mind" and "kenotic mood," the mark of Christ's voluntary self-

38. This applies to most of his writings, including personal letters.

39. From a letter to *igumena* (abbess or superior) Maria Tuchkova. PBvP, p. 736.

40. In questions of *duty* and *obedience,* towards the state for instance, even in such delicate and for us remote subjects as the question of physical punishment for crimes or amendment of recidivists, Filaret addressed the issue from a "Christian point of view" and in biblical faithfulness: ". . . The Savior transmits a spiritual law (codex) to suffer and not to demand punishment for an insult (Mt 5:38-39)." If the state finds it necessary and justifiable to use physical punishment, the church does not contradict so long as it is a just and appropriate one and provided it safeguards the person's human dignity (referring to Moses in Deut. 25:3). Moreover, it shall serve the person's redemption, which is what Filaret understood under the *Christian point of view:* "It is good to *love* the sinners, but it is even more important not to burden the innocent ones. Though one is created in the *Image of God* we cannot conclude that physical punishment is not admissible. It shall, however, serve the amendment and thus be a cause of the *salvation* of the person and his soul." Cf. "O telesnykh nakazaniakh s khristiianskoi tochki zreniia" (1862) in *Sochinenie Mitropolita Filareta,* in *Chtenia v Imperatorskom obshchestve istorii i drevnostei rossiiskikh pri Moskovskom universitete,* 4 (Moskva 1867), pp. 11-15. The need of mercy for sinners was a generic need applied to all social layers as we can read in a letter to *igumen* Evgenii: "One is rich not only by truthfulness to the righteous, love to the good ones, but also by mercy for the sinners. We all are poor, and the person who fuller knows and perceives his own poverty is closer to such riches." Cf. PBvP, p. 722.

abasement during his earthly life. This *kenotic mood,* according to Gorodetzky, was present both in Christ's earthly and premortal life, as it can be inferred from Philippians 2:5-11 and 2 Corinthians 8:9.[41] The above-mentioned kenotic notions represent the true basis of Christianity and so for Filaret they are the very foundation of his writings and teaching. Moreover, he was a true master of the Russian language who rendered Orthodox dogmas concisely but also remained "integral and harmonious" in his texts, which certainly does not simplify the work of a translator.[42]

1.4.1. God's Presence in the Heart as Moral Indicator

The attentively guarded "purity of heart" and of the inner person along with the right form of love, hope, and forgiveness (as given so received) were themes of fundamental importance to Filaret, which in fact represent a deep human side of our faith, a divine-human love of God. In a letter to Countess E. V. Novosiltseva, Filaret writes: "Search attentively your heart and have nothing in it against a person; nothing that is of animosity, so as it may not take the place from Christ, who yearns to abide in hearts filled with faith and love."[43] In another letter, Filaret invokes trust in his relative towards God's providence that is unceasing under any life-circumstance: "God's providence does not leave anybody. How could one be alienated from those whom he loves? The One, Who loves us truly more than all people together, is always with us. He continues to perform good to us even if we did not wish so. . . ."[44] And as others need our forgiveness so are we in need of repentance, reconciliation with God and with our fellow neighbors. Progress in love does not consist in solely receiving it, but precisely in loving those who are most in need of it, so to speak in *generating* love, as explained in the letter to *igumena* M. Tuchkova:

> You wish to be instructed in love for the Lord. Now, did anybody teach us how to love those dear to us? Do we not love them strongly without having ever learnt it? Consequently, is it not more convenient to love what is less worthy of love [in greater need of love]? "Her sins, which are many, are forgiven for she loved much" (Luke 7:47). Where did she learn

41. Cf. Gorodetzky, *The Humiliated Christ,* p. ix.

42. "His sermons are impossible to paraphrase; it is only possible to reread and repeat them." Cf. WoRT I, p. 217.

43. PBvP, p. 297.

44. PBvP, p. 38.

> to love with such abandon? She carried tears of repentance instead of oil.[45] God's love to the repenting soul is similar to heavenly fire that descends on them and ignites their lamps.
>
> You remarked correctly that God draws us together with good and reconciled souls for our own edification. Let us love Him and our fellow human beings through these instruments [of good and reconciled souls]. . . .[46]

Filaret not only lived but constantly led and inspired others to a deep Christian humanity, especially when it came to bringing one's proper judgments over the guilt of others. What you do not want to suffer yourself, do not inflict on others, or to put it simply: apply *God's divine* measure of fairness and mercy also to others:

> They say: "Guilty!" . . . Love, however, wants to pull out this root [of accusation]. For love says: "Whether this person is truly guilty is known to the One who is the true *knower of hearts (serdsevedets);* . . . I, as a human being, can be wrong and partial. . . . If he is truly guilty, he is guilty in front of God, just like me in so much. Yet it is necessary to live in peace with him for I too wish that others may live in peace with me and in this consists love to our neighbor. For I do not wish either that in someone may remain a harsh judgment of my own guilt.[47]

One of the evidences of a true Orthodox theologian is the concept of *theosis (divinization)* present in his treatise. Filaret describes the transformation of human love into a divine one when it gets redirected from another human being towards a celestial realm: ". . . Presumably if someone lived a long life loving a creaturely person — even though it was not an illicit love, and then came to know the duty and yearning to live a life dedicated to loving the Uncreated [i.e., God], such person shall endure with patience the feeling over the poorness of his previous love. . . . At first the creatural love has to die away so the Divine love can be born. . . ."[48]

45. The talk is about the repenting woman who with great devotion anointed Jesus' feet in Luke 7:38.

46. PBvP, p. 738.

47. From a letter to E. V. Novosiltseva. PBvP, p. 322.

48. From a letter to *igumena* Maria Tuchkova. PBvP, pp. 726-27.

1.4.2. The Simplicity of an Immense Mystery

Filaret's *sermons* are deeply sensitive, systematic in structure and broad in their range of subjects. They mostly stretch over a couple of dense pages, are rich in (preferably) biblical and patristic quotations, and relate to the theme of *love* in its diverse aspects.[49] One of Filaret's preferred *love*-related sermons was the mystery of *Christmas,* in which he would associate the *kenotic mind* of Christ with the event of Incarnation.[50] So in the Christmas homily from 1812 based on Luke 2:12 we read: "Bethlehem — means house of bread — and of what [kind of bread] if not of the *living bread, descending from heaven?* (John 6:51)." In order to be "transformed into the New Jerusalem," first each faithful has to "become this Bethlehem . . . to become the very *dwelling place of God* (Rev. 21:2-3). God wants to *reveal His Son* in all of us (Gal. 1:16) by means of our own blessed birth."[51] And the Word of God humiliated himself and became a man just like one of us:

> Do not place into your hearts other ascents to God, besides the one on which the Son of God descends to the human being: "Have this mind among yourselves, which is yours in Christ Jesus, who, though he was in the form of God, did not count equality with God a thing to be grasped, but made himself nothing, taking the form of a servant, being born in the likeness of men [Phil. 2:5-7]." Do not pass speedily by the sign that has revealed itself with(in) such an unadorned simplicity in the Judean Bethlehem — for with this same simplicity is sealed the mystery of your own Bethlehem: in the external [visible] sign of the incarnated Savior is enclosed the inner sign of saving birth.[52]

It is no easy task to render the richness of language and imagery that Filaret uses in his refined, sensitive, yet persuasive depicting of the narrative scene and of the theological reality. His homilies, however, always related to

49. Prayer, sacraments, church as body and ecclesial entity, angels, spiritual reality, incarnation, Mariology, silence, prophecies, wisdom, progress, ecclesial administration (rather richly), freedom, just to mention some. They also have been written and given at different occasions. They are organized mostly chronologically rather than topically in the diverse editions.

50. Cf. Gorodetzky, *The Humiliated Christ,* pp. ix, 177.

51. Cf. Sviatitel Filaret Moskovskii, *Prizovite Boga v pomoshch: Sbornik pisem* (Moskva: Izd. Sretenskogo monastyria, 2006), p. 94 (PBvP).

52. Cf. PBvP, p. 96.

the concrete human being and his salvation, which is unattainable without the cross and suffering: a way that Jesus paved for us by his example. The cross as a mystery of redemption was another central element in Filaret's homilies, yet never aloof from the divine love, never just as a means of punishment and extermination but as revelation of the "divine glory," the *divine love* of God.

1.4.3. As for Today: What Is Love?

His famous homily from Great Friday of 1816 based on John 3:16 bestowed on the following generations of theologians a precious and often-repeated legacy in regard to the intra-Trinitarian love-relationship.[53] Filaret introduces the Johannine "For God so loved the world. . . ."[54] with a pertinent question of his time: "Today some may ask [doubtfully]: what is love like?"[55] This "today" is the today of all epochs and times, "when the Son of God is suffering in the world, abandoned without any consolation (Matt. 27:46)" and even without a "fatherly answer."[56] So today, what can be said about love? Filaret defines the death of the "Beloved one" on the cross as the "fruit of hatred . . . the day of hatred and horror, the day of fury and vengeance."[57] God countered this by a "threefold manifestation of love,"[58] revealing that light comes through darkness (Isa. 60:1-2), an experience that a Christian can attain only through entering "the inner Sanctuary of Jesus' afflictions":

> Christian! Let *darkness cover the earth! Let gloom be on the nations! Rise* from fear and perplexity! *Glow* by faith and hope! It is through darkness that *comes Your light* (Isa. 60:1-2). Walk the path that the torn veil of

53. Cf. PBvP, p. 125.

54. "that he gave his only Son, that whoever believes in him should not perish but have eternal life."

55. PBvP, p. 124.

56. Cf. PBvP, pp. 124-25.

57. From a sermon on a different occasion (1825): "Let them slander the truth; let them hate love; let them kill life; truth is justified by herself, love triumphs, life resurrects." PBvP, p. 214.

58. To this Florovskii: ". . . Filaret emphasized that the Cross of Christ is rooted in the inscrutableness of Divine benevolence. The mystery of the Cross begins in eternity 'in the sanctuary of the tri-hypostatic Godhead' which is inaccessible to the created world. Thus, Christ is spoken of in Scriptures as the Lamb of God, forewarned or even crucified from the time of the world's creation." This elucidates Filaret's historical perception of the Bible as God's *and* humankind's common (hi)story. Cf. WoRT I, p. 117.

> mysteries opened for you, enter the inner sanctuary of Christ's suffering and leave behind the external court delivered to the scorn of the gentiles. What is in there? Nothing, except the blessed love of the Father and the Son and the Holy Spirit towards the sinful and the damned human race.
>
> The Love of the Father — in (the act of) the crucifying.
>
> The Love of the Son — (who is) the crucified.
>
> The Love of the Spirit — triumphant by the power of the cross. *Thus how God loved the world!*[59]

The immensity of this sacrificial love cannot be verbalized, therefore the "Word of God itself grew silent on the Cross."[60] This *silence of the Logos on the cross* follows a profound reflection on the kenotic aspect of Christ's obedience to the Father's will, dying on the cross, a sort of doom where one feels only the "shock of God's righteousness" and less "the sweet love of His *love*." This, however, does not prove the "absence of love" as perceived by us; much to the contrary, it shows our own unwillingness to accept the mystery that the Father's love which, even though hidden, *is* present: it can be contemplated yet solely through the eyes of faith. Thus "we shall fear only the *imperfection* in learning how to love," that is, to comprehend what *is*, or even more precisely, *Who is love* (cf. 1 John 4:18). Filaret guides us into the depths of this mystery:

> Let us clean and open wide our eyes by love and there where they have shut themselves in fear of God's judgment we shall sweeten ourselves in contemplating the love of God. *God is love* — says the Contemplator of love himself (1 John 4:16). God is love by being (essence, *sushchestvo*) and is the very essence of love. All His qualities are but robes of love; all actions are expressions of love. In it dwells in all fullness His almightiness; it is His truth when He is realizing the beloved [creation];[61] it is His wisdom . . . bounty . . . and finally it is His justice. . . . Come close and contemplate the terrifying face of God's justice, and you will truthfully recognize in it the gentle face of God's love.[62]

Just as two extremities of the infinite, in apparent contradiction, God's justice and his immense, incomprehensible, and all-encompassing love, as-

59. Cf. PBvP, p. 125.
60. Cf. PBvP, p. 125.
61. . . . *kokda osushchestvuet vozliubliaemoe.*
62. PBvP, p. 127.

tonishingly are abiding side by side. And true enough: love is not just an attribute of God but his "very essence."

1.4.4. The Principle of Divinization — and Humanization

Once more in his sermon, Filaret returns to the specifically kenotic aspect of this love: "If God out of love hands over his only begotten Son, in just the same way the Son also hands over Himself out of love for the world, and the way of love leads to crucifixion *(raspinaet),* thus love is being crucified *(raspinaetsia).* For the Son is not searching His own will but acts eternally as the follower and fulfiller of the Father's will."[63] The entire sermon is saturated with *love* — specifying anew of what sort of interaction *love is.* About the relationship between Father and Son, which inspires Christianity from its early beginnings, Filaret says:

> The love for God is jealous of God — the love for humankind loves the human being. . . . The love for God desires to defeat the enemy of God — the love (of God) for the human being humanizes the Divinity, so that through the love of God [our] humanness may be divinized, and meanwhile the love for God *raises from Earth the Son of Man* (John 12:32-34), the love for the human being tears open the embrace of the Son of God for the mortals.[64]

Filaret exhorts his readers to perceive these realms "in the spirit of truth." His entire homily, like countless other ones, is focused on the self-sacrificial love of God,[65] leaving in his audience not a spark of doubt about

63. Cf. PBvP, pp. 127-28.

64. Cf. PBvP, p. 128. Gorodetzky summarizes the whole dogmatic scheme of *the humiliation* and *redemption* in Filaret's theology in what she calls a "circulation of the glory" of God in the Trinity and Trinity and creation. This has been "disturbed" by the fall of Adam that Christ through his incarnation, suffering, and resurrection, his divine and human nature, restores and introduces "Adam's children" to the realm of his grace and the kingdom of God: becoming children of God again (John 1:12). "Thus the disturbed 'circulation of Glory' is restored through the humiliation of Christ." The central, staurological moment of the deepest self-abasement becomes the final turning point of the glorification of his human nature, and Christ's hidden, premundane glory becomes eminent and visible in his *glorious* resurrection that restores relationship between God and humanity *in love.* Cf. Gorodetzky, *The Humiliated Christ,* p. 112.

65. For instance, as shown in the following homily from 1822: "Christian, who can love you so much and be so much worthy of your love and gratitude, if not the One, Who

how much God did love — and *still loves* the world, for *Love* simply cannot do otherwise.

Conclusion

To possess erudition in theology is crucial for any spiritual person, let alone for a metropolitan. Nevertheless, to pair this knowledge with the capacity of transmitting it into a pragmatic-pastoral realm is equally indispensable. As the most eminent ecclesial authority of the Russian Orthodox Church and society of his time, Filaret knew how to address basic human anxieties and misconceptions of God: for instance, to present God's commandments as duties, yet as *duties of love* — as towards God, so towards one's neighbor. Even more so to deconstruct the distorted image of God's terrifying wrath and base it instead on Christ's revelation of the intra-Trinitarian love — the basis and essence of relationships — to depict the *gentle face of God's love.* We are called to learn the relationship of love from the Trinity, which invites creation to grow in divinization and thus become holy, i.e., whole, fully restored. Love is being learned gradually and there is a gradation even in love, everything measured on the scale of our unconditional love for God until we completely forget ourselves and *bring* the love of ourselves *in sacrifice in the love for God* and our fellow human beings. Christ's self-abasement — as in the act of Incarnation, so on the cross of Golgotha — can be seen as God's death by the hands of humans, or as the Father's embrace in His Son through the Holy Spirit. Only the Trinity could and had to accomplish this threefold and yet single kenotic act; it had to because of its perfect, unceasing, and tender love for His creation. For to love, to *be* love and to share love is God's inmost nature, it *is* God's divine-human face.

2. Makarii Bulgakov: *Lexicology of Dogmatics*

2.1. Biography

Metropolitan Makarii (Mikhail) Bulgakov (1816-1882), a native of Surkovo, had a career of rapid ascent. At the age of twenty-six he already was a profes-

---

out of love for you abandoned His heavenly glory, tasted all suffering and earthly bitterness, suffered on the cross, went through the torture of hell in order to retrieve humanity from hell and to return it into the Glory of God?" PBvP, p. 183.

sor at the Theological Academy of Kiev where he had previously obtained his baccalaureate degree (in 1842). In the same year, however, he was summoned to St. Petersburg to replace professor Afanasii on the faculty of theology. In 1859 Makarii became bishop of Charkov and in 1879 Metropolitan of Moscow.[66] As a young *hieromonakh*,[67] Makarii had a clear preference for history over theology.[68] He gained fame above all for his publications on the history of the Russian church, *Istoriia russkoi Tserkvi* and *Istoriia Khristianstva v Rossii do ravnoapostolnogo kniazia Vladimira, kak vvedenie v istoriiu Russkoi Tserkvi (The History of Christianity in Russia until the Equal-Apostolic Prince Vladimir as Introduction into the History of the Russian Church)*. His bent for history becomes especially evident in his interpretation of theology as a continuous interaction between God and humanity. Makarii's real merit lies in having *composed* the first Russian manual of dogmatic theology, preceded by an *Introduction (to Orthodox Theology)*[69] published in 1847, which gained him his doctoral title. The *Pravoslavnoe dogmaticheskoe bogoslovie*[70] *(The Orthodox Dogmatic Theology)* appeared in five volumes subsequently from 1849 till 1853 and was republished many times. A French translation, approved by the author himself, was soon published (1860) and remained in use for a long period.[71] Also a manual, or rather a textbook (in the form of an excerpt designated for education in schools), appeared later under the title of *Rukovodstvo k izucheniiu khristianskogo, pravoslavno-dogmaticheskogo bogoslovia (Manual for the Study of Christian, Orthodox-Dogmatic Theology)*.[72]

66. Cf. WoRT I, p. 255. An extensive biography and description of Makarii's works that surpasses 800 pages can be found in Makarii's ex-alumni book: F. Titov, *Makarii (Bulgakov): Mitropolit Moskovskii i Kolomenskii (istoriko-biograficheskii ocherk)* (Kiev: Tipografiia I. I. Gorbunova, 1895-1903).

67. A monk who was also an ordained priest.

68. In the academic year of 1841-42 he lectured on church and civil history at the Kiev Academy. In the following year he was sent to St. Petersburg where he worked for fifteen years and strolled the path from a bachelor to a doctoral degree, inspector, and finally the rector of the St. Petersburg Theological Academy in 1850.

69. Makarii (Bulgakov), *Vvedenie v pravoslavnoe bogoslovie* (Sankt-Peterburg: Tipografiia Departamenta Udelov, 1852) (VvPB).

70. Makarii received for his *Dogmatic Theology* the first prize of the Academy of Sciences. Cf. Makarii (Bulgakov), *Introduction à la théologie orthodoxe* (Paris: Joël Cherbuliez Librairie-Éditeur, 1857), pp. v-xi.

71. Cf. G. Cioffari, "Breve storia della teologia russa," *Quaderni di O Odigos* 6, no. 4 (Bari 1987): 34.

72. The book could be implemented in education only after Metr. Filaret's death

Makarii's dogmatic works received praise for their completeness and rigorous methodology. The uniqueness of his dogmatic manual was in its historic perspective, and according to Florovskii, in introducing to the realm of Russian theological literature "for the first time such a rich and strictly researched material expounded in a commonly understood Russian style."[73] Yet there was a lavish abundance of criticism for its *cold, scholastic,* and "soulless" style, in particular from Kireevskii, Khomiakov, and Khrapovitsky (and numerous other scholars).[74] For Vvedenskii, according to A. Palmeri, it

---

(1867), who by "silently condemning it" did not grant his approval. (Also opposed to Makarii was the new arrangement of the manuals of dogmatic theology proposed by Protasov, already in 1844.) Filaret's approach was, as we could see, an arrangement based on the *Ecumenical Symbol of Faith* that he considered correctly nothing less than a "brief system of theology," emphasizing the "ecumenical and apostolic branding" of its origin. Cf. WoRT I, pp. 256 and 259. The *Rukovodstvo* has an introduction of the basic concepts, and two further parts, each containing two sections subsequently: 1. "God and His General Relation to the World and the Human Being" with the subchapters of "God" and "God as Creator and Provider (Promyslitel')"; 2. "God-Savior and His Particular Relationship to Humankind" with the subchapters on "God-Savior" and "God as Sanctifier" as well as "God as Judge and Remunerator." Since this basically is a brief summary of his big *Dogmatic Theology* for class education, we shall disregard it in our present inquiry.

73. Cf. WoRT I, p. 257.

74. Florovskii also brings a series of serious criticisms especially on Makarii's *Dogmatic Theology* for its lack of originality that "consciously did not go beyond a simple compilation of texts." In fact, he points out that what Makarii did was merely copy and compile existing biblical and patristic references from the "Latin tradition." Makarii did not search the dogmatic text itself, falling short in terms of up-to-date interpretation. He did not transpose the message into a "living dogmatic conception, into a spiritual life" because he simply remained *unreceptive:* "There was something bureaucratic in his writing style and exposition. His dogmatic theology lacked precisely a 'sense of Church.' He dealt with texts, not with evidence or truths. Hence he had such a lifeless and uninspired style which carried no conviction. There are only answers without questions, but they cannot answer what they are not asked. Some might see this as a virtue. . . . Makarii had no personal views. . . . Many were irritated by the inner indifference and soullessness in Makarii's books from the day they appeared. Khomiakov found Makarii's *Introduction* 'admirably stupid.' Filaret Gumilevskii reacted in the same way: 'A nonsensical morass, there is neither logical order nor force in the arguments.' One might repeat about Makarii's theological books what Giliarov-Platonov wrote about Makarii's *History:* 'a workman-like construction with the trappings of scholarly apparatus. . . .' Giliarov-Platonov was emphatic. Makarii's *History* has all 'the appearance of a history book, but it is not a history, only a book. 'Not a history and not even a book, but merely a construction.'" Cf. WoRT I, pp. 257-58. We found it worthwhile to reproduce this somewhat extensive list of critical insights for its plasticity of description and the rendering of the epoch's perception of such an important and widely divulgated publication of its time in Russia. Therefore we shall see one more harsh yet illustrative review of Makarii's "schol-

was "confused" and "inaccurate," etc. In Cioffari's view Makarii's theology marks "a return to the para-catholic school of Kiev," where lecturing was still done with the scholastic methods.[75] Indeed, it is an Orthodox rendering of Catholic manuals, omitting "non-Orthodox" topics such as the question of the *Papal Primacy,* the question of *Filioque,* and partially the subject of *Purgatory* — and with major insistence on the Fathers and the Councils.

In his manuals, the most important topic for Makarii was the affirmation of *faith,* as already his mottos demonstrate,[76] finding confirmation in the Scriptures, the (patristic) tradition of the church, and their dogmatic implementation. He concluded every part of his manual with a *Nravstvennoe prilozhenie dogmata,* i.e., a *Moral Implementation of the Dogma,* a scholarly conceived and described summary of the discussed subject for a spiritual and pastoral implementation.

2.2. Introduction to Orthodox Theology

The "Latin influence" is undeniable in Makarii's works, perhaps even more so since the Kiev Academy had already followed a strictly Latin pattern of education in the previous centuries.[77] The different editions of his *Introduction*[78] are practically identical in their textual corpus. We encountered a somewhat surprising reference to Filaret of Moscow at the end of §5, where Makarii explicitly mentions that what was "admitted" in his *Introduction to Orthodox*

arly books" from the succeeding rector of the St. Petersburg Academy, Ioann Sokolov: "with their thousands of citations they contribute like nothing else in these critical times to the final stupefaction and stagnation of the religious beggars in our schools, precisely because they aid the omission of any worthwhile thought, fresh insight, sense of evidence, and inward drive." Florovskii rounds it up by adding: "Makarii's book was outdated the day it first saw the light, and it remained unneeded and without a role to play in Russian theological consciousness. It could not satisfy those devoted to a spiritual life and raised in ascetic awareness or traditions" (p. 259).

75. Cf. Cioffari, "Breve storia della teologia russa," p. 34.

76. Cf. Eph. 2:20, 1 Tim. 3:15, 1 John 4:1.

77. This later is due also to the fact that a very influential and capable Metropolitan of Kiev, Peter Mogila (1596-1647), was not opposed to including in the curriculum "what was found in Latin books as traditional and Orthodox," which eventually strengthened the presence of the Latin language and of "Latin elements" in theological education up to the point that theology in Russia was taught in Latin. Cf. WoRT I, pp. 60, 66, and 72.

78. At our disposal were the editions from 1852 and 1863 published in St. Petersburg and the French edition from 1857 published in Paris.

Theology is equally present in the introduction to the *Catechism* of Filaret, "which [the *Catechism*] is a brief Orthodox theology and shall serve us as a model."[79] What is missing from both Russian editions is an addition in the notes of the French version that testifies about a deep respect of Makarii towards Filaret and his distinction, and the esteem in which Filaret was already held during his lifetime. The text equates Filaret's rare wisdom and spirit with the Cappadocian Fathers Basil and Gregory of Nazianzen as well as Chrysostom.[80] The French edition also has a proper foreword, which fulfills a certain apologetic explanation for the western reader. It states that among other things, "the schism" in the church of East and West has "replaced the peace of God" and that this work is not meant to criticize or judge others as much as to "defend the Orthodox teaching against illegitimate attacks." The same introduction admits, interestingly, that Makarii's work, being a "succinct" résumé of lecture material, "has a *bit of scholastic form* which, however, with this kind of serious work was inevitable."[81] Indeed, after the sensitive yet eloquent and elaborate language of Filaret, Makarii's *Introduction* sounds like dry encyclopedic entries on dogmatics.

2.2.1. A Systematic Quest for Faith

After a general definition of the purpose of an introduction to a science and scientific research in the broad sense, in §6 Makarii defines "the Christian faith" as the primary purpose of (Orthodox) theology.[82] Nonetheless, he does it in such a scholarly way that it would have made a representative of late neoscholasticism pale with envy. In the following paragraph he clarifies what is understood under *Orthodox Theology* per se, again a description that best characterizes his style and method: ". . . understood is a systematic explanation of the Christian faith based on the Word of God: the Holy Scrip-

79. Cf. VvPB, p. 12.

80. In note 23 of the French edition: ". . . Ce doyen [Filaret] de nos prélats, d'une instruction tout à fait supérieure, d'un esprit et d'une sagesse rares, est l'auteur de plusieurs ouvrages historiques et dogmatiques fort estimés en Russie. Il a composé aussi de nombreux sermons et homélies, qui, par l'élévation de leur style et leur importance dogmatique, ne peuvent être comparés qu'aux écrits des S. Bazile, des Grégoire de Nazianze et des Chrysostome." Cf. *Introduction à la théologie orthodoxe*, p. 12.

81. "Résumé succinct de leçons du professeur, cet ouvrage a retenu de sa destination primitive une forme quelque peu scolastique. C'est le résultat inévitable de la méthode qu'impose tout enseignement sérieux sur un sujet aussi important." Cf. *Introduction à la théologie orthodoxe*, IX.

82. Cf. VvPB, p. 17.

tures and Holy Tradition under the direction of the Orthodox Church. We say — *a systematic exposition:* this is the general character of the Orthodox theology through which it relates to the other (classes of) sciences and without which it could not be entitled as a science."[83]

It is a systematic, at times rigidly meticulous exposition, with references and indications[84] that are surpassed only by the ones in his *Dogmatic Theology.* His narrative language at the *Introduction* is certainly one of the reasons why one is taken by surprise at its strong textbook-flavor and definition-dryness, a text that lacks barely any reference to the humanity and love of God, let alone an evident *agapic* foundation of God's acting in history and in the salvation of humanity. In the first chapter there is not a title dedicated to *love* or *agapē.* It gives the impression that these topics are not scientific enough, thus theological, and are mere sentiments rather than the very *essence* and attributes of God. The work is based on logical reasoning, yet not as in Filaret's *Catechism* or *Dialogues* with questions and answers, in both a direct and indirect sense, but in a systematic exposure of facts. Descriptive, as any nonspiritual science could be, if there are such, but lacking human warmth and relationship at its very core. For instance, in §10 with the elaborate title of *The Certainty of the Existence and Immortality of the Human Soul,* the topic is treated with the same numb and impersonal distance as any other subject. In rare occasions, Makarii ventures timidly to a more, if not poetic, at least prosaic and spiritual expression. There is an "intelligent and free soul," and Makarii goes through a list of pragmatic argumentation as to why and how its derivation from God can be experienced and proven. The proof by excellence is reflected in a "pious life": by "living piously the soul goes above the reality of the body, dominates it and becomes aware of its celestial destination." Living in God, it "perceives the presence and breath of the Holy Spirit," thus already gets a foretaste of a different, purely spiritual existence.[85]

83. Cf. VvPB, p. 7. Makarii divides his *Introduction* as follows: The first part examines the object of Orthodox theology with subsections on religion and revelation in its various aspects, and the Christian religion as the sole true revelation; the second part is dedicated to the sources of Orthodox theology, addressing the subjects of the Holy Scriptures, the Holy Tradition, and the Orthodox Church; the last part regards the system of the Orthodox theology itself in its various aspects.

84. Makarii quotes or refers frequently to the Scriptures, both AT and NT, and the Fathers, but cites or refers also to the *Talmud, Cabala, Alcoran,* and some classical and pagan thinkers such as Cicero, Plato, etc.

85. Cf. VvPB, pp. 21-23.

2.2.2. *The Motivation for Moral Effort*

In the second chapter, dedicated to the subject of *revelation,* Makarii asserts that revelation is one of *the* Christian elements that makes this religion, thanks to its divine origin, what it is: Christian. Revelation, also exemplified in scriptural stories (Moses, the prophets, etc.), is granted to us out of the infinite "justice" and "goodness of God," through the "might of His word." Makarii addresses even the notion of *mystery* with its "luminous and obscure" face, i.e., with a comprehensible and an incomprehensible side. In this context the Incarnation with its visible and invisible dimension is based on the *kenotic self-humiliation,* self-abasement of the Son of God, "without which we could have never been saved." It is conspicuous that he does so without mentioning even a single time the name of Jesus Christ.[86] We do not claim or even insinuate that Makarii omitted it on purpose; nevertheless it is surprising in an introduction to dogmatic theology, in a chapter dedicated to the question of revelation, since for Christians the utmost "concept" of God's revelation to humanity has a *Name,* and it is the personal Name of "God saves" *(Yeshuah)* and the "One who is anointed" *(Christos):* Jesus Christ (not to mention that "Christian" means "Christ-like," i.e., Christ-inherent). Again, to claim that Makarii's theology is not Christocentric may sound overstated, but while reading his exposition chapter after chapter, the question of "how much?" or "with all the scholastic apparatus, why so hazy and indirect in a manual of dogmatic theology?" involuntarily arises in the reader.

It is in the above-mentioned context of Christ's kenotic action that Makarii speaks, in one of his rare occasions, of *love* as the means of God's infinite care for humanity:

> The Son of God Himself deigned for the sake of our salvation to take on the form of a slave and to die on the cross: what a prompting for an endless gratitude and love to the divine Savior and for the observance of all his commandments. We are the temple of the Holy Spirit that accomplishes in us the work of sanctification: what a motive for us to turn away from all impurity of the flesh and spirit, even all the evil thoughts, desires and feelings.[87]

86. He eventually mentions "Christ" at the end of §27 when comparing revelation in Christianity with other religions. Cf. VvPB, pp. 35-46.

87. Cf. VvPB, p. 40.

Herewith, not to be misled, we already have reached the furthest spiritual-pastoral insight to which Makarii would take his reader. At first, he recommends "piety of life" as the maxim of virtue and certainty of faith — before returning in the shortest possible way to uncreative textbook reasoning. To his credit, however, is his epistemological clarification of the "mystery of revelation" that cannot be comprehended by reason alone, as the first one simply surpasses the second.[88]

2.2.3. *The Infinite Love(s) of the Three Hypostases*

"The Christian religion . . . is a restoration of the original alliance with God" in the death of His incarnated and crucified Son (Eph. 2:18), all of which is rooted in the "triple hypostasis" of God. And in order to "represent more distinctively the nature of this new alliance," Makarii examines it in its relations to the essential characteristics of all alliances in the subsequent paragraphs. The fallen human nature as well as the old alliance with God could be renewed only in "Christ's sacrifice on the cross." The human being has not lost entirely the image of God through his fall and has a "sincere desire to reconcile with his Creator." The solution that Christianity offers, as Makarii puts it, is repentance and amendment of life-conduct (Matt. 4:17 and Acts 2:38).[89] This is the human contribution; the divine part consists in:

> . . . solely the supreme [God's] good will for humanity, and in particular the love of God the Father for us, poor sinners, for whom He has given His only Son, *so that whoever believes in Him may not perish but may possess eternal life* (John 3:16); the infinite love of God-Son, who has given His life for us (Matt. 20:28); the infinite love of God–Holy Spirit who generously lavishes on us His precious graces (1 Cor. 12:7) and through charity being poured into our hearts (Rom. 5:5).[90]

The providence of God foresaw the fall of the human being and the need for salvation, which He accomplished in the death of His Son in *His infi-*

88. Yet, that there is an emotional, emphatic, spiritual perception and comprehension of the revelation and God's presence, again, he spends not a single word on, as if the *image of God* was merely composed of brain and intellect, and Jesus Christ was a static historic reality, a Word spoken and sounded, yet with no ongoing living interaction, let alone human warmth.

89. Cf. VvPB, p. 71.

90. VvPB, p. 71.

nite love (Eph. 1:4-5): "In time, the fulfillment of this *predetermination* of the infinite love of God for us began in the very moment of the fall of man."[91]

In order to reestablish relationship between God and humanity, to bring them back from fall and sin to happiness, God in his "fatherly tenderness" fulfilled all conditions that humanity was not able to fulfill "abandoned to its own forces." God's providence implemented three means to achieve this: 1. Instruction of the true religious doctrine through supernatural revelation; 2. The act of reconciliation of humanity to himself in the voluntary incarnation of the only Son of God, with the full consequence of his self-abasement; 3. The "moral reform" of the fallen human generation by making them "advance in piety and sanctity" (grace and sacraments). Humanity's share is to contribute its "own effort" in order to be "renewed."[92] Nevertheless the decisive means is God's mercy and care for fallen human nature, and the goals of the (to be) *renewed humankind* are equally threefold. At this point, finally, a clear Christocentric concept can be distinguished in Makarii: 1. "the mystical/sacramental union" *(tainstvennoe soedinenie)* of the Christian faithful with God, yet only *through* Jesus Christ and *in* Jesus Christ; 2. "the Glory of God" — in and through all; and 3. finally, "the happiness of the Christian faithful." What makes up this "happiness" is the "appreciation of the sweetness that comes from virtue (Matt. 5:3-12), it is the peace of God that surpasses *all thoughts* (Phil. 4:7), it is the foretaste of heavenly goods through hope, it is the sweet spiritual union with Jesus Christ, *God of all consolation* (2 Cor. 1:3), it is the *joy in the Holy Spirit* (Rom. 14:17)." Carried away with this narration, Makarii brings his audience quickly down to earth: "there won't be Christians of true happiness except in eternal life, only when *seeing God face to face* (1 Cor. 13:12)."[93] Again, this is one of the very few prosaic parts of Makarii's exposition from which he promptly draws further moral conclusions. Naturally there are paragraphs dedicated entirely to the person of Jesus Christ, the Messiah, and biblically founded systematic reflections and expositions of origin, dealing with different aspects of Christ's life and

91. With the sentence of condemnation of humankind, God gives the promise of salvation in the "holy seed" that generates "true Christians," of the woman who steps on the head of the snake — therefore, our faith in Jesus Christ as the one who saves the human generations (Heb. 11:2, 23; 12:2). Makarii takes the idea of the holy seed from St. Irenaeus *(Contra haereses)*. Cf. VvPB, pp. 71-72. At the last reference Makarii adds further Fathers such as Chrysostom, Eusebius, Gregory the Great, St. Augustine, etc.

92. VvPB, pp. 72-74.

93. VvPB, pp. 74-75

work.[94] Yet again, there is not the slightest notion of a spiritual exposé or an emotional involvement, and there is no reference to *agapē* or *agapic relationship,* apart from the above-mentioned kenotic aspect, but more of a biblical commentary. The most poetic parts in his treatises are in fact the biblical quotations.

2.3. The Orthodox Dogmatic Theology

The two volumes appeared successively in 1856 and 1857[95] with the same mottos[96] referring to the church being rooted in the Apostles and them in Christ, moral conduct in the House of God (the church) and discernment of the spirits; the fourth epigraph in the introduction regards a quote from St. Cyril of Jerusalem: "The greatest of all acquisitions is the science of the dogmas." These quotes render anew precisely Makarii's attitude and understanding of the dogmas — and perhaps his somewhat strict rendering of handing them down, very similarly to his *Introduction,* in a scholastic and rather jurisdictional style.[97]

Makarii divides the history of dogmatic theology into three "rather distinctive" periods: The first begins at the second century CE lasting until

94. The Messiah as prophet, supreme sacrifice, the type, and concepts such as justice, power, mission, alliance, etc. Cf. VvPB, pp. 137-46.

95. The French edition (1860) is an exact reproduction of the original.

96. The same as the ones he used for his *Introduction* (Eph. 2:20; 1 Tim. 3:15; 1 John 4:1).

97. The first volume is composed of two parts that follow the introduction. Part One: "On God in Himself and on His General Relationship to the World and the Human Being," with chapters on "On the Essence of the Unity of God" and "On God Who Is Trinitarian in His Persons"; Part Two bearing the same heading with the following chapters: "On God as Creator" and "God as Provider." The division of the second volume, which nevertheless creates one unity with the first one, is in three parts. Part Three: "On God as Savior," with the chapters "On Our Lord Jesus Christ in Particular," "On God Savior in His Particular Relationship with Humankind," and "On God as Sanctifier"; this part also contains an article dedicated to ecclesiology. Part Four contains an article "On the Divine Grace Considered as the Force through Which the Lord Sanctifies Us" and an article "On the Sacraments of the Church as Means of Communication of the Divine Grace," with an exposition of the sacraments. Part Five deals with the remaining sacraments of "Marriage," "Holy Orders," and "General Remarks on the Holy Sacraments," and a separate chapter is dedicated to "God the Judge and Rewarder/Avenger (Mzdovozdaiatel') for the Whole Humankind." Cf. Makarii Bulgakov, *Pravoslavno-dogmaticheskoe bogoslovie,* vols. 1-2 (Sankt-Peterburg: Tipografia Koroleva, 1856-57) (PDBo I-II).

the mid-eighth century, namely from the apostolic period till John Damascene (730-745), the second from this period till the mid-seventeenth century, that is, until Peter Mogila the metropolitan of Kiev (1631-47), and the third from then until the present. Meanwhile in the first period a proper "dogmatic theology in the form of a teaching or system" still cannot be found, but merely a *method;* the second, medieval period, brings along "right at its beginning the first system of Orthodox dogmatic theology," though still not perfect yet with all the characteristics of a system. It is at last the publication of Peter Mogila's *Pravoslavnoe ispovedanie Katholicheskoi i Apostolskoi Tserkvi Vostochnoi (The Orthodox Creed of the Catholic and Apostolic Eastern Church)* that is "the first introduced . . . teaching of theology in such extent, in which it had been taught in the European educational institutions of the time."[98] To prove whether this is a correct historical analysis of Russian Orthodox dogmatic theology's development is not our task; nevertheless it could be considered again as Makarii's contribution to the subject.

2.3.1. Moral Unity *through Theological Virtues*

As much as Makarii's *Introduction* appeared to lack an explicit Christocentric concept at times, this vagueness does not hold for his *Dogmatic Theology.* He makes clear from the beginning with the "inner motto" (1 John 5:7) that the unity of the tri-hypostatic person and "the knowledge of the invisible God the Father" — though never fully comprehensible to us by reason — can be attained "solely through the Son." Our whole existence is directed towards the Father: in and through His Son. Nevertheless he leaves this relationship between the Father and the Son (through the Holy Spirit), and between the Trinity and the created world, on a purely gnosiological level.[99]

Every unit in its concluding article contains a "moral implementation of the dogma," destined for the benefit of the faithful's everyday life, with an exhortation to "learn" the lessons and "to increase one's piety." Though still written in a rather dense, scholastic style and language, these concluding parts are the most spiritual ones in his work.[100] Unfortunately, again, there is

98. Cf. PDBo I, pp. 24-46. Makarii supports his argumentation with a detailed historical overview in the development of theology and an enumeration of historical facts, ecclesial personalities, and theological realms with special regard to Orthodoxy.

99. Makarii quotes richly the Fathers, especially in disputable or heretical questions, with the appropriate scientific apparatus in the notes. Cf. PDBo I, pp. 47-53.

100. For instance the subject on the essence of God has in his moral implication a threefold impact, "lessons" to be learned: firstly by relating to God so as to recognize him as

not a single chapter or article dedicated to the theological virtue of love, the concept of *agapē* or the form of agapic relationship, neither in the tri-hypostatic being of God nor between God and the creation in the divine economy. All one would find, mainly in biblical quotations, is the general Christian understanding of a love-relationship, presented yet not underscored or exalted. We witness once more a search for proofs through the Holy Scriptures, the Sacred Tradition, and the Fathers, in confrontation and textual analysis, a systematic procedure and an apparently complete, self-contained encyclopedia rather than a living, spiritual treatise. There is no expression of relationship *in* or *out of* love but an impressively elaborate and encyclopedic listing of theological truths that lacks any poetry or lyricism.[101] The exceptions confirm the rule, as for example in one of his *moral implementations* he exhorts to a "moral unity" that is possible through the "triple Christian unity of faith, love and hope" (Eph. 4:3-6; John 13:34; 17:21) and twice he reaffirms that this can be achieved thanks to "full devotion" through love (John 1:12-13; Luke 8:21; and John 14:23).[102] The practice and matter of *faith* remain throughout his dominant leitmotiv along with *piety of life*.[103]

2.3.2. Admirable Remedy: *Reconciliation through Christ's Obedience*

The second volume has more to do with the *mediation* of Jesus Christ[104] (introduced by 2 Cor. 5:19), for no man could reconcile with God and bridge the gap that was created through humankind's fall — to reconcile, to re-

---

the only God and to "love him with all our heart" (Deut. 6:5); secondly through believing in this God, relating to our neighbors "in brotherly love"; and thirdly in relationship to ourselves — the call, based on this knowledge, to reestablish the primordial unity in us: between the inner and outer, the spiritual and fleshly person. Cf. PDBo I, pp. 66-67.

101. Well exemplified, for instance, in the second chapter §24-§30 — regarding the Trinity of God. Cf. PDBo I, pp. 115-59.

102. Cf. PDBo I, p. 159.

103. For instance, to the question of why and how did God create the world, Makarii gives the following answer: "God did create the world not out of need but entirely out of free will . . . and since He could have not created it, but did so in His reason and intelligence, He certainly had a reason for it." How can we be certain of this? "Through *faith* we learn that God did so in His bounty for the good and happiness of the creatures which He called into being for His glory and for partaking in His goodness. In this also the Fathers and the Doctors of the Church concur unanimously: God did so out of His infinite goodness." Cf. PDBo I, pp. 283-86, 252-56.

104. Section I: "On God as Savior."

establish the union, destroy sin, to render clarity to reason, reform the human will, etc. Only God himself could "fulfill all these conditions" and reform the "deformed image of God" in us. At this point Makarii finally arrives at the kenotic concept of Christ's self-abasement as "the only means to fulfill all those conditions." It happens for the sake of reestablishing the *former alliance* between God and humanity, and re-creation of the world to its primordial state; and it happens (with)in the alliance between the Father and the Son and for the sake of this alliance.[105] This alliance is the "admirable means or remedy *(sredstvo)*":

> Remedy, the most worthy of God and of His perfections! Here His infinite bounty has been revealed: "For God so loved the world, that He gave His only Son, that whoever believes in Him should not perish but have eternal life" (John 3:16). Here His infinite truth *(pravda)*[106] has been manifested, when for His satisfaction such an extraordinary and remarkable victim was necessary: the death of the God-Man, "whom God put forward as propitiation by His blood, to be received by faith. This was to show His righteousness, for the forgiveness of former sins" (Rom. 3:25).[107]

The "infinite wisdom of God" saves what was lost; a wisdom that is a mystery hidden since the beginning of the world (Col. 1:26), the "divine allmight" that is being revealed in the God-Man. Makarii reviews the story of God's incarnation and "Christ's divine dignity" that he gave up for our salvation, thus removing "the greatest obstacle" between God and humankind. He mentions the unique role of the Mother of God, Mary, in whose "chaste womb" the *Word,* the "only friend of men," was incarnated from the Holy Spirit and became "mediator" between God and humankind.[108] Makarii sees solely the concept of *justice* in Christ's Incarnation and mediation, a justice that was needed and required by God in order that reconciliation may occur. Thus the heart of the event is not the self-abasement of Christ out of

105. Cf. PDBo II, p. 10(-13).

106. The French version at this point speaks of "justice." Cf. Makarii (Bulgakov), *Théologie dogmatique orthodoxe,* vol. 2 (Paris: Librairie de Joël Cherbuliez, 1860), p. 11.

107. . . . *whom God put forward as a propitiation by His blood, to be received by faith. This was to show God's righteousness, because in His divine forbearance He had passed over former sins* (Rom. 3:25).

108. Then, according to his consuetude, he reviews the opinion of the Fathers in this regard. Cf. PDBo II, pp. 13-16.

love but out of *obedience*. The final aim is the pacification of God's justice, "not because He breathes vengeance" but because no action contradicting God, such as sin, can be derived from His own attributes. Therefore without "fulfilling this condition" (i.e., the abyss of division caused by the fall) *reconciliation* and *union* between God and humanity would have never been possible and we would have remained, in the face of God's desire for justice, "children of wrath" (Eph. 2:3) and "children of damnation" (Gal. 3:10).[109] In a later passage, he returns to the same concept at Philippians 2:6 and highlights the "incomprehensibility" of Christ's descent from heaven, His Incarnation, but talks only about the "infinite omnipotence of God," not His love.[110]

The paragraph where Makarii unfolds somewhat the meaning and significance of love is §127: *The Motive of Redemption and the Reason Why the Son of God Came on Earth.* "Why did the tri-hypostatic God deign to save us? There is but one reason for that: His infinite love to us, sinners." Makarii quotes two very nice love-related texts (Rom. 5:8; Eph. 2:4-5, 7)[111] and with further quotes remarks that the "love of God" manifested itself particularly in each person as follows: 1. "through the Father who manifested His love to the world by sending His only Son" (1 John 4:9 and John 3:16); 2. through the Son, who proclaimed that one's greatest love sacrifice is the one for his friends (John 15:13) and that His love for His own will remain till the end of the world (John 13:1) since He has given His life for them; 3. through the Holy Spirit that unites us in God (Eph. 2:18) and brings about the re-birth and the renewal (Titus 3:5). The final act of Redemption came through *grace* in the virtue of faith (Eph. 2:8), that grace which appeared to all human beings (Titus 2:11). Both with the Scriptural texts and the Fathers' comments Makarii favors the concept of grace over that of love, when talking about the *economy* of salvation.[112] In the *moral implementation* of this chapter, Makarii returns a couple of times to the actual reason of our salvation: God

109. Cf. PDBo II, p. 10. The last quotation is a paraphrasing or an incorrect rendering. The exact quote says: *For all who rely on works of the law are under a curse; for it is written: Cursed be everyone who does not abide by all things written in the Book of the Law, and do them* (Gal. 3:10). Makarii's exact biblical sources are unknown to us.

110. Cf. PDBo II, p. 13.

111. . . . *God shows His love for us in that while we were still sinners, Christ died for us* (Rom. 5:8); . . . *But God, being rich in mercy, because of the great love with which He loved us, even when we were dead in our trespasses, made us alive together with Christ — by grace you have been saved* . . . (Eph. 2:4-5, 7).

112. Cf. PDBo II, p. 19.

knew that man could not bridge the gap created by the fall, and so he actuates the redemption that has been prepared before the centuries in his infinite bounty and love for us. Therefore "we need to reciprocate" this love of God: "Let us love God for it was He who loved us first" (1 John 4:19)[113] and extend it to others: "Beloved, if God so loved us, we also ought to love one another" (1 John 4:11).[114] The latter aspect he picks up anew in the third part where Jesus, the "author" of our faith,[115] gives us a new, more perfect commandment than that of Moses: "A new commandment I give to you, that you love one another: just as I have loved you, you also are to love one another" (John 13:34).[116]

Conclusion

It is almost astonishing that with all that effort and reflection right at the "sources of all-love," Makarii, apart from meagerly pointing out its existence, does not disclose any proper concept of love. What is the meaning of a supreme *sacrifice* and *self-abasement,* the "infinite wisdom of God," without a true motive that gives the final Revelation its full comprehensible meaning — its full and primordial image that is God's love? The teaching on God and of God should never be reduced to a science that misses the essence of His message, the *essence* of his very being, i.e., God Himself: *God is love* (1 John 4:16). Makarii was at the source but got so preoccupied by the moral implications that he simply does not have the overview of the divine-human love of God and His Son, Jesus Christ. Thus it never becomes clear that *this* is the true Image of God, this is the *dogma* of the Church.

Certainly, it would not do justice if we did not recognize Makarii's firm intention to create a complete manual of dogmatic theology, just as it would be unfair not to comprehend the criticisms on it. Then: If Christian faith is being defined and rendered merely encyclopedically and not based on a life-giving and sustaining divine-human relationship, the heart of God's matter lacks God's very heartbeat.

113. *We love because He first loved us* (1 John 4:19).
114. Cf. PDBo II, p. 32.
115. Cf. PDBo II, p. 33.
116. Cf. PDBo II, pp. 96-100.

3. Filaret Gumilevskii (Archb. Chernigovskii): *To Taste Theology*

3.1. Biography

Similar to Makarii, Filaret (1805-1866) was also a historian and dedicated various works to the history of the Russian church, for instance *Istoria russkoi Tserkvi* (1848),[117] treatises on spiritual literature such as the review of Russian spiritual literature from the very beginnings of Christianization of Russ till modern times *Obzor russkoi dukhovnoi literatury (Review of Russian Spiritual Literature)* in 1859, speeches and sermons,[118] and traditions in the Greek church. Various hagiographies of Russian and Slav saints appeared posthumously as *Zhitia sviatykh, chtimykh Pravoslavnoiu Tserkoviu (The Lives of Saints Venerated by the Orthodox Church)* in 1892 and *Sviatye iuzhnykh slavian: Opisanie zhizni ikh (The Saints of the Southern Slavs: Description of Their Lives)* in 1894, and *Besedy o stradaniiakh Gospoda nashego Iisusa Khrista (Colloquies about the Sufferings of Our Lord Jesus Christ)* in 1884. His theological vision, transparency, and exposition of arguments are diametrically opposed to Makarii, whose work Filaret criticized unsparingly.[119] Filaret's rootedness in life and spiritual pragmatism is reflected in his thoughts, teaching, and writing (especially in his letters, sermons, etc.). His intellect and his heart were equally involved in his theology, revealing much about his own "Imago Dei" that he managed to transmit with such bravura in his lectures as professor.[120] Florovskii called him the "most influential teacher of dogmatics" of his time, "a man of outstanding gifts, a restless mind and an anxious heart." He made a deep impression on his audience with his vitality and "the organic blending of intellectual curiosity and the faith of the heart."[121] Filaret's method was a healthy combination of a philosophical inquisitiveness, theological reflection, pastoral sensitivity, and a well-founded biblical/

117. With repeated translations and editions in German (1872) and Greek (1885-87).

118. For instance: *Slova i besedy Filareta Arkhiepiskopa Chernigovskago i Nezhinskago* (Chernigov: Ilinskii Monastir, 1863). A collection of talks *(besedy)* and speeches *(rechi)* on different, primarily liturgical, occasions and feasts arranged in separate sections.

119. "A nonsensical morass," see the previous title. Filaret was a contemporary of Makarii, and many of their works appeared in each other's lifetime.

120. Zernov collocates him among those gifted scholars who faced bravely the challenges of the time and the procurators' influence on the Synod: ". . . Bishops Filaret (Gumilevsky) of Chernigov (1805-1866), Makary (Bulgakov) of Moscow (1816-1882), Metropolitan Antony (Khrapovitsky) (1864-1936) and Sergy (Stragorodsky) the Patriarch of Moscow (1861-1944). . . ." Cf. RRR, p. 51.

121. WoRT I, p. 262.

patristic knowledge. In examining his scientific method, it soon becomes apparent that dogmas were not just unquestionable proofs from the past, but possessed a systematic foundation formulated by revelation and reason. Further, they were designed not only to be believed in but to increase faith, when exposited with proper heed. Theological reflection and investigative epistemology were integral parts of his courses when lecturing at the Moscow Theological Academy where, without hesitation, he applied available methods of historical-source criticism, as well as proper philosophical considerations. Indeed, all these methods can be found in his works too, so that some believed "a new era" was dawning in the Academy. As a young monk he was called to serve the bishop, a service that left him no space to work on publications, as he would recall later. On his initiative, the Moscow Academy decided to publish the Holy Fathers in Russian and (with significant delay in 1859) his patristic textbook *Istoricheskoe uchenie ob otsakh tservki (Historical Teaching on the Fathers of the Church).*[122] Filaret always carefully distinguished between the teachings of the Fathers, which he considered with great respect, and the teachings about the tradition of the church as such.

Two more important aspects need to be considered about Filaret: first that he was greatly inspired by the spirit of the Alexandrine statutes. One was his preference to awaken "thoughts and self-motivation in the students rather than to bind them with previously prepared formulae and phrases." The other was that he actively advocated for a new translation of the Slavonic Bible with the use of the Septuagint and the Old Slavonic Bible, giving both their "dogmatic merits." His note in this regard was given to the Holy Synod and became the guideline for the work on the renewed translation.[123]

3.2. *Filaret's* Orthodox Dogmatic Theology

The *Pravoslavnoe dogmaticheskoe bogoslovie* (mentioned in the title)[124] of Filaret, in contrast to the somewhat dramatic prelude of Makarii's manual,

122. Cf. WoRT I, p. 263.

123. WoRT I, pp. 264-65. It is interesting to note that despite his meticulous attention to detail, and obvious high regard for Filaret, Florovskii does not even mention Filaret's manual of *Dogmatic Theology.*

We were not able to identify a dedicated biography of Filaret Gumilevskii.

124. We have used the third edition of F. Gumilevskii, *Pravoslavnoe dogmaticheskoe bogoslovie,* vols. 1-2 (Sankt-Peterburg: I. L. Tuzov, 1882) (PDBG). The first edition appeared in 1864 in Chernigov.

opens without mottos. It has an explanatory foreword for the reader about the "on-growing influence of German rationalism," the ideals of which had started to spread in Russian society and were "now appearing also in Russian translations."[125]

The arrangement and the respective lengths of the parts disclose where Filaret's main attention lies: while not neglecting *theology*, more attention is granted to *economy* and *soteriology*. Regarding structural differences from Makarii's manual, Filaret addresses first the topic of the Sacrament of Orders instead of Matrimony and interestingly places the subject of the church after the sacraments, "less coherently than Makarii" according to Cioffari. The reason for this could lie in Filaret's focus on humankind's need of salvation (most imminent and perceivable in the sacrament); besides, he considers the sacraments as means or parts of such salvific action, which seems to be proven by the title of the part on "The Means of Sanctification (Sredstva osviashcheniia)" in the chapter "God the Sanctifier of Human Being (Bog-Osviatitel' cheloveka)."[126] The locating of these topics before ecclesiology, as well as his abundant use of scriptural references, strengthens the general view that, although he used "largely Catholic manuals" in composing his *Dogmatic Theology*, it was a Protestant audience that he had in mind.[127] The other possible argument is that this arrangement linked more logically to eschatology in the final passage.[128]

125. The content is divided between two principal parts, preceded by "An Introduction into Orthodox Dogmatic Theology." Part One, "God in Himself (Bog Sam v Sebe)," has two chapters: 1. "God Unique in Essence (Bog edinyi po sushchestvu)" and 2. "God Trinitarian in His Persons (Bog troichnyi v licach)," both dealing with the respective implications of the titles. Part Two, titled "God in His Manifestations to Creatures (Bog v iavlenii tvariam)," is almost double in length of Part One (225 pages to 115) and contains chapters 1. "God — the Creator of the World (Bog Tvorets mira)"; 2. "God Creator and Sustainer of the Non-Corporeal Spirit-World (Bog Tvorec i Promyslitel' mira beztelesnykh dukhov)"; and 3. "God — Creator and Sustainer of the Human Being (Bog Tvorec i Promyslitel' cheloveka)." The complex concept of *Promyslitel'* includes the theological notions of God as *Sustainer* as well as *Provider*, i.e., of an ongoing divine immanence and lasting care for the creation.

126. The preceding chapter is titled "The Son of God — The Savior of Man" and contains a part entitled "On the Acts of Savior for the Salvation of People."

127. Cf. Cioffari, "Breve storia della teologia russa," p. 34.

The Protestant "audience" would make even more plausible the frequent use of biblical quotations, if we ignored the reality that Filaret was a biblical scholar and patrologue at the same time.

128. See the table of contents, vol. 2.

3.3. The More Desired — the Higher Knowledge It Is

In §1 we find the definition of dogmatic theology as a systematic presentation of God's truths revealed in religion and in the spirit of Orthodoxy. Helpful is the distinction provided by the author between a) the subject of study; b) the spirit of study; c) the scheme of composition; and d) the parts of study — each of them treated separately.[129] Filaret is thorough and precise yet not rigid in his definitions, not just referring to the Scriptures and the Fathers but laying them as a foundation of his reflection. This becomes especially apparent with the scriptural quotations and analysis in the ancient languages that carry the necessary scientific apparatus throughout his entire manual. As for the question of "how much the human being and the human understanding can know of God," Filaret guides his reader in a careful and well-founded reasoning but at the end of the chapter leaves no doubt that "only the Son saw," i.e., knows the Father and that "true knowledge of God" proceeds from the *Savior* "through God's Spirit." The Son of God appeared in flesh in order to "reveal His Father to us" and this God is not merely the God of the Jews, but also that of the Gentiles.[130] All the topics and their sequences addressed by Filaret have a logical pattern that fall into their place and involuntarily invoke the question of an imaginary interlocutor that Filaret sometimes factually completes with a question mark in the subtitle. At the headword *Trinity* he reverts to a gnoseological principle that not all mysteries can be understood from their very beginning. Comprehension is related to the complexity and depths of a given mystery, while our knowledge is always rooted in the prerequisite of the Savior's knowledge. Further, he affirms the codependence of human desire and disposition for acquiring a profound spiritual insight with that of the goal itself: "Of course, the higher is the object of [desired] knowledge the higher will be the knowledge itself."[131] In his reflection on the Trinity, Filaret states that there is a "tight relationship" among the three Divine Persons, yet regrettably does not review the actual *quality* and *kind* of this union. The first of such hints, even though an indirect one and still aimed more at the individual attributes of each Person, is from 1 Corinthians 13:13.[132] It was clearly Filaret's intention to eluci-

129. Cf. PDBG I, pp. 1-18.

130. The argument is accompanied by a rich array of Scriptural quotes. Cf. PDBG I, pp. 20, 27-29.

131. *Konechno chem vyshe predmet vedeniia, tem vyshe samoe vedenie.* Cf. PDBG I, pp. 20, 70-71.

132. Cf. PDBG I, pp. 20, 73-74.

date the union of the Trinity as a God of one-Being, but he fails to point out their singular attributes and above all their full divine entity (the evidence of which he may have simply taken for granted).[133] Although he follows up on this theme with the Fathers and the development of the Trinitarian concept in the history of theological reflection and in ecclesiology, at this point of his treatise there is missing a clear expression of the explicit or implicit love-relationship in the Holy Trinity.[134]

3.4. *Invisible Perfection Visible through Love*

At "God in His Revelations to the Creatures," in part two, Filaret emphasizes that though God dwells in an "inaccessible world" (1 Tim. 6:16) "and has used the darkness as His cover[135] . . . (yet) He is love and life and therefore He deigned to reveal Himself, His invisible perfections in the world." God's true care for and interest in the creation are visible in nature and in the soul of the human being, and it is the work and task of human reason to elucidate fully the proper implications of this care, to perceive and understand God in His cosmic as well as personal dimension as Creator and Sustainer in His various relations to His creation.[136] In this section Filaret dedicates §96 to the "Subjects of God's Providential Love (Predmety promyslitel'noi liubvi Bozhei)," which embraces all that was created by God, "not excluding the smallest things in the world." There is a logical gradation of knowing God according to each entity's place in the order of creation.[137] God in His goodness and providence takes care of all that is needed, and His goodness is best seen in the contemplated creation. And for "the blessed accomplishers of God's will" there is a yet deeper insight attainable "since they open up themselves even more to God's caring [providence]."[138] In this divine care for the creation and above all humankind lie God's love and the economy of salvation (§120): "If humankind desires to understand what kind of relationship the Divine has for the spiritual and the material world, then it needs to comprehend intrinsically the quality of relationship

133. Cf. PDBG I, pp. 20, 93.

134. Cf. PDBG I, pp. 20, 74.

135. . . . *i t'mu polozhil Svoim pokrovom* (Ps. 17:11 in LXX); *He made darkness His covering, His canopy around Him the dark rain clouds of the sky* (Ps. 18:11, NIV 2011 US).

136. Cf. PDBG I, p. 117.

137. Cf. PDBG I, p. 146.

138. Cf. PDBG I, p. 148.

that God sustains towards each singular human being." Such comprehension is fundamental even on the level of an individual in order to "better know who for him God truly is":[139]

> God has shown His love to man in different forms. His very first relationship to him is the relationship of the Creator and Sustainer. The Creator fashioned him perfect. The Sustainer allowed the fall of the first man, nevertheless continues to care for all human beings. Behold the first works *(deistviia)* of God's love for humankind! They are followed by the works of the Redeemer and Sanctifier.[140]

The fullness of this *relationship* and *love* is revealed in God's utmost care for our salvation, which He realizes with and through His Son's kenotic act of love-sacrifice.[141]

3.5. *Restored to Be Children of God*

Thus §148, dedicated to the question of *restoration,* initiates with the very words: "The human being fell: but God wished to raise him up." Such was his design since the beginning of time:

> The teaching of the revelation about God's (pre-)eternal council *(predvechnyi soviet)*[142] regarding humankind's salvation consists in the following: a) The Heavenly Father decided since before time to raise the fallen human being through His eternal Son and the Holy Spirit; b) this notion of God's primordial design was an act of God's unique love; c) this predestination concerns all people, no one stands in the shade of doubt. Revelation shows that since eternity God the Father decided that the Son of God, having taken up human nature, remedied by His death God's justice and acquired for humankind the right to be the sons of God.[143]

139. Cf. PDBG I, p. 180.

140. . . . *deistviia Iskupitelia i Osviatitelia.* Cf. PDBG I, p. 180.

141. Cf. PDBG II, p. 3.

142. A concept that could stem from St. Basil or simply from Filaret Gumilevskii himself.

143. Cf. PDBG II, p. 3.

3.5.1. *The Mutual Agreement in a Family Bond*

The "reestablishment of sonship" occurs by sending (ἐντολήν) the *Son of God,* in full awareness of the price that He has to pay, where the concept *entolēn* denotes an obedience according to a mutual agreement (διαθήκη).[144] What we are witnessing here is not a blind martial obedience, as often understood in the past, but much more an intimate relationship, conformity in love and respect, so to speak — a tender family bond and *blood relationship* between Father and Son.[145] "The covenant empowers the Son with royal authority to enable others to become anew participants of His might" and thus to restore them into their full dignity as children of God. The *entolēn* and *diathēkē* transmit to us an affectionate Father-Son relationship expressed in an intra-Trinitarian kenosis that God Himself is setting in front of our inner *and* outer sight. Our "Blessed God" decided to take on Himself the task of salvation of the fallen human race (1 Tim. 2:3-4; Luke 1:68):

> . . . revelation shows that God resolved to take on Himself the act of humankind's salvation solely out of love and consequently in complete freedom and not out of any [His] necessity. Thus the Son of God, reflecting on His attitude to His salvific act for humankind, utters: *For this reason the Father loves me, because I lay down my life that I may take it up again. No one takes it from me, but I lay it down of my own accord. I have authority to lay it down, and I have authority to take it up again. This charge I have received from my Father* (John 10:17-18).[146]

For Filaret, the "utmost freedom" on Christ's part in the process of decision to fulfill the Father's will — as between "two equal partners" — is a sublimely important momentum, similar to the divine equality between the two *eternal* Persons. So the will of the Father indeed, and naturally, becomes the will of the Son. The beauty of this tender yet complete union is expressed with grace in the following thought: ". . . The Heavenly Father, contemplating the will of the Son who takes upon Himself the work of humankind's redemption, is gladdened by His will [of the Son], — and by that He expresses His love towards the human being that is being saved *(spasaemu cheloveku)*."[147]

144. Διαθήκη — agreement, covenant; cf. PDBG II, p. 3.

145. Filaret does not expressly mention the Holy Spirit in this agreement, but elsewhere it can be deduced as implicit.

146. Cf. PDBG II, p. 5.

147. Cf. PDBG II, p. 5.

We observe a flow of grace, an unfolding of the anthropological dimension in the Divine, the icon of God's humanity. This also means that *divinization* is an intrinsic concept of our human existence, for if God planned our salvation through His Son from *eternity,* then He preplanned also the means for it and thus divinization naturally is nothing less than the revelation and restoration of God's image in the human being to its former beauty and perfection — to its divine origin and destination. Love cannot be forced; therefore utmost freedom of reciprocity reigns within the Trinity. Reciprocal *love* is the sole way of communication and union that equally embraces the three divine Persons' will, bringing about one faultless and divinely perfect harmony.

3.5.2. The Healing Power of the Trinity's Love

The Trinity's "inner love," exteriorized in God's creating act, in His *Logos,* Jesus Christ, possesses a restorative, healing power.[148] God does not need to destroy the world and humankind in order to mend what was corrupted. This proves the all-encompassing and invincible might of God's love: "At a different occasion the Son of God says: . . . *so that the world may know that I love the Father, I do as the Father has commanded me* (John 14:31). And the apostle Paul teaches: *God, being rich in mercy, because of the great love with which He loved us, even when we were dead in our trespasses, made us alive together with Christ* (Eph. 2:4-5)."[149] The other *istina (truth)* that Filaret addresses repeatedly is the *universality* of salvation in Jesus Christ applying to the entire humanity: even though "initially He came to *His own,*" His redemptive mission is universal for all and every human creature, granting more than a fair chance to every individual *sinner.*[150] This is an evident aspect of theological reasoning today, yet by far not the case with all dogmatics of the epoch, and in the case of Filaret it indicates a refined perception and comprehension of God's *true* care and all-inclusive providence moved by His *love for the world* (John 3:16-17).[151]

148. Healing also our distorted and limited human reason.

149. Cf. PDBG II, p. 5.

150. "People usually like what is theirs, their thoughts, also their prejudices; this is where their favoritism comes in: the love of God is equal, as the Scriptures teach us, to all people. He is impartial *(ouk prosōpolēmptēs)* (Acts 10:34)." PDBG II, p. 6.

151. PDBG II, pp. 5-6.

3.5.3. A Soteriological Predestination

God extends His love and free will to His *created image;* thus this created image of God, the human being, possesses the freedom to accept salvation or refuse it. Therefore in accord with His very nature and essence it is never God's will that a single one of His children should perish, but is always a result of a denied cooperation on the part of Adam's children. Filaret knows and uses the term *predestination,* but in a universal context: ". . . the predestination of God's love consists in saving all under the condition of a living love for Christ and for one's neighbor."[152] It is noteworthy that God is treating us as partners — granting, sustaining, respecting our free choice and never giving up on humankind. No wonder that such a pattern of love exceeds any comprehension, and only the Son's sacrifice — who "sees the Father," that is, "knows Him" — could restore communication between God and creation. God's Logos, Jesus Christ, *is* the communication, the bridge over the abyss of the sin-fall: "Jesus Christ suffered for us, and it is not His teaching or our strict conduct of life but solely His death that constitutes the means of our reconciliation."[153]

Conclusion

Filaret's methodology on the teaching of the church is considering it from diverse epistemological aspects, examining OT and NT references, as well as spiritual and everyday experiences. He takes a look at some of the prophecies, as for instance about the suffering of the Messiah,[154] or His priestly vocation, in the different books of the Scriptures, applying frequent quotes in Greek or even Hebrew, as well as comparing the views of the Fathers. His methodology

152. PDBG II, p. 6.

153. PDBG II, p. 83.

154. A very dear theme to Filaret, as he dedicates various sermons to it as well as an entire collections of talks *(besedy)* of almost 500 pages: *O stradaniiakh Gospoda nashego Iisusa Khrista (On the Sufferings of Our Lord Jesus Christ).* The book is a narrative catechesis in two parts based on the Christian kerygma, with meditations on various aspects of Christ's last days (e.g., prediction of His sufferings, establishment of the Eucharist, His prayer to the Father, death) and the consequences for the apostles and the church. Though Filaret ends his reflections at the "Pogrebenie Spasitelia (The Burial of the Savior)" and does not complete the Christian *kerygma,* his last reflection leaves a hope-filled conclusion for those who entrust themselves fully to Jesus Christ in an eschatological finale, or opening. Cf. *Besedy o stradaniakh Gospoda nashego Iisusa Khrista, Govorenyia Filaretom (Gymilevskim), Arkhiepiskopom Chernigovskim,* ed. I. L. Tuzov (Sankt-Peterburg 1884) (and a reprint: Arxiep. Chernigovskii Filaret [Gumilevskii], Moscow 2000).

searches for the "reason" and a "reasonable understanding" of a presented dogma so that the results are not unreflected facts from the tradition and the Fathers, but rather results of a human-divine interaction, of which human *reason* is meant to be a partaker.[155] Filaret's manual may not be complete or comprehensive, from one or the other point of view, but his approach to dogmatic theology does not even evoke such a claim. Much more, it is a narrative stroll through the fertile, life-giving gardens of theology sustained by a solid methodological and scientific work. His reasoning is freshly inspiring, an exhortation to dare and to undertake further reflection, autonomous thinking, and a love-bond interpretation of the dogmas. It is less an aspect of a spectator that is being offered, as it is a call to become active partakers: to grasp the revealed harmony of God's immanence in His creation, to contemplate God's ongoing care and love for the world and its salvation; to perceive God's fully revealed humanity which became one of us. Salvation is carried out, including our free consent, in order to reestablish communication between the fallen human race and the Divine, to secure salvation to *all God's beloved children*, a path bridged by the Sustainer Himself.

4. Bishop Sil'vestr Malevanskii: *Perceiving God in the Heart*

4.1. Biography

Stefan Vasilievich Malevanskii (1828-1908), later known as Bishop Sil'vestr Malevanskii, was born into a Russian clerical family and concluded both his primary and seminary education in Volin in 1847. Fragile in health, after his ordination in 1848 he was assigned to be a village priest, and in 1856 Stefan became *hieromonakh* Sil'vestr. In 1857 after the death of his wife, Sil'vestr relocated and began to pursue further studies in the Kiev Theological Academy. Soon he excelled in his studies and was encouraged to settle down and lecture in the academy, an offer compliant also with the needs of his poor health. In the period between 1857 and 1898 Sil'vestr fulfilled diverse tasks: a theology professor, inspector of educational institutes (1857-98), and ultimately a rector of the Kievan Academy (1883-98). In 1885 he was ordained bishop and named third Vicar of the Kiev eparchy. The structured life at the Academy enabled him to dedicate himself to serious academic work and to produce numerous publications: *Kratkii istoricheskii ocherk ratsionalizma v ego otnoshenii k vere (A*

155. This complies with S. Anselm's famous: *fides quaerens intellectum*, or *faith seeks to understand.*

Brief Essay on the History of Rationalism and Its Relation to Faith); research on *Istoricheskoe razvitie noveishego panteizma, kak dokazatel'stvo ego nesostoiatel'nosti (The Historical Development of Later Pantheism as Proof of Its Inconsistency); Nesostoiatel'nost' noveishego panteizma v reshenii sushchestvenneishikh dlia cheloveka voprosov (The Inconsistency of Later Pantheism in Resolving Man's Existential Questions)*, all published after 1860 in Kiev; and his doctoral dissertation on *Uchenie o Tserkvi v pervye tri veka khristianstva (The Ecclesiology of the Church in the First Three Centuries of Christianity)* in 1872. In 1874, at the revision on the state of education at the Kiev Theological Academy, inspector Makarii Bulgakov gave an "utmost negative" evaluation of Professor Sil'vestr and his didactical methods, and raised some serious concerns about Sil'vestr's abilities as a professor of dogmatic theology, which, given Makarii's position, had a fatal impact on Sil'vestr's teaching career in the Academy. This "cloud with a silver lining," however, eventually turned into an opportunity enabling Sil'vestr to devote more time to research and publication. He consequently published a series of *Otvet Pravoslavnogo . . . (Answers of an Orthodox . . .)* on various disputed topics with the Old-Catholics (on good deeds, the Blessed Virgin, the Holy Spirit).[156] In 1877 Sil'vestr's writing reached a pinnacle with the publication of an extensive manual of Orthodox dogmatic theology in five volumes: *Opyt Pravoslavnago dogmaticheskago bogosloviia (An Experience of Orthodox Dogmatic Theology)* with a contribution — and the revealing subtitle: *S Istoricheskim izlozheniem dogmatov (With a Historical Exposition of the Dogmas)*.[157] It received lavish appreciations denoting its humanity, spiritual sensitivity, and its form that "liberates the spirit," thus truly minimizing Makarii's criticism of Sil'vestr's personality and methodology.[158] There was also a later translation into Bulgarian.[159]

156. Cf. "Introduction," in Episkop Sil'vestr, *Pravoslavno dogmatichno bogoslovie s istorichno izsledvane na dogmite*, vol. 1(-3), ed. S. M. Staikov (Sofia: Sv. Sinodna Balgarskata Tsarkva, 1912-14), pp. 3-6. Unfortunately, proper biographical material on Bishop Sil'vestr Malevanskii, apart from the above-mentioned introduction in Bulgarian, is apparently nonexistent.

157. At our disposal was the second edition published between 1884 and 1891.

158. For a historic contextualization we needed to read some of the reviews on Sil'vestr's dogmatic theology from his contemporary colleagues. Prof. Titov: "The mentioned works of bishop Sil'vestr are a real pride (lit., ornament) of Russian theological literature of the XIX century." Prof. Vvedenskii: "He has revealed that spiritual matter, which is contained in the dogmatic formulas and has freed the spirit and the truth of its verbal husk." M. Skaballanovich: "The dogmatics of bishop Sil'vestr has not been outstripped till today. . . . As for its tone so for its content this is a perfectly scientific dogmatics, with which eternal praise has been secured for him. . . ." Cf. "Introduction," in Episkop Sil'vestr, *Pravoslavno dogmatichno bogoslovie*, I:6.

159. Identical with the original (there were only the first three volumes of this edition

4.2. An Essay of Orthodox Dogmatic Theology

It is precisely what Sil'vestr humbly denominates "an essay" on *Orthodox Dogmatic Theology* that is of our chief interest. The development of each teaching is first researched in the Scriptures, then followed over the centuries through the teaching of the Fathers, in the ecumenical councils, the tradition, and the actual teaching of the church. Major units conclude with an *obshchii vyvod,* a *general conclusion,* a part on implications for the intellect and life.[160]

---

at our disposal), approved by the Bulgarian Synod, with a brief biographical introduction on Sil'vestr. Cf. PDBM, pp. 3-6.

160. The first half of volume 1 is dedicated to an introduction on dogmatic theology, its concept, methodology, principal terminology, development, and a brief review of Catholic and Protestant dogmatics; the second half enters into the question of God's entity and the gnoseology of God. Volume 2, which builds on unity with volume 3, is titled *On God in Himself (O Boge v Samom Sebe)* with two unevenly large chapters: 1. "On One God in Essence (O Boge Edinom v Sushchestve)," with topics regarding the existence and entity of God ("O sushchestve Bozhiem, O edinstve sushchestva Bozhia"), and 2. "On the Trinitarian God in [His] Persons (O Boge Troichnom v licakh)," addressing topics concerning the Trinity — history of development of the dogma, different teachings in the church up to the ninth century, and the rapport of such teaching with human reason and intellect. Volume 3 consists again of two, more evenly distributed, chapters: 1. "On God — Creator of the World (O Boge — Tvortse Mira)" in general and in particular as "Creator of the Spiritual World (O Boge — Tvortse mira dukhovnogo)," of the human being and all the human race, and all that it concerns; 2. "On God — Sustainer of the World (O Boge — Promyslitele mira)," in general and particular, and on "God — Sustainer of the Spiritual World's Entities (O Boge — Promyslitele sushchestv mira dukhovnogo)," of the sensible-reasoning beings or humankind, of the human being till and after the fall and the sin-fall of the first people with its proper nature and the nature of their offspring, and finally the "Image of Supernatural Providence (Obraz promyshleniia sverkhestestvennyi)." For some reason in volume 4 there is a swapping of terms, thus the "chapters" now become "articles," suffering somewhat in the transparency of the structure. This volume has three unevenly distributed *articles* introduced with a reflection on the primordial divine decision to save the fallen human being fulfilled in Christ: 1. "On God — Prearranger of Human Salvation (O Boge — Predustroitele chelovecheskago spaseniia)" addressing the *Preparation of God's Chosen Nation;* 2. "On God — Accomplisher of Humankind's Salvation or on Their Redeemer (O Boge — Sovershitele spaseniia liudei, ili ikh Iskupitele)," with teachings on the person of Jesus Christ; "On the Redeeming Act of Humankind Accomplished by Jesus Christ (O dele sovershennago Iisusom Khristom iskupleniia roda chelovecheskago)"; 3. "On God — Dispenser of Salvation to Humankind, or Sanctifier (O Boge — Razdaiatele liudiam spaseniia, ili Osviatitele)," with parts "On Sanctification of the Human Being and What Brings It About (Ob osviashchenii cheloveka i proizvodiashchikh evo prichinakh)," "On the Church as Mediator in the Sanctification of Human Being (O Tserkvi, kak posrednice v osviashchenii cheloveka)," and "On the Existing Means in the Church for the

4.3. *The Perceived and Felt Truth in the Heart*

The very first *istina (truth)* Sil'vestr presents for consideration is the *truth* of God's existence. That the faith in God is transmitted by revelation and the "teaching of the ancient shepherds of the Church . . . is a concluded and in-advance given truth." It is the origin of all subsequent *faith* and the condition for believing and confessing any of God's attributes.[161] Sil'vestr then pointedly places the origin of the "irresistible and by non-eradicable conviction in this truth" as deeply rooted in the human spirit. Without hesitation he involves human perception and senses in his reflection, for human feeling is the basic anthropological notion with which "every human being is born and without which no human child would survive." It is so intrinsic to the "God-like" *(bogopodobnoi)* nature of the human soul that it makes the human being close to God and causes the soul to yearn for a deeper knowledge of God by getting ever closer to Him. The Spirit of the Divinity itself, through which God is continuously revealing Himself and communicating "an undoubted belief about His existence,"[162] is closer to the human being than to other, nonrational creatures. According to St. Paul it is the task of every person, all created by God, to "search for and to find" God, who is not only "not distant but is close to us, in fact, as close as nothing else can be; *In Him* (ἐν αὐτῷ) *we live and move and have our being* (Acts 17:28). And so, as much as we feel in us our very own life, we are all the more designed to *sense*

Sanctification of Human Beings (O sushchestvuiushchikh v Tserkvi sredstvakh k osviashcheniiu cheloveka)," with treatises on the sacraments. Volume 5 first concludes the remaining two sacraments of reconciliation and unction, and inconsistently in numeration (yet topically connected to volume 3) introduces chapter 3: "On God as Fulfiller of His Last Judgments of the World and the Human Being (O Boge, kak Vypolnitele konechnykh sudeb Svoikh o mire i cheloveke)," then proceeds with the last two remaining articles: 1. "On God — Judge and Rewarder of Each Human Being Separately after His Death (O Boge — Sudii i Mzdovozdaiatele kazhdogo cheloveka porozn' po ego smerti)," with "On Retribution after the Particular Judgment (O mzdovozdaianii posle chastnogo suda)" and "On Veneration of the Relics of the Saints (O pochitanii ostankov sviatykh)"; 2. "On God the Judge and Avenger at the Last Judgment of Whole Humankind (O Boge Sudii i Mzdovozdaiatele na poslednem sude vsego roda chelovecheskago)," with the eschatological themes of the second coming of Christ, resurrection of the dead, restoration of the world, the universal judgment with its consequences, and concluding on the eternal torments of hell destined for sinners, the devil, and his angels. See also the tables of contents of the separate volumes.

161. Cf. S. Malevanskii, *Opyt pravoslavnogo dogmaticheskogo bogosloviia: S istoricheskim izlozheniem dogmatov*, vol. 1 (Kiev: Tipografia G. T. Korcsak-Novickogo, 1884), pp. 173-74 (OPDB).

162. Cf. OPDB I, pp. 175-76.

or *perceive (chuvstvovat')* in us the presence and nearness of the One, from Whom it flows and to Whom by its lawful affinity is uninterruptedly rushing [back] . . . *(ustremliaetsia)* (Rom. 14:7-8)."[163] This nearness is a life-giving and sustaining divine stream that can and should be perceived above all as we perceive our own life, for our own life is part of the *Divine life,* not just by origin but by continuous providence. All life is from and *in* God, in any current moment of history. Sil'vestr dwells long on and applies a very fine procedure in introducing basic concepts. "Reason by itself — the force of our intellect — is incapable either of aspiring to the supernatural, or directly feeling its actions. The *heart,* however, is capable of all that, which according to the word of the *Wise One (Premudrago), longs for (the springs of) life* (Prov. 4:23)." A current translation of the verse says: *Above all else, guard your heart for everything you do flows from it.*[164]

The heart can perceive and transmit what is distant or even unattainable to reason, and that is not mere gnosis or simple knowledge but a *life-giving* and *sustaining Wisdom* in which "the heart is gifted by an irresistible force of attraction and appeal to the Divinity, contemporaneously guiding towards Him the entire soul."[165]

What Sil'vestr is presenting to us is a *theology of heart* in the proper sense of the word, not a sentimental but a sensible one, not excluding the intellect, but much rather and duly assisting it, placing the focal point of force that attracts the soul unflaggingly towards God *into* the human heart. The heart has the capacity not only to deal "with the danger of superficiality in spiritual life but to dive into its very depth," connecting us with the very "source of *Life*" and the conviction of God's existence. The requirement for true epistemology is "a healthy and normal life" of the heart — and Sil'vestr comes swiftly to the core of his reflection, as it is the heart where decisions of faith are made: "This is the reason that God Himself chooses the human heart to be the place of His word and love (Dt. 30:14), and His natural law, indispensable for everybody in order to bear witness of God. Truthfully God does not write on anything else but on the hearts of men (Rom. 10:10). . . ." Conversely, it is due to the unbelieving, petrified, stubborn heart that faith and the certainty of knowledge perishes (Ps. 13:1-3; Rom. 1:21; Matt. 13:15, etc.).[166]

The human heart is presented as the epicenter of God's action, a place

163. OPDB I, p. 176.
164. Compare to Matt. 15:18-19; Mark 7:21-22.
165. Cf. OPDB I, pp. 176-77.
166. Cf. OPDB I, p. 177.

where discernment of belief and disbelief in God's existence, fidelity and faithfulness, God's love and the love for God as well as the decision to follow His law or not, take place simultaneously and so interact with each other. Yet it is not a static realm but one fitted with a *telos*, a notion of faith to grow and to expand "into a doubtless evidence and unshakeable conviction of God's existence." According to the promise of Christ, *those of pure heart shall see God* (Matt. 5:8). And *whoever loves*, following the words of the apostle John, *knows God* (1 John 4:7). *Whoever loves God*, says the apostle Paul, *will be granted knowledge by Him*[167] (1 Cor. 8:3).[168] In our modest opinion, what Sil'vestr is discussing here, whether out of a proper spiritual experience or out of inspiration, is *contemplation*. Enabled by a pure heart and induced by love, the result is faith that has matured into a conviction. Thus the purity of heart gains knowledge of God, a space and disposition that enable the Divine to become a reality in the human being. The persuasion is also inspired by looking at the visible world and seeing "nature as a perfect work of God's hands" that was purposefully created to strengthen the weak human faith, "so as to illuminate it with brighter light, if it was dark." The beauty of nature is to reveal God's immanence in it.[169]

4.3.1. Applied Anthropology

None of the manuals so far had made plain such an anthropological momentum in recognizing God's being, the knowledge and reality of which are *existentially* planted in the human heart, let alone before even reviewing any OT or NT narrative of revelation. Eventually, Sil'vestr establishes a straight association between the human heart and the "human spirit" when he states that the ability (or lack thereof) to recognize and know God's existence and being is in the final analysis caused by the human spirit, in its "moral integrity or its moral depravity." His conclusion is as simple as it is profound: it is through the depravity of the heart that the human being loses the capacity to recognize God.[170] And we can freely add: to recognize Him *as* He truly is. Sil'vestr continues his reflection by considering the teachings of various Fathers, ecclesial traditions, even (western) philosophy and relevant scriptural references also in Greek, yet far less numerously than Filaret Gumilevskii or

167. An English translation would render it with "But whoever loves God is known by God"; therefore I have used my own translation from Russian.

168. OPDB I, p. 178.

169. Cf. OPDB I, p. 179.

170. Cf. OPDB I, p. 182.

Makarii Bulgakov did. This is consistent throughout his work, and in return his own reflections have more of the consistent, meditative flow of a spiritual retreat,[171] demonstrating that applying a contemplative narrative style of reflection, a method used previously by the ancient Church Fathers, can be equally valid for a modern dogmatic manual.

4.4. God as Loving Father of All

In the second volume, dedicated to *The Trinitarian God in His Persons,* we are presented two "external" ways of knowing God, by the means of his visible attributes: a) through revelation and b) in God's relating to the world in its creation. Both, according to Sil'vestr, are accessible within our earthly realm solely to the human intellect. Consequently he asks whether God's attributes, as humans describe them, have any "inner relationship," whether they are connected intrinsically to the entity of God. Sil'vestr is looking for a *living relationship* in the rapports between the attributes of God and his very "being,"[172] as well as between the three divine Persons, rather than a sterile rational definition.[173] In the NT part, it is at the baptism of Jesus in the Jordan that he indicates the first qualitative reference of this Trinitarian relationship: "This is my beloved Son, with whom I am well pleased" (Matt. 3:16-17; Mark 1:10-11; Luke 3:22), focusing on the ontology of the three Divine Persons in the Trinity. In §89, titled *The Teaching of Jesus Christ Himself on the Three Persons of God,* the quality of their interrelatedness becomes more evident when Jesus presents "God-Father" as the "Father of all people" instead of a mere *Creator* and *Ruler:* ". . . He is also kindred *(rodstvennyi)* to humankind and is its loving Father. For instance in the teaching on love for all, not excluding even enemies, He [Jesus] was showing humankind the love of *its* Father, as the most elevated ideal of such love, a Father whom it is

171. In §37 introducing the "teaching of revelation," Sil'vestr takes up the issue of God's transparence and incomparability to anything created, or better put, the forceful limitations of our understanding in comprehending God's full entity. Cf. OPDB I, pp. 245-50.

172. Cf. OPDB II, pp. 3-6.

173. Sil'vestr has the right intention yet he rarely, if at all, becomes explicit about the quality or means of relating, when reflecting on the relationship between the three divine Persons of the Trinity. "Just as any limited and finite spirit exists as single being, the Endless Spirit exists in three persons and this does not mean three, separate parts in the being of God, for that would mean three gods in the same being. In their inner relating they show their distinct and different person." Cf. OPDB II, pp. 205-6.

called to imitate so as to be worthy children of His (Matt. 5:44-45)."[174] This elucidation of love is meant to be also an example of trust for all humanity that all is contained in the loving providence of God, of the "same Heavenly Father" who knows our needs and grants them before we even utter a request (Matt. 6:1-4, 6-8, 14-15, 18). This becomes manifest when Jesus "addresses God in a human way, calling Him Father (Matt. 11:25; John 20:17) and giving to all people the commandment not to pray diversely, as: *Our Father, who art in heaven . . .* (Matt. 6:9)."

Sil'vestr, too, arrives at John 3:13-18, revealing God's love-message for the world in the sacrifice of His beloved Son. The Son markedly has the "same character" as the Father at whom He points; they "share the same life" and therefore only the Son truly knows the Father. He knows that the Father loves Him (John 3:35), "speaks the words of God" (John 3:34), and the Son loves the Father (John 14:31). They are one in being yet different persons, "differing like a friend from a friend, because the loving one cannot remain undistinguished from the beloved one, just as the beloved one cannot confound himself with the loving one," referring to the distinct personal identities of the three hypostases.[175] There is a perichoresis of love, an emitter and a receiver, so that love may be reciprocated in an eternal motion of love — giving and receiving in one Deity with diverse Persons. The procession of love applies also to the relationship between God and the world through the Holy Spirit. It is out of *this* love that the Son is fulfilling the will of the Father (3:16-17; 5:30; 6:38-40; 8:42).

4.4.1. Jesus' Teaching on the Holy Spirit

"Christ's teaching" on the Holy Spirit is first considered in its attributes as "Spirit of truth, Consoler," etc., and then as distinction in the Trinity — "the Spirit of truth that is also a Son of God" and the "fulfiller of the Son's glory" who acts on the apostles after Jesus' ascension.[176] Even though the "Holy Spirit proceeds from the Father only," yet in His acts of redeeming humankind, the Spirit is "perfectly one with the Son's intention," just as the Son is inseparable and "undivided" from that of the Father. In this union the Spirit shall not be mistaken for a mere attribute of the Son, but seen as His true reality: a proper Person, fitted with a proper will, self-knowledge, awareness,

174. Cf. OPDB II, pp. 234-35.
175. Cf. OPDB II, pp. 237-38.
176. Cf. OPDB II, pp. 243-44.

and act. This teaching "uncovered and unfolded" by Jesus to his apostles was not an end in itself but was destined beyond the apostles for future disciples "and all the nations" of the world, "for their baptism," i.e., *salvation.*[177]

4.5. God's Primordial and Unique Image

In §29 of volume three, there is a clear distinction between the "general creation," even of the "spiritual beings," and the human being. In the last one "God's creative action is very much differing" from that of the previous creations: "Man was shaped in His image and resemblance . . . which He placed above all earthly creatures." And since "solely man has been adorned with the resemblance of God's image," being a "primordial image" *(pervoobraz),* it stands "incomparably higher than anything earthly and material."[178] Sil'vestr's methodology is very systematic yet in some cases, such as the origin of the human being, while all is based on a scriptural foundation, the anthropological aspect of the creation is surprisingly less evident.[179] God breathes life and with it a "living soul" into the human being (Gen. 2:7), in an act of a unique and life-sustaining intimacy that introduces us into the second chapter on "God as Sustainer of the World." This *undescribed intimacy* was certainly a missed occasion to lay bare why God continues to care for the human being. In §50, on *God as Sustainer of the World in General,* Sil'vestr presents a series of "God-images" from the Scriptures. Among other things, God "is not an indifferent and uninvolved spectator of all that is occurring in the world" but is much more a "father in his household" (Matt. 5:45; 6:26-32), as well as a *Supreme Ruler* and *King* in his kingdom (1 Chron. 29:11-12; Ps. 102:19):[180] "He loves the righteous ones (Ps. 145:8), and hates all the evil-doers (Ps. 5:6), He protects the first ones as the apple of His eyes (Ps. 16:8; 33:18), and does everything to their benefit (Rom. 8:28). . . . Yet He does not leave even the sinners without His providence, just as He commands His sun to rise above the evil and the good ones, sends His rain on the righteous and the unrighteous (Matt. 5:45)." God has sent His Son into the world to invite sinners (Luke 5:32), and though He "rebukes their wickedness with the rod" (Ps. 89:32), because of His mercy His anger does not last for eternity

177. Cf. OPDB II, pp. 244-48.
178. Cf. OPDB III, pp. 185-87.
179. Cf. OPDB III, p. 188.
180. Cf. OPDB III, pp. 340-41.

(Ps. 103:8-9), "but His patience is without end *(dolgoterpit i dolgoterpit)* so that by means of His goodness He may bring them to repentance (Rom. 2:4)." And if the just have to suffer and the wicked do not, in everything "He proceeds not out of a certain reason, but follows the inspiration of His truth and love" in order to purify them like silver from all impurities (Prov. 25:4).[181] Should anyone have doubts about God's wise providence, St. Paul's exclamation shall serve as a reassurance: *Oh, the depth of the riches and wisdom and knowledge of God! How unsearchable are His judgments and how inscrutable His ways!* (Rom. 11:33).[182]

4.5.1. Straining for Perfection in Communion

In an original contribution, Sil'vestr distinguishes in §56 and §59 between God's providing care for humankind before and after its fall. The first human being was created in perfection, but a perfection to be reached and gained, as it were, a "perfection in prospect and through progress" that the human being was meant to strain for (Matt. 5:48). Therefore the first human being was in constant need of God's providence for his survival *(sokhranenie);* so also for the development of those "deposits *(zadatok)* of his God-like nature in which his high vocation and destination was predetermined."[183] There was a direct dependency on God: his present life and future were continually sustained by his relationship with God. His heart was pure, thanks to which he could strain by all his forces after the "utmost happiness," but again, this purity of heart was granted and sustained out of a loving, fatherly-providential care by God.[184] In His providence, and to develop man's capacities, God gave him a soberly pragmatic commandment to avoid the fruit of knowledge of good and evil in the Garden of Eden (Gen. 2:17). This commandment was meant to strengthen him to follow God's will, which again was meant to become for him the "perpetual law, ideal and measure" of all things and relations. The access to all the other trees testifies about God's generosity and care, as well as their "closeness and the rightness *(pravota)* in relating to God," whom they used to see face to face.[185] All "the blessedness of the first humans," characterized by a reciprocal intimate relationship between them and the loving and providing God, ended with the

181. Cf. OPDB III, pp. 342-44.
182. Cf. OPDB III, p. 345.
183. Cf. OPDB III, pp. 402-3.
184. Cf. OPDB III, p. 404.
185. Cf. OPDB III, pp. 405-8.

fatal sin-fall. This brought about a change in God's providence for them and their descendants[186] and crystallized eventually in the saving act of Jesus Christ, who *is* the *Providence* of God in the Holy Spirit. God "in His endless love" from eternity had a *solution* to save fallen humankind, which He created "for an inner and free communion with Himself. Therefore even after their fall God did not cease to look for such a communion with them,"[187] through salvation:

> It consists in nothing else than in God's unique love for humankind of which Christ Himself has witnessed, teaching about God who *so loved the world that He gave His only Son so that whoever believes in Him should not perish but have eternal life* (John 3:16). In the same direct and clear way the apostles John and Paul taught, pointing out love as the main and only inducement predisposing God for salvation of humankind through His Son (1 John 4:9-10, Eph. 2:4).[188]

Sil'vestr returns anew to stress the universality and inclusiveness of this *plan,* for God does not want the death of even a single one (Ezek. 33:11).[189] Nevertheless salvation requires our free consent "and an active participation . . . under the condition of a living and acting faith in Christ," which requires an active repentance and an amended life.[190] The Christocentric character of this chapter is more than evident.

4.6. The Freedom of the Kingdom's Heirs to Love and to Be Beloved

In §95 of volume four, *The Revelational Teaching on the Prophetic Service of Christ,* Sil'vestr presents further "liberating moments" out of Christ's teaching with regard to the right image of God the Father:

> God, in Himself, is not only a Father when relating to His Son and the Holy Spirit, but also, in a moral-beneficial sense, He is the same loving Father in His relationship to humankind. He does not solely bestow upon them all goodness (Matt. 7:11) but regardless of all their sinfulness

186. Cf. OPDB III, p. 426.
187. Cf. OPDB III, pp. 495-96 and pp. 496-505 (also 490-95).
188. OPDB III, p. 497.
189. Follows a list of NT references on Christ's universal mission of salvation.
190. OPDB III, pp. 499-500.

> He loves them so much *that He gave His only Son, that whoever believes in Him should not perish but have eternal life* (John 3:16). The conception that such is God, evidently, could not help but invoke in humankind a new, sonship-like feeling towards God, rather than a slavish one, and through this to start a new, higher religious relationship to Him that the apostle Paul transmits to new believers in Christ as follows: *you did not receive the spirit of slavery to fall back into fear, but you have received the Spirit of adoption as sons, by whom we cry, "Abba! Father!"* (Rom. 8:15). *So you are no longer a slave, but a son, and if a son, then an heir through God* (Gal. 4:7).[191]

Such knowledge has a direct impact on interhuman relationships as well, since now they have one common creator and sustainer, a God with a fatherly relationship (Matt. 5:45) to whom they all pray in unison "Our Father." Thus Christ gave them the *new commandment* on love (John 13:34) "and namely of such a love that, similarly to the Heavenly Father's love, shall not fence itself in with those loving us or being friendly to us, but include also those who hate us or are our enemies (Matt. 5:44-47)." Further, our love is to "extend into the fullest self-renouncing *(samootverhenie)* for the salvation of our neighbor," an example that was given by Jesus Christ Himself (John 13:34; 15:13). Obviously this most elevated teaching of Christ had an immense impact on the moral lives of His followers, as in relation towards God so towards their neighbors.[192] Christ's high priestly role and function was indispensable to remove the weight of sin even at a rational-emotional level.[193] Christ's action was guided by His *kenotic love* as described in Philippians 2:6-8 and in the apostles' teaching on Christ (1 John 4:10; Rom. 8:32; Eph. 5:8; 1 Cor. 2:8 — kenotic mind; Acts 20:28; 1 John 1:7).[194]

The teaching of Christ is carried on and out by the church as the task of humankind's sanctification through the sacraments. No one can lay a different foundation in relating to God than Jesus Christ Himself did — a foundation that rests at the very heart of the Trinity.

191. Cf. OPDB IV, pp. 110-11.
192. Cf. OPDB IV, pp. 110-11.
193. Cf. OPDB IV, pp. 111-13.
194. Cf. OPDB IV, pp. 113-14.

Conclusion

With Sil'vestr's (Malevanskii's) dogmatic manual we witness a strong anthropological notion in(to) the field of dogmatic interpretation, including legitimately (and legitimating) human senses and feelings. *The perception of God's existence in my heart is as real as the feeling of my proper life.* How could one contest this on an epistemological level? Especially since our reason is aided by our perceptions, intuitions, a *feeling* of faith. . . . *The wisdom of heart* is an inner compass and trustworthy indicator to believe in and to contemplate God as He was revealed to us in His visible icon — Jesus Christ. Sil'vestr gave us more than just a hermeneutical key by pointing towards the human heart. The prophets, Scriptures, Fathers, and tradition speak of the divine wisdom of love that resides in the human heart, reflecting — and being reflected — the wisdom of God seated at His right. But by *love* not merely as sentiment but above all as imitation of the Holy Trinity's relations, we learn to know God better. Since *love* is God's essence and we were formed in His image, love was planted in the human heart so that it may yet grow further in(to) the Divine.

5. Nikolai Platonovich Malinovskii: *We Love Whom We Know*

5.1. Bibliography

N. P. Malinovskii (1861-1917) received his education in the Theological Academy of Moscow. He composed the last major treatise on dogmatic theology, which was his doctoral dissertation *Pravoslavnoe dogmaticheskoe bogoslovie (Orthodox Dogmatic Theology)*.[195] It appeared in a four-volume edition in Kharkov between 1895 and 1903.[196] Various editions of it were published,

195. The biographical data on N. P. Malinovskii are scarce, basically reduced to a listing of his works. Cf.' *Polnyi pravoslavnyi bogoslovskii enciklopedicheskii slovar*, ed. P. P. Soikin (Sankt-Peterburg, n.d.); and cf. *Russkie mysliteli vtoroi poloviny XIX — nachala XX Veka: Opyt kratkogo biobibliograficheskogo slovaria*, ed. B. V. Emeliianov and V. V. Kulikov (Ekaterinburg: Ural, 1996), p. 196. We know that he was ordained a priest and later became an archpriest, fulfilled functions of the rector of the Podol'sky Theological Seminary (1906), inspector of the Stavropol' Theological Seminary (1895-1908), and rector of the Vologodsky Theological Seminary (1909-10), according to the information and dates found on the cover pages of his manuals.

196. For the sake of completeness we shall use *Pravoslavnoe dogmaticheskoe bogos-*

mostly with slight changes in the grouping of content,[197] and even an *Ocherk pravoslavnogo dogmaticheskogo bogosloviia (An Essay of Orthodox Dogmatic Theology),* which has a proper introduction as it was destined to be a textbook for theological seminaries approved by the Holy Synod.[198] Another pertinent work of Malinovskii, a dogmatic essay on *God the Savior, O Boge Iskupitele: Dogmaticheskii ocherk (On God Redeemer: A Dogmatic Essay),* appeared in 1906 and is basically an excerpt from the third volume in *Pravoslavnoe dogmaticheskoe bogoslovie.*[199]

---

lovie, vols. 1-2 (Sergiev Posad: Tip. Sergievoi Lavry, 1910); and volumes 3-4 from the 1909 edition, as only this was available for us (PDBM). To the three mottos of the first edition (John 17:3, 1 John 4:1, Col. 2:8–Eph. 4:14 — with apparent dogmatic concerns) have been added others (John 1:3; Col. 1:16-17; John 3:16; Matt. 16:27; 1 Cor. 2:9), where the first (John 3:16) and the last (1 Cor. 2:9) refer to God's love for the world and concern for humankind's salvation. According to Cioffari, Malinovskii is aware of the criticisms against the manuals of his predecessors for their "coldness and scholasticism," a criticism from the *Khomiakovian stream.* For this reason Malinovskii attempted a synthesis between Makarii's manual and the new approaches, as well as to insert the "scientific-positivist" demands of his time, between *science and faith.* While more successful in the latter, according to Cioffari, he was less so in the first intention, giving an impression rather of a "juxtaposition instead of a synthesis." This would be the case especially in the "role of the hierarchy and the distinction in the Church between an *ecclesia docens* and an *ecclesia dicens.*" Cf. Cioffari, "Breve storia della teologia russa," p. 35.

197. As for instance in volumes 1-2 of *Pravoslavnoe dogmaticheskoe bogoslovie,* published in 1895-1903, and volumes 1-4 in 1909-10.

198. Its introduction mentions that it was destined for the future clergy in formation in the seminaries from whom the current times require a "broad theological knowledge," and also presents the proper characteristics of the Catholic and Protestant confessions. Cf. *Ocherk pravoslavnogo dogmaticheskogo bogosloviia* (Sergiev Posad: Sv. Troickaia Lavra, 1911), p. ii.

199. Malinovskii's *Orthodox Dogmatic Theology* is divided as follows: volume 1 has the usual introduction on dogmatic theology, its concept, methodology, principal terminology, development, and a brief review of western dogmatics. Part one on "God in Himself," with subchapters one, "On God Who Is One in Essence," and section two on "God Who Is Trinitarian in His Persons." Volume 2 carries the title of "On God in His Relations to His Creatures," with subchapters on: "God as Creator of the World, God as Sustainer of the World" (with three subparts relating to the topics of "Good" and "Evil Spirits," "Human Being," and on God's unique relationship to the human race). Volume 3 has two main parts and topics: "On God Savior," with chapters on the person and work of Jesus Christ, "On God Sanctifier" with chapters "On Grace as a Sanctifying Power," and "On the Church as Mediator of Sanctification." Volume 4 is dedicated to the "Sacraments," and the remaining part is "On God as Accomplisher of His Plans for the Entire World and Humankind."

5.2. Theology and Faith

Malinovskii's methodology is scientific yet sensitive, using scriptural, patristic, and even non-Christian references with quotations in Latin, Greek, or other original languages where required. In §1 he provides a very lucid definition of theology and dogmatics in general, based on the derivation of the term *bogoslovie (theology),* from the original Greek θεολογία used by "Christian authors who took it over from the ancient Greeks." However, in "current times" it is used in a very broad sense; he thus gives the following concise definition of dogmatic theology: "Dogmatic theology is a science whose object is the systematic presentation of the whole sum of Christian dogmas."[200] Malinovskii renders the meaning and development of dogmas through the centuries beginning with the early Church Fathers, even mentioning ancient statesmen and philosophers such as Demosthenes or Plato, biblical as well as patristic quotations. At the end of this historical review in §2 an enriched view of dogmatics is outlined: ". . . dogmas are the divine revelations of the truth, containing in themselves the teaching on God and His relationship to the world and especially to the human being, preserved, formed and taught by the Orthodox Church, as unquestionable, unchangeable and binding for all who believe the rules of faith, for all believers."[201] From the very beginning Malinovskii leaves no space for doubt as to the Christocentricism of his dogmatics and refers constantly in different passages to Christ's central place, especially when it comes to the subject of revelation (§3). He proves in numerous passages from the Scriptures the necessity and verity of faith in Jesus Christ as Savior.

5.2.1. An Intrinsic Love Soteriology

After identifying *salvation* as a requisite characteristic of Christian faith, Malinovskii identifies *love* as equally intrinsic to the Christian concept of salvation, for love proceeds from the *intrinsic* nature of God Himself. *God is spirit* (John 4:24) ". . . and consequently all that is spiritual — truth, bounty, justice, reconciliation . . . shall be placed by a Christian higher than any perceptible-material things"; "*God is love* (1 John 4:8-16). It is in the reciprocal love-relationship that the internal, hidden life of the Divinity consists. From here is drawn the conclusion that love is meant to constitute a higher

200. Cf. PDBM I, pp. 5-6.
201. Cf. PDBM I, pp. 18-19.

law *(zakon)* also for our moral being. God is the *Father of all* (Matt. 5:45; 23:9) and therefore we too are supposed to form one family and establish among ourselves family-type relationships/blood-relationships *(rodstvennyia otnosheniia)*."[202] The *imitation of God,* i.e., the adaptation of our moral ideals to God, through the revelation and teaching of Jesus Christ, is the full consequence of the above-acquired comprehension. *Your Heavenly Father is perfect, so be you* (Matt. 5:48); *God is merciful, so be you merciful* (Luke 6:36) — all these are simultaneously dogmas.[203] However, it would be false to think that the "dogmas of faith have no special importance and meaning because the essence of Christianity consists *in the teaching on love.*" This misconception apparently was a widespread opinion, since Malinovskii felt it needed to be addressed. There is an epistemological reciprocity between the commandment to love and the knowledge of God, which once more confirms the necessity and legitimate existence of dogmas since the first is rooted in the second: "Therefore, the *love for God* becomes impossible if one is denying the importance of the dogmas, which grant us the understanding of God, His perfections and His relating to us: we only can love someone whom we know and thus have an inducement to love; whom we do not know, we have no urge and cannot love."[204] In and through dogmas we obtain a proper knowledge of God and concurrently the urge to:

> . . . love above all God *with all* our *heart, with all* our *soul, with all* our *understanding* (Matt. 22:37). Dogmas revealed that God in His relating to the human being is a Creator, Sustainer and a most loving Father *(liubveobilneishii)* who has sent His only begotten Son for the salvation of the fallen human being and then the Holy Spirit, who is aiding humankind to put off the old and to put on a new person, and that with conviction and peaceful joy so as to complete the work of salvation. . . .[205]

This wealth of God's care extends from the past, through the present, beyond the last judgment, where those "loving Him" will receive their inconceivable glory.

202. Cf. PDBM I, pp. 29-30.
203. Cf. PDBM I, p. 30.
204. Cf. PDBM I, p. 31.
205. PDBM I, pp. 31-32.

5.3. The Image of Christian Love Purified in a Cognitive Process

There is a logical equation in this relationship exposed in the dogmas. It reflects the nature of the covenants that God made with humankind: "If such is God in His relationship to the human being, (then) it is natural, that the human being owes a response to this love of God with the most faithful and the most grateful love towards Him." Conversely, if one discards "such a teaching on God and His relationship to the human being, then for the human being there remains no motive to love God."[206] Reflecting on the proper image of God, Malinovskii questions what love, with a pantheistic idea of God, would be like, where God is impersonal, a creator that creates the human being in order just to turn indifferent to his fate, abandoning him without further providence. This juxtaposition is a good proof of Malinovskii's anthropological sensitivity: the question is not regarding primarily creation in general, or the world and universe, but focuses on the *human being,* and therefore even more concretely on the *relationship* between God and the human being: precisely, a *relationship* that grows out of love and yearns to be reciprocated. Just as God's love is poured out into the creation, human love, constantly fed from its Origin, needs to be shared with our fellow human beings. The dogmas exhort us to "*love our neighbors,* as *ourselves* (Matt. 22:39; Luke 10:27; Gal. 5:14),"[207] for "we all descend from the same couple and we *are* (and not merely *supposed* to be) siblings,[208] united in life, death and final judgment, wherefore love for each other is a matter of course." The commandment and concept of love for one's neighbor is essentially linked to the Christian image of God who is:

> . . . a God of love in Himself *(Bog liubvi v Samom Sebe)* as well as in His relationships to people. Since we all are created in the image of God, each person is called to imitate His way of relating. Ultimately this commandment, being divine and the commandment of God, constitutes an inseparable part of the love for God, as the Savior said: *If anyone loves me, he will keep my word* (John 14:21, 23; 1 John 4:20-21). Being so conceived, the Christian commandment on love is comprehensible and natural to humankind and does not evoke misunderstandings. However, if we negate this latter dogmatic evidence, it also loses its proper sense.[209]

206. Cf. PDBM I, pp. 31-32.
207. Cf. PDBM I, p. 32.
208. Malinovskii uses "brothers."
209. PDBM I, p. 32.

And with it we lose *the* point of reference also for how to love our neighbors as our very self.[210] In this, Christian love fundamentally differs, for instance, from the view of the ancient "great intellects" such as Plato or Aristotle, who by distinguishing between "aristocratic Greeks" and "barbarians," and even among Greeks and Greeks, run the risk of creating animosities resulting in rules such as "homo homini lupus est." Christian love, equally in contrast to humanism or altruism, is a love that is called "to be all-embracing" and inclusive, even with one's enemies (Matt. 5:43-47), and "be willing to be all-forgiving and self-sacrificing for the good of one's neighbors (John 15:12-13; 1 Cor. 13:1-6; Eph. 4:30-32)."[211]

Malinovskii insists on the ontological foundation of love in the knowledge of God and His salvation. The described "traits of Christian love cannot be comprehended outside the dogma on salvation, since they are entirely imbedded in the love that has manifested itself in the mystery of salvation."[212] An acute observation completes the characterization of divine love, which streams from the ontological foundation of "God's image within the human being." There is a need and obligation to love our very self, yet not in an egoistic way but for the sake of God's image that is in our very souls and that makes us into *God-bearers.* The love of our very self, in the proper meaning of the word, is a love of God which is present in his image within us, as God's permanent presence in our being. Thus, *the* true love for one's very self is a love that is charitable, providing, and cooperating in salvation. To transmit this cognition of truth and distinguish it from egoism is one of the tasks of dogmatic theology: "Without the idea of perceiving our *self* as a bearer of God's image, nothing remains. Without the ordinary love for our self, i.e., to love the image of God in ourselves, the character of love for one's self exteriorizes in the form of a coarse self-love (egoism)."[213] Indeed, this is a most noble task of dogmatics.

5.4. *Dogmas as Interpretation*

Malinovskii undertakes a spiritual leap in scrutinizing Schleiermacher's view on Christ. For Schleiermacher, Christ was "solely a morally-perfect and holy person, who thanks to the might of His unique God-awareness *(bogosoz-*

210. Cf. PDBM I, p. 32.
211. Cf. PDBM I, pp. 32-33.
212. PDBM I, p. 33.
213. . . . *v forme grubago samoliubia (egoisma).* PDBM I, p. 33.

nanie)" stood in closest union with God, in a measure that "no one from among human beings can achieve." Malinovskii picks up the thread where Schleiermacher left it and states that out of this precise reason "is Christ for us an example that we are called to follow," and since "Jesus is Redeemer and Savior," our faith does not depend on "metaphysical attributes of His existence and the supernatural events from His life (miraculous birth, resurrection, ascension and others)" but rather ". . . is a faith of experience *(vera opyta);* a communion with God by the way of imitation of Christ."[214] Accordingly, there are logical boundaries even for the dogmas since they have their origin in *faith.* Faith itself, however, stands at the birth of theology and therefore is not subject to the formulas of theology:

> Dogmas are not objective divine truths, but subjective interpretations of Christian experience expressing that which is common in the Christian experience of all who believe in Christ or the Church. The adogmatics *(adogmatizm)* of Schleiermacher, therefore, stands on a mystical ground. Such an attribution of utmost importance to feelings, pious aspirations and dispositions of heart in religious life — together with rejecting the importance of dogmas — is common for all mystical teachings of antiquity and of modern times.[215]

Feeling as cognition, the human heart, cannot be and is not meant to be excluded from the process of faith, just as true gnosis and epistemology are not. In that sense, to *know* and to *love* are one motion of the spirit, stretching the heart and expanding the horizons of the intellect to grasp the mysteries of divine revelation.

5.4.1. "As Long as the Heart Is Not Involved . . ."

Even though these may appear to be daring statements, Malinovskii's reasoning does not sound artificial; he proceeds organically and in a structured way, based on the given dogmatic truths and his own reflection. When he places faith through living experience and gives love a central role in an inner relationship with God, it is not sentimentalism but rather raising the debate to a different epistemological level, perhaps granting us an insight into his proper

214. . . . *putem podrazhaniia Khristu.* A formulation that sounds conspicuously similar to the Russian title of Thomas à Kempis's *Imitation of Christ.* Cf. PDBM I, p. 34.

215. PDBM I, p. 35.

faith-experience with God. That senses have a role of utmost importance in religious-moral life, according to him, is evident from the Revelation (Matt. 5:8, Eph. 5:19; Ps. 23:3-4). "As long as the heart is not involved in contemplating the religious truths," these latter bear a "cold comprehension of reason and do not exercise any influence on the life of the human being" but end in a mechanical fulfillment of religious duties, turning the person into a hypocrite. This, once more, gives credit to the *senses* in the concept of religion and a proper relationship to God and the quality of this relationship:[216]

> We (too) are not supposed to say in an abstract way: "there is God" *(Bog est')*, "God exists" *(Bog sushchestvuiet)*, but rather: God is love; Christ has revealed Him to us as the Father, who desires our salvation. We do not know how the son of Mary has obtained the knowledge of this most high revelation; but it is indisputable that solely through Jesus we have obtained the knowledge of the Father, because the charity *(miloserdie)* and might *(mogushchestvo)* of God . . . have been revealed to us solely through the work of Jesus Christ.[217]

This "obtained knowledge," subsequently recognized as a revealing divine truth, is being transmitted to us by the dogmas in the form of logical explanation.[218] The knowledge of God's existence, unrelated, is not sufficient. *True knowledge can be attained only by acquiring the knowledge of the essence of God.*

5.4.2. Reasoning Moral-Beings Filled with Beatitude

In §12, on the *Truth of God's Existence,* we find that this ontological truth is planted deeply in the human being, first by a God-like nature of the human soul and second by the most particular relationship of the Divine to the human soul. "The idea of God is directly inherent or innate to the human being . . . in the depths of his soul he carries the perception/feeling of God's existence . . . for God is closer to the human soul than to any of the irrational creatures."[219] Malinovskii does a detailed scriptural analysis of his postulates while his theology remains fully Christocentric. The proper knowledge of

216. Cf. PDBM I, p. 35.
217. PDBM I, p. 37.
218. Cf. PDBM I, p. 41.
219. Cf. PDBM I, pp. 143-44.

the Father equals eternal life; ergo salvation is revealed by the arrival of Jesus Christ: *And this is eternal life, that they know you the only true God, and Jesus Christ whom you have sent* (John 17:3). But the life Jesus brings revives equally the *reason,* the *will,* and the *heart.* "Without the knowledge of God there is no life for the soul, and because there is no truth for the reason, there is no bounty for the will and there is no blessedness for the heart. God is the *source of life* to our soul (Ps 35:10)."[220]

In §23, in the second part when treating the subject of the *Endless Goodness and Blessedness,* i.e., *God's Love for His Creatures,* it is the first time we encounter the expression of love in one of the titles of the current manual. "God reveals Himself in an all-blessed *(vseblagim)* and all-loving *(vseliubiashchim)* form to those who love the utmost bounty *(verkhovnoe blago)* and grants them so much blessedness and happiness as they can bear and need in order to be content." Malinovskii cites for precision St. Gregory the Great, who to a hypothetical question "What do we celebrate, what do we worship?" provides the following explanation: ". . . we honor love, for according to the uttering of the Holy Spirit: our *God is love* (1 John 4:8-16)." This indescribable beatitude was what moved God to create the world along with "the reasoning-moral beings . . . capable of loving Him and finding for themselves blessedness in Him (Eph. 1:5, 9; John 14:23; Matt. 25:34)."[221]

5.5. *Selfless Love and the God of Justice*

In numerous NT quotations, our author displays how profound the caring relationship of God is. For instance: on the image of the mother that cannot forget her child, but even if she presumably did, God will never forget His children (Isa. 49:15); similarly the *Father images* revealed by Jesus (Matt. 23:9; 7:9-11). Others follow the Acts and the apostolic letters, concluding that the greatest act of mercy was and remains the act of our salvation through the death of His only begotten Son (John 3:16). Malinovskii adds what he calls "the explanation of John" to the previous passage about the *how,* the *quality*

220. Cf. PDBM I, p. 161. Ps. 35:10 referring to Ps. 36:9: "For with you is the fountain of life; in your light do we see light."

221. All of God's works and creation are signs of His bounty and beatitude, but the human being has a privileged, special place since it carries His image in itself, and therefore, once again: "In particular His bounty and love God revealed and keeps revealing in His relationship to the human being." Cf. PDBM I, p. 245.

of God's love for the world: "*In this is love, not that we have loved God but that He loved us and sent His Son to be the propitiation for our sins* (1 John 4:10; cf. Rom. 5:6-8).[222] So unbounded and unutterable is the grace of God in His relationship to created beings!"[223] It is not about the capability of the created "restricted beings" (i.e., beings with limitations) to love but that their love is "never entirely free of self-interest." The selfish, egoistic love is the contrary of the Christian concept of love: "Even in increasing the well-being *(blago)* of the other, there is always a strong self-interest in increasing our own well-being. God's love is not of this kind, since He has, and is, the fullness of *goodness* and *well-being,* but His love is boundlessly and selflessly extending on the whole world — not just a part of it — but all that exists in it."[224]

5.5.1. *Moral Applications of Diverse Attributes*

On the moral level, to some, "with a one-sided religious-moral disposition of mind," there is a discrepancy between the above-described image of God and a God who "strongly rebukes" evildoers. Thus for some of the ancient heretics (the Gnostics, Manicheans, and the like) the two *attributes* in God, that of *justice* and of *love,* could not coexist in one God; hence they spoke of two gods. This danger is not fully banned and there are still Christians who have an "image of God of love" while they "exclude from Him" the aspect of justice.[225] Both concepts are naturally one-sided and lacking an essential attribute of God. Malinovskii condenses it to the point that if God did not have both aspects in Him, His love would not be *just* and consequently not *true* either: "Naturally, God is love *(Bog liuby est'),*[226] but His love is just, equally as His truth is true, animated by love: love without truth would not be a true love (it would manifest itself by a simple susceptibility and complacency).[227] Equally, truth without love would not be a veritable truth (it would turn into coldness or soullessness, it would be close to cruelty [*zhestokost'*])." Revelation, however, does not divide these attributes in God and presents Him both as the "loving Father" and the "just Judge" (Ps. 98:8;

222. The originally quoted text of Malinovskii says: ". . . ap. Ioann poiasniaet tak: *o sem est liuby, ne iako my vozliubikhom Boga, no iako Toi vozliubil nas, i poslal Syna Svoego ochishchenie o gresekh nashikh* (1 Jn 4:10; Rm 5:6-8)." PDBM I, p. 246.

223. Cf. PDBM I, p. 246.

224. Cf. PDBM I, pp. 247-51.

225. Cf. PDBM I, pp. 246-47.

226. Here he applies a quote in Church Slavonic.

227. . . . *iavlas by prostoiu chuvstvitelnostiiu i blagodushiem.*

cf. 24:8-10; 84:11; Sir. 16:12; Ezra 3:11-12; etc.).[228] It is a balanced image of God, an image that allows and challenges the faithful Christian to grow humanly and divinely, in all dimensions of love. *Justice* is not an outside attribute or accompanier of love, but a fruit of charity, of divine, self-sacrificing love: in order to safeguard the necessary space for each human being. Malinovskii places God's "punishments" along with the concept of the Fathers — as "medicine and remedy" for the salvation of the soul.[229]

5.5.2. The Trinity of Love and More Epistemology

On the topic of the "Trinitarian God in His Persons (O Boge Troichnom v licakh)," in §29 Malinovskii reverts to the symbol of St. Athanasius on the equality of the three persons in the Holy Trinity: "Nothing is first or last, nothing more or less, but all the Three Hypostases are existing co-eternally and are equal among themselves."[230] While equality in the Trinity is a fundamental teaching of Christianity, the incomprehensibility of the Holy Trinity applies not only to the human intellect but also to heavenly creatures such as the angels, for "*no one knows the Father except the Son and anyone to whom the Son chooses to reveal Him*" (Matt. 11:27).[231] Solely the Spirit of God knows the answers: *for the Spirit searches everything, even the depths of God* (1 Cor. 2:10).[232] In the following passage, Malinovskii undertakes a well-researched review of the historical development of this dogma. In §31 he returns to Athanasius's teaching on the Trinity, in which the dogma is expressed with the "greatest completeness" and where all the fundamental aspects of it are reviewed: "So as the Father, such is the Son, and such is the Holy Spirit too; nevertheless, they are not three gods, but one God . . . ,"[233] thus revealing about love that all of the Hypostases are united in "one will, one love, one action . . ." for the created world and the human being.

For the world it was the incarnated Word of God that brought the possibility to know God the Father such as He is. The first NT quote comes from Mark (Mark 1:11) and from Luke's Gospel (Luke 3:22) comes the story of Je-

228. Here many biblical attributes with their references are indicated: *for who God loves, him He chastises* (Prov. 3:11-12; cf. Heb. 12:5-8) or *Those I love, I reprove and discipline, so be zealous and repent* (Rev. 3:19; cf. 1 Cor. 11:32). Cf. PDBM I, pp. 247-49.

229. Cf. PDBM I, p. 249.

230. . . . *soprisnosushchny sut i sebe ravny.* Cf. PDBM I, pp. 287-88.

231. Cf. PDBM I, p. 288.

232. Cf. PDBM I, p. 289.

233. Cf. PDBM I, p. 327.

sus' baptism in the Jordan, in which the Father talks about His *beloved* Son: *"You are my beloved Son; with you I am well pleased."*[234] First things first — and this is Malinovskii's point too: if this was the most urgent message that the Father had to reveal about His Son to the world right at the beginning of His public ministry, confirming it by the peaceful presence of the Holy Spirit in the form of a dove, then it *is* crucial and essential to God. What begins with a love-message ends in the same way, as the second testimony, which Jesus reveals to His disciples shortly before his martyrdom on the cross: *"I love the Father,*[235] *and he will give you another Helper, to be with you forever. . . . But the Helper, the Holy Spirit, whom the Father will send in my name, He will teach you all things and bring to your remembrance all that I have said to you"* (John 14:16, 26).[236] This passage renders even more apparent the Three Hypostases in the Trinity.

5.5.3. *The Divine Economy*

After these premises and key epistemological concepts on the interaction between love and knowledge, Malinovskii reviews all the other listed topics in the subsequent volumes with the identical scientific approach. So in the second volume of his dogmatic theology he treats broadly anthropology in its various aspects: the human being in composition of soul and body — their origin, relationship, and sustenance by God.[237] God's loving care is visible in His providential and providing love to the first created human being, present already in the primordial nature of the human being. It is interesting to note that God's plan foresaw a further development of their capacities even in Eden.[238] The sin-fall, which arose from a yet not-fully-understood concept of freedom, however, changed all this, for they were supposed to reach full maturity through growth in freedom.[239] God desired, in His eternal wisdom and bounty, to save fallen humankind, yet not without or against the gift of their free will. The totality of God's grace-acts as Savior of humankind

234. Cf. PDBM I, p. 340.

235. This part was added by Malinovskii or is a different, to us unknown, translation. Another possible explication is a free paraphrasing, which, in sight of the Gospel used, that of John, and the chapter in question, is not such a "deviation" from a proper method of quoting. It could be equally cited from John 14:31: *"I love the Father."*

236. Cf. PDBM I, p. 340.

237. Cf. PDBM II, pp. 140-204.

238. Cf. PDBM II, pp. 292-94.

239. Cf. PDBM II, p. 309.

is called the "divine economy (*domostroitelstvo,* οἰκονομία, e.g., Eph. 1:10; 3:2, 9; Col. 1:25) of salvation of the human being." It was accomplished by His Son, Jesus Christ, and is being carried out to the end by His Church, which "has been granted all the indispensable means (sacraments)[240] for a blessed sanctification of the human being."[241]

Even though Malevanskii initiated the topic of "God as Savior" in the second volume, it is really developed in volume three in the light of the NT world. Jesus Christ is *the* Messiah for the reception of whom humankind has been prepared during many centuries and who came "for the salvation of *all* the nations."[242] Malinovskii makes a side-by-side listing and comparison of the prophecies and their fulfillment in Jesus Christ in the Scriptures, reviewing concurrently the other nonprophetical scriptural references.[243]

At last in §73, "The Lord Jesus Christ Is a God-Man," we read: "According to moral life — Jesus Christ is the living example of morality and demonstrates the completeness of the human being. He is the primordial image of the Divine *(pervoobraz),* after which the soul of the human being was formed." Even here the key concept and point of reference is "the love of God, love for the neighbor till self-sacrifice (John 15:13) regardless of their vocation, position or even nationality."[244] A message from the past century for our era: to respect our neighbor is not an option but an invitation to encounter God in His image.

Conclusion

"The dogmas revealed that God in His relating to the human being is a Creator, Sustainer and a most loving Father who has sent His only begotten Son for the salvation of the fallen human being. . . ." The centrality of the *loving Father* as God's image revealed in Christ's person and work is the core of Malinovskii's *God-image.* He simply founds his dogmatics upon the concept of love: on God's relationship to the human being, the imitation and *reciprocation* of the divine love. What sometimes had to be looked for through en-

240. To which he dedicates the fourth volume of his *Orthodox Dogmatic Theology.*

241. Cf. PDBM II, pp. 387-88.

242. Cf. PDBM III, pp. 3-4.

243. Cf. PDBM III, pp. 4-9.

244. Cf. PDBM III, p. 25. In this volume Malinovskii fully develops the question of the relationship between Son and Father, Christ's human yet divine life, His salvific and sanctifying role in and through His death and resurrection as well as the church's divine origin.

tire volumes in most of the previous manuals, Malinovskii lays down at the beginning like a bridge to an immense citadel — a bridge of *teaching* and *perception of the divine* that one simply has to cross in order to reach its inner chambers and find a safe haven. This plan seems not to omit anything that is essential for the Christian faith — even a clear exposure of the need for a self-sacrificing love for others, if we want to grow ever more into God's resemblance. *The knowledge of God* through *love* is the closest *union with God* one can hope for. Who knows, understands, and who understands, loves. This image is of a *loving* God-Father who bends down to the fallen human being, so much so that we can even *feel Him*. Thus there are two epistemological moments — or perhaps only one yet legitimately involving the entirety of the human person: *reason and the senses*. The anthropological dimension rendered by Malinovskii is one of the most profound we have encountered so far in any Orthodox manual of dogmatics of the past century, making it a unique spiritual type. Dogmas finally may become what they really are: earthly *renderings* of the Trinity's divine realm and its sacred economy, an invitation to know and love more, to reciprocate and share the only life-creating and sustaining tender love of God revealed to us in Jesus Christ's sacrificial love.

III. The Birth of Lay and Ecclesial Modern Theology

1. Alexei Stepanovich Khomiakov: The Church as a Living Organism of Truth and Love

1.1. Biography

To describe A. S. Khomiakov's life (1804-1860) and original personality is not a simple task, first due to the complexity of themes and events he addressed during his lifetime and second because of the array of personalities with whom he was in intense personal contact and correspondence. Khomiakov found himself frequently in the midst of intellectual and theological circles, with delight especially where the debate was heated and controversial.[1] This was especially true for the 40s and the 50s of his century, a time in which the Slavophil movement was shaped and modern Russian religious thought was formed: in all of them Khomiakov played a significant role.[2] For these rea-

1. "Les Kirêevski et Kochélev, les Aksakov et Samarine formèrent, groupés autour de Khomiakov, le véritable noyau de cercle nationaliste moscovite. De cette pléiade, Alexis Stéphanovitch est incontestablement le centre. Il a mieux saisi que les autres la vraie signification du mouvement. Avec 'son esprit lumineux qui, dit Samarine, jetait des rayons dans toutes les directions,' avec 'l'unité intérieure des ses initiatives, en apparence sans lien,' et 'l'intégrité strictement maintenue de ses points de vue,' il en a éclairci, fortifié, défendu tous les aspects; et c'est à lui qu'il faut recourir pour en avoir l'intelligence complète." Cf. A. Gratieux, *A. S. Khomiakov et le mouvement Slavophile: Les hommes* (Paris: Cerf, 1939), p. 95. Even though the above description is referring to Khomiakov in the Slavophil movement, it is equally valid for Khomiakov's personality in general. In addition Khomiakov married Katherine Iazykov, the mother of his nine children, the sister of the famous poet N. M. Iazykov.

2. References of earlier biographical studies can be found in Gratieux, *A. S. Khomiakov et le mouvement Slavophile: Les hommes*, p. xx. Gratieux's work itself has a biographical

sons we shall dedicate a more detailed introduction to Khomiakov's personality and work, similarly to A. M. Bukharev, the second theologian featured in this chapter.

Born in 1804 in Moscow, the young "Alexis" Stepanovich was brought up in a milieu where he learned to maintain with care the ancient traditions of his origin. His father Stepan was an intellectual who equally enjoyed collecting books and playing games of chance, assembling a respectful amount in the first case and losing a proverbial fortune in the second. His mother Maria Alexeeva was an energetic woman who ran the household and later the whole Khomiakov estate in an attempt to save it. She passed her moral imprint to her children and the entire household, and it was she who took care of the children's education along with their religious formation.[3] On their estates the Khomiakovs lived for generations in an exemplary and respectful symbiosis with their peasants and domestic servants, which made the concept of "nation" and later the meaning "Slavophil" real and *palpable* to the young Alexis.[4] Thus *slavophilism* for Khomiakov was not a mere "na-

---

framing. N. Berdaiev dedicates a book to Khomiakov and his thoughts and N. Zernov a part in *Three Russian Prophets, Khomiakov, Dostoevsky, Soloviev* (London: SCM Press, 1944), pp. 48-82; T. I. Blagova, *Rodonachal'niki slavianofil'stva: Aleksei Khomiakov i Ivan Kireevskii* (Moskva: "Vysschaia shkola," 1995); V. Tsurikov, ed., *A. S. Khomiakov: Poet, Philosopher, Theologian* (Jordanville, NY: Holy Trinity Seminary Press, 2004); V. A. Koshelev, *Aleksei Stepanovich Khomiakov: Zhizneopisanie v dokumentakh, v rassuzhdeniiakh i razyskaniiakh* (Moskva: Novoe literarnoe obozrenie, 2000).

3. It is interesting to note for the genesis of modern Russian thought that Maria Alexeeva came from the Kireevskii family, which means that the Kireevskii brothers (Ivan and Peter) and her son Alexei were cousins and cultivated their family ties from early childhood. Maria Alexeeva was well versed in European culture: Alexei's French émigré tutor Abbé Boivin is the proof of her interest in giving a solid knowledge to her nine children of the finest that Europe could offer at that time. This care Alexis perceived as "decisive" for his life orientation; in particular when he mentions his mother's prayer for the "unity of the Church . . . of all Christianity." She insisted on a strict observance of all the rites of the Orthodox Church and remained unwavering in questions of morals throughout. Some of this early formation and views made Khomiakov later an "outsider" in his life setting, for instance in the royal horse guards, the elite of the Russian army, that stood for all that was thriving and progressive in the modern world of the era. Cf. Zernov, *Three Russian Prophets,* pp. 49-52.

4. As a child, for instance, he used to play with children of peasants. Even Khomiakov's premature death on September 23, 1860 was due to a cholera infection caught while treating his peasants during the epidemic. Cf. Zernov, *Three Russian Prophets,* p. 50. Also cf. G. Grabbe, "Introduction," in Khomiakov, *The Church Is One* (Seattle: St. Nectarios Press, 1979), pp. 6-10, 14-16. (Archpriest G. Grabbe was a direct grandchild of Khomiakov's daughter Anna, who most likely provided him with firsthand insights into the Khomiakov family

tional sentimentalism" or nationalism but rather a carefully studied, well-reflected, and above all co-shared Russian realm that he lived out in his life.[5]

By the age of seventeen, Khomiakov, a student of mathematics, had completed most of his higher education at Moscow University. Among his extraordinary skills were an outstanding knowledge of classical and numerous modern languages, great love for books and studies, a prodigious memory, and an artistically gifted, unceasingly curious spirit of research and creativity.[6] Among his talents, his poetry needs to be mentioned as one highly appreciated by the "poet of the nation," Pushkin.[7] Khomiakov's deepest interest, however, lay in the "study of theology, philosophy, history and philology," and he loved to be engaged in discussions, as mentioned before, preferably controversial ones.

Though Khomiakov was a "retired cavalry captain and a layman with no official theological standing," he was an intellectual and a man of fervent prayer, someone of a devoted spiritual life. Iu. Smarin witnessed him at times spending entire nights in prayer and considered him along with I. Aksakov as "a doctor of the Church." "He did not believe in a faith abstracted from life" and "an abstracted theology did not appeal to him,"[8]

---

history and A. S. Khomiakov's personality. However, some of the dates regarding our author's bibliography in his introduction differ from the ones indicated generally.)

5. "Les Slavophilisme se tournait vers le passé pour y reconnaître ses racines; mais il ne regardait pas moins vers l'avenir, pour y préparer l'épanouissement de son idéal. Cet idéal était avant tout spirituel, sans méconnaître cependant la nécessité de certaines réalisations dans l'ordre temporel. Il rayonnait autour d'une idée centrale qui en était l'âme, la lumière et la vie: l'Église." A. Gratieux, *A. S. Khomiakov et le mouvement Slavophile: Les doctrines* (Paris: Cerf, 1939), p. 102. Of course it was not solely Khomiakov who shaped the movement at the beginning, but his contribution was decisive, and conversely he, too, was profoundly influenced by it. Cf. Zernov, *Three Russian Prophets,* p. 52.

6. After joining the army in 1822 he "he served with distinction" in the Turkish-Russian war of 1828-29 as a cavalry officer, yet willingly abandoned the armed forces once the war was over. Cf. Zernov, *Three Russian Prophets,* pp. 49-50.

7. A further example of his skills is that without any philological degree the Russian Imperial Academy of Science published his dictionary of Sanskrit, an undertaking for which Khomiakov was regarded as a pioneer in this field. Cf. Grabbe, "Introduction," pp. 6-9.

8. This fact may well accord with the idea that Khomiakov with his theological work responded to "an external challenge, a crisis." Cf. P. Valliere, "The Modernity of Khomiakov," in *A. S. Khomiakov: Poet, Philosopher, Theologian,* vol. 2, ed. V. Tsurikov (Jordanville, NY: Holy Trinity Seminary Press, 2004), pp. 130-31. Also: "It is significant that both Sergei Khoruzhii and Paul Valliere single out the concept 'life' as the essential characteristic of Khomiakov's thought, rooted in a sincere belief in God's gifts and humanity's potential. Khomiakov's theology results from his personal care for the world in which he found him-

which may well justify Grabbe's assertion: "He was full of love for God and men. All his conceptions and actions flowed from that love,"[9] an observation as significant as unassuming. By some he was considered the "first original theologian of the Russian Church,"[10] one whose ideas were picked up later by such thinkers as Solov'ev and Dostoevsky and discussed by many to follow.[11] It was precisely his *laity*, a disadvantage in the sight of some, that provided him with a fresh view and approach to theology. Khomiakov was and remained Orthodox, but his laical status was the reason his writings took such a long time to be published and to become popular in Russia.[12] More importantly, however, Khomiakov like other Russian religious philosophers of the nineteenth and twentieth century was not a traditional thinker: "They were modern thinkers, and modern concepts profoundly conditioned the traditional element in their thought." This certainly is one of Khomiakov's novelties identified by Valliere. The other "unprecedented" and *revolutionary* newness was that, in spite of his epoch, Khomiakov as a layperson first engaged in theology, and second he even started to produce it.[13] Another

---

self alive." R. Bird, "The Knight of Russian Theology," in Tsurikov, ed., *A. S. Khomiakov: Poet, Philosopher, Theologian*, p. 202.

9. Grabbe, "Introduction," pp. 5-6 and 9-10. Also: "One cannot pass hours in prayer if one does not love God. There is no doubt that Khomiakov loved God with all his heart. This love was the essence of his spiritual life." Grabbe, "Introduction," p. 10.

10. Cf. Zernov, *Three Russian Prophets*, p. 56, n. 1.

11. "What Pushkin had done for Russian poetry (and would do for fictional prose), Khomiakov set out to do for Russian philosophy and theology. [And] if the name of Petr Chaadaev were added to those of Pushkin and Khomiakov, we would gain a full picture of the genesis of modern Russian thought in the pointed but inconclusive debates of the early 1830s. . . . Innovative and wide-ranging as it is, the Russian religious-philosophical movement created little that could not be traced to Khomiakov's own writings. Certainly, the entire tradition is unthinkable without Khomiakov's founding impetus and gesture." Cf. Bird, "The Knight of Russian Theology," pp. 198-99.

12. A view shared among others by Metropolitan Antony of Kiev. Cf. Grabbe, "Introduction," p. 13.

13. Until then theology was a "business of hierarchs and monks"; laity and secular clergy abstained from dealing with theology (except perhaps for the theological training they received in the seminaries or theological academies). More important is to note that the "verbal theology" was not the key one in Russia until then, but rather it was "iconography, *umozrenie v kraskakh* (contemplation in colors)." Cf. Valliere, "The Modernity of Khomiakov," pp. 129-30. N. Zernov, too, just as many others, connects the "birth of the first true Russian theology" to the revival of the nonpossessor tradition that continued in the Slavophil movement. He considers A. S. Khomiakov "the first original theologian of the Russian Church, the first to formulate in terms of modern thought the experience of his mother Church." Cf. N. Zernov, *Moscow the Third Rome* (New York: AMS Press, 1971), pp. 86-88.

significant observation of Valliere in Khomiakov's originalities is "his application of the adjective 'living' to the categories of unity and tradition. . . ."[14] Contemporary to Khomiakov's concerns was the Orthodox identity of both the Russian church and society, a matter that would condense in his influence on the Slavophil movement. In addition, "with him Orthodox theology and Russian philosophy became inextricably intertwined,"[15] partly due to the family ties and "sympathy" with the Kireevskii brothers (considered also as founders of modern Russian philosophy), elaborating and positively fusing the Kireevskiis' thoughts with or into his theology.

Khomiakov's first literary works were poetry, which even later he never gave up composing. Initially it was his father who published his poems together with his two tragedies *Ermark* and the *Dimitrii Samozvanets (The Impostor Dmitrii)* in 1844. Because of the censure in Russia some of his works were written in French and published abroad; others appeared only after his death. In the last twenty years of his life Khomiakov worked repeatedly on *Zapiski o vsemirnoi istorii (Notes on Universal History),* also called *Semiramida,* which he never finished. By far the most important are his theological works, among them *Tserkov' odna (The Church Is One)*[16] published in Russian and in English in *Pravoslavnoe obozrenie (Orthodox Review)* in 1864. Further letters (some in French in the review *Union Chrétienne,* or in English to W. Palmer,[17]

14. ". . . hence also in the implication that unity and tradition may be 'dead'" in the sense of a *"zhivotvoriashchii (life-giving)"* Holy Spirit confessed in the Creed. Cf. Valliere, "The Modernity of Khomiakov," p. 134.

15. Bird, "The Knight of Russian Theology," p. 200.

16. Though writing in 1844 or 1845, according to G. Grabbe, Khomiakov worked on this document improving it for many years. A different view is that "Khomiakov's masterpiece *Tserkov' odna* . . . had been written by 1846, because in a letter from 18 July of that year Khomiakov complained that Vasilii Andreeevich Panov had locked it up at his house." Further revelations bring more to light about the author's wit than the actual work: "Khomiakov intimated that the work had been written in Greek, but there are indications that in fact he only translated it into Greek as part of a plan to present it as a newly discovered ancient manuscript. . . . In other words, Khomiakov seems to have treated this text in a somewhat cavalier fashion." R. Bird's comment is based on V. M. Lur'e's historical commentary in A. S. Khomiakov, *Sochineniia v dvukh tomakh,* II:344-45. Cf. Bird, "The Knight of Russian Theology," pp. 197-98. The genesis of this fundamental work is that soon after its publishing it was banned by the ecclesial censure and rehabilitated only in 1879. The premier edition of Khomiakov's theological works was done by Iu. Samarin, which appeared in 1867 in Prague and was reproduced repeatedly thereafter. A. Cavazza, *Cerkov' odna di A. S. Chomjakov, Edizione critica del manoscritto OPI GIM,* Excerpta ex Dissertatione ad Doctoratum (Bologna: Pontificium Institutum Orientalum, 2002), p. vi.

17. Palmer translated some of Khomiakov's poetry dedicated to two of his deceased

and pamphlets in German aimed at Protestant audiences) were addressed to diverse personalities of his time. His polemical brochures titled *Quelques mots d'un Chrétien orthodoxe sur les confessions occidentales* appeared in 1853 in Paris and in 1855 in Leipzig, just to mention some of the more significant ones.[18]

The context in which Khomiakov thought and lived was the church. His intellectual horizon and all his social and religious ideas moved and existed in her. For this reason *Tserkov' odna,* written in the form of a catechesis for Orthodox readers, and therefore intentionally in Russian,[19] represents his theological work of major significance and fame and shall serve us as the principal point of reference. One can find the concepts of *unity and love* as well as *love and prayer* and their reciprocal interactions in the church, a fundamental notion for Khomiakov that he describes repeatedly.[20]

---

sons, a work of Palmer that initiated an important correspondence and friendship between the two theologians.

18. Cf. Gratieux, *A. S. Khomiakov et le mouvement Slavophile: Les hommes,* pp. xvi-xviii. Volume 4 of *Sochineniia* is dedicated entirely to it.

19. As mentioned above it appeared soon in English. Khomiakov's thought was affected in its substance by confrontation with western society and Christianity. Most of his theological writings were directed to non-Orthodox Western European interlocutors (Catholic and Protestant). Valliere mentions here the "pronounced Pauline features" in Khomiakov's theology from the German Protestant exegetes (e.g., the comment on Phil. 2:6), or the significant influence of a contemporary Catholic theologian J. A. Möhler (1796-1838) noticeable in *Tserkov' odna.* Cf. Valliere, "The Modernity of Khomiakov," pp. 131-32.

20. We can only speculate whether Khomiakov's inspiration flows from his own fervent prayer life and is being projected onto the institution of church or proceeds from church liturgy and is channeled through his proper reflection. The interaction of both notions is not excluded and perhaps is the accurate interpretation. On a general note regarding Khomiakov's works that were at our disposition:

The first two editions of *Polnoe sobranie sochinenii Alekseia Stepanovicha Khomiakova* (PSSK) appeared between 1861, a year after Khomiakov's death, and 1882. The 3rd edition from 1900 (vol. 1-8) and all later editions at our disposition proved to be identical. The 3rd edition was edited meticulously by M. Dmitri Khomiakov, who was eager to present as complete and "definitive" *Works* of A. S. Khomiakov as possible; thus it was significantly supplemented in comparison to the first two editions with the addition of Khomiakov's poems, two tragedies, and various letters. Cf. *Polnoe sobranie sochinenii: A. S. Khomiakov,* 3rd ed., vol. 1 (Moskva: Universitetskaia tipografiia, 1900); cf. Gratieux, *A. S. Khomiakov et le mouvement Slavophile: Les hommes,* p. xvi. The 4th and 5th editions of volume 2, which contains works of theological character, have an explanatory note to the Russian translation. It appeared first in Berlin in 1867 thanks to Iu. Samarin, and by the decree of the Holy Synod from February 22, 1879 it was "allowed to circulate in Russia." The editor remarks that the inconsistency of certain expressions originated in the author's lack of theological preparation, a note that was placed as a condition for publishing by the authority. Cf. 5th ed., vol. 2, 1907. Here in addition

1.2. The Law of Love

One of Khomiakov's determined intentions was to give his ecclesiology a logical definition, to show the church in its different manifestations, "the church that had doctrines but is not a doctrine and is not an institution. . . . *The Church* is a living organism, the organism of truth and love, or more precisely: *the truth and love as organism,*" which is according to Iu. Samarin the theme of all Khomiakov's theological articles.[21] The "discussion, refutation, explication and definition" of what is true and false, is not the task of the church but rather of the school that exists in the church, "of the ecclesial science otherwise called theology."[22] We agree with Zernov that to Khomiakov's "basic intuition," perhaps even "the driving power behind his religious, political and economic ideas," belongs the notion of "universal laws of willing reason or reasoning will *(voliiashchago razuma ili razumeiushchei voli).*"[23] Nevertheless Khomiakov's focal point of spiritual and intellectual optics was *love,* as a "living path that leads the human being forward to his higher goal . . ." found in the second part of the very same phrase. Khomiakov defines it as *law:* "From the universal laws of the acting reason or the reasoning will (for such is the definition of the very spirit) the first, the highest, the most perfect [among them] to the uncorrupted spirit appears the law of love."[24] Thus as noble and necessary as *will* and *reason* are *(will* stands in a straight relationship with *reason* and true *knowledge* is dependent on *love),* highest and most noble is the "law that governs the universe," *the law of love:* "Therefore to live in accord with it [*the law of love*] strengthens and enlarges our mental vision *(myshlennoe zrenie).* We are to submit ourselves to it and attune the persistent disorder *(upornoe neustroistvo)* of our intellectual powers *(umstvennykh sil).* Solely after the ac-

---

one finds a part of A. V. Gorky's remarks on Khomiakov's theological works. Cf. *Polnoe sobranie sochinenii Alekseia Stepanovicha Khomiakova: Sochineniia bogoslovskiia,* 5th ed. (Moskva: Tipo-litogr. T-va I. N. Kushnerev, 1907), pp. 517-40. For consistency and for its completeness we used the 3rd edition of volumes 1-8 in our research (except vol. 2 from the 4th edition). The 2nd volume, dedicated to theology, underwent major changes after the 3rd edition when the letters of W. Palmer were discovered and added to it. It begins with the introduction of Khomiakov's disciple Iu. Samarin.

21. Note 1: "C'est la thème de tous les articles théologiques de Khomiakov." G. Samarine, *Préface aux oeuvres théologiques de A. S. Khomiakov* (Paris: Cerf, 1939), p. 58.

22. Cf. Samarine, *Préface aux oeuvres,* pp. 57-58.

23. Cf. Zernov, *Three Russian Prophets,* p. 57.

24. *Polnoe sobranie sochinenii Alekseia Stepanovicha Khomiakova,* vol. 1 (Moskva: Universitetskaia tipografiia, 1900), p. 283 (PSSK I).

complishment of this step can we hope for a fuller development of our intellect *(razuma)*." Be it *intellect* or *reason*, the point is that any process of cognition is only an intermediary step towards knowledge, as Khomiakov explains. It borrows the thought of Kireevskii that "philosophy is nothing but a transitional notion of human intellect from the realm of faith into a diverse application of everyday thoughts."[25] Human intellect is interim since eventually it has to return to faith as its source and its new beginning. Love becomes "indispensable" if we want to obtain true *knowledge:*

> Love is not a uniform striving:[26] it requires, finds and creates responses and communion *(obshchenie)* and grows, strengthens and is being perfected through responses and communion *(obshchenie)*. Thus communion of love is not only useful, but entirely indispensable for the perception of truth, and the understanding of truth is based on communion of love and cannot be achieved without her. Incomprehensible to isolated reasoning, truth is accessible only to the totality of thinking *(tol'ko sovokupnosti myshlenii)* joined together by love. . . .[27] What has been said about the higher truth stands also for philosophy. Apparently attainable to only few, yet in reality it is the creation and possession of all.[28]

This reflection of Khomiakov was found on an annotated fragment of conversations in the papers of I. V. Kireevskii.[29] The critical conclusion that Khomiakov draws is that even the "philosophical thought with its strict conclusions returns to the firm truths of faith" and that, logically, "the understanding of the Church is higher than human understanding." Moreover it is said about Kireevskii's separate note that it denotes an *existential unity* of all

25. PSSK I, p. 283.

26. *Liubov' ne est' stremlenie odinakovoe,* i.e., *Love* is a complex, multifaceted aspiration and thriving. Zernov's rendering "Love is not a tendency towards unification . . ." is not correct, and can be even misleading. Also in the rest of this passage's translation there are minor conceptual discrepancies; therefore we shall provide, as usual, our own translation. Cf. Zernov, *Three Russian Prophets,* p. 58.

27. Khomiakov remarks "that this trait sharply distinguishes the Orthodox teaching from all the other ones: from the Latin standing on external authority, and from Protestantism, releasing personality into freedom in the deserts of rational abstractness *(. . . otreshaiushchago lichnost' do svobody v pustyhiakh razsudochnoi otvlechennosti)*." PSSK I, p. 283.

28. PSSK I, p. 283.

29. It deals especially with German philosophy (in particular Kant and Hegel) and its implications on the human faculties of *will, reason,* and the virtue of *faith.* Cf. *Po povodu otryvkov naidennykh v bumagakh I. V. Kireevskago,* in PSSK I, pp. 263-84.

human beings,[30] that is, a result achieved by common effort, something an individual on his own cannot achieve, for we were created in and for interaction and community. The stream of life flows between human beings as a communion and is not an event of isolated, *private* character. Kireevskii asserts: "Veritable convictions are beneficial and powerful only in the totality and development of a social self-consciousness."[31] Thus "philosophical sciences, understood in their entire life-extent, [that is] departing necessarily from faith and returning to it, provide contemporaneously freedom to reason *(razsudok)*, force to inner knowledge and fullness to life."[32]

1.3. The Church Is One

The concept of *unity* is very dear to Khomiakov, be it as an epistemological result of the reason that searches for truth and knowledge, as seen previously, or as a spiritual and mystical experience of the *Truth* deriving from the Trinitarian unity that is meant to be reflected in the church. Therefore the very first statement of the first paragraph is: "The unity of the church originates necessarily in the unity of God, for the Church is not a multitude of persons in their separate individuality, but a unity of God's grace that is living in the multitude of rational creatures who are submitting themselves to God's grace."[33] Therefore any division in the church into a "visible and invisible" part is simply a human construct, as in God there is no division and the church's "unity is true and absolute."[34] A tender moment of spiritual insight, and perhaps Khomiakov's intimate spiritual life, is this glimpse into God's timeless presence in creation when our author says that the church embraces also the invisible creation: ". . . and God hears the prayers knowing the faith of those whom He has not yet called out of nonexistence into existence." Khomiakov defines from the outset what is to be understood under the concept of *church* and whose "entity" the *church* is, namely "the Body of Christ."[35] Two repeatedly discussed concepts are "inner holiness" *(vnutrenniaia sviatost')*, which is linked to the "spirit of truth" that *lives* in the church,

30. Zernov terms it "organic unity." Cf. Zernov, *Three Russian Prophets*, p. 58.

31. *Istinnyia ubezhdeniia blagodetel'ny i sil'ny tol'ko v sovokupnosti i v razrabotke obshchestvennago samosoznaniia.*

32. Cf. PSSK I, p. 284.

33. Khomiakov indeed uses a capital for Church in the original text.

34. Cf. *Tserkov' odna*, in PSSK II, p. 3 (TsOD).

35. Cf. TsOD, p. 3.

and the "external immutability" *(vneshniaia neizmennost')* that comes from her "head, Jesus Christ." The *inwardness* is where her *inner* knowledge of faith derives — as opposed to the *external* knowledge that can never comprehend the former one — for it is where *unity* and the unchanging character of spirit are nesting in the "spirit of God."[36] This is the Church's source of truth and inevitability, or as Khomiakov puts it, she does not err, "for she is the truth . . . she is holy"[37] as expressed in the Creed about the *one, holy, catholic and apostolic* church,[38] ". . . for in the apostolic writings and doctrine all the fullness of her faith, her hope and her love is contained."[39] The three theological virtues express her unity, which surpasses any geographical, national, or social boundary. This is meant to be a source of joy to all Christians in order to comprehend and to share that which is the *crown* and *glory* of the church: "Every Christian ought to set a high value upon unity in the rites of the Church, for in it is manifested, even for the unenlightened, the unity of spirit and doctrine, while for the enlightened person it contains the source of life and Christian joy. Love is the crown and glory of the Church."[40]

The matter of knowledge remains pending in a continuum of reflection for practically the rest of Khomiakov's writing. He keeps returning to its essence, the differentiation of the *inner* and *external* knowledge, its sources, and the *one* true source, i.e., "the one Spirit of God," a crucial gnoseological momentum by which a Christian discerns what truly matters in the end: "For a Christian knowledge is not a work of an inquisitive intellect *(razuma pytuiushchago)* but of a living faith filled with divine grace. Scripture is ex-

36. Cf. TsOD, p. 4.

37. Cf. TsOD, p. 5.

38. It is in this instance that Khomiakov begins to distinguish in his writings between "catholic" and "*sobornaia*." Although he does not use the noun *sobornost'* here, yet he uses its above-mentioned adjective, and returns to the argument more extensively in his later writings. Here for distinction Khomiakov puts "catholic" and "universal, ecumenical" in a bracket after *sobornaia:* "Tserkov nazyvaetsia *edinoiu, sviatoiu, sobornoiu* (katolicheskoiu i vselenskoiu) *apostolskoiu. . . .*" Cf. PSSK II, p. 6. Also: "The title under which we know the text was introduced only in later reprintings. The term *sobornost',* with which the text is most closely associated, is not used in it (or in any other of Khomiakov's extant writings), and in any case it has long been shown that the idea was not really original to him. And yet, despite all of these vagaries of composition and publication, 'The Church Is One' and its concept of *sobornost'* have permeated Russian culture and have changed the landscape of Christian theology the world over." Bird, "The Knight of Russian Theology," p. 198.

39. TsOD, p. 6.

40. TsOD, p. 6.

ternal and tradition is external and works are external — that which is inner in them is the one Spirit of God."[41] Once again the final and "unifying element" in the church and of all her external works is what we encounter at the end of the chapter as a seal of wisdom: "Yet in the Church there has not been, nor ever will be any contradictions, either in Scripture, or in tradition or in works: for in all three is Christ present, one and unchangeable."[42] The "full completeness" of the gifts granted by the Holy Spirit is in the virtues of "faith, hope and love," which are "inseparably united in one holy and living unity." While "works pleasing God" stand for *love,* an active, charitable dimension, "prayer pleasing God" relates more to *hope,* and the "Creed pleasing God" to *faith.* Thus while unity is being built by these three constituting elements, unity on the other hand maintains them through their reciprocal relationship in the Church, sustaining the unceasing awareness that "they are true and perfect."[43]

1.3.1. The Creed

Further reflection on the Creed shows, repeatedly in the light of an *inner* and *external* discernment of knowledge,[44] that any deviation from the true Creed[45] is a consequence of an uncharitable action "not inspired by a spirit of love" towards the brethren. Khomiakov refers here to the changes adapted into the Nicene-Constantinopolitan Creed and the Catholic Church. One may agree or disagree with Khomiakov's view on the western churches and the causes of schism,[46] but his discernment is of universal value since faith and love cannot be separated and ". . . faith is not preserved there, where love has grown weak. . . ." Similarly in the context of the *Filioque* controversy:

41. One of Khomiakov's criticisms on the Protestant as well as Catholic Church is that Scripture and works are only external actions if the illuminating and unifying "Spirit of God" is missing from them. It is the task of ecclesiology to assure that this does not come about in the church. Cf. TsOD, pp. 7-8.

42. TsOD, p. 8.

43. Cf. TsOD, pp. 8-9.

44. Virtually speaking of an "inner and living, not a dead and external, knowledge," which contains in itself nothing less than "the mystery of the existence of God, not only in relation to His external action upon creation, but also to His inner, eternal being." Cf. TsOD, p. 10.

45. Addressing the schisms between the western and eastern churches.

46. Though we have to remark that Khomiakov's vision of the *one* Church is at times more compassionate and merciful with the "nonbaptized" and those "not yet in communion with the Church" as with other churches. Cf. TsOD, pp. 4 and 13.

"Renouncing the spirit of love and divesting oneself of the gifts of grace, it is not possible to possess inner knowledge, i.e. faith, but merely one limited by external knowledge; such a person can know only externally and not the inner mysteries of God."[47] All this needs to be understood in its setting of *unity* and communion among faith, hope, and love,[48] ergo unity of the Church and her decision-taking in an ecumenical setting in "the Spirit of God" who is "the very Spirit of love." The Church acknowledges herself to be "the instrument and vessel of divine grace" that is the pledge of the "knowledge concerning her essence," a gift and grace from above, "accessible to faith alone and not to reason," as also the understanding that she cannot err, for "the understanding of God dwells within her." This *dwelling* is more sacramental than merely historic, for she relates as "sheep" to the "Divine Pastor," as a flock that has "never been deprived of its Divine Pastor," underscoring the church's unity with Christ.[49]

1.3.2. The Prayer of Love

Towards the end of *Tserkov' odna* the references on love increase exponentially until they crystallize *love* with faith and hope in the very center of the church and her oneness. This cohesion of a communal and mutual support takes up a soteriological dimension: "We know that when any one of us falls, he falls alone, but no one is saved alone. Anyone saved is being saved in the Church, as a member of her and in unity with all her other members. If one believes, he is in the communion of Faith; if one loves, he is in the communion of Love; if one prays, he is in the communion of prayer." This unity goes beyond what is visible and is perfected in our conforming ourselves to Christ in order to "glorify all whom God has glorified and is glorifying": ". . . for how should we say that Christ is living within us, if we do not make ourselves similar to Christ?"[50] The glorifying and prayer happen in the "spirit of love." In order for the prayer to be true: ". . . we pray in the spirit of love, knowing that no one will be saved otherwise than by the prayer of all the Church, in which Christ lives . . ." and where prayers and glory are being rendered unceasingly until the *eschaton*.[51] This prayer needs to be pure and

47. TsOD, pp. 10-11.

48. Whenever referred to, the theological virtues in *Tserkov' odna* are being presented in one line as symbol of one inseparable unity.

49. Cf. TsOD, pp. 12-13.

50. TsOD, p. 21.

51. Cf. TsOD, p. 22.

holy, "a true expression of love and not merely diverse forms of words," an attitude that from a mere anthropological dimension of "not being able to love all" and therefore praying only for those "whom we love" matures into the desire to be Christ-like, i.e., all-inclusive and all-relational, therefore: "we pray God that we may be able to love all and pray for all without hypocrisy." From human to divine, from earthly to heavenly, divinization in our intimate prayers and feelings, in front of God: What better instance to start with as prayer? We are interdependent, interrelated, and the quality of our being is defined by the genuineness of our prayer, our relationship to God: "Mutual prayer is the blood of the Church, and the glorification of God is her breath. We pray in the spirit of love, not for benefit, in the spirit of filial freedom, not in the law of a day-laborer demanding his pay. Anyone asking: 'What use is there in prayer?' acknowledges himself to be in bondage of a slave [who expects payment in exchange]. True prayer is true love."[52]

1.3.3. Love in Liturgical Art

In the final instance *Love* becomes predominant since the unity of the church is not merely defined by it: "Love and unity are above everything, but Love expresses itself in many ways: by works, by prayer, and by spiritual songs."[53] The freedom of these love-expressions shall be safeguarded in the church: "The Church imparts her blessing upon all these expressions of love. If you cannot express your love for God in word, but you express it through a visible representation, that is to say, by an *icon,* will the Church condemn

52. Cf. TsOD, p. 23.

53. Or *icons.* Cf. TsOD, p. 23. It is useful to consider Gratieux's reflection on behalf of the concept of "internal unity and love," which do not exclude or contradict the church hierarchy: "L'unité intérieure de l'amour n'exclut pas l'unité extérieure de l'organisation hiérarchique. Jésus-Christ lui-même, l'a voulue, mettant la charité à la base de l'organisation, et faisant de l'autorité, et aussi de l'obéissance, un service d'amour." Additional remarks also regarding the Slavophil movement in this context can be found in the corresponding notes. Cf. Gratieux, *A. S. Khomiakov et le mouvement Slavophile: Les doctrines,* p. 235. The Slavophil notion of authority was perceived as too "external and too abstract," and this was considered to be "its weak point" as well as: "Aux partisans de l'autorité comme à ceux de la liberté il manquait, pour résoudre le problème, de faire intervenir un moyen terme, l'amour. L'amour est la justification de l'autorité comme il est le contenu positif et la garantie de la liberté. Il est le mot suprême de la vie sociale comme de la vie personnelle. Il donne l'intégrité et la plénitude qui permettent d'arriver à la vérité totale et vivante. C'était le dernier mot de la pensée slavophile. L'Occidental croyait à l'ordre, à la logique, à l'organisation, à la discipline, le Russe croyait à l'amour" (p. 237).

you? She won't; but she will condemn the one who condemns you for he is judging your love." One can be saved without icons, statues, and other visible representations, but what one cannot survive is when a brother *condemns the love of his brother* by listening "without a feeling of reverence to a prayer or spiritual song composed by his brother," or looks "without reverence at the image his love and not his art has produced." This approach is not an acquisition of the "inner knowledge," as it is not from the "Spirit of God."[54] And one final defining note on art and liturgy: "An icon (i.e., the Name of God painted in colors), or a representation of His Saints, created by Love, is not forbidden by the spirit of truth. . . . The Church accepts every rite which expresses spiritual aspiration towards God . . . but she recognizes as higher than all rites the holy Liturgy, in which is expressed all the fullness of the doctrine and spirit of the Church. . . . Above all [purpose] stands the union of Holiness and Love."[55]

1.3.4. Salvation

The above reflection culminates in the last but one, yet theologically supreme chapter on salvation. It is collocated between the "last judgment" when "our justification in Christ will be revealed in its fullness and grace which is given freely and to all." Thus all merit shall belong to God and only the "nonresistance to grace" shall be the human being's claim. And as it is supposed to be, following the teaching of St. Paul, among the three — faith, hope, and love — there will be only one left untransformed as the "seal of Salvation." The other two will change by attaining their fullness:

> All is accomplished in the fulfillment of the general judgment, and the Spirit of God — the Spirit of Faith, Hope and Love — will reveal Himself in all His fullness and every gift will attain its utmost perfection: but love will be above all of them. One shall not think that faith and hope, which are gifts of God, will perish (for they are not separable from Love), but Love alone will preserve its name, while Faith arriving here at its perfection, will then have become a fully inner knowledge and vision; Hope will have become joy; for even on earth we know that the stronger it is, the more joyful it is.[56]

54. Cf. TsOD, pp. 23-24.
55. Cf. TsOD, p. 24.
56. Cf. TsOD, pp. 24-26.

Khomiakov further develops in his writings (especially in his letters), his ecclesiology and within it some advanced implications of love.[57] Among these letters are the *Encore quelques mots d'un chrétien orthodoxe sur les communions occidentales, à l'occasion de plusieurs publications religieuses latines et protestantes* (1858) and a brief essay, *A Letter to the Editor of "L'Union Chrétienne" on the Meaning of the Words "Catholic" and "Sobornyi."* The first letter, particularly in its second half, contains some beautiful Christological reflections illuminated by soterology.[58]

1.4. Christ (in) the History

In his unfinished three-volume *Zapiski o vsemirnoi istorii,* Khomiakov begins with basic definitions before addressing the core message:[59] "In this time [when the world remained without God] appeared in Judea a man by the name of Jesus . . . telling about himself to be the Messiah, the Son of God . . . announcing the fulfillment of the Old Covenant, inviting to repentance, to a life of spiritual purity, establishing a new law of perfection, a precept of universal love that defies all worldly goods and power, promising his followers the inheritance of endless beatitude. . . ."[60] Consequently Khomiakov develops his idea on the function of love of a "noncomplicated covenant" transmitted by a "once Jewish now universal Teacher" as a unifying element and a necessary step towards true freedom ("in a spiritual sense") that offers

57. For this reason some tend to distinguish among Khomiakov's recognizable progress of thought and style in his ecclesiology up to three successive "phases," or "stages," as for instance E. Ch. Suttner in the initial chapters of his *Offenbarung, Gnade und Kirche bei A. S. Chomjakov* (Würzburg: Augustinus-Verlag, 1967).

58. Cf. *Neskol'ko slov pravoslavnago khristianina o zapadnykh veroispovedaniiakh: Po povodu raznykh sochinenii Latinskikh i Protestantskikh o predmetakh very,* in PSSK VI, pp. 163-248.

59. Geographical definitions, nations, customs, traditions, myths, linguistic development (all that can be sociologically relevant for a culture and tradition) from the earliest times of humanity up to medieval times and then to nineteenth- and twentieth-century Sweden. At the history of the Roman Empire in the Middle East Khomiakov places *The Apparition of the Messiah* as a historical milestone in a separate title. It was an event long awaited by Israel, collocated in the context of the Roman-Jewish conflict of occupation and the era of Augustus where the Roman and Hellenistic worldviews came to the end of their wisdom and the "world remained without God." Cf. Khomiakov, *Zapiski o vsemirnoi istorii,* in PSSK VI, pp. 406-8.

60. Cf. Khomiakov, *Zapiski o vsemirnoi istorii,* pp. 409-10.

humankind "the inner possibility of endless perfection." This occurs by "handing over" one's proper will into that of the "human-divine will . . . and so the human being enters into the interior of the Divinity *(Bozhestvo)* by means of a voluntary union of love with the spiritually perfect human being. In this consists all his liberation, all his greatness, all his reward."[61]

1.5. The Letter to Filippov, the Editor of Russkaia Beseda

The trigger of this, for our topic extremely relevant, letter was George Sand (pseudonym for Amantine Lucile Aurore Dupin, later Baroness Dudevant), mainly her thesis about the emancipation of women and the concept of love presented in an article by Filippov.[62] Khomiakov, as a part of his criticism on the "erroneous" article in Filippov's periodical,[63] first exercises a severe criticism on western society and its moral habits, whereupon he reviews the concept of love, of "true love," and its implications in some profound yet prosaic lines of thought.

Filippov in his article asserts that "love's self-esteem" to itself puts limits to its rights not because it follows some kind of external law but precisely in consequence of its own respect to itself.[64] Khomiakov feels the urge to address this concept of "love's self-esteem" *(samouvazhenie liubvi)* first of all because of "the duties that result from it." Khomiakov agrees with Filippov that "true love renounces its own rights to happiness every time when this happiness would be acquired by a shameful bargaining with the conscience" in which case "love's self-denial *(samootrechenie liubvi)* is a natural consequence of its respect to its proper shrine." Despite his preliminary agreement, Khomiakov points out that Filippov "did not develop his thought to its full logical extent."[65] From this point on Khomiakov takes over and initiates his proper reflection by equating a love that searches itself and its proper happiness in the other person with simple egoism — no matter how

61. Cf. Khomiakov, *Zapiski o vsemirnoi istorii,* pp. 410-11.

62. Among the other themes were: injustice in the society, still with regard to women, the "merciless" denial of their rights "in the domain of sentiments," which men, on the contrary, lavished upon themselves. Cf. Gratieux, *A. S. Khomiakov et le mouvement Slavophile: Les doctrines,* p. 179.

63. Khomiakov lists three points of "accusation" against Filippov and his article but also other contributors. *Pis'mo k T. I. Filippovu,* in PSSK III, pp. 243-45.

64. *Pis'mo k T. I. Filippovu,* p. 245.

65. Cf. *Pis'mo k T. I. Filippovu,* p. 248.

fervent and zealous it may appear. "This is a stage in which it neither contains nobleness nor moral dignity . . . and she [love] yet does not deserve the name of love," comparing it to the sentiment expressed in English by "to like" something. This latter expresses merely a love to "lower, soulless or irrational things" whereas "true love has a different, higher meaning. The object of love is not a means anymore:[66] it becomes an aspiration and the loving person puts it equal to himself if not even above himself. Put it diversely: by not claiming it to be means any more but an aspiration, he transfers on it his own rights, a part of his own life, for its sake, and not for his own self."[67] Here we already are in the sphere of an elevated concept of love, of a "privileging-the-other" not for a selfish advantage but out of a selfless, caring relationship, not out of self-realization but allowing the other to become a full reality, fully present, even if it means putting one's proper interests in the shadow of oblivion. The higher stage of love, which in its essence is "the *true human love,* already encloses indispensably in itself the understanding of a spiritual self-sacrifice." Surely, so long as it is a human action there always will be some element of "egoistic character." Even this egoism, however, shall be transformed: "In love it is passing to a higher level, to a level of *self-denying egoism (samootritsaiushchii egoizm).* This love is — and only because of this love — the highest moral sentiment that a spiritual being is capable of, the highest a human being can strive for." If there is anything higher, nobler and truthful in the world it is "undoubtedly love the supreme law, which is supposed to define all relations in general of a human being, or that of a rational individual to its entire species. . . ."[68] "When recognizing the beauty of this elevated law and not finding enough strength in himself, the human being starts to look for external help (though within tight limits) in order to achieve it. He encounters this external help in the earthly happiness that is given to him in the union with a person of the other gender in virtue of that primordial law *(pervonachal'nyi zakon)* which divided the human race into two halves that complement each other as in the material so in the spiritual relationship."[69] "Happiness [as such] is not the aim of the union, but a support granted to the coarse human egoism for a fuller realization of the supreme law of love, receiving an other/a different human being not as a means of enjoyment but as an aim of a fuller moral life . . . in order

66. . . . *predmet liubimyi uzhe ne est' sredstvo.*
67. Cf. *Pis'mo k T. I. Filippovu,* p. 249.
68. Cf. *Pis'mo k T. I. Filippovu,* p. 249.
69. Cf. *Pis'mo k T. I. Filippovu,* p. 250.

to await the self-denial of egoism *(samootritsanie egoizma),* which is a candid, true and acting love. . . . As to the few who can live up to the law of active love for all humankind[70] without any external help, it would be erroneous to enter a union, useless for the higher aim of their life." It would achieve the contrary; instead of elevating them and the aim, it would lower both parties of the union, and the means that served for a higher end would become again a source of abasement. "That which elevates the average being would cause the fall of a superior one." On the other side it is the "family circle" where for the "majority of humankind . . . true human love is being practiced and does develop"; and what is equally important, it is where the passage from a "distant concept" towards "a living and acting manifestation" transpires. "It is evident that violating in any way the sanctity of the family equals to violating the very law of love"[71] — a phrase and concept so important to Khomiakov that he repeats it twice within the same paragraph. The reason is that the sanctity of the family is also for the relations of love that are happening in its circle:

> It is in the children that love becomes alive and, so to speak, the reciprocal love of parents settles down; and it is surely not exaggerated to say that it is in their children they love not themselves but rather each other. At the same time the reciprocal love between parents and children represents that type of elevated human love, which in the human race unites the generations among themselves. Therefore a rupture between the parents destroys also the rapport with their children that represents the hideous and immoral phenomenon of the break between human generations. For one shall not forget that the inner morality *(vnutrenniaia nravstvennost')* of each generation consists mainly in the benefit of love and of hopes that it directs towards the forthcoming generation. Just tell me: If the human being looked only at his present environment, if he did not hope, with a warm sentiment of love, that all human truth *(chelovecheskaia istina)* will more fully illuminate the coming generations, who would not fall into despondency and would not beg God to shorten the ungrateful task of [his] terrestrial life? And thus to violate the sanctity of a family is a violation of all human laws of love.[72]

70. . . . *dlia zakona deiatel'noi vsechelovecheskoi liubvi.*
71. Cf. *Pis'mo k T. I. Filippovu,* pp. 250-51.
72. *Pis'mo k T. I. Filippovu,* p. 251.

Khomiakov says that he wanted to show love's "full identity with its conclusions" based on a "healthy sense and reason that derive from the moral definition of love." For in the conviction of Khomiakov, these "unreachable highs of the Christian teaching" manifest themselves "by never putting up any arbitrary and external rule that, so to speak, would be external for the human soul."[73]

Hereupon Khomiakov returns once again to the primary trigger of his letter to the editor: the situation of women in the society, their emancipation, moral and social principles, the hypocrisy in the society (especially by "granting shameful privileges" for corruption to men), the false sense of the male superiority and their various implications,[74] whereby some sarcasm peeks through at the end of his valuation of certain anti-Christian teachings to which he compares "Sand's school."[75]

1.6. The Exegetical Note on the Letter to the Philippians 2:6

This note is, apart its exegetical character and message, a sort of a proof for Khomiakov's strong bent for the Pauline theology "that cannot be simply explained as an 'elective affinity' between him and the apostle although a spiritual kinship certainly existed." According to Valliere this is also "the early evidence of 'kenotic theme' in Russian theology, which in this case, can accentuate the word *theology*.[76] Khomiakov in his *note* focuses on verse 6 in Philippians 2 *(Who, although He was in the form of God, did not regard equality with God something to be grasped),* comparing the Russian with French, English, and New Greek translations, but bases his own analysis on the NT Greek text, and comes to the conclusion that "all the new translations known to him are completely equal."[77] For various reasons related to "the pauline meaning" of the text, Khomiakov "rejects" the addition of "хотя" *(khotia), although.* Khomiakov in his own interpretation distances himself from all authorities,

73. Cf. *Pis'mo k T. I. Filippovu,* p. 251.

74. Cf. *Pis'mo k T. I. Filippovu,* pp. 249-55.

75. Exemplifying the ephemeral character of some, in their time popular, anti-Christian teachings of the "encyclopedeians of the XVIII century": ". . . years gone by; about them as of the teachers [of these ideas] nobody talks anymore, except for some French mummy, that death has forgotten [to take away], because it never perceived active signs of life in it. . . ." Cf. *Pis'mo k T. I. Filippovu,* p. 258.

76. Cf. Valliere, "The Modernity of Khomiakov," pp. 131-32.

77. Cf. *Zametka na tekst poslaniia apostola Pavla k Filippiitsam,* in PSSK II, pp. 422-24.

claiming that his "translation is absolutely independent from any authority," a judgment supported by the fact that the examined "Slav translation was done by Greeks."[78] Khomiakov's new translation renders it in the following way: ". . . he did not think to grasp (appropriate) for Himself willfully equality with God, but . . . etc." According to our author, this is "in full accordance" with the character of Paul's "course of thought in the letter to the Philippians" and is an allusion to the juxtaposition of the old Adam, who having been created in God's image, wanted to "appropriate the divine willfully to himself."[79] This has changed with the "new Adam, Christ, who humbled Himself *(smirilsia)*" and united the divine and human in Himself.[80] Apart from the comparison between the *old* and the *new Adam,* this would appear more of a philological work if not for Christ's *kenotic* action of *self-abasement* that restored the primordial relationship between humankind and God.

Conclusion

Khomiakov, with his straightforward argumentation, is the first lay theologian to grasp the essential, which we can summarize as *communion in love.* Our cognition is truthful if it is primarily based on an internal knowledge of *love* and *union,* the first and basic principle that the human being needs to learn from God who is union of three different Persons. Even though Khomiakov does not mention the Trinity explicitly, the notion is evident: The salvific action and message of Jesus become comprehensible to our reason only if we fully cooperate with divine grace and with each other; first when humankind places its proper *will* into the *divine will* following the example of Christ, only then will it live fully and become *communion,* that is, *Church.* The *Church is love* as it stems from God; yet our personal *love-aspiration,* our way of relating, needs to be divinized in order to become *candid* and capable of the highest transformative sacrifice: *self-sacrifice.* Self-sacrifice, *kenosis,* is the cornerstone of any lasting unity, let alone of the divine-human union. Therefore Christ set in our history a *new precept of perfection,* a truly *supreme law* of this highest example of love. Now we know that *true prayer* to God *is true love,* and therefore our *inner knowledge-vision* reveals that the *true Church* is *union* in *true love.*

78. Cf. *Zametka na tekst poslaniia apostola Pavla k Filippiitsam,* in PSSK II, p. 423.
79. . . . *zakhotel svoevol'no prislovit' sebe bozhestvennoe.*
80. Cf. *Zametka na tekst poslaniia apostola Pavla k Filippiitsam,* p. 424.

2. Alexis Matveevich Bukharev: Living Communion with the Sovereign Love

2.1. Biography

Alexis (Alexander) M. Bukharev (1824-1871), also known as Archimandrite Feodor,[81] was born into the family of an impoverished village deacon.[82] In his childhood Alexis experienced poverty and at the age of thirteen he was sent to the Tver' seminary (1837-42), soon becoming its "best pupil." His formation he completed by 1846 at the Moscow Theological Academy, again excelling in his studies. Metropolit Filaret "turned his attention" to the talented young man and even "became his promoter."[83] In the same year Bukharev became a monk and received clerical orders,[84] taking on the religious name of Feodor.[85] The young hieromonakh remained at the academy to lecture at the Cathedral of the Holy Scripture on biblical history, Greek, and Scriptures, and was promoted in 1852 to "extraordinary professor of the academy." In these eight years of professorship he began to write what he considered his "life's work," the *Apocalypse*.[86] In 1854 Bukharev was transferred to Kazan to lecture on different subjects (dogmatics, morals, and pastoral) where

81. Biographical material can be found in N. Gorodetzky, *The Humiliated Christ in Modern Russian Thought* (London: SPCK, 1938), pp. 116-26; an excerpt for biographical materials by his wife in: A. S. Bukhareva, "Alexander Matveevich Bukharev (Arkhimandrit Feodor): Iz materialov dlia biografii," in *Svobodnaia sovest', Literaturno-filosofskii sbornik*, vol. 1 (Moskva: Tipografiia T-va I. D. Sytina, 1906), pp. 1-20; *Vmesto vvedeniia: O hizni i trudakh A. M. Bukhareva (In Place of Introduction: On Life and Works of A. M. Bukharev)* by P. Znamenskii in Arkhimandrit Feodor (A. M. Bukharev), *O pravoslavii v otnoshenii k sovremennosti* (Sankt-Peterburg: Synodal'naia tipografiia, 1906) (this article is missing in the 1860 edition); and a standard work that is also an excellent guide for biographical as well as theological references: P. Valliere, *Modern Russian Theology: Bukharev, Soloviev, Bulgakov; Orthodox Theology in a New Key* (Grand Rapids: Eerdmans, 2000), pp. 19-106.

82. Cf. *The Humiliated Christ*, p. 116.

83. Cf. *O pravoslavii v otnoshenii k sovremennosti* (1906), p. vii.

84. Cf. K. Koksheneva, "V svetlom prostore istiny," in Arkhimandrit Feodor (A. M. Bukharev), *O dukhovnykh potrebnostiakh zhizni* (Moskva: Izdatel'stvo Stolica, 1991), p. 9 (ODPZ). Here can be found also an article by V. V. Rozanov from 1922 on A. M. Bukharev under the title *Askochenskii i Arkhimandrit Feodor Bukharev*, pp. 24-37.

85. According to Gorodetzky, Bukharev "was persuaded to take Orders. The Academy considered it a failure if some of the pupils did not become monks. For some it was also the step to a promising career impossible for a member of the secular clergy. In this case it was obedience to the elders and the desire to consecrate his life to the service of Christ as fully as possible." Cf. *The Humiliated Christ*, p. 116.

86. Cf. "V svetlom prostore istiny," in ODPZ, p. 9.

"right from the start students loved him from their heart, because his entire being was impregnated by love."[87] Unfortunately, it was also a place where he became melancholic due to the "harsh atmosphere . . . where discipline was based on fear and punishment," a setting that a person of his gentleness, "goodhearted and dreamy man" that he was, could not cope with.[88] Though a monk, Archimandrite Feodor was not a person attracted by "traditional monastic ascetics"; indeed it was "utmost alien" to him.[89]

In 1855 Bukharev became a member of the editor's committee for the newly established *Pravoslavnyi sobesednik (Orthodox Interlocutor).* In 1858 he was appointed by the Hl. Synod to become the ecclesiastical censor at St. Petersburg, a post from which he very soon tried to resign and finally succeeded in 1861, officially for reasons of "poor health."[90] The truth was that few were less suited for this task than the "sensitive-spirited Archimandrite Feodor," who initially hoped through this post to get into closer touch with the world. In 1862 the Synod denied the publication of his *Apocalypse;* Bukharev was deeply disappointed and shaken, a disillusion that eventually led him to request release from his monastic vows.[91]

87. Cf. *O pravoslavii v otnoshenii k sovremennosti* (1906), p. XII.

88. Gorodetzky adds further commentary but the most significant is her kenotic hermeneutical key: "He tried 'to take upon himself the form of a student and considered the very faults of them as his own.' As we see, the very wording of this witness of one of his students reminds us of Phil. ii. Bukharev 'was ill two or three days after some misdeed of a student.'" Cf. *The Humiliated Christ,* p. 117.

89. His wife Anna Sergeevna (whom he married shortly after having been released from his vows) describes Bukharev's monastic vocation as certainly not ascetic-bound: ". . . In monasticism he saw the possibility to serve the work of disclosure of Christ's truth without scattering, in the spirit of the Orthodox dogma *(verouchenie).* Upon entering monasticism there was only one feeling that moved and dominated him — the love for Christ's truth and a zealous desire that all living reality may be penetrated by it." He intended to do it "by lessons and theological works; and he dedicated himself to this service, consecrating to it the best years of his life, all his thoughts, intentions and his whole heartfelt youthful ardor." Cf. Bukhareva, "A. M. Bukharev (Arkhimandrit Feodor)," pp. 1-2.

90. Cf. *V svetlom protosre istiny,* in ODPZ, p. 9.

91. Bukharev narrates it personally in his letter to his old acquaintances Antonina Ivanovna Dubrovinova and a lifelong friend and supporter (even after his laicization) Varvara Vasil'evna Liubimova. Here he mentions that the publishing of *Apocalypse* "was already approved by the censor, yet forbidden by the Synod" as well as describes his feelings of ". . . restraint in the middle of monasticism in the very service to the word of God; I do not need such monasticism, because I joined the monastic life for the (sake of the) truth of God's word." Cf. *Pis'ma Arkhimandrita Feodora (Aleksandra Matveevicha Bukhareva) k kazanskim druz'iam: V. V. Liubimovoi, A. I. Dubrovinoi i protoiereiu V. V. Lavrskomu,* ed. P. Florenskii (Sergiev Posad, 1917), p. 14. More on this subject with a broader theological context can be

The reasons for such a "shocking move," naturally, were more profound and can be understood only in connection to his vocation as he perceived it. Bukharev felt for a long time a vivid interest in the events of the secular world, especially its cultural, intellectual, and spiritual developments, despite the traditional, and the secular world-denying attitude of Metropolitan Filaret (Drozdov).[92] Bukharev was often misunderstood in his intentions,[93] in his "spirit of sonship," and "was often mocked as a sort of innocent" or naïve.[94] One of those who looked at him with suspicion was V. I. Askochenskii (1813-1879), among others editor of *Domashniaia beseda (The Domestic Debate)*, who accused Bukharev of Hegelianism and of being a representative of the philosophical course of the Moscow Theological Academy.[95] Bukharev's true intention and desire, however, was to establish a link between the secular life of the world and the "(ap-)proved" forms of religious life. In this light are to be seen his *Tri pis'ma k N. V. Gogoliu (Three Letters to N. V. Gogol')* from 1848. Bukharev designated these epistles as a help for the readers in their moral and spiritual orientation besides being a genuine appraisal of Gogol's faith.[96]

Bukharev's core desire to "sanctify each act of life" flowed from his de-

---

found in the letters to Valerian Viktorovich Larskii (himself priest and professor) and Aleksandra Ivanovna Larskaia. Cf. pp. 88-89, 100-104.

92. Again Gorodetzky with her empathic perception gives a nice résumé on this point: "Bukharev wrote to and about Gogol', he grieved about the anti-religious attitude of Belinsky, and in the following years noticed the painting of Ivanov [A. A. Ivanov, *Iavlenie Khrista narodu (The Appearance of Christ to the People)* — was an event on its own] and the works of Turgenev, Chernyshevsky and Dostoevsky." Cf. *The Humiliated Christ*, pp. 116-17. All of this perhaps would be less special and unusual about Bukharev if we were not talking of a *hieromonakh* in a mid-nineteenth-century Russia who would not deprive himself of works of western thinkers. N. Zernov lists him among "the outstanding priests and theologians" of the nineteenth century who "were in no way obscurantist" in difficult times of state-church relationship. Cf. Zernov, *Moscow the Third Rome*, p. 89.

93. Cf. Bukhareva, "A. M. Bukharev (Arkhimandrit Feodor)," pp. 18-20.

94. He owed much of his character and ponderous spirit undoubtedly to his father who led and encouraged with his children at their earliest age deep spiritual discussions in the family. We can find a beautiful example of it in Bukhareva, "A. M. Bukharev (Arkhimandrit Feodor)," pp. 14-15.

95. Cf. ODPZ, p. 12.

96. Cf. ODPZ, p. 13. His wife also mentions in this context that Bukharev's "development of thought" was very fast, given the fact that he wrote these letters only two years after becoming a monk (i.e., at the age of twenty-four) and that his Weltanschauung *(miroserzanie)* was already fully reflected in them. Soon afterwards he composed those articles that "entered the book on Orthodoxy in its relationship to modernity . . . which then served primarily as the cause for the persecution of the author." Cf. Bukhareva, "A. M. Bukharev (Arkhimandrit Feodor)," p. 4.

sire to unite the church and the secular world "in the common task of the sanctification of life as whole." Yet it was too innovative and suspicious for its time.[97] Also in the eyes of Metropolitan Filaret, Bukharev's language and style in the *Apocalypse* could have caused misunderstandings and confusion, which eventually led to the above-mentioned denial of permission of publication.[98] Bukharev's request to be relieved from the monastic state was without precedent, and it was not until 1863 that he was finally released. Bukharev did not want to accuse anybody and accepted fully the consequences of his choice, which eventually reduced him to a life of dire need and involuntary renunciation mainly because of the omnipresent and omnipotent censor in his life. Anna Sergeevna proved to be his "faithful disciple";[99] together they had a child that died at a very young age.[100] Bukharev himself died on April 2, 1871, of consumption, and although his orthodoxy[101] and that of his writings were never questioned, his works were published only after he "resumed his monastic dignity." Shortly before his death, Bukharev was most impressed and inspired by "the humiliation of Christ and the redemption of the world,"[102] a crucial bit of information in trying to comprehend our author, his life-decisions, and his work.

Beyond the mentioned works, Bukharev in 1864 published among others a series of commentaries on OT books (mainly prophets); in 1865 *O*

97. Anna Sergeevna describes one of Bukharev's reflections induced by a lecture of W. Scott: ". . . his imagination worked in such a direction as to search for the reflection of the heavenly in the worldly, the image of God — in people, and in the reality of life — the presence of God's divine grace." Cf. Bukhareva, "A. M. Bukharev (Arkhimandrit Feodor)," p. 3.

98. Interesting is also Herzen's view on the controversy in favor of Bukharev. Cf. *The Humiliated Christ,* pp. 117-18. Filaret liked Bukharev and when he did not allow Bukharev's works to be published it was not out of questions about his orthodoxy but rather because Filaret "did not let his student go further than those limits that he set up for himself." This statement, of course, could be considered controversial. Cf. ODPZ, p. 14.

99. Anna Sergeevna renders in an excellent summary the "principal ideas" of Bukharev's Weltanschauung using "his authentic expressions." Cf. Bukhareva, "Alexander Matveevich Bukharev (Arkhimandrit Feodor)," pp. 5-14.

100. "Sasha" died on the very day of Easter in 1869, a trial that deeply marked the couple.

101. ". . . speaking of Orthodoxy Alexander Matveevich called it often treasure, gold." Bukhareva, "Alexander Matveevich Bukharev (Arkhimandrit Feodor)," p. 18.

102. "Life is meant to be sanctified, 'enchurched,' embraced in all its forms by the spirit of Christ. The mode of this sanctification must be that chosen by the Lord who humbled Himself. In his work on the Revelation he wrote: 'Our Russian task is to serve the purification of thought, of knowledge, of literature, of the whole civilization of the world,' but we should act and be ourselves 'in the spirit of condescension of this Bride of the Lamb,' Rev. xxi.9. The world should reflect 'the New Jerusalem *coming down* from heaven.'" Cf. *The Humiliated Christ,* pp. 118-19.

sovremennykh potrebnostiakh mysli i zhizni, osobenno russkoi (On Modern Needs of Thought and Life, in Particular the Russian One) appeared, a collection of theological reflections related to actual issues; in 1866 various pamphlets: *O podlinnosti apostol'skikh poslanii (On the Authenticity of the Apostolic Letters); Moia apologia po povodu kriticheskikh otzyvov o knige: O sovremennykh potrebnostiakh mysli i zhizni (My Apologetics Regarding the Critical Reactions to the Book: On the Modern Needs of Mind and Life); Ob upokoenii usopshikh i o dukhovnom zdravii zhivykh (On the Rest of the Deceased and on the Spiritual Health of the Living).* His *I. Khristos v Svoem slove (J. Christ in His Word)* was evaluated by his censor Archimandrite Mikhail as "the most clear and understandable of Bukharev's works."[103] He liked to quote from and comment on other authors' writings that greatly inspired him. Some later authors, for instance V. V. Rozanov, saw in Bukharev's works his own predecessor — especially "in questions of Christianization of the secular life *(mirovaia zhizn')*, the illuminating of all sides of life and activity of the human being by the light of Christ. . . ."[104]

If we had to briefly characterize Bukharev based only on the written testimony of his widow, the dominant notions in his thought were Christocentrism (as) God's immanent and transcendent presence and care for humankind; Christ, the "Lamb of God" in whom and through whom heaven and earth are united and reconciled — ". . . who has taken on himself all responsibility for the sins of the world, and for whom love is the spirit of all His earthly existence" — an attitude that each Christian is called to reflect in his life.[105] In addition, there was the already-mentioned *kenotic disposition* of Christ as God's sign of care for the salvation of His creation.

2.2. On the Spiritual Needs of the Russian Mind and Life[106]

In his address to the reader our author reveals that the following letters were written while Gogol' was still alive.[107] Although "only some brief passages"

103. Cf. *O pravoslavii v otnoshenii k sovremennosti* (1906), pp. xxi-xxiii. Currently there is still no complete collection and description of his works, mostly published posthumously.

104. Cf. *O dukhovnykh potrebnostiakh zhizni,* p. 306.

105. Cf. Bukhareva, "A. M. Bukharev (Arkhimandrit Feodor)," p. 8.

106. *O sovremennykh dukhovnykh potrebnostiakh mysli i zhizni, osobenno russkoi (On Modern Spiritual Needs of Thought and Life, especially in Russia)* published in 1865, mentioned in Gorodetzky's book on p. 119, was equally not available.

107. Arkhimandrit Feodor (A. M. Bukharev), *Tri pis'ma k N. V. Gogoliu, pisannye v 1848: K Chitateliu (To the Reader),* in ODPZ, pp. 253-56.

were eventually read to Gogol', the addressee did refer to them on different occasions. Further, Bukharev mentions importantly that despite the fact of Gogol' being a secular person *(svetskii chelovek),* he attributed the merit and sense of his work to Christ, the "sovereign Lord whom we all serve." In consequence we all are called to spread God's grace, which we have received in and through Christ.[108] In Bukharev's comments, the reader quickly encounters in a refined Russian language what Gorodetzky defined as the *kenotic mind of Christ:*

> The present theological point of view is to look at everything in the spirit of Christ who is the foundation, the Word of God, who created and carries everything by the word of His power.[109] He has become a human being for the salvation from straying and sins of all that is human. He took on Himself the guilt of the human being and carried it (in)to death on the cross thus sowing on all and everything His love, a love that abolishes evil and generates life that leads out from death.[110]

Bukharev's mind is set to accept nothing but what can be turned into a service for Christ: "For we need to know, that everybody and everything that alienates itself from Christ, the Son of God, becomes alienated from the love of His heavenly Father." Only someone who accepts Christ's unique mediating role can "accordingly to the amount of his faith . . . enter into the spirit of Christ's love that has been revealed to us."[111]

2.2.1. The First Letter

In *Pis'mo pervoe*[112] Bukharev announces, addressing Gogol', that he intends to show "his own point of view" on Gogol' based on the author's *Perepiski s*

108. Cf. *K Chitateliu,* in ODPZ, pp. 253-54.

109. . . . *nosit vsiacheskaia glagolom sily Svoeia.*

110. Bukharev mentions that he ceased to follow just "the letter of the texts," but his understanding is "faithful to the teaching of Faith" and he tried to "enter into the very force of dogmas," and the teachings "of the holy Fathers" were for him those "of living *(zhivoi)*" authorities. In fact he mentions in context of theology and teaching repeatedly the concept of *zhivoi (living, alive).* Cf. *K Chitateliu,* in ODPZ, p. 255.

111. *K Chitateliu,* in ODPZ, p. 256.

112. Metropolitan Filaret read the *First Letter to Gogol'* and did not approve its publication; the other two letters were written after this disapproval (no other works of Bukharev could be published in his lifetime either). In the first letter Bukharev quotes and comments or "freely renders" from the *Selected Passages from the Correspondence with Friends* of Gogol's, in

druziami (Correspondence with Friends),[113] talking "simply and directly."[114] Bukharev's intention is to comment à la "how I understand you," but soon after the initial pages his own reflection becomes prevalent, leaving interpretation secondary.

Gogol' understands that God as "Father of all who is love Himself" unites all "in a close and beautiful kinship" and is the source of all wisdom. "All that lives is a work and reflection of His love" and the human being is granted an access "into His love," obtaining from Him, just as His child would, all possible graces.[115] "The day of Christ's resurrection," which is nothing other than a full revelation of God's restoring love, the "living communion with the Sovereign love[116] that creates life even in the reign of death," appears "majestic and beautiful" in the supreme sign of resurrection and makes human beings "into siblings of the same family again." The timelessness of God's essence becomes visible against the contrasting background of worldly human existence. "The emptiness and the vanity in the world," into which the "living and life-giving Eternal love descended" in order to save fallen humankind, there this *Eternal, life-giving love* descends even into "the last depths of our evil, i.e., hell." No one is righteous enough to accomplish such an undertaking but God Himself in His Son, who equals God's essence, His *love:* "The Resurrection of our Savior or the love of God embraces in the resurrected Savior absolutely all, even sinners, calling together all into one family, one house of the heavenly Father."[117]

2.2.2. Divine Wisdom Conferred by Christ

"The love of God . . . bestows on an obedient person . . . an elevated look at himself [i.e., divine discernments] that enables him to raise in himself a shield against all that is obscure."[118] And since love is a living relationship,

---

the second he reviews in what relation were the last works of Gogol' to his first ones, and in the third letter Bukharev mainly exposes his own "theological system." Cf. ODPZ, p. 316.

113. It needs to mentioned here that Gogol' by his loyalty and open confession to his faith and the Orthodox Church, suggesting it as *the* solution to social problems and discords in Russia, caused especially among his friends and admirers much rumor and suspicion at its time. Cf. *Modern Russian Theology,* p. 22.

114. Cf. Arkhimandrit Feodor (A. M. Bukharev), *Pis'mo pervoe,* in ODPZ, p. 257.

115. Cf. Arkhimandrit Feodor (A. M. Bukharev), *Pis'mo pervoe,* in ODPZ, p. 258.

116. . . . *v zhivom soprikosnovenii k Vsederzhavnoi liubvi.*

117. Cf. *Pis'mo pervoe,* p. 260.

118. Cf. *Pis'mo pervoe,* pp. 260-61.

not a static matter, for those "who turn honestly to this Divine love which saves us" the strong will be more strengthened and the enslaved one shall be revived in spirit. "Thus God's saving love in Christ," after having accomplished the work of reconciliation, will spur in the person all faculties towards "one unanimous hymn to the Highest Being." It is the light, which, while opening up the person to faith, "permeates[119] entirely the human being in all his forces; behold the cleansing fire through which the whole nature of the human being has to pass." And when the soul truly yearns for this love of God, it "arranges its entire spiritual household [according to it] bringing it into full order and concord." Into such a soul the "heavenly guest" moves in and the soul becomes "wise by wisdom that cannot be acquired by education, is not inborn to us, but conferred by Christ." For an individual disposed this way, everybody, even "the most insignificant person can become a teacher and the most foolish thing can show its wise aspect to him; and a whole universe lies as a single, open book of doctrine before him."[120] *Love* and *wisdom* with Bukharev are interlinked and similarly to Khomiakov stand in direct relationship: "The listener is a disciple of his inner teacher . . . of that love of God that extends itself to all and embraces all." Such a disciple obtains the capacity to turn everything into good, for "there is no such tool that could not be assigned to the service of God." And the more such a person is exposed to the "enlightening, permeating light and fire of this love of God," the more his capacity to love truly his brothers *(siblings)* grows, treating them and delighting in them as in his dearest friend.[121]

2.2.3. Humility *as the Call for God's Saving Intervention*

These and the following pages are full of beautiful description of selfless, self-sacrificing, empathetic, Christ-imitating love, of those who allow their hearts to be partakers of that "heavenly love" which transforms, illuminates, permeates, and reunites humanity with(in) itself and with God. In this reflection *love* in its *heavenly form* is the point of reference, the beginning and completion of salvation and reconciliation on all levels, between all created

119. *Prosvetliaet* could be rendered here as *shines through* and *enlightens,* or illuminates, at the same time.

120. Valliere underlines the "theme of divine pedagogy, or *paideia*" prominent already this early in Bukharev's writings. (The last quoted phrase is Valliere's translation.) Cf. *Modern Russian Theology,* 27-28.

121. Cf. *Pis'mo pervoe,* pp. 262-63.

and the supreme entity of the Creator. Humankind is brought together "in one beautiful organism of concordant harmony."[122]

An element that Bukharev mentions repeatedly is *poslushnost' (obedience),* whereas we see this reference more as an obedience to the Spirit of God, obedience to the love of Christ, obedience in the sense of *humility* and *humiliation* for the sake of love and out of love, as a mere slavish submission or duty. Humility, in this context, is a need for God's salvific intervention, a precondition for entering and abiding in the "love of Christ" as well as a result of a "spiritual development or progress" *(dukhovnoe razvitie).* Everything, even the most noble and pure intention, stems from the *living* "spirit of [Christ's] love," for nothing good can be done or created without this mutual abiding: *it* in us and we in *it.* Without God's life-giving presence, *good* becomes a mere illusion.[123]

After several dense pages Bukharev summarizes: "These are the very fundamental thoughts of your 'Correspondence with Friends,'" all of which were directed to enlighten every aspect of human life and the secular world, which is "heading towards Christ's truth." The "truth of Christ" shall be revealed in "its spirit of truth" or "truthful spirit," i.e., "in the very spirit of Christ that loves humankind.[124] . . . Who revealed Himself to all in His life-giving love, power and wisdom." Thus the ideas of Gogol' on Russian and universal history disclose that "the life-giving love of God in Christ" played a constant and fundamental role helping humankind to open up to "the heavenly saving grace."[125] In the following pages Bukharev uses the same methodology for identifying in Russia's (divine) task the traces of divine intervention, which always actuated through *"Bozhestvennaia liubov" (Divine love).*[126]

122. . . . *odin prekrasnyi soglasnoiu stroinostiiu organizm.*

123. Cf. *Pis'mo pervoe,* pp. 264-65.

124. The literal rendering of *v chelovekoliubivom dukhe samogo Khrista* would be: "in the man-loving spirit of Christ" (where *man* naturally is the generic and genderless equivalent of *human being*).

125. *Pis'mo pervoe,* p. 266.

126. Cf. *Pis'mo pervoe,* pp. 266-305. Noteworthy is the language, which Bukharev uses to describe the "unique call of a well-known ancient nation [Israel] *into* the love of God" (p. 267). Bukharev also explicitly mentions having reached the point in the interpretation of Gogol' at which "the spiritual sphere *(dukhovnaia oblast')* of God's saving love in Christ" has been "revealed in full light," an "empire" that is not from the current world but rather "the apostolic, Universal Church which is the holder of the life-giving love." Solely she is capable of granting sacraments and creating equilibrium even between opposed forces and tendencies. In her is space "not only for the soul and heart of the person, but also for its intellect in its highest capacities so long as it wished to fit into her [the church's] sphere and surren-

Among Bukharev's topical preferences in his comments on the text of Gogol' are the underlying themes of "God's love in Christ," a love of a "Father for his children," for the entire humankind, the world, a love rediscovered through *obedience* and imitation (even though he does not use the term) so that the particular person and the entire humankind, and finally the world, *permeated, enlightened,* and *transformed* by the light and fire of this divine, self-sacrificing love, may become united with each other and with God through and in his essence, which is *love.* Bukharev dedicates entire densely composed pages to the notion of love, illuminating it from different theological perspectives. Less of a dogmatic and more of a catechetical and pragmatic-spiritual approach is offered, in a high-styled, eloquent Russian language. Hence when Bukharev intends to show Gogol' the way he perceives him, these elements constitute the most relevant and conspicuous part of his correspondence.[127]

2.3. On Orthodoxy's Relationship to Modernity[128]

This work regarded by some as naïve[129] (the part on *Dvanadesiatye tserkovnye prazdniki, The Twelve Ecclesial Feasts,* will be our principal interest) be-

---

dered itself entirely to the Divine love through obedience and faith. In one word, in her is the Divine saving love with all its Divine treasures." An entire ecclesiological and sacramental discourse is developed at this stage, the church as the conjunction of visible and invisible, an ascertainable presence of God's grace in the world with a unique task in history and even more so in the history of Russia (whereby the concept of *church* here naturally refers to the Russian Orthodox Church). Cf. *Pis'mo pervoe,* pp. 269-78. For Bukharev *love* and specifically *the Divine love of God* is the hermeneutical key for reviewing Russian authors and their works. Cf. *Pis'mo pervoe,* pp. 293-305.

127. Unfortunately we did not have access to the following two letters.

128. *O pravoslavii v otnosheniik sovremennosti.* As to the differences between the two editions: The 1860 edition contains "Pedagogicheskiia zametki o prigotovlenii i obrazovanii blagonadeznykh deiatelei dlia obrashcheniia zablizhdaiushchikh" in chapter 12. This is missing from the 1906 edition, where, however, besides his works and the author's foreword from 1860 (apparently first edition) a twenty-four-page introduction on Bukharev was added. In our research we have used the version from 1906 since it is a collection of writings, as indicated by his wife. Cf. Arkhimandrit Feodor (A. M. Bukharev), *O Pravoslavii v otnoshenii k sovremennosti: V raznykh stat'iakh Arkhimandrita Feodora* (Sankt-Peterburg: Tipografiia Torgovago Doma S. Strugovshchikova, 1860) (OPOS) and Arkhimandrit Feodor (A. M. Bukharev), *O Pravoslavii v otnoshenii k sovremennosti* (1906) (Sankt-Peterburg: Synodal'naia tipografiia, 1906).

129. Cf. *The Humiliated Christ,* p. 124.

gins with "To the reflecting *or* reasoning one" *(razmyshliaiiushchii)* and leads into a guided meditation on Matthew 13:44: *The kingdom of heaven is like treasure hidden in a field.* The *field* is a synonym for the human being into which the Holy Spirit descends in the sacrament of baptism and doing so brings "with His breath a treasure: the imperishable seed of rebirth, new life from God."[130] Bukharev invites the reader into a "written conversation" based on an icon of the twelve feasts of the Orthodox Church and encourages readers to join in asking the Holy Spirit for help.[131] From this "recorded conversation" we will render only some illuminating examples regarding our topic, since each of the main Orthodox feasts, beginning with the "Nativity of the Blessed Mother of God" and ending with the Resurrection, Ascension of Christ to heaven and the Dormition of the Theotokos, reflects God's love in different aspects.

2.3.1. The Receptacle of Christ's Heart

The text has a strong pietistic character yet in clear relationship and care for the world introduced by St. Paul's confession in Philippians 1:8: *For God is my witness, how I yearn for you all with the affection [love] of Christ Jesus.*[132] It is necessary that the "spirit of the Theotokos' love for perishing sinners . . . so to say may be born in our world — for instance in our soul. . . ." This spirit of "God's love for humankind" is always accessible to those who believe "especially in the miraculous icons of the Mother of God." She is in "the receptacle of Christ's heart that embraces the entire world with infinite love. Therefore we can say that in Christ's body, in the Church, the Mother of God constitutes the very heart, beating solely with the Divine love." It comprises all the sufferings and needs of believers. The "closer in spirit" one moves to this heart, the more fully the person enters into the suffering of others. Facing such compassion, Bukharev uses a moral exhortation to "suffer with love and to [perceive] the sickness of others as if they were [our] proper ones." Such love inspires and is modeled after Christ's love; and learning from the Mother of God protects one from "the danger of spiritual death" through the Holy Spirit that alone "vivifies our faith."[133]

130. Cf. *Dvanadesiatye tserkovnye prazdniki,* in OPOS, p. 3.
131. Cf. *Dvanadesiatye tserkovnye prazdniki,* in OPOS, p. 5.
132. The Russian original uses *love* in place of *affection.*
133. Cf. *Dvanadesiatye tserkovnye prazdniki,* pp. 6-7.

2.3.2. *The Temple of the Father's Love*

The feast of Mary's presentation in the Temple is compared to the "New Jerusalem . . . the Bride of the Lamb" where the Lord himself prepared a Temple and this Temple is the *Lamb* itself based on Revelation 21:22. Christ is the Word, the Glory of God, the Holy of Holies, the Lamb of God in whom "the fullness of the Father's kindness and love can be contemplated," a divine-fatherly love that is "resplendent in the Son." Mary is being introduced precisely into this "Temple of the Father's love." Bukharev's pointed usage of the *Lamb of God* is not merely a personal preference, as we shall see later, but an image that expresses his perception of Christ's kenotic love and relationship with the Father.[134] Quoting the high priestly prayer of Jesus from John 17:24 and 26, Bukharev points out that the beatitude and glory of the saints — for only they can enter the Temple of the Lamb — is nothing other than "an open delight of the Father's love in the Holy Spirit."[135] And since the fullness of love and of the Holy Spirit is in Christ, there is no love of the Father "outside of Christ, the Word of God."[136] Our participation in Christ's love is consummated through the Holy Spirit — this clear realm of Pneumatology is of a subtle yet decisive importance. Finally the one who enters the *Temple of the Lamb, the New Jerusalem,* is reinvigorated and "renewed in faith and love," regardless of what condition the soul has been in previously.

2.3.3. *God's Universal Salvific Offer*

God desires to give us all that is necessary for our salvation, which is the reason why "His glory and splendor," Jesus Christ, became one of us and yearns to transmit "the Father's love" if we "only accept and receive Him." Thus the love of the Father is an *offer* of relationship that requests a response from our side, Bukharev asserts, while commenting on the feast of Visitation.[137] Whoever receives Christ, receives the "Lamb of God" who has taken our sins away, whom the Father "so to say made to be sin for us," for all of us, and through whom we discover the "incarnated truth" in each other. God's love

134. According to Gorodetzky: "The writings of Bukharev, with his constant appeal to follow the 'humiliated Lamb,' and his own strange and sorrowful destiny could be explained from his desire for personal self-abasement on the lines of foolishness for Christ's sake." *The Humiliated Christ,* p. 177.

135. Cf. *Dvanadesiatye tserkovnye prazdniki,* pp. 8-9.

136. Cf. *Dvanadesiatye tserkovnye prazdniki,* p. 10.

137. Cf. *Dvanadesiatye tserkovnye prazdniki,* pp. 12-14.

in Christ is being revealed in charity and compassion similarly to the parable of the Good Samaritan; in order to be saved one needs to exemplify "love for his neighbor."[138] The entire reflection is based on this relationship; the saving grace and love of God go beyond national affiliation or borders. A great opening towards the heathen from the side of the primitive church, in this case to the Samaritans, is a sign of God's care for *all* His children. "The division that separated the primitive Church from the nonbelievers and Samaritans . . . was destroyed in Jesus Christ. . . . If you turn away from a Samaritan — you are turning away in his face from Me — your Savior." Again, this Savior is "the Lamb of God who also took the sins of the Samaritan together with the sins of all the world: this very Samaritan, now repulsive to you, will become in Me, (as) your most beloved brother, and even closer than a brother."[139]

The Lamb of God represents "the glory and splendor of God," His salvation and reconciliation. The believer animated by "the spirit of [Christ's] love" brings the Samaritan to the church, thus fulfilling towards him "[God's] act of mercy." Therefore: "Enter into the spirit of My love towards this outcast sinner." On the example of the apostles, who converted countless heathen, Bukharev reflects in a missionary zeal on how many could be converted to the Orthodox Church, regardless of their fault, if following Christ by taking up for them their sins "as if they were our own," faithful Christians shared with them Christ's attitude of love. It is the first hint towards the universality of God's saving love in Christ for the *entire* humanity, or as Bukharev would put it: for the world, patterned on Mary's humble obedience as a *maiden of the Lord* and on her intermediation *(bringing to the King the virgins in many-colored robes she is led to the King, with her virgin companions following behind her* . . . cf. Ps. 45:14).[140] The "Lamb of God (who takes away the sins of the world)"[141] and the "spirit of Christ, of Christ's love," are frequently used concepts with Bukharev.[142]

138. Cf. *Dvanadesiatye tserkovnye prazdniki,* p. 16.

139. Cf. *Dvanadesiatye tserkovnye prazdniki,* pp. 17-18.

140. Cf. *Dvanadesiatye tserkovnye prazdniki,* pp. 18-19, 23.

141. Bukharev links it with the "mind of Christ" in Philippians 2:5: "Have this mind among yourselves, which is yours in Christ Jesus." We assume that this could have served as foreshadowing or even model for Gorodetzky's concept on *Christ's kenotic mind.* Also in this regard: "Kenosis begins, according to Tareev, long before the Incarnation. There was in Bukharev already a foreboding of this thought: creation as a kenotic act." Cf. *The Humiliated Christ,* pp. 144-45.

142. Cf. *Dvanadesiatye tserkovnye prazdniki,* p. 27.

As for the Trinity, Bukharev describes the relationship in the Holy Trinity with John 14:17, 23 as a love-relationship that was reflected also among the apostles, in particular in the Feast of Pentecost: it is the entire Trinity that descends within the fire of the Holy Spirit.[143]

2.3.4. Multilayered Communion and Redemption of the Intellect

At the *Khimesis,* the Dormition of the Theotokos, Bukharev says that death is "nothing but a final and complete union with Christ's death" and subsequently with the glory of his resurrection (reflecting on Phil. 1:21, 23). "Yet the spirit and strength of Christ's death is His love for the sinful world, as of a Lamb, who takes away the sins of the world and is sacrificed for the sins of the world." The Mother of God entered into this same transforming power of Christ's death.[144] "There is salvation for all and everything from the all-destructive worldly evil, salvation which is in the cross of Christ." This salvation was fulfilled in the death and resurrection of the Lamb of God, "the strength of Christ's love to the world and for me," quoting repeatedly St. Paul in Galatians 6:14. God's care, love, and salvation for the *whole world* is a deep concern to Bukharev, in fact one of the greatest concerns, and it can be achieved only by *Christom Bogom Slovom:* "by Christ, the Word of God, the beginning and end of all things," in whom all is being renewed.[145] Therefore at the center of the contemplated icon of salvation is "Christ's descent into the Netherworld" in order to restore life to Adam and his descendants. Sharing is indispensable for salvation, for salvation does not occur as a private event but is embedded in the community, in the human family, in the church. "By sharing in common faith and the mutual love of Christ" we share the burden of each other's guilt; "in Christ we are members of one body."[146]

One of Bukharev's phenomenal novelties is creating a liaison between gnoseology and soteriology based upon Luke 2:52, Hebrews 1:1, and John 1:3. The incarnate Word of God descended and redeemed also the *human intellect,* which relates to *good* and *evil* like anything else in the human being. ". . . The only begotten Word of God received our human existence including our human comprehension, heart and mind into a personal conjunction

143. Cf. *Dvanadesiatye tserkovnye prazdniki,* p. 36.
144. Cf. *Dvanadesiatye tserkovnye prazdniki,* p. 37.
145. Cf. *Dvanadesiatye tserkovnye prazdniki,* pp. 39-40.
146. Cf. *Dvanadesiatye tserkovnye prazdniki,* pp. 41-42.

(edinolichnoe soedinenie) with Himself, into the oneness of his 'I' *(Ia)*."[147] And if that is the case, Christ uniting two natures in himself, all that is united in the *Me* of the Word is lifted up, transformed, divinized, i.e., saved. Yet, naturally, Christ's love-sacrifice saves the entire human being, the entire world — descending, in *"the power of His love,"* even into the Netherworld.[148] It is "the spirit of Christ's love" that concludes Bukharev's reflection and remains the leitmotiv of his thought.

2.4. *Modernity in Its Relation to Orthodoxy*

The truth of the Lord prevails forever, for he himself *is* the truth (John 14:6), and the martyrs of Christ "did suffer out of love and fidelity" towards their Lord, for this truth. It was "the sweetness of the experienced divine love" that made them rejoice even amidst martyrdom, and the "strength of His love" accompanied their words and (miraculous) deeds.[149] The described understanding is meant to help the contemporary reader in following "the spirit of Christ and in order not to become alienated from Him." Imitating the martyrs, "in the spirit and strength of the love of the Lamb of God," in a response to "His love for the human being" the Christian is to become "the martyr of the Lord's love for us sinners" and to "endure many of the spiritual burdens of his neighbors." The probable epicenter of the texts is that "without partaking in the spirit and disposition (of mind) of God's love," and all of what he underwent for our salvation, the faith of a Christian can be trapped by "spiritual self-complacency" and of judgment over the weaknesses of others.[150] Instead we are to imitate the "tender forgiveness of the *God who loves the human being (chelovekoliubiiashchii Bog)* and who died on the *cross of love for the human being (krizh chelovekoliubiia): Father, forgive them, for they know not what they do* (Luke 23:34)."[151]

147. Cf. *Dvanadesiatye tserkovnye prazdniki,* pp. 43-44. Also: "Bukharev insisted upon Christ's sacrificial taking upon Himself of the sin of human ignorance." *The Humiliated Christ,* p. 169.

148. Cf. *Dvanadesiatye tserkovnye prazdniki,* p. 47.

149. *O sovremennosti v otnoshenii k pravoslaviiu,* in OPOS, pp. 52-53.

150. Cf. *O sovremennosti,* in OPOS, p. 54.

151. *O sovremennosti,* in OPOS, p. 55.

2.5. *The Reciprocal Perfection of Faith and Love*

Bukharev continues by quoting at length Metropolitan Filaret Drozdov[152] in his reflection on a right appropriation or internalization of Orthodoxy that goes beyond simply confessing, or as he puts it, "having it in the word of God and the symbol of faith . . . what belongs to God, His Prophets, Apostles, Fathers of the Church, but yet not to you. . . . The fervency for Orthodoxy unites us with that spirit of the holy Fathers through which they laid down their lives for it and were equally fully prompt to lay down their lives for the salvation of souls."[153] One can appropriate the sentiment of Orthodoxy that is "imbedded in his thoughts and memory" yet in a further step he should move on from "a deposit to receiving a treasure, namely the living strength of faith." How can this be obtained? asks Filaret in a rhetorical question, and answers with St. Paul in Romans 10:10: "By heart," for it is *with the heart that one believes*[154] and faith received by the heart will lead to *abiding in love* as again St. Paul says in Ephesians 3:17: *So that Christ may dwell in your hearts through faith — and you may be rooted and grounded in love.*[155] Then the love of Christ himself becomes the actuating force in a person: "One begins to love all people by nothing other than the love of Christ. . . . Out of love and gratitude for the One who suffered and died for you, you will be ready even to die for those saved by His love and redeemed by His death. In brief, by the extent of perfection in faith you will be perfect in the love to your neighbor."[156] Similarly to the epistle of St. James, faith and its manifestations can be measured by the integration and internalization of love to God and one's neighbor.

Subsequently, Bukharev's main and original point is not merely an external but much rather an internal, internalized commitment "in the same strength" for Orthodoxy "according to the needs of our [current] times," acting in "Christ's love for human beings which expressed itself in His sufferings and death for them. . . ." The full interpretation of it became plain only "to the children of the Holy Church" where Christ "entered and abided *(vselialsia)* in their souls, as the supreme principle *(verkhovnoe nachalo)* of all their actions and life, as God of their mind, feeling, desires, all their ac-

152. Pronounced at the consecration of Prince Alexander Nevskii's church.

153. *O sovremennosti,* in OPOS, p. 56.

154. ". . . and is justified, and with the mouth one confesses and is saved."

155. Filaret quotes only the first part of the phrase and develops his homily on the second one.

156. *O sovremennosti,* in OPOS, p. 57.

tions so as to unfold in them his holiness, wisdom and love."[157] Christ is the initiator and fulfiller of divinization: "All God's fulfillment is disclosed to the human being in Christ," and if divinization could not be accomplished yet, it is only due to the division that occurred in the church.[158] Here dominates an anthropological aspect of God's proximity to the human being in Christ's love and wisdom, in the God-Word. Without this divine soteriological initiative and loving proximity, the human being cannot be saved (Heb. 1:3).[159] The fullness of Christ's divinity is being revealed to us bodily (Col. 2:9) thanks to his blessed mother, Mary. As the unity of Christ's divinity and humanity is a *oneness,* so is our joining in Christ's incarnated "I" — thanks to his mother — eternal.[160] In Christ nothing human is being "swallowed up" by the divine but rather united with it.[161]

"Christ comes into the world in the mindset and dispositions of the Lamb of God," taking on all the sins of mankind and the responsibility for them: "Love is the spirit of all His earthly life, of all His being and actions; precisely in such spirit of His is supposed to be our own spirituality, all our internal dispositions and thoughts as well as external relations and actions." Christ became fully human for our sake, "in thoughts, desires, perceptions," and beyond: there's a unique value of each human being, when he talks in general about the "human nature," because the Son of God came to all levels of our society, that of the family, nation, social, and not only spiritual or ecclesial.[162] And to the aforementioned "spirit and disposition of the Lamb

157. *O sovremennosti,* in OPOS, pp. 57-58.

158. Relating to the great schism and ongoing division between East and West, taking, naturally, the side of Orthodoxy.

159. *O sovremennosti,* in OPOS, p. 59.

160. Cf. *O sovremennosti,* in OPOS, p. 60.

161. Cf. *O sovremennosti,* in OPOS, p. 66.

162. Cf. *O sovremennosti,* in OPOS, pp. 67-69. Bukharev is faithful to this concept of God entering into our "earthly order of things" for our sake, and he returns to it also in his article "Iavlenie Khrista miru" on Ivanov's famous painting. Following the introduction, where he describes the task of an artist, namely to "reflect God's love" in the world, Bukharev describes God as "the Heavenly Father who is the all-creating and all-sustaining, eternal and hypostatic (in person existing) all-wise/all-knowing Love, revealing Himself in His consubstantially hypostatic Son-Word and breathing with/in the consubstantial and hypostatic life-giving Holy Spirit." Our life, world, and all events are in the power of this God, who in all His attributes and known revelations is above and beyond all *Love.* To perceive and to render somehow this, "the strength and power of the Father's love" fully revealed in "His Son — the Lamb of God," is the task of the artist, as it precisely happens in the painting of Ivanov. All relations in Bukharev's interpretation (not solely of the painting) are animated by the love streaming from the Father, through the Son and reflected or yearned

of God" we are to conform our own mind, lives, and intentions to the "love that was the spirit of all His earthly life," which Bukharev calls "the spirit of the Lamb of God," reflecting and pointing to his heavenly, meanwhile fully grounded in his earthly, existence and mission. The true fidelity to the Orthodox faith and church in words and acts "can be only in conformity to this disposition and spirit (spirituality) of Christ's love in order to fully reveal the Image of God in us."[163]

Conclusion

If Khomiakov lived the church and theology, so Bukharev lived universally applied love. The love that streamed from the Father through the incarnation and acted *in the spirit of the Son-Word* in the world, as at the moment of creation, so even *in modern times,* Bukharev understood as a form of dialogue between God and his entire creation. His theology is Trinitarian yet his attention rests primarily on the fatherly love of God and the fulfillment of His will in the love-response of the Son. Again a language of communication unfolds in front of our eyes, a model to be transmitted and/or encountered in the communion of church but equally in our societies, our culture, the secular world. For that matter, can anything be truly *secular* for God in his own creation? Bukharev provides a bridge over the ideological chasm with all that is sacred on one side and all that is secular on the other side. Then, if being consistent, what is more secular than time? Yet he takes the liturgical calendar and shows how each remembrance of the past creates a present immersion in the eternal *Love* that *is* God. Similarly, by loving our neighbor in the world, in imitating Christ's all-inclusive love and bringing heaven to earth, an *enchurching* of the *secular* occurs in transforming it into the heavenly and divine *reality,* into the Temple of the New Jerusalem, where the *Lamb of God* awaits all of us with His *sovereign love.*

---

for by the other figures present in the painting. And the Lamb of God, by taking upon Himself all the illness and alienation of humankind, "leads it back into the Father's love." Cf. *Iavlenie Khrista miru,* in OPOS, pp. 222-29, 243.

163. . . . *v nastroenii i dukhe liubvi Gospodnei.* The text carries on: "For as Christ came in the disposition of the Lamb of God into the world taking [upon Himself] the sin of the world and the responsibility for human sins, His love is the spirit of His entire earthly life, His entire status *(sostoianie)* and deeds: precisely in such Spirit of His shall consist the spirituality of ours, as of internal attitude and awareness, so of external relations and procedures." *Iavlenie Khrista miru,* in OPOS, p. 69.

IV. The Concept of *Love* with the Two Founders of Russian Religious Philosophy: N. F. Fedorov and V. S. Solov'ev

1. Nikolai Fedorovich Fedorov: *Brotherly Love*

1.1. Biography

N. F. Fedorov (1828/29-1903) was a highly original and controversial Russian religious thinker. Born as an illegitimate child of a prince (P. I. Gagarin) and raised by his mother, he inherited the name of his godfather. After finishing his secondary schooling in Tambov (1849), he could not conclude his study of jurisprudence in Odessa (1852) because his uncle, K. I. Gagarin, who was supporting the family as well as Fedorov's studies, died. Two years later, Fedorov began teaching history and geography in various school districts, transferring to seven different towns in thirteen years. In 1867, after having met N. P. Peterson,[1] he moved on foot to Moscow where he served in the Chertovskaia Museum. From 1874 until his death, he was a librarian for twenty-nine years in the Rumiatsev Library.[2] It was there, on Sundays, that the catalogue room where he worked became "a discussion club attended by many illustrious persons of that period."[3]

Possessing a mind of vast erudition[4] while being a thinker of undoubtedly audacious creativity, Fedorov led an austere, ascetic life. He possessed an unwavering sense of duty, which he expressed in his library-work and in

1. Peterson was at that time a teacher in Tolstoy's school in Iasnaia Poliana and became Fedorov's friend, disciple, and eventually editor of his works.

2. Today the Russian State Library in Moscow.

3. Cf. O. Kolesnikov, "Moskovsii Sokrat," in N. Fedorov, *Filosofiia obshchego dela,* vol. 1 (Moskva: AST, 2003), pp. 5-6 (FOD I-II).

4. There was a general view that he had read all the books that he catalogued.

sharing with others virtually all he possessed. Though considered by some as the founder of a neochristian outlook and (co-)initiator of Russian cosmism,[5] Fedorov never wrote down or published his ideas, apart from some articles that appeared under a pseudonym. What posthumously appeared was a collection of writings, talks, and lectures given to, and eventually assembled and edited by, his disciples under the title of *Filosofiia obshchego dela (The Philosophy of the Common Task)* in 1906, reprinted in 1913 with limited copies.[6] The reasons for the limited number of publications were, first, a lack of financial resources and, second, the fact that Fedorov fervently promulgated free access to knowledge.[7]

Fedorov's work and personality are of a notable interest because of his long-term interaction and philosophical exchanges with the great thinkers of his time, such as F. M. Dostoevsky, L. N. Tolstoy, V. S. Solov'ev, A. A. Fet, and many others.[8] From their correspondence, as well as from the articles written on Fedorov by many of the modern Russian religious thinkers, it is clear that some Fedorovan ideas influenced Dostoevsky, Tolstoy, and Solov'ev, even though they did not agree with all or incorporate all of his ideas into their proper works. Fedorov enjoyed high regard and appreciation from their part since he was a religious thinker who built his ideas on Christian teaching and adhered to an exemplary high standard of Christian ethics and morals in the conduct of his own life.[9]

5. At the library having closely followed and academically coached the hearing-impaired K. E. Tsiolkovsky, who is seen as the forefather of Soviet space rocketry.

6. The first edition numbered only 480 and the second 620 copies. They were not for sale but were distributed for free among friends and libraries. There is an edition of his complete works in four + one volumes, which appeared in 1994-2000 by Traditsia, Moskva.

7. He even dedicated a proper reflection to the question of copyright, requesting change in this matter — an apparently trivial detail yet of unfading interest even in our times. See FOD II, pp. 424-29.

8. There is a famous sketch by L. O. Pasternak titled "The Three Wise Men," which depicts Fedorov, Solov'ev, and Tolstoy in a friendly conversation. The image of Fedorov was drawn secretly by Pasternak while he pretended to read in the library, as Fedorov shunned all fame and would not allow any picture or drawing to be produced of him.

9. For further reading on Fedorov's biography and work we recommend the abovementioned complete works in four and one complementary volumes edited by I. I. Blauberg; the extensive and well-researched standard work of S. Smenova, *Filosof budushchego veka Nikolai Fedorov (A Philosopher of the Age to Come: Nikolai Fedorov)* (Moskva: "Pashkov dom," 2004); the voluminous two-book edition of the anthology *Pro et Contra* (Sankt-Peterburg: RKhGA, 2004-8); in English the translated and abridged works of N. F. Fedorov with a brief yet excellent introduction to the complex realm of Fedorov, his

Regarding the textual corpus, there was much criticism of Fedorov's ideas, which apart from being at times eccentric and exceptionally bold, suffer from a lack of consistency in their presentation and from a "heavy repetitive style." The inconsistency may be due to the posthumous compilation by the editors N. P. Peterson and V. A. Kozhevnikov, who "put them together in some sort of order." Furthermore, Fedorov himself seemed incapable of presenting his work in a "systematic and streamlined form," making it difficult to edit.[10]

1.2. The Cause of Suffering

Fedorov dedicated his initial question to the existing incongruity between peace and the world: "Why are 'peace' and 'world' not synonymous?" Philologically and in Fedorov's time Russian orthography "мiр" and "мир" (today both spelled "мир") stood for "peace" and "world" separately. Thus, his question phrased literally would be: "Why does peace not mean [or equal] world?"[11] Peace or, conversely, the lack of it, is a precise indicator for the status of relations. Therefore, Fedorov embarked on addressing the various causes for the "unbrotherly and nonkindred relationship" *(nerodstvennoie otnoshenie)* towards our neighbors: calamities resulting in crop failure,[12] the country-dwellers' lack of knowledge on one side and the abstract, life-distant, and speculative reasoning of the town-dwellers on the other, and the dissociation of thought from action are some of the most important causes — and at the same time results — of a "hateful division of the world."[13] This "immaturity of humankind" is the cause of wars and ongoing "mutual annihilation." Thus, instead of using our God-given gifts of knowledge and means for general prosperity and peaceful coexistence, humankind develops means of destruction, society becomes further militarized,[14] and weapons are invented or further improved. This is radically opposed to what

ideas, and time: *What Was Man Created For? The Philosophy of the Common Task: Selected Works,* ed. E. Koutaissoff and M. Minto (London: Honeyglen Publishing/ Lausanne: L'Age d'Homme, 1990).

10. "Which was not an easy job, since Fedorov wrote in response to a variety of contemporary events." Cf. *What Was Man Created For?* pp. 13-14, 17.

11. "Почему мiр не мир?" Cf. FOD, p. 9.

12. Referring here to the disastrous year 1891. Cf. p. 9.

13. Cf. FOD I, pp. 9-14.

14. It was one of the urgent problems of the late nineteenth and twentieth centuries. Eventually, as we know, it led to WWI and WWII.

God created and intended for humanity, and it takes its toll "most heavily" on the "unlearned and simple ones." The educated class, which "exhibits alienation from its kin in an extreme form," has "the duty, ability, and responsibility to restore kinship" yet fails to do so.[15]

1.3. The Duty of Love and the Common Task

How can this *unbrotherly* and *unkinly* trend of "juridical and economic relations, class distinctions, and international strife," which merely reflects egoism[16] and a lack of love, be mended? The concepts of "citizenship, civilization, and loyalty" also represent the misuse of love for other aims: "Loyalty to the land of the fathers is not 'patriotism,' which replaces love for the fathers with pride in their achievement, the substitution of the vice of pride for the virtue of love, and self-love and vanity for love of the fathers. People who take pride in the same object can form an honorable order but not a brotherhood of loving sons."[17] Fedorov's answer to the former problem was a unifying task, a *task of duty (out) of love* to the ancestors that would amalgamate humanity into unity. The "common cause or task" *(obshchee delo)* would, through focusing humankind's efforts and applying the means of knowledge and science, lend it the unique capacity to master nature's "death-bearing" and "blind forces."[18] Consequently, wars would no longer be a priority as famine and energy needs would be resolved and humanity would reach "adulthood,"[19] that is, being united in attaining the same goal.[20] Yet this "goal" is nothing less than that which includes and regards *all* and

15. Cf. FOD I, p. 13.

16. For the confrontation of egoism versus love and duty, see N. F. Fedorov, *Sobranie sochineniia v chetyrekh tomakh,* vol. 3 (Moskva: Traditsiia, 1997), pp. 347-48.

17. FOD I, p. 17.

18. "Serving the God of ancestors consists in transforming the blind, death-bearing force into a life-giving one," by controlling it. Cf. FOD I, pp. 18, 59.

19. An idea imbedded in the concept of *supramoralism* (a term coined by Fedorov himself), which is the highest form of Christian morals leading to general unification of humanity with itself and its deceased ancestors through the resuscitation of the latter ones. Cf. FOD I, pp. 456-536. *Supramoralism* and Easter are closely interlinked for Fedorov; see *Vertikal'noe polozhenie, ili Paskha (Supramoralism, ego sushchnost' est' Paskha) (The vertical Position, or Easter [Supramoralism, Its Being Is Easter]),* Fedorov, *Sobranie sochineniia v chetyrekh tomakh,* vol. 3, pp. 317-20.

20. "The search for meaning is the search for a goal, a cause, a common task." For *Common task* in relation to universal history, see FOD I, pp. 150-55.

everybody, and that final goal for Fedorov cannot be merely self-preservation but the "restitution of life" to the ancestors, which leads to a completed unity of humankind.[21] For Fedorov, it is a question of "duty/debt *(dolg)* towards them, to all deceased fathers"; he assigns the resuscitation of the dead as the final goal of the *sons and daughters* of the human being.[22] All Fedorov's reflection drifts in one way or another towards his idea of resuscitation of the deceased ancestors and an earthly, even interstellar, utopian paradise. His veneration of the deceased fathers and ancestors truly borders on a cult.[23]

One of Fedorov's eccentric ideas is steeped in a deep *agapic* symbolism, in which he nonetheless conceives Christianity still merely in view of his system:

> [Christianity is an] association of the living for the resuscitation of the dead, i.e., an assembly of those eating and drinking in love with the purpose of returning the departed ones to the (dining) table of love *(trapeza);*

21. ". . . the unity of the Common Task — that of resuscitation — is the highest form of unity." FOD I, pp. 150-55.

22. Cf. FOD I, p. 18. The resurrection, more precisely the "resuscitation *(voskreshenie)* of the fathers and deceased ancestors," is Fedorov's main concern, to which he keeps returning up to the point of nausea. Its obsessive repetition is most probably connected to Fedorov's childhood trauma of losing his father and grandfather at the age of four. His deviation from Christian dogma with these ideas is more than evident. Solely the One who himself *is* the Resurrection has the might to bring about *resuscitation,* which is included in resurrection: *I am the resurrection and the life* (John 11:25), says Jesus to Martha at the occasion of her brother Lazarus' death. Ironically, Lazarus' resuscitation is one of Fedorov's main arguments regarding the subject in question; nevertheless, after his *resuscitation,* Lazarus died, which proves that the final *raising* of the dead is an eschatological event and inevitably connected to Christ's second coming, thus the Last Judgment. *This is indeed the will of my Father, that all who see the Son and believe in Him may have eternal life; and I will raise them up on the last day* (John 6:40); And an agapic-eucharistical discourse closely related to this reflection: *Very truly, I tell you, unless you eat the flesh of the Son of Man and drink His blood, you have no life in you. Those who eat my flesh and drink my blood have eternal life, and I will raise them up on the last day* (John 6:53-54) — another fundamental scriptural proof and dogmatic truth, which, for some strange reason, Fedorov's erudite mind overlooked or simply ignored. Consequently, despite his other ideas, acute observations, and brilliant intuitions, these deviations from the fundamentals of Christian doctrine cast unfortunately yet comprehensibly a shadow on his entire work.

23. Fedorov in fact calls it "the cult of ancestors/fathers" even though under explicitly different, namely Christian, rather than pagan prerequisites: "God Himself confirms the truth that religion is the cult of ancestors by calling Himself the God of the fathers." FOD I, pp. 58, 156-57. One can find a somewhat different approach, yet with the same result of common goal in FOD II, pp. 144-46.

> for they eat and drink as to have strength to return to life the deceased. Christ at His departure united the commemoration [of the dead], or love for Him (that means to all departed), with feeding [meal], with that which gives life and strength for the [upcoming] toil. He commanded to gather all the living to this supper of love (*vechera liubvi* [*agapē*]), a love for Him, as well as all deceased, to such love that consumes all life's strength in order to see and hear Him with all the departed ones.[24]

Leaving Fedorov's eccentric religious ideas aside, his observation on the danger of substituting a false concept of progress for love and respect for the ancestors builds on a comparison and presumption of superiority over the predecessors, which, in turn, deceives society by a nondurable and misleading contempt that in fact shall further diminish:

> And in future, with further development of progress, contempt will gradually decrease. Yet not even the diminishing of contempt will engender love and respect for one's predecessors, i.e., the feelings that really ennoble the descendants. Therefore, can progress give meaning to life, let alone any purpose? For only what can express the noblest forms of love and esteem gives meaning and purpose to life.[25]

Indeed, this seems to be a central element of propulsion in his project: the need for a "lofty form of love" and healthy esteem founded in the model of the Holy Trinity, as we shall see next.

1.4. The Moral Law of Unity

Unity is paramount to Fedorov's understanding of God, which is why God's unity in the Trinity is the best model for humanity as well:[26]

> The Divine Being that Himself is the perfect model of community (society), a Being that is a unity of independent, Immortal Persons, fully perceiving their eternal and thus by death unbreakable unity (a unity that even excludes death) — such is the Christian idea of God. In other

24. FOD I, pp. 154-55. See also p. 162.

25. Cf. FOD I, pp. 27-31.

26. See for example Fedorov's reflections on the pragmatic use of the (concept of) Trinity for a moral evaluation of an agreement, etc. FOD I, 82-84.

> words in the Divine is revealed what humanity needs [in order] to become immortal. The Trinity is *the Church of Immortals,* and it shall be alike on the human side a *church of the resurrected.*[27]

Based on this paradigm, Fedorov proceeds to the quality of this intra-Trinitarian relationship defined as the "law of unity," which equals the "law of love." Fedorov uses a sensitive spiritual discernment when speaking of a divine *plan* instead of *will* or *idea:* "Thus does it not represent (this idea or, more precisely, plan) the very law of love, i.e., the very being of Christianity? In unity, in mutual fidelity, paternal and filial love, the communion of immortal persons is not bound in death as it is with us, in the community of mortals. To be more accurate and to express it more distinctly, there is no death in them because their faithfulness and love are boundless."[28] This certainly is a worthy and more than a valid theological reflection.

The importance of this intra-Trinitarian paradigm raises once more the core-question: "Will the Christian idea of God realized by humanity be also that of the law of love?" In other words, will humankind understand that if it is to grow up and reach full *adulthood,* it has to see *love* as an indispensable prerequisite for a truly faithful image of God, without which it cannot prosper? The love and respect of law, indirectly or in its final consequences, applies to *this* "law of love." In comparison to non-Christian religions: for a Christian to mourn the loss of this love has to do with the loss of unity and vice versa; or should we speak of integrality? "Repentance is the recognition of one's guilt over disunity and admitting one's duty in the unification of universal love which eliminates the consequences of disunity."[29] Since God is a unity of distinct Divine Persons, a *multi-unity,* yet fully and truly united, and we are images of God, perhaps we should start to consider *disunity* the factual root of all *un-love* in creation.[30] The force or quality of

27. FOD I, p. 85.

28. FOD I, p. 85. Yet the Trinity's unity respects the individuality of each person, and equally human unity is meant to be a "multi-unity" *(mnogo-edinstvo),* not far even in expression from V. Solov'ev's "all-unity" *(vseedinstvo).* "For the understanding of the Divine Trinity the human all-unity *(vse-edinstvo)* is an indispensable condition (we say it by all- [with a hyphen] and not allunity, wishing to express the unity of persons and not an allunity *in abstracto*)." FOD I, p. 86.

29. FOD I, p. 90.

30. "Christianity does not know at all the other [person in singularity], it is altogether not altruism, it knows only [the concept of and relation to] *all.*" Remarks to note 5, FOD I, pp. 47-48.

this unity is eternal or death-transcending. This aspect of the Trinity is what Federov has in mind for the common task of humanity — humanity can participate in the love force of unity to transcend death.

Unity, and the way to it, includes natural moral purity and the *trust* of children who are the heirs of the Kingdom. Yet it is about growing from a childlike love into *adulthood* instead of regressing into some kind of childishness, the consequences of which are already well known.[31]

Conclusion

It is true that in some of his ideas, for example his endlessly repeated concept of *resuscitation* of the ancestors by humanity itself, or in the question of procreation (which we did not address), Fedorov fell into the trap of religious eccentrism. Yet on the other side, one has to contextualize his thoughts, which again is not easy for the reasons mentioned in the introduction. As Berdiaev puts it: "He was a monoideist entirely taken by one idea — by the idea of defeating death by returning life to the deceased. And in this model of his idea there was something austere *(surovoe)*."[32] Death would be eradicated by the united effort of humanity — a duty done out of filial love, following the First Risen and on the example of the first raised from the dead — Lazarus.[33]

Although he explicitly mentions Christ in his role of "Resurrector," yet at the same time he is not conclusive about Christ's unique role in this regard. The Christian teaching on resurrection leaves no space for ambiguity that this task is assigned to Jesus Christ and His heavenly Father. No one has the knowledge let alone the might to actuate it — in none of Fedorov's interstellar worlds: cf. Colossians 1; 2:12-20; Revelation 7. Fedorov starts off with *Alpha* but, in the proper sense, does not finish with *Omega*,[34] as if avoiding the eschatological aspect of Christ's second coming.[35]

31. Cf. FOD I, pp. 71-74.

32. N. Berdaiev, *Russkaia ideia* (Sankt-Peterburg: Azbuka-klassika, 2008), p. 253.

33. "Christ is the resurrector *(voskresitel')* and Christianity is resuscitation *(voskreshenie);* the fulfillment *(sovershenie)* of Christ's service was the resuscitation *(voskreshenie)* of Lazarus" (FOD I, p. 161). The theme of Lazarus and his resuscitation is fully discussed in FOD II, pp. 162-66 and 167-71. As mentioned, Lazarus died anew; therefore Fedorov's equation is not conclusive even on an epistemological level.

34. *"I am the Alpha and the Omega," says the Lord God, "who is and who was and who is to come, the Almighty."* Cf. Revelation 1:4-8.

35. Unless perhaps he understands Christ's return in the form of all humanity united in purpose and love, but he fails to say so explicitly.

Among Fedorov's merits is his virtually endless optimism in humanity, a strong anthropological and social aspect, for a possibly brighter future if only humanity would cooperate with God, regain its proper unity, and fulfill its duty. He offers a solution, a system based on Christian values — above all, love formed on the intra-Trinitarian relationship which, despite Fedorov's excesses, is very accurate. The other important aspect in Fedorov's *Common Task* is that all and everybody is needed; no one is left behind. This indeed is an inspiring concept of *multi-unity.*

By working in concord in a Common Task, everything would be achievable to the children of God. Because he witnessed the technical-industrial marvels of his time[36] as well as the frightening reality of growing militarism and wars, it is understandable why Fedorov slipped into such wishful thinking.[37] Most importantly, however, Fedorov understood that the love modeled on the Trinity's inner relationship, and by cooperating in God's plan, is a transformative love, an *action* in union with *knowledge* that brings about things that human *eyes have not seen nor ears heard.*

2. Vladimir Sergeievich Solov'ev: *The Meaning of Love* and *All-Unity* in the Divine

2.1. *Biography*

Having already dedicated part 4.1 in Chapter I to a broader introduction of V. S. Solov'ev (1853-1900) and his work, we shall refrain from repetition. Moreover, in Solov'ev's case, there is an abundance of excellent monographs, articles, and other diverse publications that could fill any gap regarding his other ideas rather than the ones addressed in this work.[38]

36. And the recent concepts of quantum physics by Max Planck (published in 1900).

37. We also wish to recall that Fedorov was not a theologian, but a philosopher and religious thinker and above all an autodidact in the proper sense of the word.

38. We shall recommend only a few for a general overview and more a specific introduction: A. Losev, *Vladimir Solov'ev i ego vremiia* (Moskva: Progress, 1990) (in a way we agree with Losev's reasoning that after having got acquainted with Solov'ev's unique biography and work it appears simpler to ask who he was *not* instead of the affirmative version of the same question; cf. p. 601); K. Mocul'skii, *Vladimir Solov'ev: Zhizn' i uchenie* (Paris: YMCA Press, 1951). For a more detailed study see S. M. Solov'ev, *Zhizn' i tvorcheskaia evoliutsiia Vladimira Solov'eva* (Brussels: Izd. "Zhizn' s Bogom," 1977); J. Sutton, *The Religious Philosophy of Vladimir Solovyov: Towards a Reassessment* (New York: St. Martin's Press, 1988). For our references of

2.2. *Love as Self-Denial*

In *Filosofskie nachala tsel'nogo znaniia (The Philosophical Principles of Integral Knowledge)* published in 1877-80, Solov'ev elaborates some of "the major ideas that would occupy him throughout his life."[39] In treating the question of the "absolute," he provides one of his initial and key descriptions of love,[40] defining first its receptacle as *the absolute* that, simultaneously, is "nothing and all." By laying down the "absolute first principle as the one

---

original quotes we used Solov'ev's collected works in the phototypical reedition of the *Sobrannye sochineniia Vladimira Sergeievicha Solovieva,* ed. Sergei M. Soloviev and Ernst L. Radlov (Sankt-Peterburg: Prosveshchenie, 1911-14), vols. 1-10, reprinted with two additional volumes and *Pis'ma i Prilozhenie* (Brussels: Izd."Zhizn' s Bogom," 1966-70) (SOS).

39. As the title already reveals, Solov'ev's principal point is the integrality of knowledge, which can be attained not by separation of fields of research but on the contrary by (re-)discovering their interrelatedness, above all in the fields of "theosophy, theocracy, and theurgy." This is the task of the true "love of wisdom" *(philosophia),* namely to connect humanity with the "absolute first principle of existence: God." Solov'ev considers the clarification of the common and final goal of human existence as the most compelling task. He identifies three "subjective bases" and three "objective principles" as a frame for his philosophical effort: feeling–beauty; thinking–truth; will–common. See chart: SOS I, p. 264 and chart: p. 373. Cf. "Introduction," by V. Z. Nollan in Vladimir Soloviev, *The Philosophical Principles of Integral Knowledge,* trans. V. Z. Nollan (Grand Rapids and Cambridge: Eerdmans, 2008), pp. 6-9. In the introduction, Nollan provides many useful insights about the importance of this work for all of modern Russian philosophy, completed by its author at the age of only twenty-four.

40. Nature, art and fine arts, poetry, music, etc. all render a transcendental beauty in our world. Yet, since we only love partially, their *form* and *content* do not match completely, and thus beauty too we perceive in parts and fragments, as apparently different reflections, nonetheless of one and the same truth that we fail to see in relationship. Solov'ev expresses it by a poem from A. K. Tolstoy titled "A Tear Trembles in Your Jealous Eyes":

> "And hungrily searching for it separately,
> We catch a reflection of eternal beauty;
> The forest rustles to us with the joyful news of it,
> Of it the stream resounds with a cold spray,
> And the flowers, swaying, speak.
> And we love with a love that is fragmented:
> The quiet whisper of the pussy-willow by the stream,
> And the dear girl's face, bent over us,
> And the sparkling stars, and the beauty of the universe —
> Yet we're unable to connect these things with each other."

SOS, p. 263. Translation quoted from *The Philosophical Principles of Integral Knowledge,* p. 30.

which possesses the positive force of being"[41] and its need for expressing itself in an "other," that is, in its own "opposition," the first prerequisite of a true relationship emerges. For "if the absolute remained only by itself, excluding all [the] other, then this other would become its negation, and as a consequence it itself would no longer be absolute."[42] In other words, the absolute needs an-other, a *not-absolute* in order to be what it is: there is no being without nonbeing, love without self-denial, a profoundly kenotic element right at the root of the very existence. It has created (or allowed into existence) an *other* relational self, and even more:

> . . . an opposition to its own self or the unity of itself and its opposite — denn Alles muss in Nichts zerfallen, Wenn es im Seyn beharren will [For everything has to disintegrate into nothing, if it wants to persist in Being]. This supreme, logical law is only an abstract expression for the great physical and moral fact of love. Love is the self-denial of a being, yet the affirmation of the other by it [the absolute]. Meanwhile, by means of this self-denial, love's highest self-affirmation is being realized.[43]

Love *equals* self-denial then, which, in turn, is not auto-deprivation or humiliation for its own sake, as one may be inclined to infer, but on the contrary: self-denial in love is a necessary means for the full realization of one's self because of the other.[44] A minimum of two poles is necessary in order to sustain the positive tension of being. Life, *Being,* and love become inseparably interrelated, almost synonymous, as revealed by the Scriptures: "Thus, when we say that the absolute first principle by its very definition constitutes a unity of itself and of its negation, we are repeating — only in a more abstract form — the words of the great apostle: God is love."[45]

Speaking of love as the essence of something or, better, *someone,* the next step is to define love as the relationship between unity and multiplicity. Since the absolute is the sum of existence and, thus, "superexistent," it is

41. . . . *chto obladaet' polozhitel'noiu siloiu bytiia.*

42. Cf. SOS I, pp. 348-49.

43. Cf. SOS I, p. 349.

44. The absence of self-denial, and thus love, is according to Solov'ev not "self-affirmation of a being" but much rather "a fruitless, unsatisfying/unsatisfiable striving or effort toward self-affirmation, in consequence of which egoism is in fact the source of all kinds of sufferings; genuine self-affirmation *(deistvitel'noe zhe samoutverzhdenie)* is attained only in self-denial. . . ." Cf. SOS I, p. 349.

45. SOS I, p. 349.

"unconditionally indivisible," yet, because of love, the absolute is also capable of plurality:

> As striving toward another absolute, i.e., toward being, love is the principle of plurality, since the absolute, in and of itself, as the superexistent is unconditionally indivisible; moreover, every kind of being is a relationship, and a relationship presupposes those which relate to it, i.e., plurality. Yet, the absolute, being the principle of its other or the unity of itself and this other, i.e., love cannot stop, as we have seen, to be its own self; on the contrary, as in our human love, which is the negation of our *I*, this *I* not only does not get lost, but even receives the highest affirmation, so here as well, in assuming its other, the absolute first principle by that very fact is affirmed as such in its own definition.[46]

The anthropological analogy is not a mere exemplification of the divine realm, certainly not for Solov'ev, but much rather a mirroring, a reflection where the full, clear *image* is in the act of becoming.[47]

2.3. *Three Modes of Being*

Love is the principle of plurality and, equally, the unifying bond, even though it can manifest itself in different ways and forms, such as *feeling, thought,* or *beauty,* for instance. Reflecting on the different aspects of unity and plurality, of "the existence and its *not-self* or essence" Solov'ev sees three basic attributes, or "modes of being," in the fact that "it desires its own essence, imagines it, feels it; hence its being is characterized as *will, imagination, feeling.*"[48] These are interrelated attributes of "three independent and integral subjects of being, or three existents"[49] that Solov'ev eventually terms "spirit, mind, and soul."[50] All three, although specific in themselves, are in-

46. SOS I, pp. 349-50.

47. In Christological terms or analogy one would think of Colossians 1:15-17: *He is the image of the invisible God, the firstborn of all creation; for in Him all things in heaven and on earth were created, things visible and invisible, whether thrones or dominions or rulers or powers — all things have been created through Him and for Him. He Himself is before all things, and in Him all things hold together.*

48. SOS I, p. 362.

49. . . . *trekh samostoiatel'nykh i tsel'nykh sub'ekotv bytiia ili trekh sushchikh.*

50. SOS I, p. 367.

terrelated and co-bearers of the attributes and specificities of the other ones, a relationship that Solov'ev illustrates in "a human experience" of two persons falling in love. Among others, the distinction demonstrated here will take on an important significance in ethics later on:[51]

> There are people who, having fallen in love with someone right away, already on the basis of this love, conceptualize a general impression of the beloved object, and likewise because of the strength and degree of this love determine also the aesthetic value of the impressions raised by the beloved entity. But there are also people in whom each given entity brings forth at first a certain general theoretical impression of themselves, and already this impression conforms to their will and feeling concerning this entity. Finally, there are people on whom first and foremost the sensual aspect of an object acts, and by means of aesthetic effects both their intellectual and moral relationships to the object are already determined. The first group at first loves or desires, and consequently already because of its love or will imagines and feels; the second group at first imagines, and by means of this imagination already desires and feels; the third group first and foremost feels, and according to feeling already imagines and desires. The first are spiritual people, the second intellectual people, the third psychic or sensual people.[52]

The difference here exemplified between *"people of one nature (odnoprirodnyi)"* and the *absolute* is — even though the former still share the "general means or forms of beings" — that the latter's very unity is in "no wise violated by this threefold-ness of subjects": form and content match in *absolute* perfection.[53]

2.4. *Self-Denial and Society*[54]

The above-mentioned concept of love as self-denial reappears in Solov'ev's famous *Chteniia o Bogochelovechestve (Lectures on Divine Humanity* [also

51. Cf. note 37, SOS, p. 368.

52. SOS I, p. 368.

53. Cf. SOS I, p. 368.

54. For more detailed treatises on the moral implementation of the "Good" on society and economics see "The Good through Human History," in *The Justification of the Good,* SOS VIII, pp. 227-511; regarding the topic of love to the nation, see "Love to the Nation and

known as: *Lectures on Godmanhood*]) held in Petersburg in 1878-81, and comes to a full and highly unique elaboration in *Smysl liubvi (The Meaning of Love)* written in 1892-94, a series of essays on modalities of love. In his *Lectures,* Solov'ev sees the Christian culture as a platform of universal and harmonious social coexistence, which already has become reality in Christ: for only He in His *Bogochelovechestvo* fully united the divine and the human.[55] In his first lecture, while laying bare the incompatibility of socialism (and its claims) with Christianity, above all in points of morality, Solov'ev agrees with the rebelling of the socialists of his epoch against "the existing social untruth." In opposition to them, however, Solov'ev remains consistent in his inquiry to determine the real "root of that untruth," which he identifies in the *egoism of individuals* from which derive "all competition, struggle, enmity and all social evils."[56] The proposed solution is a Christian message of a deeply kenotic character (even though Solov'ev does not mention God explicitly): "In order to realize that truth, each individual member of the society must set a limit to his exclusive self-assertion, must adopt the point of view of self-denial, renounce his exclusive will, [and] sacrifice it."[57] It would be a self-deception to believe that the comrades of post-Bolshevik Communism would have been eager to agree with Solov'ev in this regard. That is, to accept "self-denial" as a pattern for the good of the other and consequently, the entire society, is possible only if the formula has a balanced equation, that is: self-denial = love = self-realization, and vice versa. Only this deeply Christian equilibrium can assure internal and external justice to all human beings as well as a spiritual and mental oneness in every individual person.[58]

---

the Russian National Ideal," SOS V, pp. 39-58, as well as the topic of theocracy in SOS IV, pp. 243-655.

55. *Bogochelovechestvo: humanity of God* or *Divine humanity,* mostly translated as "*Godmanhood.*" The expression of *Bogochelovechestvo* is also related to the concepts of *divinization* or *deification, obozhenie* (*theosis* in Greek), further to the idea of Sophia, the Wisdom of God, the creative love of God as well as the church and society, finally to the whole world as creation.

56. SOS III, p. 9.

57. SOS III, p. 9.

58. Out of this simple yet profound truth of self-denial as an inalienable means of self-realization, socialism or communism remains but a caricature of Christianity and cannot serve as a foundation for a real society. Yet more importantly Solov'ev's inner, spiritual understanding of *Bogochelovechestvo* is well transmitted in his poem that he composed in the first year of his famous lectures (11 March 1892) — titled "Emmanuel":

> Into the darkness of the ages had the night
> Receded when, worn out with evil and care,

2.5. The Will of God as Law[59]

Fear and respect of the law alone are not sufficient to conform one's will freely and willingly to a higher, more powerful will, even if that will is the will of God. Moreover, even religious ceremonies and sacrifices, as in the case of ancient Israel, could not establish an inner relatedness to God's will: ". . . As absolute, this will [of God] cannot be connected with any external object, and no external action can satisfy it."[60] This brings to collapse the entire concept of any "satisfying" or "pacifying" sacrifices instead of an inner relationship of love (Isa. 58:6-10). It is refreshing to observe Solov'ev's systematic yet elegant argument "liberating" the image of God from misleading anthropomorphisms: "God's will, as absolute, cannot exclude anything from itself or, what is the same thing, desire anything *exclusively:* Knowing no privation, it knows no envy. It equally asserts the being and the good of all, and therefore she herself [the will of God][61] is determined as absolute goodness

---

> The earth found rest in heaven's arms
> And God-with-us was born in the stillness.
>
> There is much that is now not possible:
> No longer do kings look up at the sky
> And shepherds do not listen in the desert
> To the angels speaking about God.
>
> But the eternal that had been revealed that night
> Is that which cannot be destroyed by time,
> And, born long ago in the manger, the Word
> Has once again been born within your soul.
>
> Yes! God is with us — but not there in the azure
> Cave, nor beyond the numberless worlds.
> Not in the evil fire, not in agitated breathing,
> Not in the dormant memory of the ages.
>
> He is *here and now.* Amidst our random vanities,
> Within the confused stream of life's anxieties
> You possess a secret wholly joyous:
> Evil is powerless. We are eternal. God is with us!

The Religious Poetry of Vladimir Solovyov, trans. B. Jakim and L. Magnus (San Rafael, CA: Semantron Press, 2008), p. 45.

59. For the interaction of law and morals, see "The Good through Human History," in *The Justification of the Good,* SOS VIII, pp. 519-721.

60. Especially in reference to Isaiah 66:1-3. Cf. SOS III, p. 76.

61. In Russian the noun "will" carries the feminine gender.

or love. 'Yes, I have loved you with an everlasting love: therefore with loving kindness have I drawn you,' says the Lord to His creatures (Jer 31:3)."[62] Sustained by the prophetic quote from Isaiah (58:6-10) in which the Lord dialogues with His chosen nation (between reproach, request, and repeated promise of protection and prosperity), Solov'ev collocates his principal idea that the fulfillment of God's will must be founded *on an inner relationship* of trust. "The will of God has to be the law and norm for the human will, [yet] not as *acknowledged despotism* [or] *tyranny (priznannyi proizvol)* but as the *consciously perceived* [or] received *good (soznannoe dobro)*. Upon this inner relationship will be established a new covenant between God and humankind, a new divine-human order which will replace the preliminary and transitional religion that was grounded in the external law."[63] Unfortunately, the "external religion," if it relates to God at all, still lives on in many facets of our societies. The new divine-human covenant "founded on the inner law of love" is all-inclusive, excluding only "arbitrary choices or condemnation of person and nations. The new inner covenant is a global, universal covenant which restores all humankind and, through it, the whole of nature."[64] This is a prophetic vision and a truly *human-divine* task for humanity that makes the concept of *divinization* somewhat more palpable for the general understanding of today.

2.6. The Meaning of Love

A question that, first and last, we all would like to have answered in *truth*, and that Solov'ev converts into a central theme of a methodical and scrupulous reflection in *Smysl liubvi*, is the proper meaning of love.[65] The subject

62. The original scriptural quotation uses the present tense. Cf. SOS III, pp. 76-77.

63. SOS III, p. 77. Also see quote with the promise of new covenant in Jeremiah 31:31-34.

64. SOS III, p. 77, with two more fitting quotes: Isaiah 2:2-4 and Isaiah 11:6-10.

65. We do not entirely agree with the view that in his *Smysl liubvi* Solov'ev "struggled to reconcile erotic love with philosophical idealism and biblical truth." First, Solov'ev talks about "sexual love," which is not "erotic," let alone in our sense of the word, and that Solov'ev circumscribed precisely (see in our text). Secondly, he follows an accurate and a methodological concept that he brings, in our modest view, to a successful conclusion and therefore does not justify the label of a "struggle," but rather one of a prereflected, even though sometimes slightly repetitive, epistemological inquiry. Cf. "Introduction," in *Politics, Law, Morality: Essays by V. S. Soloviev*, ed. and trans. Vladimir Wozniuk (New Haven: Yale University Press, 2000), p. xxiii.

of love is latently or immanently present in many if not all of his works.[66] For instance, the reflection upon the meaning of life[67] makes the genesis of this original piece of work more comprehensible. Solov'ev remains faithful to a transparent, meticulous methodology, building his argument from modes and models of lower or basic forms of *love-patterns* and behaviors in flora and fauna to their higher and highest forms in the human society, between individuals up to the love-relationship between human beings and the Divine.

2.6.1 Sexual Love *and Anthropology*

To begin, Solov'ev confronts some of the misconceptions regarding love, in particular, "sexual love"[68] *(polovoi liubvi)* and the "propagation of [the] species" *(razmnozhenie roda),* in which the latter would be the (sole) scope of the former, thus proving the exact contradiction and inconsistency of this theory.[69] Similarly, "feeling in love" in human beings cannot be just a "cun-

66. Of particular interest is Solov'ev's rich and expressive poetry, which alone, according to Sergei Bulgakov, reflects all that is in Solov'ev "absolutely authentic, so that his philosophy can and must be checked against the poetry" and what cannot be found there "must be considered artificial, scholastic, or accidental in his philosophy." Cf. *The Religious Poetry of Vladimir Soloviev,* p. 155. The essay under the title "The Poetry of Vladimir Soloviev" by Sergius Bulgakov first appeared in the journal *Russkaia Mysl' (Russian Thought)* in 1915. To the representative and famed poems belongs what Solov'ev calls his "short autobiography" narrating his three encounters with "the beautiful Lady . . . Sophia" in *Tri svidania (Moskva-London-Egipet 1862-75-76) (Three Meetings [Moscow-London-Egypt 1862-75-76]),* in SOS XII, pp. 80-86.

67. The very meaning of life, including the question of love, and its worthy, "good and just" conduct is the underlining argument of Solov'ev's *Opravedenie dobra: Nravstvennaia filosofia* (*The Justification of Good: Moral Philosophy* [1897]).

68. "Sexual relations" or "love" meaning "for a want of a better term" the principle of sexual poles and their natural attraction, "between persons of different sexes, which makes possible the relation between them of husband and wife" (also "nuptial love"). On no account does Solov'ev wish to "prejudge . . . the importance of the physical side of the matter." Cf. Note 6, SOS VII, p. 22. Also: "The external union, earthly and in particular physical, does not possess any specific relation to love. It exists without love, and love exists without it. It is necessary for love, not as its indispensable condition and independent end, but only as its final realization. If this realization is set as the end in itself, ahead of the ideal concern of love, it ruins the love. Every kind of external act or fact in itself is nothing; love is something only thanks to its meaning or idea as the restoration of the unity or integrity of the human personality, as the creation of an absolute individuality." SOS VII, p. 29.

69. Cf. SOS VII, pp. 3-5. For the English translations we consulted *The Meaning of Love,* ed. T. R. Beyer (Hudson, NY: Lindisfarne Press, 1985).

ning . . . delusion employed by nature or the will of the universe in order to achieve her own specific ends."[70] The theory in which the "will of the universe" awakens a special passion or higher bliss in two individuals to create "an earthly genius" that would possess an extraordinary significance in the historical process of humanity also does not hold true.[71] Solov'ev sees *sexual love* both in animals and in humans as "the highest flowering of individual life." The "worth of the human being" is nothing less than the "indubitable presence of the absolute form (image) of *rational* consciousness in him. His awareness above the phenomena of life is determined in addition by the wisdom [meaning] of truth."[72] Thus, the human being, who represents "the real end" in the process of the creation of the world,[73] is at nature's center and, as such, in direct relation with the Creator: "[The human being] is revealed as the center of the universal consciousness of nature, the soul of the world, the potentiality of the absolute unity-of-the-all coming to realization, and, consequently, above him there can be only this same absolute in its perfect act or eternal being, that is God."[74] The reference of absolute human desire becomes a logical orientation to the source and goal of all unity, in the absolute, or all-unity *(vseedinstvo)*. Each human being possesses the capacity to "recognize and realize the truth, each may become a living reflection of the absolute whole," an instance where *truth* for Solov'ev is a synonym for the "image of God."[75] Consequently, love cannot be outside of this divine realm, and the rational character of human consciousness plays a key role in determining the quality of this relationship:

> Truth, as a living power, that takes possession of the internal being of a human person actually rescues him from the false self-assertion that is

70. Cf. SOS VII, p. 5.

71. Cf. SOS VII, pp. 6-8. Very interesting are some of Solov'ev's conclusions in this regard (based on observations of nature and history): 1. A powerful love quite often remains unshared; 2. A mutually shared or perceived powerful passion leads to a tragic end and does not produce posterity; 3. Happy love, if it is very powerful, usually also remains unfruitful (or in those rare cases where this is not true, the posterity is an ordinary one). Cf. SOS VII, p. 9. Highly interesting is the exemplification of some of these rules in the "sacred history" of the Bible. Cf. SOS VII, pp. 10-11.

72. . . . *ego soznanie sverkh iavlenii zhizni opredeliaetsia eshcho razumom istiny.*

73. Cf. SOS VII, p. 12. This latter affirmation of the absolute value or *worth* of the human being regains its vigor in the light of love as relationship and not just a mere act of procreation, be it with or without selection or improvement of the species.

74. SOS VII, p. 14.

75. Cf. SOS VII, p. 14.

> termed love. Love as the actual abrogation of egoism is the real justification and salvation of individuality. Love is greater than rational consciousness, yet without the latter it could not act as an internal saving power, elevating and not abrogating individuality. Only thanks to a rational consciousness (or, what is the same thing, a consciousness of the truth) can the human being distinguish his very self,[76] i.e., his true individuality from his proper egoism, and sacrificing this egoism, surrendering himself to love, he finds [in love] not merely a living, but also a vivifying/ life-giving power. And he does not lose his individual being together with his egoism, but on the contrary eternalizes it *(uvekovechivaet ego)*.[77]

Once more it is proved that egoism[78] is a false self-assertion claiming what it cannot provide, but, on the contrary, what the human being obtains gratuitously if he conforms himself to his creational vocation "to become a living reflection of the absolute whole." Negative egoism is *the* mortal malady of humankind, which can be cured solely by the antidote of love, and this argument is clearly of a soteriological importance: "The meaning of human love, speaking generally, is *the justification and salvation of individuality through the sacrifice of egoism*."[79] Solov'ev brilliantly collocates what he believed to be his "particular task," explaining the need of love to express itself and to interact. "For good reason, sexual relations are not merely termed love, but are also generally acknowledged to represent love *par excellence*, being the type and ideal of all other kinds of love (cf. the *Song of Songs* and the *Apocalypse*)."[80]

2.6.2 Vseedinstvo — *Unity of All or All-Unity*

Sexual or *nuptial love* as the ideal removes those "internal boundaries" that cause separation and impede "*vseedinstvo*," in English, rendered often as *all-unity* or *unity-of-the-all*.[81] "Only together with others can an individual real-

76. . . . *chelovek mozhet razlichat samogo sebia.*

77. SOS VII, pp. 15-16.

78. Solov'ev distinguishes between negative and positive egoism, where the former "unjustly refuses to others the same significance" as it attributes (justly) to itself. It is an "exclusionary self-assertion" through which the human being "cannot be in reality what he affirms himself to be." Cf. SOS VII, p. 17.

79. SOS VII, p. 16.

80. SOS VII, p. 16.

81. A renowned concept elaborated by Solov'ev representing the interconnectedness

ize his absolute significance — becoming an inseparable and irreplaceable part of the universal whole, an independent, living, and original organ of the absolute life."[82] Only through and in love can we learn and maintain the relationship that unites and creates unity, and thus gain the capacity "to transcend the borders of our factual phenomenal being, in our capacity not only to live in ourselves, but also in another."[83] For some reason, again not stated explicitly but conceptually implied, Solov'ev lends this idea a *kenotic quality*, the life-sharing empathy to live in another. Beyond feelings and emotions, there is a *core-shift* from the individual's self (in)to the center of the other, and such transition must occur in one's interest. "Love is important, not as one of our feelings, but as the transfer of all our interest in life from ourselves to an-other, as the shifting or transposition of the very center of our personal lives. This is characteristic of every kind of love, but predominantly sexual love. . . . Only this love can lead to the real and indissoluble union of two lives into one; only of this love the word of God says: 'They shall be one flesh,' i.e., shall become one real being."[84] Connecting to the senses is a further task of love to *"justify in deed"* that feeling, which can be achieved only in "such a union of two given finite natures as would create out of them one absolutely ideal personality," a restored, "integral human form" that will be capable (and willing) to accommodate the "absolute content" which is the "eternal life or kingdom of God." Unity, or integration of the two separated halves,[85] is the prerequisite and "immediate *task* of love," which, Solov'ev believes, has never been stated consciously.[86] Similar to the belief held by N. Fedorov, the significance of love lies, above all, in the concrete act that must surpass bare emotions. Only then can love create and become reality.[87] The reality herein and for which love is to become laborious is the "restoration of the Divine image" in the human being. This process requires "active faith, moral effort" and, surprise: "hard work." They are necessary to "keep

---

of all, an all-encompassing, all-inclusive, universal unity of creation with its Creator. SOS VII, p. 17. "There is only one power which can from within undermine egoism at the root, and really does undermine it, namely love, and chiefly sexual love." SOS VII, p. 18.

82. SOS VII, p. 17.

83. SOS VII, p. 18.

84. SOS VII, pp. 21-22.

85. A clearly Platonic idea discussed in *Eneades*. An original contribution on the concept and understanding of *Erōs* in the role of a bridge and mediator can be found in "Zhiznennaia drama Platona," in *Vestnik Evropy* 3-4 (March-April 1898): 334-56 and 769-93 respectively, which we shall address later.

86. Cf. SOS VII, p. 22.

87. Cf. SOS VII, p. 26.

for oneself, to strengthen and develop this gift of luminous and creative love, through it to incarnate in oneself and in another the image of God, and to create out of two infinite and perishable natures one absolute and immortal individuality."[88] Yet it is not about a restoration of the lost Paradise but rather a new creation that is being completed, a process that is being brought to its due fulfillment.

2.6.3 Three Bonds and Spiritual Love

The "very impulse of love" compels us to restore the lost unity. In *truth,* we assert our own individuality, paradoxically, by asserting through the emotions, "the feeling of love," the absolute significance of the other's individuality.[89] Eventually, Solov'ev lists three kinds of unions, "physical" (in animal nature), "legal in social-moral order," and, most importantly, the "union in God," which he considers the highest form, "wholly *natural* to a human being, in his entirety as a being, for it partakes in the supreme divine principle and forms a link between it and the world."[90]

Fulfilling the role of a liaison between the divine and the world, "spiritual love" belongs to the loftiest forms of love under the condition that there is no division between the spiritual and the "sensuous" to which such love aspires. Such a love undergoes the high scrutiny of soteriology: "True spiritual love is not a feeble imitation and anticipation of death, but a triumph over death, not a separation of the immortal from the mortal, of the eternal from the temporal, but a transfiguration of the mortal into the immortal, the acceptance of the temporal into the eternal. False spirituality is a denial of the flesh; true spirituality is the regeneration of the flesh, its salvation, its resurrection from the dead."[91] It is evident that Solov'ev aims at *vseedinstvo* even in theosophical questions, i.e., at complete, all-inclusive solutions.

88. Cf. SOS VII, p. 27.

89. Cf. SOS VII, p. 31. In this chapter, Solov'ev dedicates a profound reflection to the relationship of love and death, the enlightenment and spiritualization of the flesh, and, consequently, the question of immortality. One cannot but think of N. Fedorov and his central idea of resuscitation and immortality. Solov'ev, however, does not follow a purely socioanthropological solution of the issue and remains with the concept of *resurrection.* Cf. SOS VII, pp. 31-32, 50 and especially note 10, p. 38. Finally, there is a passage where he indirectly, though distinctly, polemicizes about the question of resuscitation. Cf. SOS VII, pp. 51-52. Yet in his "Seven Paschal Letters," Solov'ev affirms, ". . . until that final resurrection, which we can obtain only through Christ." *Politics, Law, Morality,* p. 93.

90. Cf. SOS VII, p. 38.

91. Cf. SOS VII, p. 40.

2.10. *The Female Side and* Triune *Faith*

Unity results from love, i.e., relatedness as well as relationship, and the integrity of the person is an essential part of this process. Human integrity has its origin in the absolute, God, who not only created the human being in His own image but also as male and female (Gen. 1:27), and the relatedness of these two aspects is meant to be fully restored. "As God is in relation to His creation, as Christ is in relation to His Church, so the husband ought to be in relation to his wife,"[92] a profound mystery of integrity and, in terms of human society, an imitation of the divine economy. While the relationship of God and Christ to their subjects is in its "absolute fullness to the pure potentiality of being," the relationship between husband and wife is that of "equally imperfect potentialities, which attains perfection only in the process or reciprocity. . . . Man and his female *alter ego* mutually fulfill each other."[93] Solov'ev insists that a man ought to "create and build his female complement" in himself, which certainly applies equally to the woman with the other gender in her personality. What may sound as inapt or abstract is an "essential analogy" between the human and the Divine in their relationship. This, as it were, personified *relationship* is conceived as the *feminine* of the Divine, His beauty, His wisdom.[94] Therefore, He created *man and woman* with different yet complementary aspects. *He created them* so that they may and need to be in unity; not a forced one, but a unity of love-bond.[95]

92. SOS VII, p. 41.

93. SOS VII, p. 41.

94. Also: "For God, His *other* (i.e., the universe) possesses from all eternity the image of perfect femininity, but He desires that this image should exist not merely for Him, but that it should be realized and incarnated in each individual being capable of union with it. Such a realization and incarnation is also the aspiration of the eternal Femininity itself, which is not merely an inert image in the Divine mind, but a living spiritual being possessed of all the fullness of powers and activities. The whole process of the cosmos and of history is the process of its realization and incarnation in a great manifold of forms and degrees." Solov'ev refers here to Sophia, a topic of immense importance not alone in Russian philosophy and religious thought, which would require a separate yet well-merited study. SOS VII, p. 46. For further material regarding the subject of *Sophia* see V. Kvarchenko, *Vladimir Solov'ev i Sofiia* (Moskva: Agraf, 2006); A. Losev, *Vladimir Solov'ev i ego vremia* (esp. *III. Uchenie o Sofii,* pp. 209-58); J. D. Kornblatt, *Divine Sophia: The Wisdom Writings of Vladimir Solovyov* (Ithaca and London: Cornell University Press, 2009); V. S. Solov'ëv, *La Sofia: L'Eterna Sapienza mediatrice tra Dio e il mondo,* trans. E. Treu (Milano: San Paolo, 1997).

95. In his earlier-mentioned highly interesting article "Zhiznennaia drama Platona

For *true love,* both *ascending* and *descending,* the goal of this human "journey" requires a firm and lasting foundation which is *faith,*[96] and without which the passage or transfer from one's own (integrated) being to that of the "center and root" of its existence "into the sphere of the Divine," to God, cannot be accomplished. In fact, an internal act of "triune faith" precedes all other notions, laying the very first basis of a true union with the Divine.[97] The image of the Creator in the human being can be restored only through union with the Creator, and this "living and immortal Image"[98] is the eternal-unity of the Three, multi-unity, all-unity.[99] Their relationship is the ideal, *fons et origo:* "This living ideal of the Divine love, antecedent to our love, contains in itself the secret of the idealization of our love."[100] Solov'ev calls the revelation of this possibility the "dawn of love," which has revealed to the human being trapped in egoism "completely different horizons."[101] It grants means for social and ecclesiastic

(The Life-Drama of Plato)," published in 1898, two years before his death, Solov'ev recurs to the theme of the unity of the "male and female principle . . . [as] true androgyny without an external mixing of the forms" (p. 234). This in his view is the highest degree and form of love. *Erōs* in the Greek mythology and for Plato was a divine force and demon, a *high priest* and intermediator, between the *One* Divine Creator, i.e., God, and the *multitude* of creation, in particular the human being. The latter participates in the process by receiving *Erōs* into its soul. Depending on which part of the soul is appropriating *Erōs,* the higher or the lower motivated, i.e., the intelligible or the irascible one, it directs *Erōs* according to its own passions and designs. Solov'ev identifies five kinds of *loves* in this process (chapters XV–XXVI) but the goal of the last and most perfect love is the "whole(some)," (re-)united person. ". . . The way of the highest love" consists in restoring the perfect *spiritual-corporal* unity and that of the female and male principle. This then is an integral part of an overall process of unification of the human being with God, "i.e. it is a divine-human process *(process' Bogochelovecheskii)*" (cf. p. 234). Although Plato obtained this unique inspiritation, as Solov'ev sees it, he failed to implement it in his own life as that by which he could have set an example. Plato turned away from the principle of the interior union of the human individual (as with itself, so with God), and thus improving society from within the individual, and instead recurred to an external solution founded on a sociopolitical approach to be implemented within the society. Plato exposed his ideas in the broad treatise of his *Republica.* Cf. SOS IX, pp. 194-241, esp. chapters XXII–XXVIII.

96. "For the emotion of love comes and passes away but the faith of love abides." SOS VII, p. 49.

97. SOS VII, p. 41.

98. SOS VII, p. 46.

99. "When we imagine the ideal form of the beloved object . . . this form is communicated to us, this same unity-of-the-all essence." SOS VII, p. 43.

100. SOS VII, p. 45.

101. Cf. SOS VII, pp. 48-49.

struggles of present and future centuries: "Against these hostile powers,[102] true faith has only one defensive weapon — endurance to the end. To earn its bliss, it must take up its cross. In our materialistic society, it is impossible to preserve true love unless we understand and accept it as a moral achievement. Not without reason does the Orthodox Church in her *marriage* ceremony make mention of holy *martyrs* and compare their crowns to the bridal crowns."[103]

2.6.5 Individual Maxim — Mystical Body

"Involuntary and immediate feeling reveals to us the meaning of love as the highest manifestation of individual life, which finds in union with another being its own proper infinity. Is not this momentary revelation sufficient?"[104] Surely it would be if not for the other side of the poise, which is *all-unity.* To this aspect, Solov'ev dedicates the conclusive part of his treatise under the following perspective: "The idea of all-unity can finally be realized or embodied only in the fullness of completed individualities; this means that the final end of the whole matter is the higher development of each individuality in the fullest unity of all. . . . We are just as necessary to the world as the world is to us."[105] Solov'ev asserts, after a brief reflection on physics, and what we would today consider quantum physics, that "the body of the universe is the totality of the real-ideal, the psycho-physical, or simply it is a *mystical body.*"[106] As such, it must be and is con-penetrable, consisting of the act of sharing: "true life is to live in another as in oneself," beginning with two individuals and aiming at the "collective life"[107] (or entity) on the example of the Holy Trinity, till solidarity with the *whole* reigns, and all-unity is fully restored.

Until then, we are *invited* to *hard work* on worldwide unity, knowing that there is an existing interrelatedness regardless of our external feelings and perceptions. Solov'ev proposes creating and cultivating a *syzygetic*[108] re-

102. Of a society that builds its dominion on animating and using "animal" and "still worse, human passions." SOS VII, p. 49.

103. SOS VII, p. 49.

104. SOS VII, p. 47.

105. SOS VII, pp. 52-53.

106. SOS VII, p. 54.

107. Cf. SOS VII, pp. 56-57.

108. From Greek συζυγία meaning "close union," an expression introduced by Solov'ev for want of any better one in contemporary terminology.

lation in the world. It would perfect relations, communities, and individuals; it would communicate to the spheres of collective and universal being a "unity and fullness of life's content and, thereby, elevate and make immortal the fundamental individual form of love."[109] All of this would be inspired by the idea of a "cosmic syzygy" for the restoration of *all-unity.*[110]

2.6.6 Agapē *as Ideal of Unity*

In an article from an encyclopedic dictionary under the entry of "Dogma," Solov'ev's concise treatment of the topic of love is similar to that in the *Meaning of Love,* based on the three basic forms, "parental love, love of the children for their parents, and sexual love (or spousal love),"[111] extending it, of course, to the various philosophical and theological mainstreams in history.[112] "The ideal principle of community [or] social relationships, according to Christianity, is not domination but love," based upon the principle rendered in the New Testament where Christ's relationship to the church is a nuptial one as in the image of the "Lamb" to His bride which is the church. This also is meant to be reflected in the relationship of the ecclesial hierarchy to and in the local communities. This is the only place where Solov'ev explicitly mentions the word *agapē,* namely, in contraposition to pagan religious concepts of love such as *fallism;* "the ideal principle of spiritual and societal unification *(obshchestvennago edineniia)* is *agapē.*"[113]

Unity, being one of the leitmotivs in Russian religious thought, on many levels, is even more significant for Solov'ev, as seen above. On a personal and, above all, spiritual, transcendental level, unity means completeness, fulfillment, joy, and, consequently, happiness, which are always rooted in *hope, faith,* and *love.* The following poem comprises both, the horizontal and vertical level, beginning and ending in the divine while not lessening the anthropological, very human element:

109. Cf. SOS VII, pp. 57-58.

110. Cf. SOS VII, p. 60.

111. ". . . *liubov roditel'skaia, liubov' detei k roditeliam i liubov polovaia (ili supruzheskaia),*" SOS XI, p. 236.

112. Cf. SOS XI, pp. 236-38.

113. The image is borrowed from the relationship between God and the chosen nation in the Old Testament. Cf. SOS XII, p. 237.

What Do People Live By?[114]

People live by God's caresses,
Which pour invisibly down upon them.
They live by God's word, that silently
Within the universe resounds.

People live by the love
That draws all things together,
That triumphs over death
And will not cease in hell.

And when, without much boldness,
I think myself a part of "people," then
I live by the thought that my darling
And I will be together in eternity.

Conclusion

Humankind's restoration of its lost integrity is its answer to God's call in Paradise to Adam, that is, the entirety of humankind that just lost its *unity* with(in) itself and with its Creator. Ever since, we have been attempting to learn this anew: the lost language of heaven that Solov'ev identifies as *love.* If *all that is authentic* in Solov'ev can be found in his poems, then "his worldview" should be expounded on the basis of them, "while considering his prose to be a philosophical commentary to them and not vice versa."[115] The following poem is a faithful rendering of Solov'ev's inner world. This portrait shows in a few lines the depth of his mystical, unceasingly inquisitive, yet joy-filled spirit, the depth of humanity, the intuition of Divine love, and the *all-unity* through love with the *absolute* that is God:

L'onda dal mar divisa[116]

Once separated from the sea
The wave can know no peace.

114. *Chem liudi zhivy?* From January 30th, 1892. SOS XII, 94. (The translation of the poem is quoted from *The Religious Poetry of Vladimir Soloviev,* pp. 26, 42.)

115. Cf. Bulgakov, "The Poetry of Vladimir Soloviev," p. 155.

116. "The Wave Separated from the Sea" (1882). The poem was titled in Italian by Solov'ev himself.

It seethes like a hot spring
Or rolls on like a river.
It grumbles and it sighs
In freedom and in chains,
Yearning for the shoreless
And fathomless blue sea.[117]

117. SOS XII, p. 8.

V. The Moralist School of Theology

1. Alexandr Dmitrievich Beliaev: *Love from Above*

1.1. Biography

In A. D. Beliaev (1849-1919), the son of a provincial priest, we encounter an authentic and productive theologian, a former distinguished student (who finished his studies in 1876), and subsequent professor of the Moscow Theological Academy.[1] Beliaev was one of those "rare academic lecturers who, from the beginning, was respected and loved for his person."[2] He dedicated an entire theological treatise to the subject of divine love titled *Liubov' Bozhestvennaia: Opyt raskrytiia glavneishikh khristianskikh dogmatov iz nachala liubvi Bozhestvennoi (The Divine Love: An Essay on Disclosing the Most Important Christian Dogmas from the Principle of the Divine Love),* which appeared in Moscow in 1880, and in a second, appended edition in 1884.[3] It was his first serious treatise — an ambitious intent to create a dogmatic system based, as the title suggests, on the single principle of *divine love* — for which he obtained his Master's degree in theology in 1876.[4] Beliaev received his doctoral degree for his other renowned work, *O bezbozhii i*

1. His life and work were inseparably connected to the Academy.

2. Cf. "A Short Biographical Sketch," in A. Beliaev, *Liubov' Bozhestvennaia: Opyt raskrytiia glavneishikh khristianskikh dogmatov iz nachala liubvi Bozhestvennoi* (Sankt-Peterburg: "Nevskaia zhemchuzhina," 2006), p. 4 (LB).

3. For its accessible language, the first edition was soon followed by an improved and complemented second one, with an additional chapter on the entity and character of Divine Love. Cf. "A Short Biographical Sketch," p. 13.

4. Cf. "A Short Biographical Sketch," pp. 3-6.

antikhriste (On Godlessness and the Antichrist) published in 1898.[5] On the far side of the thematic scale of the first book, this work is an elaborate compilation of views on the subject of atheism and the antichrist from "the apostolic period," including Orthodox, Catholic, and Protestant sources. Interestingly enough, the latter work seems to have enjoyed an even broader promulgation and popularity than the former. In his fifty years of academic activity, Beliaev addressed most of the current ecclesial, historic, and dogmatic issues of his period in his numerous lectures on biblical topics and his journals *Vera i razum (Faith and Reason)* and *Russkoe obozrenie (Russian Review)*,[6] such as Pope Leo XIII's exhortation to the Orthodox and other churches to return to the Catholic Church. Also among his better-known works are his dissertation titled *Ideia edinobozhiia v Vetkhom Zavete (The Idea of Monotheism in the Old Testament)* and *Istinnoe khristianstvo i gumanizm (True Christianity and Humanism)* from 1893, on L. N. Tolstoy's and V. S. Solov'ev's views on Christianity. Yet most of his works still await elaboration.[7]

1.2. Liubov' Bozhestvennaia — The Divine Love[8]

A single glance into the content of this work reveals Beliaev's consistent intent to found his theological system on the principle of love. Yet he meant it less as an independent system and more as a supplement to the existing dogmatic

5. Reprinted in two volumes by "Palomnik" (Moskva, 1996).

6. See also *O soedinenii tserkvei: Razbor entsikliky Papy L'va XIII ot 20 iunia 1894* (Sergiev Posad: Tip. A. Snegirevoi, 1897).

7. Cf. LB, pp. 3-6, 9-14. Unfortunately the biographical material on A. Beliaev himself and his intellectual work is very scarce and fragmented; thus for further reference, apart from his own books, we can mention only indirect sources: I. V. Popov, *Otzyv na dokt. dis. A. D. Beliaeva,* Zhurnaly Soveta MDA (za 1899 g.): 39-51; S. S. Glagolev, Zhurnaly Soveta MDA (za 1899 g.): 51-70; G. Florovsky, *Puti russkogo bogosloviia,* pp. 436-37; V. Sabodan, *Ekkleziologiia v otechestvennom bogoslovii* (Kaliningrad, 1997), pp. 190-203; S. Golubtsov, *Professura MDA v nach. XX v.* (Moskva, 1999), pp. 17-18; *Pravoslavnaia entsiklopediia,* vol. 4 (Moskva, 2002), pp. 586-88; B. V. Emeliianov and V. V. Kulikov, *Russkie mysliteli vtoroi poloviny XIX — nachala XX veka: Opyt kratkogo biobibliograficheskogo slovaria* (Ekaterinburg: Ural, 1996), p. 43.

8. Beliaev gives an insightful explanation why he kept the adjective "divine" instead of "God's" love in the title despite some "recommendations" to change it. He wanted to show the love as a relationship of and among *each* person of the Holy Trinity, as well as their relationship of love towards the creation as opposed to that of one God in general. The Trinitarian aspect of love was crucial, and therefore a fitting alternative to the existing title, according to the author himself, could be: "The Love of the Triune God." Cf. LB, pp. 13-14.

manuals.[9] In a way, this book could represent the formal center of our thesis, as its own double-motto paves the way with the words of the "apostle of love": *Bog est' liubov', God is love* (1 John 4:16) and *Liubov' ot Boga, Love from God* (1 John 4:7).[10] Beliaev's main and almost exclusive source is the Holy Scripture, especially the New Testament,[11] with occasional quotations from the Fathers and some western authors.[12] Since the "love of God in itself, just as God Himself in Himself, remains for humans inscrutable" *(nepostizhimaia)*,[13] Beliaev focused his attention instead on the "manifestations *(proiavlenia)* of the Divine love" in order to deduce from them their "characteristic traits."[14] Directly, God's love can be recognized and known by its action but barely, if at all, in its abstractness.[15] This explains the surprising fact that in Beliaev's book, according to the author himself, there is "not much discussion about the very love of God" except for one chapter. It is rather about the "nature of the Divine love," as the subtitle indicates and as the author himself elucidates.[16]

1.3. The Cornerstone of Dogmatics as a New Hermeneutical Key

At the end of the current edition, we have a unique and precious testimony in the *Magisterskii disput,* a sort of minutes from the master's degree defense, along with the candidate's defense speech. The former displays his intelligence,[17] whereas the latter provides valuable methodological insights into

9. Cf. LB, p. 10. See also the subtitle.

10. LB, p. 8.

11. From which he apparently extracted all love-related references and other relevant quotes.

12. He complained about the lack of relevant material besides "two or three books" that advert "more or less" to the subject in question. Cf. LB, p. 483.

13. LB, p. 479.

14. LB, p. 480.

15. Philosophy and the human mind in general are powerless in exploring the love of God directly. Cf. LB, p. 479. To illustrate the challenge, Beliaev uses an analogy with the fundamental role of atoms and our very limited knowledge of them, speaking for the epoch. Cf. LB, pp. 27-28, 482.

16. Cf. LB, p. 30.

17. Among the criticisms was that Beliaev did not always indicate (correctly) his sources. Cf. LB, p. 499. In fact, an important unidentified quotation from Filaret Drozdov is on p. 306: "Come near and contemplate the terrifying face of God's justice, and you will truthfully recognize in it the gentle face of God's love." Sviatitel Filaret (Drozdov), *Izbrannye trudy, pis'ma, vospominania* (Moskva 2003), p. 127. The other significant quote from Filaret is indicated: "The Love of the Father — in (the act of) the crucifying. The Love of the Son —

the genesis of this work.[18] For instance, while doing the preparatory work for the book, Beliaev realized that, thus far, any research on the love of God was inevitably connected to moral theology or simply to the concept of generally accepted theological virtue. He himself never considered "reading nor even seeing any special dogmatic or philosophical research on the love of God as a [possible] metaphysical principle of being and life." Nor has anyone thought of "making it into a subject of special dogmatic research and that the teaching of it [love] can be laid as a cornerstone of the entire dogmatics."[19] If this is the case indeed, one needs to speak of a "new hermeneutical key" that Beliaev (re-)discovered and applied. Thus, when looking anew on scriptural quotes which "at once broaden and clarify our view, . . . [we] obtain a completely new meaning to many scriptural texts, which we [previously] knew only in a literary sense without having penetrated profoundly into their inner sense." Thanks to the new hermeneutical key and the above-mentioned experience during his research, Beliaev makes a further crucial realization regarding the entire Christian teaching: "Here, for the first time, we realize [for ourselves] in all clarity an indubitable idea that Christianity is not only in moral *(nravouchenie)* but also in religious doctrine *(verouchenie)* a proclamation of God's love, that love entirely permeates this religion, like an all-acting, omnipotent force *(vsedeistvuiushchaia sila)*."[20] This love-message "is being proclaimed to humankind by God Himself who also speaks and acts like love *(kak liubov')*," transforming the listener into a "love-tuned" person in whom this facilitated "love becomes an organon of cognition of God *(Bogopoznania)*."[21] Equipped with such a methodological apparatus, Beliaev hopes that his exposition will become more comprehensible if it is subdivided into major areas of reflection in his book.[22]

(who is) the crucified. The Love of the Spirit — triumphant by the power of the cross." *Izbrannye trudy*, p. 125. Both quotes can be found in our chapter on Filaret.

18. Most of these ideas of Beliaev can be found also in his meticulous introduction to his book. Cf. LB, pp. 15-44.

19. Cf. LB, pp. 476-77. For a more detailed and methodological reflection about this argument, see Beliaev's introduction: LB, pp. 23-26.

20. Cf. LB, pp. 477-78.

21. Cf. LB, pp. 18-19, 24.

22. 1. "The Being and Characteristics of the Divine Love" *(Sushchnost' i svoistva liubvi Bozhestvennoi)* — a chapter introduced into the second, improved edition; 2. "The Divine Love as an Inner Life Activity of the Triune God" *(Liubov' Bozhestvennaia kak vnutrenniaia zhiznedeiatel'nost' triedinogo Boga)*; 3. "The Creative or Omnificent (All-Creative) Divine Love" *(Liubov' Bozhestvennaia tvoriashchaia ili vsesozidaiushchaia)*; 4. "The Divine Love That Saves or Re-creates (Renews) Humankind" *(Liubov' Bozhestvennaia spasaiushchaia ili*

1.4. The Being of God Manifested as Love

Before any reflection on the manifestation of God's love can be done, one needs to know more about its entity and traits or attributes, which are best described in the first letter of St. John. Apart from revealing the following love-triangle of relations — God, the human being, the fellow human being, and back to its origin — the letter reveals God's very entity twice as love (1 John 4:8 and 16).[23] Knowing and "seeing" God and His attributes are qualitative and quantitative differences in this epistemological process between the Son of Man and the rest of humankind.[24]

Though the Son of God ascribes the knowledge of God to human beings, this knowledge differs from his knowledge of God. First by its source *(po istochniku)*, for the Son of God has a knowledge of God by His very Self *(imeet znanie o Boge Sam po Sebe)*, and humankind receives this knowledge through the Son; secondly by His very own being because the Son sees God and knows who God is, i.e., knows the very Being of God, while humankind cannot see God and therefore cannot fully grasp His nature.[25]

With 1 Corinthians 2:7-11[26] (especially the last verse: *No-one knows the thoughts of God except the Spirit of God*) in mind, Beliaev argues that the Spirit of God alone knows God's being; for instance, when revealing the hidden wisdom of God, the being is not revealed but only "the meaning of its actions in relation to humanity, the meaning of the economy of salvation of humankind *(smysl domostroitel'stva spasenia liudei)*."[27] For centuries, Christianity has been familiar with the struggle for the appropriate name or attribute that would most faithfully render God's being. Yet all of the known attributes reflect only an aspect of God's being and never the full reality, which is equally true for the "expression *God is love*." Nevertheless, "*love* is such a property/characteristic *(svoistvo)* in God, in which His being and life come to express themselves in a specially broad and multifaceted way. For in

vossozdaiushchaia chelovechestvo); 5. "The Divine Love That Sanctifies or Re-creates (Renews) the Human Being" *(Liubov' Bozhestvennaia osviashchaiushchaia ili vossozdaiushchaia cheloveka)*. Cf. LB, p. 44.

23. He also quotes Plato and St. Anselm of Canterbury who, as philosophers, considered "God's being as the highest good." Cf. LB, pp. 45-46.

24. 1 John 4:12; John 4:24; 6:45-46; and a long series of other scriptural quotes.

25. Cf. LB, pp. 46-47.

26. In the edition used by us incorrectly indicated as chapter "21" instead of chapter "2." Cf. LB, p. 48.

27. Cf. LB, p. 48.

His great deeds — His incarnation, redemption of humankind from sin and its unfortunate consequences, and sanctification *(osviashchenie)* of the human being — God prefers to reveal Himself as the God of love" even more so in the New Testament.[28] After some reflection on the biblical quotes, Beliaev comes to a double conclusion regarding the relation of love and God's nature: "The love of God is not identical with the very being of God" since it does not combine in itself the "fullness of being and life of the Divinity." On the other side, love is "the most important and most universal characteristic of God," and reflects better and more than any other trait "God's nature."[29] Whether consciously or not, Beliaev with his stressing of love as an attribute instead of an essence of God stands in the ranks of the apophatic theologians.

1.5. *The Continuous Unveiling of God's Love*

The love of God is continuously revealed in the inner life of God and in the world, namely in the creation, and thus also in the human being. The greatest revelation "in boundless fullness is the incarnation of the Son of God for the salvation of humankind" who through his earthly life granted to humanity the insight on God's love: "God's love was and is being manifested first in the inner life of God Himself, second in the world and third in the human being . . ." but above all was revealed in Christ's incarnation "in an unlimited fullness . . . for the salvation of the human race. . . .[30] The person, life, sufferings and death of Jesus Christ are the most important witnesses of the Divine love and its action — as of its inner, so the external manifestation."[31] For in the final analysis, "love which abides in the human heart as a feeling, manifesting itself in his life as a physical and spiritual, personal, universal and familial one, [or] as a creative strength, is but a reflection, although [perhaps] a weak and dim one, of the Divine love. Therefore the examination of the traits and manifestations of human love can provide us with some understanding of the traits and manifestations of the Divine love."[32] Love in human beings, even in its loftiest and most spiritual forms, in fact all forms of true love, strives for God not only from the action of a (free hu-

28. Cf. LB, pp. 48-53.
29. Cf. LB, p. 54.
30. Cf. LB, pp. 54-55.
31. Cf. LB, p. 55.
32. LB, pp. 55-56.

man) will but as an intrinsic, natural human need.[33] "This yearning to live in God and for God is an aspiration that comes through the most profound discovery in ourselves, that there is a divine principle [of the desire] for nearness to God, and [this aspiration] is love."[34] Similarly, "the love for artistic creativity aims at embodying, incarnating *(voplotit')* the idea of beauty in a form accessible for the external senses, and which cannot be achieved without love for beauty, and love for beauty is love of the divine," that is, God.[35] If the object of the human love-desire is God, what is God's love-desire if not "God Himself"? This does not exclude the world from His love; however, "it is not of the same meaning." God loves the world as His creation, "as the reflection of His perfections . . . and also in the world God loves only what is divine."[36] This is an apparently consistent and logical argument, yet our author, with the very best intentions, strolls into a metaphysical contradiction.[37] Of course, God does not approve wrongdoing and evil, yet all that is in being can subsist only in God, not outside of Him; thus His sun shines on good and evil equally (cf. Matt. 5:45).[38] In fact, this is one of God's mysterious, unfathomable, and incomprehensible *traits,* His divine love or, better yet, the *divinity* of His love. It is incomprehensible for our human mind, but not so for God. To love unconditionally is a matter of an integral, all-encompassing comprehension that is inclusive yet beyond earthly senses or intellect — precisely a divine predisposition, a godly quality implanted to grow in every human heart.

33. Cf. LB, pp. 59-62.

34. LB, p. 61.

35. LB, pp. 62-63.

36. LB, p. 63.

37. Similarly, on a dogmatic level, ". . . it goes without saying for instance that God loves the less worthy less than the more worthy ones." Cf. LB, p. 253. Either it would have required a different formulation (with an open end towards divinization, for example) or else the Christian axiom about God's exceeding love for the world for which He gave His only Son (cf. John 3:16) becomes unsustainable.

38. Thus on the other hand, Beliaev perceives and describes beautifully God's special care for the fallen human being, sinners, and especially His love for His enemies. God's love is beneficial above all to them: "The love for enemies is the highest degree of love. This love is so elevated and perfect, that all who possess it become similar to God." Cf. LB, pp. 245-46. Further regarding this subject: "Therefore, we can repeat again, that the fall of the human being in sin has served as a ground for a greater and more glorious revelation of the love of God, and the remnants of good in him [the human being] made this revelation possible." Cf. also note 83, LB, p. 266.

1.6. The Ideal of Love

Beliaev adds "self-deliverance, communication (co-relation or co-sharing), and participation (or assimilation)" *(samopredannost', soobshchenie, uchastie)* to the substantial characteristics of the divine love. By "self-deliverance," he intends "a willingness out of love for God, human beings, or some kind of idea, to sacrifice the proper person, to give up even one's own life if it is required."[39] Evidently, this is a *kenotic* concept, although Beliaev does not use the Greek term.[40] The second point is about sharing in and out of love as "to give to the other from oneself: to share [both] sorrow and joy," not out of self-love but for the sake and prosperity of the other, to "multiply in him the good and to strengthen the divine principle."[41] The third point, participation — assimilation *(uchastie, vospriiatie)*, aims at taking part in the "perceptions, desires, thoughts and efforts, sorrows and joys" of the other. It is a complementary part of co-sharing in which the loving person receives from the other party through an empathetic sharing.[42] These "proofs" that God is love, that the human being abides in Him through love and thus resembles Him, Beliaev derives from 1 John 4:9-10, 13, and 20-21:

> In our proper love for our neighbors, and equally in our love for God, as this latter is inseparably connected to the love for fellow human beings, we see or cognize the love of God similarly to how we see our face in a mirror. Our love is a reflection of God's love so that through love the human being becomes similar to God, just as the born [one] is similar to the begetting one. *Whoever loves,* says the Scripture, *has been born of God* (1 John 4:7). Once, however, being similar to God through love, the human being can impossibly not know God and the love of God. Possessing love for God and for his neighbors, he knows and experiences intimately and directly the state of love *(sostoianie liubvi);* and knowing love, he knows God as well: God who is love. . . .[43]

39. LB, p. 64.

40. "In a deep and ardent love, the [loving] person as if transferred altogether his self into the heart of the person whom he loves, while his own person(-ality) does not vanish in the other one." LB, p. 65.

41. Cf. LB, pp. 66-67.

42. Cf. LB, p. 67.

43. Cf. LB, pp. 70-71.

We reflect the One who is the Primordial Image *(pervoobraz)*, the Fountain of Love, and by becoming similar to God (by reflecting Him and His love) love becomes a gnoseological means for knowing Him *as* He is, i.e., as a "loving Being."[44] Within all forms and varieties of expression that a true love can take on, only a few among humans reach the summit of love, which is to lay down one's life for his brothers (John 3:16), as the God-man/God-human *(Bogochelovek)* Jesus did for us (1 John 3:16; 4:17).[45] The ideal-love is manifested in the highest sacrifice for the good, for the life of the other, and in imitating our tender God's action for the redemption of others: for they carry the precious Divine Image in themselves, just as we do ourselves.[46] The very "ideal of love," though unreachable, will always be the goal of our final yearning, and the human being will not cease to strain after it, for this ideal is God Himself.[47]

1.7. Holy Union and Strain of Re-creation

When it comes to the "reciprocal relationship of each Person" in the Trinity, Beliaev leans on *De Trinitate* of St. Augustine and quotes his threefold "reflection" of the Trinity in the human soul.[48] The inner life of the Trinity can be known only through the *economy of salvation (domostroitel'stvo)*,[49] the Trinity's relationship to creation, and, above all, through the revelation received in Jesus Christ, His love-relationship to His Father, and vice versa.[50] Based on what we know, we can see how this affects our human existence: "If God is love that means that His life consists in love. . . . The life of God consists above all in love and since life resides in the heart, the strength and activity of the heart is in love. In whom there is no love, in him the senses are asleep or have even died away; and where feeling is dead or absent, there is no life either."[51]

44. Cf. LB, p. 71.
45. Cf. LB, pp. 72-73.
46. Cf. LB, p. 75.
47. Cf. LB, p. 76.
48. "Imo vero vides Trinitatem, si charitatem vides. . . . Ecce tria sunt: amans, et quod amatur, et amor." *De Trinitate,* VIII, 8, 10. LB, pp. 89, 109. Beliaev mentions St. Augustine a couple of times in his work, as well as Leo the Great and St. Thomas of Aquinas, in a positive note. He repeatedly refers also to St. Anselm of Canterbury, as well as occasionally to some other, Eastern Church Fathers.
49. For the subject of economy of salvation in the context of Christ's kenotic love see LB, pp. 301-7.
50. Cf. LB, pp. 93-97.
51. LB, p. 101.

Beliaev raises an intriguing question, namely whether God loves Himself as well. The answer is affirmative and founded: "He has to love Himself in the first place since He is most unique and the most perfect of all that there is," and this love is not egoism but much rather a "holy love *(sviataia liubov')*."[52] This *holy love* for the perfection in good and bounty is therefore humankind's inspiration granted in the incarnated revelation of God's love-message to His creation. The proof that the world is a creation of God is in the very scope of the world's existence: "The purpose/destiny of the world *(tsel' mira)* lies in the union with God. The way to this goal is in the yearning of creation to become (re-)connected to the Creator, and the means for it are [in] the progress of betterment/perfection *(usovershenstvovanie)*, i.e., in becoming God-like *(Bogoupodoblenie)*."[53] This intrinsic effort leads to what Beliaev terms a "union of love *(soiuz liubvi)*."[54]

After the fall, if God did not want to destroy the world and let humankind perish, re-creation became inevitable: "To re-create the world *(vossozdat' mir)* needed a greater strength of love than the creation at the beginning did. To make the rebellious obedient, the evil good, the sinners holy, and the enemies friends, behold in what the grandeur of the Divine love — in renewing the world — is truly manifested."[55] The transformative force of God's saving Love takes flesh.

1.8. Gratitude and Prosperity

Gratitude is a characteristic of love, the wish to be beneficial to all. "The characteristic of love is to be beneficent to all. However, it can be beneficent only to those who do not reject its help but, on the contrary, voluntarily supplicate for it and accept it" — only to those who do not depreciate but rather request it.[56] A fundamental condition for the intervention of God's love is that one's life be at God's disposition, the "need and desire for it." Asking and recognizing the need for the divine-love's intervention is complementary with acknowledging the proper sinfulness and act(ion) of repentance. This, along with faith, is what Christ requested when performing a healing. All is God's gift, so that we may not boast (Eph. 2:4-9). Nevertheless, we can ask

52. Cf. LB, pp. 105-6.

53. *Bogoupodoblenie* and *obozhenie* are the Russian synonyms for the Greek *theosis.*

54. Cf. LB, p. 188.

55. Cf. LB, p. 246.

56. Cf. LB, p. 262.

for conversion, faith, and full participation in God's inner life already here on earth,[57] which in final consequence will lead us to "immortality."[58] The seriousness of this "offer to humankind" proves God by the death of His Son for us sinners (1 John 4:10; Rom. 5:8).[59]

All blessings and prosperity come through the salvific action, re-creation, or restoration of the primordial order, thanks to the sacrifice of the Son of God. Beliaev discerns three distinctive elements here that we can term *kenotic* (although again he does not use the Greek term): a) the love for the Son as a sacrifice or self-denial; b) the love for the Father as an act of obedience to Him; c) the love for human beings as a communication of graces to them.[60] Importantly for the sake of God's image, this sacrifice was not required by the wrath of God for the sins of humanity as an atonement, but "in effect it was the love for humankind that brought the Son of God to the cross." Apparently, this is one and the same message, but the perspective has been inverted, rendering now a positive, loving image of the Father.[61] There is no doubt about the sacrificial character of Jesus' death. The fact that it was "an act of love out of freedom does not lessen its character as a heavy, terrible sacrifice" through which salvation became possible.[62] "Christ is the love of God revealed in person, sacrificing Himself for the human being; He is the Divine that unites [Himself] in person with humankind."[63]

1.9. Fullness of Divine Participation

From the side of humanity, the union in its "telos," i.e., the full realization of the union between the human and the divine, has its most visible and palpable form in the sacraments of the Church. The Eucharist among all other sacraments represents the summit of this union:

57. Cf. LB, pp. 263-66.
58. Cf. LB, p. 288.
59. Cf. LB, p. 289.
60. Cf. LB, p. 307.
61. Cf. LB, p. 357.
62. Cf. LB, p. 385.
63. LB, p. 388. When we look at it once more from a social aspect Christianity indeed is a religion of love: "The love among people appears as a consequence of Jesus Christ's love to humankind. The Christian religion is a religion of love and as such a true religion, a perfect one. The religion of Christianity made people human. Humanness *(chelovechnost')* assuredly is the greatest good for the entire human society and each member of it." LB, p. 340.

> We know that for the human being on earth there is no closer possible relationship with God than that which he enters through a worthy communion of the Body and Blood of Christ. We know that this relationship is the holiest by entity, the greatest by its fruits of union between God and the human being. We know that the communion is an indispensable criterion of humankind's eternal union with God and through it also the eternal life of the human being. Yet no matter what kind of union between the human being and God there would be, one thing is doubtless, namely that the foundation and the primordial image *(pervoobraz)* of this union is a hypostatic union in Christ of the Divine and human nature. Because the union between God and the human being is a union of holy love, pouring out from God on[to] the human being, and from the human being striving back to God, Jesus Christ is the exact reflection of God's love and concurrently the primordial image of the human love.[64]

The belief that this union goes beyond death is again best illustrated in the relationship of the terrestrial and heavenly church, where union has an ever-present and eternal character:

> The heavenly church, i.e., the pure spirits *(dukhi)* and the souls of saints departed to God, is in such close and inseparable union with the terrestrial church as the members of the one and the other church are among themselves. Bodily death is a difference in the form of being (or existence) and life; separation by space or time cannot isolate *(otluchit')* one soul from the other [because they are] united by the bond of holy love. Truly, no present nor future, no heights nor depths can separate them from the love of God.[65]

Conclusion

Beliaev's line of thought is disciplined — first analytic then synthetic, as he himself described his scientific procedure, though at times it is repetitive and extensive in style. Certainly, he has created a unique piece of work merely by extracting love-related texts from the Scriptures and using them as a main thread for his reflections especially on dogmatic themes. His text is

64. LB, p. 390. Similarly on the Eucharist as sacrament of life in God, cf. LB, pp. 421-25.
65. LB, p. 461.

very spiritual and devout, and his intuition to ground dogmatics on the foundational principle of *divine love* is undoubtedly exceptional, if not even possessing a primacy in modern theology, certainly not with such extensive elaboration. It is a pity that Beliaev did not continue in developing this concept further in his doctoral thesis and instead switched topics completely (see above). Given the magnitude of this work, though, it is somewhat surprising to find a lack of Greek original quotations, let alone the Hebrew of the OT. In the few cases where he does cite the original, the examples are neat but mostly trivial.[66] The whole work is basically built up around the biblical citations, at times giving the impression of a spiritual treatise in the form of a retreat. Beliaev is very eloquent about all aspects of love that he could address (even that of the pagan *erōs*),[67] yet he never mentions *agapē*, not even when treating the sacraments as a means of love and salvation through, with, and in the church.[68] The closest aspect of this is in the kenotic expression of love, which again, Beliaev does not term *kenotic*, even though it is accurately described and placed on the highest rank of love. Although Beliaev struggled somewhat with the Trinitarian concept of love, yet his is the most extensive treatise on love as a dogmatic-exegetical subject that we have encountered thus far in modern Russian religious literature.

Most importantly, however, Beliaev manages to present God *as* love, the divine love as his proper and most accurate manifestation and the example to be imitated and cherished by humankind and all God's creation, in order to live in *a union of God's divine love.*

2. Mikhail Mikhailovich Tareev: The Temptations of Christ and Kenosis

2.1. Biography

M. M. Tareev (1867-1934) is known as an Orthodox religious philosopher, exegete, above all a theologian, and someone who was eager to create an "original Russian interpretation of Christianity."[69] Born into the family of a village

66. Cf. LB, pp. 96 or 108, for instance.

67. "Eros is love for beauty . . . in its eternal birth/generation *(rozhdenie)* and progress *(razvitie)*. Eros is not a person but an idea . . ." etc. Cf. LB, pp. 192-93.

68. Perhaps for distinction between *agapē* and the Eucharist made by St. Paul.

69. Further biographical data as well as a thorough analysis of Tareev's work from a kenotic aspect can be found in H.-J. Röhring, *Kenosis: Die Versuchungen Jesu Christi im*

priest, Tareev graduated from the Moscow Theological Academy in 1891, where he himself later taught. Here he received his master's degree in 1892 for *Iskusheniia Bogocheloveka*[70] *kak edinyi iskupitel'nyi podvig vsei zemnoi zhizni Khrista, v sviazi s istorieiu dokhristianskikh religii i khristianskoi Tserkvi (The Temptations of the God-man as the One [Sole] Redemptive Act of Christ's Whole Earthly Life in Relation to the History of Pre-Christian Religions and of the Christian Church)*. Eleven years later he received his doctoral degree for his *Filosofiia evangel'skoi istorii: Zhizn' Iisusa Khrista — slava Bozhiia (The Philosophy of the Gospel-History: The Life of Jesus Christ — the Glory of God)*. Due to his broad erudition, he taught a great variety of subjects in diverse educational centers. Among his more important publications are *Unichizhenie Gospoda nashego Iiisusa Khrista (The Humiliation of Our Lord Jesus Christ)*, *Tsel' i smysl zhizni (The Goal and Meaning of Life)*, *Zhizn' i uchenie Khrista (Life and the Teaching of Christ)*. Between 1908 and 1910 appeared his five-volume work titled *Osnovy khristianstva: Sistema religioznoi mysli (The Foundation of Christianity: A System of Religious Thought)* which contains some of the above-mentioned works, and in 1916 and 1917 his *Filosofiia zhizni (Philosophy of Life)* and *Novoe Bogoslovie (The New Theology)* respectively. There are further works regarding ethics, morals, socialism, monasticism, as well as works related to the most prominent authors and thinkers of his lifetime.[71] Tareev's theological epicenter is collocated in the temptations and sufferings of Jesus Christ the God-man, his self-denial and self-limitation, and the *kenosis* of the Godhead or the Divine that was manifested in and through the Son of God,[72] a

---

Denken von Michail M. Tareev (Leipzig: Benno-Verlag, 2000); a popular booklet in Russian that claims to be the first investigation of Tareev's work from A. I. Brodskii, *Mikhail Tareev* (Sankt-Peterburg: Izd. Sankt Peterburgskogo Universiteta, 1994); a concise listing of works and brief biography in *Russkie mysliteli vtoroi poloviny XIX — nachala XX veka: Opyt kratkogo biobibliograficheskogo solvaria*, ed. B. V. Emeliianov and V. V. Kulikov (Ekaterinburg: Ural, 1996), p. 320; similar yet with a summary of principal ideas in P. V. Alekseev, *Filosofy Rossii XIX-XX stoletii, biografii, idei, trudy* (Moskva: "Akademicheskii Proekt," 2002), pp. 960-61; the electronic theological portal www.Bogoslov.ru provides selectively further useful information: http://bogoslov.ru/persons/44563/index.html. A very brief yet important input on Tareev and "the moralist tendencies in Russian theology" is available in N. Zernov's *The Russian Religious Renaissance of the Twentieth Century* (London: Darton, Longman & Todd, 1963), pp. 50 and 94.

70. In its second edition (1900), following the request of the Synod, the alternate title was *Iskushenie Gospoda nashego Iisusa Khrista (The Temptation of Our Lord Jesus Christ)*.

71. For an extensive list of publications, see Röhring, *Kenosis*, pp. xiii-xviii.

72. "Beides jedoch, das Sprechen von den Versuchungen und von der Kenosis, bildet bei Tareev eine Einheit." Röhring, *Kenosis*, p. 27. According to Röhring, Tareev created the "first kenotic system in Russian theology" including the "fetching home of the patristic

theme that by some is considered central par excellence in nineteenth-century Russia.

2.2. *The Temptations of the God-Man* (Bogochelovek)[73]

Tareev's intention was to give theology a fresh start by bringing it to "an undoubtedly fruitful way" as opposed to the path on which theology had thus far traversed. The novelty of Tareev consists in his reinterpretation of Christ's temptations "in dogmatic systems of all directions *(vsiakikh napravlenii),*" a one-time occurrence, yet an exceptional one. The fundamental question regards the matter of how Christ with "His *humanity*" related to sin, a quest that, according to Tareev, "did not and could not bring precise or positive and fruitful results," precisely because they were understood *merely* as "temptations of His humanity."[74] Tareev makes a distinction between a sin of a *moral* character and that of a *religious* or *relational* character, which stands in relationship to God. According to Tareev the bodily temptations bear no significance for "the growth of the religious-moral character of the human being" but rather are "pedagogical means for the strengthening of the will." It was a *religious* temptation[75] that Jesus had to endure for our sake.[76] Salvation was a "redemptive act" that God worked on humanity, and the centrality of this mystery for Tareev lies precisely in the

---

kenosis," psychology, etc. "Während Solov'ev der russische Philosoph ist, der das kenotische Denken zu einem prinzipiellen Element seines metaphysischen Denkens gemacht hat, ist Tareev der russische Theologe, dessen Theologie insgesamt vom kenotischen Denken durchdrungen ist. Er hat die Idee der Kenosis, wie er selbst eingesteht, 'aus dem metaphysischen Bereich' — wohl eine Anspielung auf Solov'ev, — 'in die reale Sphäre der geistlichen Wirklichkeit übertragen.'" Cf. *Kenosis,* pp. 234-53.

73. The Russian expression *Bogochelovek,* in Greek *Theanthropos,* can also be translated as God-man, God and Man (Christ), God incarnate, God-become-man, the Incarnate Christ, and the like. We shall use here the traditional rendering, *God-man.*

74. Yet, being one hypostasis of the Trinity, how could he possibly have sinned? Moreover, he who cannot sin nor has an inclination to sin cannot be tempted. Cf. M. M. Taarev, *Iskusheniia Bogocheloveka kak edinyi iskupitel'nyi podvig vsei zemnoi zhizni Khrista, v sviazi s istorieiu dokhristianskikh religii i khristianskoi Tserkvi,* Izd. Obshchestva Liub. dukh (Moskva: Prosveshcheniia, 1892), pp. 1-4 (IB).

75. *Religious temptations* are the ones conducting into the sin of "religious self-justification . . . they consist . . . in *relating* of the human being to God" whose image he is and "in the limitation of factual being of the human person." Under moral temptation, "we understand the temptation as lust or lasciviousness" and its diverse manifestations. (Cf. IB, p. 7.)

76. Cf. IB, p. 4.

temptations of the God-man as they contain "an existential question on the anthropical person of Christ," namely the mystery of unity between Divine and human in Him. Thus, these temptations have not only a *historical, chronological, and psychological* link but also a "dogmatic link" *(sviaz)* to Christ's entire earthly life,[77] not just a one-time occurrence but a *dvizhenie,* i.e., a motion or progress to salvation: "The dearest act to a heart of a Christian, warmed by the breath of divine Love, is his salvation from suffering and all evil of life by the God-man.[78] The redeeming work of Christ is the 'medial as well as focal' point of Christian theologizing."[79] It is a pity that Tareev here implicitly limited the benefits of the divine Love in his soteriology to the present life and does not complete it with *salvation from sin* as well as the ultimate enemy, *death.*

2.3. Kenosis *in the Incarnation and the Logic of Divine-Human Life*

When treating the "sense of pre-Christian history of humanity," we find for the first time in Tareev (and among our other authors) an explicit use of the Greek term κένωσις as expression and concept.[80] The human-divine union became possible because of "self-denial" *(samootrechenie),* and "self-limitation" *(samoogranichenie)* was needed from both sides — human and divine alike, and was fully realized in the incarnation of the Son of God. "The Divine *(Bozhestvo)* limits himself already at the act of creation of the human being, inasmuch as the creation of a godlike being was a manifestation of the Divine in the conditions of a life of creational-limits. And this self-limitation (κένωσις)[81] is not meant to be understood in a subjective-human sense: since it was the *Divine* itself who accepted fully the human condition, it was an authentic and effective one *(deistvitel'nyi).*"[82] To accept

77. Cf. IB, p. 5.

78. "His taking on the human sins — this is the essential sense of His redemptive service," yet not as a "sinful lusciousness but as evil and distress in human life." Cf. IB, p. 18.

79. IB, p. 20.

80. Tareev dedicates an entire book based on acute historical research to the theme of *kenosis* in *Osnovy khristianstva,* vol. 1, "Khristos," *I. Unichizhenie Khrista,* which he intends to be seen as a unity with his later work *Filosofiia evangel'skoi istorii,* i.e., Christ's incarnation and death out of *kenosis* as one unifying and redeeming act in the history of humankind.

81. In the book erroneously spelled with an initial "φ." Cf. IB, p. 30. For the biblical context of κένωσις, cf. 1 Corinthians 1:17 and Philippians 2:5-11.

82. Cf. IB, p. 30.

and understand this requires a mental move from a "deistic" to a "theistic" idea of the Divine who also grants proper freedom (of decision and action) to the creature that "remains in God's hands."[83] Yet what good would be any sacrifice, any *kenosis,* performed out of or for creating fear; in fact, this could never reflect the true image of the God whom Christ addresses as *Father,* nor God's true intention in His *unfading glory:*

> We shall not be frightened by the thought of such self-limitation of the Divine for the sake of man, for it is not an external and negative self-limitation . . . but an enamored one *(liubovnoe),* inner and, therefore, positive. Yes, an affirmative self-limitation: such is the logic of divine-human life *(zhizn' Bogochelovecheskaia).* By self-limiting Itself out of love for the human being, the Divine manifests Its glory not only in Itself, but through the other and for the other and thus gains this other, the human being, for Itself. Not negating the glory of the human being by an exclusive assertion of Its own glory, but permeating him lovingly by Its proper glory, placing into the human being not a glory alien to Itself but Its own through which It makes the human being into Its guest.[84]

Because of our human fear, even such an ultimate act of God as His self-limitation calls for tenderness and the gentlest manner of God. He effectuates it through a *loving, affirmative* incarnation in order to restore His creature to its former dignity. Then what possibly could be more self-limiting than becoming an infant in complete dependence on human love? So much about God's self-limitation. But in what consists human self-limitation? How can God's glory be manifested in "the other," i.e., the human being? Man has to "renounce his exclusiveness, his *(from the beginning unfailingly recognized)* contraposition to the Divine" in order to appropriate this offer of divine glory. He shall act thus "through a loving appropriation, so that he may place his glory into the glory of God and [that] glory of God[85] be incremented in him; he has to be aware of God *(soznat' Boga),* not merely as someone along his side, or at his level *(ne kak drugago na riadu s*

83. Here Tareev explicitly uses *God (Bog)* instead of the term *Divine (Bozhestvo).* Cf. IB, p. 31.

84. IB, p. 31.

85. Here again Tareev uses specifically the word *God,* though, considering the text in its entirety, he is apparently using the two terms as synonyms.

soboiu), but to be aware of Him in His very self." By placing His proper glory in the human being, God makes man "into His bearer."[86]

Self-denial and *faith* are just as indispensable in reaching this "endless ideal"[87] as are "free will" and the "strength of love."[88] Faith opens the person for the "disposition of the Son of God" *(bogosynovnee nastroenie),*[89] a transformative attitude that enables one to "believe in God's love for the human being."[90] The temptations of Christ are to be understood in this key of Christ's *disposition* or *kenotic mood,* and Tareev insists on a distinction between God's self-limitation out of love in the incarnation and His self-limitation as a "redemptive act or notion of Christ's earthly life." He elucidates it as follows:

> This is the reason why we distinguish the self-limitation of the Divine that occurred in the birth of the God-man as a criterion of the temptation of the God-man from the self-limitation of the Divine, as the redemptive act of Jesus Christ's earthly life. That which, at the self-limitation of the Divine in the birth of the God-man was a dispassionate act *(bezstrastnyi akt)* of the divine love, in the human-divine deed of the incarnating son of God was a work of struggle and victory. God in His love desires since eternity the salvation of the human being and, consequently, wishes His own self-limitation for the sake of the human being. Also the Son of God personally, as the Father's only nature [or essence], from eternity and during the time of His earthly life, desires both the salvation of the human being and the self-limitation of the Divine.[91]

By now, it is evident how crucial *kenosis* is, and how inconceivable it would be in Christian terms without divine love that streams forth and flows back to its *origin.* Love is a salvific notion of which *kenosis* is the proof; it is not just an action, a one-time occurrence but rather a lasting happening of a *gerundive state,* a nominalized infinitive, an ever-resounding Logos of God's essence.

86. Cf. IB, p. 31.

87. This ideal helps the human being to realize "in his very self the image of God" and to contemplate the limits of his own being.

88. Faith, i.e., the "essential expression" of the human being's free and reasoned relationship to God. Cf. IB, p. 34.

89. A *form of mind* or *disposition* defined by Gorodetzky as the "kenotic mood of Christ."

90. Cf. IB, p. 35.

91. IB, p. 177.

2.4. *The Conquering Love of Sonship*

To "regenerate" and thus liberate the human being from his sinful tendencies,[92] it was the Son of God who had to take upon Himself evil and suffering, to be tempted by them, in order to defeat them definitely. This required a specific divine force: "The power with which Christ reconciled Divine and human was love: it [love] conquered evil and the suffering of human life; indeed evil and suffering were accepted by love in Christ, just as only love can substantiate *(obosnovat')* sacrifice and self-denial." And since love *is* self-sacrifice and self-denial, it is at the same time the "source of an all-conquering faith . . . and it stipulates faith" that is indispensable for the actual self-sacrifice. Therefore, the temptations of Christ were temptations of His love and His faith, both towards God and towards the human being. What follows is certainly one of Tareev's original insights where he renders a spectacular anthropological vision and visualization of Christ's temptations:

> The human-divine religious temptations of Christ, caused by the evil and suffering of human life, which was perceived *(vospriniaty)* and defeated by His love, related to the divine-human love of Christ [and] were *temptations* of [directed at] His *love.* Love is self-sacrifice and self-denial; from one side, the source of all-conquering faith, from the other, it determines and generates *(obuslovlivat' i vyzyvat')* the heroic act of faith *(podvig very),*[93] both intrinsic elements of self-denial: the all-conquering faith is attainable only for someone who loves and offers an action of faith out of self-denial. Therefore, the temptations of Christ, in Whom love united God and the human being, were . . . temptations of [directed at] His love, as well as *temptations* of His *faith.* For all that, since Christ's heroic act of faith was twofold, divine-human, and His temptations were related from one side to His *love and faith in God the Father,* and from the other to His love and faith in the human being, for which . . . His victory over the temptations was an acquisition of the Father's love for the human being and the victory over the evil and unbelief of the human being. Because the heroic act of Christ included all humankind *(vsheobshchechelovecheskii)* and, above all, was conditioned by His relationship with the historic human being as the indwelling of the Son of

92. Tendencies that deceive and lure him into the "sin of self-justification." Cf. IB, p. 177.

93. Could be rendered also as an "ascetic act of faith."

> God in the human heart, His temptations related above all to His love and faith in the human being, to the faith that the incarnation [or indwelling] *(vselenie)* of the Son of God into the human being was possible, [and thus] his divine-sonship *(Bogosynovstvo)* [could be restored].[94]

By becoming one of us and spurred by his love-faith for the human being, Christ transformed the temptations of "*human faith* in *His divine-sonship,* so that through His indwelling truth He confirmed the divine-sonship, [and although] conditioned by creational-limits and full of the evil and sufferings of terrestrial life, by this very act generated the all-conquering and saving *human faith and human love,* i.e., faith in the divine-sonship of the Son of man and love to the Son of God." Thus transformed (or transfigured), Christ defeated the "evil spirit of self-justification by human powers *(chelovecheskimi silami),*" shared His self-awareness of divine-sonship with His fellow human beings, and restored their unity with God. Tareev is consistent in his reasoning and adds that since Christ's temptations were human-divine, they involved all aspects of this realm, including the temptation of Christ's faith in His own divine, i.e., God-sonship.[95]

2.5. Agapē, *the True Love*

Tareev dedicates an extended and mature reflection to the essence and attributes of the *divine love.* That it is addressed in the middle of his book is more than symbolic, because the matter of love, especially that of divine love, is at the heart of Tareev's theology: "Love is a divine force *(sila bozhestvennaia),* a creative power. It is the beginning of all life and especially of life in its true unity and perfect fullness, it is the source of sanctity and beatitude, harmony and beauty."[96] It "strengthens" the soul for the good and "shields" it from the stain of sin and any evil, and all that is noble comes from love.[97] The power of love is an "acting power" that can raise the dead and heal divisions, through which "ugliness regenerates into harmony, beauty engenders in place of desolation and abomination . . . with its unique

94. Cf. IB, p. 197.

95. Cf. IB, p. 198. For further love-related reflections in this regard, see also "Istoria iskushenii Khrista," IB, pp. 222-318.

96. Cf. IB, p. 207.

97. Tareev makes a Pauline reflection on love similar to the one in the Corinthian letter. Cf. 1 Corinthians 13:4-8.

source residing in God." Yet since the human being sinned, "by deviating from his original Source he has also lost the tenure of love. As the primary expression of the divine ('God is love'), it became, in its unselfish purity, the least intrinsic/inherent to the sinful human being."[98] Yet any sort of reduced or selfishly motivated love is better than none, for love, even as much as a scintilla, carries an indelible token of its heavenly origin, and even though divine love became unreachable to the human being, "from time to time it illuminates him temporarily from high above with its warm ray."[99]

Gently, Tareev steers *("kak by")* towards the sensible, personal experiences of the divine love that appears to "chosen natures" in "dreams" *(snovidenie)* and is expressed in "selfless conduct" *(samootverzhennykh postupkakh),* finally reaching perfection in "an ecstatic state [or condition]" *(ekstaticheskoe sostoianie).* Love is a relationship, yet it expresses itself through that which is sensible and perceptible; therefore our senses have to be involved. How can any love, let alone the divine, be experienced if the very fundamental human element of perception is banned? "The supersensible world *(sverkhchustvennyi)* was captured in the realization of artistic images, whereas supernatural reason was grasped in profound philosophical conceptions; the classical world did not yet know love — the true love (ἀγάπη) — it did not rise above worldly love (ἔρως)."[100] Thus, the contraposition between *agapē* and *erōs* is much deeper than just a hermeneutical or moral one — it is ontological: true love from true Source (light from light, true God from true God). How we live our loves, relationships, and sacrifices, whether *agapē* or *erōs,* is not "a product" of our actions, but we do act in line with our choices, a *yes* — in and with faith — divinely if we choose divine love or, as Tareev puts it, *true love,* i.e., *agapē.* God Himself plants His love into the human heart:

> The One, Who alone can according to our prayers infuse the spirit of love into our hearts,[101] Who alone could awaken in the human being his

98. . . . *ona stala mene vsego svoistvennoiu — v svoei bezkorystnoi chistote — grekhovnomu cheloveku.*

99. Cf. IB, p. 207.

100. "This is the reason why the God-chosen nation, for its faith deserving the Savior of the world, still did not comprehend love; and even in our Christian times when it is so much easier in comparison . . . is so hard for the proper forces of a person even the slightest revelation of true love." Cf. IB, p. 208.

101. Here Tareev is paraphrasing St. Augustine, which he duly and meticulously indicates in the notes. Cf. IB, p. 208.

> best divine gift, resurrect in him the defunct love and make it vital and acting, the One Himself was the first and full revelation of divine love on earth. The love of Christ for God the Father and the human being acquired the love of God for the human being, and that of the human being for God united truly intrinsically *(istinno vnutrenne)* the human being with God. Christ was able to generate (literarily *to give birth, porodit'*) love in the human heart because He Himself was the full and absolute manifestation of love; yet for Him love was *a heroic act* [of salvation] *(podvig).*[102]

The goal of this *heroic act of faith (podvig)*, the *redemptive action of* Christ, was to assert the divine love and regain its full dignity in creation by taking the only place worthy of its dwelling: the human heart. In Tareev's view, there was no qualitative or quantitative difference between Christ's love towards His heavenly Father and the fallen human being.[103] He came out of love, His message was the divine love, His redeeming deed was *kenotic,* self-sacrifice out of love, and His return to the Father a proof of love for both: the Father and humankind.[104] Christ has set the highest standard by revealing the sole *true love,* the *divine love, agapē,* whose only worthy dwelling is the human heart, a heart that cannot be satisfied by anything less than the vivifying streams of this *divine agapē.*

For some reason, Tareev does not mention the Holy Spirit, not as a Hypostasis, and not in any active role in this intimate economy of salvation. His Pneumatology appears to be conspicuously modest for an eastern theologian, which naturally raises also questions about his Trinitarian concept.[105]

102. IB, pp. 208-9.

103. Cf. IB, p. 209.

104. Tareev further develops this theme. Cf. IB, pp. 210-22.

105. This would be an investigation that deserves a separate frame of research. There were also doubts about Tareev's ecclesiology as well as his concept of relationship between *church* and *the secular world.* He was one of Bukharev's critics in this regard as exposed by Gorodetzky:

> The secular life — body, nature, history — must be set free as well and left to its own development. This would allow the religious world to be preserved in its fullness and purity. This idea of Tareev aroused lively controversy and gave occasion to some of accusing him of heathenism and even immorality. Such accusations are obviously harsh and wrong; but if Tareev had an organic view of the church he could overcome the difficulty. It is the more astonishing, as he in his turn criticized Bukharev's "monastic" outlook. If even the world was for Bukharev a sinful world, he saw it on the way to salvation through the Incarnate, sacrificial Lamb.

The interaction of love and faith[106] plays a decisive role and is a thought that is further developed in *Iskusheniia Bogocheloveka* and in *Tsel' i smysl zhizni* when treating the theological virtues in the chapters on *Spiritual life.*[107] As for the interhuman relationship, the "same love that is meant to unite the human being with God is destined to unite human beings among themselves," the dignity in service to God and each other in freedom of choice and faith.[108]

Conclusion

We could closely examine only some of Tareev's original insights, covering the most pertinent areas of his interest, namely the temptations of Christ and the notion of *kenosis.* Although his thoughts are often multilayered, he does not get lost in overcomplex reasoning. Tareev proves himself as possessing a solid knowledge and competent use of the Scriptures and patristic texts, offering frequent quotations in the original language. Having worked as an exegete, he was well aware of the importance of a correct methodological procedure, especially when making a historical overview, as in the case of *Unichizhenie Khrista,* for instance. Tareev identified *agapē* with the *true divine love,* not veiling his personal spiritual journey of someone who has come to know love and to know to be loved. He certainly offers a new hermeneutics of Christ's temptations constituting them *as one sole and continu-*

> Tareev, who considers the world and natural life neutral or even good, almost excludes it from the realm of grace. His clear-cut method shows both extremes of the Russian kenotic mind: its evangelical pureness and desire to cling faithfully to Christ's ways and commandments and also its social dangers. (*The Humiliated Christ,* p. 154)

106. "Love, it is the soul that will remain for the life beyond, after the sanctification of the earthly body; faith, it is the body of soul." IB, p. 212. There are numerous similar pairings of *faith* and *love.* Again, much less to none of *hope.*

107. Cf. "Khristianskoe mirovozzrenie," in *Osnovy Khristianstva,* vol. 3, *I. Tsel' i smysl zhizni,* pp. 78-157, esp. 107-37. The edition of M. Tareev, *Tsel' i smysl zhizni* (Pushkino: Izd. Dom Graal', 2002), has some inconsistencies at the end of the booklet that appeared to be unfortunately abridged from the original (for example, pages 146-56 in the version used here are entirely missing). For freedom in human choice of *Love* made possible by Christ first choosing freely the cross: cf. *Tsel' i smysl zhizni,* p. 278. For the conditions of discipleship: cf. *Tsel' i smysl zhizni,* p. 283.

108. Cf. *Tsel' i smysl zhizni,* p. 293. In the notion of freedom: in primitive religions, a person afraid of God does not want Him to be close, but makes a sacrifice to keep the Divine at a distance from himself. Cf. *Tsel' i smysl zhizni,* p. 86.

ous redemptive act of Christ as opposed to a *one-event occurrence* in the Savior's life. If Tareev had done nothing other than this, his merit would still be noteworthy.[109] He points out a "soteriological change" by Christ's restoration of *faith* and *love,* and thus a renewing *unity* between God and the human being. Perhaps the absence of references to the Holy Spirit can be explained by his eagerness to exemplify the uniqueness of the divine love revealed in Christ. Explained yet not justified, which stands also for the missing representation of God in his Trinitarian aspect.

Tareev's theology is profoundly Christocentric. Precisely for this reason, the factual goal of his theology lies beyond the mere acts of temptations — namely in the *salvific act,* the essence of which is God's *divine love, agapē,* revealed in Christ's self-sacrifice.

3. Pavel Iakovlevich Svetlov: Golgotha as Veritable Explanation of Love

3.1. Biography

P. I. Svetlov (1861-1945), the son of a priest, received his theological formation at the Moscow Theological Academy, which he finished in 1886. Afterwards he taught philosophy and the history of philosophy at a seminary and secondary school while ministering as a priest. In 1897, he became a professor of theology at Kiev University and the Nezhin Institute of History and Philosophy and was an ardent advocate for establishing theological faculties at universities. In 1896, he defended his master's thesis in theology with the work *Znachenie khresta v dele Khristovom: Opyt iziasneniia dogmata iskupleniia (The Meaning of the Cross in the Work of Christ: An Essay of Explanation of the Dogma on Redemption),*[110] which appeared in Kiev in 1892. In 1902 he became a doctor of theology. Svetlov was a prolific writer and published richly in almost all theological magazines on the subjects of dog-

109. In his *The Goal and Meaning of Life,* for instance, Tareev makes equally lucid epistemological insights, for instance: Without faith there is no Christian love; only someone who has been loved by Christ's love can know this love; the Christian love is a believing love; and numerous other ones. To the question, what is the meaning and goal of life, he concludes: to understand life's goal is its meaning. This goal includes all that is true, divine, and solely of meaning: *agapē. Tsel' i smysl zhizni* (Moskva 1901).

110. It is a criticism of the popular scholastic teaching on salvation, promoting instead a biblical-ethical explanation of this dogma.

matics, moral theology, apologetics, and biblical history. Among his numerous books are *Istochniki khodiachego mneniia o vere kak protivopolozhnosti razumu (Sources of Current Thought on Faith as a Juxtaposition to Reason),* which appeared in 1896; *Khristianskoe verouchenie v apologeticheskom izlozhenii (Christian Dogmatics in an Apologetic Exposition),* which was reedited four times and republished as a two-volume dogmatic theology;[111] *Mistitsizm kontsa XIX v. v ego otnoshenii k khristianskoi religii i filosovii (Mysticism at the End of the Nineteenth Century in Its Relation to the Christian Religion and Philosophy)* in 1897, an original survey of mysticism and mystical tendencies in the nineteenth century; *O meste bogosloviia v sem'e universtitetskikh nauk (On the Place of Theology in the Family of University Sciences)* in 1897; *L'Eglise orthodoxe orientale et l'Eglise ancienne catholique* in 1899; *Kurs apologeticheskogo bogosloviia (A Course of Apologetic Theology)* in 1900 (1905, 1914 reprints); *Un prétendu obstacle à l'union des églises ancienne catholique et orientale* in 1903; *Ideia Tsarstva Bozhiia v ee znachenii dlia khristianskogo mirosozertsaniia (The Idea of God's Kingdom in Its Meaning for the Christian Worldview)* in 1905; and *Religiia i nauka (Religion and Science)* in 1914.[112]

3.2. The Idea of Kingdom of God in Its Meaning for the Christian Worldview[113]

In the introduction[114] to this apologetic theological research, Svetlov explains his intention to illuminate the truth of "sacrificing earthly goods for

111. First appeared as *Opyt apologeticheskago izlozheniia pravoslavno-khristianskago verouchenia,* T. I. Nezhin 1896 and Kiev 1899. In vol. 2, Svetlov dedicates two substantial chapters to Christology and soteriology ("Otdelenie II. O printsipakh ucheniia ob iskuplenii i Khristologiia ili uchenie o litse Iskupitelia," pp. 319-756). Cf. *Khristianskoe verouchenie v apologeticheskom izlozhenii* (Kiev: Tipografiia S. V. Kul'zhenko, 1912-14), vols. 1-2. The entire work shows solid erudition, confrontation with other authors, and good research methodology.

112. A concise biographical description and an apparently complete bibliographical listing of Svetlov's works can be found in *Russkie mysliteli vtoroi poloviny XIX — nachala XX veka: Opyt kratkogo biobibliograficheskogo slovaria,* ed. B. V. Emeliianov and V. V. Kulikov (Ekaterinburg: Ural, 1996), pp. 283-84; and P. V. Alekseev, *Filosofy Rossii XIX-XX stoletii, biografii, idei, trudy* (Moskva: "Akademicheskii Proekt," 2002), pp. 860-61.

113. P. I. Svetlov, *Ideia Tsarstva Bozhiia v ee znachenii dlia khristianskago mirosozertsaniia* (Sviato-Troitskaia Sergieva Lavra 1905) (ITsB).

114. Cf. ITsB, pp. 3-7.

the sake of the Kingdom of God" in the spirit of the gospel, while discerning what really corresponds to the *Christian roots*[115] of this renunciation. Svetlov argues that the "alienation of the Church"[116] from its ideal of communion and action in love, through the sociopolitical development of society along the centuries, had to be justified by "an ideal of 'beyond the grave.'" The "reigning spirit of bureaucracy"[117] and individualism is meant to be opposed by the apostle's[118] vision that "members of the Church are being perfected by reciprocal unity *(vzaimnoe edinenie)* and edification in faith and love" (1 Cor. 14:3-4, 12, 26; Eph. 4:16; 1 Thess. 5:11, etc.). For the sake and success of the church's special task — *dushespasenia,* which is the salvation of souls, the church has to return to its spiritual "origins and laws."[119] More than symbolically, he placed his introduction and work under the epigraph from the Gospel of St. Luke: *"Leave the dead to bury their own dead. But as for you, go and proclaim the kingdom of God"* (Luke 9:60). To Svetlov, the kingdom of God enjoys an "exclusive and particular place" in Christianity,[120] despite all the importance of doctrines such as "salvation or love as chief principles of morality . . . [that] yielded their place to the universal and grand idea of the Kingdom of God"[121] brought to us by the gospel. It possesses this primacy because it "contains all the gospel teachings as the dogmatic thus the moral one," and "salvation and love as chief moral principle." For this reason, Svetlov considers the idea of the kingdom of God as the *central* one.[122]

115. Which, for Russia, Svetlov understandably collocates into Byzantium.

116. Literally *omertvenie dlia zhizni, mortification* [or: *deadened*] *for life.*

117. Svetlov specifically mentions the religious censure that sacrifices the "higher interests of the Christian religion to transient and haphazard interests of church politics." Cf. ITsB, p. 5.

118. St. Paul.

119. Cf. ITsB, p. 5. Svetlov expresses a growing interest for the question of whether and how the church and the individual Christian should relate to earthly life and its goods, especially in the West, and lists numerous current German publications, from A. Harnack to Br. Ankermann. Many of these, one way or another, relate to L. N. Tolstoy's approach of "renouncing earthly life and earthly goods." Cf. ITsB, pp. 6-7.

120. And higher than any other religion.

121. The author in his work spelled *Kingdom* with a minuscule.

122. Cf. ITsB, pp. 9-11. In the rest of the introduction, Svetlov delineates his methodology, the exegetical foundations of the kingdom of God, and the different (primarily theological) aspects of it, especially that of dogmatics. He also touches upon the question of Christ's temptations. Cf. ITsB, p. 24. On pages 34-41 he lists a considerable, in great part foreign, bibliography used in his research. Cf. ITsB, p. 24.

3.2.1. Rationality and Freedom for Perfection

In his first chapter, when addressing the subject of foundation and restoration of the kingdom of God, Svetlov describes the relationship between God and creation in poetic words, God as the origin and final aspiration of everything, all created and uninterruptedly sustained by "the inexhaustible graces of Divine love" to which creation responds:

> Creation originated from the love of God, it exists and is sustained by the love of God, and it was created for the love of God: originating from love, also for love is it created. At the creation of the world the love of God established for its objective [or: goal] *(tsel')* the benefit and happiness of rational creatures. The latter ones, however, shall obtain this objective when, in a grateful response of love to the Creator which was planted into their souls at creation, they forget about themselves and their proper happiness, and consign their goal and the very purpose of their existence in God, His glory and the service to Him. Therefore, the teaching on the purpose [*tsel'*] of the world and the meaning of the human life can be formulated briefly and precisely as follows: *the human being, like all that exists, was created for the service of God — a reason-guided and voluntary one.*[123]

Svetlov adds that *rational creatures,* by their very nature, are called to a "*free* service to God,"[124] which is participation in the kingdom of God, "the last and concluding sense of the world's creation . . . the glory of God." For a "full participation in perfection," which can be experienced only in God, freedom is an ontological fundamental and extends to the whole visible and invisible world.[125] This kingdom exemplified and conveyed through Jesus

123. In addition, he lines up a series of OT quotations. Cf. ITsB, pp. 42-43.

124. To the subject of *freedom* and *unity* in the human relating to God, where *unity in freedom* is an equivalent of *love,* Svetlov dedicates an extensive and refined reflection under the subtitle: *Tri tipa otnoshenii cheloveka k Bogu: Edinstvo bez svobody, svoboda bez edinstva, edinstvo v svobode (liubov'), i ikh mesto v istorii* (Three kinds of relations of the human being to God: Unity without freedom, freedom without unity, unity in freedom [love], and their place in the history). Cf. P. I. Svetlov, *Znachenie Khresta v dele Khristovom: Opyt iziasneniia dogmata iskupleniia,* 2nd ed. (Kiev: Tip. C. V. Kul'zhenko, 1907), pp. 261-78, esp. 267-72 (ZKhK).

125. This is more than "a mere theological conclusion," being the very "teaching of the Word of God" (Matt. 25:34). Svetlov develops the argument based on intense exegetical research. Cf. ZKhK, p. 43.

Christ is based on the "just love of God" that includes all and is reciprocated among human beings again "by the strength of truth and love" (Matt. 8:10-12; 21:28-32; Luke 10:16-24; 13:25-30; 14:23; 15:11-31; John 10:16, etc.).[126] "The Kingdom of God in Christ is affirmed *(utverzhdat'sia)* by a unique force: the force of truth and love. The Kingdom of God in Christ is affirmed by the Cross."[127] The Son of God did not appear for "the establishment of the Kingdom of God on earth in bliss and heavenly glory but in the humble image of Jesus the Galilean from Nazareth,"[128] who did not wish to attract people "by might, nor by riches or power" but by "truth, love, so that through love for Him He could bring us back to God," which is why He "hid the treasures of His nature *(estestvo)* in the weakness of our own [human] nature."[129] As evident from Svetlov's reasoning both *truth* and *love* are ontologically interrelated, such as *faith* and *love* are for other modern Russian thinkers. The first two are the nearest attributes describing God's true nature, the latter ones are the human recognition and interaction with the divine realm.

3.2.2. The Foundation of Love: Definition of Reason and Love

Therefore, the *foundation* and *goal* of the kingdom cannot be anything else but "truth and love, the free and rational service to God in truth and love" (John 15:15), where *truth* is a "deed of persuasion of the intellect and is acquired by the free research of it," and *love* "is an act of the heart's free attraction *(vlecheniie)* and is the fruit of the moral independent action or spontaneous activity of the human being, i.e., a work or deed of his free, spiritual, ascetic labor." In this sense, *truth* and *love* are also two anthropological aspects and cornerstones "of the inner nature" of the kingdom of God.[130]

126. Cf. ZKhK, pp. 52-53. For Svetlov those Christian nations that wish to grow into the kingdom of God under the "protection of the gospel" act as follows: "Christian nations are embellishing themselves by humility, peace and love, and not by the sentiment of national pride, especially in the religious sphere. They are strong [and] valiant in thanksgiving, holding in remembrance God, the Father of all, and His Kingdom — that Kingdom, where those who consider themselves first are always the last." Cf. ZKhK, p. 53.

127. ZKhK, p. 62.

128. Cf. ZKhK, p. 63. Svetlov also applies a series of Christological titles and attributes, such as "man of sorrows" and "the slave of YHWH," or "the Lamb of God."

129. Cf. ZKhK, pp. 64, 66.

130. Cf. ZKhK, pp. 66-67.

Svetlov in his book recurs fervently to the theme of *love* and its aspects, e.g., *self-denial (samootrechenie)*,[131] or the condition of *acting* and *true love (istinnaia liubov')* expressed in the love of Christ and His kingdom. His theology is unambiguously Christocentric: "From what was said about the inner nature of the Kingdom of God so far, the following conclusion emerges: *the kingdom of God is a life with God granted in Christ to the human being, a Communion with God (bogoobshchenie)*."[132] Also, "*the kingdom of God is the fulfillment of Christ's commandments on earth*" and "*a brotherly union of people with Christ (bratskoe edinenie liudei vo Khriste).*"[133] The core and essence of Christ's commandments is in the love for God and one's neighbor, an attitude "that represents a distinguished and true sign of the discipleship of Christ" (John 13:34-35; 15:12-14, 17; 1 John 2:7-11; 3:23). Both loves reflect in each other the other (1 John 3:16-18; 4:19-21) because *communion* and *unity* are intrinsic attributes of this kingdom in which people are "bound together by the power of love" (John 17:21-23). This communal *bond* brings about a shift from "the sphere of individualism into a social domain."[134] Svetlov perceives and allows others to perceive clearly the significance of love, posing some direct questions:

> What is love? Love is the totality *(sovokupnost')* of all perfections and the peak of perfection, for it is through [love] that we become alike to God (Matt. 5:48; Luke 6:36; 1 John 4:8, 17; Col. 3:14 etc.). Love is light because in [love] there is the highest truth of life and of the Gospel (1 John 2:9-11). Love is life, and through it "we have passed out from death into life" (1 John 3:14).
>
> Love — is perfection,
> love — *is light,*
> love — *is life.*
>
> The *Kingdom of God* is created by love. It *is summum bonum, the highest good, serving the goal and being the limit of all our aspirations, desires, and deeds* (Matt. 13:44-46). The Kingdom of God is being estab-

131. "Self-denial is a condition of love; it is [all] the greater, the greater the love is." Since there is "nothing higher than the love for Christ," this love requires self-denial and "renunciation of the world." Cf. ZKhK, pp. 78-79.

132. In Russian, *bogoobshchenie* is composed from the words *God* and *fellowship, communion,* or even *communication;* in that sense *bogoobshchenie* is understood as a *communion with God.*

133. ZKhK, p. 80; also previously in p. 77.

134. Cf. ZKhK, p. 80.

lished once and for all by the power of Christ's Spirit (Gal. 4:6; Rom. 5:5) and it includes all the gifts that Christ's coming will bring about.[135]

Moreover, Svetlov sees Christianity "as a religion of love" and equates ignoring love to ignoring the inmost verity and identity of Christianity. In this sense, he exemplifies definitions of Christianity based on love:

> To ignore love — not deriving absolutely everything from it, its worthy royal place in one's heart and life — means to ignore Christianity in its very holy of holies, to negate Christianity. Christianity is a religion of love where everything is subject to love and obtains a God-pleasing value *(bogougodnaia tsennost')* only in [its] relationship to love; even charity, knowledge, the heroic effort for good *(podvig dobra)*, and all our toils have only true moral value inasmuch as they flow from love. Love is a distinctive sign of Christians shown by the Lord Himself (John 14:23-24). Love contains all the essential matter of Christianity. In love there is the fulfillment of the [ethical or moral] law, i.e., the morals of Christianity; in love is the principal and essential content of the Christian theoretic teaching or doctrine of faith. The entire Christian theology, in its core, is sutained by two propositions: *God is love,* and *He loved the world so much, that He gave His only Son* for its salvation (1 John 4:8; John 3:16). The royal primacy of love in Christianity cannot be expressed better than it is in the words of the apostle Paul: *And if I have prophetic powers, and understand all mysteries and all knowledge, and if I have all faith, so as to remove mountains, but have not love, I am nothing. If I give away all I have, and if I deliver up my body to be burned, but have not love, I gain nothing. . . . So now faith, hope, and love abide, these three; but the greatest of these is love* (1 Cor. 13:2-3, 13).[136]

135. ZKhK, p. 81. On the relationship of the state and Christianity: Christianity is a "religion of love . . . yet not a sentimental and flabby one that lacks justice, but one of a rational *(razumnoi),* holy and just love." Cf. ZKhK, pp. 208-9. Svetlov also dedicates refined reflections to the concept of love in the chapter "Tsarstvo Bozhie v vozzreniiakh Gogol'ia, Dostoevskago i Tolstogo (The Kingdom of God in the Views of Gogol', Dostoevsky and Tolstoy)." Cf. ZKhK, pp. 216-72, esp. 221-22, 250; further on Tolstoy, p. 368, on Tolstoy and Dostoevsky, pp. 379-80. For love as the "core of Christianity," cf. ZKhK, pp. 377-79.

136. ZKhK, pp. 377-78. In chapter 9, "Ideia tsarstva Bozhiia v russkom bogoslovii" (pp. 326-467), Svetlov also quotes Dostoevsky and Tolstoy on the subject of love. Cf. ZKhK, pp. 379-80.

3.3. Course of Apologetic Theology:[137] *Suffering and Cross as Means to the Goal*

Unlike in his major dogmatic manual written a couple of years earlier,[138] here Svetlov explicitly introduces the theme of love in his Christology under the title of *Otkroveniie Bozhestvennoi liubvi vo Khriste Iisuse (The Revelation of the Divine Love in Christ Jesus).*[139]

One of the great challenges to our faith and love was and remains suffering, which Svetlov sees as following:

Suffering is a consequence of sin and serves for our purification. Ultimately, it is a "means of our reconciliation with God." Christ came and showed us how to suffer, "but even the Stoics taught that." More importantly, "He gave us the strength to get above the necessity of evil and transform *(prevratit')* this bondage into a personal, free heroic deed *(podvig)* of life by the revelation of the mystery of suffering. . . . Up to [the time of] Christ and outside of Christ," suffering appeared "as the denial of Divine love, as a result of God's disregarding the human being, [God's] enmity and alienation, or as a terrible, merciless justice."[140] These are very human thoughts, familiar even in our times, a temptation probably as old as humankind itself, caused after the fall through the loss of the true image of God and alienation from the source, the Creator. Therefore, Svetlov offers a twofold answer, addressing what God is like as well as the profound meaning of suffering in our lives: "In the suffering of the Son of God for us, God reveals Himself through His boundless love, a holy love for the happiness of every human being, a love that corrects and renounces sin in him. For man there is no other way to happiness than the way of sanctity, i.e., loving God and averting sin. There is no better means for being purified from sins than suffering."[141] Christ, as the "Lamb of God" and through his suffering and cross, fulfilled this transforma-

137. P. I. Svetlov, *Kurs apologeticheskogo bogosloviia,* 4th ed. (Kiev: Tipografiia S. V. Kul'zhenko, 1912) (KAB). With an epigraph from Schiller's *Die Räuber* (1781), fifth act, first scene: "Es ist nur eine Wahrheit, es ist nur eine Tugend! Wehe, wehe, wehe dem zweifelnden Wurme!"

138. Cf. P. I. Svetlov, *Khristianskoe verouchenie v apologeticheskom izlozhenii* (Kiev: S. V. Kul'zhenko, 1912-14).

139. With the epigraph from John 3:16: *For God so loved the world, that He gave His only Son, that whoever believes in Him should not perish but have eternal life* (in comparison to Rom. 5:8: *God shows His love for us in that while we were still sinners, Christ died for us*), and he addresses love also in other chapters. Cf. KAB, pp. 275-320.

140. Cf. KAB, p. 276.

141. KAB, p. 276.

tion, and this is the "central meaning of Christ's suffering" from where we receive all our graces. "On the Cross, in full and ultimate light, is God's love [a] holy Love of the suffering Divinity." This *holy Love* comes naturally through Christ who saves us and the world.[142]

3.4. The Cross of Christ and Salvation

The subject of staurology is certainly among those most dear to Svetlov's heart and mind, as he frequently addresses it, especially in the association of *soteriology* and the *love of God* manifested as His divine nature. For instance, he returns to it systematically in his manual on apologetic theology *Otkrovenie bozhestvennoi sily vo Khriste Iisuse ili o khreste v ego torzhestve nad mirom (The Revelation of the Divine Power in Christ Jesus or Concerning the Cross in His Triumph over the World).*[143] Thus, in his magisterial work *Znachenie khresta v dele Khristovom: Opyt iz'iasneniia dogmata iskupleniia (The Meaning of the Cross in the Work of Christ: An Essay at Clarifying the Dogma of Redemption),*[144] Svetlov attempts to illuminate this dogma, dogmatics being one of his fields of excellence, as seen above. He subdivides it into two major parts: 1. A historic-dogmatic analysis of the "Catholic-Protestant doctrines on redemption and their consequences for the very dogma on redemption" and "the teachings of the holy Fathers on redemption." 2. An analysis "on the essence and image of humankind's redemption accomplished by Our Lord Jesus Christ" with a strong anthropological accentuation and an elucidation of Christ's work founded on a relational level of love.[145]

142. Cf. KAB, p. 277. Svetlov dedicates an engaging reflection to the theological notions of *satisfaction* and (pacifying) sacrifice based on the proposition that "God is love" from an anthropological point of view. Cf. KAB, pp. 278-80, 281-92. This is one of his principal conclusions: "Yet God in His being, as we saw it, is best comprehensible to our understanding through the idea of love: *God is love,* the character of justice is not an independent character but rather a manifestation of love, since in God [love] is always pure, holy. *God, as Love, cannot be satisfied by anything exterior, not in any sacrifices, but [solely by] our love for Him.* God requests not the external renunciation in the sense of deprivation of some sort of material goods in sacrifices but an inner self-denial of my '*I,*' essentially united with a love for God." KAB, p. 285.

143. Cf. KAB, pp. 321-76.

144. *Znachenie khresta v dele Khristovom: Opyt iz'iasneniia dogmata iskupleniia,* 2nd ed. (Kiev: Tip. S. V. Kul'zhenko, 1907) (ZKhK).

145. See *Oglavnenie (Content).* Cf. ZKhK, pp. i-iv. Again, Svetlov addresses the need of a relationship to God founded in love and not a sort of "reconciliation with God [that] is an

3.5. God's Love in Salvation

In this text that carries the epigraph of 1 John 4:9-10,[146] Svetlov reviews different approaches to God's love in salvation. One is regarded as "Catholic-Protestant," although in fact it was a widespread misinterpretation, where a reconciliatory sacrifice of Christ was needed for the renewal of God's love for humanity because of its grave sin. "God has ceased to love man," so Christ had to bring himself as a sacrifice "for a *right* to the benefit of God's love."[147] A burdened conscience leads to the inner approach where the sacrifices of the human being become a mere confession that "God does not love me, I am not worthy of his love, and I must buy his mercy through the price of self-denial" and thus pacify him.[148] This Svetlov considers a "dogmatic-objective" view. He links this evidently OT approach to the notion that God always revealed to the human being only as much as society could cope with since "a full and complete revelation of the God of love in the OT was premature (see John 16:12)" precisely because of the juridical understanding of relationship with God.[149] Christ's love is not and cannot be based on this kind of relationship.[150]

According to the "dogmatic-subjective" view on the other hand, "God is love, and love does not require sacrifice: [love] sacrifices all [what it is and what it has]. The love of God indeed brought an infinite sacrifice: it ascended on the Cross in order to deliver humankind from its 'illusions' (i.e., sinfulness in front of the court of the Divine truth) and from the sufferings caused by them."[151]

---

external jurisdictional relationship and not an inner one in a spirit of love" (quoting a.o. Metr. Filaret Drozdov). The entire introduction is, so to speak, love-related, love as a turning-point of theological hermeneutics, preannounced by a joined, moral concept of love-freedom: "The criterion and guide of conscience . . . is not an external law but an inner principle, i.e., the very conscience, by a moral force — not the sensation of fear for an external good or a mere perception of cold duty — but the inner perception of love for the good, love; the substance *(sushchnost')* of love or of moral force is freedom; the external becomes an expression of the internal, which is its principle and foundation." Cf. ZKhK, pp. 10, 11-24.

146. In this the love of God was made manifest among us, that *God sent His only Son into the world, so that we might live through Him. In this is love, not that we have loved God but that He loved us and sent His Son to be the propitiation for our sins.*

147. Cf. ZKhK, pp. 279-80.

148. As in the case of burnt and sacrificial offerings. Cf. ZKhK, pp. 282-85.

149. Cf. ZKhK, p. 288.

150. Cf. ZKhK, p. 289.

151. ZKhK, p. 290.

Svetlov disagrees with the latter statement on *illusion* since it "obscures the true sense of the Cross," Christ's salvific action and its sense. God's dying for an illusion, in effect, would have been nothing more than a mistake: "No, the heart did not deceive humankind, the sacrifice was necessary." Yet this sacrifice was not requested by God out of justice or justification, but "because God is love . . . an immense mystery revealed on Golgotha. To Love Golgotha will be more comprehensible because Golgotha is the revelation of God's love, its mystery is the mystery of love."[152] On this track, Svetlov arrives at the mystery of the cross that is imbedded in love and makes no sense without God's divine, forgiving, restoring, and vivifying love. Svetlov consistently refuses the idea of justification as a diminution and limitation of the true relationship between God and the human being.[153]

Svetlov sticks to his primary intention and theologizes competently, but unlike Tareev for instance, at least in this last work, it is an *apologetic* theology that is less of a proper original thought and more of a contestation of different theological views *(subjective* and *objective).* It is a well-constructed and correct (counter)argument, and many of his thoughts are repeated in his later works, especially the dogmatic ones.[154] Eventually, he comes to the conclusion that both approaches, the *subjective* as well as the *objective,* require the notion of *satisfaction (udovletovenie):*[155] "If the need for salvation would not be satisfied *(udovletvorena),* there would be no way humankind could be saved. Satisfaction is indispensable for a) the *subjective* side of salvation that consists in restoring in humankind the love for God, and also for b) the *objective* side that restores God's love to humankind in the form of forgiveness."[156]

152. *Liubvi budet poniatnee Golgotha, ibo Golgotha — otkrovenie Bozhiei liubvi, taina eia — taina liubvi.* Cf. ZKhK, pp. 290-91.

153. Cf. ZKhK, pp. 292-94. "The readers can see that salvation or reconciliation between God and humankind is not a juridical act, *but an act of a free bond in mutual love of God for humankind and of humankind for God.*" Yet this bond between God and humankind did not come along because God "saw a mathematical equation" in humankind's sins and Christ's redeeming sufferings, "but in the fact that this suffering of the Savior was an expression of humankind's love for God and of God — anticipating us with His invitation — for humankind, and that the love of God and humankind here on the Cross found for itself a mutual support of each other; the place of love was Golgotha; love can be measured by no mathematics." Cf. ZKhK, p. 309.

154. For instance, the relating of *good* and *love* as synonyms (Cf. ZKhK, pp. 296-99), or the doing of *good* being a *moral instance.* Cf. ZKhK, pp. 302-5.

155. Cf. ZKhK, pp. 305-8.

156. ZKhK, p. 305.

Even though there is a chapter on *God's love in salvation,* missing is an allusion to the love of the human being for his neighbor as a part of this love-communication between the human being and God, and missing also are the concepts of *samoogranichenie* and *samootrechenie (self-limitation* and *self-denial).*[157] Yet the beauty of the *Golgotha-Love* concept as a reconciliatory encounter of the divine and human, *God* and *the human being,* compensates the reader abundantly in the search for a profound and *true* image of a loving God.

Conclusion

Similarly to Tareev, Svetlov's research and argumentation are based on a solid methodology and perspicuous exegetical work. Most of his insights are original and profound, especially regarding the kingdom of God and its relatedness to Christianity as *communion* and the everyday life of the faithful. The fundamental role of freedom in participation in the kingdom of God and thus the divine perfection could be seen as an ontological turning point in the concept of freedom — as opposed to the merely passive anthropological asset. That the center of this kingdom is love is self-evident yet distinctly elucidated. Through Christ, humanity has regained faith in God and also in itself: Christ, through His sacrifice, *the mystery of love on Golgotha,* showed the way of a *true* and fruitful relationship to the Creator — and to one's neighbor. If fellow humans are not included in our sacrifices, they will miss the point of *true love* — one that is not based on fear (of pacifying sacrifices, for example) but a freedom that leads to perfection in God. The prototype of *true love* comes from God. We do not have to (re-)invent it, but rather to relearn it by following Christ's example. Svetlov undoubtedly touches the substantial traits of love when dealing with its kenotic nucleus in the final and decisive self-sacrifice of Christ on the cross. Although Svetlov does not mention the Holy Spirit explicitly, the words and acts take place *in the Spirit of Christ.* Thus, we assume that the Trinitarian aspect of this relationship is at least implicit. The dogma on salvation for Svetlov is to be comprehended in the key of sacrifice, whereas the highest sacrifice is *love,* the one that Christ has revealed to us.

157. Cf. ZKhK, pp. 305-10. Svetlov adds four pages of patristic and scriptural data regarding the latter subject, among others citing also Filaret's famous threefold kenotic love definition as one of the central references. Cf. ZKhK, pp. 311-14.

4. Metropolitan Antonii Khrapovitskii: *Love as Pastoral Care*

4.1. Biography

A. P. Khrapovitskii (1863-1936), later known as Metropolitan Antonii, was born in Batagino of the Novgorod region and died exiled in Serbia.[158] A diligent and pious student, he entered the Theological Academy in St. Petersburg in 1885 against the will of his father, and there, after having completed his studies, he became a hieromonakh. In the following years, he taught numerous subjects including homiletics, liturgy, and canon law in different educational centers, seminaries, and academies, eventually becoming a docent of the chair of the OT department in Kholm seminary (1887-89). At the end of the 1880s he met and got acquainted with Ioann Kronshtandtskii, who inspired him to create a course of pastoral theology presented as "a path of love and suffering."[159] Because Khrapovitskii was a born pedagogue, teaching and proper pastoral care of the faithful, of which he was a living example, were of the utmost concern to him. This concern, along with a strong monastic ideal, continued even after his appointment as rector of the Theological Academy in St. Petersburg in 1890.[160] Numerous other academic nominations followed. In 1897, he was ordained bishop, and in 1912, he became a stable member of the Holy Synod. Forced to leave for the Island of Vallaam in 1917, Khrapovitskii wrote there the *Dogmat iskupleniia (The Dogma on Redemption)* and in the same year became the most favored candidate among the three proposed ones for the new patriarch.[161] Arrested and interned in 1918,

158. For more detailed biographical material see Mitropolit Antonii (Khrapovitskii), *Molitva russkoi dushi,* ed. T. A. Solovova (Moskva: Sretenskii monastyr', 2006), pp. 5-20; Mitropolit Antonii (Khrapovitskii), *Sobranie sochinenii (v dvukh tomakh),* vol. 1 (Moskva: Izd. Dar", 2007), pp. 5-17 (AKSS I-II); Mitropolit Antonii (Khrapovitskii), *Zhizneopisanie: Pis'ma k raznym litsam 1919-39 godov* (Sankt-Peterburg: Izd. Olega Abyshko, 2006), pp. 7-129. This last one is endowed by a hagiographical touch.

159. Metr. Antonii saw also "in the grace of the priesthood" a "gift of compassionate love" modeled on Christ's love for the fallen human being. "All life-interests *(zhiznennye interesy)* of Metropolitan Antonii, all his deeds, derived from how he understood the entity of ministry, namely as 'the way of love.'" Evidence of this is his booklet dedicated to pastoral ministry: *Uchenie o pastyre, pastyrstve i ob ispovedi (Teaching on the Minister, Ministry and Confession).* Cf. AKSS I, pp. 12-14.

160. In his view, only monasticism could resist the evil in the world. One of his former *postrizhennikov* (a monk whom he tonsured), Metr. Evlogii Georgievskii, used the daring expression of "fanatic of monasticism" in his regard. Cf. Mitropolit Antonii (Khrapovitskii), *Molitva russkoi dushi,* p. 9.

161. The decision was made by drawing of lots, and Metropolitan Tikhon became the

Khrapovitskii had to abandon Russia definitely in 1920 and settled as a refugee in Serbia in Sremski-Karlovtsi. There he presided at the *Sobor Russkoi Pravoslavnoi Tserkvi Zagranitsei (The Synod of the Russian Orthodox Church Abroad)* that began on May 23, 1923, and he addressed the principal organizational question of the Russian church in the Diaspora.

Among his better-known works are: *Tolkovanie na knigu proroka Mikheia (Commentary on the Book of Micah)* published in 1890; on his initiation in 1891 appeared the *Bogoslovskii vestnik (Theological Messenger);* also in 1891 appeared his *Nravstvennaia ideia dogmata Presviatoi Troitsy (The Moral Concept of the Dogma on the Holy Trinity)*. For his *Psikhologicheskie dannye v pol'zu svobody voli i nravstvennoi otvetstvennosti (Psychological Evidence in Favor of Freedom of Will and Moral Responsibility)* Khrapovitskii obtained in 1891 his master's and, subsequently, doctoral degrees. After 1900, his complete works gradually appeared in various editions.[162] Among his favorite authors were Pushkin and Dostoevsky,[163] while Tolstoy and "modern philosophers" such as V. S. Solov'ev belonged to the (sometimes harshly) criticized ones.[164]

4.2. The Moral Idea of the Doctrine of the Church[165]

Metropolitan Antonii's sensibility for pastoral care in the church was firmly imbedded in moral doctrine and its implications for the everyday

---

new Patriarch. At the end of his time in Moscow, Khrapovitskii also met Metr. Sergei Stragorodskii, the later short-lived patriarch of Russia. In 1933, from exile, Khrapovitskii wrote a rebuking letter to Stragorodskii for his loyalty (and his exhortation to the Russian faithful to decline loyalty) to the Bolshevik regime. Cf. Mitropolit Antonii (Khrapovitskii), *Molitva russkoi dushi,* pp. 237-48.

162. For a list of his works see AKSS I, pp. 13-14. The editor of this last edition claims to have included "works of all his working periods." Cf. AKSS I, p. 14.

163. Khrapovitskii offers the reader splendidly assembled excerpts and comments on the love-related texts and concepts in Dostoevsky's works. His insights and exemplification of thought are worthy of a true authority and connoisseur of the author in *Pastoral Analysis of People and Life according to F. M. Dostoevsky.* Especially captivating is the material under the titles of *In Service of Renewal* and *The Servers of Renewal and Love.* Cf. *Molitva russkoi dushi,* 188-209. To our astonishment, this superb literary and spiritual analysis is not extant in the *Collected Works,* AKSS I-II, published in 2007, a year successively to the pocket edition of the *Molitva russkoi dushi.* The same stands for the missing analysis of Pushkin's works, although the collection is explicitly introduced as "our collected works" in AKSS I, p. 12.

164. Cf. AKSS II, pp. 5-204 and 223-90.

165. *Nravstvennaia ideia dogmata tserkvi.* AKSS II, pp. 457-78.

life of the faithful. The ancient Christians understood that "to love one another is the most demanding task of life" and as a stipulation, the way *par excellence* of enhancing their spiritual life, which Khrapovitskii equates to the process of salvation. Christians drew the strength to fulfill this task from the very entity of the Church which, despite its high ideals and "shining examples," would be powerless if not for "uniting its members into a single living entity of love"; indeed, they would die spiritually as soon as they abandoned this bond. Based above all on Christ's word and that of His apostles, namely on apostolic succession,[166] it is in the communion and unity through which God's saving grace acts. "[The Savior] granted His truth and grace not to each faithful separately but to the unity of faithful in the Church which is a body animated by the Spirit of God." The essentialities of the church are in its unity and in being an entity of love with a distinctive purpose to uphold the "spiritual growth of the Christian faithful."[167] In this constellation, for the salvation of the human being, for its "spiritual enhancement *(usovershenstvovanie)*" as an intermediary step, the three indispensable participants are God, the human being, and the church.[168] The tool for forging *unity* is prayer.[169] The prayer models the entity of the church, not after earthly patterns "where there is no unity but division," but after a heavenly one where the three Persons are united into one Being "so that there are not three Gods but the One God who is living a sole life [or who is alive by one life] *(zhivushchii edinii zhizn'iu)*."[170] The "new entity," the church, is not an end in itself but is called "to relate to each of its constitutive parts, that is to say to the personhood of the human being: '*I desire,*' says the Lord, '*that also those whom you have given me may be with me where I am to see my glory which you have given me . . . that the love with which you have loved me may be in them, and I in them*' (John 17:24, 26)."[171] This is the final goal and purpose of the church, and the immediate, indispensable, intermediary step is the "spiritual growth of the

166. Even though he does not explicitly use this term.

167. "Our contemporaries have lost this comprehension and are in need of a theoretical interpretation of [the question] what meaning the doctrine on the Church has for the spiritual enhancement of a person." Cf. AKSS II, pp. 459-60.

168. Cf. AKSS II, p. 461.

169. Prayer is a spiritual activity frequently referred to by Metr. Antonii. See *Pis'mo k sviashchenniku o nauchenii molitve (A Letter to a Priest on Learning to Pray)*. Cf. AKSS II, pp. 652-60.

170. Cf. AKSS II, pp. 461-62.

171. Cf. AKSS II, p. 462.

human being in the Church" formed after the intra-Trinitarian relationship in God.[172]

While discerning among various kinds of love ("sexual love" or "the highest expression of natural love, the maternal one," etc.), Khrapovitskii speaks of a "law of love" since there is a "natural inclination" in the human being to love, but the human is equally inclined to "self-centered love or the love of self" *(samoliubie)*. Nevertheless, the human being can never "achieve the fullness of Christian love and will never become a true Christian" as long as he remains in the bonds of his natural inclinations. Torn between them, some he will love, others hate, because love and self-love create a juxtaposition of "*I* and *not I*" and act in the inner person like "two irreconcilable enemies."[173]

4.3. The Moral Attractiveness of the Feat of Love[174]

The inner contradiction of these two kinds of love is well known from art and life itself,[175] a contradiction that even our human understanding cannot resolve and that is strengthened by "abandoning the unique notion of free personhood" which is a prerequisite for "the high demands of strict morals."[176] This is how Khrapovitskii comments upon the new philosophical tendencies of his time:

172. "And this principal idea (for one's proper increment of love) is already disrupting the image of the body that knows no love, with which it points out again that the idea of the Church is the idea of an exceptional being *(bytie iskliuchitel'noe)*, contrary to everything earthly." Cf. AKSS II, p. 462.

173. Cf. AKSS II, pp. 463-65.

174. *Nravstvennaia privlekatel'nost' podviga liubvi.* Cf. AKSS II, p. 465.

175. Khrapovitskii names as examples Pushkin's "Egyptian Nights (Egipetskie nochi)," Dostoevsky's "Crumbs (Kroshki)," and Nekrasov's "Mother (Mat')." The English titles here are my literal translation from the Russian originals.

176. Khrapovitskii refers to the stoics and Kant who, by abandoning it "along with the teaching on justice, chastity (virtue), [and] uprightness, preferred to proclaim a haughtily and cold, juridical and formal way of relating to one's neighbors." This approach has also denied the sense of "the virtue of love" *(dobrodetel' liubvi)* and proposed to replace it with the "principle of respect of one's neighbors." Such alteration eventually led, introduced by "scholastic-theologians," to the substitution of "love to one's neighbors" for the concept of a "moral debt" and "an invented teaching of one's love to his very self [self-love]," which besides the interhuman relationships also impacts "the teaching on God and the Savior." Cf. AKSS II, p. 464.

> The latest humanistic moral jointly with the rationally headed Protestant moral came to the conclusion that in order to strengthen the principle of love it is indispensable to renounce the scholastic concepts of personhood, freedom of will, retribution as well as the substitution of these concepts that are safeguarding egoism *(okhraniaiushchikh egoizm)*. [Moreover it is necessary] to strengthen the opposite view, namely of sharing one [united] Divine life effused in all creatures and aspiring to merge anew into one blessed fullness. Thus the sole principle of reason and life must be the principle of unity and love.[177]

As convincing as it may sound, for Khrapovitskii it is merely a switch from "spiritualism" to "pantheism," which he considered the stream of European philosophy and the rational theology of his time, all of which nurtured the rejection of *free will*. Khrapovitskii argues that the juxtaposition between *I* and *not I* "has been eliminated" and with it also the human being as an entity or personhood. Apart from such an *oxymoron*, an ethical and spiritual issue emerges: If there is no free will, there consequently is no difference between good and evil, and the "moral responsibility of the human being" has been eliminated, along with "the moral appeal of love's heroic deed *(podvig)* and its moral indispensability."[178] That would make the need of any action of charity and love simply superfluous.[179]

In order to find a solution for this confrontation between "our proud sensual egoism and the principle of love kindred to our heart," it is not sufficient to rely on philosophy, pondering within the boundaries of natural life, or the nature of our earthly life. Yet again, it is precisely our everyday life and our reason that intermediate the solution of reconciliation:

> Reconciliation [occurs] between an unrestrained self-appraisal, the principle of self-denial and the life for others, where these others, this *not I*, would not be something of an antagonism of myself, of my *I*, [but] where the freedom of each person would mingle with the metaphysical unity of their proper being, contrary to pantheism *(vopreki panteizmu)*. Such is the principal concept presented about the Church in the definitions that we delineated above, when we collocated her foundation on the Word of God. And, in fact, we observe that a person who evolves in

177. AKSS II, p. 464.

178. Cf. AKSS II, p. 465.

179. And he quotes St. Paul: *Let us eat and drink, for tomorrow we die* (1 Cor. 15:32).

> the Church merges a fullness of self-denying love with a high degree of individual will.[180]

The foremost examples of the last statement are the saints of the early Universal Church and later Eastern Church,[181] namely the "martyrs, ascetics, and holy hierarchs *(sviatiteli)*." In all three, we find the unification of the two contradictory positions of love: they lived entirely and died for the ecclesial brotherhood and the glory of God, and if they voluntarily gave up their free will, it was motivated by a "higher scope." The inspiration by the example of the Holy Trinity revealed by Christ, especially in his prayer, is an image that the Church is called to reflect on earth. Similar to so many other Orthodox writers, in Khrapovitskii, too, we find a strong emphasis on Christ's incarnation for the sake of restoring the "original image of God" in the human being (and thus revealing him as he was before the fall). Khrapovitskii, however, establishes a neat link between the founding of the church by Christ and his proper intention to actuate the restoration of the original image of *a triune God* with and through it.[182]

4.4. A Fragile Source

The human forefather's fall into sin by "self-enamored disobedience" against God's will "weakened his nature."[183] Christ, however, restores the fullness of the human nature by obeying and remaining in the Father's love: "*I have kept my Father's commandments and abide in His love* (John 15:10)." Therefore all that one needs to do is to freely concur "with the fragile source of love (charity), virtue (graces), reason(-ableness), and joy within him." There is a potentiality that can come to flourish in the church, and we dare to hope that one day this vision would apply to the Universal Church of Christ: "Ex-

180. Cf. AKSS II, p. 465.

181. Given the striking exclusiveness it needs to be remarked that in Khrapovitskii's writings we encountered very little appreciation, if any at all, for other Christian churches or denominations, which apparently was even truer for other religions.

182. Cf. AKSS II, pp. 466-67.

183. Khrapovitskii considers the monks, quoting the eighteenth chapter of St. Basil's *Ascetic Rule,* to be those who by their lives are "wiping out the sin of the forefather Adam in themselves" and thus are restoring the "primordial goodness" that reigned before sin that caused divisions, wars, and evil by "interrupted unity." Unquestionably, this would be a praiseworthy ideal and monastic vocation to be lived out. Cf. AKSS II, p. 469.

ploring together the beautiful creation of God and the Creator Himself, delighting their hearts in reciprocal love and joy, all people would be more and more permeated by the consciousness of their [proper] unity, and one could hardly speak of the actions and thoughts of Peter, Paul, and John but simply speak of and judge the actions of the human being."[184]

It is a markedly Christocentric ecclesiology coined by a strong hesychast spirituality that characterizes Khrapovitskii's thought. At the end of his chapter dedicated to ecclesiology and personhood, it is evident that liberating humankind from "self-centered-love," ergo egoism, is what reestablishes the unity in love of humankind and God, in the heart of the human being, made possible thanks to Christ's love and obedience. On a spiritual plain, *freedom, virtues, purity, prayer, charity,* and *joy* in the heart of the individual (yet always within the ecclesial community which is the place of conversion and the remodeling of a relationship) are the elementary building blocks of any spiritual progress.[185] The Church, as defined in her role above, possesses an indispensable role in the mediation between God and the human being, as well as for the dispensation-mediation of grace.[186]

4.5. *Pastoral Care*

In his numerous sermons and speeches, Metropolitan Antonii emerges as a caring pastor of his flock(s); as such, he not only discerned but also taught and reminded his hearers of the necessity for spiritual discernment.[187] Al-

184. Cf. AKSS II, pp. 468-69.

185. In an article titled "Tserkov' kak khranitel'nitsa i istolkovatel'nitsa Bozhestvennogo otkroveniia (The Church as Custodian and Interpreter of the Divine Revelation)," interestingly not present in AKSS I and II, Khrapovitskii again discerns between forms of "exclusively individualistic or personal love" *(liubov' iskliuchatel'no lichnaia)* or a "self-lover" *(sebialiubets)* and "communal or universal" charity *(liubov' vselennaia)* based on the exhortation from Matthew 25:44-45. With it, he warns against certain current "sectarian streams" of personal and individualistic interpretations: "We are to love Christ and to live only for Him, yet not [for] such a Christ that knows only you, and you Him, not [for] such a one that is only your bridegroom, but [also] the bridegroom of the Church. We are to love Christ in His body [in flesh] *(liubit' Christa vo ploti),* yet not solely in the glorified one, but in the one about which the apostle says: *For just as the body is one and has many members, and all the members of the body, though many, are one body, so it is with Christ* (1 Cor. 12:12, 21)." With specificity to Orthodoxy: "The Orthodox love of Christ is a love of constant existential self-denial, benevolence, and humility." Cf. *Molitva russkoi dushi,* pp. 66-68.

186. Cf. AKSS II, p. 470.

187. For spiritual discernment, see *O Sviatom Dukhe: Uchenie Tserkvi o Sviatom*

though the issue in question is the discernment of a priestly and/or monastic vocation of an individual based "on his feeling to be called," or "on the love for the vocation" (or, on the contrary, the lack of it), the decisive aspect for Khrapovitskii is in being a good and faithful pastor.[188] Thus, often what is being perceived as "the voice of God in the heart[189] . . . appears to us mostly, if not always, as nothing but a voice of self-delusion *(samoobol'shchenie)*." To avoid this and grant the genuineness of the call, the candidate must be one presented by the church, because the human "self-love" can take on different, "blatant or subtle" appearances.[190] The degree of love needed for a vocation can be discerned for Khrapovitskii by a quote from "a less-known part," Simeon the New Theologian:

> [It is a person who] possesses such a love for God that by merely hearing Christ's name to be mentioned, he gets ignited by love and sheds tears crying for his neighbor as well, and considers the trespasses of others as

---

Dukhe (On the Holy Spirit: Teaching of the Church on the Holy Spirit). Cf. AKSS I, pp. 686-706. Especially on pages 698-705, Khrapovitskii performs a fine discernment based on aspects of love, "which is the *totality of perfection* (cf. Col. 3:14), and the Spirit of God." He states that "the love of self" in the sense of self-centered egoism is the "main enemy of our salvation" and becomes especially dangerous when united with "delights" *(prelest')* or "self-delusion" *(samoobol'shchenie).*

188. Cf. AKSS I, pp. 63-65. There is a profound spiritual reflection on faithfulness and a "pastoral conscience," where also Christ's life, especially its conclusion, is defined as a "sacrifice" (cf. Phil. 2:17 and 2 Tim. 4:6), which is being quoted as an example of the "pastoral conscience," i.e., responsibility, realized through self-denial modeled on Christ's sacrifice for the benefit of "the [new] spiritual family." Cf. *Ispoved' pastyria pred krestom Khristovym (The Confession of a Pastor in Front of Christ's Cross),* AKSS I, pp. 174-77. In conclusion: "We shall weep, fathers and brothers, over the neglect of our pastoral service, so that through our repentance we would draw nearer to Christ, resurrect Him [in our] heart, and with it obtain a new pastoral unction: *Simon, son of John, do you love me? . . . Feed my sheep* (John 21:17)." It is noteworthy to remark that from the threefold question on Peter's love of Jesus, Khrapovitskii chooses the last question as if to indicate the definitiveness of this bond. Cf. AKSS I, pp. 177-78, 337. When discussing homiletics, Khrapovitskii brings up an example of love for Christ by "abandoning sin and taking up good habits in the name of a personal love for Him." Cf. AKSS I, p. 188.

189. Here the bad example is provided once more by the Catholics.

190. The view, however, that "self-appraisal or evaluation, [i.e.,] the way the candidate for priesthood feels about it, shall possess no importance at all" is even for that epoch a bit far stretched. Cf. AKSS I, pp. 65-66. A very nice and realistic criterion we find towards the end borrowed from St. John Chrysostom's work on priesthood: "There are people who can remain indifferent when [they] pass by the beauties of nature, yet not so when encountering human distress and vice." AKSS I, p. 68.

> his own . . . knows the infirmity [or frailty] of the human nature, sets his hopes upon the [divine] grace and its strengthening of [the human nature] . . . renounces any human design and would willingly and gladly lay down his very soul [or life] for the sake of a single commandment of God and the love of his neighbor.[191]

These qualities are needed in order to "establish love and truth in the candidates' proper souls and the hearts of the people" of the entire nation. Whoever "senses such a desire" should not doubt the authenticity of his vocation.[192] Yet, clearly, charity and love of a kenotic degree is required in order to be a good steward of the Church's sacraments and for the sanctification of its members.

"Not the one who prays to God is Christ's follower, but the one who loves his neighbor. All that makes up Christianity consists in the love of one's neighbor." This was one of the concurrent ideas that Khrapovitskii vehemently disagreed with as a pastor, questioning from "which edition of the Gospel had our humanists subtracted such [an] aphorism."[193] In correction, he quotes the double law on love (Matt. 22:37-40), which requests first a full devotion and adherence to God and thus forms the model for the second one to one's neighbor. Therefore, "the love for God, as a living, us-hearing Creator and Savior is the principal content *(soderzhanie)* of a Christian's life. . . . [This love] manifests itself first of all in prayer. . . . The one who loves God cannot live without prayer." Prayer is not an end in itself, but a stream of communication (or, if you like, communion); it is also the best conceivable support in the spiritual struggle for those "loving God" as well as those "who wish to love Him." The tradition of the holy Fathers, whose customs the church approved and handed down, is to be of inspiration and encouragement for our spiritual journey.[194]

4.6. On Love of One's Neighbor[195]

A touching testimony of *kenotic* and *agapic* love can be found in a brief Maundy Thursday sermon from 1897, which carries the epigraph: *I have ear-*

191. Trans. from Russian (here indicated as "word XII, izd. 1869 g."). Ibid. The original text is in *Symeon Neotheologus Catecheses* 1-34, Oration 18, v. 285-90.

192. Cf. AKSS I, pp. 68-69.

193. "Iz pastyrskikh besed (From Pastoral Talks)," in *Molitva russkoi dushi*, p. 215.

194. Cf. *Molitva russkoi dushi*, p. 216.

195. *Slovo v Velikii Chetverg o liubvi k blizhnim.* AKSS II, pp. 564-67.

nestly desired to eat this Passover with you before I suffer (Luke 22:15). Christ's love for His disciples went to the ultimate (John 13:1). The fourth liturgical day of Holy Week is a day of remembrance, albeit not joyous, yet a consoling one: "Not sorrow but a quiet, reconciling hope and humble gratitude are taking root in our hearts *(vseliaiutsia):* in the awareness of our own weakness we bow down *(prekloniaemsia)* in front of the greatness of Christ's love," that despite the horrendous events of those days and hours could still "in all divine beauty [and] fatherly tenderness, effuse onto the disciples of Christ. This is the exultant, triumphant, solemn love *(torzhestvuiushchaia liubov')* which is why the Church still possesses joy in [the] days of sorrow."[196] While the disciples are frightened of what is happening, the Lord "prepares a festive dinner [and] washes their feet, like the lowest of all slaves."[197] Among His last words are "friends" and the request to "love each other," inviting them into a communion just as He is in communion with the Father in the Trinity.

As an example in an extreme situation, this "holy, Divine, Christ's love . . . flares up with a primordial flame of holy zeal for the sanctification of His disciples and proclaims them the holy Sacrament of Eucharist, teaches them meek, mutual love, hope in God, the endurance of distress, and the consolation from the Holy Spirit."[198] God's embrace of love in Christ goes beyond the apostles, thereby including all of us.[199] Thus, Khrapovitskii repeats again and again the obligation to "love one another" (John 13:34); for seeing such a love from God's side, "which conscience, let it be even the most wretched one, can liberate itself from such a debt of love?"[200] Christ, in His "all-forgiving love [and] by his self-abandonment for all times, condemned all sin, each [instance of] self-love or selfishness *(sebialiubie).*" There is no other way but the one Christ demonstrated to us, to love one another: "He, Whom the two-faced Pilate could not acquit in front of His enemies, took away all justification from our two-faced heart, in case it coveted to liberate itself from the boundaries of love and of self-crucifixion."[201] *And I, when I am lifted up from the earth, will draw all people to myself* (John 12:32).[202]

Khrapovitskii concludes with Romans 8:38-39, assuring his faithful

196. Cf. AKSS II, p. 564.

197. Cf. AKSS II, pp. 564-65.

198. Cf. AKSS II, p. 565.

199. At one point Khrapovitskii expressly indicates the disciples with a masculine and a feminine gender, so as to abolish any possible segregation or classification.

200. Cf. AKSS II, p. 565.

201. AKSS II, p. 566.

202. Cf. AKSS II, pp. 566-67.

that nothing can separate us from the love of God that was revealed and given to us once and for all in Christ.[203]

Conclusion

Metropolitan Antonii's reasoning shows a well-versed and applied biblical knowledge, a pastoral, moral, and spiritual discernment — since taken for granted — measured by love and charity. He also proves that pastoral work, apart from being essential to the goal of applied theology (for if not fulfilling a soteriological mission in the final instance, what purpose does it serve?), can be exercised professionally without dreariness, and is deeply anthropological for the human need of sanctification, i.e., spiritual enhancement, piously immersed in a prayer-life and thus opened to the Divine. Grounded in Christ and centered in His Church, His teaching and very life-example of self-sacrifice out of love and charity are the compass for any spiritual discernment. In front of such divine generosity, who can elude the debt of love? For as a current intercessory prayer says, "Let us be mindful of loving our neighbor, for first, it is he who becomes alienated from our love, and then the next to follow is God."

5. Sergii Stragorodskii: *Loving God as Love — Joy from the Divine Love*

5.1. Biography

Ivan Nikolaevich (1867-1944), best known as Metropolitan and later Patriarch Sergii Stragorodskii, was born into a priestly family and grew up within the walls of the monastery where his family lived. After completing his studies in 1890 at the St. Petersburg Theological Academy and where he subsequently taught NT exegesis, Stragorodskii became its inspector in 1899 and a year later its rector. After becoming a hieromonakh he spent three years in missionary work in Japan. In 1895, he defended his master's thesis, which was titled *Pravoslavnoe uchenie o spasenii (The Orthodox Doctrine on Salvation)* and published the same year, leading to his becoming one of the most prominent theologians of his time.[204] During his St. Petersburg period, Strago-

203. Cf. AKSS II, p. 567.

204. A comprehensive interpretation of biblical soteriology was seen among his greatest contributions.

rodskii was an active member of the religious-philosophical meetings organized by Merezhkovskii. In 1901, he was ordained bishop, in 1905 archbishop, and in 1911, became a member of the Holy Synod. In 1917 followed a new teaching assignment as well as participation in the last council; afterwards, Stragorodskii made great efforts in 1927 as the deputy of the Patriarch's locum tenens in conciliating the relationship between the church and the Soviet rulers. In 1934, as the Patriarch's locum tenens, he was in charge of the Russian Orthodox Church, and in 1943, a year before his death, he was elected Patriarch of Moscow and Russia.

Among his works are the pastoral and missionary letters, *Po Iaponii, Zapiski missionera (Around Japan: Notes of a Missionary)* and *Na dal'nom Vostoke: Pis'ma iaponskogo missionera (In the Far East: Letters of a Missionary of Japan)*; a comparison of the doctrine on salvation between Catholic, Protestant, and Orthodox churches in *Vopros o lichnom spasenii (The Question on Personal Salvation)* in 1895; an original pastoral writing, *Vechnaia zhizn' kak vysshee blago (Eternal Life as Highest Good)* from 1895; as well as *Zakon Bozhii, napisannyi v estestve cheloveka (The Divine Law Written Down in Human Nature)* in 1904. In his biography of Patriarch Sergii, M. I. Odintsov chose an epigraph from Stragorodskii's writing that speaks volumes: "To be a pastor means not to live one's proper life but that of the flock, to be ill with its illnesses, to carry its sicknesses with one sole goal: to serve its salvation, to die, so that it may live."[205]

5.2. The Orthodox Doctrine on Salvation[206]

The first text to be examined is *The Orthodox Doctrine: Teaching on Salvation*, which Patriarch Sergii Stragorodskii wrote in the late 1890s and it saw four

205. A brief yet moving biography (along with that of Patriarkh Tikhon) can be found in "Krestnyi put' Patriarkha Sergiia (The Way of the Cross of Patriarch Sergei)," in M. I. Odintsov, *Russkie patriarkhi XX veka* (Moskva: Izd. Rags, 1999), pp. 147-203. Additional documents and correspondence, pp. 204-317. *Aktovaia rech' MDA* on the life and works of S. Stragorodskii by V. Saboran, ZhMP *(Zhurnal Moskovskogo Patriarkhata)*, 11 (1973); G. Egorov, *Literaturnye trudy Patriarkha Sergiia*, ZhMP, 5, no. 7 (1954); *Patriarkh Sergii i ego dukhovnoe nasledstvo* (Moskva 1947); Arch. Feognost, *Pamiati vydaiushchegosia rus. bogoslova-ekzegeta*, ZhMP 10 (1960). As to his pastoral sensitivity, perhaps his staying behind and not abandoning Russia through the Bolshevik Revolution and into the Soviet era can be seen as a testament to his solidarity as a pastor with his people.

206. *Pravoslavnoe uchenie o spasenii: Opyt raskrytiia nravstvenno-subektivnoi storony spaseniia na osnovanii Sv. Pisaniia i tvorenii sviato-otecheskikh* (OS). The 2nd and 4th edi-

subsequent editions. As the book's subtitle suggests, it is a moral (-subjective) approach to the question of salvation based on an erudite, exegetic, and patristic foundation.[207] The vital question on "personal salvation" *(lichnoe spasenie)* that leads to this work regards the ancient quest for the "meaning of life": What should be one's life conduct in order to live a "true life," a question that appears to be the "alpha and omega of both the philosophical and religious life"? Unless it leads to life, any system of thought or religion remains fruitless;[208] therefore, to know God most assuredly provides a meaning for a human being when God first becomes for him "the solely Holy." And the measure of *knowing* God will reflect in the kind of relationship that reigns between one's self and his neighbor: *If anyone says, "I love God," and hates his brother, he is a liar;* and there is not truth in him (cf. 1 John 4:20). The *inner* and *outer*, invisible and visible, in relationships are just two faces of the same coin.[209] Stragorodskii returns repeatedly to this axiom of love in a sort of defense speech of the *divine life* that was transmitted in God's Word, as "not a mere metaphysical foundation but a direct prototype/model and source of human life."[210]

---

tions from 1898 and 1910 appear to be identical. We shall use the 2nd edition. There is a n.d. abridged edition of eighty pages with an extract, *V mesto predisloviia — Vopros o lichnom spasenii,* and the part on *Spasenie.* Furthermore, there is also an identical reprint of the 2nd edition (Moskva: Izd. "Prosvetitel'," 1991), including an article from *Bogoslovskii Vestnik,* ed. Moscow Theological Academy, July 1895, on the resonances to S. Stragorodskii's *Pravoslavnoe uchenie o spasenii.* OS, pp. 257-64.

207. Cf. *V mesto predislovia: Vopros o lichnom spasenii. Rech pred zashchitoi magisterskoi dissertatsii,* in *OS,* pp. 3-11.

208. This explains the epigraph of this book: *I am the vine; you are the branches* (John 15:5).

209. Cf. OS, pp. 3-4.

210. See 1 John 4:7-8 and John 1:4. Cf. OS, p. 6. For Stragorodskii the fundamental differences between the Catholic, Protestant, and Orthodox churches are to be found less in their teachings and rather in their concept of "life and personal salvation," meaning of life, and the concept of "higher good." He compares the difference between "orthodoxy and heterodoxy" *(pravoslavie i inoslavie)* and exemplifies them as self-love of the old human being that lives following the world's customs and that of the "self-denying love" *(samootverzhennaia liubov'),* a life of the renewed human being following Christ: two incompatible worldviews. Stragorodskii builds his case on a personal-moral view of God and how to relate to Him as opposed to the impersonal view of God in the West, which is "locked into His absoluteness," and from the theological point of view of salvation as seen from the "aspect of *satisfaction*" is a juridical and formal approach. Stragorodskii reverses the case: God shows us that "nobody can and shall live for himself," which is His will. That way the foundation of each personal life is "not self-love anymore but 'the love of truth' (2 Thess.

"We believe that we are being saved only through Jesus Christ" are the initial words and line of argumentation based on Stragorodskii's exegesis and patristic research. Yet he goes on to say that we are still called to act with good deeds and so to cooperate with God, for only "those who take efforts" can reach the kingdom of heaven (Matt. 11:12) and as we receive good, so we are called to share it (Eph. 6:8). Thus, *good* is not just a fruit of salvation but also one of its direct causes and an access to "the eternal kingdom of Our Lord and Savior Jesus Christ (2 Peter 1:11)" that consists in "an active akolouthia of Christ (Col. 3:1-14)." For "our earthly life is the act of sowing, and the one beyond the grave is that of a harvest (Gal. 6:7-10)," which is one of the other reasons for doing good: in order to receive our reward from God in the end by becoming similar to him as opposed to an egoist or self-lover living only for his proper "me" and "in his soul being God's enemy (Rom. 8:7; John 8:44)." Doing good is, in a way, a condition of salvation, better yet a cooperation in it.[211] "God's just and all-encompassing, unconditional love" is present to all, the righteous and sinners, all who want to be inspired by it and grow in likeness to it (Matt. 5:36-47; 1 John 4:10; Rom. 5:8).[212] The essence of the Christian life is in love, which is "the fulfillment of the law": *Love does no wrong to a neighbor; therefore, love is the fulfilling of the law* (Rom. 13:10). Yet true love has gone and still goes beyond merely fulfilling the law. It is more than just non-wrongdoing, it is actively desiring what is best for the other and doing good, placing Christ in the center of our life instead of our own "I."[213] To know God, to love and serve Him, as well as our neighbor, is one unifying notion occurring in and through Christ, exempli-

---

2:10)." Guided by such maxims the relationship with God and neighbor, in every human life, is imbedded in love and not self-love anymore. Thus, salvation is inseparably linked to one's "worldview" *(zhizneponimanie)* and moral life-conduct on earth. Cf. OS, 8-10. His general conclusion is that "the true life of a human being is . . . in relationship with God," and participation in this life is possible only by becoming alike to God, which again can occur only if God comes to a soul that welcomes him and believes in Jesus Christ. Cf. OS, p. 11. In *Vvedenie (Introduction),* Stragorodskii thoroughly analyzes the current approaches and their past development, a legal and scholastic approach of *jus* (law) of fear, merits, and *Gerechtfertigung* versus a "spiritual approach" built on a personal relationship and *love* of God in Jesus Christ, as evident in the Scriptures (when interpreted in context) and in the Church Fathers. The latter one is what according to Stragorodskii corresponds to the Orthodox view. Cf. OS, pp. 12-55.

211. Cf. OS, pp. 56-58. Stragorodskii examines the Scripture and the *Predanie* (Church Tradition) and the Fathers in this regard. Cf. OS, pp. 60-112.

212. Cf. OS, pp. 79-81.

213. Cf. OS, pp. 81-85. "Voluptuousness *(slastoliubie)* is the root of self-love." OS, p. 91.

fied in his relationship to the Father.[214] "The peak of Christian perfection" is in a "self-forgetting love," for only a person "permeated with such love will become similar to God and acquire that knowledge of God, in which consists the essence of eternal life."[215] Stragorodskii is profound and very pragmatic at the same time. For him, the blessing of "Communion-with-God" *(Bogoobshchenie)* does not consist in pleasure *(v uslazhdenii)* but rather in holiness, which requires self-denial *(samootrechenie)* in the name of the unconditional good that brings about a true knowledge of God. "And so the primordial image of sanctity is incarnating in God, and [it] is love; that self-denial in the name of good, eventually, is granted *(razreshaetsia)* into an unselfish delight in the presence of God, compelling the human being to live only for God and to see God alone, forgetting everything else. God is love, and Christianity, which is an 'imitation *(podrazhanie)* of the Divine nature,'[216] also places its highest good into love."[217]

5.3. *Retribution*

Based on the above conclusion, Stragorodskii considers "the highest good and virtue as identical notions. The essence of eternal life consists in moral perfection, in [the] real experiencing of the Divine good in one's self."[218] Eternal life, however, does not mean "to move from one sphere of being into another, but to acquire a distinguished spiritual disposition. That way, eternal life is not only being received but gradually grows in the human being. Therefore, one can pray to God: 'May my heart be a good soil for Thee, receiving [into itself] the good seed, and may Thy divine grace bedew me with the dew of eternal life.'"[219] Christians already in this earthly life are to begin their eternal life, "to pre-begin their life of blessedness" that will reach its perfection,

214. The second chapter on "Vechnaia zhizn' (Eternal life)" is in its initial pages identical with the initial pages of *Vechnaia zhizn' kak vysshee blago,* yet here it possesses a more scientific character in elaboration, especially the patristic quotations. Cf. OS, pp. 94-111.

215. Cf. OS, pp. 109-10. He adds, quoting St. Gregory Nazianzen: "Who loved, will be loved; and who is loved, in him abides God. And in whom God abides, cannot be unworthy of the light; and the first benefit of the light is to get acquainted with the very light. Thus love brings about knowledge." OS, p. 110.

216. Quoting St. Gregory of Nyssa (*De profess. Christ.,* Migne. t. XLVI, 224).

217. Cf. OS, p. 111.

218. In the Orthodox dogma, it is a continuation of terrestrial life, founded in faith in Jesus Christ. Cf. OS, pp. 112-13.

219. Quoting Ephraim the Syrian (Sl. 127 on repentance, vol. V, 105). Cf. OS, p. 114.

when their love will be perfected, namely after they renounce every self-love, ergo egoism, evil, and sin.[220] In the OT we find expressions such as the Lord "loves to show kindness" *(liubit' milovat')* (Mic. 7:18), and "He does not like to punish," but does all in order to bring the human being back to the right path of relationship and salvation through the grace of baptism granted to all in the Holy Spirit.[221] Stragorodskii takes all his time and effort to underline the difference between a *selfish,* not life-giving love, and that of God's saving love which brings the *highest good,* and he does so with great eloquence and scholarship. This is the message of Christianity: "The Lord is love, and He forgives the human being everything, if he only repents and accepts the gift that is being offered to him." The other insight of his is that "the truth and love of God are never in confrontation,"[222] an idea that reappears in various forms when treating the subject of salvation and, especially, that of faith. Salvation is God's love, an offering based on repentance mediated through Christ: a notion away from egoism towards communion with God.[223] God's love and grace are "all-forgiving," and thus this relationship can never consist in fear.[224] Faith[225] is the "only criterion of salvation," yet it is understood as being conditioned on the love of and for God,[226] revealed to us through Christ: "*The love of God we know is that He has laid down His life for us* (1 John 3:16). Thus, the love of God can dwell only in one who believes that Jesus, who suffered and was crucified, is truly the Son of God. And when one believes that Christ truly suffered for us, can any trace of fear before God and of alienation from Him remain in that person?"[227]

5.4. Eternal Life as Highest Good[228]

In this booklet Stragorodskii examines *eternal life* from a soteriological point of view as the highest salvific good in terms of four different aspects:

220. Cf. OS, pp. 116-20.

221. Cf. OS, pp. 121-22, 133.

222. Cf. OS, pp. 141-45.

223. Cf. OS, pp. 163, 187.

224. "The consciousness of past sins only teaches the human being to understand grace and the all-forgiving love of God, and does not awaken in him horror of God's wrath." Cf. OS, p. 167.

225. Also explicitly treated in *Spasenie i vera po pravoslavnomu ucheniu* (Moskva, 1913).

226. Cf. OS, pp. 228-33, 239.

227. Cf. OS, pp. 229, 239.

228. *Vechnaia zhizn' kak vysshee blago.*

(1) its traits, (2) its virtue and beatitude, (3) as the love of God and neighbor, and (4) in relationship to present, earthly life.[229] "Eternal life is an experiential knowing of God, a sensation [or perception], experiencing the Divine life in one's self," a reflection based on the Savior's words in John 17:3.[230] It is accomplished when a person achieves Bogo*podobie* (God-*likeness*), in Bogo*obshchenie* (Communion-with-God).[231] Eternal life is definitely not a static condition but a dynamic happening, a progress: "Eternal life is constantly evolving." The very theme of love, even though it may not be omnipresent, enjoys a central place in Stragorodskii's reflection, which he treats in a concise yet thorough way and always with exegetic and patristic input.

Based on a quotation from St. Isaac the Syrian on what love is and how it manifests itself in a person, that is to say love that transforms the *interior* and *exterior* of a person as well as his relationships,[232] Stragorodskii underscores: "It is not a cold accounting and acknowledging of debts, but [much rather] the soul's aspiration towards the unity with God, an aspiration that gushes from [the soul's] very essence and is strengthened by the awareness of the reciprocated yet undeserved love of God."[233] The trait of "true love" in God's love and communion is often compared to that of a mother's love for her child and can be encountered in the Scriptures and in the Church Fathers. Therefore, the "power of bodily love" *(sila liubvi plotskoi)* should serve as an example and inspiration of striving of "a person in love who desires so much the beloved one that he constantly contemplates the image of the other in his soul," as expressed in the Song of Songs for instance.[234] "The love for God is meant to reach the intensity of bodily love. It is meant to be of such yearning for God, of such a self-forgetfulness *(samozabvenie)*, or *'rapture of soul,'* as Ioann Lestvichnik described it." Accordingly, the nature and essence of *eternal life* is in the union with God, in placing our "highest good" into God and not into ourselves, yet not out of some selfish reason, as for instance "personal happiness," but for the mere "blessed union with God."[235] The "blessedness of love" makes sense solely in the union with God: "love alone" and not deeds of love, as St. Paul points

229. Arkhiepiskop Sergii, *Vechnaia zhizn' kak vysshee blago* (Moskva: Pechatnia A. I. Snegirevoi, 1917), pp. 22-33 (VZVB).

230. VZVB, p. 4.

231. Cf. VZVB, pp. 6-7.

232. Slovo, p. 73-e.

233. Cf. VZVB, p. 23.

234. Stragorodskii quotes Sr. Ioann Lestvichnik. Cf. VZVB, p. 23.

235. Cf. VZVB, p. 24.

out the danger of a possible misunderstanding.[236] What Stragorodskii is trying to transmit is that the deeds and actions of love, including *self-sacrifice* and *self-denial,* cannot be performed by compulsion and force, just as "the divine love cannot be learned externally," as the great hesychast St. Basil put it.[237] "Therefore, in order to be the foundation and essence of eternal life, the love of God must not be a commandment but a *'rapture of the soul';* it has to be an inevitable, nonmodifiable aspiration, one that directs the entire human being towards God, with delight *(vostorgom)* in His presence leading up to self-forgetfulness."[238]

5.5. Moral Progress

Love, just as with *eternal life,* aspiring to "the ideal . . . is endlessly perfecting itself [in the process of]" *(bezkonechno usovershaetsia),* and this is also true of its moral aspect by cultivating an attitude or virtue. Once a person steps on the path of *true love,* he gradually sacrifices all for this love in order to make it "as similar to the Divine Love as possible, for such love never ends (1 Cor. 13:8)." And the closer one moves to this love, the more such a person will be attracted by it, and the "more it will appear worthy of his love." This gradation has no end "until eternity," yet not as a source of eternal frustration but as a progression of "unending improvement" in which the person finds "his eternal blessedness." Stragorodskii leaves the door open, so to say, for an increment *of* and *in* love, which is fair enough, as it is a love of the "Infinite" and, therefore, cannot become less than equally infinite.[239] Again, the fundamental condition remains that it is not a self-oriented but a self-sacrificing love. Every imperfection discovered on the path of this "love-ideal" is but a further spur to get even closer to the source and an opening for a yet deeper and happier relationship. *Joy* is one of the sure signs that it is the Divine love we are encountering,[240] joy in the relationship, the re-

236. *If I give away all I have, and if I deliver up my body to be burned, but have not love, I gain nothing* (1 Cor. 13:3).

237. Cf. VZVB, p. 25. "The work of love, including even self-scarification, can, naturally, be forced, be realized with suffering and violence towards one's self; yet with force nobody can be made to love, including your very self." As St. Basil the Great says, "It is impossible to acquire love by learning God's love from outside [i.e., as imposed]."

238. VZVB, p. 25.

239. "To love him into infinity." VZVB, p. 26.

240. In this point, Stragorodskii is leaning on the following: "The love of God, says

gained union with God — the more one has of it, the more one desires to receive.[241]

5.6. The Most Profound Foundation of Self-Sacrificing Love: God as Triune Love

"God inside of His Being is Love," not only because He has loved the human being and His creation, but first and foremost because "He loves Himself." Yet since God is a Trinity, this love can by no means be an egotistic love as "in the systems of rigid monotheism" or deism. The self-sufficiency of deism is excluded from this *Love,* which is "a real, living reciprocal relationship of Three Persons, united since eternity," sharing even the will, glory, and might of the other two. This implies that *self-sacrifice* and *self-denial of individuality* for the advantage of the other two is intrinsic to the Being of the triune God.[242] In the fundamentality of the Trinity is contained the mystery of God's essence: "It is out of this reason that God's being is called more than anything else the God of *peace,* namely of unanimity in diversity, of unity in multiplicity. . . . Incomprehensible is the Love in God without the Trinity and [the] Trinity without love. God is Love because He is Triune."[243] In Stragorodskii we have encountered this latter affirmation for the first time in our research.

5.7. The Love of Neighbor

In order to be God-like in love, meaning *divine,* the human being has to express his love in self-sacrifice towards "finite creations" just like himself. Even more, the other has to become part of his (of the first-loving) very self as an intermediate way to love God who remains invisible (1 John 4:12). The *kenotic* aspect of self-sacrifice is at the very foundation of love, be it a love of

---

St. Tikhon Zadonskii, without joy cannot exist. And as many times as one perceives in his heart the sweetness of God's love, as many times he is rejoicing at God. For love as sweet virtue, without joy cannot make itself felt" (vol. 5, p. 235). VZVB, p. 27.

241. Cf. VZVB, p. 27.

242. Cf. VZVB, pp. 28-29.

243. VZVB, p. 29. Here Stragorodskii leans on the teaching of St. Gregory Nazianzen who says that God has to be triune in order to share love; one or two would be scanty. Cf. VZVB, p. 29.

God or one's neighbor. Yet only a love expressed in charity for one's neighbor gives an immediate feedback and, therefore, the possibility of correction.[244] For in relating to God, loving and serving Him, we do not act as mere separate entities, but are helping each other in this aspiration and thus giving a possibility for charity to others. Only by actively loving our neighbors can we progress on the path of and to the Divine Love, within a *team-work,* so to say.[245] In fact, God's invitation to love Him extends to all of us as a community, and community *is* a reflection of the heavenly realm, a God-like state, a fellowship and communion with God.[246] One of the traits of the self-sacrificing and self-renouncing love is that, by renouncing egoism, it creates community. And where there are two or three in my name. . . .[247]

Stragorodskii reveals the principle of Divine love: that the more one "loves *God as Love,*" and because He is love, i.e., by the same divine, selfless, unselfish, disinterested love as God, the more one becomes similar to the Trinity.[248] What he is describing briefly yet meticulously is the process of divinization, though he never uses the very term. It is a simple catechetical text, probably for the everyday faithful, therefore composed in a simple language, which also makes it so transparent and enjoyable.[249] Great truths are simple in their core: "Love like God, and you will be like God." Remain faithful to your effort, and it will transform you into what you are meant to be: heir of His kingdom.[250] The highest example and proof of this is Christ Himself and His self-sacrificial love that precedes everything and everybody. By imitating the Divine ideal how to love each other and God, we discover in loving *God as Love* our "final blessedness."[251]

244. Cf. VZVB, p. 30.

245. Cf. VZVB, p. 31. Needless to say that the expression of *team-work* is an anachronism introduced by us, yet as a concept of sharing or common research was well known to many of the Russian intellectuals.

246. Cf. VZVB, pp. 31-32.

247. *For where two or three are gathered in my name, there am I among them* (Matt. 18:20).

248. His argumentation is based on 1 John 4:7-8: *Beloved, let us love one another, for love is from God, and whoever loves has been born of God and knows God. Anyone who does not love does not know God, because God is love.*

249. Often no sources indicated.

250. Romans 8:15.

251. Cf. VZVB, p. 33.

Conclusion

To Stragorodskii, indisputable merits are deserved for showing to the Orthodox faithful of his time that salvation and a Christian relationship with God cannot be founded in a juridical-formal attitude, nor in justification by faith alone, but both: faith and deed persuaded by the love of God and for one's neighbor. Christ has revealed the primordial pattern of this relationship in the Holy Trinity, the infinity of this merciful love that is an invitation to become *God-like* through *God-fellowship* and thus regain com-*union* with God. Stragorodskii's pastoral sensitivity assured that the reader perceives the *process* and *progress* in this relationship, a constant growing and evolving *of* and *in* love, thus of comprehension of *eternal life,* which is but a continuation of our earthly life. His argumentation is dense and methodologically well founded, although it sometimes obfuscates his own opinion and inhibits original ideas in the massive lineup of patristic and scriptural quotations. Nonetheless, perhaps it is most striking to see that a true pastor never forgets his primary call, that of care for the salvation of his flock. And the image of salvation presented by Stragorodskii's writing is one imbedded in God's caring and merciful love in the image and example of Jesus Christ, already available in the present life. To love in *God as Love* is one of his few, yet crucially original ideas that overlap in soteriology, epistemology, ecclesiology, and many more fields of theology. Namely, it presents an image of God as the merciful Father of Jesus Christ to those who stray, and God's justice to fearful human beings — precisely *God as Love.*

VI. The Mystical-Wisdom Stream of Theology

1. Pavel Alexandrovich Florenskii: *Knowledge Becomes Love*

1.1. Biography

In P. A. Florenskii (1882-1934), we encounter not only a married priest and father of five, but a multifaceted genius: an expert in the sciences, a key person in the electrification of Russia in the early twentieth century, an inventor of a noncoagulating machine oil, a mathematician and physicist, a linguist, man of letters, philosopher and theologian of highly refined insights, and overall, a tenuously creative spirit, and a martyr for his faith and his church.

Florenskii was born on January 9, 1882 in Evlach, Azerbaijan, and grew into a sensitive child who experienced moments of mystical intuition for nature and science that would accompany him throughout his life. He attended secondary school in Tiflis (Tbilisi), Georgia, where he immediately showed extraordinary mathematical skills. In 1900, he commenced his studies in physics and mathematics at Moscow University while simultaneously studying philosophy at the philosophical faculty. He attended the lectures of N. V. Bugaev, S. N. Trubetskii, and L. M. Lopantin, the noted mathematician, philosopher, and psychologist, respectively. Despite his love for the exact sciences, and maintaining a lifelong fascination for mathematics, upon graduation, his attention turned more to theology and philosophy. In 1904, he decided to enter the Theological Academy in Moscow, and, after his master's exam in 1908, he was appointed the chair of history of philosophy, where he also lectured. Shortly thereafter he married A. M. Giacintova and was ordained priest. In 1914 he published his dissertation and masterpiece titled *Stolp i utverzhdenie istiny: Opyt Pravoslavnoi teoditsei (The Pillar and Ground of Truth: An Essay in*

Orthodox Theodicy [in Twelve Letters]),[1] which had a unique influence on modern Russian theological thought for its rich content and absolute novelty of style. Some of the significant interest that it attracted for its "bold statements" was not uncritical.[2] In the prerevolutionary times, he published diverse studies in *Bogoslovskii vsetnik (Theological Herald),* for instance *Obshchechelovecheskie Korni idealizma (The Universally Human Roots of Idealism)* or *Smysl idealizma (The Meaning of Idealism).* During the Bolshevik Revolution of 1917 and the years following Florenskii decided to remain in Russia where he continued to be engaged in pastoral and scientific work. Gradually his person and academic activity were forced to vanish from public life. Considered to be a threat to the Soviet regime, in 1928 he was arrested and transferred to Nizhnii Novgorod where he actuated research on radioactivity and eventually was released from prison due to his scientific competence. Further scientific nominations followed,[3] until he was arrested a second time in 1933 and condemned to ten years of forced labor in Skovorodino (Amur). The second incarceration was due to the widely held notion that clerical status was incompatible with service to the Soviet government.[4] In 1934, Florenskii was transferred to the Solovki camp (an island in the White Sea) where he worked on obtaining iodine from the agar-agar sea algae. On December 8 of the same year, he was executed by a firing squad with five hundred other inmates in the Leningrad area. His final resting place remains unknown. Although Florenskii was rehabili-

1. This was preceded with an earlier version from which the later-supplied five chapters were still missing and was titled *The Pillar and Ground of Truth: An Essay in Orthodox Theodicy* (1908). The entire work "grew out of his candidate thesis *On Religious Truth* (1908) and his master's dissertation *On Spiritual Truth* (1912)." Cf. F. F. Gustafson, "Introduction," in P. Florensky, *The Pillar and Ground of the Truth: An Essay in Orthodox Theodicy in Twelve Letters,* trans. B. Jakim, p. x (PGT). Unless there is some adaptation in the text (indicated), we shall consult B. Jakim's translation for quotations while using the original in the Russian edition: P. Florenskii, *Stolp i utverzhdenie istiny. Opyt Pravoslavnoi teoditsei* (Moskva: "Izd. ACT," 2002) (SUI). The title refers to the church and is taken from 1 Tim. 3:15.

2. "The book was also congenial to the romantic and mystical tendencies in Russian society. . . . Even its external appearance — the unusual type-face, vignettes, sketches, and numerous unexpected 'lyrical' digressions, as well as the 'oppressive scholarship' of its innumerable footnotes — was all to the taste of the period. The author's pretentiousness in expounding his *own* ideas as firm ecclesiastical truth repelled some readers, although it attracted others. In any case, the book was an immense success." Cf. V. V. Zenkovsky, *A History of Russian Philosophy I* (London: Routledge & Kegan Paul, 1953), p. 876.

3. He was appointed as the deputy director of the electro-technical institute K. A. Krug for the research into electro-conductive and isolating materials.

4. "Throughout this period [of the Bolshevik regime] he remained a priest and appeared at government offices in his cassock." Gustafson, "Introduction," in PGT, p. xi.

tated in 1958 and 1959 successively by the Moscow and Archangel tribunals, and his theological and philosophical works were published from the 1970s on in the Soviet Union and Russia today, there are still numerous unedited manuscripts awaiting publication.[5]

Among his numerous works are *Smysl idealizma* (*The Meaning of Idealism* [1915]), *Pervye shagi filosofii: Iz lektsii po istorii filosofii* (*First Steps of Philosophy: From Lectures on the History of Philosophy* [1917]), *Zakon illiuzii* (*The Law of Illusion* [1971]), *Iconostas* (*Iconostasis* [1972]), *Ekkleziologicheskie meterialy* (*Ecclesiological Materials* [1974]), *U vodorazdelov mysli* (*At the Watersheds of Thought* [1990]), and *Detiam moim* (*To My Children* [1992]). A great number of technical articles appeared while he served as editor of the *Soviet Technical Encyclopedia,* along with further liturgical works, historical essays, and linguistic researches.

1.2. The Pillar and Ground of Truth

Because this work represents Florenskii's fundamental research on the concept of love, it shall be in the focus of our attention. That this work is a composition of two previous writings and of material jotted down in different moods and occasions[6] poses both a help and a challenge. It is also an artistic creation rich in poetry and lyrics. In addition, Florenskii's mathematical genius comes to light in the oeuvre through all the arithmetical equations from logic, drawings, tables, and sketches. The text reveals a strong bent toward the symbolic movement of which Florenskii himself was a member. Thus, the twelve letters can be grouped into three spheres of interest or, ac-

5. There are also numerous publications on P. A. Florenskii and his broad field of work; therefore we shall indicate only some with bibliographical notes: A moving visual-text documentary from Igumen Andronik (Trubachev), *Obo mne ne pechal'tes' . . . Zhizneopisanie sviashchennika Pavla Florenskogo (Do not grieve for me . . . : Biography of the Priest Pavel Florenskii)* (Moskva: Izd. Sovet Russkoi Pravoslavnoi Tserkvi, 2007); a classic book on Florenskii by R. Slesinski, *Pavel Florensky: A Metaphysics of Love* (Crestwood, NY: St. Vladimir's Seminary Press, 1984), pp. 21-48; an outstanding monographic work on Florenskii and his guiding ideas: L. Zak, *Verità come ethos: La teodicea trinitaria di P. A. Florenskij* (Roma: Città Nuova, 1998); the anthology *P. A. Florenskii: Pro et Contra* (Sankt-Peterburg: Izd. Russkogo Khristianskogo gumanitarnogo instituta, 2001); a work with comprehensive bibliography: M. Zust, *À la recherche de la vérité vivante: L'expérience religieuse de Pavel A. Florensky, 1882-1937* (Roma: Lipa, 2002); *Abitando la Trinità: Per un rinnovamento dell'ontologia,* ed. P. Coda and L. Zak (Roma: Città Nuova, 1998), esp. pp. 5-27 and 123-33; P. Coda and A. Tapken, *La Trinità e il pensare: Figure, percorsi, prospettive* (Roma: Città Nuova, 1997).

6. Cf. SUI, p. 33.

cording to Gustafson, "controlling ideas" delineating the following structure: *epistemological* in letters two, three, and six; *relational* between human beings and between them and God based on love in letters four, eleven, and twelve; and, finally, *ontological* in letters five, nine, and ten.[7]

It is a gnoseological inquiry that Florenskii sets out upon — perhaps with no finalized definition yet — as if not sure where his search for the ultimate criterion of *Truth* in the first chapters would lead him. The epigraph over his work, a phrase borrowed from St. Gregory of Nyssa, however, speaks volumes: ἡ δὲ γνῶσις ἀγάπη γίνεται *(Knowledge becomes love)*,[8] and beneath the initial image of the book is a Latin inscription: *Finis amoris, ut duo unum fiant (The Scope of Love Is That [the] Two May Be [or Become] One).*[9]

1.2.1. *Ecclesiality*

"Living religious experience as the sole legitimate way to gain knowledge of the dogmas — that is how I would like to express the general theme of my book,"[10] for only a "purified heart" can experience the true realm of the Church's beatifying sanctity in her saints and, through their example, God.[11] These initial thoughts, along with an elated description of the transcendent realm of the Church, are directed to the reader and are setting the right mood and receptivity for the lecture: it is the "pure heart" that hears the "invitation." This realm of the Church Florenskii calls "ecclesiality" *(tserkovnost')*, "that is the name of the refuge where the heart's anxiety finds peace, where the pretensions of the rational mind are tamed, where great tranquility descends into our reason," meanwhile admitting that neither he nor anybody else can really define what *ecclesiality* truly means. Undoubtedly, this "resting peace and harboring security" is imaginable solely in a pragmatic

7. Cf. SUI, pp. xiv-xx. Of the remaining letters, *One* is an introduction directed at the reader, *Seven* is on sin and *Eight* on Gehenna. The twelve letters are directed to an unidentified person invoked under different names: *brother, friend, winged Friend, elder, Guardian* (cf. SUI, pp. 82, 317), and each of the letters carries a proper epigraph.

8. Cf. SUI. Florenskii dedicates his book to the Blessed Mother: "To the Most Fragrant and Most Pure Name of the Virgin and Mother." SUI.

9. We prefer our translation to the rendering "The Limit of Love: Two Are One" in PGT since the Latin uses a subjunctive introduced by *ut.* On the other hand, the latter rendering rhymes and thus is perhaps closer to the symbolic-artistic spirit of the author. Cf. PGT, p. 2.

10. SUI, p. 33.

11. "The ascetic saints of the Church are alive for the living and dead for the dead." Cf. SUI, pp. 33-34.

and profoundly lived-out spiritual life, a liturgical ecclesialism so treasured as proper to Orthodoxy.[12] Thus, understandably, the center of the Christian community's as well as the individual's life is (the life in) the Church. *Ecclesiality* is: ". . . a new life, a life in the Spirit. The criterion of the rightness of this life is *beauty.* Yes, there is a singular beauty of the spirit,[13] and she cannot be grasped by logical formulas; it is at the same time the only true path to the definition of what is orthodox and what is not orthodox." This divine beauty of ecclesiality is best reflected in the lives of the "spiritual elders, the *startsy,* masters of the 'art of arts' as the holy Fathers call asceticism. The *startsy* were adept at assessing the quality of spiritual life."[14]

From this starting point, Florenskii ventures into his discovery of *Truth* and its ontological realm, first in metaphysics and philosophy, with the full involvement of as many sciences as possible, including humanities, in the following chapters. We shall examine those that concern our subject most closely, proposing that it is Florenskii's inner methodical (re)search that leads him to the *answer of love* regarding the existential question of *what or who Truth is.*

1.2.2. Through Doubt to Certainty and Trinitarian Ontology[15]

The first direct notion of love is provided in the concluding phrase of the first letter. Florenskii humbly defines himself as a "pupil" vis-à-vis a teacher in his personal approach to the task. The unknown teacher he addresses ini-

12. In this context, the Church as "body of Christ" and "the fullness *(to plērōma)* of him who fills all in all" (Eph. 1:23) is also in juxtaposition "to the narrow coffin of logical definition." Cf. SUI, pp. 35 and esp. 36.

13. In place of ". . . a special beauty of the spirit." Cf. PGT, p. 8.

14. Cf. SUI, p. 36.

15. All of my following reflections on the ontology of the Trinity, the ontological and intrinsic dimension of love in the Trinity, as well as the epistemology of love have been inspired and decisively influenced by Prof. L'. Žák from the Pontifical Lateran University in Rome and his work *Verità come ethos: La teodicea trinitaria di P. A. Florenskij,* pp. 224-78, and esp. 267-70. One example for many: ". . . Il problema è che sia Leibniz che Spinoza privano l'amore della sua natura di valore oggettivo: sia nell'uno che nell'altro, cioè, l'amore non guida metafisicamente nessuno verso nessuna meta, non unisce realmente qualcuno a qualcun altro. . . . Ciò che decisamente manca a una tale concezione leibniziana e spinoziana dell'amore è la dimensione personalistica, relazionale: essa non è sufficientemente attenta al fatto che, da una parte, l'amore è possibile *solo* verso una persona, che esso può 'accadere' — come atto — solo (nel rapporto) tra le persone, e che, dall'altra, l'amore *introduce* le persone che si amano in una 'nuova realtà' *trans*-empirica. Tale attenzione, invece, è uno dei tratti fondamentali che caratterizzano il concetto dell'amore pensato, nel modo più radicale, alla luce della Rivelazione cristiana e, dunque, di una visione di Dio come Amore e Trinità. Ed è, difatti, in questa

tially with "my meek, my radiant friend," which once more allows the importance of personal religious experience to surface:[16] "And I, after all, am nothing more than a pupil who repeats after you the lessons of love."[17]

What follows in the second letter, aptly named *Doubt,* is a proper and systematic unfolding of gnoseology, imbedded in a critical reflection on the search for *Truth* with the capital "T." It includes reexamining the etymology of Truth, its definition of identity, accessibility, attributes, and above all, as we shall discover gradually, its proper ontology.[18] The principal analogy of a given fact or its "givenness," i.e., truth, in modern philosophy is the logical formula of A = A, the "law of identity,"[19] which transposed into a personal domain reads "I = I." This is based on "a judgment that is given directly [which] is the self-evidence of intuition." After examining the three kinds of

---

prospettiva che Florenskij spiega la sua concezione *ontologica* dell'amore . . . — siccome la Verità è la SS.ma Trinità — conoscere significa 'entrare realmente nelle viscere della Triunità divina'. Il che, allo stesso tempo, significa che la conoscenza di Dio-Trinità è possibile 'solo attraverso la *transustanziazione* dell'uomo, la sua divinizzazione', solo attraverso 'l'acquisto dell'amore quale sostanza divina'; chi non è con Dio — per essere *come* Dio — non conosce Dio" (pp. 269-70). Of equal importance in this process (including for the above-mentioned aspects in Bulgakov and Karsavin) served my research Prof. L'. Žák's earlier, excellent contributions and articles: "P. A. Florenskij: Progetto e testimonianza di una gnoseologia trinitaria," in Coda and Tapken, *La Trinità e il pensare,* pp. 193-225, esp. 219-27, as well as: "Verso una ontologia trinitaria," in P. Coda and L'. Žák, *Abitando la Trinità: Per un rinnovamento dell'ontologia* (Roma: Città Nuova, 1998), pp. 5-25; L'. Žák, "Kenosi di Cristo e mistero della Chiesa nella teologia di Pavel A. Florenskij," in *La Sapienza della Croce,* Anno XX, N. 4 and Anno XXI, N. 1 (Roma: Pamom-Città Nuova, 2004).

16. Which will become even more evident when he discusses Pilate's (religious) blindness and vain attempt to grasp the Truth while interrogating Jesus about the Truth: "The Living Answer stood before him, but Pilate did not see the Truth's truthfulness." And even if Jesus answered him, Pilate still "would have remained without an answer, for he would not have known how to recognize the Truth as truth, could not have been convinced of its genuineness. The knowledge that Pilate lacked, the knowledge that all of mankind lacks above all, is the knowledge of the conditions of certitude." Cf. SUI, p. 47.

17. Cf. SUI, pp. 37, 40. As we shall see later, Florenskii's arguments are virtually imbedded (or supported by numerous notes) in a wealth of patristic, scriptural quotations and analyses, all of which are in their respective original languages. Further philological comparisons and etymological analyses include equally modern European languages.

18. Florenskii mentions up front Solov'ev's definition of Truth: "The Truth, according to the philosopher [V. Solov'ev], is the 'all-one existent' *(sushchee vseedinoe)*"; however, in his notes Florenskii leaves no doubt that he intends to use it "only formally, emptying it of its interpretation." Yet more importantly he adds that his "entire work, in its antinomian spirit, opposes Solovyov's conciliatory philosophy." Cf. SUI, p. 41, and n. 4, pp. 468-69.

19. . . . *zakon tozhdestva,* SUI, p. 50.

self-evident *intuitions* that derive from the above analogy (namely, "sensuous-empirical, transcendental-rationalistic, and subconscious-mystical" or to put it concisely the self-evidence of *sensuous, intellectual,* and *mystical* experience), Florenskii comes to the conclusion that they all bear "one insufficiency in common: their naked, unjustified givenness."[20] Their *givenness* namely would in final effect exclude any spatial, chronological, or other kind of relationship: "The law A = A becomes a completely empty schema of self-affirmation, a schema that does not synthesize any real elements, anything that is worth connecting with the '=' sign. 'I = I' turns out to be nothing more than a cry of naked egotism: 'I'! For where there is no difference, there can be no connection. There is therefore only a blind force of stagnation and self-imprisonment, only egotism."[21] In the following lines it will become evident that since relationship is the basic ontological-building element in any given entity, A = A (or I = I) is not only lacking relationship, but is its own exclusion and therefore cannot be true:

> Outside of itself, *I* hates every [other] *I*, since for it this *I* is *not-I;* and hating, *I* strives to exclude this *I* from the sphere of being. And since the past *I* (*I* in the past) is also considered objectively, i.e., since it also appears as *not-I*, then it too is irreconcilably subject to exclusion. *I* cannot bear itself in time and negates itself in all ways in the past and future. Thus, since the naked "now" is pure zero of content, *I* hates the whole of its concrete content, i.e., the whole of its life. *I* turns out to be a dead desert of "here" and "now." But what then is governed by the formula "A is A"? Only a fiction (an atom, a monad, etc.), only a hypostatized abstraction of a moment and a point, which, in themselves, do not exist. Yes, the law of identity is an unlimited monarch. But its subjects do not object to its autocracy only because they are bloodless phantoms, without reality, because they are not persons but only rational shades of persons, i.e., things that do not exist. This is sheol. This is the kingdom of death.[22]

Subsequently, the *criterion*[23] of *self-evidence* provides no certainty under any of the above-mentioned three intuitions and therefore becomes a

20. . . . *golaia ikh dannost', ikh* neoprav-*dannost'.* Cf. SUI, pp. 47-49.

21. SUI, p. 51.

22. SUI, p. 51.

23. "The problem of the certitude of truth is reducible to the problem of finding a criterion. The entire demonstrative force of a system is focused, as it were, in the answer to this problem of finding a criterion." SUI, p. 48.

"radical condemnation of all philosophical dogmatic systems, not excluding that of Kant, for which sensuousness and reason with all its functions are simply givenness."[24] On the following pages, in a similar manner and with the premise that the "love of the Truth demands precisely truth and nothing else,"[25] Florenskii thoroughly examines "*mediate* judgment" in skepticism with its refraining or incapability of making a judgment, *epochē*,[26] originated from its "absolute doubt," a circle and result of nonending negations.[27] Nevertheless, this road "also leads to nothing"[28] and thus Florenskii undertakes, with the same scrutiny of an investigator, the adventure of *trust* and *hope,* since there is no certainty that reason (alone) would find the way to Truth: "If the Truth exists, it could be sought. Perhaps we could find it by taking some road at random and then it would perhaps announce itself as such, as the Truth." An answer to this venture could be the simple: "Why not?" As abstract as it may sound, for Florenskii *hope* with *no logical expression* becomes a method and way, hope as *"gift,* as *gratia quae gratis datur*" or as St. Seraphim of Sarov identified it, "a wise hope . . . if a man, out of love for God, does not overmuch concern himself with himself. . . ."[29] In this domain of *probabilism,* even though only as an experiment, Florenskii postulates three propositions: the absolute Truth exists; it is knowable; and it is given as a fact. In quintessence it means that "Truth is intuition" and that "Truth is discursion," which renders the final formula: "Truth Is Intuition-Discursion."[30] *Revelation,* a new yet not

24. Cf. SUI, p. 52.

25. SUI, p. 56.

26. "Epochē or the state of refraining from all statement is the last word of skepticism." SUI, p. 56.

27. Cf. SUI, pp. 56-59.

28. "We demand certitude, and this demand is expressed in the decision not to accept anything without proof. But at the same time the very proposition 'not to accept anything without proof' must be proved. . . ." SUI, p. 59.

29. Cf. SUI, pp. 59-60. In the last quoted phrase we changed the order of words: the initial subject separated by dots is at the end of the original phrase.

30. Cf. SUI, pp. 61-62. Further: "Truth is intuition that is provable, i.e., discursive. In order to be discursive, intuition must be intuition which is not blind, not obtusely limited. . . . Discursive intuition is intuition that is differentiated to infinity, whereas intuitive discursion is discursion that is integrated to unity. Thus, if the Truth exists, it is real reasonableness and reasonable reality. It is finite infinity and infinite finitude . . . the Infinite conceived as integral Unity as one Subject complete in itself. . . . The Truth is a sun that illuminates both itself and the whole universe. Its abyss is the abyss of power, not of nothingness. The Truth is immobile motion and moving immobility. It is the unity of opposites, *coincidentia oppositorum.* . . . The Truth is always 'answerable.' To every 'why' there is an an-

surprising element, is introduced next in this series of probabilities as a possibility of synthesis of the infinite: "series of grounds into a finite intuition."[31] The substance of this "self-proving Subject," the Truth, consists in its ontological relatedness to its other*ness,* or other-self of each element, which Florenskii defines as its "substantial relationship" or even more precisely a "relationship-substance."[32] If therefore Truth is a *relationship-substance,* then A must relate to a non-A (and not an A, i.e., very self) "in which it finds its affirmation as A. More precisely, A is A, because it is not-A . . . through the affirmation of itself as not-A, through the assimilation of everything and the likening of everything to itself."[33] This latter implies also that there is a dynamics of and in relationship itself, in the Truth itself. And therefore the non-A (which Florenskii for the sake of simplifying designates as "B") must have its own identity, or it would be a mere "blind B." Consequently B needs its non-B to which to relate, or it would be simply identical to A, and not its other*ness.* Non-B (for simplification being designated as "C") does not need a non-C, for it finds its other*ness* in A. In such manner Florenskii closes the circle of relational-substance by A-B-C on an ontological level and thus effectively as a threefold relationship, or "triunity of relationship."[34] Conveyed into a person-like and Trinitarian constellation, based on the proper entity of each above-mentioned "not it . . . [but] hypostases," we receive the following presentation:

> The self-provenness and self-groundedness of the Subject of the Truth, *I,* is the relation to *He,* through *Thou.* . . . The Truth contemplates Itself through Itself in Itself. . . . Truth is the contemplation of Oneself through Another in a Third: Father, Son and Spirit. Such is the metaphysical definition of the "essence" *(ousia)* of the self-proving Subject, which is, as is evident, a substantial relationship. The Subject of the Truth is a relationship of the Three, but this is a relationship that is a substance, a relationship-substance. The Subject of the Truth is a Rela-

---

swer, and all these answers are not given separately, are not linked to one another externally, but are woven into an integral inwardly fused unity. A single moment of perception of the Truth gives the Truth with *all* its grounds. . . . The blink of an eye gives all the fullness of knowledge." SUI, p. 62.

31. Cf. SUI, p. 64.

32. . . . *otnoshenie-substantsia.* ". . . then the law of identity, eternally violated, is eternally restored by its very violation." SUI, p. 64.

33. Cf. SUI, p. 64.

34. Cf. SUI, pp. 65-66.

tionship of Three. . . . the *ousia* of the Truth is the Infinite act of Three in Unity. . . . The Truth is [therefore] *one essence with three hypostases.*[35]

The above-demonstrated and broadly quoted gnoseological journey is an indispensable intermediary step to Letter Three, and the successive ones, where the *relationship-substance* obtains its proper definition in the Trinity, again not a mere logical proof but rather an ontological dimension that reveals the unique role and place of the divine love, so in the transcendent as in the immanent realm of God and thus of Truth.[36]

1.2.3. The Truth as Dogma of Triunity

The following patristic definition of the Trinity, "Trinity unisubstantial and indivisible, unity tri-hypostatic and consubstantial," shifts our author from the philosophical to a theological quest for Truth. He also considers it as the only solution, if there is one at all, for skepticism's last word, *epochē,* and in fact the only possible comprehension of the Truth.[37] We do not need per se to enter the questions of consubstantiality, hypostasis, ousia, homoousios, which involved a great number of council Fathers at the Nicene and following councils. The crucial momentum that Florenskii points out in this context, however, is the early Church Fathers' *faith* by which they *defeated rationality* when "daring to use terms that were completely identical in con-

35. SUI, p. 66.

36. An important and sincere consideration is added to the *deductibility* of "the triune number of the Divine Hypostases" in Florenskii's *XXIX Remarks to the Trinity.* In essence he admits that even though he made the attempt, yet this number is an "'infinite fact,' apprehended in the everlasting light of the spirit, but not derivable *logically,* for God is above logic," nor can be said "*a priori*" anything about it. In Florenskii's own view he basically just repeated what already had been said in and through the Trinitarian dogma (see also note 1037, p. 620). In the rest of these remarks, however, he provides some beautiful and insightful examples of the fundamental and self-sufficient character of the number three that in his understanding illustrates "the absoluteness of Divinity, characterizes all that possesses relative self-sufficiency. It characterizes self-contained kinds of being. In a positive sense, the number three appears everywhere as a kind of fundamental category of life and thought" (such as three basic dimensions, three time realms, etc.). Cf. SUI, pp. 457-60. Florenskii ponders briefly over the hypothetical question of a fourth hypostasis, which would, however, introduce into the first three hypostases some "order," where there is no order in sense of sequence, chronology, etc., as there is "absolute unity of the Three," and thus such idea must be discarded. Cf. SUI, p. 67.

37. Cf. SUI, p. 68.

tent."[38] Precisely this *step of faith* shall become the next, a new stage of philosophizing, even a "*new* norm." Rationality can impossibly "encompass Trinity in Unity and Unity in Trinity"[39] and it needs to renounce its limitedness.[40] Ascesis, again the art of arts, is required even in intellectual investigation: "Ascesis, for what is required is an effort, an exertion, a self-renunciation, a casting of the 'old Adam' from oneself while everything that is given — 'natural,' infinite, familiar, conditional — attracts one to itself. What is necessary is self-overcoming, faith. If the 'untrembling Heart of immutable Truth . . .' for which Parmenides yearned is at all possible, the path to Him cannot avoid the Gethsemanic ascesis of faith."[41] This faith will turn into "total trust" for the rest of the new epistemological approach, or rather its deeper, by reason not graspable level: "Sweating drops of blood, I will say: '*Credo quia absurdum.* I believe despite the moans of the rational mind."[42] Therefore the remaining two steps are in accord with St. Anselm of Canterbury's "Credo ut intelligam"[43] and "worship to the 'Known God' . . ."[44] in which "the boundaries of knowledge and belief merge" and "all of rationality is transformed into a new essence." This last stage renders the new experience and reversed formula of: "Intelligo ut credam!"[45] To accept the "Truth of dogma," or the dogma of Truth, as described above, one has to pass through the ascesis of faith, i.e., to renounce the (already) experienced and investigated certainty of reason, that renders no solution, and to undertake the uncertain path of *total trust,* namely faith, which presupposes also a complete personal participation leading to *living faith* in the *Known God.*

38. As a result they acquired "the power to express — even with purely verbal clarity — the inexpressible mystery of the Trinity." Cf. SUI, pp. 69-70.

39. One shall not oversee the capital "U" in Unity: "'Troitsa vo Edinitse i Edinitsa v Troitse.'" Cf. SUI, p. 74.

40. "Reason must reject the closedness of rational constructions and turn to a new norm. It must become a 'new' reason. A free act of ascesis is required here." Cf. SUI, p. 74.

41. "*. . . to put' k Nemu ne minuet gefsimanskogo podviga very.*" Cf. SUI, p. 74. This *ascesis of faith,* as it will become evident later, is a notion away from an "assertoric truth of the world to the apodictic, but not yet given, Truth of dogma." Cf. SUI, p. 76.

42. ". . . I have seen already that if I remain with rationality I will die in epochē. I now wish to be irrational." SUI, p. 75.

43. Preceded by the affirmation: "Now I see that my faith is a source of higher understanding, and my rational mind gets its depth in this faith." Cf. SUI, p. 76.

44. Quoting 1 Corinthians 13:12: *Now we see but a poor reflection as in a mirror; then we shall see face to face. Now I know in part; then I shall know fully, even as I am fully known.* SUI, p. 76.

45. SUI, p. 76.

1.2.4. The Inexhaustible Light of Truth

Before our author places his further reflection on Truth and its relationship to love under the dictum of *Inflammatur (I burn but I do not exhaust* or *consume myself)* he discards Tolstoy's solution of "rational faith" that "does not desire to reject selfhood" and counterbalances it with Mary's bearing, "who humbly accepts eternal deification from the Truth: 'Behold the servant of the Lord! Let it be for me according to Thy word.'"[46] Florenskii's personal and epistemological journey reaches its new horizon at the point where *living* and *faith* become indispensable notions of *love:* "This cry of ultimate despair is the beginning of a new stage of philosophizing, the beginning of a living faith. I do not know if the Truth exists or not. . . . Perhaps it does not exist, but I love it. I love it more than anything that exists. . . . For its sake, I renounce everything, *even my own questions and my own doubt.*"[47]

This horizon lies beyond the identity of a singular entity, beyond a believed "center of philosophical seeking" and therefore cannot be reached solely out of proper forces: "The triple act of faith, hope, and love overcomes the inertia of the law of identity. I stop being I, my thought stops being my thought. By an unfathomable act I renounce the self-affirmation I = I. Something or Someone helps me escape my self-enclosedness." What we witness then is an existential-ontological turning point at which all philosophy ceases its place for an *incarnating* theology: "Previously, sinful selfhood had put itself in the place of God, but now with the help of God I put God in my place, God, whom I do not yet know but for whom I yearn and whom I love." This is a definite step of faith, "the first hint" out of "ultimate despair," cognition of a life-preceding love.[48]

1.2.5. The Mystery in the Divine Triunity and Love as Epistemological Category

Being a fine narrator, our author knows the importance of the right setting for a pacified mind — in a silent, oil-lamp-illuminated room with an icon, while "the snow lies deep beneath the window" and "all is quiet." There is a perceivable sacredness in this inviting space, and we empathize with his experience acquired *in prayer:* "Having made strenuous effort over myself for

46. Cf. SUI, p. 78.
47. SUI, p. 80.
48. Cf. SUI, pp. 80, 82.

love of the Truth, I entered into personal, living communion with the Truth." *Personal, living,* and *communion:* three fundamental constitutive elements of any relationship, the more so with the divine.[49] Most importantly, however, at this point Florenskii introduces, or better ascertains *love* in its *absolute,* i.e., ontological dimension, in his quest of Truth and thus the image of God. The *substantiality* of love in God is a question of his *truthfulness,* ergo of Truth in its absoluteness:

> Love for people has somehow become connected with this [personal process of cognition], and in love I found the first stage of the intuition that I had long desired.
>
> If God exists, and for me this was becoming unquestionable, then He necessarily is absolute love. But love is *not an attribute*[50] of God. God would not be absolute love if He were love only for another, for the conditional, for the corruptible, for the world. For then God's love would depend on conditional being and would thus be accidental. God is an absolute being because He is the substantial act of love, act-substance. God, or the Truth, not only *has* love but, above all, "God *is* love, ὁ θεὸς ἀγάπη ἐστίν" (1 John 4:8, 16), that is, love is God's essence, His [very] own nature, and not only His providential relationship, which is proper to Him. In other words, "God is *love*" (more precisely "Love"), and not only "the Loving One," even if the "perfectly Loving One."
>
> In this proposition is the summit of theoretical ("negative") knowledge and the passing [or crossing] to the practical ("positive") knowledge.[51]

The "intuitive-discursive" knowledge, which effectively eliminated the condition of "if God exists at all," now yields its place to "ascetic action" and that of personal experience. With this, at the same time, a mere philosopher would have terminated his *"experimentum crucis,"* or his quest for the Truth: he shall not return to "the idolatry of blind intuition, nor to the self-willfulness of proud discursion." From here on nothing but the "KNOWN GOD" can satisfy Florenskii's yearning for Truth.[52] Out of this realization he examines Abraham, the Old Testament figure of faith (Gen. 15:6 = Rom. 4:3),

49. Cf. SUI, pp. 82-83.

50. The Russian original uses the noun *priznak,* literally "sign" or "indication" but in context *quality, trait,* or *character* is understood.

51. SUI, p. 83.

52. Cf. SUI, p. 84.

whose "knowing of God" was still based on a personal engagement, an encounter of the Invisible, the obedience to "the mysterious call of the Unknown Truth."[53] Abraham's example of "faith" (Heb. 11:8-9) serves as an illustration of "*going* of the knower *out* of himself . . . *into* the known, a real unification of the knower and what is known."[54]

There is no "essential knowing of the Truth, i.e., communion . . . [without] entering into the interior of the Divine Triunity. . . ." This inner touch — for an *outer,* superficial, never does suffice to bring about *essential knowledge* — can occur "only through transubstantiation *(presushchestvlenie)* of the human being, through his deification *(obozhenie ego),* through the acquisition of love as the Divine essence: he who is not with God does not know God. In love and only in love is real knowledge of the Truth conceivable. On the other hand, knowledge of the Truth is also revealed by love: he who is with Love is unable not to love." Put simply, the one who *knows,* loves, and the one who loves, *knows,* because "manifested truth is love," whereby the initial impulse obviously derives from God. Thus, "Truth, Good, and Beauty" are constitutive parts of the same "spiritual life," diverse only in our perceptions, but in fact "one principle" that Florenskii defines as "metaphysical triad." The description of love's ontological *nestling* in the Triunity, as well as in its economy of interaction, also as truth, requires from us anew a full quotation: "Manifested truth is love. Realized love is beauty. Love is God's action in me and my action in God. This co-activity is the principle of my communion with Divine life and being, i.e., with essential love, for God's absolute truthfulness reveals itself precisely in love." With this assertion Florenskii introduces unambiguously *love* as the essence of action and interaction, as well as the cognitive and epistemological path that reveals fully God's truthfulness, and thus the Truth that abides in God. It must be *love* since joy and knowledge are di-

53. And later we shall recall that *Abraham believed God, and it was counted to him as righteousness, and he was called a friend of God* (James 2:23).

54. This reflection then unfolds in context as follows: "That is the fundamental and characteristic proposition of Russian and, in general, of all Eastern philosophy. We deduced this proposition previously in a somewhat different and more certain way, directly indicating that the heart and soul of this 'ongoing out of oneself' is the act of faith in the religious sense, in the orthodox sense, for the true 'going out' is precisely faith. Everything else may be an illusion and a temptation. Thus, knowing is not the capturing of a dead object by a predatory subject of knowledge, but a living moral communion of persons, each serving for each as both object and subject. Strictly speaking, only a person is known and only by a person." Cf. SUI, pp. 84-85. The latter phrases remind us of Khomiakov's vision of ecclesial communion in his *Tserkov' odna.*

rected towards a subject, whereas love is a relationship of interaction — indeed a divine essence.[55]

One of Florenskii's great gifts is to be an artist of words while being synthetic and organized. Often, all essentials are placed on the same or the following page(s), as they are here: "Contemplated objectively, by a third, love of another is beauty."[56] The relations among the Three Divine Hypostases and the economy of salvation reveal to us the "hypostatic Divine Love" based on the "communicability" of love; meanwhile, surprisingly, this is not the case with knowledge and joy: "God's love goes over to us, but knowledge and contemplative joy abide in Him. For this reason, it is not the Hypostasis of the Father or the Hypostasis of the Holy Spirit (Paraclete = Comforter or Giver of Joy) that became incarnate, but the Son-Word, the hypostatic Divine Love, the Father's Heart. If it is permissible to use Jacob Boehme's powerful phrase, the Son of God is 'the heart in the Father *(das Herz in dem Vater)*.'"[57]

To the question of how "the Truth *concretely* reveals itself," Florenskii

55. Cf. SUI, pp. 84-85. Also, let us note the differences of dynamism in the concepts of *knowledge, love,* and *joy* depending on the divinization or transubstantiation in the person and his relationship to God's very love. This is an excellent demonstration of the *divine love's* unique role also in the cognitive process: "God actively knows, loves, and rejoices in me, for I am given to Him. Here, the source of knowledge, love, and joy is God Himself. But my knowledge of God, my love of God, and my joy in God are passive, because God is only partly given to me and can be given only to the extent of my God-likeness. The likening to God's love is active love of what is already given to me. Why love precisely, and not knowledge and joy? Because love is a substantial act, going from the subject to the object and having support in the object, whereas knowledge and joy are directed toward the subject, and the subject is the point of application of their force." Cf. SUI, p. 86.

56. Cf. SUI, pp. 85-86. (Of course, we rearranged the "flow" of Florenskii's text here according to the need of our presentation.) The subject of *beauty* is intrinsically connected to knowledge and "active love." Especially the latter one is a condition for a "spiritual life" directed towards the "creatures" but also "as an object of contemplation, love becomes beauty." Florenskii's thought goes beyond aesthetics, since contemplation, or any act of loving God, is an opening up of "one's heart" to the "energy of Divine love," the energy of divinization. Yet any transformation is proved in and by life, in the love to one's "brother." Cf. SUI, p. 92.

57. We encountered a grammatical mistake, most probably a misprint, in the German original: "im dem Vater" (a redundancy of dative, which should be as indicated above or "im Vater"), also present in the 1990 reprint of the 1914 edition, vol. I/1 (Moskva: Izd. "Pravda," 1990), p. 76. Cf. SUI, p. 86. There is a concluding thought at the end of the fourth letter on Christ's "Hypostasis in the Trinity" as unique possible mediation and "absolute vision" (as opposed to the one described by Plotinus) based on Christ's "self-renouncing love, on immaculate purity, on unfathomable beauty, and on infinite wisdom." Cf. SUI, p. 109.

answers with St. Paul's hymn of love (1 Cor. 13:4-7) "which says everything." He also ascribes to each Hypostasis a particular "spiritual life . . . organization . . . character of path to God" (knowledge, love, and delight) that illumine through nuances how they demonstrate their love: "Thus, the love of the first Hypostasis is fiery and jealous; the love of the second is meek and sacrificial; the love of the third is enthusiastic and trembling."[58]

1.2.6. Identities and Similarities — to Commune *and to* Abide

Florenskii leads his reader through different significant philosophical approaches, especially the western ones, with particular attention to the "concept of person," i.e., the human "identity" that can be only a "numerical identity, *homoousia (numericheskoe tozhdestvo, homoousia),*" whereas the "generic similarity, *homoiousia (genericheskoe tozhdestvo, homoiousia)*" regards "pure things" and not human beings. (This distinction shall play its proper role when treating the subject of "jealousy" in the last letter, since love-relation is possible only to a person; to a thing it is but "a desire.")[59] The progress from the "one" or "I" to a dual-relationship "I-Thou" is just a transitory state into its completion in a human-divine trinity. *Communion* is not an option, but rather true love. Thus *true love* and *life* are the intrinsic sense of inquiry for Truth, which is "abiding" in the Trinity. The same is true for the personal *spiritual life* and *experience,* none of which is real if not *lived* in God. We recognize distinctly St. John's handwriting in these reflections:

> Only one who has come to know the Triune God can love with a true love. If I have not come to know God, have not come to commune with His Being, I do not love. And, contrarily, if I love, I commune with God, know Him. But if I do not love, I do not commune with Him and do not know Him. There is a direct relationship between knowledge and love for creatures here. The center from which this knowledge and this love proceed is my abiding in God and God's abiding in me.[60]

58. Cf. SUI, p. 100.

59. Following the upper distinction, Florenskii juxtaposes "Christian philosophy" to "rationalism" as such: "*Christian philosophy,* i.e., the philosophy of idea and reason, the philosophy of persons and creative acts, is based on the possibility of overcoming the law of identity and can be characterized as a *homoousian philosophy.* It is a spiritual philosophy." Cf. SUI, p. 89.

60. Cf. SUI, p. 92.

The *abiding* explains, among others, Florenskii's deep appreciation of liturgy[61] where one of the central ideas is that "mutual love alone is the condition of 'unity of thought,' *homonoia,* the one thought of those who love one another," for the goal is to achieve through communion "'consubstantiality' [which] is precisely 'wisdom.'"[62] Thus, knowledge is never self-purpose but is meant to lead to wisdom, and reaching its Origin it becomes what St. Gregory of Nyssa defined as *"Knowledge becomes love."* Florenskii completes: "Therefore, the mutual love of Christ's disciples is the sign of their learning, their knowledge, their walking in the truth. Love is the characteristic sign, by which a disciple of Christ is recognized, and, if we like, so is their wisdom: *By this all people will know that you are my disciples, if you have love for one another* (John 13:35)."[63] The substantiality of the triune character of the divine love, as well as the title of our book, will become evident again in about the middle of Letter Nine on *Creation.* Comparing the *impossibility* of love between gods and humans in antiquity, Florenskii founds the unity of the antinomies between creational freedom and God's providence precisely on the concept of *God as Love:*

> Theologically speaking, it was necessary to introduce two dogmas in man's consciousness: the dogma of the Providence of One God and the dogma of the creation of the world by a Good God, that is, the dogma of the giving of its own independent being to creation. The providence of God and the freedom of creation form, in their antinomy, *one* dogma, the dogma of God's love for creation, a dogma that has its foundation in the idea of God as Love, namely, the idea of the Triunity of Divinity.[64]

61. For more on liturgy see SUI, p. 103.

62. In the part on "consubstantiality," Florenskii refers to the baptismal formula and the Creed, which are "no more and no less than an expression of the dogma of the consubstantiality of the Holy Trinity." Cf. SUI, p. 94.

63. The Russian original text puts it literally, "if you have love — ἀγάπη — among yourselves" (p. 95). On the contrary, no activity without true love — or by the "so-called love," which is a "love outside of God" or any outward "appearance or skin" of love of nondivine origin — can suffice and replace truthful intentions and the essence of love or charity, as St. Paul teaches in 1 Corinthians 13:1-3. Cf. SUI, pp. 95-96.

64. "This antinomy, in all its decisiveness, is the foundation of modern science. Without this antinomy, there is no science. Thus, if previously it was demonstrated that the dogma on Trinity is the first principle of philosophy, here it is revealed that this dogma also serves as the rule for the development of science." Cf. SUI, pp. 233-34.

1.2.7. Kenosis, *i.e., Sacrificial Love*

The truthfulness and completeness of this love is measured by self-sacrifice, by "overcoming of the naked self-identity 'I = I' and in going out of oneself," i.e., *kenosis* as taught and lived by Jesus himself, by His very life that reflected the intra-Trinitarian relationship, but also by St. Paul's "sacred hymns," for instance, in the letter to the Philippians (2:7). In the *kenotic* love-sacrifice the "not-I" *freely* "empties, exhausts, ravages, and disparages"[65] itself by "rising above the logical, empty, contentless law of identity and becoming identified with the beloved brother."[66] This knowledge put into action, which is the love of charity or charitable love, is also the *light* of Truth revealed, because Truth becomes manifest in its very essence: love implied in communion.[67] The basic foundation of the communion, consisting in a "transfer" of the lover's "I" into the loved one's "I" through a third "I," which is the "love in God,"[68] occurs in "mutual self-surrendering, self-exhaustion, and self-disparagement

65. . . . *opustoshaet, istoshchaet, obkhishchaet, unichizhaet sebia.* Florenskii provides also the mode of "the interrelationship of the Hypostases" in the Trinity that is not based solely on kenosis (defined by love), i.e., the "intra-Divine self-depletion of the Hypostases," but that of "eternal restoration and affirmation of One by Another, as glorification and kingship." To put it in different terms, the two notions complete each other: "the tragic, sacrificial love" with the "reverse current of . . . *answering love,* triumphant love, glorifying the Loving one and restoring Him, . . . [a] transfer of glory from Hypostasis to Hypostasis." Cf. SUI, 131-32. On God's selfless, kenotic love, "voluntary limitation of Himself" for the sake of His creation see also Letter Nine on *Creation,* SUI, pp. 241-42, and Letter Ten on *Sophia,* SUI, pp. 265-66.

66. "Thus, the impersonal 'not-I' becomes a person, another 'I,' namely 'Thou.' But in this 'impoverishment' or 'exhaustion' of 'I,' in this 'emptying' or 'kenosis,' there occurs a reverse restoration of 'I' in the norm of being proper to it." Cf. SUI, p. 98.

67. For a detailed discourse on *light, beauty,* and *love* and their reciprocal manifestations, see SUI, pp. 101-3. For instance, Florenskii heavily relies on Ephesians 5:13 in his reflection-meditation regarding the subject: "Thus, if beauty is precisely manifestation and manifestation is precisely light, then, I repeat, beauty is light and light is beauty. Absolute light is the absolute beautiful. It is Love itself in its perfection, and this Love makes every person spiritually beautiful." Cf. SUI, pp. 102-3.

The highest and purest forms of it, while still being granted from above, require "self-purification, or self-correction" in asceticism, "the art of arts" of the Fathers. For "the light of Divine knowledge is the possession of a purified person." Cf. SUI, p. 104.

68. To this: "Friendship is not only psychological and ethical in nature but, first and foremost, ontological and mystical in nature. In all ages, all the profound contemplators of life viewed friendship in this way. What is friendship? Self-contemplation through a Friend in God. Friendship is the seeing of oneself with the eyes of another, but before a third, namely *the Third.* The 'I,' being reflected in a *friend* (Russ. *v druge*), recognizes in the friend's 'I' its own other *(drugoe).*" Cf. SUI, p. 350.

(vzaimnye samo-predaniie, samo-istoshchanie, samo-unichizhenie) of the lovers," and is what Florenskii calls the *dvoitsa*, a "di-unitary being," which is a *biunity* or *dyad*. This mutuality of a *dvoitsa*, a "di-unitary being," has the principle of its unity in God: "*Finis amoris, ut duo unum fiant (The scope of love is that [the] two may be one).*" How this biunity, or *dyad*, becomes "consubstantial" with the Eternal, Florenskii demonstrates in a poetic and magisterial merging of metaphysics into theology:

> Rising above the bounds of its nature, "I" goes out of temporal-spatial limitedness [by transferring his "I" into the "I" of the beloved] and enters into Eternity. There the whole process of the interrelation of the lovers is a single act in which an infinite series of individual moments of love is synthesized. The single, eternal, and infinite act is the consubstantiality of the lovers in God, where "I" is one and the same as the other "I," but also different. . . . Furthermore, every "I" sees in the Divine image of another "I" its own Divine image as in a mirror.
>
> This dyad has love by its very essence and, as concretely incarnate love, it is beautiful for objective contemplation.[69]

Of essence is the merging of these earthly "tri-unities or trinities" into the "Church, the Body of Christ," by an organic process of *growing* together into "a consubstantial whole." That implies sharing bounty, love, and beauty with others without any elitism or separatism whatsoever, based on norms or identifiers of charity such as described by St. Paul in 1 Corinthians 13:4-7.[70]

69. SUI, pp. 98-99. We took anew the liberty to rearrange Florenskii's text in order to highlight those elements that may appear conclusive only in a broader textual context. Following the last quoted phrase Florenskii exemplifies how the *dyad* becomes a trinity in and through love contemplated in the Divine and then these "trinities grow together into a consubstantial whole, into the Church, or body of Christ, as an objective disclosure of the Hypostases of Divine love. Each third I can be first in the second trinity and second in the third, so that this chain of love, beginning with the Absolute Trinity (which by its force holds everything together as a magnet holds together a pattern of iron filings), extends farther and farther." In this context he mentions St. Augustine and J. Scotus Eriugena's concept of love as a "bond" and unifying element. SUI, pp. 98-99.

70. Cf. SUI, pp. 99-100. On the margin of "moralism" without overcoming the proper "naked self-identity, 'I = I,'" it needs to be mentioned that it remains but "a vain, inwardly insane attempt at a human, extra-Divine love" for which, we know, Florenskii has not much appreciation. "Even moral activity (philanthropy, etc.) is, taken in itself, an absolute zero" (p. 96). Cf. SUI, pp. 97-98. Florenskii further develops his metaphysical argument on the *dyads* and *triunity* on p. 99.

1.2.8. On Friendship

Florenskii's treatment of friendship as philosophical and psychological occurrence still raises notable discussion. One reason may simply be that friendship to him has an equal if not superior theological as well as spiritual imprint.[71]

Under the epigraph of *Faustum praelium (Happy Battle)* and an analogous meditative setting as of letter four, Florenskii addresses a "Distant Friend and Brother," describing what we would consider a spiritual yet, by and large, uneventful memory. In reality, however, here is hidden the hermeneutical key to everything that Florenskii yearns to share on friendship out of proper experience. Two friends shared a monastery visit in "fasting [and] common prayer before the large crucifix," eventually jointly participating in Eucharist: "You and I took communion together. That was the seed to everything that I now have."[72] An outstanding description of how spiritual friendship can nourish, unite, and fortify.

With no delay, Florenskii reconnects to the core of his inquiry, as well as to its result grown through experience and in wisdom: "The spiritual activity in which and by which knowledge of the Pillar of the Truth is granted is love. This is love full of grace, manifested only in a purified consciousness. It can only be attained by a long (O how long!) ascesis. In striving to attain love — unimaginable for creatures — it is necessary to receive an initial impulse and then to be sustained in one's further motion." This sustainment in motion, like the "initial impulse," comes from the Divine. And while further discussed as *love,* it is different from the *love* alluded to in *Letter Four,* yet "a foreshadowing of that love, the expected love."[73]

1.2.9. Agapan *and* Philein: *Higher Forms of Love*

Through thorough research, Florenskii undertakes a rigorous philological analysis of the "four categories of love" in their comprehension, *erōs, storgē, agapē,* and *philia.* Since ancient times in the Greek language these were "the

71. After *Sophia, Friendship* is the longest and concluding Letter (11), to which the following Letter, *Jealousy* (12), serves as a kind of appendix.

72. "For it is not for nothing that our Abba Isidor told us so many times (only now, after his departure, do I begin to understand the secret meaning of his repeated, persistent words): 'A brother helped by a brother is as strong as a fortress' (Prov. 18:19). That is what I wish to elucidate to some extent in the present letter." Cf. SUI, p. 318.

73. Cf. SUI, p. 319.

surging *erōs,* or sensuous, passionate love; tender, organic *storgē,* or the love of kith and kin, attachment; the dry, rational *agapē,* or the love of valuation, respect; and cordial, sincere *philia,* or the love of inward acceptance, personal insight, friendliness."[74] The arrival of the "Holy Scriptures . . . gave them a new concept," their meanings altered or developed, especially of the two dynamic ones: *philein* and *agapan.*[75] Florenskii describes the results of his investigation:

> In the Holy Scripture, *philein* was filled with spirit and came to express Christian relations of love based on personal inclination and personal communion. Finally, the formerly colorless and dry *agapan* was filled with spiritual life, and in the newly formed, expressly biblical *agapē* it began to communicate profound universal love, the love of higher, spiritual freedom. In some cases *philein* and *agapan* are almost interchangeable; in other cases they are differentiated. Thus, when it is a question of the *commandment* of love for God and for one's neighbors, the word *agapan* is always used; however, concerning love for enemies, *only agapan* is used, never *philein.*[76]

This last distinction is of great interest to Florenskii, as he differentiates between the significance of living and dying for enemies or for friends.[77] Even-

74. "But in fact, none of these words expresses the love of friendship that we are considering in the present letter, a love that combines the aspects of *philia, erōs,* and *agapē,* a love the ancients attempted to express in some degree by the compound word *philophrosynē* (φιλοφροσύνη). In any case, the most suitable word here is *philein* with its derivates." SUI, pp. 322-23. The concept of *philia* that fascinates Florenskii so much, and judging by the description he gives us with good reason, can be found soon after the initial pages of this chapter: "Beyond the moment of *erōs* in the Platonic sense of the word, *philia* revealed in the soul is the highest point of earth and the bridge to heaven. Constantly revealing in the person of the loved one the glimmer of primordial beauty, *philia* erases . . . the bounds of selfhood's separateness, which is aloneness. In a friend, in this other *I* of the loving one, one finds the source of hope for victory and the symbol of what is to come. And one is thus given preliminary consubstantiality and therefore preliminary knowledge of the Truth. It is upon this peak of human feeling that the heavenly grace of *that* love descends." And in order to avoid confusion Florenskii begins to clarify the love-concepts of the Greeks and their development in later "scriptural times" (OT, NT) with occasional patristic exceptions (Gregory of Nyssa, Nicholas Cabasilas, and others who used *erōs* and *eran* "to designate higher love for God"). Cf. SUI, pp. 319, 324-25.

75. Meanwhile, *eran* and *erōs* are virtually absent from the OT and "completely excluded from the books of the NT." Cf. SUI, pp. 324-25.

76. SUI, p. 325.

77. According to Florenskii's view, *agapan* in the NT is used "in all cases where it is a

tually, he returns once more to the philological and historical interpretation of the noun *agapē,* underscoring its "self-negating and passive self-surrender" character for others, and thus possessing "Divine and absolute" quality.[78]

1.2.10. Are You My Friend?

Florenskii offers an accurate and revealing exegesis (perhaps less of a novelty nowadays) on the dialogue between the Resurrected Lord and Peter in John's last chapter (John 21:15). The first two of the three questions of the Resurrected Christ to Peter about his love for Him "indicate to Peter that he violated friendly love — *philia* — for the Lord and that henceforth one can demand of him only universal human love, only that love which every disciple of Christ necessarily offers to every person, even to his enemy. It is in this sense that the Lord asks: '*Agapais me?*'" Florenskii's point is precisely the tie of friendship, *philia,* between Christ and Peter before the tragic events, a friendship that Peter utterly betrayed. Therefore, Christ's initial two questions are formed with "*agapais me,*" i.e., do you love me at least with the love due to all other people? It is this question that Peter ignores, answering twice with "*Philō se*" ("*I am your friend,*" that is, *I love you as your friend).* The last question of Christ comes with "*Phileis me?*" ("*Are you my friend?*"). This is where Peter becomes sad, aware that it was a friend or, more precisely, *the Friend* whom he betrayed.[79] We have to admit that the New Testament text speaks with utmost clarity, and Florenskii makes a point about a long-

question of direction of will (Mt 5:43, 44, etc.), as well as where inclination rests on a decision of the will, on the choice of the object of love (Heb 1:9; 2 Cor 9:7; 2 Pt 2:15; Jn 13:19; Jn 12:43; Jn 21:15-17; Lk 6:32)." Cf. SUI, p. 325.

78. "As for *agapē,* it is a word that, as we have said, is wholly alien to the extra-Biblical, ancient secular world. It signifies a love that, through a decision of the will, selects for itself its object *(dilectio),* thus becoming a self-negating and passive self-surrender *for* and *for the sake of* the object. Such sacrificial love on a secular basis is known only as a fleeting feeling, an inspiration from another world, not as a determination of life-activity. The Biblical *agapē,* therefore, has features that are not human and conditional but Divine and absolute." For the medieval comparison, Florenskii uses Arnold Geulincx's *Ethics,* where the author lists and describes four types of love (and in parentheses we indicate Florenskii's own complements): *Amor affectionis:* love of feeling *(= philia); Amor benevolentiae:* love of benevolence *(= agapē); Amor concupiscentiae:* love of attraction *(= erōs); Amor obedientiae:* love of respect *(= stergō).* Geulincx also mentions a "*fifth* type of love, which he calls *amor spiritualis*" but which Florenskii perceives as not quite conclusive since bordering on esotericism ("astral," mediums, etc.). Cf. SUI, p. 327. On the subsequent pages, he provides an overview chart.

79. Cf. SUI, pp. 325-26.

ignored sacredness (or sacrament) of *philia* ("*personal, friendly* love"), Friendship being a term he deliberately spells with a capital *F.* The entire conversation is woven so much in the tenderness of a personal encounter that initially "the immeasurable delicate reproach" in Christ's words, this "figure of silence" understood only by true friends, does not even dawn on Peter. It is not about restoring Peter's apostleship, "but what Peter really needed was the restoration of friendly, personal relations with the Lord."[80]

1.2.11. Philia *in* Agapē

Only the personal character of a relationship can give a more unique character to *agapē.* This is not meant to be directed towards further divisions or elitism but should lead towards the large community, the Church and its communal and "highest aspect of *agapē,*" the Eucharist:

> The *agapic* aspect of a Christian society finds its embodiment in the early Christian ecclesia, in a parish, in a monastic cenoby (*koino-bia* = communal living). *Feasts of love (vechera liubvi)* or *agapēs,* culminating in a clearly mystical, even mysterial, co-partaking of the Sacred Body *(Prechistogo Tela)* and Precious Blood *(Chestnoi Krovi),* are the highest expression of this agapic aspect. This *blossom* of ecclesial life contains the source that nourishes all other life-activity of the ecclesia, from the everyday torment of the mutual bearing of burdens up to bloody martyrdom. Such, then, is the agapic side of life. By contrast, the *philic* side is embodied in relations of *friendship.* These relations blossom in sacramental *adelphopoiēsis (brato-tvorenii,* literally: *a brotherhood-creating)*[81] and the *co*-partaking of the Holy Eucharist, and are nourished by this partaking for *co*-ascesis, *co*-patience, and *co*-martyrdom.[82]

According to Florenskii, brotherhood and friendship are equivalent to the "agapic and philic aspects of church life" as two currents, and they even "strive to merge fully" when reaching their "highest significance, at their peaks."[83] Once again, the Eucharist as the maxim of divine-human commu-

80. Cf. SUI, p. 326.

81. On this and on *druzheskoe bratotvorenie, adelphopoiēsis* of friends, and various liturgical rites in this regard, see SUI, pp. 364-67.

82. SUI, p. 331.

83. Florenskii once more implements his philological sensitivity by illustrating that "a brother (*brat* in Russian) is a taker *(bratel')* of the burden of life upon himself, one who

nion on earth becomes the ultimate realm since "the communion with Christ through the sacrament of the Holy Eucharist is the source of *all* spirituality."[84] However, for Florenskii, the *philia* and *philic aspect* of love is the highest and most desirable one, even if at times it may appear uncertain or inconclusive: "In order to live among brothers, it is necessary to have a Friend, if only a distant one. In order to have a Friend, it is necessary to live among brothers, at least to be with them in spirit." For some, this is a contradiction, for others, simply two complementing aspects. Although Florenskii insists so much on friendship, or a *philic love,* brotherhood appears to be, as seen above, of equal importance, also for the sake of a healthy spiritual balance.

There are numerous other quotes that we would like to include for their direct relationship to the topic of *love* as *agapē* and their implementation in human-divine relations, but our space is limited. Nevertheless, we would not do justice to the topic and Florenskii's views if we did not quote one more concise yet deeply spiritual synthesis from his pen on *agapē* and *philic love,* i.e., Friendship, towards the end of this letter:

> FRIENDSHIP gives the loftiest joy but it also demands the strictest ascesis. Every day, hour, and minute, ruining my soul with sorrow for the sake of my Friend, it is in joy that I acquire this soul restored. Just as *agapē* toward a person gives birth to *philia* toward him, so here too, in friendship, sovereign *agapē* is embodied in *philia* as in a living medium. Divine, agapic love transubstantiates philic love, and on this summit of human feeling, like clouds brushing against the twin-peaked Ararat, the heavenly swirls above the earthly: *Greater love (agapēn) has no one than this, that someone lays down his life for his friends (hyper tōn philōn autou)* (John 15:13). The greatest agapic love is realizable only in relation to *friends,* not in relation to all people, not "in general." The greatest agapic love consists in the laying down of one's soul for one's friend. . . . Dying for friends is only the final (not the most difficult!) step on the ladder of friendship. But before dying for one's friend, one must be their friend, and this is achieved by long and difficult ascesis.[85]

---

takes *(beret)* upon himself the cross of another" regardless of whether the origin of the word corresponds and is equally true for a friend. "On the other hand, if a friend (*drug* in Russian) is another 'I' *(drugoe Ia),* can one not say the same thing about a brother?" At this latter example, *drugoi — another I,* or a *not-I,* is already more of a philosophical than philological interpretation, nevertheless still valid. Cf. SUI, p. 331.

84. Cf. SUI, p. 331.

85. SUI, p. 363. We find a similar idea with "mystical unity" as a qualifier of *philic* love,

1.2.12. The Role of Jealousy

Florenskii considers Jealousy an indispensable element of a unique friendship. There "definiteness of connections" and "constancy of unions" are so necessary that he concludes his *Letters* with *Letter Twelve* on the subject of jealousy, again with an eloquent epigraph: *Mersus ut emergam (I immerse myself in order to emerge).*[86] Jealousy is a different face, or the other side of love and friendship, though not in a negative sense as the "revolutionary intelligentsia *par excellence*," namely that of the eighteenth century, saw it.[87] Rather, Florenskii relates to Spinoza's views where "jealousy . . . is a necessary *equivalent* of love, appearing when relations take a turn for the worse. Love does not disappear but is transformed into jealousy." The difference is that in Spinoza's system, love is conceivable without jealousy, *in* or *as* a "perfect reciprocity,"[88] but this is not the view of Florenskii. Love is not a desire, which is only a relationship to things, as elucidated previously.[89]

Therefore, "to understand jealousy in its proper nature, one must connect it more intimately with love. One must introduce it into the very heart of love, and, having underscored the *personal* nature of love, one must disclose that *jealousy is love itself, but in love's 'alter-being.'* One must disclose that *jealousy is a necessary condition and inevitable side of love, but a side that is turned toward sorrow, so that to destroy jealousy would be to destroy love.* In the same way, desire always contains hate with envy."[90] To support his argu-

---

being also the "leaven" and *agapē* the "salt that keeps human relations from spoiling." Cf. SUI, p. 332. We need to mention that Florenskii had his moments of struggle with the "*agapē-philia* antinomy," especially in the Old Testament, but he eventually returned to what he called the "community molecule," which is "a pair of friends." Strangely he did not consider family in this context (especially as he himself was a family man), which he understands as "a kind of molecule for the pagan community." However, this also could simply mean: ". . . since they knew nothing better." Nevertheless, this proposition of his would need further investigation. Cf. SUI, pp. 335-37. A strong argument behind his reasoning about the pairs of friends is Jesus' "pairing of the apostles" before sending them off "by two and two," also based on their "relations of kin, blood, even brotherhood," and character traits — being consequent with Florenskii's reasoning — calling them out from their families. Cf. SUI, pp. 341-43.

86. Cf. SUI, p. 368.

87. Cf. SUI, pp. 368-70. In Russian *revniv,* from Old Slavonic *v'v-n'iv-',* is in the same family as *rvenie, revnostnyi, revnitel', zeal, zealous, zealot.* There are further philological analyses on the following pages. Cf. SUI, pp. 378-80.

88. Cf. SUI, p. 369.

89. "Jam, cigars, cards, and so forth cannot be loved; they can only be desired." Cf. SUI, p. 371.

90. Cf. SUI, pp. 371-72.

mentation based on the Scriptures as an example *par excellence,* Florenskii brings up the nation with "the purest God-consciousness, the chosen Jewish nation" that knew and understood "the love of God more clearly than any other nation." The Israelites experienced divine jealousy and knew it as no other nation, just as no other nation had the knowledge and description of human love as the "genius-nation" Greeks did.[91] Based on their experiences and the knowledge that jealousy is positive, Florenskii draws his own definition of jealousy:[92] "It is one of the aspects of love, the foundation of love, the background of love, the primordial darkness in which the ray of love shines."[93]

Freedom and *choice, dilectio* (the latter also means *love* and *affection* in Latin), are two key concepts that are bestowed upon the human being at creation in an act of divine power. This makes us truly "divinizable" as we are to return to our own love, which possesses "a selective [or a selecting power] — *dilectio.*" And selecting is coupled with "chosenness," i.e., what is being "affirmed and protected." This is what jealousy acts upon — the "purity, genuineness, and preservation of my love. . . . *Thou* hast grown into *me,* hast become part of me. To stop loving is to lose a part of myself. To forget is to cut a piece of living flesh from myself. This is what happens when, respecting the freedom of another, one finds it necessary to tear love from one's breast together with one's heart."[94] Even if this may sound somewhat pathetic, our author writes from his proper experience, and, therefore, we can credit him with being genuine. At times, we can perceive the latent danger of *exclusive-*

91. Cf. SUI, p. 372.

92. He quotes Nietzsche: "The ennoblement of jealousy, the Greeks — they are the most jealous nation." Cf. SUI, p. 372.

93. The reflection goes on: "Love is free choice. From many persons, I, by an act of inner self-determination, choose one person, and to this person, one of many, I establish a unique relation, become attached in my soul to this person. I wish to view this person, who is ordinary, as extraordinary. I wish to view this person, who is gray and drab, as festive. I wish to view this quite average person as a triumph. This person stands in a crowd, but I summon him, and, from the city square, I lead him into the cozy room of my heart. I inscribe this person's image on a gold medallion." SUI, pp. 372-73. This poetic description may sound like an exaggeration, and perhaps it is, yet Florenskii is pointing to a metaphysical relationship and transformation of a "beyond-human" implication. "It is rather an image of the Divine image, an icon" than just a simple "portrait" of exclusiveness, and the "chosen person becomes Thou for me. Friendship, I repeat, is *exclusive,* just as conjugal love is exclusive." This last indication is as much as a hint to Florenskii's understanding of Friendship in sacred or even sacramental terms. Cf. SUI, pp. 372-73.

94. Cf. SUI, p. 374.

ness growing into isolation or separation, but Florenskii always makes sure that "communion" and community stand above all — or, at the end of his reasoning: "One should be doing everything, should do everything in friendship to overcome the wall standing between persons. One should not spare one's strength; one should struggle strenuously for communion — unto the blood of the martyr, unto death. One should lay down one's life for one's friends, for the first thing that one's friends should be delivered from is insincerity, coldness, and self-closedness." Thus, "friends" here means community and vice versa, while still respecting the uniqueness of *the Friendship.* Communion is about building and maintaining unity despite anything that may qualify it as impossible: "A person must free himself from what is impossible, and what is impossible here is to show another person that the impossible, i.e., love, is possible."[95]

Finally, jealousy is not only positive and the other face of love, but its weakening can be a warning sign, a symptom of "spiritual cooling" or "self-reliance and pride." This is definitely an interesting spiritual insight. To conclude are Florenskii's own words reconnected to his initial inquiry: "Thus, a striving to attain the Pillar and Ground of the Truth is realized and preserved by jealousy, this force of our spirit that is persecuted and held in contempt by the contemporary consciousness."[96] God is jealous of His chosen ones; so should we be jealous of our relationship with God and protect it by multiplying it through sharing. For sharing in the Divine realm is not loosing and diminution but increment in relationship, i.e., in faith, hope, and love.

Conclusion

Although he may sound commonplace at times, some of Fr. Florenskii's scientific-lyrical reflections on the phenomenon of love often say more than other authors do in entire volumes. He is the first author in our inquiry to address the "matter of love" in a methodologically systematic and theological way, starting in metaphysical gnoseology, scrutinizing the etymological origins of terms before and after Christianity (proving a real sense for its historical development in philosophy and theology), and implementing virtually all scientific tools and knowledge at hand, all while remaining an authentic narrator. The system of his notes — extensive, exhaustive, and meticulous, total-

95. SUI, p. 377.
96. Cf. SUI, p. 381.

ing 1,056 (impressive even today, let alone in 1914!) — as well as the supplements at the end of the book offer a spectacular reading and reflection on terms of *agapic* and *philic love,* adjectives so crucial to qualify and sort the value of relationships, both human and divine. The four types of love presented are interconnected, or at times serve as a stage to a higher degree or quality of love. Florenskii is the first to unfold on a philosophical and theological (i.e., *theosophical*) level their full impact and interactions, beginning with a metaphysical search for the Truth and then organically "outgrowing" its limits, yielding deliberately and justly its space to theology.

An even more important, in fact fundamental, intuition of our author is the introduction of *love, the Divine essence,* the *relationship-substance,* as a proper and only true ontology of Truth in the Trinity, i.e., knowing God is possible only as a *Love-Unity of three Hypostases,* and therefore this cognition can occur only through *love* as well. This knowledge which is communicated, ergo *revealed,* by Truth Itself, is further acquired by means of living faith and most importantly solely through sharing and abiding in the *divine love.* The process occurs through transubstantiation and deification of a person, which is the acquisition of and entering into the "love as the Divine essence." To know God, one has to be with God, and love is the only way to enter and participate in the mystery of the Trinity. Although Florenskii presents a proper and full-scaled epistemology to the cognition of Truth's intrinsically Divine and Trinitarian ontology, he is to be credited for having the modesty and consistency to admit that in the final instance, and/or *a priori,* our knowledge of this divine realm is based solely on *revelation,* epistemologically best approachable through the *Intuitive-Discursive Method.* This latter may serve in understanding the legitimate place of speculative theology, or in other words, the right of theology to ponder beyond the boundaries set by different schools and tendencies of theology, whatever *per se* does not oppose the Church's teaching.

One of the highly original aspects of Love for Florenskii is the *philic love, Friendship,* which he describes in a profundity that borders on mysticism. Or is it mysticism that borders on true and divine-human Friendship, *the Friendship* with the capital *F?* If cared for properly and to the very last sacrificial asceticism, "the art of arts," it is a secure vehicle that is meant to be a co-sharing and coexistence in the Trinity — and the Church that leads both and all towards salvation. Why two and not three, remains a legitimate question. A possible answer is that relating in two is the "basic element" of any community, streaming from the natural inclination of the human being, before heading out to the third and so forth. Admittedly, some of Florenskii's ideas on friendship are somewhat outlandish for a current reader, but are they therefore forcibly wrong? Somewhat boldly, we could speak of a "sacrament of Friendship," or at least of the "sacramentality" of it, but, certainly, of the "sacredness" of Friendship that Florenskii delineates for us. His monastic contacts, ideals, and (possible) vocation are the key to some of his statements: the sort of spiritual yet deeply human friendship that Florenskii ideates is one of the monastic approaches for a common journey towards salvation. On the other hand he himself did not choose to become a monk, but rather a priest with wife and children.

Never outside the *communion,* the Church, or exclusive, but, on the contrary, the zealously heeded *philia* in *agapē* is meant to *abide* in the Church, the *consubstantiality* with the others, the visible and actuating earthly presence of God, that is, *Love* in humanity. For did not "*the friend* of tax collectors" (Matt. 11:19; Luke 7:34) redefine His disciples' status because of co-sharing, i.e., communion? *I have called you friends, for all that I have heard from my Father I have made known to you* (John 15:15). Thus *knowledge* indeed becomes *Love.*

2. Sergei Nikolaevich Bulgakov: God's Love-Humility for His Creation

2.1. Biography

S. N. Bulgakov (1871-1944) was an acknowledged economist, philosopher, and above all a brilliant theologian, known especially for his treatises on sophiology and intra-Trinitarian kenosis. As a youth, he was a typical representative of the Russian Intelligentsia and the Silver Age. Bulgakov was born into the family of a provincial priest and a mother of noble origins. They resided in the small town of Livnyi in the province of Orlov. His life followed that of his father and ancestors who had been priests for about six preceding generations. In Livnyi, he received his theological education, and in 1884, he moved to the theological seminary but abandoned it in 1888 after the loss of his "religious faith" (a complex experience that turned him towards the Intelligentsia).[97] At that point Bulgakov dedicated himself to the secular study of political economy and law at Moscow University (1890-94), and added two more years of graduate studies at the Moscow Commercial Institute where he

97. Bulgakov describes his experiences in his *Autobiographicheskie zametki (Autobiographical Notes)* (Paris: YMCA Press, 1946).

also began to publish his first articles. Although he was more inclined to literature and science, he chose these subjects out of a desire to contribute better to the "salvation of his country," which included an active opposition to "tsarism and autocracy."[98] From 1898, he spent two years in Western Europe gathering material for his dissertation which was published under the title *Kapitalizm i zemledenie (Capitalism and Agriculture)*. Despite its massive volume and vast research, the work did not take root in Russia.

The years from 1900 to the Bolshevik Revolution were a period of strenuous existential search that was crucial for the rest of his life, traces of which are evident in *Dva Grada* (*The Two Cities* [1911]) written in his midlife and *Svet nevechernii* (*Unfading Light* [1917]). The latter work is "a type of spiritual autobiography or confession"[99] that was written "slowly, with long interruptions,"[100] and is a true philosophic-theological masterpiece, inspired by his return to the Orthodox Church. Prior to that, Bulgakov adhered to the ideas and ideals of Marxism but soon discovered its flaws and shallowness, which turned him resolutely against it. In 1903, he published *Ot marksizma k idealizmu (From Marxism to Idealism)*, which also marked his rapprochement with the Orthodox Church (similarly to P. Struve, S. Frank, and N. Berdiaev). In 1906, Bulgakov was granted the chair of political economy at the Polytechnic University of Kiev and successively at the Polytechnic University of Moscow, which he held until 1918. During these years, he actively collaborated with N. Berdiaev on the *Vekhi (Signposts)*, a compilation of articles on and by the Russian Intelligentsia; in addition he started the editorial board of *Put' (The Way)*. Growing in idealism and firm in faith, eventually Bulgakov was ordained a priest in 1918 and gained importance in ecclesial circles. He took part in the All-Russian Sobor of the Orthodox Church that reestablished the Patriarchate in Russia, electing Patriarch Tikhon of Moscow. Bulgakov opposed the Revolution and after 1918 he moved to the Crimea to teach political economy and theology, eventually to be expelled from the USSR in 1922 with some 160 other prominent intellectuals. In the 1920s Bulgakov composed his important philosophical treatise *Tragediia filosofii* (first published in 1927 in Germany as *Die Tragödie der Philosophie)*. He made a critical reflection on the limits of (primarily) western and modern philosophy, revealing its inability to express Christian dogmatic truths, especially on the Trinity. It also marked his turning

98. Cf. C. Evtuhov, *The Cross and the Sickle: Sergei Bulgakov and the Fate of Russian Religious Philosophy, 1890-1920* (Ithaca, NY: Cornell University Press, 1997), pp. 25-28.

99. S. N. Bulgakov, "Ot avtora (From the Author)," in *Svet nevechernii: Sozertsaniia i umozreniia* (Sankt-Peterburg: Izd. Olega Abyshko, 2008), p. 10 (SVN).

100. SVN, p. 7.

away from philosophy. From this point forward Bulgakov dedicated his full attention to a theology that was profoundly imbedded in systematic metaphysics. He explicitly addressed the subject of the Trinity and the relations of the Father, Son, and Holy Spirit on a metaphysical-theological level with his *Ipostas' i ipostasnost'* (*Hypostasis and Hypostaticity* [1925]) and *Glavy o Troichnosti* (*Chapters on Trinitarity* [1928/30]).

The tragic events during and in consequence of the Bolshevik Revolution due to which Bulgakov lost his two sons and found out about a grave and humiliating crime committed against his daughter Maria, marked decisively Bulgakov's faith as priest and father, his mystical insights and intellectual output, best reflected in his personal diary *(Dnevniki)*. After a brief teaching sojourn in Prague, Bulgakov moved with his family to Paris where, together with other Russian exiles, he co-founded the Theological Institute of St. Serge and was appointed dean and the chair of dogmatic theology. Bulgakov remained in Paris until the end of his life, teaching, publishing, and actively interacting with students and other Russian intellectuals, with vivid interest and involvement in ecumenical dialogue.

Bulgakov's sophisticated philosophical and theological work and his systematizing of Orthodox religious thought in a modern approach are regarded as an epitome of modern Russian theology, even though his treatises on *sophiology* may still raise debates with some. Among his more important works from the period of exile is a trilogy, *Kupina neopalimaia: Opyt domgaticheskogo istoklovaniia nekotorykh chert v pravoslavnom pochitanii Bogomateri (The Burning Bush: A Dogmatic Interpretation of Some Features of the Orthodox Veneration of the Mother of God* [1927]). In the same year was published *Drug zhenikha (Io 3:28-30): O pravoslavnom pochitanii Predtechi (The Friend of the Bridegroom (John 3:28-30): On the Orthodox Veneration of the Forerunner)*, and two years later *Lestvitsa Iakovlia: Ob angelakh (Jacob's Ladder: On Angels)*. These three are also known as *The Small Trilogy*. Between 1933 and 1945 appeared his second *Great Trilogy: Agnets Bozhii* (*The Lamb of God* [1933]), *Uteshitel'* (*The Comforter* [1936]), and *Nevesta Agntsa* (*The Bride of the Lamb* [1945]), the latter published posthumously, as well as the following works: *Apokalipsis Ioanna* (*The Apocalypse of John* [1948]) and *Filosofiia imeni* (*The Philosophy of Name* [1953]).[101]

101. There are numerous publications on Father S. Bulgakov and his work; therefore, we shall indicate only some here. Besides the previously quoted standard work of Catherine Evtuhov, for a fresh approach to modern Russian theology and Bulgakov's role in it see P. Valliere, *Modern Russian Theology: Bukharev, Soloviev, Bulgakov: Orthodox Theology in a New Key*

2.2. Unfading Light

Bulgakov's work, written during the First World War, was finished in turbulent revolutionary times and contains all of the significant seminal ideas later developed individually. His introduction to the book states that his intention was to "reveal through philosophical thought or to incarnate in reflection some religious meditations" regarding Orthodox life. This path leads him through an analysis of and confrontation with the western thought "that gained predominance" and its impact on Orthodoxy.[102] Bulgakov sets out by establishing a "liaison" among his initial ideas that he would revisit and develop in his successive works: "The guiding ideas of this work do not merge into one 'system' but rather in a *syzygia,*[103] in an organic gathering, in a symphonic liaison."[104] The decisive impetus was the overstressed "transcendentalism" of the West that "justifies a dialectical antithesis" of God's "immanentism."[105] Just as it happens "in some sects," this occurs when "prayer is replaced by devotion or meditation, the gaze of faith by the intellect, the sacrament by ecstasy, [and] religion by mysticism," leading to false concepts of religiosity. Precisely here is a "dialectically justified degree of religious [auto-]consciousness," of an encounter between the "sectarian man-god" and "God-man" *(khlysta-chelovekoboga . . . s Bogo-chelovekom),* where "the claims of 'gnosis' that seeks to *replace* [with itself] the threefold unity of faith, hope, and love needs even more to be countered by the humility of the believing love, which alone 'never ends — as for prophecies, they will pass away; as for tongues, they will cease; as for knowledge, it will pass away' (1 Cor. 13:8)."[106] Bulgakov defines *the humility of believing love* as the securest guard

(Grand Rapids: Eerdmans, 2000), pp. 225-372; on political theology, the anthology edited and commented by Rowan Williams: *Sergii Bulgakov: Towards a Russian Political Theology* (Edinburgh: T. & T. Clark, 1999); for autobiographical notes and diaries: Prot. S. Bulgakov, *Dnevniki (Diaries)* (Orel: Izd. Orlovskoi gosudarstvennoi teleradioveshchatel'noi kompanii, 1998), as well as *Bratstvo sviatoi Sofi: Materialy i dokumenty 1923-39 (The Brotherhood of the Holy Sophia: Materials and Documents 1923-39)* (Moskva: Russkii Put'/Paris: YMCA-Press, 2000); Prot. S. Bulgakov, *Dela i dni (Works and Days)* (Moskva: Sobranie, 2008), esp. "Memuarnaiia i dnevnikovaiia proza (Prose of Memories and Diaries)," pp. 325-412; M. Campatelli, "Nota introduttiva (Introductory Note)," in S. N. Bulgakov, *La luce senza tramonto* (Roma: Lipa, 2002), pp. xvii-lii.

102. Cf. SVN, pp. 5-10.

103. A term coined or revived by Solov'ev; see our chapter on him.

104. SVN, p. 6.

105. SVN, pp. 9-10.

106. SVN, p. 9.

against the straying and false promises of gnosis, which claims to replace personal relationship to God with itself. Such an attitude is neither true knowledge nor true religion and therefore cannot be a path to salvation. Faith and knowledge are to be of mutual enrichment as encountered in the teaching and tradition of the Church.

2.2.1. Through Faith to Truth: Gnoseology by Love

On a cognitive level, Bulgakov opposes the "gnoseologist advocates of 'mystical empirism'" who reduce faith to a mere "existential judgment" obstructing the way of true mystical knowledge. "Faith is not abstract but concrete, which means that *faith indispensably generates dogmas* . . . or, the other way round, the dogma is the expression of that which faith acknowledges as transcendental being *(transtsendentnoe bytie)*."[107] Truth — referring to the *Divine Truth* — cannot allow another truth to exist parallel to itself; it guards its primacy and uniqueness jealously, "or it is not truth anymore." Thus, it is thanks to *faith* but primarily and uniquely through *love,* that *truth* is revealed. This is a proper ontological statement, fundamental also for Bulgakov's later reflections on the Trinity: "Faith is love because truth cannot be known without loving it: truth reveals itself only to love. On the other hand, faith is substantially nothing other than love, yet a love striving, burning, and burning to ashes all that is alien to it." Bulgakov quotes Luke 12:49, the Song of Songs, and Florenskii when defining the quality of this love as *jealous.* "Jealousy is the power of love, for love cannot be non-jealous, even if love transformed into jealousy loses its sweetness and tenderness and becomes demanding and severe."[108] In the Old Testament, God revealed Himself as a "jealous God" and a "consuming fire."[109] Bulgakov highlights the negative side of jealousy (more so than Florenskii) as well as its transforming, even distorting, impact on love — unless, of course, jealousy is understood as a "protective approach" or attitude of protection. Love can be demanding and severe, but only if a major good of the loved one requires it. Even though we are looking more intently on the aspects of theology and di-

107. "The dogma is a truth that is being gained through a wearing effort of the soul's strength." Cf. SVN, p. 78.

108. Bulgakov quotes from the concluding part of the Song of Songs, adding his explanation in brackets: "Set me (says love) as a seal on your heart; as a ring on your arm; for stern as death is love, relentless as the netherworld is jealousy, its flames are blazing fire. Deep waters cannot quench love, nor floods sweep it away (Song 8:6-7)." Cf. SVN, p. 79.

109. Cf. SVN, p. 79.

vine economy in Bulgakov's thoughts, his work bears a strong metaphysical branding, especially in its gnoseology and sophiology.

2.2.2. *In the Heart of the Trinity*

In Bulgakov's view, Sophia (one of the dearest concepts to him — one he would define in a successive step) and creation are intrinsically connected. He describes this with a transition from the metaphysical concept of "God as the Absolute," as a transcendental, to a personal realm of God as "Creator" who reveals Himself to the creation in a kenotic action of love by "giving space in Himself to the relative *(otnositel'nyi),* with an inexpressible act of love-humility *(liubov'-smirenie).* He places it alongside yet outside of Himself, limiting Himself through His creation. With this very act, the Absolute becomes God,[110] and from the unconditional Absolute becomes a relative [or better, relational] Absolute *(otnositel'noe Absolutno),* or the Absolute for the relative *(Absolutno dlia otnositel'nogo),* which appears thus as a mirror of the divine absoluteness." With His auto-revelation to creation, God "renounces His absolute transcendence," which is, at the same time, the first manifestation of kenosis, i.e., self-limiting "love-humility" of God towards creation through the actions of "His energies."[111] God's *love-humility* through his energies "reveal[s] the inner-divine life *(vnutribozhestvennaia zhizn'),* making knowable what is unknowable," and shows the interconnectedness of all: just like the diverse rays of light that all derive from a unique source, the sun. Creation carries God's seal, and the Christian faith "does nothing else but to unveil what is written in the heart of creation."[112] Bulgakov does not solely describe but, like an artist, he depicts ontology. The unveiling of God's heart in creation reflects the Trinity, and the Trinity's "heart is Love," which concurrently constitutes its *Identity,* the mystery of absolute Love in the Trinity:

> In the Christian revelation, it is taken for granted that the intra-divine life is the triunity, one [unique] Divinity in three Hypostases that are one in the eternally realized love of God. God is Love. [This] Love is not a quality or attribute, not a predicate, but is the very substance *(sushchestvo)* of God. And in this Divine Love, each Hypostasis, offering Himself in love, finds Himself in the other Hypostases and realizes (the)

110. . . . *Absoliutnoe tem samym delaetsia Bogom.*
111. Cf. SVN, p. 290.
112. Cf. SVN, p. 291.

> one Divinity. In the Holy Trinity, the absolutely personal character of the Divinity, His hypostatic nature, unites with the absolute-supra-personal character of His trinity:[113] 'Trinity in the Oneness (Monad) and the Oneness in the Trinity.' . . . To the first Hypostasis is proper [the quality of] the divine Paternity, the substantiality, the source *(iskhod);* to the second Hypostasis is proper the discernment, Logos, knowledge: He is the Heart of God in which the Father loves the Son; the third Hypostasis, the Holy Spirit, feels/perceives *(chuvstvuet)* as the Father so the Son, is in Them and rejoices of the Divine Love. . . . In the Divinity cannot be admitted any succession or gradation of development because the Holy Trinity is an eternal *supra-being (sverkh-est')* in one unique, fluent act of Love and Identity *(Tozhestvo)*.[114]

As the nature of light is to emanate, so is the nature of the Divinity to "illuminate the obscurity of nonbeing" out of its profusion with "Its rays of love," a love that Bulgakov defines as a "gift of free, generous love — of favor, of grace and mercy." In this sense, creation, as the nondivine, is at the same time *invitation* and *invitee* of the Divine to participate in Its love: by Its "divine condescension and self-denial out of love, the Divinity wants the non-Self, the non-Divinity, and empties Itself in creating it."[115] The outer life of the Trinity revealed in creation finds its conclusion in and through the economy of salvation: another form of divine kenosis, of self-denial out of love, restoring the fallen creation to its primordial beauty and dignity.

2.2.3. God's Delight, Joy, *and* Play

It is at this "limit" between, yet at the same time overlapping the realms of the Absolute and creation, the Divine and the world, where Bulgakov perceives the place and role of the *Holy Sophia.* She is an intermediary "living being," the messenger of the Message, "love of Love," and receives here sublime delineation of her position:

> By force of definition, collocated *between* God and the world, between the Creator and creation, such border is neither the one nor the other, but something particular that contemporaneously separates and unites these

113. [or trinitariety] . . . *s absoliutno-sverkhlichnym kharakterom Ego troichnosti.*
114. SVN, pp. 291-92.
115. Cf. SVN, p. 292.

two realms (a sort of Platonic μεταξύ). The Holy Sophia is the Angel of creation and the Beginning of God's ways. She is the *love of Love.* The Divine Triunity, God-Love, in His closed *(zamknutyi),* self-contained [or integral] *(samodovleiushchyi),* eternal Divine act, extra-collocates *(vnepologaet)* (in the sense of metaphysical extra-collocation) the object of this Divine Love, loves it, and, by doing so, effuses on it the vivifying power of the tri-hypostatic Love *(sila triipostasnoi Liubvi).* Certainly, this object of love is not merely an abstract idea or a dead mirror, but it can be solely a living being, possessing a personality, hypostasis. And this love is Sophia, the eternal object of God's Love, "delight," "joy," [and] "play." Sophia, the "Idea" of God, cannot be merely thought of as an ideal representation, lacking any living concreteness and force of being.[116]

The concreteness, or "*ens realissimus,*" of Sophia lies firmly in her origin and mission, being the "Idea of God" fulfilling her purpose in the divine theology and economy as the *love of Love,* as well as in the interchange of loving and being loved. In his effort to denominate appropriately the role and place of Sophia, Bulgakov ventures on "thin ice" by expressly using the theological term *hypostasis* and by enumerating Sophia as the "fourth" one. This implementation of a theological formulation raised in the past notable criticism with some, even though Bulgakov unmistakably states in the very same phrase that she "*differs* from the Hypostases of the Holy Trinity" and "is a hypostasis of a different order *(inogo poriadka),*" not participating "in the intra-divine life," and that she "is not God," and more.[117] There is a unique beauty in Sophia's substance and relationship of love. Her main attributes, and essence, are to be the revelation of God's glory and of the inner-outer life of the Trinity that consists in *kenotic love:*

Sophia is not only the loved one but also loves with a reciprocating Love, and, in this reciprocal love, she receives all and *is* ALL. As the love of Love

116. SVN, p. 292.

117. Bulgakov also clearly uses a minor case for the hypostasis of the Sophia and a major case for the Hypostases of the Holy Trinity, while one of his concerns was to grant a personality to the being of Sophia. Some of the issues concerning the sophiology of Bulgakov raised questions about his orthodoxy, for which, along with some other arguments, he was rigorously condemned by the Russian Orthodox Church in 1935 at the Karlovtsi Synod. Yet the synodal commission of the Orthodox Church convoked by Metropolitan Evlogii in 1937 exonerated Bulgakov and his writings of any charges and suspicion of heresy previously raised by V. Losskii, G. Florovskii, and Sergius Chetvernikov.

> and the love for Love, Sophia possesses a personality and countenance *(lik)*, she is a subject, a person or, to use a theological terminus, a hypostasis; of course, she *differs* from the Hypostasis of the Holy Trinity, is a hypostasis of a different degree, the fourth hypostasis. She does not participate in the intra-divine life, *is not God,* and, therefore, does not convert the tri-hypostasis into tetra-hypostasis, or the trinity into quaternity. Yet she is the beginning of a new, creaturely multi-hypostaticity, for, after her many other hypostases follow (that of the human beings and of the angels), being in a sophianic relationship to the Divinity. Nevertheless, she remains *outside* of the Divine world, does not enter the absolute and self-containing fullness. Yet she is granted an access out of the inexpressible condescension of God's love.[118] Thanks to this, she reveals the mysteries of the Divinity and His depths and rejoices (plays) with these gifts in the face of God. The life of the Holy Trinity is an act of eternal self-surrender *(samootdanie)*, self-depletion *(samoistoshchenie)* of the Hypostases in the Divine Love. Also, the Holy Sophia yields herself to the Divine Love and receives its gifts, the revelation of its mysteries.[119]

While the Divine Hypostases have consubstantial shares in the Trinity, Sophia participates passively by merely "receiving" or "assimilating" *(priemlet)* "since she has nothing to give and contains only what she has received."[120] Bulgakov recognizes in this the "feminine principle" of Sophia at the beginning *(archē, bereshit)* of the world that was "conceived before being created." The kenotic notion is intrinsic to Sophia, as the realization of creation occurs through her "*presenting* [or *handing over*] herself to the Divine Love, with which she gives, beginning in herself, to everything. In this sense, she is *feminine,* receptive, and 'Eternally Feminine.'"[121] The eternal femininity of Sophia, which is more than "merely female," next to her intrinsic relatedness to Love, is

118. A similar reflection deals with the relationship of Sophia to *time* and *Eternity:* she is between the two continuums, participating in both, being above time, yet herself not being Eternity, while participating in the latter as "love of Love, yet not because of her substance but out of Love's grace." Certainly, one of her closest aspects and descriptions is that of an *intermediary.* Cf. SVN, p. 296.

119. SVN, p. 293.

120. This is once more a proof that the idea of the "fourth hypostasis" is not an attempt of heresy on Bulgakov's side but rather a description of Sophia's being and function.

121. "At the same time, she is the ideal, intelligible world, ALL, the genuine *en kai pan,* the all-unity." At these thoughts in his notes, Bulgakov refers to the works of V. Solov'ev and P. Florenskii. Cf. SVN, pp. 293-94.

one of Sophia's fundamental attributes effused by the Holy Spirit on Mary, the Mother of God, whom Bulgakov calls the "heart of the Church."[122]

2.2.4. *The Divine in the Human Being*

The image of God in the human soul is a kind of "*repetition* that does not mean identity with the Archetype."[123] Nevertheless, a substantial participation in God's nature "is realized" *(osushchestviaetsia)* in the human soul above all because of its "positive participation in the mystery of the Divine, of Its tri-hypostasity." Based on John 14:23,[124] this participation "has been marked in our spirit with sacred letters," the proof of which is also the threefold structure of the human soul: *will, intellect,* and *feeling (perception),* corresponding to the divine *Good, Truth,* and *Beauty.*[125] Man has been created as male and female (Gen. 1:27) and, therefore, the "fullness of God's image" correlates with man's "sexual duality" *(dvupolost'),*[126] the latter being the mystery and explanation of human relations among themselves. Other Fathers and medieval philosophers, such as St. Gregory of Nyssa, St. Augustine, Scotus Eriugena, etc., see this from a different perspective, but, above all, from the Old Testament tradition: after the separation of the two, the *hermaphroditic nature* leaves behind an "erotic tension as the profoundest principle, as its condition of creation so of creative energy." This explains why "the personal experience of love" can grant so many revelations about the mysteries of this world.[127]

122. Furthermore, Sophia is "the ideal soul of creation, beauty, and is all this together: Daughter and Fiancée, Wife and Mother, the trinity of Bounty, Truth, and Beauty, the holy Trinity in the world." In the Orthodox liturgy, the feast of the Holy Sophia is "formally linked" to the principal feast of the Mother of God, *Kimesis,* the Dormition. Cf. SVN, pp. 294-95. Bulgakov's creativity reflected in his Mariology would definitely deserve more attention, for instance: "For the Christian mind, it is indispensable to be aware of the fact that the femininity, precisely maternity, is glorified by the Mother of God (*Blessed is the womb that bore you, and the breasts at which you nursed!* [Luke 11:27])." Cf. SVN, p. 397. Bulgakov fully develops his sophiological argument in *O Sofii premudrosti Bozhiei (On Sophia the Wisdom of God)* (Paris: YMCA Press, 1935).

123. Cf. SVN, pp. 378-79.

124. *If anyone loves me, he will keep my word, and my Father will love him, and we will come to him and make our home with him.*

125. Cf. SVN, p. 382.

126. The term *bisexual nature* would have been a proper English rendering, yet, for its one-sided connotation in our times, we refrained from its usage. Cf. SVN, p. 391.

127. Cf. SVN, p. 399. Again, it is through Sophia that God reveals Himself, and Sophia

The "sexual duality" in Adam split into male and female, Adam and Eve, explains the sense and vocation of "the mystery of marriage: [where] the two are one in one body." Bulgakov correctly adds that, "like any religious mysteries, this one too is an antinomy for the intellect, [because of its] abolishing the law of identity."[128] He reviews the three forms of celibacy from Matthew 19:10-12, and the so-called "third sex" (mentioned here is V. Solov'ev and "his articles in *The Meaning of Love*"), i.e., those who "recognize the being in love or the 'spiritual matrimony' *(dukhovnaia brachnost')*, but despise matrimony itself and especially procreation out of diverse ideological reasons," an attitude that Bulgakov decorates with labels of "militant Don Giovanniism," "spiritual haeterism," and "belle deformity." This approach is to be found frequently in "artistic natures, painters, poets, who not seldom breed their children in an 'astral' world, which they confuse with the spiritual one." Bulgakov rejects any form of "third [kind of] sexuality," besides that of virginity and matrimony, since "the integral image *(obraz)* of the human being is that of a man *and* woman in union, in spiritual-corporal matrimony." On their own, each of them is a *half*-person, while remaining still "an autonomous personality, a hypostasis." The goal lies beyond our physical concepts without abolishing the person's identity (hypostasis), yet surpassing the *human* polarization: in Jesus Christ, "there is neither male nor female" (cf. Gal. 3:28).[129] Behold, once more the noble and necessary goal of *unity* as an imitation of the Holy Trinity's love-relationship revealed in the Eternal Logos, Jesus Christ.

2.2.5. The Sin-Fall and the Saving-Kenosis

The children of God both have sinned: she in her passive, feminine, and he in his active, male, nature. They sinned against "chastity and knowledge"

"receives this revelation in a feminine way. She is the 'glory of God' (the *Shekinah* of the Qabbala). Sophia is the feminine principle that receives the power of the Logos, and this union is described in the Word of God as the 'Wedding of the Lamb.'" Saint Paul referred to this mystery when comparing the husband-wife relationship and hierarchy to that between Christ and the church (Eph. 5:22-23). Cf. SVN, pp. 389-99.

128. Cf. SVN, p. 400. The concept of family and its purpose is one of the various occasions where Bulgakov refers to N. F. Fedorov and his line of thought. Cf. SVN, p. 403.

129. In his very depth, "every person remains hermaphroditic or his life would be impossible." On a spiritual level "the highest expression of religious consciousness that it [a soul] possesses of itself, an attitude when the soul is turned towards God," is usually defined by the religious authors and mystics as "spiritual matrimony." Cf. SVN, pp. 411-14.

(tselo-mudrie) as a state of *integral* or, more precisely, *integrity of knowledge (tselnost' mudrosti)* — a play on words in Russian with an evidently existential content. The *integrity of knowledge* and the *integrity* of the *human being* consist in imitating to perfection the Trinity's kenotic notion of love, within and outside. Chastity becomes not a goal but a result and fertile ground of such "love epistemology," love-wisdom:

> The human being could grow, realizing in himself the Divine likeness *(podobie Bozhie),* solely by the power of love. By sacrificing his hypostasis [and] going out of himself in love, following the example [image] of the tri-hypostatic God, the human being finds in himself his proper being. The wisdom of integrity *(mudrost' tsel'nosti)* and the integrity of wisdom become for him the law of life — *tselomudrie,* chastity *(tselo:* integral, *mudrie:* wisdom, knowledge, i.e., chastity is *the wisdom of the intact state),* which is, contemporaneously, as the condition, so the consequence of love.[130]

In "the law of integral being," Adam first related to God as to a Father, in a "childlike, trusting, and loving obedience" that, with Adam's *growth* or advancement, was meant to become more "comprehensive and joyous," a state equal to the "pure love of spouses who were living in their conjugal relationships the erotic ecstasy of the universe." The latter Bulgakov considers *tselomudrie.*[131] Since Adam was still in an infantile stage in his development, the evil undertook its attack: the antithesis of the *integral state of being* ("love's wisdom-cradle") caused the fall of humanity by corrupting the world and "mingling being and nonbeing." Into this "attempt of chaos" enters God with a saving kenotic action of love similar to that at the moment of creation: a "sacrificial love [of] His boundless divine humility," revealing simultaneously his "boundless wisdom and omnipotence."[132] This salvific

130. SVN, p. 424.

131. Cf. SVN, p. 424. It is somewhat beyond the context of this text, nevertheless important to note that for Bulgakov *obedience* was and remained a deeply pragmatic and universal call: ". . . He repeated insistently all through his life Dostoevsky's demand for 'spiritual denial, for sacrifice of the proud ego' of the intelligentsia. It is a return to the Christian and Russian ideal of obedience, humility, repentance. All life should become 'the holy obedience,' because, like Bukharev, Bulgakov sees in the Incarnation the foundation of culture in its fullness." N. Gorodetzky, *The Humiliated Christ* (London: SPCK, 1938), pp. 172-73.

132. Cf. SVN, p. 425. The dynamism of the fall, besides being "evidently" connected to the "ambience of sex," Bulgakov sees as a result of the evil who, in the "appearance of Lucifer,

action Bulgakov allegorically and liturgically calls "the light in the darkness" (cf. John 1:5). This light shines despite human narcissism, which is "incapable of comprehending the incommensurability of God's love-humility, His self-humiliation *(samounichizheniie)* out of love for the creation, just as [humanity] could not appreciate the nobility of the human spirit, in which immortally shone the beauty of God's image."[133]

God's creative omnipotence "is inseparable" from His "love-humility." Therefore, creation can be only a work of love, in His very foundation a sacrificial love through self-limitation, and Bulgakov explicitly uses the term *kenosis.* God's self-abasement "in the blessedness of sacrificial love" already at creation contained "another kenosis, a concrete one: the incarnation of the Son of God and the sacrifice of Golgotha (John 3:16-17)." At creation, God decided to hand over His Son, the Son decided to obey His Father's will up to death, but it was humankind's choice whether to "send Him to Golgotha; this depended [upon] the freedom of the human being."[134] We can recognize a trinity of love-action(s) in God (in the creation, provision, and restoration or salvation), a generosity and "unlimitedness of love" towards the world that "even the evil would not have deemed possible." Bulgakov supports with scriptural evidence the notion that God definitely restored and renewed the world with the divine incarnation *as kenotic action.*[135]

---

the Gnostic master," falsely promises knowledge through a "cold development," i.e., without love and relationship, and the "consolidation of one's *ego*": ". . . The abstract gnosis is a function of the *ego;* meanwhile, the commandment of God has ordered to overcome such egocentrism in the spousal love, [which is also] cosmic, divine *(v liubvi supruzheskoi, kosmicheskoi, bozhestvennoi).* The awakening of sensitivity and concupiscence of knowledge had a common origin in the human being's abuse of his proper hypostaticity *(ipostastnostiu).* Turning away from God, the human being turns his attention to the world, to creation, and falls into a one-sided *cosmism* ('immanentism'); he already thirsts only for the world, not for God, and betrays the divine love." Cf. SVN, p. 428.

133. Cf. SVN, pp. 432-33. This argument Bulgakov considers as the starting point of religion in which God revealed himself; its symbol is the "ladder of Jacob," a theme to which he dedicates a separate book and where he develops his angelology as well. Cf. SVN, pp. 434-35. See also: "The incarnation of God was realized, the ladder of Jacob between heaven and earth was raised, the salvation of the world is a concluded fact. Christ became absolutely immanent to the human being and thus to the world. He [Christ] is the deepest foundation, the most intimate essence of the human being." SVN, p. 459.

134. Cf. SVN, pp. 452-53.

135. Cf. SVN, pp. 456-57. He also connects the sacrifice on Golgotha to the sacrifice of the priest in the liturgy of Eucharist: the sacrifice on Golgotha that is offered by "the perfect Human Being" *(sovershennyi Chelovek),* who is the *High Priest, the Nonhuman Being, the New Adam, God-become-man, Jesus Christ.* Cf. SVN, pp. 464-66. As an expression of a rela-

2.3. Excursus: Trinitarian Ontology

The ontological foundation of the dogmatic truth on God as Trinity, as well as the inner and outer life of the Trinity, were concepts that Bulgakov addressed in a sequence of dedicated works, on a philosophical, metaphysical, and finally theological level.[136] His reasons for doing so are related to gnoseology as such, but also to personal religious experience. All forms of knowledge on the Trinity are dependent on revelation and thus on the dogma, the two of which alone can provide a true ontological insight on the Trinity. To this task, however, modern philosophical systems cannot step up because they ignore revelation and by doing so they abandon the path of discovering the truth about the *ontology of Truth,* which is intrinsically Trinitarian. Thus, they fail to provide a full and satisfying solution, let alone a *wholistic* answer. In his dialogue with the major philosophical systems, Bulgakov "presents the Trinitarian dogma as a new principle of rationality capable of presenting the law of identity not in static but rational terms."[137] Contemporaneously it displays *divine love* as the means and essence of this insight and comprehension.

2.3.1. Die Tragödie der Philosophie

It is not by chance that this magisterial work on philosophy by Bulgakov appeared first in German and in Germany, although originally composed in Russian. Apart from the historical events that would have made publishing after his exile (1922) in Russian and in Russia impossible, Bulgakov, like most of his contemporary intellectuals, was greatly inspired by I. Kant,

tionship to Christ, Bulgakov borrows some of Florenskii's reflections on friendship, whereby the "other" (*drugoi* from *drug — friend* in Russian) is not a "non-I"; rather, one finds his self in this "Other, the Friend, and this Friend is Christ," a friendship where the two hypostases commune in "reciprocal love." Cf. SVN, pp. 471-72. A most valid review of friendship in its various love-aspects, especially with regard to P. Florenskii, can be found in P. Valliere's *Modern Russian Theology.* Cf. pp. 368-71.

136. This somewhat artificial segregation of his approach is true in its principal implementation, although Bulgakov remains metaphysical in his analysis throughout his oeuvre.

137. Cf. L'. Žák, "'Experientia crucis' come luogo teologico. Fondamenti staurologici del pensiero di Bulgakov," in *La Sapienza della Croce,* Anno XIX, n. 4 (Roma: Pamom-Città Nuova, 2004). See also L'. Žák, "Kenosi di Cristo e mistero della Chiesa nella sofiologia di S. N. Bulgakov," in *La Sapienza della Croce,* Anno XX, nn. 2.-3 (Roma: Pamom-Città Nuova, 2004).

J. Fichte, F. Schelling, G. F. Hegel, and German Idealism in general. Nevertheless, initially he was also greatly inspired by Solov'ev, and one can discover parallels in pointing out the strengths and above all the outer limits of western philosophy.

The weakness and failure of philosophy consists in the "spirit and pathos of the System" that tries to (re-)present truth as a "logical monism," raising the claim of being an "absolute philosophy" (be it the system of Schopenhauer, Hegel, or even of Kant), meanwhile not being able to provide a satisfying metaphysical or philosophical solution for the ontology of truth, nor its gnoseology. Therefore Bulgakov ascertains: "The history of philosophy is a tragedy."[138] If reason does not want to be involved "in a sheer pondering over the world," and thus existence as such, but strives to explore its first cause *(Urgrund),* it cannot ignore "its dependency on a certain mystical-metaphysical experience" that is attained not by a "mere chain of logical conclusions" but is "a revelation of the World itself in the human conscience; a very peculiar knowledge." And since the question whether despite such mystical-metaphysical *revelation* human reason is capable of absorbing the revealed knowledge remains pending, "empiricism," according to Bulgakov, is the path to be taken: "Empiricism is the proper gnoseology of life, the revelation of all mysteries. . . ."[139] And although an adequate philosophical system given the premises is not conceivable, it does not imply that philosophy is not needed or desired. Yet any lingering in monistic systems lessens reality, and impedes seeing that "the revelation of the world is an auto-revelation of God." To admit the limits of reason and reasoning is to avoid pure *rationalism,* which on its terms "derives from the pride of reason."[140] Each, even the most seminal, philosophical judgment is expressed with(in) a logical-grammatical phrase containing three elements that are the "subject *(Satzgegenstand, Subjekt),* the copula [conjunction] *(Kopula)* and the predicate *(Satzbestimmung, Prädikat),*" based on which Bulgakov un-

138. S. N. Bulgakov, *Die Tragödie der Philosophie* (Darmstadt: Otto Reichl Verlag, 1927), pp. 11-14 (TPh). This tragic side of philosophy, though, had already been fully perceived by some great individual intellects of antiquity such as Heraclitus and Plato. Cf. TPh, p. 14.

139. "Als einzig mögliche Folgerung hieraus ergibt sich ein eigentümlich gearteter, von aller beschränkten und falschen Auslegung befreiter und in der ganzen Tiefe einer lebenserfüllten und mystischen Erfahrung erfaßter Empirismus. Der Empirismus ist die eigentliche Gnoseologie des Lebens, der Offenbarung aller Mysterien, als die sich stets alle Erkenntnis der Wirklichkeit und alles Denken über sie darstellt." Cf. TPh, pp. 15-17.

140. Cf. TPh, pp. 18-19.

folds his philological and philosophical reasoning of the *triune* character of any basic truth, soon adding a pneumatological insight: "The Spirit is a living and itself always realizing phrase."[141] Similarly to Florenskii, Bulgakov too takes the philosophical "law of identity" $I = A$ for the outset of his investigation, displaying the hypostatical character of I and, subsequently, the nonsustainability of such monistic equation. "Each judgment therefore is ontologically founded in a generic relationship of subject and object that are nothing other than an I (= Hypostasis) and its nature . . . brought to expression through its copula of being *(Seinskopula).*" And this is precisely where all philosophic systems stray: one of the above elements is defined as principal and the remaining two are then derived from or led back to it, ending, eventually, in monism and denying the intrinsic triune character in each judgment (for $I = A$ is threefold in its phrase judgment, as above). "This axiom, however, is false . . . as the substance is not uniform *(einheitlich)* but triform *(dreiheitlich).*"[142] The logic searched and applied by philosophy lies for Bulgakov in the relationship of the hypostasis as subject to the predicate through the conjunction of *being (Seinskopula),* the *is,* while admitting that the "hypostatical *I* is a living Spirit (which, by the way, is a synonym), the vitality *(Lebenskraft)* of which cannot be exhausted in any definition."[143]

The above-mentioned law of identity *I am A* $(I = A)$ is not only a tautology leading at best to a barren repetitiveness of $I = I = I = I \ldots$, but is a direct denial of identity, an "auto-entanglement of *I*." In reality the predicate of the hypostatic *I*, a second *I*, becomes its *non-I*, following an "illogical, more precisely extra-logical *(außerlogische)* synthesis," and since this *non-I* is the same yet different than the *I-hypostasis,* just as with Florenskii, it can be identified as a *B*.[144] *B* is the (auto-)revelation of *A* that is realized in and through the conjunction *is* representing the process of *thinking* or (self-)*reflection* of *A* in the "ontological sense of origin."[145] Completed with the cop-

141. *Der Geist ist ein lebendiger, ständing sich realisierender Satz.* TPh, pp. 18-19.

142. Cf. TPh, pp. 20-22.

143. "Er offenbart sich in der Zeit, steht aber selbst nicht nur über der Zeit, sondern auch über der Zeitlichkeit. Für die Hypostase gibt es kein Entstehen und kein Vergehen, keinen Anfang und kein Ende. Indem sie außerzeitlich ist, ist sie zugleich auch überzeitlich, ihr gehört die Ewigkeit, sie ist ebenso und im selben Sinne ewig wie Gott, der Selbst, aus Sich, dem Menschen bei dessen Erschaffung Seinen Odem eingehaucht hat. Der Mensch ist Gottes Sohn und ein erschaffener Gott, und das Bild der Ewigkeit ist ihm unverlierbar und unauslöschlich eigen." Cf. TPh, pp. 24-25.

144. Cf. TPh, pp. 29-31.

145. Cf. TPh, pp. 31-32. "Jedes 'ist' hat nicht einen grammatikalischen und logischen, sondern einen ontologischen Sinn zum Ursprung: in ihm verwirklicht sich die Selbstoffen-

ula of being *(Sein)*, the *substance* is "so to speak an equilateral triangle"[146] always presupposing the other two angles regardless of where one starts out and thus the *substance* is a "metaphysical triunity *(Dreieinheit)* that finds its expression in the phrase." Crucial is the cognition that their "relation" is not of logical but of "ontological nature." Reason necessarily has to deal with "antinomies," and Bulgakov comes to the conclusion that "all philosophy is philosophy of revelation — a revelation of the Divine *(Gottheit)* in the world . . ." and following this line, "all philosophy, as a science *(Lehre)* of the world, universe, is necessarily, at the same time, also a theologizing."[147]

The above-discussed Trinitarian principle of judgment is, of course, valid also in anthropology since the human being was modeled in the image of God: "It means that he carries in his entire spiritual nature the form/character *(Gestalt)* of the Holy Trinity," which is already apparent in the Scripture when God, in creating human being(s), refers to Himself in the grammatical plural.[148] The implication is far-reaching also for philosophy: if the Trinitarian aspect intrinsic to God is the same to, and in, the human being, *truth* as such can be comprehended only through knowing and reflecting on the divine, i.e., God, and thus through theology. In fact "the triune nature of the human spirit is a living symbol of the Holy Spirit and, contemporaneously, its revelation, a Church dogma, the sole postulate providing the idea to comprehend the human spirit."[149] Precisely on this anthropological level it is essential to remember that given the above considerations it is through an "immediate mystic-intuitive act" that the human personal *I* gains cognition of the *divine hypostatic I* (and its triunity) as well as of all of its manifestations, the latter of which relates also to the idea of *uncreated Sophia*.[150] The

---

barung der Hypostase, es ist die Brücke über den Abgrund, die die Essenz mit dem Sein, den Satzgegenstand mit dem Prädikat verbindet; es begründet die Wirklichkeit, die Existenz. Die Kopula 'ist' ist das Leben des wahrhaft Seienden. Und so ist denn die Substanz, d.h. der Geist, die in actu seiende Dreieinheit von Subjekt, Objekt und des Zusammenhanges zwischen ihnen, ihres Seins, wobei alle drei Momente weder voneinander getrennt noch auch miteinander verschmolzen werden können." TPh, p. 32.

146. Bulgakov in his book provides a depiction of a triangle with letters A, B, C at each angle.

147. Cf. TPh, pp. 33-36.

148. Cf. Genesis 1:26-27.

149. Cf. TPh, pp. 133-35.

150. ". . . Und nicht nur das psychische Subjekt, als ein Komplex in ständiger Wandlung begriffener Zuständlichkeiten, sondern auch das gnoseologische Ich, die Gesamtheit aller Formen, Schemata und Kategorien der Erkenntnis, ist in bezug auf das noumenale Ich Prädikat. Daran, diese Wahrheit nicht genügend klar erkannt zu haben,

predicate is the herald, and "speaks of everything, is an all-encompassing Word, the Worldlogos *(Weltlogos)*. This Logos rises from the depth of the Hypostasis' nature." This dyad of subject and object, i.e., Hypostasis and nature, is where the act of judgment, ergo thinking, occurs, yet the dyad does not remain a dyad "but leads to a triunity *(Dreieinigkeit)* . . . through the vivifying potency, which is the existence, a living life, reality, being."[151] The decisive passage, or bridge, from the metaphysical realm to theology lies in the potency of being: "Through the fact that there is a vivifying potency of being *(Seinspotenz)* that grants participation in the reality to all, the Hypostasis descends (in)to the level of being *(in die Ebene des Seins)*, altogether becoming actually accessible to it."[152]

2.3.1.1. The Dogma of the Trinity as Postulate

The dogma's challenge for philosophy is contemporaneously its strength and justification for theology: "The dogma on Trinity is a divine mystery that becomes accessible to the human being solely through a divine revelation and discloses itself to faith alone." It is less of a formula of comprehension as a signpost, a guide to "truth and goal of all religious life." More importantly: "The human being's acquaintance/dealing with God sets [the person] free from the constraints of reason(ing) *(Vernunft)*, which implies that the dogma's standing above reason(ing) is of no obstacle."[153]

---

krankt die Philosophie Kants und die ganze von ihr ausgehende gnoseologische Bewegung. . . . Auch das Wollen ist nur eine Hülle des Ich, sein Zutagetreten im Sein, denn der starke, autonome Wille, den hier die Metaphysik des Schopenhauerschen Voluntarismus einführt, ist nichts weiter als hypostasierter Psychologismus." Cf. TPh, pp. 139-41. In this context see with regard to Schelling, Hegel, and Cohen, respectively: TPh, pp. 145-46, 150.

151. TPh, 147-48. "Die Realität hat scheinbar keine eigene Stimme und Gestalt, ist nur das *Wie* eines *Was*, gleichsam dessen Modus." TPh, p. 148.

152. "Dadurch, daß es eine lebendigmachende Seinspotenz gibt, die alles an der Realität teilhaben läßt, steigt die Hypostase in die Ebene des Seins hinab, wird ihr diese überhaupt erst zugänglich." TPh, p. 149.

153. "Man lebt sich in das Dogma hinein, und das Leben in der Kirche ist nichts weiter als dieses Sichhineinleben in die Dogmen, das Teilhaben am Mysterium des Göttlichen Lebens, an dessen Fülle: 'Wer mich liebet, der wird mein Wort halten; und mein Vater wird ihn lieben, und wir werden zu ihm kommen und Wohnung bei ihm machen' (Jn 14:23). Der Umgang des Menschen mit Gott befreit von den Schranken der Vernunft, führt aus der Vernunft heraus, was auch der Grund dafür ist, dass das Über-der-Vernunft-Stehen des Dogmas kein Hindernis bedeutet." Cf. TPh, p. 189. Once more with regard to the relation of dogma-philosophy from a different viewpoint: "Das Dogma hat einen philosophischen Sinn, und die Erschließung dieses Sinnes ist es, worauf die Bemühungen der philo-

2.3.1.2. Self-Limitation and the Fullness of the Other

The *non-I* is the reflection of the *I* and its self-limitation at the same time. Although here expressed only implicitly, the theological principle of *kenosis* applies even to metaphysics. Bulgakov points out that the *non-I* "limits the substance of the Absolute" as long as it does not become, while still reflecting *I*, also equal to the *I:* hence $A = B$. On a theological and ontological-trinitarian level it reflects that God the Father begets his Son, the Logos, who is the revelation and expression of the Father's self-limitation at the same time, "which is possible in a spiritual begetting, and in which consists the mystery of the Father's and Son's hypostasis" (John 10:30; 14:7, 11). Love, again, figures as the link in this most ontological of all relationships and exemplifies, first in the form of a dyad, the unique bond "of full identity" while preserving the difference of two hypostases: "The Father reveals Himself, yet He does it in begetting His only-begotten Son from Himself. Father and Son are united through the unity of Divinity and as Hypostases united through love."[154] The reciprocity of this love-bond is ontological and existential, i.e., substantial; meanwhile a dyad,[155] naturally, "does not exhaust the substance that is triune in its auto-determination . . . for with begetting the Son, also the outgoing *(Ausgang)* of the Holy Spirit is a given fact." And truly, the Holy Spirit, the "hypostasis of Being is in its ontological destination the third Hypostasis that closes the circle and binds the first two Hypostases with each other, conferring form/character *(Gestalt)* to the first and the potency of being *(Potenz des Seins)* to the second." And while all of this is a mystery "hidden in the depths of the Divine life," Bulgakov is convinced that the "philo-

---

sophischen spekulativen Dogmatik, die somit zugleich auch allgemeine Metaphysik ist, gerichtet sind. Die Analyse der Substanz hat uns ganz unmittelbar zu dem Postulat der Dreieinigkeit hingeführt. Die Frage ist so gestellt: wenn das Absolute dreieinige Substanz ist, so wird durch diese dem Menschen seine eigene geistige Natur verständlich. Ob diese dreieinige Substanz ist — darauf kann die Vernunft selbst keine Antwort geben und muß die Antwort des Glaubens annehmen, und sie harrt dieser Antwort, die vom ganzen Wesen des Menschen, das ohne sie ein unentwirrbares Paradoxon ist, gefordert wird. . . . Die Vernunft gibt eine logische Projektion des Dogmas, gleichsam einen Schatten, aber auch dazu muss sie in ihrer Struktur, in ihrer Problematik einen Zugang zu ihm finden, dasselbe Problemschema aufweisen. . . . Das Dogma ist ein wesentlicher Ausweg für die Vernunft, eine Rettung vor ihren Antinomien und Aporien." TPh, pp. 189-91.

154. Cf. TPh, pp. 192-93. Bulgakov dedicates various pages to the topic of *begetting* of the Son by the Father underlined with scriptural quotes, while also admitting the very *act of begetting* would naturally remain "abnormal" to human comprehension. Cf. TPh, pp. 194-98.

155. For more on the relationship of dyad and triad see TPh, pp. 203-5.

sophical sense" of it can be comprehended by reason.[156] Critical for our passage from metaphysics to theology is the fact that the *triunity* does not consist in the equality of three units, but of "concrete, living Hypostases,"[157] where the "*third I . . .* makes a dyadic egoism impossible," and the communion of *us* is imbedded in life-giving and vivifying love, to be reflected in the church.[158] The constitutive bond of love in the Trinity is the life-giving and life-creating act for the world and all creation, "acts of grace and love to humankind of the giving, nothing but giving Divine Love" and under no circumstances a "metaphysical necessity."[159]

2.3.2. Hypostasis and Hypostaticity

Bulgakov's passage from *absolute* as *transcendent* to *absolute* as *personal God* and *Spirit* occurs in this work on the very first page. The *I* represents the hypostatic, relational *I* of God (as opposed to a self-enclosed love), a *Oneness in Trinity* and *Trinity in the Oneness:*[160] "The limitedness of *I* is authentically overcome by love in which *I* preserves itself through self-sacrifice *(pogubliat' sebia)*, going beyond its limits towards the other *I*, thus becoming the image of the Absolute Spirit, as in relationship so of its own hypostatical being."[161] The next step is establishing the relationality in the Trinity: "*God is love* (1 John 4:8) as a triunity *(triedinstvo)*, in which the primordial act of reciprocity and self-surrender *(samootdanie)* in love is being realized. A single Absolute subject reveals its absoluteness in the reciprocal love of the Three, overcoming by it the limitedness of *I*, goes out (in)to the other *I* through self-surrender and self-depletion *(samoistoshchenie)* in sacrificial love and finds in it anew its given-up *I*. Thus the three Hypostases are realized in their unity *(v edinii)*, [which is] a revelation of one absolute *I*." Apart from having introduced *samootdanie* as a concept and expression

156. Cf. TPh, pp. 199-201.

157. Cf. TPh, p. 203. Also: "Die Dreiheitlichkeit der Gestalt Gottes ist uns durch unsere eigene Natur, durch die dreieinige Substantialität unseres Geistes vertraut und verständlich. Das Geheimnis und die Unfassbarkeit der absoluten Substanz beruht nicht auf der Dreieinigkeit, sondern auf der Dreihypostasheit und, infolgedessen, auf der Hypostasierung der drei Momente der unteilbaren Substanz und auf der Entstehung der Hypostasen durch Zeugung und Ausgang." TPh, p. 211.

158. TPh, pp. 215, 217.

159. Cf. TPh, pp. 218-20.

160. . . . *Edinitsa v Troitse i Troitsa v Edinitse.* Cf. S. N. Bulgakov, "Ipostas' i ipostasnost'," in *Trudy o Troichnosti* (Moskva: OGI, 2001), p. 21.

161. Bulgakov, "Ipostas' i ipostasnost'," p. 20.

of self-sacrificial love,[162] Bulgakov again provides scriptural references of God, the "Absolute subject, the three-hypostatically existing I" who addresses himself in the plural. The tri-hypostatic God's life is in His love among the three, to his very self and to the creation. The dynamism, and functionality, if you like, of this "proper and *non*-proper . . . humble, self-denying, and limitless" love is best exemplified in the Son-Father relationship, opening up our comprehension of the Trinity's life, as mentioned previously. "This love of God is not only the primordial *act* of life, but also its *content (soderzhanie),* inseparably united among themselves. Included in this tie is the reason of God's revelation (in)to creation, the transition from transcendent to immanent."[163] The latter, God's revelation in(to) His creation, and God's love for his very self, "is Sophia who is the love of Love, the primordial subject and content of God's love," a subject to which Bulgakov dedicates further clarification.[164]

2.3.3. Chapters on the Trinity

Chronologically seen, Bulgakov links the above-mentioned *sacrificial love* to the cross placing it ontologically into the center of the Trinity — as its love and relationship. This staurological concept was part of a homily on the *Power of the Cross* composed and published in Prague in 1925, and Bulgakov reverts to it in his *Chapters on the Trinity* as well. There are numerous flashbacks to his previously examined *Tragediia filosofii* and the *Ipostas' i ipostasnost',* but the accent in general would shift from the gnoseological level more towards ontology, as well as theology and anthropology: "The human being out of his own forces cannot know God, unless He [God] reveals Himself to him. . . . *The Divine Image* in the human being, even though obscured by sin and aberration, is an ontological principle of revelation. Anthropology is a natural principle of revelation. Of course, she cannot substitute for revelation, yet grants the possibility of its acceptance."[165] One of the

162. For the very first time though in his *Svet nevechernii.*

163. Cf. Bulgakov, "Ipostas' i ipostasnost'," pp. 21-23.

164. Cf. Bulgakov, "Ipostas' i ipostasnost'," pp. 26-33. Bulgakov's solution introduced here with regard to the being and entity of Sophia is its "capability of *hypostasizing, to belong to* a hypostasis, to be its revelation, *to surrender* to it." Thus in her passivity and receptivity she is what mystics called the "eternal feminine" *(vechnaia zhenstvennost').* Cf. Bulgakov, "Ipostas' i ipostasnost'," p. 28.

165. Cf. S. N. Bulgakov, "Glavy o Troichnosti," in *Trudy o Troichnosti* (Moskva: OGI, 2001), p. 54.

novelties is the aspect of "*us*" introduced as a summary of *I-you-he* relatedness, united yet not mixed, a "bonding triune self-consciousness of *I*, unity, revealed in three.[166] . . . *Us* is an *ontological love* in *I*, which lives not solely in itself, but also in *you* and in *he*, since love precisely is life in the other and with the other." Nevertheless, Bulgakov asserts that even this "self-determination of *I*" eventually leads to aporia, as the dyads of *I-us* and *I-you* are antinomies.[167] This can be overcome only on the ontological level of *I-You-He* of the Absolute Subject: "Unity as Trinity, and Trinity as Unity; the triunity of the Divine Spirit *(Bozhestvennogo Dukha)* is the answer to all postulates and end of all aporias."[168] The final gnoseological step to the mystery of the Trinity follows a reflection on the "hypostatic love" as a relation between *I-You-He* in the *Us:* "God is Love, love not as 'property' but the very substance *(sushchestvo)*. It is from love and through love that one can gain access to the contemplation of God's mysteries.[169] The tri-hypostaticity *(triipostasnost')* of the Divine can be comprehended only as a pre-eternal act of Love,[170] it establishes the triunity *(triedinstvo)* of the Divine Subject as an eternal reciprocal love."[171] The self-sacrificial element of the relations in the Trinity, encoded in the metaphysical aspect of the Absolute Subject, is of such fundamental importance that only through self-sacrifice, a "sacred circle" of sacrifice of love, is it possible that self-realization, self-affirmation, self-awareness, and self-revelation, as well as that of creation, of each Hypostasis can occur. Only the relatedness of three can break the "ontological egoism" of *I-I*.[172] It is redeemed by a different ontology, a staurological ontology of love:

> The Divine *I* in the act of self-positing [or self-constitution] *(samopolaganiia)* as *I*, goes out from itself and self-posits itself *(samopolagat'sia v drugom)* in the other *I*, removing any disparity and thus revealing itself as absolute. But, such self-positing *(samopolaganie)* of itself in the other and

166. . . . *nekoe vnutrennee i, skrepliaiushchee troistvennoe samosoznanie ia, edinstvo, otkryvaiushcheesia v trekh;* ". . . unity revealed in three" is a different yet similar aspect of the "Trinity revealed in one" of the previously quoted work. Cf. "Glavy o Troichnosti," pp. 60-61.

167. Cf. "Glavy o Troichnosti," pp. 60-61.

168. Cf. "Glavy o Troichnosti," pp. 67-68.

169. . . . *sozertsanie tain Bozhiikh.*

170. . . . *predvechnyi akt Liubvi.*

171. Cf. "Glavy o Troichnosti," p. 80. "The Absolute Divine Subject Is Hypostatic Love" (p. 81).

172. Cf. "Glavy o Troichnosti," p. 96.

> through the other is *Love as true act*, the ontology of love. God is love, and as Love, He is the Holy Trinity. Love is the assertion *(utverzhdenie)* of oneself and of one's [proper] self not by self-assertion but by self-surrender — self-positing through self-denial *(samootrechenie)* — these are higher forces and a higher beatitude of love. And if the *cross* is the symbol of sacrificial love in general, thus the Holy Trinity is the power of the cross *(krestnaia sila)* of the reciprocal self-denial in the bosoms of the tri-hypostatic Subject. And the Holy Cross is not only the symbol of our salvation but equally of the Holy Trinity's life. This explains the place and reverence that is granted to the Cross and the Power of the Cross in Christian piety. . . . The mutual depletion by the cross *(Krestnoe vzaimoistoshchenie)* and the mutual fulfillment by the cross *(vzaimovospolnenie)* express the life of the tri-hypostatic Divinity as in the relation of hypostatic self-consciousness *(samopoznanie)*, so of natural self-revelation *(prirodnoe samoraskrytie)*. God is Living Love, which means sacrificial, a Love that acquires itself in sacrifice and therefore also eternal life, for Life is Love, just as Love is Life (any defectiveness of love is defectiveness of life too). The power of the cross is an infinite divine power by which are surmounted all boundaries not only outside but also within itself and in its self-realization. Solely the tri-hypostatic Love is [an] *absolute* Being. . . .[173]

It is indeed justified and worthy to end the excursus on Bulgakov's gnoseology on the Trinitarian love-ontology with the staurological concept of the fullness of sacrificial love in the Holy Trinity — insights that undoubtedly require the mystical experience our author repeatedly referred to.

2.4. Jacob's Ladder — *The Need for Personal Love*

Perhaps somewhat surprisingly to a reader of our times, Bulgakov develops a systematic reflection on love in his book dedicated to angels, primarily inspired by the story of Jacob's dream (cf. Gen. 28:10-12, and following). The explanation for this we find in the introduction of the author, "The Heavenly Friend," initiating the first paragraph with some fundamental divine and anthropological observations on love:

173. "Glavy o Troichnosti," pp. 97-98.

> God-Love created the human being for love. The heart of the human being wants to love and desires to be loved. It suffers when it does not love or is not loved. It wants to expand, accommodate in itself, in its life, other lives, many lives, all lives; going out from itself, it tries to melt [or fuse, *rasplavit'sia*], to lose itself in the other, to become the *other* to himself, to be lost in the ocean of universal love. To lose one's own soul *(dushu)* in order to save it, such is the precept of love admonished by the Word, by whom it [the soul] is penetrated.[174]

We notice that "God-Love" is the very first word and, as such, gives clear purpose to the progress of the love-relationship that the angels serve, the progress of human nature towards its perfection. The character of this maxim of love, found in the "poorness of spirit," is entirely self-offering and self-sacrificing, capable of making a "non-I" in itself, a "non-mine" on its own, "to be fulfilled in emptying itself, to be elevated by humiliating itself, to live in love, to become love according to the image of the Holy tri-hypostatic, consubstantial, and indivisible Trinity: such is the destination of the human nature." This sharing and learning impedes the human being to act in what is against his nature — the "auto-isolation . . . because there is no life, nor eternity in nonlove." Meanwhile, in *Unfading Light,* the strength of love is its jealousy; here it is the capacity implanted into the human being to become someone else, which consists in abandoning one's *self* for someone else, to merge with him and to be "filled with the universal life." The auto-sharing and self-sacrificial love, uniquely proper to God-Love, reveals the mystery of "universal life" through our earthly life: "The human being lives only in the measure in which and in how much he loves, and dies in the measure in which and how much he does not love."[175] Thus *life* and *love* are, again, essentially same, the same realm.[176] The self-sacrificial character of this love-life cannot be enough emphasized, for our understanding of, i.e., acceptance of — and cooperation with, God-Love, depends upon it, just as

174. S. N. Bulgakov, "Lestvitsa Iakovlia: Ob angelakh," in *Malaia Trilogiia* (Moskva: Obshchedostupnyi Pravoslavnyi Universtitet o. Prot. A. Menem, 2008), p. 395 (LVI). This is a reprint from the 1929 publication in Paris.

175. Cf. LVI, p. 395.

176. For Bulgakov, this also is true on an epistemological level. In one of his earlier articles, he corrects Descartes' *cogito ergo sum* into *amo ergo sum,* shifting the ontological statement from epistemology into the realm of existential truth of relatedness, from *ratio* to *relatio.* Cf. S. N. Bulgakov, "Priroda v filosofii V. Solov'eva," in *Sbornik pervyi o Vladimire Solov'ove* (Moskva: Put', 1911), p. 10.

do our very life and salvation. As "God is Love — not impersonal but hypostatic, tri-hypostatic," so *love* in the divine Trinity is equally fully "personal, completely impregnated with personal qualities" — equally is our vocation to respond in a whole, integral, all-embracing, yet still fully personal way, as in the example of Christ: "Christ in His human nature, as the New Adam, establishes the possibility of an all-human love [or love for all humankind] *(vsechelovecheskaia liubov')*." Love for one's neighbor remains planted in each human being's likeness of God, his love of his very self, which, however, is not an egoistic self-love. Very importantly, the "need of a *personal* love, to love and to be loved, is deposited in the human being as his ontological character"; and as such, it streams back to the metaphysical Absolute and, beyond that, the personal tri-hypostatic God through whom human nature is divinized in Christ.[177] The adjective *personal* safeguards our personality, our freedom of choice to love. The fullness of sacrifice is in the auto-diminishing of our proper self at the realization of our proper *I* in the *drugoi (the other)*, who thus can become a *drug*, or a *friend*.[178] This need for a dyadic and personal form of relationship is underlined by the "psychosomatic *(dukhovno-telesnyi)*, spiritual-corporeal *(dushevno-telesnyi)*" reality and the need in human love for "its concreteness," which is to be realized in a concrete space and time.[179]

2.4.1. *The Spiritual — Guardian Friend*

In monasticism, we find a particular form of love's realization in the "refusal of any *personal* terrestrial love" for the "absolutely personal love for God."

177. Cf. LVI, pp. 396-98. "Omnis individuation est negation. . . . In the deification, in the love of grace, the creature so to speak loses its creatural character and with it its [own] limitedness and unites with the divine love. Nevertheless, in this love there is no place for a metaphysical depersonalization through the death of the hypostasis." Also, Bulgakov treats the subjects of "syzygic love" and "dyads and a series of dyadic persons" in the "chain of worldwide love," which is about the communion-building character of love. Cf. LVI, p. 399.

178. Bulgakov points out the nonaccidental common root of friend(ship) and love in Greek *(philos* deriving from *phileō)*, Latin *(amicus* from *amo)* and, of course, the "genius of the russian-slav" realm looking for a *drug*, a friend in the *drugoi*, the other, this latter being of particular importance to him. Cf. LVI, p. 398.

179. Cf. LVI, pp. 402-3. At the same time, this "human love carries in itself the sign of fatal" incompleteness because it is subdivided into "multiple relations of love," goes into fractions and "particular manifestations," even though they all are but a color range of a "multicolor spectrum of love's white light." Cf. LVI, pp. 404-5.

The ideal of monasticism, for Bulgakov, consists in the "assumption of the angelic image."[180] The capability to love, which is a grace, is destined to love the *other,* in this case a personal and *spiritual* Friend given to every person: one's guardian angel. He lives "one and the same life" with that of the person looked after. The coexistence occurs *in silence* when we are taught and inspired "in a celestial pedagogy"[181] to undertake an inner and ongoing initiative of sanctification.[182]

> The guardian angel is a friend who loves the person that he is entrusted with, and this love is also for him [the angel] personal. . . . He scrutinizes our soul with a gaze full of affection, tenderness, cordiality, light, and joy, which shines [with] all the power of love. In this love is hidden not only our salvation, but also, as in each love, his own life. This love possesses a vital force not only for us, but also for him. He is a being in the spiritual world who lives one [and the same] life with us, shares our fate, and looks for our reciprocity. The guardian angel is this friend who loves us and, therefore, lives with us. His relationship with us is determined not by an external service, but by an interior link of love that already testifies about an ontological union.[183]

The ontological union conditioning the very existence of a being is one of the strongest expressions of selflessness, whether in a human or angelical sphere, and again "the force that establishes the link between the two spheres is love." The novelty that Bulgakov introduces is the kenotic quality of the angelic love. As all kenotic love, it is based on "voluntary self-abasement" and "metaphysical auto-impoverishment," and its supreme quality is in the sacrifice of abandoning the "beatitudes of the angelic spheres" in order to assist the world and unite its life to that of the entrusted person:

> The angels serve the world because they are sent into it by God. Moreover, they love the world which they serve, just as the guardian angel loves his human double *(chelovecheskogo dvoinika).* And since there is

180. . . . *priniatie angel'skogo obraza.*

181. The theme of *divine paideia* or *pedagogy* has already been addressed by F. Bukharev in his *Three letters to N. V. Gogol'* and pointed out in its broader context by Valliere in his *Modern Russian Theology,* pp. 27-29, 180-90.

182. Cf. LVI, pp. 405-7.

183. LVI, pp. 408-9.

> no love without sacrifice, in which consists the strength of love, the guardian angel's love towards us is a sacrificial love [which is] not merely involuntary, [granted] by the divine disposition, but also a freedom of consent, the *kenosis* of the angelic nature. . . . For the non-corporeal spirit, this means a metaphysical auto-impoverishment, an ontological kenosis, thanks to which his life gets united through love to the life of the carnal human being.[184]

There is no love without sacrifice, for true love implies self-sacrifice, a theme that Bulgakov rightly likes to reiterate. Further there is a quality expressed through the *patience* of our heavenly *Friend* and companion, a patience that for us humans is a reward of spiritual consolation and inner peace.[185]

2.5. The Lamb of God — *The Victorious Power of Love*

Since Bulgakov develops his ideas on love mostly as presented in *Unfading Light,* as well as in the following oeuvre *The Comforter,* we shall merely highlight some of the relevant and novel notions in his most remarkable book on Christology. The author's attention lies with the kenotic aspect of love and relationship of Christ, since the "sonhood is already [an] *eternal kenosis,*" having its beginning before the creation of the world. Love through sacrifice and joy through suffering in the divine economy are apparently contradictions for human logic:

> The Son's love is the sacrificial, self-renouncing *(samootvergaiushchii)* humility of the Lamb of God, "foreordained before the foundation of the world" (1 Peter 1:20). . . . [Christ the Father's Word] being rich, He makes Himself poor, becoming sacrificially silent in the bosom of the

184. Cf. LVI, p. 411. We find a beautiful summary of the *angelic kenotic love* in its "metaphysical auto-renunciation" in the book's conclusion. Once more, the strength of love "consists in its sacrificial character," and the love of the angels is selfless since they serve by their very nature; they "live outside of themselves, not their proper life but a metaphysical kenosis. By their nature, they are *only* angels, hypostatic *metaxu.* . . . The world is wrapped from the wings of the angels. . . . In the presence of God's throne, they live one commun[al] life with us, united with the union of love." Cf. LVI, pp. 561-63.

185. The two aspects, *inner peace* and *spiritual consolation,* describe Bulgakov himself based on one of his own mystical experiences. Cf. LVI, pp. 414-15.

> Father. . . . The sacrifice of the Father's love consists in self-renunciation *(samootrechenie)* and in self-emptying *(samoopustoshenie)* in the begetting of the Son. The sacrifice of the Son's love consists in self-depletion *(samoistoshchanie),* in being begotten *(rozhdennosti)* by the Father, in the acceptance of birth as begottenness. These are not only pre-eternal facts but also acts of both, the one and the other. The *sacrifice* of love, in its reality, is pre-eternal suffering. . . . If God is love, He is also sacrifice, which manifests the victorious power of love and its joy only though suffering.[186]

This highest sacrifice would miss its point if it remained self-enclosed and self-sufficient, if it was not based on mutual love of the dyad between the two Hypostases. The third Hypostasis is the "*joy* of sacrificial love, the bliss and actualization of this love," a theme that Bulgakov further develops in *The Comforter.* The *Beauty* of this relationship reflects the fullness of its *Truth* in the *Revelation.* Importantly, there is *one* love in the Trinity and not three separate ones.[187] Here again Bulgakov underlines the fundamental truth in the relationship between multiplicity and oneness, which is "the copula *is* [, which] signifies not a relation of formal logic but the ontological link of love."[188]

186. S. N. Bulgakov, *Agnets Bozhii* (Moskva: Obshchedostupnyi Pravoslavnyi Universtitet o. Prot. A. Menem, 2000). Cf. pp. 130-32 (AGB).

187. Bulgakov discerns between Ousia-Sophia and the Creational-Sophia, a refined and, at times, rather complex reflection that we cannot further pursue here. Yet, as an example: "Ousia-Sophia is the Life of life and the proto-ground of all creaturely life. She is the divine life in God, who is love. Therefore, divine life too is love, which is the power of this life: The *All* — multiform, multidiverse, but also one — is linked in the *All-unity* by the power of love as one in the many and the many in the one, as all in all." This postulate would elucidate the link between the one and the multiplicity on a metaphysical level: "Love in God's life is an all-permeating, all concrete multi-unity, as a spiritual organism. This form of unity is not given to us in our rational logic, which corresponds to the corrupted state of the sinful world. This all-unity is, nevertheless, a necessary ontological postulate for our thought and feeling in relation to life, not as this relation is given, but as it is proposed — the universal cosmic *sobornost'* of concrete all-unity in divine love." Cf. AGB, pp. 134-35.

188. Cf. AGB, p. 135. On the following pages, Bulgakov also differentiates between the various "forms of love" in their expression: 1. The hypostatic love; 2. God's love for Sophia, his self-revelation and love for the divine world; 3. The Sophia's response in love to God; 4. The love as "centering force of the spiritual pan-organism," a sort of impersonal love, "as the connecting and organizing principle, as the universal mutual attraction and order of divine ideas existing in the divine world." Put simply: "Love here is the natural order of the divine world." Cf. AGB, pp. 136-38.

This is a beautiful exemplification of God's love for the world, which God *needed* to create, a love based on "personal communication" with the human being,[189] an image and description that can help us overcome the "divine versus world" antagonism once perceived from God's point of view: "God comes even into the fallen world; God's love is repulsed neither by the infirmity of the creature nor by its fallen image. . . . The Lamb of God, who takes upon Himself the sins of the world, comes into the world. God thus gives everything for the deification of the world and its salvation; there is nothing that is not given. Such is God's love; such is love. Such is love in the intra-Trinitarian life, in the mutual giving of the three Hypostases; such is love in the relation of God to the world."[190] When one thinks there is nothing more that could be said about God's love and His care for the world, the human intellect simply needs to be challenged further to open up for the divine sphere.[191]

2.6. The Comforter — *Agapē the Gift of Love*

Pneumatology in Orthodox theology enjoys some well-merited, particular attention, not the least so with Bulgakov who intrinsically connects love on an ontological level with the Holy Spirit in the Trinity. The Scripture "attests that God is . . . a tri-hypostatic Spirit: Father, Word, and Holy Spirit. It also attests that God is love (1 John 4:8, 16)," not only loving and possessing love, but that "love is His very being . . . a definition that is not descriptive but ontological in character." Bulgakov draws the conclusion that "God is Spirit-Love," and, in a consecutive step, he describes "the Holy Trinity as Spirit whose life is Love."[192] Since Bulgakov identifies the Holy Spirit with love,[193] there are numerous references to the subject of

189. Cf. AGB, pp. 195-96.

190. AGB, pp. 197-98.

191. The union of love among the Hypostases is so unique that, following Metropolitan Filaret's theology, Bulgakov speaks of the redemptive act — the "kenosis of the Divinity" — of their *co-crucifixion,* where "love itself is co-crucified. . . . The sacrifice of the Son presupposes the co-sacrificial love of the entire Holy Trinity: 'God so loved the world' (Jn 3:16), and love has no power without sacrifice." Cf. AGB, pp. 372-73.

192. S. N. Bulgakov, *Uteshitel'* (Moskva: Obshchedostupnyi Pravoslavnyi Universtitet o. Prot. A. Menem, 2003). Cf. p. 78 (UTE).

193. See especially chapter three, "On the Spirit of God and the Holy Spirit." UTE, pp. 200-23.

love in this present work, as well as the ontology of its presence in the Holy Trinity.[194]

New, and somewhat surprisingly not encountered so far, is the concept of *agapē* as that which we encounter in the fifth chapter, i.e., towards the end of the book in the part on "The Gift of Love."[195] Bulgakov provides a deep anthropological insight by inverting our perspective of the image of God in the human being based on the ontological foundation of love, by stating that "the capacity to love is the seal of God's image in the human being," a gift granted most gratuitously to those who seek and have the *will* to seek.[196] The specific kinds of love granted by the Holy Spirit as "a gift of love in Pentecost" is what Bulgakov calls *"churchly love" (liubov' tserkovnaia),* which converts society into "churchliness" through its "ontic power," creating *koinonia,* communion, in the end result.[197]

Alongside *philia* and *erōs* and leaning very much on Florenskii's *Pillar and Ground of Truth,* the first brief mentioning of *agapē* is virtually a definition in a single phrase: "Agapic love is love in general, which includes various forms and nuances of love, whereas philic love is qualified, individualized, personal love, love as friendship." Bulgakov also highlights the positive sides of *erōs* (in historical context) present in most kinds of love as "inspiration, transcendence of oneself, ecstatic love," being a constitutive part of friendship's *syzygic* relationship as well.[198] Moreover, he understands "churchly love" as containing both *agapē* and *erōs* contemporaneously and in antinomy:

> In the dual character of churchly love as *agapē* and *erōs,* there is manifested the antinomic duality of the Christian path as ascesis and creative activity, of repentant humility and creative inspiration. Self-renunciation is realized in *agapē:* an individual dies in his egoism in order to live in and by the whole. In *erōs,* an individual, experiencing

194. Some of which can be found already in the *Lamb of God* (indicated by the author himself) and the previously examined *Tragediia filosofii* and "Glavy o Troichnosti."

195. Cf. UTE, pp. 346-63.

196. Yet another approach: "The capacity for love, or the vocation of love, in which the fullness of life is being realized, is a feature of the image of God in the human being and thus is above all a gift of *natural* grace as the *postulate* of love." The gift of natural grace is built on or can be traced in the "Trinitarian composition" of the human being: "spirit, soul, and body." Cf. UTE, pp. 364-65.

197. Cf. UTE, pp. 369-70.

198. Cf. UTE, pp. 371-73.

> inspiration to the point of self-transcendence, ascends to creative self-revelation. *Agapē* can be realized even by a solitary individual; it even presupposes a certain spiritual isolation, with withdrawal into the inner cell of the heart. By contrast, *erōs* is the going out of oneself, a certain opening of the heart by the power of inspiration, which is given by the *erōs* of love. In syzygial connectedness, an individual person comes to see himself in and through another. . . . Friendship as spiritual "syzygy" (to use the Gnostic expression employed by Vladimir Solovyov) is the most general expression of love as *erōs,* without regard to distinction of gender.[199]

Nevertheless, *erōs* is "transfigured" by *ascesis,* the discipline of love being a truly monastic task, yet not solely[200] because, in the end, transfiguration is accomplished solely by the Holy Spirit.[201] After all, "love lives by sacrifice; and the kenosis of the Holy Spirit is a sacrifice of love, brought by the very hypostasis of Love." The only thing that can stop this outpouring is *unlove,* the "limited receptivity of creation." Thus, God restrains His love in the name of love, and His sacrifice of love is to suffer the imperfection of the world: "He must suffer and — wait."[202] Bulgakov is correct: this is *kenosis,* yet kenosis *is* an aspect of God's sacrificial love, *agapē.* However, he avoids such a conclusion, and we do not wish to commit an *eisegesis.* For Bulgakov, kenosis is *not* an aspect but the very principle of the tri-hypostatic love. This may be the reason why *agapē* appears in his writings so rarely and, rather, as one aspect of love.

In Bulgakov's concluding page dedicated to the person of the first

199. UTE, p. 373.

200. Cf. UTE, p. 373. When talking about *erōs,* Bulgakov makes his position clear: "*Erōs* is enslaved and oppressed by sex to such an extent that the latter has appropriated and thus distorted in the eyes of many the very name *erōs,* which is usually understood only sexually, although it is not really such." On the other side, he argues that the monastic "mortification" of "flesh," i.e., sex, and also of *erōs* would be a "spiritual suicide." Evidently, he is not speaking against chastity but about *a* denial of one's proper "sexual identity," for, based on the Scriptures, "the Church, as well as its foundation, churchly love, is represented in Revelation not only by images of agapic and philic love, but also by images of spiritual *erōs,* of inspiring and inspired love, of a certain divine ecstasy." (For instance, in the Song of Songs, the "true subject" is not the couple, the bride and bridegroom, and their love, "but *Love* itself.") Cf. UTE, pp. 376-77.

201. Cf. UTE, pp. 394-95.

202. UTE, p. 405. In the part on the *Father,* we can read Bulgakov's mystically poetic, kenotic hymn on the Father's love. Cf. UTE, pp. 442-43.

Hypostasis, the Father, we find the final, mystical closing of the circle on the initial quest of the metaphysical *Absolute Subject:* "The Absolute *loves;* He is the Father. That is the idea that unites the entire absoluteness of the Heavenly God and the entire power of His revelation in the relative, for this power is *Love.* Metaphysics finds fulfillment in this divinely revealed doctrine, for it actualizes all its postulates in the latter."[203]

The final image is God *as* love founded on a genuine metaphysical and theological reflection just to reach a long-known ontological realm: "All that we know and love in the Son is the Father, for as the Son is, so also is the Father. All the love and inspiration that we have in the Holy Spirit are also the Father, for as the Father is, so also is the Holy Spirit, who proceeds from Him, His own Spirit. . . . If the Son and the Holy Spirit are Love and the revelation of Love, the Father is Love itself, the very Heart of Love and, truly, the Will of Love." Love and trembling walk hand in hand in front of the Almighty's face as we "*bow [our] knees before the Father of our Lord Jesus Christ* (Eph. 3:14), we, His creatures and His children."[204]

Conclusion

Protoierei Bulgakov dedicated decisive parts of his work to the subject and theme of love, and scrutinized them with a unique systemization and consistency in their connotation, the latter aspects surpassed, perhaps, only by P. Florenskii. Bulgakov also implemented his personal, spiritual, and mystical experiences, but clung, above all, to the methodology of metaphysics and theology as if keeping in mind the members of the Intelligentsia of his time and times to come who would read his reflections. In fact, he addresses love in its most varied forms, like the different-colored rays that are parts of the divine light of Love which may appear under diverse aspects but with singular characteristics, as one unique source of Love that God (unlike the Absolute, personal and tri-personal) communicates through the divine Sophia — a being and entity, God's divine idea and messenger, the love of Love, a personality outside the Trinity, and yet in a unique relationship with it.

203. "But this is also the only possible and true fulfillment of the postulates of the religious consciousness, which simultaneously requires that the heavenly God be remote from us and that He be near and accessible to us. These two things are harmonized in the revelation of God and the Father, heavenly by His Divinity and near to us by His Fatherhood." UTE, p. 451.

204. UTE, p. 451.

Bulgakov's gnoseological examination of Trinitarian ontology is unique and substantial: the Absolute Subject, the personal and tri-hypostatic God whose substance and inner and outer relationships consist in Love, can be known only through love. We witness a gnoseology of principal judgment — law of identity — by means of and in the divine substance of the Trinitarian love engraved in the being and character of the human being who was formed in the image of God-Trinity, i.e., God-Love.

For some reason, Bulgakov does not give broader consideration to the concept of *agapē* as such, other than a rather general acknowledgment, referring primarily to Florenskii. This is somewhat surprising, for *agapē* has a unique position and role in the message of the New Testament and of Christianity. Though we could theorize that Bulgakov took this for granted and did not wish to reenter the topic anew, or simply that his attention was focused on the entity and role of Sophia, and, certainly, on *kenosis* as one of the maxims of God's love.

Bulgakov showed impressive depth of thought and daring speculative originality, and not least a novelty of approach, drawing on his personal spiritual experience, at times, as with Sophia, angelic love and the intra-Trinitarian life, venturing into less examined or unexplored realms. His main focus lies in the integrity *(koinia, katholicity,* or *sobornost')* of love's vocation, and rightly so: imitating the tri-hypostatic kenotic love-union, the relationship in the Holy Trinity, the human being is called to learn and apply this *oneness* of love, so that through willing self-sacrifice for the good of the other, division may disappear, and, through grace and divinization, humankind may regain its *integrity* with(in) God-Trinity.

3. Lev Platonovich Karsavin: Love as a Dialogue of Suffering

3.1. Biography

Lev Platonovich Karsavin (1882-1952) was born in St. Petersburg into the family of a famous ballet master.[205] Karsavin, too, was an exemplar of Russia's religious intellectuals par excellence, entering "organically the tradition of Christian philosophy which in Russia began with the works of A. Khomiakov and V. Solov'ev."[206] He approximated them as an author in

205. His sister, Tamara Karsavina, also became a renowned ballerina.

206. Cf. S. S. Khoruzhii, "K chitateliu," in L. P. Karsavin, *Malye sochineniia* (Sankt-

style, and was a gifted philosopher, historian, and religious writer. His chief formation and primary field of work was in medieval history,[207] and to this period are connected his first works, including his doctoral thesis in history, *Osnovy srednevekovoi religioznosti v XII-XIII vekakh, preimushchestvenno v Italii (The Foundation of Medieval Religiosity in the XII-XIII Centuries, Principally in Italy* [1915]). Due to the Bolshevik Revolution, his research shifted exponentially to other fields, such as metaphysics, philosophy (of history), ecclesiology, theology, and the question of the fate of Russia — the euroasian idea and movement. Karsavin proved himself in a variety of literary styles in these above-mentioned domains, stretching from scientific research to poetry and mystical insights, the latter deriving from his personal faith experience.

In 1922, Karsavin found himself among the philosophers expelled from Russia. Initially, he lived in Berlin and, from 1926, in Paris where he participated in the religious-philosophic academy initiated by Berdiaev. Later in 1926, he moved to Lithuania where he taught at Kaunas University. From 1931 he began publishing in Lithuanian his *Istoria evropeiskoi kul'tury (The History of European Culture)*, a multivolume work that has never reached its conclusion. In 1940, Karsavin was transferred to Vilnius, where, in the mid-1940s, he focused on a course of esthetics, yet was removed from the cathedra after the 1940s annexation of Lithuania to the USSR. Eventually he assumed a position of director at the local museum of art. After the invasion of Lithuania by the Soviet troops, Karsavin was arrested in May of 1949 for his previous criticism of Stalinism and the same year deported to the polar labor camp of Abez' in Kom ASSR for the disabled. It was there that he spent his last years, and died in July 1952 of tuberculosis. Up to his death, despite the hostile circumstances, Karsavin did not give up on his work as well as teaching and debating philosophy and theology, which he led with his prison mates.[208] A

Peterburg: AO "Aleteiia," 1994), p. 7. See also S. S. Khoruzhii, "Zhizn' i uchenie L'va Karsavina," in L. P. Karsavin, *Religiozno-filosofskie sochineniia*, vol. 1, "Renessans" (Moskva: SP "EWO-S&D," 1992), pp. v-lxxiii.

207. Having spent a couple of study-years in France and Italy (1910-12), his master's degree was *Ocherki religioznoi zhizni v Italii XII-XIII vekov (Essays on Religious Life in Italy of the XII-XIII Century).* These study-stays may have provided Karsavin with a more benevolent and objective view of the Catholic Church than what one might usually have found in Russian ecclesial circles of his time.

208. A collection of these valuable works and memories appeared, written and edited by his fellow inmate A. A. Vaneev: *Dva goda v Abezi: V pamiat' o L. P. Karsavine (Two Years in Abez': In Memory of L. P. Karsavin)* (Moskva: Izd. "Zhizn' s Bogom"/Brussels: La Presse Li-

truly original feature in Karsavin's professional career, and unique for the epoch, was the degree of doctor of theology conferred on him while he was a layman by the St. Petersburg Theological Academy.[209]

Among his numerous works are *Monashestvo v srednie veka* (*Monasticism in Medieval Ages* [1912]); *Metafizika liubvi (Metaphysics of Love)* published in *Russkaia mysl' (Russian Thought)* and *Saligia* (1918); *Katolichestvo* (*Catholicism* [1919]); *Vostok, Zapad i russkaia ideia* (*East, West and the Russian Idea* [1922]). Also in 1922 his first systematic exposition of his metaphysics of all-unity *(vseedinstvo)* and love appeared: *Noctes Petropolitanae (Petersburg Nights).* Further: *O nachalakh: Opyt khristianskoi metafiziki* (*On Principles: An Essay on Christian Metaphysics* [1925]); *Peri archōn. Ideen zur christlichen Metaphysik* (1928); *O lichnosti* (*On Personality* [1929]); and *Poema o smerti* (*A Poem of Death* [1932]).[210]

---

bre, 1990), and contains, among dialogues and poetry, Vaneev's memories on Karsavin and also a brief introduction to his biography and works *(Ocherk zhizni i idei Karsavina).* Vaneev himself was a man of letters, a well-versed thinker, and was rehabilitated by the Soviet regime in 1955. Cf. *Dva goda v Abezi,* pp. 7-19; similarly, Iu. B. Melikh, *Personalism L. P. Karsavina i evropeiskaia filosofiia (L. P. Karsavin's Personality and the European Philosophy)* (Moskva: Progress-Traditsiia, 2003), pp. 9-18. This latter book provides in four chapters a well-structured overview of the different aspects in Karsavin's philosophical works. Chapter three is dedicated to the "theme of love in L. P. Karsavin's philosophy of personality." Cf. pp. 155-77. A standard work on "history and metahistory" as well as translations of Karsavin's *Sonnets* and a detailed bibliography we find in A. D. Siclari, *I Sonetti di L. P. Karsavin: Storia e metastoria* (Milano: Francoangeli, 2008). A work dedicated explicitly to the bibliography of Karsavin: *Lev Platonovich Karsavin: Bibliografiia — Bibliographie des oeuvres de Lev Karsavine* (Ru-Fr), ed. A. Klementiev (Paris: Institut d'Études Slaves, 1994). An essential source in our quest on Karsavin's Trinitarian ontology and kenotic aspect of love in the Trinity were the contributions of Professor L'. Žák, especially his article,"Kenosi di Cristo nell' 'età d'argento' dell'ortodossia russa: La prospettiva di L. P. Karsavin (1882-1952)," in *Il crocifisso e le religioni,* ed. P. Coda and M. Crociata (Roma: Città Nuova, 2002), pp. 209-29. Zernov designates Karsavin as "one of the most original Russian religious thinkers of the century." Cf. RRR, p. 342. Also: Khoruzhii, "Zhizn' i uchenie L'va Karsavina," pp. v-lxiii; G. A. Wetter, "L. P. Karsawins Ontologie der Dreieinheit: Die Struktur des kreatürlichen Seins als Abbild der göttlichen Dreifaltigkeit," in *Orientalia Christiana Periodica* IX, nn. 3-4 (Roma 1943): 366-405.

209. Karsavin became an extraordinary professor at this university in 1913. Cf. G. A. Wetter, "L. P. Karsavin," in *Dva goda v Abezi,* p. 9, also pp. 10-19.

210. Zernov lists the latter work under the title *A Poem of Death: Doubt, Science and Faith,* published in Paris, 1925. Cf. RRR, p. 342. A 1992 edition of this work indicates 1931 and the journal of the Lithuanian philosophical circle "Eranus" as the year and place of its first publication. Cf. Notes in *Pamiatniki religiozno-filosofskoi mysli,* Lev Karsavin, *Religiozno-filosofskie sochineniia,* vol. 1 (Moskva: Renaissanse SP "Ewo-S&D," 1992), p. 321.

3.2. Saligia[211] — *or Evolved Christian Metaphysics*

Although Karsavin does not seem to have a high appreciation of metaphysics as a science, considering it *cold* and *remote,*[212] with *Saligia,*[213] he places himself among the finest Christian metaphysicians of modern times. His initial phrase sets faith as a benchmark for relating to God, a God whose image is "All-one and All-good," an image of hope and compassion: "Beloved reader, to you I turn in [the] hope that you believe in God, sense His breeze *(veianie)* and hear His voice, that resounds in your soul. And if my hope is not deluded, we shall reflect together on the thoughts that I have put down and shall take comfort in the All-one and All-good God."[214] It is evidently a gnoseological "journey to know God"[215] on which the author, applying a refined literary language, invites his reader. This gnoseology is founded upon the proper hermeneutics of the relationship between *Creator-creation* and that of a personal *I-You.*[216] An essential concept in this journey is *dvizhenie,* a love-propelled *notion, development,* and even *motion,* which strives towards *union* and *unity; dvizhenie* is the aspiration of creation and the individual *towards* and *into* the Divine. "I pursue God *(vzyskuiu Boga),* i.e., I love God, striving towards Him and into Him as all creation strives towards Him. My love's desire is to become fully merged *(sliianie)* with the Divine. . . ."[217]

211. The acronym *"Saligia"* stands for the first letters of the seven mortal sins in Latin: *superbia, avaritia, luxuria, invidia, gula, ira,* and *acedia.* Karsavin has chosen this acronym in order to help the reader memorize "the order of the seven deadly sins," for *innumerable sins* descend from them, and in order to discover their interrelatedness. But the final purpose of it, indicated by Karsavin, reveals the author's brilliance in metaphysics, which we shall discuss in the main corpus of our text. Cf. L. P. Karsavin, *Put' Pravoslavia* (Moskva: Izd. Folio, 2003), pp. 65-66 (PPR). (This edition of Karsavin's chosen works follows the previous editions, *Religiozno-filosofskie sochineniia,* vol. 1, and *Malye sochineniia.* Cf. PPR, p. 4.)

212. He appreciated most meditative prose and poetry: "Poetry is the meaning and system. Poetry is metaphysics lifting up 'meta, beyond' the boundaries of nature. Metaphysics lives in poetry; poetry, revealing its meaning, dies in the cold light of metaphysics." PPR, pp. 460, also 461, 466. He perceives this similarly in the person of the philosopher and, yet even worse, in theologians. Cf. PPR, p. 518.

213. And his subsequent metaphysical works.

214. ". . . *v Boge Vseedinom i Vseblagom.*" The former presumably resonates with Solov'ev's concept of *vseedinstvo.* PPR, p. 23.

215. . . . *put' Bogopoznaniia.* Cf. PPR, p. 25.

216. Cf. PPR, pp. 26-29.

217. Cf. PPR, p. 30. The divine voice that speaks in every human soul says: "Your goal is not in fighting some kind of ruling evil but rather the fullness of *our* love for God and with God." Cf. PPR, p. 62.

The talk here is about the *quality* of the relationship with the Divine precisely through the Divine's unity, i.e., its rootedness in Love.[218] *Love* nourishes and sustains the unity in the "Triunity" itself, which on its turn is the ideal model of (any) love-relationship. Thus Karsavin means the *unity of love with(in)* God that is searched and strived for, yet meanwhile strictly respecting the individual characteristic and identity of each person, like the distinctions of the Divine Persons within the Trinity. His reasoning is metaphysically consistent and the divine dynamism is valid also in our terrestrial realm. Unity and diversity/distinction are a creative tension where love is born and thrives:

> For there is none, will not and cannot be any love, where there is no distinction between the loving [one] and the loved [one] and their unity is undistinguished. Love germinates in differentiation,[219] derives from splitting, is conditioned and [re-]created by Unity. . . . And tell me, is God Love, if He has none or is not in Him His Son, who is different from Him and [yet] one with Him? Consequently, some kind of opposition *(protivostoianie)* or divergence of creation from God is indispensable. Yet be mindful, that currently we are talking only about the indispensable condition of love, and not about the indispensable condition of perfect love,[220] which can be only in the Triunity *(Triedinstve)* and the image of the Triunity. Further note, that to our love, eternally unsaturated by the terrestrial [love], is granted an authentic pledge of our eternity.[221]

218. Karsavin employs a conscious alternation of capitals and minuscules, especially with the word *love.*

219. . . . *liubov' zarozhdaetsia v razdelenii.*

220. *Perfection,* and *imperfection* as its juxtaposition, is an important concept to which Karsavin recurs frequently, even more so towards the end of his life in the prison camp. Cf. L. P. Karsavin, "O sovershenstve: Metafizika sovershenstva v traktate khristianina-uznika (On Perfection: Metaphysics of Perfection in the Treatises of a Christian Prisoner)," in *Bogoslovskie trudy* 39 (Moskva: Izd. Sovet russkoi Pravoslvanoi Tserkvi, 2004), pp. 269-96.

221. PPR, pp. 30-31. To reflect, to some extent, upon the matter of *unity* and *diversity* in God and His creation requires a metaphysic-philosophical construct that may appear contradictory and yet perfectly true: "To put it differently, if the creation is something [i.e., exists], and all that *there is,* is God (a vsio, chto *est',* est' Bog), creation cannot be creation. Creation is not creation, if it is creation; and the Absolute is not absolute, if it is Absolute." Karsavin dares and apparently enjoys venturing into similar reflections while remaining pragmatic and spiritual, and pragmatically spiritual, when he notes that it is the true discovery of God, through one's heart, which bestows joy upon the human being: "Don't you see how much and how lofty you know by your not knowing? What a joy fills you when ap-

Karsavin proceeds with great caution and subtleness when defining unity and multiplicity, as their relationship reflects humankind's relationship to its Creator and, consequently, God's providential care for the human being. God gives rise to the multiple, or creation, by "self-determination, i.e., self-limitation and self-finalization,"[222] the latter expression apparently coined by Karsavin himself, based upon what he discerns between "God-Revelation" *(Bogoiavlenie)* and "God-Existence" *(Bogobytie)*,[223] the former being the visible side of the hidden latter.[224] It renders a character of an existential unity (in essence) with God:

> [Consequently,] all our reason, perception, desire or action, is nothing other than God, and besides God we cannot see anything else in them. Therefore comprehend, human being, how exalted you are and with what reverence you are to relate to that which you mistakenly consider to be yours; understand how you are [obliged] to take care of the gift that has been sent down upon you and with what circumspection you are [obliged] to relate to those similar to you, remembering the Gospel words: "Don't judge!"[225]

In the context of non-judging, Karsavin understands *love* as the human being's attraction to the *good* moved by the Divine within him.[226] "The initial attraction[227] is grounded and conditioned by the self,[228] in which lies its great beauty." The self-determination of the Divine attraction, being "God's image," and while never disregarding the individual's "free will," establishes the

---

proaching the true mystery of God and His creation, as inscrutable as the most high mystery of the Triunity!" Cf. PPR, p. 31.

222. . . . *samoopredelenie, samoogranichenie, samookonechivanie* — respectively.

223. Once more, most probably Karsavin's own expression.

224. Cf. PPR, p. 32.

225. PPR, pp. 32-33, 62.

226. In this Divine motion/notion he counts also "anger, envy, hatred," where the fundamental idea is that they are "just" or righteous as long as they represent God's true design with creation. Cf. PPR, p. 33.

227. We encountered some philological challenge with rendering the concepts of *vlechenie, stremlenie,* and *dvizhenie,* all of which have their precise nominal translations yet also overlap in the given context as *attraction, aspiration,* and *motion* or *impulse.* This is caused by the metaphysical character of the text and concept, in which *attraction* and *aspiration* (causing in the final instance *the motion* towards and into God) are, in their essence of *movement,* identical.

228. . . . *pervoistochnoe vlechenie samoosnovno i samoobuslovlenno.*

sense of love in itself: "'Why do I love?' St. Bernard of Clairvaux asked himself, and answered: 'I love because I love.' Behold: the best and most devout answer!"[229] The more rapid this motion becomes,[230] the more "divinized" one grows, which God actuates through Christ; and we can discover in the course of history that there are many free, reasonable individuals who consented to this process. "The relative being of the universe[231] is nothing other than the motion *(dvizhenie)* created by God, and only by God, a motion towards Him and in Him of every free 'I,' differentiated only by the pace of their motion, namely, by the degree of their free-reasonable communion *(priobshchenie)* with God's own motion and thus composing a glorious panegyric song to the Creator of variety *(vsiacheskogo)*. Look how wisely everything is established in the beautiful creation of God."[232] The ultimate sense of this *motion* is unity and existence in "the Divine life," where the proper "I" searches its delight in God and in the multitude of the "other I."[233]

How truly God is interested and involved in (the personal) human history becomes literarily visible in His suffering, which Karsavin refines into suffering *with us:* passion — compassion *(stradanie — sostradanie)*. "Pain,

229. "Why is aspiring the free-reasonable 'I'? — Well, because it is aspiring, or if you like because it is the image of God and God is aspiring and [there] is no 'why' and no 'for what.'" Karsavin illustrates that *motion* and/or *aspiration* is intrinsic to love as it is intrinsic to God. Yet the crucial point is not why it is happening but rather why it is happening "insufficiently," something that he considers as "sinful." His answer is as precise as simple: because we are lazy *(lenivyi)*. Cf. PPR, pp. 45, 191, 492. Also: ". . . the world is lazy to die," i.e., to live in love. Cf. PPR, p. 59.

230. As fast as "endlessly-fast, i.e., absolute quietude." Cf. PPR, p. 50.

231. . . . *otnositel'noe bytie vselennoi.*

232. Cf. PPR, p. 46.

233. Karsavin builds his reasoning gradually from the *"pervoe ia," the first I,* to the *"vtoroe Ia,"* the *"second or other I."* Cf. PPR, pp. 49-56. Allusions to this differentiation and inseparability of the two entities, just as of the "ia," "I" in relation to God as "All-Unity," are very present in this work. One can easily derive the ecclesiological dimension of humankind's interrelatedness and necessity in the common struggle. The tie between the various *"I's"* is, in God, love, where the well-being of the other "delights more [than one's own], as a pledge and agent of unifying love . . . selflessly donating myself to them." Cf. PPR, pp. 55-56. Karsavin readdresses the theme of "hatred and anger" towards the "otherness of the other" in the existing multiplicity of the creation, which, in the final result, is God Himself: "Envy, hatred, and anger also reflect the shining Sun of Love and lead us . . . to His infinite light, in which 'the righteous are shining like lights.'" Yet, a "sick and blind person" misses his true goal and "does not see himself as love." Cf. PPR, pp. 56-57. Only one thing can be worse than anger — which, in fact, is needed — and that is "*toska,* melancholy — the worst of all deadly sins." Cf. PPR, p. 58.

torments, and suffering" are the lack of felicity or beatitude, yet at the same time are indubitable signs of existence; "consequently, as of itself so by the unbreakable tie with beatitude, suffering is the Divine or Theophany."[234] Through his staurology Karsavin exemplifies what Christ meant by demanding us to be "like children," to live and trust like children of God, even (or precisely) in times of suffering: "Turn swiftly to the cross, look at the bleeding wounds of the Crucified, hearken to His moaning, look how He is suffering even today in His innocent little children, and then tell me — is the Divine not being compassionate with you?"[235] In this sense of supreme sacrifice demonstrated by God in becoming human and saving us by his suffering and death on the cross, Karsavin exhorts his fellow believer to follow the divine example of salvation by *self-sacrifice* if an intercessory word or action cannot stop injustice or crime:

> If the word of exhortation does not help, place yourself between the sacrifice and the tormentor and lay down your soul for your brothers, for it will be of great benefit as for them so for you when together with your body also your otherness from them will be destroyed and you will resurrect in them and in God. And the more you are yourself, the more selflessly and distressfully you are dying for the other, the more significant and needed is your death, for the more is then in you, and through you and in them Christ Himself defeating death and turning it into life. . . . However, your anger shall be holy, that is, cultivate your anger till it is not transfigured into a blazing love that consumes the otherness of the other from you.[236]

Otherness is a transitory state that can be overcome solely by transformation through self-sacrifice and not purely death. That means that passivity will not do it, and cooperation is indispensable. "Now, therefore, aspire to cognize only the good, for there is no evil, and its appearance [or illusion] ceases, burned by redeeming suffering." The appearance that remains is that of the *Creator* "on whose face the images of all His creation are being reflected."[237] This is

234. Cf. PPR, pp. 48 and 49. On "Highest Theophany" as "Divine-Suffering" that expresses itself in the terrestrial suffering by its proper incarnation and thus transforms the terrestrial one "into suffering-gratification [or suffering-delight] *(stradanie-naslazhdenie),*" see PPR, p. 58.

235. PPR, pp. 48-49.

236. PPR, p. 63.

237. Cf. PPR, p. 66.

the *image of God's love* that Karsavin offers. If we were looking for a definition of the kenotic mystery of God's love in metaphysics, his description certainly would be among the most empathetic ones.[238]

3.3. Noctes Petropolitanae[239]

As the title suggests, this is a sequence of meditatively philosophical or, better, metaphysically meditative reflections in nine "Nights" on both kinds of *loves:* that with the lowercase and that with the uppercase initial.[240] Through his artistic soul and medievalist formation, Karsavin at times is inclined toward a somewhat "baroque" form of expression that has been contested by contemporary reviewers as stylistic and contextual "contradictions."[241] This piece is a link between *Saligia* and *A Poem on Death,* as in context, so stylistically and chronologically. Therefore, some of the reflections, such as the examination, meditation of, and aspirations towards love in the *Third Night* for instance, are repeated or subsequently developed.[242]

In the *First Night,* Karsavin initiates from his personal experience. "My heart is filled with love," and invoking *Love's* return, he claims: "More oppressive than death is the thought that you would not return, worse yet is the thought that you did not exist within me." Love has uprooted his "previous life, which was not life but a pale dream," also realizing in *Love* that truth is attained through an other, beloved, person, as well as life and the way that "solves all riddles." It is a shared walk of common struggle full of sacrifice. Karsavin invokes *Love* "who loved us yet in whom I loved in accord and united with you" and whom he entitles with *Vladychitsa Liubov', Our Lady Love.* She is "an all-possessing, invincibly moving element . . . alive by her freedom."[243] Therefore, freedom as personal choice of a subject is being safeguarded also on

238. As an endnote to Karsavin's reflection, it needs to be mentioned that he brought his reasoning to the extreme human realm of destruction, which is war. He remains consistent in his "kenotic love-solution," in an awe-inspiring manner. We deliberately decided to omit commenting on it, since without the strict context of his line of thought woven from a delicate thread it could be easily misinterpreted.

239. *Petersburg Nights.*

240. The first standing for a relationship, and the second is the personification of Love, God.

241. Cf. PPR, pp. 69-72.

242. Cf. PPR, pp. 111-16.

243. Cf. PPR, pp. 73-74.

an anthropological level: "Love, she is me,[244] and she is all [that is] not me. I can decline her, close my soul. I also could not acknowledge the precept that is evident to me and not make it my duty. Yet freely and of my own choice I align myself with her and in merging with her *(slivaiasia s nei),* I do not differ anymore. My Love is not a mere feeling!"[245] The resulting relationship, since respecting the otherness of the other, yet being fully merged, becomes a "mysterious biunity" *(tainstvennoe dvuedinstvo).*[246] Similarly to St. Augustine, not recognizing love's most intimate proximity but meanwhile yearning for it, for Karsavin *Love* reveals herself first in his personal love-relationship to a woman. He perceives *Love* "looking and pouring out of her precious eyes" at him. These moments are of such profound oneness that the world around disappears and the concept of human *unity* reaches entirely new dimensions: "I do not know anymore where I am, where is the loved one [she] and where is Love? All has merged into one inseparable unity."[247]

Naturally, human love, which is being reflected in the other, derives from divine Love. Intimate, unique, universal, and all-connected at the same time: "I hear the harmony of your soul. Yet this harmony is the very law *(zakon)* of Love that has become audible and alive in you, the law of the universe, in you finally revealed to me."[248] Further: "Love, it is I and you, indissoluble from it. You are revealing me, Love, and by Love I am disclosing myself in you and you in me." The *Love,* which and in which one is disclosed, is the "great mystery of the All-Unity *(Vseedinstvo).*" Yet before arriving at this point, during a blizzard in the harboring quiet of his room, Karsavin discovers and spells out the "triune" *(triedinyi)* character of any life-unity: "Love it is I and she, my beloved, and this is more than us: the very All-one Life/the Life of all-unity *(Vseedinaia Zhizn'),* that descended into us, uniting us and being one with us."[249] At this point we find the first proper gnoseological suggestion of Love as means of comprehending the divine mysteries: ". . . We shall never doubt the cognizing power of Love: she *is* the Cognition itself *(Poznanie).* Nonetheless, it is difficult to appropriate and to describe what is known by her, since neither definitions nor words suffice: all expressions are

244. In Russian, the noun "love" (like "sophia") is of feminine gender, so Karsavin, in Russian, naturally keeps referring to it as "she," with an undercurrent of tenderness and intimate personification that may be lost in translation.

245. Cf. PPR, p. 74.

246. PPR, p. 75.

247. Cf. PPR, p. 75.

248. PPR, p. 76.

249. Cf. PPR, p. 78.

endlessly less than what we may try to say." The knowledge of Love, and to be known by Love, is beyond words. The solution is offered in the following paragraph: That which is "elusive and inexpressible in words is being known through/by love." Yet it occurs in a mystical notion: *knowledge,* the spiritual gaze of our understanding, has to go beyond Love's "bottomless abyss of forgetting and knowing, beyond all excellence, there, where unity is being acquired." Anything less than that is but "a reflection, a dream of a biunity *(dvuedinstvo),* which in its mutability merely copies reality."[250] For: "[This divine] Reality is even deeper than that of life. In it contradictions are extinguished and the ineffable truth *(neskazuemaia istina)* is revealed." Karsavin leads his gnoseology of the actively *knowing Love,* and thus knowing the *truth,* through human love back to the bosom of interhuman relationship. A relationship of physical union where two souls "found each other and compenetrated each other *(vzaimoproniknovenie),* in which spirituality and corporeality are one unity."[251] Such intensity and wholeness of union in this conjugal spirituality is meant to lead to a "new true body in Christ and in the Church, [where] the incarnation of the Logos in His Bride is being repeated."[252] This is why with(in) Love this biunity finally becomes a "triunity" as imitation of a divine triunity, as we shall see later. The experience of "triunity" about which Karsavin speaks here is incorporating his "entire empiricism" of interhuman, divine-human, personal yet shared relationship and therefore refers to it as "our triunity."[253]

The *Second Night* and *Third Night* build upon this human aspect in a logical sequence, and an approach to Love exemplified in Dostoevky's *Brothers Karamazov,* introduced by "Love is a universal power, 'l'Amor che move il sole e l'altre stele.'"[254] The example of a couple's biunity of love and its instantaneous transition to a triunity, which thus co-builds the Church in order to be full of Love, possesses a social aspect and applies to all of humankind. "Each and all triniunity is built up by a biunity,"[255] yet those languishing ones who yet have not encountered their chosen ones and "cannot lift themselves above the corporality of love" are like reflections of "the Sun of

250. Cf. PPR, p. 79.

251. . . . *ediny dushevnost' s telesnost'iu.*

252. Cf. PPR, p. 80.

253. Cf. PPR, pp. 83-84. "Remember the triunity of your love; do not forget it even for an instant." PPR, p. 85.

254. Quoting Dante, *Il Paradiso.* "Move" is a poetic and antiquated verbal form of the Italian "muove." PPR, p. 85. Cf. PPR, pp. 85-101.

255. Cf. PPR, p. 112.

Love" and not light itself. Such persons are "people of moonlight" *(liudi lunnogo sveta),* without true light and true life. In the "subtle and powerful attraction of Love" that Karsavin perceives in the "All-Unity," he believes in the indispensability of personal love in order to reach the universal one. And without spelling out the name of this "Son of Love" who "by His creating-word made the world in me and my beloved one," the one "who is close to my soul," Karsavin affirms: ". . . I love Him, but I neither desire to, nor have to love without my beloved."[256]

The *Fifth Night,* being collocated in the center of this work factually represents its metaphysical climax:[257]

> Love is eternity Itself. She is the absolute, perfect, true being, and outside of Love there is no existence *(bytie).* And we, too, who may be participating only to some extent in her, perceive in the experience of our love our indivisibility from her. I did not exist until she did not descend and call me from nonbeing. I cannot find in me anything "proper": all is being granted to me by the absolute Being, the inexhaustible Good, by the very Love.[258]

Though being a "nothing," in our nothingness as creation (i.e., not being God), in our "participation" and "otherness" Love is being reflected in us and, moreover, becomes a *reality.* All is attracted into the being of *Love;* she summons everything into herself, all the multiplicity of creation, which too reflects the *one* "Endless Love," God:[259] "[It is proper to] every unity that it not only constitutes itself and summons all into itself, but it also surrenders itself to everything, disintegrates *(razlagaetsia),* in order to be present in all. This self-surrender *(samootdacha)* is the dying of unity *(umiranie edinstva);* this is Love, as the beginning/principle of death and death itself."[260]

256. Cf. PPR, p. 116.

257. From here, Karsavin moves to an explicit Christology, sophiology, and Mariology in the *Seventh* and *Eighth Night.* Cf. PPR, pp. 163-83.

258. Cf. PPR, p. 131.

259. Cf. PPR, pp. 132-35.

260. PPR, p. 132, also 133. Karsavin in his meditation on *Love* is certainly inspired by the concepts and descriptions of mystical love that he gained during his previous studies. Cf. PPR, pp. 136-37, 141. Inseparably to *death* is related the eschatological expectation of the "Kingdom of God on earth, which, however, is awaited in time only by those who are lazy and do not think: for it is inside of us, drawn already near to us, and we can enter it at every instant." Another aspect of this eschatological momentum is the fundamental "unsaturatedness" and inexhaustibility of Love: "If it gets saturated, it will be Love no more." Cf. PPR,

Once more Karsavin's gnoseology reverts to the notion of *cognition equals love,* yet this time more extensively:

> Knowledge *(poznanie)* is love. And in the love for the Divine the same thing becomes evident as that which is in the knowledge of God. The limit and aim of Love is in the merging *(sliianie)* of the loving ones, yet Love is possible only if they are distinct. One aspect of Love, [namely] unity as goal, appears to be the full identification with Love. But Love without separation *(raz"edinenie)*[261] is not Love anymore, just as knowing without it is not knowing. Therefore on the heights of mystical love God is being perceived as *nonlove.* "And I did not see Love there, and have lost that Love, that I carried in me earlier, and I became non-Love."[262] God is non-Love, yet He is Love, Love All-Unity *(Liubov' Vseedinaia).* And therefore that which loves in me, my love, is God Himself, the very Divine Love, so is my knowledge of God, God's self-knowledge. God loves me, and that is why I am distinct *(otlichen)* from God and God from me is distinct: I love Him as much as I know Him.
>
> I see you in God's Love, love for my beloved one![263]

Again Karsavin employs anthropological insights in order to mine the wisdom of his personal love experience and to explicate the process and interaction of love-cognition in the realm of divine economy.[264] Similarly to Florenskii and Bulgakov, Karsavin too elaborates his own metaphysical human-divine interrelational paradigm. He exemplifies it as relating within the Divine: "Yes. You are above Love. You are non-Love and Love, yet in your unity Love is absolute and, one with You, I am distinct in her. If you love me, I am non-You, You are non-me; if You are absolute — you are united with

---

p. 142. Similarly, he addresses the aspect of growth and progression in Love taught by Love herself, which is established in the progress "from biunity to triunity" and which necessarily has to include and involve interhuman relationships. Cf. PPR, pp. 143-45.

261. G. Wetter renders *raz"ediniat'* with "enteint" and *raz"ediniaetsiia* with "Enteinung" and "Enteinheit." Cf. Wetter, "L. P. Karsawins Ontologie der Dreieinheit," p. 371, n. 3. Another possible rendering in English could be "disuniting."

262. An undefined source of quotation.

263. PPR, p. 138.

264. Cf. PPR, p. 138. He concludes: "My own personality *(lichnost')* is only a reflection of the Divine image, and I can find my perfected self only in God. If the goal of all earthly love consists in our being essentially one *(edinosushchie)* while safeguarding distinction, the aim of love for God is in becoming like Him while safeguarding our essential difference [of personal identity] *(inosushchnost').*" PPR, p. 138.

me, You are me myself, I myself am You. I am You and non-You; You are me and non-me."[265] Karsavin's reflection about the absolute character of Love continues on a metaphysical level, yet always anchored in a personal experience: "My love for God is God-Love that descended into me and seized me. . . ." To *Him* he aspires, in *Him* he lives and exists,[266] and through his earthly love of biunity, "triunity comes into being."[267]

If we designated the previous *Night* as the *metaphysical climax,* the *Sixth Night* certainly merits being considered the *climax* of Karsavin's *Trinitarian ontology* in this work.[268] First we encounter St. John's ontological truth on God's Being.[269] With the reflection upon it Karsavin introduces the divine relationship of God to God, i.e., God to Himself, laying the foundation for the ontological divine bi- and triunity, previously exemplified on an anthropological level:

> God is Love, an all-one and sole Being,[270] perfect, self-contained, and self-sufficient *(samodovleiushchii).* If He is love, He loves. However, there is no love without the loved and loving one. Yet whom can the infinite Being love so much as to pour into him all His infinity and thus to fill him with it, in order to become perfect Love? . . . If God is Love, He loves the infinite and that with an infinite love, pouring Himself entirely into him and entirely receiving it into Himself. Yet there cannot be two equally absolute infinities, two Gods: the endless does not know boundaries and nowhere reaches its limits. If God is Love, He loves a God different from Him, yet this God, from Him distinct, is He Himself. The Divine is One, one and only; and It is bipartite, like Love, and dual.[271] True and full is His unity, yet true and full is also His biunity *(dvuedinstvo).* So am I united to my beloved one in my love, nonetheless [remaining] fully distinct.[272]

265. Cf. PPR, p. 141.

266. Cf. PPR, pp. 142, 143.

267. Cf. PPR, p. 144.

268. The in-depth elaboration of the subject, especially the staurologic and kenotic aspect of the intra-Trinitarian relationship, we find in *O Nachalakh,* especially chapters 3, 4, and 5, a work that appeared three years later. See L'. Žák, "Kenosi di Cristo nell' 'età d'argento' dell'ortodossia russa." Also Wetter, "L. P. Karsawins Ontologie der Dreieinheit."

269. Yet without an identification or indication of the source.

270. . . . *vseedinoe i edinstvennoe Bytie.*

271. *Edino Bozhestvo, edino i edinstvenno; i dvoistvenno Ono, kak Liubov', dvuedino.* PPR, pp. 147-48.

272. Cf. PPR.

God, of His very nature, must love Himself in a perfect way, and, on the path of divine economy, we learn like children to observe and imitate this perfect relationship within the Divine. It is as logical as beautiful that we are participants in *this Divine Relationship* before gaining consciousness of its Presence in our lives: "Living by Love, by possessing, unveiling her in our earthly love, we are learning from Love Herself, who She truly is, what is Her nature. The world is an Epiphany *(Bogoiavlenie),* theophany; and each one of us is a theophany too, and a veritable *I,* a biunity — a revelation of God-Love."[273] And since there are only two forms of love we know, that to a "fellow human being," and the one "for God and of God for us," also expressed as "between those equal in being *(mezhdu edinosushchnymi)*" and "between those distinct in being *(mezhdu inosushchnymi),*"[274] Karsavin insists on the indispensability of the anthropological dimension of love in order to know the divine one, eventually that of the tri-hypostatic God, introducing an epistemological reflection into his Trinitarian ontology:

> Our love, the loving love of those equal in being *(edinosushchnyi),* shows us the path to the comprehension of God-Love, to Love absolute in himself. The one who has not found his chosen one, who has not known love, will not [come to] know God either. The one who proudly rejected earthly love will not penetrate the mysterious life of the Divine. For such person the Divine will remains but a single.[275] Enveloped [obscured] by a perennially shining cloud, such person will not find himself in the Divine. Alone Love herself, triune in biunity, has the power to reveal her triunity. And she reveals it only to someone who, loving her and in her, loves his [proper] beloved one. She is reflected in him as the Love of the one essence of the tri-hypostatic God.[276]

In God's one essence Karsavin discerns between *God-Loving* and *God-Loved,* two Hypostases that are "absolutely individual, the fullness of God's self-disclosure *(samoobnaruzhenie),*" meanwhile maintaining their full unity. They are "one in being, biune in their hypostaticity," and Karsavin names ex-

273. . . . *dvuedinyi — iavlenie Boga-Liubvi.* PPR, p. 148.

274. This could be rendered also as "between those essentially one" and "between those essentially different."

275. That is, with no relationship, a monad.

276. *V nem otrazhaetsia ona, kak Liubov' edinoi sushchnosti triipostasnogo Boga.* PPR, p. 149.

plicitly the Father and Son of the Trinity.[277] God and His love are revealed because of His sharing *(razdelenie svoe)* and by giving to the Son who is reciprocating it. The love of the Father and the Son must be the same and yet distinct in order to be a proper response, and therefore it has its own personality, and without spelling it out Karsavin identifies it with the third Hypostasis, the Holy Spirit. This Love, the third Hypostasis, "unites the Father and the Son and itself." The fullness and absoluteness of Love and non-Love is in the Triunity of God's Hypostases, as "the Holy Spirit does not possess the fullness of Love in Himself. The Spirit is Love that unites, restoring what is separated: He is Love-Life that opposes Love-Death" and since He is part of both, Father and Son (through the Son), He has His fullness of Love in uniting the other two Hypostases.[278] "The consubstantial Divine, not alternating, nothing losing and nothing gaining, is eternally disclosing itself as Love in its tri-hypostatic being." And Karsavin goes on with a dedicated reflection on the intra-Trinitarian life,[279] returning to the gnoseological notion of Love:

> Love knows *(poznaet):* she is knowledge itself as the union *(edinen'e)* of the one who knows with the one who is being known by her. And the beginning of knowledge, as the beginning of Love herself, lies in separation *(raz"edinen'e)*,[280] in the "Father of Truth." The living Truth Itself, as the reciprocal *(otvetno)* known and knowing, is that which is being born by the Father — the Son, Eternal Wisdom, Logos, Reason *(Um)*. In Logos there is Truth, the only dividing/splitting of the All-Unity, the Father as the dividing/splitting, the Spirit as the union.[281]

Love is the mediator of the knowledge about the ontology of the Trinity, the intra-Trinitarian life and relationship. For Karsavin the interhuman intimate love-relationship-union is the intermediary step to immerse in the Divine's third Hypostasis and so to receive divine knowledge: "Thus immersing with my biunity in(to) Love, in the hypostatic Love or in the Holy Spirit, I reach the threshold of infinity and I see myself 'in the Most Holy Trinity, in the middle of It.' And then the very Love of God in her [Love] un-

277. Cf. PPR, p. 149.
278. Cf. PPR, pp. 150-52.
279. Cf. PPR, pp. 153-54.
280. Again, "disuniting" would be the possible alternative English rendering.
281. PPR, p. 154.

divided unmingled *(nesliiannost')* state of the hypostases opens up for me: Infinite Love in the tri-hypostatic darkness of unity *(v mrake edinstva)*."[282]

The reflection goes on: "The All-perfect Love *(Vsesovershennaia Liubov')* . . . is above delight and suffering, life and death, love and hatred. She is their multi-unity, detracting nothing from them; She is their perfection," as well as the perfection and completion of freedom, "which is the necessity of the Trinity's nature."[283] And that the "darkness" or "veil" in which the unity of the Trinity is enveloped may be pierced and the mystery contemplated: "Behold, light shone in the darkness over the abyss: the Divine reveals in Itself the tri-hypostatic unity of Love. And along with the passing of the Divine from the darkness into the light, we, too, enter light: with the birth of the Son, our knowledge is born too; in the shining of the Spirit, shines also our love."[284]

By re-cognizing in ourselves the utter dependence and emptiness that can be filled only by God, as creations of God, "we cognize God as Love," a knowledge that is natural and freely outpouring in the form of "Bounty and Infinite Goodness."[285] The divine principle of *free, unrestrained* giving and receiving is a constitutive part of all levels of Love-relationship leading to a sacrificial completion: "To receive God wholly, i.e., to live truly, means to deliver one's self fully to God, i.e., to renounce one's own self and to die."[286] These sound as prophetic words some thirty years before Karsavin's own sacrificial completion in the gulag.

In the *Seventh Night,* the hypostatic Love appears under different forms and expressions, such as *Sophia,* the *Wisdom of God, Adam Kadmon,* the *Virgin Mary, Sophia the Church,* etc.[287] In this meditation Karsavin explicitly mentions the concept of "agapē" as a synonym for "dilectio," i.e., "election," an option or choice, to and for someone, and which requires an answer of free consent. "Love is always an election, 'dilectio' or 'agapē,'[288] always reckons the beloved and unique one, always reveals itself in a cou-

282. "Darkness" is to be understood as a *veil of mystery* in which this unity is shrouded. PPR, p. 155.

283. Cf. PPR, pp. 155-56.

284. PPR, p. 156.

285. Cf. PPR, p. 156.

286. Cf. PPR, pp. 157-59.

287. Cf. PPR, pp. 163-73, esp. 167.

288. In his footnote Karsavin specifies the origin and definition of the terms: "Dilectio — election (Lat.), agapē — love (Gr.); the meaning of the Greek word includes in itself also the aspect of assessment or preference." Cf. PPR, p. 556.

ple."[289] This love safeguards its authenticity only as long as it is "incarnated" by Jesus Christ Himself and Karsavin's mariology, sophiology, and ecclesiology are united in this fulcrum of mystical relationship.[290] "Above all stands the love to the supreme and perfect human being Jesus, the son of Mary" — the anthropological complementary to Karsavin's high Christology, seen previously.

In the *Eighth Night,* Karsavin mentions the role of "Beauty" revealed through love,[291] and, also in the symbolically last *Ninth Night,* we find a profound reflection on God's Love revealed in and through the sacrifice of Christ on the cross, based on Philippians 2:5-11.[292]

Though this conclusion is at the end of the last but one, i.e., *Eighth Night,* the following lines sum up well the whole work's ideal and epicenter: "Everything accomplishes its journey around One Sun. . . . Only in the Love for Jesus is our universal Love full and perfect *(vselenskaia Liubov').* He is the sole true center of the entire created world. He is the Unchanging Sun of Love."[293]

3.4. Poema o Smerti — A Poem on Death

"A poem on death. . . . Why, after all, should it not be a poem? We sing to lighten our spirit."[294] This is a work in which Karsavin reflects not only on death, but also on the essentials of life and death,[295] completed with occasional poetry almost as an ornament; yet the text is, in great part, written in lyrical

289. . . . *vsegda iavlaet sebia v chete.*

290. Cf. PPR, p. 172.

291. Again personified with a capital letter. Cf. PPR, pp. 181-82. Before that, he further develops some of the previously addressed aspects of love and also dedicates space to the relationship of Jesus and His mother Mary as the example of "pure Love."

292. Once more, Karsavin does not indicate the scriptural source, but he bases his reflections on Philippians 2:5-11. Cf. PPR, pp. 183-85.

293. Yet another close and implicit description of *agapē* even in its Eucharistic implication: "In love is to us being revealed Beauty, Truth and Bounty. Without them we cannot love, without them there will not be us, you and me. They are necessary for us, necessary as air, as ambrosia — the food of the immortals." PPR, p. 182.

294. PPR, p. 457.

295. It becomes evident on the initial pages when Karsavin refers to his "book on love" *(Noctes Petropolitanae)* printed a decade earlier in 1922 as a "rather tasteless, yet not uninteresting" one. He admits that the book raised harsh criticism at its appearance despite or precisely because of its subject, and that "the mentioned book . . . brought me to an inner decomposition, i.e., to spiritual death." Cf. PPR, p. 459.

prose. "The poet is a child" who "grew up" into the wisdom of the old (and) wise through suffering and "bitter tears," yet still knowing what joy meant.[296]

Being forcibly unjust to the artistic side, and viewing death as part of life, namely one of its essentials, Karsavin returns to the subject of love that led him to reflect on death. Often in dialogue with a person identified as "Elenite," with whom Karsavin is in love, he professes: "I love you because of you yourself; and we together shall compose some sort of very deep and beautiful theory of love." Clearly, it is a love inspired by human attraction, similarly, as in the beginning of *Noctes Petropolitanae*. However, the final destination, as well as the source, is beyond physical and beyond the human realm: it is the Divine and, thus, for us, divinized human.[297] Karsavin sees in the [hi]story of Israel a reflection of ours, namely, the human fate described as a "slavery of insuperable necessity." Yet, having created us so mercifully, could God enjoy seeing us enslaved? "This must be said: good is mercy, good is the Divine love!" And once openly interacting with us out of compassion, God must be a loving God: "He who revealed Himself by Love had to take compassion on me."[298] As we progress through the book, and in reflection, the essentiality of life-death is gradually permeated by thoughts of the soul's confusion, fear, and hope,[299] eventually reaching the Old Testament and its perpetual truth the author affirms: "God does not put any-

296. Karsavin juxtaposes the child-spirit of a *poet* with that of the *metaphysician*, who, although being an old man, "knows no pain and no joy anymore." He comprehended and turned all into wisdom: "Yet where is all this, since he is not alive anymore?" Cf. PPR, pp. 460-61.

297. Therefore, Karsavin immediately adds, "Don't, don't believe a poet, lady; Do not call him — yours; And more than the Divine wrath; Fear the poet's love."

298. Cf. PPR, pp. 483-84.

299. For example,

> Yes, all is Yours, all is You. Even my freedom, even my love for You: all is — only You. There is nothing that belongs to me. Spare me! I am scared to comprehend Your words. . . . I did not know that non-existence was so terrifying! . . . Yet You are right again: I love life — I love You. And I am afraid: [that] I do not exist.
>
> Poorly, I love you? Distantly? — But how distantly, if You are in me?
> If I hold You as I do hold myself?
> If only by You, I move, breathe, live, and desire?

Eventually, the dialogue reaches its pacifying harbor:

> I myself do not know whether I want or don't — or both at the same time. . . . Yet I feel by some kind of an inexplicable and infallible knowledge the truth of Your Love.

Cf. PPR, pp. 486-87.

body to death *(umershchvliat')*, God is [the God] of the living and not of the dead, for He is Love." Yet this is not enough, not reflecting sufficiently the relational character of love. There, birth, life, and death are redefined, revealing the fruits of Karsavin's previous works, reflections, and personal spiritual struggle:

> The Divine Love is God. He is the eternal birth of the Son in the bosom of the Father, i.e., His eternal dying and death for the Father, but also His eternal resurrection by the Holy Spirit. God is eternal life through the perpetual self-sacrificing Death, the unity and quiescence of His unending motion. Yet God is a greater Love as the Divine one. For the sake of what did not and does not exist? For the sake of the world, for me, yes — even for me, sacrificially, God is dying and died. What, in front of such self-immolation of the Divine [God], are the howls and groans of the world, the infernal torments, the rage of the elements?[300]

Karsavin, unlike some of our previous authors, is very explicit about the Holy Spirit and His role within the prevailing kenotic aspect of God's love.[301] The theme of Divine Love, the *Love* with the capital letter, representing the maxim of sacrificial Love in the person of Jesus Christ, occupies Karsavin's spiritual, if not mystical,[302] reflections and convictions up to the last page of the book.[303] The final questions effectively regard the greatness of this gift of the *Cross and the Crucified:* "What shall I give you, my God, for this Sacrifice?"[304] The *Cross* is the "Perfect [or Concluded] Love" by which God re-created our "imperfect being," an imperfection that resulted from our partial, a non-full *yes,* a sin of nonconformity to God's self-sacrificial Absolute Love.[305] This absolute Love alone can defeat death, being the full-

300. PPR, p. 491. Here, Karsavin also introduces an interesting view of the underworld conditioned by earthly conduct and the future of the time as continuum: "Then there will be no underworld. Use [take advantage of] the time: time is the currency of eternity." PPR, pp. 486-87.

301. Also, "In the world, and not in God, is love absent, the sacrificial one — why, what other love does exist?" PPR, p. 492. Similarly, on human hesitancy to "embrace God's Love," since it "shuddered at spotting the shining Cross." PPR, p. 492.

302. "Only on the heights of love is the gloomy suffering being elucidated and does flicker the Divine light." Or: "If God desires to die entirely, by His sacrificial Love He entirely divinizes the world." Yet Karsavin likes to point out that God respects the free will of the human being up to its utmost limits. Cf. PPR, p. 503.

303. See especially the chapter on "Raspiatyi (The Crucified)." Cf. PPR, pp. 494-508.

304. PPR, p. 523.

305. . . . *Sovershennaia Liubov'.* Cf. PPR, pp. 527-28.

ness and timelessness of Life. Perhaps, this way we can better understand the last phrase of this meditation on death, which starts markedly in the present tense: "God innocently suffers for me and in me. Do I not want for His sake, for the sake of His Fullness *(Polnota)*, to also suffer innocently? Do we not eventually settle the accounts of our mutual love?[306] And will I not soon . . . will I not 'soon' die by His Death?"[307]

3.5. Katolichestvo

Although the treatise on *Catholicism* is a "general sketch,"[308] as in its style so in its content, and certainly does not belong to the major philosophical works of Karsavin, in it he displays his fundamental concepts on ecclesiology and Christology founded in love. True faith relevant for the cohesion of the *One Church*, whether according to the Scriptures or Tradition, "can be revealed only through an inner personal experience." Unable to resolve the question of why the separation of churches occurred, since it is the "visible body of Christ," Karsavin very pragmatically prefers rather to ponder on "when and how the disturbed unity can be restored" and become truly *catholic:* "Only this is clear: if the earthly expression of unity of all in Christ is concluded in the unity of the Catholic Church, or loving unity of all Churches,[309] only through such unity of love of all believers, regardless of what denomination, becomes a transition from fragmentation to unity of all in one body and one spirit possible."[310] One can hardly be more specific and more elucidating than this about the substance of cohesion.

3.5.1. Love Mysticism

Apparently, one of the motives of Karsavin's attraction to the historic Catholic Church is the theology of its love-mysticism,[311] which can be clearly traced

306. *Ne svodim li my, nakonets, schety nashei vzaimnoi liubvi?*

307. PPR, p. 528. On the theme of sacrifice, love, and "life through death" we find touchingly deep poetry from the time of Karsavin's imprisonment in the labor camp: Cf. Vaneev, *Dva goda v Abezi,* p. 273, for instance.

308. L. P. Karsavin, *Katolichestvo: Obshchii ocherk* (Petrograd: Izd. "Ogni," 1918).

309. Karsavin uses a minuscule for church and churches.

310. Cf. *Katolichestvo,* pp. 9-10.

311. He means Love-mysticism again with the capital "L" and dissociates from any erotic one, which he sees as a deviation and distortion of a true (mystical) love-relationship.

in his numerous writings.[312] In the present work he illuminates this mystical love and love-mysticism, ideally implemented and manifested on an anthropological and ecclesial level in the Catholic Church, where it streams from the Trinity and represents a dialogue between Creator and creation, a "Loved and the loving One." It passes from the Trinity through the love for one's neighbor to a "trinitariety" of a human-divine relationship, finally to the entity of Church, which is the "unity of love for God in God." His definition of love and its manifestation grants us an insight into Karsavin's own views on the subject. Karsavin mentions repeatedly "God's will" and "God's love" in Christ as synonyms or equal attributes, both participating in the same measure in God's "self-forgetfulness," that is, His kenotic saving action:

> Love is conceivable only if contrasted [contemporaneously] with the Loved and the loving one — of God and the soul. Yet not without reason is the loving soul God's likeness *(podobie)*. God is love, and in love is the mystery of the Trinity. However, the love of God [and, consequently, that of the human being] reaches its fullness only if there is a loving, a loved one, and one participating in love, i.e., the love of God is complete only in the Trinity, and so the human love is complete only in the participation of God, of the soul, and of one's neighbor. On the other hand, God's will or God's love in Christ turned self-forgetfully to humankind that became His brothers, according to the flesh, and His sons. Therefore, likening to God *(upodoblenie Bogu)*, [just] as likening to Christ, is a transformation *(prevrashchenie)* of the human being's will into the will of Christ, namely an acting love to one's neighbors. That way, the analysis of [the] comprehension of love brings us to the idea of Church as a

312. Karsavin comments on the development of what he calls a "full theory of love for God and one's neighbor" in the Catholic Church, already in the twelfth century, especially with St. Bernard of Clairvaux and the Victorines *(viktorintsy)*. He carries on: "Love — it is God; the human being's love for Him is the generation *(porozhdenie)* and gift of God's love, or God. The loving one aspires for the union with the Loved one in order to become one in spirit with Him. Therefore, the extreme of love is the full merging of the soul with God, its deification, yet in a way that the entity [or individuality] of the human spirit all the same does not become God but only likened to Him in righteousness, beauty, knowledge, and beatitude, concording entirely his will with that of God. The will of the human being becomes that of God while remaining also the will of the human being and not losing its freedom. This is a very fine yet principled differing of the creation from God; a juxtaposition of creation-soul to Creator-God *(protivopostavlenie tvoreniia-dushi Tvortsu-Bogu)* protects even in the [very] supreme act of love the heights of Catholic mysticism from deviating into pantheism." Cf. *Katolichestvo,* pp. 15-16.

> union of love for and in God. Catholicism has expressed fully and vividly such a comprehension of church.[313]

The "best example" of how to *imitate Christ* for Karsavin is "the seraphic order of St. Francis." He remarks once more that this concept of love is "an active love,"[314] a love that cares for the "spiritual and corporeal needs" of one's neighbor, in a "selfless service *(samootverzhennoe sluzhenie)* to God's church."[315]

Conclusion

In *Saligia* and all the other works treated here, in addition to providing a deeply empathic and yet methodologically solid and well-styled reflection on the relationship between *Unity* and the *multiplicity* of creation as the revelation of God, Karsavin offers the reader a sublime reversal of the role and understanding of evil, the essence and meaning of Love, and, thus, of death and life. Evil is a misunderstanding, an intolerance for the otherness of the other. Still, and unceasingly in service of God, suffering is one of life's notions, and where there is life, there is God, and where there is God, there is Love. Karsavin does not justify evil and wrongdoing, but he perceives that the tragedy of its misconception has much deeper roots and robs the human being of a precious chance to grow and become truly free. One spontaneously recalls St. Paul's words from Romans 8:35-39: *Who shall separate us from the love of Christ? Shall tribulation, or distress, or persecution, or famine,*

313. *Katolichestvo,* p. 16.

314. For the concept of "active love" in the "living members of the Body of Christ, the Church," see the booklet: L. P. Karsavin, *Tserkov', lichnost' i gosudarstvo* (Paris: Evraziiskoe knizoizdatel'stvo, 1927), esp. pp. 3-7 and 27.

315. Karsavin is not blind to some "straining tendencies" or ideas taken from Protestantism and the ones not genuine to the Catholic tradition or spirit (as is the popular "mechanical" comprehension and use of good deeds for the salvation of souls, for instance) within the Catholic Church. Yet he adds that "a religion should not be evaluated by its lows but rather its heights." Cf. *Katolichestvo,* pp. 16-17. Karsavin's view of Catholicism is evidently founded on a detailed study of the subject and its history, is balanced ("not having any polemic or apologetic goals," p. 131), and rather positive, as the following pages (especially with regard to our theme of love) prove. Cf. *Katolichestvo,* pp. 17-27. Interesting is his perception of Orthodox and Catholic concepts of *Tradition,* where, in the first, it is "fixed or consolidated" *(zakrepleno),* and, in the latter, it "flows and is alive to the present times *(ono techet i zhivo do sikh por).*" Cf. *Katolichestvo,* pp. 27-28.

or nakedness, or danger, or sword? As it is written, "For your sake we are being killed all the day long; we are regarded as sheep to be slaughtered." No, in all these things we are more than conquerors through Him who loved us. For I am sure that neither death nor life, nor angels nor rulers, nor things present nor things to come, nor powers, nor height nor depth, nor anything else in all creation, will be able to separate us from the love of God in Christ Jesus our Lord.

Karsavin dared to formulate and transpose this into metaphysics while returning consistently to the centrality of the sacrificial character of Christ's love, enthroned in the heart of the Trinity. He does not deny God the chance that God, "in fact and truly," can and *does* use everything to the benefit of our salvation, and by that Karsavin means *illimitably everything.*

Other sublime and profound treatises we find with this author in his reflections on the gnoseology of the Trinitarian ontology imbedded in Love. Love, attained and received through the anthropological dimension of interhuman love-relationship, is the thirdness to its duality, or as frequently quoted, its *biunity.* The latter is indispensable, nevertheless not a self-purpose: human love is the space and in the space of the Divine Love, the Divine Third that gives it its transcendental character and the comprehension of it. In the image of the love-relationship of the Father and the Son constantly united by the Holy Spirit, the hypostatic or hypostatized Love of the two former, the human family — not just the individual biunities, and more so the Church — is called to imitate and *reflect* the Trinity. The sacrificial character of this Trinitarian relationship and its utmost value Karsavin affirmed with his own death. The earnestness and solemnity he felt about sacrifice and transformation into the *true Likeness of God* were fully demonstrated by the last years of his life in the gulag.

VII. To Ponder and to Pronounce *Love* in Exile: Between Philosophy and Poetry

1. Nikolai Alexandrovich Berdiaev: *Creative Amorousness*

1.1. Biography

N. A. Berdiaev (1874-1948) undoubtedly belongs to those modern Russian philosophers who, by now, require little introduction in the West.[1] Born into a military family, he received a military education in his native city of Kiev where he completed his studies. Not deeply rooted in religion at home where his spiritual evolution began, Berdiaev soon adhered to Marxism. In 1898, however, his university studies were forcefully and permanently interrupted because of his participation in the social-democrat movement and various student initiatives. His social-Marxist activities led to his deportation to Germany by the tsarist regime. While in exile in Heidelberg, he studied philosophy and became acquainted with the thought of J. Böhme, F. Schelling, and S. Kierkegaard. As with other gifted members of the Intelligentsia, Berdiaev's fascination with Marxism was not enduring, leading him to contest Marx's teachings. Eventually, he turned his attention toward transcendental idealism and became actively involved in the publications *Vekhi* and *Problemy idealizma (The Problems of Idealism).*

In 1920, upon his return to Russia, Berdiaev was appointed professor

1. M. Meerson considers Berdiaev the "chief Russian architect of the existential philosophy of the Trinity," constructing the love paradigm of the Trinity based on a personalist understanding of the human person. Berdiaev perceives, with a modern vision, the thoughts of medieval mystics, including Angela of Foligno, Angelus Silesius, and Hugh and Richard St. Victor. Cf. M. A. Meerson, *The Trinity of Love in Modern Russian Theology* (Quincy, IL: Franciscan Press, 1998), pp. 99-100.

at the University of Moscow. In 1922, he was exiled permanently, this time by the Bolsheviks for his opposition to Marxism. After a brief and academically active stay in Berlin, in 1924, he moved to Paris where he got acquainted with French existentialism. In Paris, he became a professor at the theological institute of St. Serge, cooperated with S. Bulgakov in editing *Put'* (1925-40), and became the editor of YMCA Press (both annals made public the articles of the Russian exiled Intelligentsia). Despite his unfinished university studies, Berdiaev gained an impressive intellectual erudition and versatility in literary genres, addressing a broad variety of topics in his writings, with a special talent in synthesis, although lacking skills in systematization. In fact, he is among the most productive writers and gives particular attention to the principles of *being, personhood/identity,* and *freedom,* while also addressing numerous other philosophic-existential issues (art, creativity, truth, revelation, and more). Berdiaev had a notable bent towards "self-stylization," his writing consistently relating to himself and his personal search. Zenkovsky's analysis illuminates some of the inconsistencies in Berdiaev's thinking by identifying four nonchronological but rather aspectual (i.e., "somewhat artificially divided") periods with different emphases in Berdiaev's work: *ethical* themes, *mystical and religious* crises (during the period of the revolution, 1918-22), *historiosophical* problems, and *personalistic* ideas. These are related to two "central ideas": *the principle of objectivization* and the *primacy of freedom over being.* Berdiaev's Christianity was dominated by the "new religious consciousness" and "neo-Christianity," both concepts coined by him, and not without contradiction, since he "showed immediate tendency to reject 'historical Christianity.'"[2] Berdiaev's death at his writing table perhaps is symbolic of his prodigious productivity and restless inquisitiveness.[3]

Among Berdiaev's more important publications are *Sub"ektivizm i individualizm v obshchestvennoi filosofii (Subjectivism and Individualism in*

2. V. V. Zenkovsky, *A History of Russian Philosophy II,* trans. G. L. Kline (London: Routledge & Kegan Paul, 2005), pp. 760-80, esp. 764-65, 772.

3. Some indicative publishing on Berdiaev and his philosophy: R. Rössler, *Das Weltbild N. Berdjajews: Existenz und Obektivisation* (Göttingen: Vandenhoeck & Ruprecht, 1956); J. L. Segundo, *Berdiaeff: Une réflexion chrétienne sur la personne* (Paris: Aubier, 1963); J. Gaith, *N. Berdjaev's Philosophy of Hope* (Leiden: Brill, 1968); D. K. Wood, *Men Against Time: Nicolas Berdjaev, T. S. Eliot, A. Huxley, and C. G. Jung* (Lawrence: University Press of Kansas, 1982); *N. A. Berdiaev i edinstvo evropeiskogo dukha,* ed. V. Porus (Moskva: Bibl. Bog. Instituta Sv. Apostola Andreia, 2007); S. A. Titarenko, *N. Berdiaev* (Moskva: "MarT," 2005); N. Berdiaev, *Samopoznanie* (Sankt-Peterburg: Izd. Dom "Azbuka-klassika," 2007).

Social Philosophy [1901]); a collection of articles in *Sub specie aeternitatis* as well as *Vekhi; Novoe religioznoe soznanie i obschestvennost'* (*The New Religious Consciousness and the Public* [1907]); *Dukhovnyi krizis intelligentsii* (*The Spiritual Crisis of the Intelligentsia* [1910]); *Filosofiia svobody* (*The Philosophy of Freedom* [1911]); *Smysl tvorchestva* (*The Meaning of Creativity* [1916]), his last work published in Russia; *Filosofiia Dostoevskogo* (*The Philosophy of Dostoevsky* [1921]); *Mirosozertsanie Dostoevskogo* (*The Worldview/Weltanschauung of Dostoevsky* [1923]);[4] *Filosofiia neravenstva* (*The Philosophy of Inequality* [1923]) written in Berlin against the Soviet ideology; *Filosofiia svobodnogo dukha* (*The Philosophy of the Free Spirit* [1927-28]), considered to be his most important spiritual book; *Smysl istorii (The Meaning of History),* which was an immense success abroad; and *Novoe srednevekovie: Razmyshlenie o sud'be Rossii i Evropy* (*The New Middle Ages: Reflections on the Destiny of Russia and Europe* [1934]), which was published in Paris and brought him international fame. This latter work inaugurated a long series of publications in Paris (here only selectively represented): *O naznachenii cheloveka: Opyt paradoksal'noi etiki* (*The Destiny of Man: An Essay of Paradoxical Ethics* [1931]); *Russkaia Idea (The Russian Idea);* and his last book, *Opyt eskhatologicheskoi metafiziki: Tvorchestvo i ob"ektivatsiia* (*An Essay in Eschatological Metaphysics: Creativity and Objectivization* [1947]). His autobiography, *Samopoznanie (Self-Knowledge)* and *Tsarstvo dukha i tsarstvo kesaria (The Kingdom of the Spirit and the Kingdom of Caesar),* appeared posthumously in 1949.

1.2. Freedom, Creativity, and Personhood

Berdiaev was a philosopher of wide interests, yet *freedom, creativity,* and *personhood* (or identity, *lichnost'*) were his particular focus, creating the framework upon which most of his (love-related) thoughts were constructed. He was a prolific writer, leaving behind an impressive number of publications, yet also a repetitive one, at times leaving the reader confronted with entire passages or formulations from his previous works. Nevertheless, there still is a marked and noticeable progression in his ideas, often purposefully consolidated with excerpts from a previous opus.

4. Here he also dedicated a study to the theme of love in Dostoevsky's works. Cf. N. Berdiaev, "Mirosozertsanie Dostoevskoko,"in *Filosofiia tvorechestva, kul' tury i iskustva,* vol. 2 (Moskva: Izd. "Iskusstvo," IChP "Liga," 1994), pp. 73-86.

1.3. The Philosophy of Freedom

In philosophy, the attainment of knowledge and faith can run parallel. Yet, an "act of faith" leading to true knowledge requires not only freedom *in* will, namely of choice, but also freedom *in* love in order to "make the invisible things visible and to make their cognition possible."[5] The difference between an *act of faith* and *cognition* is that the first includes "a notion of renunciation" because it is "an act of free love" or, more precisely, "an act of *freedom of love*."[6] Thus, "pure" or "scientific" cognition yields its place to a personal, kenotically conditioned experience of knowledge: "I believe in my God" not because of proofs but because "I love Him." On this epistemological level, Berdiaev speaks of a *need* to "choose a new object of love," leaving the old one behind, and "to be born to a new life, [in]to a new, different reality," a higher level of cognition through faith.[7] In a Pauline interpretation, *love* is indispensable for understanding Christ's act of resurrection and, in the final instance, his act of salvation: "One has to love the Savior so that the mystery of his resurrection may be revealed. . . . On the example of faith in the resurrection, one can clearly see the nature of faith in general. Faith in resurrection is an act of freedom, of free choice *(izbranie)*, of freedom in love for Christ and, along with it, an act of renunciation of one's proper limitedness and that of the world." This not only demonstrates the "nature of a miracle" *(chudesno)*, but it always calls upon "human freedom and human love" in order to be grasped.[8] The notion of *ontological gnoseology* further intensifies with the mystery of the Trinity, which Berdiaev coined the "mystical dialectic" *(mysticheskaia dialektika)*. The history of the world began in the mysti-

5. Cf. N. Berdiaev, *Filosofiia svobody* (Moskva: Izd. "Act," 2005), pp. 56-57 (FSV).

6. . . . *akt svobodnoi liubvi*. The literal translation is the former one, i.e., "free love," yet because of its modern misleading connotation of false sexual freedom and promiscuity, we shall render from this point on the meaning of *svobodnaia liubov'* as "freedom of love" which, co-understood with the notion of "freedom *in* love" and "freedom to love," corresponds best to the proper meaning of the term.

7. Cf. FSV, pp. 58-59. On a level of *psychological characterization* of faith, he mentions Tertullian's dictum of paradox (or attributed to him), "credo quia absurdum est" ("I believe because it is absurd"), as the (only) way to obtain higher knowledge. Cf. FSV, p. 59.

8. Cf. FSV, pp. 66-68. On the contrary, the source of incomprehension, that is, "the defects of knowledge," is rooted in wrong choices of the will, "in nonlove" *(v neliubvi)* for God and in love to a limited "organizational reality" given by our human comprehension, especially that of our social condition. Cf. FSV, p. 70. Here, Berdiaev arrives at the concept of "ontological gnoseology" to which he dedicates an entire chapter and is significantly inspired by N. O. Losskii. Cf. FSV, pp. 119-55.

cal dialectic of the Trinity, created by "God in Logos, through Meaning [or Sense] *(Smysl),*" which is the "Son of God, the Son-Love" who, from eternity, is the "bearer of the Creator's oneness *(soedinennost')* with creation, the love uniting the Divinity with humanity." This is true knowledge, which includes the sense that the universe coexists with and is carried in the divine Sense of Love — that is in Christ.[9]

1.4. The Third Covenant or "Falling in Love with God"

Creation is a result of the love-relation between the Father and the Son. All was created "in the name of Christ in order that it may resemble Christ, [who is] the image of [the] Cosmos revealed in a person."[10] Christ is the guarantor of human freedom, which humanity had lost through sin-fall. He is the personification of that "*freedom of love* of the creation which is the affirmation of [the] being in the Trinity." Since Christ is the sense and scope of creation and the entire world, the Holy Spirit is the "synthesis-moment" in the mystical dialectic, the bearer of the divine principle of freedom of love. It is in three, the Trinity, that the mystical dialectic is "fully and eternally concluded" (and reflected in the Church on earth).[11]

Given the intrinsic character of freedom in our very existence, the "religion of Christ" cannot be that of "bloody sacrifices" but is a "religion of love and freedom." Bloody sacrifices, as well as others, were fully substituted by the Eucharist, and the ancient "*Law* was replaced by [the] freedom of love. God does not want sacrifices and tortures but desires the human being to freely love — a free union of human [being] with the Divine. [Therefore,] the New Covenant is a covenant [or commandment][12] of the human being's freedom of love for God." Discontented with the Christian, ecclesial, moralistic reading of the New Testament, Berdiaev claims that it is a "teaching on Christ as Redeemer and Savior" and not the actual teaching *of* Christ, meaning it is to be "the path of salvation and not of evangelical morals *(evan-*

9. "With God there is the Son-Logos, Son-Love, and He creates the world realizing the fullness of being in love and sense." Cf. FSV, pp. 184-85.

10. Cf. FSV, pp. 185-86.

11. Cf. FSV, pp. 186-87.

12. Berdiaev also calls it the "Third Covenant," criticizing "historical Christianity" for having failed to implement and realize in everyday life the "covenant [or precept] of love," which alone reflects "true anthropology," or, we could add, it reflects it *truly.* Cf. FSV, pp. 236-37.

gel'skaia moral'), nor Christian moralizing."[13] Berdiaev's criticism on such *moralizing* evolved over the years, especially in regard to the incompatibility of such moralizing with the image of God revealed by Christ, who humbled Himself and became one of us: "The sense of creation is that the human being and after him the whole world may [fall in] love [with] God-Love and not fear God-Might." If Christ had appeared with the royal power and might of a king, it would have impeded humanity from further historical progress, just as if God had created a human being incapable of sin, for only a free person is capable of committing a sin. Without freedom, there is no "divine love," and, consequently, no union with the Divine is possible. "The Son of God had to be crucified and tormented in the world so that the child-world *(ditia-mir)* could love the Father and, freely saved, return to His Bosom" through and in the love of Christ.[14] The logic of gnoseology of the divine proves once more that it works with the parameters of love along with faith, which goes beyond comprehension, transcending immanence: "Christ died on the cross — this weakness sees the whole world; Christ has risen — this power sees only someone who loves Him and believes in Him." We shall remain blind so long until power does not yield to a love completed in freedom, or freedom is fully permeated by sacrificial love;[15] behold the *Third Covenant.*

1.5. Mystical Marriage *as a Sacrament of Love*

Freedom, as seen above, is not an option but a divine offer, a "duty and obligation," a condition of human existence, but also a "burden" that the human being "has not the right" to cast down: "God accepts only free persons. . . . The Christian religion is freedom in Christ. Salvation by force is not possible and not desired." Being a divine gift, an existential human right and duty, freedom in Christianity is unlimited, except for the boundaries of love. Christianity is a religion of "freedom of love and of loving freedom." These two dogmatic notions, as two sides of the same coin, exhaust the content of New Testament faith.[16] Freedom in such a dimension is materialized *(osushchestvennaia),* or lived in the realm of ecclesial unity. Nothing but *freedom*

13. Cf. FSV, p. 200.

14. Cf. FSV, pp. 203-6.

15. Cf. FSV, pp. 205-6.

16. Cf. FSV, pp. 254-56. Berdiaev names A. Khomiakov, Iu. Samarin, and I. Aksakov (the "fathers of Slavophilism") as advocates of this view. Cf. FSV, pp. 254-56.

and *love* constitute the Church since it is "a divine-human *(Bogochelovecheskii)* organism and divine-human process."[17] Even the mystical life of the Church can properly be reflected only in freedom; its philosophy is a "philosophy of freedom."[18] Freedom is a qualifier of love, its depth, and a transcendental trait intrinsic to mystical life.

Yet for Berdiaev, any authentic "mystical world-feeling" *(mirochuvstvie)* is intrinsically linked to *Erōs:* "The mystical perception of the world is in the higher sense of this word an erotic perception" because the question of sex [as gender] *(pol)*[19] is fundamental in the secret of a person's unity and thus of his fullness or completeness, namely, in "androgyny."[20] The fullness of God's image in the human being, its secret and sacrament, is in the union of the two genders, yet it is well beyond the *archaic* concepts of matrimony, especially if its (sole) purpose is understood merely as procreation (or other practicalities of social character) distant to love.[21] Only

17. Cf. FSV, pp. 261-62. For Berdiaev, the concept of the Church is a broad, universal, "cosmic, catholic" one, beyond ascetic practices, on the foundations of love, freedom, and mystical union, with "theurgy," which he perceives as the constituting element of community. "Theurgy" and the concepts of *Erōs,* etc., indicate here Berdiaev's usage of Greek terms and concepts, later fully developed in his works, and mostly understood by him as "truths" or "pre-concepts" fully developed in Christianity, or rather, that which Christianity failed to develop. Cf. FSV, pp. 301-3. Also cf. FSV, pp. 296-97.

18. "Freedom is not only the goal and end of mystical life but even its foundation and principle." FSV, pp. 293-94.

19. A similar and more developed review of the theme of sexuality as well as of the *male* and *female principles* reflected in the divine Logos and the Church can be found in Berdiaev's *Smysl tvorchestva* (Moskva: Izd. Khranitel'/Ast, 2007), pp. 186-211 (STV). Here, he indicates besides the Church's Fathers, modern psychology, especially Freud, as one of his scientific sources, although he does not remain entirely uncritical to him (cf. STV, 186-89). Sexuality *(pol)* possesses a constituting role not only in human life but also in the transcendent, cosmic entity of the human being: "Sexuality is a cosmic power and can be comprehended only from a cosmic aspect." Or: "Sexuality is not only an intersection of two worlds in the human being but also an intersection of the human being with the universe, of the micro- and macrocosms" (cf. STV, p. 190), and therefore the human being is *called* to a higher form of love.

20. Berdiaev draws his inspiration from Plato, J. Böhm, and Fr. Baader. Cf. FSV, p. 296.

21. In this regard, Berdiaev returns to the ideas of N. Fedorov and his vision of resuscitation of the deceased ancestors, which implies humanity's maturation and transformation of sexual energy to such a scope that procreation would be unnecessary, even undesired: "The resuscitation of the deceased ancestors which N. Fedorov exhorts presumes the transfer of sexual energy from procreating children to the resuscitation of the fathers." Cf. STV, pp. 202-9. Similarly, when treating the question of matrimony, he underscores that love is

"mystical matrimony" *(mysticheskii brak)* can bring a true union of the two genders and create a complete union, such as the Church and the Logos. The fullness of personhood, *androgyny,* is revealed only in the sanctity of love *(sviatost' liubvi),* a completeness that restores "God's Image" in the human being. Only this *new love,* the *sacrament of love,* the *mystical matrimony* can and will restore union with God, which is at "the peaks of Christian mysticism," uniting the male and female principle. Yet to transpose the "categories of sexual eroticism" *(polovaia erotika)* into the (intra-Trinitarian) life of God is a "lie," since these categories are relations merely in our world.[22]

1.6. The Tragedy of Love

Creativeness, a divine-human privilege, reveals new perspectives, especially regarding gender and sexuality.[23] Much has been said about the "sexual act," however, hardly anything about "sexual love," and Berdiaev underscores that true "love under no circumstance is a sexual act," although the mystery of sex *(pola)* "is . . . revealed only in love." Berdiaev perceived that much "hypocrisy" has been committed through social sciences but also in theology, including Christian morals and ethics. Sexual love is an aspect of love; love as such is a

---

"more tightly linked to death than to birth," and because of this there is a "deep antagonism between love and childbirth." Cf. STV, p. 219; similarly in: "O rabstve i svobode cheloveka," in N. Berdiaev, *Eros i lichnost': Filosofiia pola i liubvi* (Sankt-Peterburg: Izd. Dom "Azbuka-klassika," 2006), pp. 185-89. Berdiaev contributes two articles to Fedorov's themes under the title "Religia voskresheniia (The Religion of Resuscitation)" and "Prorochestva N. F. Fedorova o voine (The Prophecies of N. F. Fedorov on War)," in his book *Mutnye liki,* Kanon (Moskva: "Reabilitatsiia," 2004), pp. 5-63, 64-70.

22. Berdiaev attributes to *Logos* "the eternal manliness," or male-principle *(muzhestvennost'),* and "the eternal femininity, womanhood," or female-principle, to the virginity *(devstvennost')* of Mary who was united with the eternal manliness. This is beyond sexuality, as such, and has a deep symbolic connotation as "the entire earth, the mother-earth is womanly or feminine (as a female-principle)." The main point here is that the fullness of personhood, which is the true and complete image of God, cannot be achieved alone or in separateness but only in a *sacrament of love,* the *mystical matrimony* that conveys itself in *androgyny (androgonizm),* meaning the full, reunited being of the two sexual-genders, manliness and womanhood. Cf. FSV, pp. 296-97. On *personhood* and its full realization in *love,* which equals the kingdom of God, see FSD, p. 312.

23. Similar reflections, but from a different perspective, can be found in Berdiaev's autobiographic book in ch. 8: "Mir tvorchestva. 'Smysl tvorchestva' i perezhivaniie tvorcheskogo ekstaza," in N. Berdiaev, *Samopoznanie,* pp. 244-63.

transcendent reality,[24] "existing in a somewhat different realm of being *(v inom plane bytiia)*. . . . Love resides beyond humanity [human existence] and its comprehension." Rather, it is "sexual depravity" that lies closer to our understanding, with which love and sexuality, i.e., "sexual love," are being confused.[25] One can get used to depravity, but true love in its ontological essence cannot be "domesticated," that is, lowered to our fallen earthly standards: "Love cannot be theologized, nor moralized, sociologized, nor biologized; she [it] is beyond all this, she is 'not from this world,' she is not a flower from here, perishing amidst this world. The growth of love is tragically impossible."[26] In this misinterpretation, there is a "tragedy of love," or, more precisely, a tragedy in the comprehension of love. "Tragic love" is mostly understood as nonfulfilled, nonreciprocated, misunderstood in intention between two persons. Yet what does one call the concept of love if it is distorted on a sociological or, even worse, spiritual level? Indeed, it is a "tragedy of love."

1.7. The Duty of Higher Creativity

Creativity is love's sacrament, as in marriage, but not strongly in the ancient concept of the family:

> The sacrament *(tainstvo)* of marriage is not the family, not the natural sacrament *(natural'noe tainstvo)* of birth and prolongation of [the] race; the sacrament of marriage is the sacrament of union in love. Only love is a holy sacrament. The sacrament of love is above and beyond the law; in it is the way out of sexuality and sexual constraint; in it is the principle of nature's transformation. Love is not submission, it is not carrying the tie and burden of "the world," but a creative daring *(tvorcheskoe derznovenie)*.[27]

Berdiaev's central point is that the creative capacity and power of "genuine love [which is] from another world" excludes or transforms the sexual act "in the name of the union," which is better expressed by the con-

24. Berdiaev does not apply this precise term.

25. *Seksual'nyi rozvrat*, sexual depravity, is one of the strong juxtapositions and arguments referred to at different occasions by Berdiaev. Cf. STV, pp. 212-13.

26. *Rost liubvi tragicheski nevozmozhen.* Cf. STV, pp. 214-15, 221-22. It is in this context that Berdiaev sees the irreplaceability of love as a matter of fact by (Christian) marriage, family, and procreation. Cf. STV, pp. 216-17.

27. Cf. STV, pp. 218-19.

cept of *vliubliennost'*, "being in love [or] being enamored." This is the true creativity of love, transcending all laws, free from all earthly constraints through its "self-sacrificing character" *(zhertvennost');* then, "only sacrifice secures freedom" and freedom of love, which is at the same time a "heavenly truth."[28] Creativity is the safeguard of love's authenticity because looking for the *other* in our life, and even beyond it, prevents it from becoming an end in itself. This "beyond," not without or outside the other, is the shift from an anthropologic to a divine level of union:

> The creative mystery of the beloved person is revealed in the creative act of love. . . . Love is the way of unveiling the mystery of a person, to co-receive his person(hood) in the depth of his existence. . . . That union of love, which creates a different, new, eternal life for the [other] person, is not achieved in a kinship nor in the sexual act. It is in God that the loving one encounters the loved one, in God does he see the loved person. . . . The nature of love is cosmic, *supra*-individual *(sverkhindividual'naia)*. . . . Love is the way through which everyone discovers in himself the androgynous-being.[29]

The higher purpose and *call* to love is linked to a "higher will." Therefore, the sacrificial character is intrinsic to it in the form of a "duty," not out of fear but in a "mystical dimension of love" directed towards androgynism, as in the example of Christ, the complete(d) or "Absolute Human Being." Berdiaev's opinion of the "Christian love" of his time is rather low, perceived as having become "distant, body[less] and bloodless, [a] 'vitreous' love" *(steklannaia liubov')*, using at various times Rozanov's expression.[30] While being a "universal and brotherly" love directed towards all, it also is impersonal and, apparently, passionless. True "Christian love" is meant to be a "reflection of heavenly erotica *(otblesk nebesnoi erotiki)*." Before getting scandalized or jumping to conclusions about this last statement, we should not forget that Berdiaev is first a philosopher and not a theologian, and secondly is referring to a quality of *Erōs* in its highest terms, free from sexual promiscuity or depravity. Berdiaev uses this term in its most refined philosophical sense as a divine-natural element existentially present in the human being

28. Cf. STV, pp. 219-21. "There is no life-sacrifice that would not be justified in the name of genuine love." Cf. STV, p. 222.

29. STV, p. 221.

30. Similarly, on this and on the quality of (Christian) love-relating, see FSD, pp. 280-83.

and his life, completed in love's "mystical sense," which is androgyny, i.e., the full restoration of God's image in the human being.[31]

1.8. Depth Calls on Depth

To the great theme of *freedom,* Berdiaev dedicates an entire opus, *Filosofiia svobodnogo dukha,* evidently experiencing a religious crisis of his own where he deepens some of his love-related, spiritual, and mystical treatises. It is a theocentric setting where "God is life and, therefore, He reveals Himself only in spiritual life."[32] The depth and "mystery of spiritual life" is unveiled in Christianity, the depths of being as "divine mystery" as well as life's tragic dimension. This divine mystery, also hidden in the Spirit, is the mystery that salvation fulfilled on Golgotha: "Golgotha is the intimate moment of spiritual life, of the spiritual path, the prolongation of all life through crucifixion, through sacrifice,"[33] and "the mystery of the cross, the mystery of Golgotha is the mystery of freedom."[34]

31. At this point, Berdiaev also briefly addresses the subject of jealousy and considers it a negative factor because it "denies the cosmic nature of love . . . for the sake of individualistic bourgeois tenure. . . . Jealous individuals believe that they possess the object of their love, meanwhile they belong to God." Cf. STV, pp. 223-24, 226-29. Berdiaev underlines *androgyny* as a guiding idea in J. Böhm, Fr. Baader, and V. Solov'ev, since "the union of erotic love with androgyny is contemporaneously its union with [the] personhood for surely each person is androgynic. Androgyny is the restored fullness of gender or sexuality in a godlike entity of personhood *(v bogopodobnom bytii lichnosti).* It is not the mystery of femininity or of masculinity that is meant to be unveiled in love but the *mystery of the human being (taina cheloveka)*." Cf. STV, pp. 228-29. Berdiaev ascribes to Solov'ev to have for the first time "in the history of Christian thought linked love-*erōs* to personhood instead of to the family *(s rodom)*" in his *Smysl liubvi.* Cf. "O rabstve i svobode cheloveka," in N. Berdiaev, *Eros i lichnost',* pp. 185-86. Some of Berdiaev's other (medieval) sources were Meister Eckhart, Angelus Silesius, the Victorines, and Angela of Foligno, as mentioned previously.

32. Cf. N. A. Berdiaev, *Filosofiia svobodnogo dukha* (Moskva: Izd. "Respublika," 1994), p. 35 (FSD). Gnostics did not come to know the "mystery of freedom and love" in Christ because they separated the "bodily" from "spiritual" instead of respecting the process of transformation of what is "lower into what is higher." Cf. FSD, p. 19. See also his discussion of "naturalization" in regard to relations between physical, spiritual, and mental states (where an exclusion of God's Spirit from what is *creational* leaves the human being with the misleading impression of being the sole "natural being, a psycho-physical monad"). Cf. FSD, p. 37.

33. "In the depth of the Spirit, Christ is born, walks His path of life, dies on the cross for the sins of the world, and is resurrected. This is an inner mystery of the spirit" that is revealed in a spiritual experience to those "born out of the spirit." Cf. FSD, p. 40.

34. Also: "Freedom is meant to lead me to love and love is meant to make me free. The

The source of *freedom* is not located in the "natural human being" since the source of life and freedom are one and the same; therefore, their origin is in God. After his sin-fall, the human being lost the capacity to "freely answer . . . God's call of love; [therefore,] it is God Himself who answers to Himself." Our freedom is guaranteed in Christ, the sole God-man *(Bogochelovek)*, "heavenly Adam, Adam Kadmon," and in Him is — He *is* — our answer to the call of God's love, which Berdiaev defines as "God's need of love" *(potrebnost' v liubvi)*. The freedom that is a part of the Heavenly Adam united with love "is free love, is freedom in love."[35] For Berdiaev, to comprehend the mystery of freedom is as great as comprehending the mystery of Christianity, the end of all dualisms and monism, or to "adhere to the mystery of unity of two natures."[36] Why would God call and answer as well? "God languishes after His *other*, after the loving and the loved one because God is infinite love. Love cannot remain self-contained; it must seek out. In His Son, God finds His friend, the loving and the loved one. The Son fulfills the answer of the other to God, of the Heavenly Human Being *(Nebesnyi Chelovek)* to the love of God. Yet love can be only free, and only free love is what God desires." This free act is carried out by the spiritual and heavenly Adam, Christ, and concluded in the "Third, the Spirit, who is realized Love *(osushchestvlennaia Liubov')*. . . . The Kingdom of love in freedom is the kingdom of Trinitarity *(Troichnosti)*."[37]

Although scarcely mentioned, Berdiaev explicitly refers to *agapē* as *the* "Christian love" in juxtaposition to a deeper, "mystical sense of love between a man and a woman (of *erōs* and not *agapē*)" which he perceived as "poorly" represented by the dogmatics of the Church. He renewed his previous reflections on gender and procreation with a conclusion inspired by V. Solov'ev: "Love according to its nature possesses the same place as mysticism. . . . It is connected to the very first idea of the human being. The religious sense of love is . . . unveiled only in the symbolism of relations between Christ and the Church."[38]

---

divine grace of Christ is the grace of loving freedom and freedom of love (free love). She [it] was revealed on the cross. In the gratuitous suffering of the God-man turned towards the freedom of the human being is hidden the mystery of Christian love." FSD, p. 101.

35. . . . *svobodnaiia liubov', est' svoboda v liubvi.*

36. Cf. FSD, pp. 98-99.

37. Cf. FSD, pp. 100-101, 111, 122-24 (especially on the theme of the sacrificial character of Christ's redeeming love).

38. Cf. FSD, pp. 138-39.

1.9. The True Identity of God

Mysticism is the closest perception and cognition of divine love or the divinity of love, and the greatest mystics strived more after the "union of love with[in] God than personal salvation." This was due to mysticism's comprehension of salvation as "enlightening *(prosvetlenie)* and divinization of creation," as (re)turning towards God. "The Love for God is the goal" that is also transformative creativity, which cannot be life-distant and disconcerned as at times Christian love has become.[39] "Love is an affirmation of the face *(lika)* of the loved in eternity and God who is the affirmation of being. The love for God is inseparable from the love for one's neighbor [and] the love for God's creation. Christianity is a revelation of divine-human love. What saves me is that which transforms my nature, which is not only love for God but also love for my neighbor." The image of God has been distorted, as has the image of His kingdom: "Yet God has revealed Himself in His Son as a Father, as boundless, unlimited love. And with this forever has been changed the understanding of God as a cruel, angry, and vengeful Master and Lord."[40] Berdiaev simply is proposing God's authentic image, namely *Love* in its most profound, existential, and ontological *sense.*

1.10. The Union between Erōs *and* Agapē[41]

The realization of "personhood is bound to love," as well as hatred; it is torn between "Eros and anti-Eros," as love "is *the way* by which personhood is . . . realized." Therefore, Berdiaev distinguishes between two basic notions: the *ascending,* which is *erotic* love, and the *descending,* which is *agapic* love, in the tension of which personhood is shaped. Berdiaev refines the image of *Erōs* by placing it in the Platonic context of the relationship of the *Ideal* and *Beauty* — things, events, acts, or being part of "constituent or selective love" *(izbiraiushchei liubvi),* as in the case of friendship, for example. In contrast, "caritative [charitable] love" does not look for its own advantage and enrichment but "gives away, sacrifices, is immersed in the suffering, in the dark of the agoniz-

39. Once more, Berdiaev reverts to Rozanov's expression; yet this time his criticism is markedly less negative in its tonality and more concerned about the right form of Christian love — relating from the perspective of a Christian faithful and challenging Christianity to live up to its vocation. We assume a strong social connotation of the epoch.

40. "Spasenie i tvorchestvo," in Berdiaev, *Eros i lichnost',* pp. 168-72.

41. "O rabstve i svobode cheloveka," in Berdiaev, *Eros i lichnost',* pp. 173-97.

ing world." Berdiaev occasionally calls this *liubov'-zhalost' (i sostradanie), love of sorrow* or *pity* (and *compassion*).[42] Since Platonism did not encounter the challenge of *person* or *identity (lichnost')*, but Christianity did, Berdiaev's solution is the union of these two complementary kinds of love. For some reason, Berdiaev's view and historic-theological cognition of *agapē* and *agapic love* appears to be rather limited: "The impersonal *(bezlichnyi)* Eros is directed at beauty and perfection instead of a concrete being, a unique person; the impersonal agapic and caritative love is directed at an impersonal other [who is] suffering and needy for help." A purely "erotic love" contains a "demonic and destructive element," while a purely caritative, impersonal love "degrades the dignity of the other person."[43] The combination of the two is the aforementioned *vliublennost', enamoredness* or *being in love*, "which is broader than just love between a man and a woman, and is an ascending love, attracting all and reaching its fullness in a creative ecstasy" or, perhaps, more precisely, ecstatic creativity. Berdiaev once more underscores that "Christian love" is not *erōs* but *agapē*,[44] and his difficulty with the latter, as well as with caritative love, is its impersonal, nonselective character: "One cannot love all people." Then, he

42. Cf. "O rabstve i svobode cheloveka," pp. 173-74.

43. Cf. "O rabstve i svobode cheloveka," p. 175. There is also a threefold division of love's aspects, most importantly depicting the *uzhas*, "metaphysical dread," and a possible despotism and slavery *in* love, something that "can be death-bearing," all these aspects of love's drama, yet not of authentic love. In conclusion, love is meant to lead towards God, freedom, and personification: "On its peak love is always contemplation of the loved one's face in God." Cf. "O rabstve i svobode cheloveka," 193-97.

44. Berdiaev states exactly the contrary in his *Opyt religioznoi filosofii obshchestvennosti*, where he creates a complete Platonic/neo-Platonic mélange of a Gnostic flavor with Christianity. (Although most probably well meant and ill succeeded as for the maxim of the ideal handed down by antiquity and representing, as Berdiaev sees it, a genuine search of the ancient writers for the perfection of love and union with God in pre-Christian times. This maxim is in Eros and its highest personification the Heavenly Aphrodite.) "Christ taught about the divine Eros, about the Heavenly Aphrodite whom already Plato has sensed, yet the teaching of Christ on love remained mysterious and incomprehensible, it did not 'get in'" *(tainstvennym i neponiatnym; ne 'vmestilos'")*. Or: "Christ is the Divine Eros, incarnated into humanity, the source of all love *(vsiakoi liubvi)*." Cf. "Metafizika pola i liubvi (Metaphysics of Gender and Love)," in *Russkii Eros ili filosofiia liubvi v Rossii* (Moskva: "Progress," 1991), pp. 232-65, particularly 244-45 and 261. In paralleling *Erōs* with the Christian concept of love, we had the impression of seeing V. I. Ivanov's influence on Berdiaev, yet it could have been, although less likely, vice versa. One way or the other, Ivanov's parallel reading is definitely organic, systematic, and more genuine (in our view, because of his background and educational formation, besides specialized publications in the field of mythology). See our chapter on Ivanov.

claims that "authentic love — eros includes in itself love-caritas *(liubov'-caritas)* and love-compassion," which again is *not* erotic love.[45]

Conclusion

Berdiaev's contribution to the dialogue of philosophy between East and West is indisputable, and the centrality of love, especially in the appearance of *Eros* in his religious thought, is self-evident. Praiseworthy also are his perception of the social phenomena of love having become impersonal, the challenge for *agapē* and *caritas* to be a truly universal yet personal love, and the aspect of *erōs* in the very essence of the human being, yet not as a pagan element but as a reflection of divine love that unites with "Christian love." Authentic "Christian love" is *called* in a *creative* process to restore through androgyny the fullness of God's image in the human being by restoring its unity with(in) itself. To that purpose, erotic love (not eroticism) is a love that shall not be absent from matrimony, or the latter no longer fulfills its primary purpose. What we do miss from a philosopher of Berdiaev's stature is the systematic research and deepening of the idea of a true Christian love, which in fact combines (or is meant to combine) the *ascending* and *descending* love, from and to God, through one's neighbor. Where we would have difficulty contradicting Berdiaev, even today, is in his criticism of his time for "the lost spark of God's divine passion," God's unlimited love for His created human image and His creation — all this on the horizon of our everyday life, and, above all, in our creative relations.

2. Viacheslav Ivanovich Ivanov: *Love Sings to Me: "You Are!"*

2.1. Biography

V. I. Ivanov (1866-1949) was a poet and an aesthete, a representative of Russian realistic symbolism,[46] a religious thinker, and a cultural expert. Born in

45. Cf. *Eros i lichnost',* pp. 179-81. He also adds that, while *erōs*-love needs reciprocity *(vzaimnost'),* "love-charity" *(liubov'-miloserdie)* does not require reciprocity; this "is its richness and strength." Cf. *Eros i lichnost',* p. 181. A basically identical rendering of these ideas with a more personal approach can be found in Berdiaev's autobiographical book; cf. Berdiaev, *Samopoznanie,* pp. 88-97.

46. As opposed to *idealistic symbolism,* the mainstream idea of his time.

Moscow to the family of a land surveyor, he received from his mother a deep and living faith in God. Excelling as a student, he proceeded to the Philological Institute in Moscow (1884-86), then to the University of Berlin (1886-91) for studies of classical languages, philology, and philosophy under Professor T. Mommsen. During this sojourn in Germany, he absorbed the thoughts of F. Nietzsche and the German Romantics, notably of Novalis and F. Hölderlin. In 1898, he married Lydia Zinovieva-Annibal, herself a poet and translator. From 1899, he lectured in Paris, but the couple also lived in Rome, Athens, Alexandria, and Palestine. While living in Italy, Ivanov became acquainted with Renaissance art, and his poetry was influenced by the nature of the regions, but mostly by the medieval poetry of Catholic mystics. After his "triumphant" return to Petersburg in 1904, Ivanov's house, the famous *Bashnia (The Tower),* soon became a fashionable literary salon, a center for encounters among members of the local Intelligentsia — artists, writers, philosophers, and scholars.[47] He soon became one of the leading figures of the Christian religious-philosophical community of his time. After a brief stay abroad in 1917, Ivanov transferred to Moscow, maintaining close relations with the critic M. Gershenzon and thinkers involved in the edition of *Put',* such as S. Bulgakov, P. Florenskii, and others. Ivanov was also actively involved in the local theatrical scene, a subject dear to his heart. From 1920 to 1924, he lived and taught in Baku, obtaining his doctoral degree in classical philosophy for *Dionis i pradionisiistvo (Dionysus and Pre-Dionysianism).* In 1924, Ivanov left Russia for good and settled in Rome (of which eight years were spent in Pavia), where he taught for many years at different Pontifical Institutes.

Greatly influencing Ivanov were Solov'ev, regarded as the first theoretician of symbolism, and St. Augustine. Ivanov considered mystical intuition (a bridge of universal perception, *sobornost'*) culturally best rendered by realistic symbolism. In his view, supernatural and rational knowledge transformed into a symbol that can be retrieved in a theatric rendering of mysteries, for instance via an artist's creativity and a religious act of *ecstasy.*

Among his works are *Kormchie zvezdy* (*Guiding Stars* [1902]); *Ellinskaia religiia stradaiushchego Boga* (*The Hellenic Religion of the Suffering God* [1904]); *Eros* (1907); *Mysli o simvolizme (Ideas on Symbolism)* and *Cor Ardens* (1911); *Trudy i dni* (*Works and Days* [1912]); *Rodnoe i vselenskoe* (*National and*

47. Berdiaev talks about these meetings in his article "Ivanovskie sredy (The Ivanovian Wednesdays)," in his book *Mutnye liki,* Kanon (Moskva: "Reabilitatsiia," 2004), pp. 123-27.

Universal [1918]); *Perepiska iz dvokh uglov* (*Correspondence from Two Angles* [1921]); *Rimskie sonety* (*Roman Sonnets* [1932]); *Chelovek: Poema* (*The Human Being: Poetry* [1939]); and works on Pushkin, Dostoevsky, and Solov'ev, as well as books of poetry and letters.[48]

2.2. You Are Mine

In order to comprehend Ivanov's work *Chelovek (The Human Being)*, a result of over twenty years of Ivanov's travails and a work of principal interest to us,[49] we need to understand the key to his hermeneutics, which is the great existential *I-You* dialogue delineated in *Rodnoe i vselenskoe (Generic and Universal)*.[50]

As often as human beings may claim that their intention is to live in harmony with nature, "in fact, [they] constantly act against Nature," and, ever since they gained self-awareness, they aim to *conquer* Nature. This is at the root of the entire drama: "'I am alien *(chuzhd)* to you,' says he [humanity] to her [his nature] and knows himself that what he says is untruth; yet she stretches her inescapable embrace to the fleeing, [by] answering, 'You are mine, since you *are* me.'[51] . . . And thus speaks the oracle: you will not conquer [the] Mother till you . . . turn around and embrace her yourself and tell her, 'You are mine because you are *me* myself.'"[52] Ivanov considers the entire ancient, pre-Christian morality "a simple hygienics of the empirical person-

48. For further biographical material, see S. S. Averintsev, *"Skvoreshnits vol'nykh grazhdanin"* (Sankt-Peterburg: Izd. "Aleteia," 2002); M. S. Al'tman, *Iz besed s poetom V. I. Ivanovym (From Conversations with the Poet Ivanov)* (Sankt-Peterburg: Inapress, 1995); F. Malcovati, *Vjaceslav Ivanov: Estetica e filosofia* (Firenze: La Nuova Italia, 1983); G. A. Stepanova, *Ideia "sobornogo teatra" v poeticheskoi filosofii Viacheslava Ivanova (The Idea of a "Conciliar Theater" in the Poetic Philosophy of Viacheslav Ivanov)* (Moskva: "Gitis," 2005); to the work and person of V. I. Ivanov has been dedicated a voluminous edition of *Symbol*, 53-54 (Paris-Moskva 2008); *Viacheslav Ivanov — Peterburg — mirovaia kul'tura (Viacheslav Ivanov — Peterburg — World Culture)* (Tomsk-Moskva: Vodolei Publishers, 2003); a concise yet well-founded introduction of M. T. Mayer in Vjaceslav Ivanov, *L'uomo* (Milano: Aquilegia Edizioni, 1999), pp. 11-28.

49. First published in Paris in 1939.

50. *Rodnoe* could also be rendered in English by *proper* or *national*. V. I. Ivanov, *Rodnoe i vselenskoe* (Moskva: Izd. "Respublika," 1994) (RIV). The book's first chapter is dedicated to the "Crisis of Individualism."

51. Ivanov uses a minuscule in spelling the "I" in Russian, "я" (versus "Я"). This plays a role in his poems, discerning between the divine "I" (of the Son of God) and the human being's "i." Therefore, we shall render the latter with *"me"* and the former with "I."

52. Cf. RIV, p. 83.

ality and empirical community"[53] related to self-preservation *(samosokhranenie)* [and] based on the proper and universal understanding of "me," as opposed to the morality of the "mystics and Christians, which is a morality of co-attraction *(sovlechenia)*." Based upon this, the character and quality of sacrifice changed from an external bloody one to an attempt to liberate "the internal personhood." Thus the mystical and Christian morals' message is "You are possessed by no one; you belong to yourself, [for] you have been redeemed [at] a precious price." This also teaches that the best means of finding oneself and saving one's soul lies in "self-dissipation" *(samorastochenie)*. Both morals are operative until current times, "fighting in the human being about the control over him and for a new type of his evolution."[54] Similarly, the life-death dualism is a dialogue where the human being evolves from "a passion that he used to call life," if he did not grasp it as "incarnation," and all around him gradually dies away up to the point where *Death* appears with a "shining face" in front of his "spiritual gaze," uttering "Look up and recall: I am life." As if correcting or completing N. Fedorov's position, Ivanov proclaims that life is lived for the deceased *and* the living, "contemporarily for the ancestors and the descendents," a union as well as an obligation to safeguard the freedom of the individual.[55]

2.3. *Me, I, and All-I*

The three "daughters of Wisdom," *faith, hope,* and *love,* "exhort to self-knowledge," enabling one to discover the evolution or, more precisely, the three stages of the perception of identity in the human being. The "highest *I*, his holy of holies, the goal of his understanding . . . the divine focus of the microcosm" is coupled to faith; the *"me"*[56] defined by the limits of "empirical personhood [or identity]" is linked to hope; finally, the *"All-I,"* a realm embracing the universe, is related to love. Ivanov calls these the "three hypostases of Life." The "precept of life" is taught by Wisdom herself, and

53. . . . *gigienoi empiricheskoi lichnosti i empircheskogo obshchestva.*

54. In this context, Ivanov mentions Nietzsche's "Pathos der Distanz" *(Pathos of Distance)* and the "depth of Nietzsche's psychic split [or division] *(glubina dushevnogo raskola Nitsshe)*." Cf. RIV, pp. 83-84.

55. "Therefore the teaching *how* to live is a false ethics." The human being is called to a free and full life, one that transforms all *No's* into a *Yes*. "Ethics is a teaching on truthful *Yes*." Cf. RIV, p. 85.

56. Still spelled "я" in Russian.

thus the three theological virtues correspond respectively to *Death, Beginning,* and *Love.* We can discover a descending motion, going out from the Divine and reaching the human being, involving him to give a proper response of love, in which *beginning* and *end* reconnect: "'Love, begin, die' is the threefold precept of Life, the infringement of which results in spiritual death. For Love is Beginning, and Beginning is Death, and Love is Death, and Death is Beginning. 'Do not grow weary to begin, do not stop dying,' this is what Love requires from the human being, which in the microcosm, just as in Dante's heaven, 'moves the sun and the other stars.'"[57] The pendant to microcosm is the macrocosm that, as "the boundless Universe," speaks to the human being: "you are me," or in the same way the *Self* utters to the *me* a relationship that Ivanov calls a "tie" or "bond" *(sviaz').*[58]

2.4. *The Substance of Religion*

In the symbolism of *day* and *light,* Ivanov interprets Adam's encounter with the macrocosm and creation, specifically in the naming of creation. This encounter simultaneously gives him joy in his space, enrichment, and enlightenment.[59] Once more, Ivanov returns to the subject of *ethics,* which he breaks down to "aesthetics" and "religion," and, principle-wise, he sees it deriving from *Eros.* Thus, "in the construction of the soul *(dusha),* ethics [in fact] is erotica *(erotika)* and more genuinely *(pravee)* could be nominated eroticism." The coupling of the definition of love to the clarification of *ethics* while underscoring the role of *Eros* is an indispensable issue for Ivanov, and most likely a burning issue of his time.[60] The substance of religion is a love of desire, formed between our *no* and *yes,* mystical yet also profoundly imbedded in the human and the sacred:

57. Cf. RIV, p. 86. The Johannine love-death equation is represented in the background of Greek mythology where the chariot pulled by the horse *Thymos* (= intense feeling) is steered by the "standing flaming Eros." Ivanov makes a smooth and logical yet delicate parallel, reading Greek mythology side by side with Christianity on various levels, as we will see further in our text. The Johannine equation applied by Ivanov: "Who does not love is dead. Life, that means love. 'And life is the light of people.' . . . Eros leads through his gardens by hand Psycheia, the planetary soul of the human being: such have seen the Word (Logos), like the artists of the catacombs." Also, Ivanov dedicates the fourth book in his "Cor Ardens" to the theme of *Love and Death.*

58. Cf. RIV, p. 87.

59. Cf. RIV, pp. 87-88.

60. Cf. RIV, p. 88.

The yearning love *(alchushchaia liubov')*, the suffering, and the passionate one[61] behold the fundamental principle of our religiosity; [it is] chilled from our implacable *No (neprimirimovo Net)*, [our] *Yes* born by our finite wanting [and] unaccepted by love, [and] the world incapable of accepting love; behold the solarity *(solnechnost')* of our transforming desire, the male principle of conciliarity *(sobornost')* coming to light in the spirit as a sacrament of love, as a sacred sacramental *(sviashchennoe tainodeistvie)* of the sexual.[62]

2.5. *The Audacity of Love*

Ivanov discerns between "theocratic" *(teokraticheskaia)* and "theomorphic" *(teomorfoznaia) ways* or *formulas* of mysticism, both equally necessary and as complementary as "Heaven and Earth, Father and Mother, [and] maleness and femaleness." The first, which is "planetary and female," receives and engraves the divine descent, whereas the second is an illumination of humanity from its inner "divine and consubstantial Logos *me* by a mystical energy" that is directed to reveal the realm in which "God will be 'all in all'" *(vsiacheskaia vo vsekh)*. The latter is "the path of prophetically anticipatory initiative, the solar and manly path of daring love."[63] Somewhere deep in the human being's struggle with God *(bogoborstvie)*[64] dozes the awareness of his broken unity with the Divine, like a seed sown in the ground waiting to sprout: "I — in You, and You — in me."[65]

61. Ivanov brilliantly uses the Russian language, employing the very same word, *"strastnaia,"* twice with two different accentuations (in the everyday usage of Russian not indicated); with an accent on the second syllable, i.e., *strastnáia*, it means "suffering," from *stradát'* (as Christ's suffering and self-emptying on the cross was a *stradánie*) and is connected with the adjective used for Holy Week *(strastnoi)*. By accentuating the first syllable, i.e., *strástnaia*, it means "passionate," from *strástnyi*. Evidently, both words take their roots from *strast', passion (for), fervor, flame.*

62. RIV, p. 88.

63. *Eto — put' prorochestvenno uprezhdaiushchego pochina, solnechnyi i muzhestvennyi put' liubvi derzaiushchei*. Cf. RIV, p. 89. A similar usage of *audacity* in connection to creativity *(tvorcheskoe derznovenie)* we encountered in Berdiaev's *Smysl tvorchestva*, pp. 218-19.

64. Could be also rendered in English with the Grecism *theomachy*.

65. Ivanov quotes from "Cor Ardens," the peak of poetic works, a collection dedicated to his wife Lydia. In this context, he also quotes from Nietzsche's *Zarathustras Nachtlied*, as well as a brief review of Kant's concept of "practical reason" based on Socrates' philosophy related to "energetism" and "erotism." Cf. RIV, pp. 89-90.

The dialogue of symbols of *night* and *day,* that is, of the masculine *(muzhestvennoe)* and feminine *(zhenstvennoe)* elements of one and the same love, reflects on the realm of microcosms and macrocosms. The first is accessible through *will,* while the second through *love.* This may shed light, at least partially, on Ivanov's parallel reading of Greek mythology and Christianity: "The will contains in itself the insight into the *me* of microcosm. Dionysius, its dynamic principle, unveils itself as the Eros of conciliarity *(sobornost').* Through love the human being enters the *I* of macrocosm — God. 'I is the way. Nobody comes to the Father if not only through Me.'" For Ivanov, volitional consciousness *(volevoe soznanie)* is the *real* one, and the "realism of mystical knowledge" can be attained by immersing the self in the mysteries of microcosm, which, of course, is also an ontological realm. Thus, "the activity of love" is the factual gaining of this mystical knowledge.[66] The fusion of "daring manliness" of the human being with the "soul of the world" *(dusha mira),* which with the night revealed itself in its femininity, occurs in the union of "the breeding ground of internal cognition";[67] it then consolidates in the union of "creative and sacrificial love."[68] Ivanov exempli-

66. "Such cognition is nightly *(nochnoe)* in juxtaposition to the daily, empirical, and rational knowledge, which is only phenomenology. Inner solarity *(solnechnost'),* surrounded by the light of diurnal cognition *(dnevnogo znania),* gives birth to idealism; and only in the night, lit by our solar torch *(solnechnyi fakel),* we recognize in the fires of heaven brotherly luminaries, only in the night the stars become a reality *(realnost')*." Cf. RIV, p. 90.

67. Ivanov considers the crisis of individualism in the misapprehension and the lack of depth (of the proper identity), leading to (further) division in the unity of personhood. The *me* finds itself in the *I* of the Divine, which he also calls *You* in different contexts. He develops this concept while still paraphrasing (mostly pre-) non-Christian religions in the chapter on "Ty esi (You are)." A particular role in all this is played by *Ecstasy,* the mystical experience of "going out of oneself," that simultaneously discloses the antinomy of personhood. Cf. RIV, pp. 91-95.

68. In a second instance, the two elements are compared or assigned to Adam and Eve (or also compared as *Psychea* and *Eros, Menade* and *Dionysius*), where the female element of "our hidden entity" can fully unfold its independent life *(obosoblennuiu zhizn')* when the "internal hearth of our manly energies is extinguished, similarly to Eve who is created during Adam's sleep. . . . Then Psychea recognizes her bridegroom, approaching in such a way to her from the depth of personal cognition in the image of the resurrected *me,* as the awakened *(prosnuvshiisia)* son of God (Lk 3:38) — Adam — approaches his newly-wedded bride *(novozdanna nevesta)*." This corresponds to the moment of Christ's birth in the *me* in the teaching of Meister Eckhart or Menade's receiving the boy Dionysius into the cradle. Ivanov sees the merging of "the personal *me* with the God-man-Son" in the Dionysian cult where it reaches its fullest expression in the representation of Bacchus. Cf. RIV, pp. 92-93. It is valid in all religions that when the soul finds the *You (Heaven)* in its *me,* then it

fies this in the concluding part of *Zavet solntsa (The Testament of the Sun),* a poem steeped in symbolism, from *Cor Ardens (The Flaming Heart* or *Heart Ablaze).*[69] The burning union of the two elements is, "according to Plato," *Eros,* and Ivanov introduces what he sees as the stoic concept for it, the *tonos.*[70] One is talking about the audacity of love here.[71]

2.6. The Human Being

Ivanov's most mature poetry, a long meditative and philosophic reflection, is dedicated to the human being, its sacred and less sacred history with God, presented often in a parallel reading of non-Christian religions and Christianity. He unfolds and puts into poetry these ideas on faith, life, love and death, and, with particular intensity, the *I-You* relationship, which we have seen. Here, it takes on an existential trait that makes it convincingly authentic and mystically profound. Above all, it is a dialogue between the Creator and his image, and excerpts from this poem illustrate this point:

> Oh, human being![72] I, human being, have measured
> your guilt and mystery: the Son of God,
> you were the first who did not believe him.[73]
> Among all the worlds alone you had plotted
> that there is no God, and you committed a parricide.[74]

---

gains the conscience that the external world, the *Macrocosm,* has been given to him to "learn the name *You,* as in the inaccessible neighbor so in [an] inaccessible God, and that the world is but a revelation of his microcosm"; in his depth eventually he discovers the Son of God. Cf. RIV, p. 95.

69. "Cor Ardens," in *Viacheslav Ivanov: Sobranie sochinenii II* (Bruxelles: Foyer Oriental Chrétien, 1974), pp. 220-358: *Zavet solntsa,* pp. 233-34.

70. The Greek τόνος corresponds to *accent, stress, tone,* or *tune.*

71. Cf. RIV, p. 90. This *audacity* in humankind could be considered a reflection or response to the totally audacious, gracious, infinite love of God. Thus, *audacity* would be an instinct — sewn into the fabric of our being by the Creator, his thumbprint left on our hearts. We possess the capacity for great, courageous love.

72. We render, as usual, with "human being" what in Russian, like here, is indicated as *chelovek.* At this point, *Chelovek* refers to Adam, but, also in this part, Ivanov makes the parallel between Adam and Oedipus.

73. Our translation is not artistic but centered on the content.

74. V. Ivanov, *L'uomo,* a billingual edition, ed. M. T. Mayer (Milano: Aquilegia Edizioni, 1999), pp. 68-70 (CHK). *Parricide* refers here to the killing of the Father.

Ivanov introduces an ontological reflection on staurology based on the *I* and *AM* of God, where the first is God's *essence,* the vertical axis, and the second is God's *existence* or *being,* the horizontal axis of the cross.[75] Only by the union of the two can reconciliation occur.[76] Life and death share a common destiny, "a common tone" in the process of redemption:

Pierced by you, I penetrated
into the ringing of the golden arch.
And as the disciple I understood
that detachment is gold,
that death is love's pledge,
that death is love's double [or twin];
that for the earthly soul
they are of one destiny
two names, two sounds.[77]

Ivanov reveals his deepest comprehension of love starting out from a human love, a proper human experience, on which he demonstrates the Creator's incommensurable care for His created image, repeatedly calling the person into existence in and through love. Our author introduces it with a

75. Another example can be found in a sonnet written to a loved person, titled properly "Love":

We are two trunks ignited by lightning,
Two flames in the midnight forest;
We are two meteors flying in the night,
The double-stinging arrow of a single fate!

We are two horses whose reins are held
By the same hand, bitten by one spur;
We are two eyes of a single gaze,
Two trembling wings of one dream.

We are a pair of shadows grieving
Over the holy marble grave,
Where ancient Beauty slumbers.

The two-voiced mouth of secrets shared,
We two make a single Sphinx.
The two arms of a single cross.

Viacheslav Ivanov, Sobranie sochinenii I (Bruxelles: Foyer Oriental Chrétien, 1971), pp. 610-11.

76. Cf. CHK, pp. 74-76.

77. Cf. CHK, pp. 84-86.

definite shift to the Christian concept of love by placing the "cross" into the "crossing" of the love-relationship:[78]

> Until I do not love, I am;
> In love, like a phoenix, I die:
> I myself make the ardent lodge,
> looking on the sun with my two eyes,
> gathering their scalding sparkles,
> I burn . . . do not put out the fire
> when I am being consumed on the stake;
> love sings to me: "You are."
>
> My captivity I share with another soul,
> my veils apart I tear,
> feed the flesh of others with my own,
> and on the flesh of another I myself hungrily feed;
> to the far extremity I am approaching
> where death crawls: "cease in [the] embrace" (*"istai v smesi"* or
> "languish in the blend")
> but I contradict the dark,
> love sings to me: "You are."
>
> The seal of "I am" is like wax, I melt
> in fire, [and] there, being born anew, I conquer;
> I boil with a fiery flux,
> Gehenna's fount I unlock *(otpirat');*
> in the purple Lethe[79] I fade away —
> and barely I whisper: "save";

78. The reflection reads, "Leader of the enamored, sidereal Amur, / as the lips of / two springs cherish the last ice / conjures [these] with the crossing of its lights: / like in the quadrate field of augurs, / stands in the center of [the] cross *(sredotochie kresta):* (N.B.: The Italian translation does not render the word *cross,* although it is explicitly mentioned, but instead, "sta al centro dell'incrocio e giunge") and binds four stars / the eyes' four stars. (Again, we find a discrepancy in the translation, "i quattro occhi dell'astro"). Still the demure lips / did not fuse the "you" in the kiss, / and the matter sight conveyed: / "I give you my soul / my well has dried up and is empty, / thirsting the spurt of your veins: / like grace, return me / my departed humor." Cf. CHK, pp. 96-97.

79. One of the five infernal rivers of Hades where the soul, forced to drink, would forget its past life.

the fury of elements I subdue,
young wings I stretch out . . .
love sings to me: "You are."

When from my front the "I am" I wipe off
and see God in Heaven, —
and while my boat floats towards Paradise,
love sings to me: "You are."[80]

Also, the entire creation and, above all, one's "brother,"[81] sings the "You are" like a reflection in a mirror, giving back again and again the same ontological truth, revealed first — and at last — by love.[82] This "love" leads to Christ and, eventually, to a Trinitarian relationship.[83] With Christ, "the Eternal Human Being," the staurological element as a passage and revelation of kenotic love, makes its way back to the scene. The "You are" receives its highest affirmation calling from the "Eternally begotten" to "Eternity":

With the Eternal about His right of firstborn
you dispute, — denying again and again
of succession in free being, —
human being, yet God: "Do not contradict,
for You are!
Carry the Royal Cross!"
Contending, their love disputes!

Sacrificial epiphany of love!
The opening of royal doors . . .
"You are" — I exhale and in the same instant
the heart's Empire begins to shine . . .
An instant — and in Heaven
I hear: "You are" —
and on the cross is pending the King of Kings.[84]

80. CHK, pp. 98-99.

81. Cf. CHK, pp. 106-7. The notion of the community and *sobornost'* are recognizable in this passage (similarly pp. 156-57).

82. Cf. CHK, pp. 100-103.

83. Cf. CHK, pp. 106-7.

84. Cf. CHK, pp. 102-3. Again, although on the margin, we need to remark some slight discrepancies in the Italian translation from the content of the Russian original,

Conclusion

Ivanov leaves no doubt about being a symbolist of realism, as he himself was rooted in the reality of symbolism. His fascination with the Dionysian cult and its parallels to Christianity can be understood based on his scholarly formation and interests (certainly, his acquaintance with Nietzsche and Hölderlin played a significant role in it). The image of a loving God appears as foreshadowing in the pre-Christian religions, and thus any effort to come nearer to the divine must be honored and seen as inspirational. At times, it is surprising how close, as in the case of Greek mythology, to a (Christian) sacrificial concept of love they approached, assuming and believing that it simply had to be present in the divine. It is Christianity that fully developed these seminal, mystical insights of ancient times. In Christ's light we see light, in His cross and His unconditional kenotic, salvific action of love. The force of Ivanov's thought is in the tenderness of a true artist who is aware of the fugitiveness of the muse — the materialness of light and tone, the sound of a voice singing us into life, like a sculptor who brings out the invisible, the spoken word that transforms transparency into immanence, or is it the other way around? The key tone is love, resounding from eternity to Eternity, the mud from which human beings have been formed and the breath that revived them. Yes, them, since every human being is a *he* and a *she,* even though Ivanov does not state it explicitly. His attention is turned towards the reverberations of love between two enamored persons, for this is the closest to paradise that one can experience on earth, and, above all, to the great Echo of Eternity that calls us by our proper names, all of us in the *All-I* and still in the personal-singular, as a unique image, a work of art, each one of us, in an eternal present: "love sings to me: 'You are.'"

3. Semen Liudvigovich Frank: *God's Love as God-with-Us*

3.1. Biography

S. L. Frank (1877-1950) is considered one of the most systematic philosophers of the Russian Silver Age and of the Russian exile. He was born in Moscow as the son of a doctor. While still attending grammar school, he

which, however, could be attributed to the translator's effort to highlight other (e.g., aesthetic) aspects of the poetry.

joined the Marxist movement, which influenced his decision to enter the School of Law at Moscow University. As a result of his Marxist activities, he was arrested and exiled in 1899, upon which he continued his studies of political economy and philosophy in Berlin, Heidelberg, and Munich. During this time, he published his first work, *Teoriia tsennosti Marksa i ee znacheniie (Marx's Theory of Value and Its Meaning)* in 1900, and the following year his first philosophic work *Fr. Nitsshe i etika "liubvi k dal'nemu" (Nietzsche and the Ethics of "Love for the Distant")*, after which his attention turned fully towards philosophic subjects. He was also involved in the editing of *Problemy idealizma* (*Problems of Idealism* [1902]), *Vekhi* (1909), the political weeklies *Poliarnaia zvezda (The Pole Star)* and *Svoboda kul'tury (The Freedom of Culture)* in 1905-6, as well as translating some of Schleiermacher's works. From 1912 to 1915 Frank lectured as a private docent of the Petersburg University, at the end of which he defended his master's degree with *Predmet znaniia* (*The Object of Knowledge* [1915]), and later his book *Dusha cheloveka* (*The Soul of Man* [1917]) was presented as a doctoral thesis. Given, however, the political upheaval of the time, it could not be defended. Two more university assignments followed, in Saratov and Moscow, until 1922 when he was exiled for good. He settled first in Berlin, lecturing from 1930 to 1937 on the history of Russian thought and literature at the University of Berlin, then moved to France and, in 1945, to England where he died in 1950 near London.

Frank was a prolific writer with a capability for a systematically developed "clear exposition," combining literary talent with "masterful analysis" of a given problematic. He developed the concept of philosophic realism, and it was in his principal philosophical work, *The Object of Knowledge*, that his own system evolved to the point where he detached himself from Solov'ev's general influence especially on the theme of all-unity. All-unity, in fact, provides the hermeneutical key to Frank's philosophic system.[85] He was also greatly influenced by Nicholas of Cusa, whom he considered "in a certain sense" his "sole teacher of philosophy,"[86] and had a great admiration for the system of Plotinus. Zenkovsky considers that "in strength of philosophic vision Frank may be called without hesitation the most outstanding among Russian philosophers generally — not merely among those who share his ideas" — defining his philosophic system as a "well-thought-out" one that

85. Cf. V. V. Zenkovsky, *A History of Russian Philosophy II* (London: Routledge and Kegan Paul, 2005), p. 852.

86. Cf. S. L. Frank, "Nepostizhimoe," in *S. L. Frank: Sochineniia* (Moskva: Izd. "Pravda," 1990), p. 184 (NPO).

touched in a profound way logic, epistemology, metaphysics, anthropology, and ethics.[87] Frank also became involved in addressing the social and psychological problems of Russian society, offering a religious approach to and interaction with the Divine and God whom we recognize through love.[88]

Some of his other works are *Zhivoe znanie* (*The Living Knowledge* [1923]); *Religia i nauka* (*Religion and Science* [1924]); *Krushenie kumirov* (*The Downfall of Idols* [1924]); *Smysl zhizni* (*The Meaning of Life* [1926]); *Dukhovnye osnovy obshchestva* (*The Spiritual Foundations of Society* [1930]); *Nepostizhimoe* (*Unfathomable* [1939]); *S nami Bog* (*God with Us* [1946]); *Svet vo t'me* (*The Light in Darkness* [1949]); and *Realnost' i chelovek (Reality and the Human Being)*, which was completed upon his death and published in 1956.

3.2. Near and Distant Loves

Frank's systematic thinking is evident on the subject of love. *Nietzsche and the Ethics of "Love for the Distant,"* his very first philosophic work, is dedicated to a reflection on Nietzsche's "most splendid and undoubtedly brilliant work," *Zarathustra,*[89] which grants particular attention to the question of the ethics of love to *far* and *near* relations. Frank was enthused about the beauty of this literary-philosophic piece, frequently commenting on direct quotes from it. He aimed at a discernment, juxtaposition, and reciprocal complementation of love's two aspects: that which is related to the distant yet not less important realities of life, and the classic, Christian presentation of love for the *near,* i.e., one's neighbor.[90] While the ethics of "the love for one's neighbor" *(liubov' k blizhnemu)* is a "moral system based on the instinct of compassion" *(instinkt*

87. Cf. Zenkovsky, *A History of Russian Philosophy II,* pp. 852-54; P. V. Alekseev, *Filosofy Rossii XIX-XX stoletii* (Moskva: "Akademicheskii Proekt," 2002), pp. 1028-29.

88. For biography and bibliography, see P. Boobbyer, *S. L. Frank: The Life and Work of a Russian Philosopher 1877-1950* (Athens: Ohio University Press, 1995), which also appeared under the same title in Russian (Moskva: Rosspen, 2001); I. M. Nevleva, *Filosofiia kul'tury S. L. Franka* (Sankt-Peterburg: Aleteiia, 2007); *Ideinoe nasledie S. L. Franka v kontekste sovremennoi kul'tury* (Moskva: Bibleisko-Bogoslovskii institut Sv. Apostola Andreia, 2009); *Russian Religious Thought,* ed. J. D. Kornblatt and R. F. Gustafson (Madison: University of Wisconsin Press, 1996), pp. 195-259; Zenkovsky, *A History of Russian Philosophy II,* pp. 852-72.

89. "Fr. Nitsshe i etika 'liubvi k dal'nemu,'" in *Semen Frank: Sochineniia* (Moskva: Kharvest; Minsk: Ast, 2000), p. 12 (NIE).

90. The book's epigraph is self-revelatory: "Die Zukunft und das Fernste sei dir die Ursache deines Heute. . . . Meine Brüder, zur Nächstenliebe rathe ich euch nicht: ich rathe euch zur Fernstenliebe." *Also sprach Zarathustra.* NIE, p. 3.

sostradaniia), "the love for the distant" is directed towards the "interests" of those same neighbors,[91] which often lie somewhat far off. This means "love for people who are for us 'distant,' fellow citizens, our descendants, humankind," but also concepts such as "love for truth, good(ness), righteousness," and simply for anything that we designate as "the ideal," or, in Nietzsche's words, "love for things and ghosts (Liebe zu Sachen und Gespenstern)." Specifically, Frank examines what he calls the "antithesis" between the "two feelings" of these love-attitudes, which at times actualizes in a struggle or even in "tragedies" between them.[92] According to Frank, it is Nietzsche's "brilliant merit" to have laid open with utmost clarity this "as old as the world" antithesis between love to the *near* and the *distant* and thus to have brought a "rough yet didactic idea" into ethics, an element that can be comprehended as "the Gospel of 'love for the distant.'"[93] This has moral consequences and creates an "ethics of love" that serves as the rapprochement to the "reality of life." Such reality naturally unfolds in time; therefore, we are talking about an "ethics of progress . . . in a formal-sociological meaning of the term."[94] Frank substantially comments on Zarathustra's ideas on love with the insight, in the middle of his commentary, that as long as there exists in the human being "a struggle between the principles of reconciliation *(primirenie)* and the principle of revolt [or rebellion] *(vozmushchenie),*" between the striving to preserve the old and to establish the new, "the rivalry between these two great moral systems will not cease in the human soul."[95] However, since these two elements are constitutive ones in human society, peace cannot come easily, nor, on a positive note, will (spiritual) progress cease because of the tension between the two of them.

As for the following philosophic works, *The Object of Knowledge* and *The Soul of Man,* Frank builds up a strict systematic-philosophic line of reasoning, mentioning love-relations rather marginally and only to underscore his epistemology.[96] Most of the ideas from these two works Frank refines, completes, and extends in a third book titled *Dukhovnye osnovy obshchestva*

91. In Russian, *blizhnyi* corresponds to the English *next* or *close,* as well as in the Christian sense *one's neighbor;* thus it is about the "distant interests" of our "close, dear ones."

92. Cf. NIE, pp. 5-10.

93. . . . *kak evangelie "liubvi k dal'nemu."*

94. Cf. NIE, pp. 11-16.

95. Cf. NIE, p. 34.

96. In the first case, it is a quote and paraphrasing of St. Augustine's *De civitate Dei,* XI, 26. Cf. S. Frank, *Predmet znaniia. Dusha cheloveka* (Moskva: Ast, 2000), pp. 571, 687.

(The Spiritual Foundations of Society), which appeared in Paris in 1930 (the three were referred to by Frank as "the Trilogy").[97] An original notion in this book is a reflection that Frank dedicates to *freedom,* which is preceded by another reflection on the "principle of solidarity." Both are founded in Christianity, specifically in the realm of the "'image and likeness of God' and its conversion *(prevrashchenie)* into the zoic *(zhivotnoe)* . . . above all the human being."[98] Thus its divine origin of *solidarity* represents a lasting challenge for the divinization of all societies that claim to be built upon a Christian foundation.

3.3. *Spiritual Emptiness and the* Encounter with the Living God

This title from *The Downfall of Idols* for Frank is more of an ontological or existential task than just a mere philosophic subject. All his works carry the trace of an inner-outer, individual-social search, a path from the empty multilayered promises of the past towards the mystical-real ontology of God's ever-present life within and among us in this work. After having analyzed the recent past of Russia with its revolting events and tendencies, or "idols" (meaning "revolution, politics, culture, ideas and moral idealism"), Frank reaches an essential development in epistemology, namely the notion from the meaninglessness of emptiness to the fullness of the living God.[99] Since none of the idols "we have served" have brought satisfaction for the soul, what then should be the "purpose of life"?[100]

In Frank's view, the more one feels oppressed and unhappy, the more one turns his love towards the uniting element of all, which (especially for Russians) was the *rodina* (homeland). It is not an idol, and the love for it is a sacred notion of "genuine love," so impressively described by M. I. Lermontov in his poem *Rodina.*[101] Yet the loftiest and most noble love or patriotism

97. Cf. S. L. Frank, *Dukhovnye osnovy obshchestva* (Moskva: Izd. "Respublika," 1992), p. 14 (DOB).

98. Cf. DOB, pp. 112-17.

99. Cf. "Krushenie kumirov," in *S. L. Frank: Sochineniia* (Moskva: Izd. "Pravda," 1990), pp. 116-60 (KRK).

100. Frank returns to Nietzsche, considering his lofty ideals also as a "brief epoch" of illusion, the belief to be free from all constraints and free for taking all the advantages of life. Even this is but an idol. Hence the question: "Freedom *from everything* in the world — for what purpose is it good for us if we do not know what we are free for?" Cf. KRK, pp. 161-62.

101. For most Russians, this is understood as the "holy motherland." Cf. KRK, pp. 163-65.

for the homeland[102] cannot and does not perform *salvation,* since love without faith (faith being something "original, fundamental, unshakeable") is lacking in "a deeper justification *(glubochaishee opravdanie).*" In hopelessness while in "anguish and spiritual desire," the soul strays on paths of diverse ideas until it finally encounters "the living God," a God appearing to us in the "very Living Truth" of Christ who proclaims the "Kingdom of Heaven."[103] Frank makes the ultimate step to bring "into focus" the image of God in us based on Plato's request to "turn the eyes of the soul *(dusha)*" and discover a new "*most profound ontological reality*" of God who lives "endlessly close to us," an image in our very souls, "the image of true God, as a God of life, God of truth and love."[104]

Therefore, this "Existent" *(Sushchee)*[105] is not a philosophical "dead scheme" but a "true, boundlessly full, eternal Being, a living endless life and the authentically real, almighty, creative power of love." This power of "endless love" not only creates but also heals "all the diseases of our organic existence."[106] Since this image is the true image transmitted to us by Jesus Christ, the very "Living Truth," the fully revealed and final ontological reality, therefore, on a principle level the soul's search has been concluded: "We have found the eternal Friend and Father, we are not alone and forsaken anymore; in silence *(tishina),* alone *(naedina)* with one's self and with God, we delight by the joy of love."[107]

3.4. *Spiritual Health*

In order for us to obtain access to this realm, we need to grant access to God by "the inner *disclosure of the soul,* [by] interrupting its reticence, its cold and debilitating being in itself," which can be achieved by the "power of boundless love and true life" streaming from God Himself. By granting access to God, the final meaning of existence is fulfilled in a "gradual learning

102. ". . . with which we share the same sickness." KRK, p. 165.

103. Cf. KRK, pp. 165-69.

104. Cf. KRK, p. 170.

105. Following Hegel.

106. Cf. KRK, pp. 171-72.

107. "In comparison with which these matters of all the failures, disillusions, and sorrows of the external life cease to exist." Frank quotes the final part of Solov'ev's famous poem titled "Emmanuel" (from March 11, 1892): "Amidst our random vanities / Within the confused stream of life's anxieties / You possess a secret wholly joyous: / Evil is powerless. We are eternal. God is with us!" KRK, p. 172.

to love all. . . . This eternal power of love that has awaken[ed] in us the love to ourselves is meant to keep giving birth in us to love for all and everything." Frank repeats Abba Dorotheus's image of God's "absolute centrality of existence and life," which means that the closer we move to God, the closer we move to each other.[108]

To the image of God as a loving Father and "Absolute source of love and life" indwelling in the individual person and whole society, Frank traces all concepts of morals, which are "nothing but some kind of *hygiene* or *technique* of salvation, preservation of one's proper life" for the future promised life of heaven.[109] In this sphere are collocated the various forms of "religious asceticism" that are meant to be a *kind* or *mellow* asceticism of salvation[110] and not a "frenzied-brutal asceticism of moral fanaticism."[111] Both are opposed to the goal of our straining, which is "personal salvation" accompanied by profound happiness and in which tenderly "breathes the spirit of love as the very entity of life and salvation."[112] This, of course, may seem like a somewhat naïve spirituality, yet once we admit life's roughness and the struggle for salvation, an encounter in *peace* and *silence* between the soul and its "Eternal Friend" appears all the more to make sense. Frank denotes this process as "a new instinct of spiritual health and self-preservation"[113] and concludes on a very positive ecclesiastic note that in our attitude towards life, thanks to our participation in the divine unity, we are "penetrated by love,"[114] and thus best disposed to encounter our *Eternal Friend.*

108. On the following pages, Frank underlines the inseparability of this love for fellow human beings from the love for God since the previous is "rooted in the awareness of brotherhood in God . . . [who is our] Heavenly Father as the Absolute source of love and life." Cf. KRK, pp. 173-74.

109. "The sphere of spiritual principles" *(sfera dukhovnykh osnov),* Pascal also calls "ordre du cœur" or "logique du cœur." Cf. KRK, pp. 174-75. For the treatise on "God of Jesus Christ — the loving Father," see *S nami Bog,* in DOB, pp. 264, 297.

110. . . . *blagostnyi asketizm spaseniia.*

111. . . . *istuplenno-zhestokii asketizm.*

112. Cf. KRK, pp. 176-77.

113. . . . *novyi instinkt dukhovnogo zdorov'ia.*

114. An evidently crucial component of the Church is to be understood as "a living universal soul of humankind, as a *sobornyi* personality through the bond of which we co-participate in the universal, cosmic mystery of Divine-Community *(Bogoobshchestvo).*" Cf. KRK, pp. 178-80. Concerning sacraments, marital love, and "church and the world," see DOB, pp. 83-98. "The love for God and love for the human being, the bond *(sviaz')* with God and the relationship with the human being, no matter even how often they differed empirically between themselves . . . in their base they are one and the same feeling *(chuvstvo),* one and the same ontological relationship *(otnoshenie).*" Cf. DOB, p. 90.

3.5. The Meaning of Life

Similarly to Frank's previous work, this booklet came about as a result of discussions and disputes with the Russian student movement, and it reflects the personal beliefs of the author.[115] The difference from the *The Fall of the Idols* is that here Frank defines *love* clearly and actively as the unique core of eternal life and quotes John's Gospel for faith in the One sent by God (John 6:28-29) along with Christ's answer to the scholar of the law on how to gain eternal life with the request of twofold love (Luke 10:25-28). These two — love for God and love for one's neighbor — are the *only* "deeds" saving and safeguarding life.[116]

In the first notion, although love enjoys full freedom, Frank gets into a slight contradiction about its self-sacrificial character in overcoming the *subjective* and *objective,* the *mine* and *yours* aspects: "Love is not a cold and drain[ing] egoistic desire of pleasure, neither is it a slavish service, self-destructing oneself for the other. Love is such an overcoming of our self-interested life that it even gives us the blessed fullness of *true life (podlinnaia zhizn'),* and with that gives meaning to our life."[117] Yet this meaning is guaranteed only beyond "the circularity of time," i.e., by the twofold love for the divine and human[118] inevitably striving for and being concluded in deification *(obozhenie).*[119] While in the process of deification, the empirical experience and cognition reach their limits,[120] yet it is "a self-evident truth for the knowledge of the heart[121] not needing any proofs and not even admitting one precisely because of its self-evidence." Frank very elegantly shows "from

115. Cf. S. Frank, *Smysl zhizni* (Bruxelles: Izd. "Zhin' s Bogom," Foyer Oriental Chrétien, 1992), pp. 5-7 (SMZ).

116. Cf. SMZ, pp. 33-34. "Faith without deeds is dead," but since God is life, "not a God of the dead, and we believe in God-Life, our faith cannot but be a faith of life and life-bearing." Cf. SMZ, p. 99.

117. "There is no greater good than life itself — yet only that of *true life* . . . of [the] creative unfolding of the absolute depths of our entity." SMZ, p. 87. Later, however, "True life is a life in an all-embracing all-unity, unceasing service to the absolute whole *(absoliutnomu tselomu);* we first truly *find* ourselves and our life when we sacrifice ourselves *(zhertvujem soboi)* and our empirical separatedness *(ot"edinennost'iu)* and seclusion *(zamknutost')* and strengthen all our being in [an]other — in God, as the primary source *(pervoistochnik)* of all life." Since we are "children of one Father," the task to love and to sacrifice is one and the same source for all. Cf. SMZ, pp. 105-6.

118. Cf. SMZ, pp. 41-42.

119. Cf. SMZ, pp. 44-46.

120. Namely that the "absolute depth of being . . . perfection, perfect happiness, blessedness and joyous [luminous] peace *(svetlyi pokoi) are one and the same thing.*" SMZ, p. 87.

121. . . . *dlia serdechnogo zhe znaniia.*

what our heart lives," and that its "feelings or dreams" are not subjective. On the contrary, it perceives and *knows* "the final depths of existence," a mystery "best represented" by the love which is God's essence (1 John 4:7-8, 16). "God is love," and all who dwell in Him dwell in love, and vice versa. As revealed by St. John, "in this is the essence *(sushchestvo)* of religious faith."[122] This awareness saves us from those two elements in the human soul that are wearing it down: "the feeling of dread" *(chuvstvo uzhasa)*[123] and "the desire of perfection, happiness, and reconciliation."[124]

As he frequently does, Frank concludes his reflection on Christology and ecclesiology in God-manhood *(Bogochelovechestvo)*, "the incarnation of Meaning in life" and "God in incarnation of God-Word,"[125] shifting the value of sacrifice to a relational level: "True life is a life in an all-embracing all-unity, unceasing service to the absolute whole *(absoliutnomu tselomu)*; we first truly *find* ourselves and our life when we sacrifice ourselves *(zhertvovat' soboi)* and our empirical separateness and seclusion and strengthen all our being in *an* other — in God, as the primordial source *(pervoistochnik)* of all life." As we are "children of one Father," the task to love and to sacrifice is one and the same source for all: "*Love* is the foundation of human life on the whole, its very essence. . . . Outside of love there is no life." So it is *bond (sviaz')* and *relationship* — instead of *separateness* and *seclusion* — *service* and *sacrifice of one's self* out of love for God and one's neighbor, that gives meaning to life, which *is* the meaning, its joy and truth.[126]

3.6. *The Relatedness of the Unfathomable*

Our life "flows" in a realm that surrounds us and is defined as "reality," *(deistvitel'nost')*, in which we are called to inquire and orient ourselves. It also is the *metaphysical* means *in* and *through* which we cognize the "Sovereign

122. "For love, authentic love, is nothing other than the joy of life, or life as the fullness of delight — an inner, undivided unity of life's bounty, an intensity of gratification *(udovletvorenie)*. It is the desire of life and being in joy, bounty, [and] happiness. And that is why we comprehend that 'God is love.'" Cf. SMZ, pp. 87-88.

123. *Uzhas* in Russian has a strong emotional charge close to *terror, dread,* and *horror.*

124. . . . *zhazhda sovershenstva, schast'ia, umirotvoreniia.* Yet "perfect love casts out fear" (1 John 4:18) and, therefore, neither fear nor dread of God should be in our love, for this excludes any "higher joy" from our life. Cf. SMZ, pp. 88-89.

125. As well as repeating his previous quotation of Solov'ev's "Emmanuel." Cf. SMZ, pp. 92-94.

126. Cf. SMZ, pp. 105-7.

Lord" *(Vsederzhitelia)*, the *Pantocrator* of the world.[127] To the "normality of the human being" pertains the fullness of being and existence, even the "starry sky above my head," and not merely the "moral imperative" of Kant but rather an all-embracing *Reality.* Pursuing his argument systematically, Frank addresses "authentic erotic love" with all its excesses and depths[128] as a "marvelous mystery *(tajna)* . . . a profound layer of existence" that cannot be explored by any "cold-cynical analysis" but rather awakes a shiver in the soul and the feeling that we face "something unfathomable" yet perceived as something very real, truly a *reality.*[129] Frank unfolds this idea between metaphysics and philosophy venturing also into the *I-You* relationship of one's self with the other. In the end, this other is the *Absolute* that, even in "my beloved self," remains a "terrifying *(zhutkii)* and incomprehensible" *you.*[130]

3.7. One-for-the-Other

Frank dedicates some separate titles to the theme of *love* — one in the perspective of its essence, others in its relatedness between God and the human being — although every one remains grounded in the *I-you* relationship.[131]

127. Cf. "Nepostizhimoe," in *S. L. Frank: Sochinenia* (Moskva: Izd. "Pravda," 1990), pp. 186-89 (NPO).

128. "Beginning from 'sodomite abysses' and ending with the 'cult of the Madonna.'" Cf. NPO, p. 192.

129. Understood is a derivative of Kant's "categorical imperative." Cf. NPO, pp. 190-92.

130. Cf. NPO, pp. 363-68. "Precisely for this reason enmity and hatred can be an expression of a secret, unrealized love, as love in general, love and hatred in some kind of form are conjugated between themselves. And erotic love striving for the very intimate union of 'I' and 'you,' in the same instance causes serious, at times tragic conflicts between its concerned parties. 'The union of a soul with one's own soul' is, according to the words of Tiutchev, also always 'their fateful duel' *(ikh poedinok rokovoi).*" Thus the *I-you* relationship is similar to what R. Otto described as a "mysterium tremendum" with "mysterium fascinosum" rendered by Frank as "union of the mystery of fear and enmity with the mystery of love." As further sources Frank indicates M. Sheller, M. Buber, and F. Ebner. Cf. NPO, p. 368. On the concept of "transcending into" *(transtsendirovaniie vo-vnutr')* the inner being of the other whom we perceive "as the loved one," into the *you* of the depth of the other perceived as *transsubjective* in the *I-you* relationship, see NPO, pp. 386-91. As for the *I* and *Us* relationship, see DOB, pp. 47-63. On the "contemporary theologian" R. Otto, Frank and his concepts, see *S nami Bog*, DOB, p. 237.

131. He examines this bond systematically not only from a philosophical but also from the up-to-date psychological knowledge of his time.

"The transrationality and unfathomability[132] of autonomy *(samobytiia),*[133] as it emerges in the being of one-for-the-other *(odnogo-dlia-drugogo),* in the being [of] *I-you,* unfolds in the deepest depth of its appearance in *love,* in which for the first time the relationship of *I-you* is being realized fully, in its completeness." The human being's proper identity, that "something undoubtedly unique and with nothing comparable meaning of *my I,*" which Frank expresses in Russian with *"ia-esm' (I am),"* seems to echo, even though not explicitly stated, a familiar *I am who I am.*[134] That the *I-you* relationship fully and authentically unfolds in the "phenomenon of *love*" is an idea that Frank will repeat numerous times and under different points of view,[135] for "love is . . . *unity,* dwelling in *unity* with the *'other,'*" and that finally will lead to the concept of *coincidentia oppositorum* — an "antinomistic monodualism *(antinomisticheskii monodualizm).*"[136] From this view, Frank underlines that the quality of love lies beyond any exclusive, romantic, ideal, erotic love, but also beyond "religiously-enlightened" *(religiozno-prosvetlennoi)* love for the human being in general as understood "in the sense of the Christian precept of love to one's neighbor, ἀγάπη." Explicitly, "The matter is a universal and original phenomenon that steers the entire human life. . . . Love in this essence *(sushchestve)* unfolds not only in erotic and marital love, in maternal love, in love towards parents, brothers and sisters, in authentic intimate friendship, but in every single [and] in general relationship to 'you' as [my] kindred (homogeneous, *odnorodnoi*), to me genuine reality — in every relationship to 'you' as towards a 'neighbor.'"[137] So the highest and all-encompassing quality of love is not identified with the Christian concept of love, *agapē,* nor with erotic love as such, but apparently with a primordial *essence* or *principle* inspiring and *occurring* in various forms in the human person and in the Divine, as well as in their interrelatedness. In a poetic-metaphysical way, we could transliterate this ontological reality by the Bulgakovian: *I am, therefore I love.*

132. . . . *transratsional'nost' i nepostizhimost'.*

133. Literally, *self-being.*

134. Cf. NPO, pp. 373-74. Frank subsequently extends the *I am* concept to the commune of *us.* Cf. NPO, pp. 378-85.

135. "Love does not make blind, but in fact turns one into a *seer*" of reality, seeing and understanding the other, *you,* as a "second I." Cf. NPO, pp. 374-75.

136. He was evidently inspired also by Nietzsche's concept of "Einsamkeit" — "Zweisamkeit," which Frank explicitly mentions. Cf. NPO, p. 376.

137. Cf. NPO, pp. 376-77.

3.8. Only as "You" Are You My God

Frank developed his presentation retrospectively, from the anthropologic towards the divine level, from the earthly-material towards the spheres of primordial, identifying the "Divine as 'you'" on a philosophical and as "God-with-us (Emmanu-el)" on a religious level, the latter being for him "in final result the *'God-with-me.'* . . . For what is being revealed in me is not only God 'as such' but precisely 'God-with-me,' a concrete completeness of the undividable and infusible *(nesliiannyi)* dual-unity *(dvuedinstvo) 'God-and-I.'*" The very personal character of this relationship is of utmost importance to Frank, and the astounding reason for it is in the following phrase: "The Divinity becomes for me 'you,' reveals [itself] as 'you'; and solely in the quality of 'you' it *is God.*" The *facing* of the Divine towards the human being, or the human being's "existential facings" towards it, *is* the space where, in the "self-disclosure of reality"[138] and the opening up for it, the *name* (as) *God* is revealed.[139]

3.9. God-with-Me as Love

"There is only one term in the human language" that expresses the "transrational nature" of the "God-with-me" relationship, and that is *love,* and here Frank means specifically the *kenotic* quality of love. "Love in [its] very self is already a mystery: the loving one surrenders self-forgetfully *(samozabvenno)* and selflessly *(samootverzhenno)* to the loved one, transfers — all the while not ceasing to be himself — the center of his being into the loved one, dwells in the loved one just as the loved dwells in the loving one; *I* lose myself in *you* and precisely by that I *find myself,* enriched by the accessioning to me [and by the] granted *you* to me." In his analysis, Frank uses deliberately means of logic to prove that it is useless even to try to create a logical formula for this interaction. The answer to this enigma is most probably the *life*

138. . . . *samoobnaruzhenie real'nosti i iz prizyvania ee.*

139. Cf. NPO, pp. 466-69. "To talk about God in the third person, to call him 'he' is — purely from a religious point of view — an intrinsic blasphemy," and as a next logical step, Frank moves from *you* to the *You* of God. Also, he would regularly return to the inseparability of the love for God and one's neighbor, where the former is "the ontological fundamental principle" of the latter (based on 1 John 4:7-8), and every "being-for-myself" is in its core a "being-with-God" and "being-for-God," consequently also a *being-for-you.* Cf. NPO, pp. 468, 471-72.

of this relationship and the *origin* of the love-notion, both of which stem from (within) God: "It [*God* as *You*] is not merely the 'loved one' and also is not merely the 'loving one' — but is *love*, the very creative love: 'God is love' (1 John 4:8)."[140] And as such, it is a mere question of time to realize that our proper love for God is nothing but a reflection of His love, or "even more precisely the reflex and manifestation of God's very Self *as* love."[141] Frank unfolds this, finally, in its Christological dimension of "God-with-me as Divine-human being" and its universal, inexplicitly ecclesial character of "with-us-God" virtually in the concluding paragraph of the last chapter.[142]

3.10. Politics of Love

Svet vo t'me (The Light in Darkness), as the title insinuates, was his penultimate book. In it, Frank's attention turns once more towards the social and soteriological aspects of love imbedded in Christ's truth, which is proclaiming the kingdom of God. This latter, however, is not an ambiguous choice between the salvation of the proper soul and the salvation of the world, an *either-or*, but an interlinked *and*, which is achieved by excluding "egoism" as an "anti-Christian mythology." Furthermore, egoism is in juxtaposition to "God who is love" and needs to be overcome by striving for "deification" *(obozhenie)* through Christ. "A person who identifies himself as a Christian can neither think of his own salvation only, neglecting the participation of his brothers, nor serenely delight in the blissful state of '[being already] saved,' contemplating with indifference the deadly torments of other souls. The very idea of salvation becomes distorted [with such an attitude], a glaring contradiction, for salvation in fact is an acquisition of a refuge and peace in *God*, God [who] after all is *love*."[143]

This love, the *light* of "Christ's truth," is presented for the first time

140. The ontological statement from St. John can be found repeatedly in Frank's major works.

141. Cf. NPO, pp. 494-98. "Even my obscure [gloomy] search for God is a manifestation of the power His love has over me." NPO, p. 497.

142. Cf. NPO, pp. 550-51, 555.

143. It is primarily based on the Johannine tradition of "God is love" (1 John 4:8, 16). Cf. S. L. Frank, *Svet vo t'me* (Moskva: "Faktorial," 1998), pp. 130-37 (SVT). *As it is, there are many parts, yet one body. . . .* [*Therefore,*] *If one member suffers, all suffer together; if one member is honored, all rejoice together* (1 Cor. 12:20, 26). Cf. SVT, p. 137 and similarly in 1 John 4:20; 2:9. Cf. SVT, pp. 138-39.

from Frank as "energy" *(energiia)* and a principle of interaction and compassion with our neighbors and the world, which is *in darkness,* meaning *lifeless* without it.[144] Frank invents an original yet logical proposal of a solution based on the *essentiality* of love for life and life-sustaining relationships, for a "Christian existence and Christian moral life" that is not a contradiction anymore but two aspects of the same "all-encompassing principle of love." This solution is the "politics of love" *(politika liubvi),* which is a "system of planned actions governed by love," including both aspects of love, the personal and the universal, but also the spiritual and the pragmatic.[145] Frank proposes love as the foundation for solutions to problems on both the micro or individual level as well as the macro or societal level.

3.11. Agapan-Philein

Based on the previous reflection, Frank had to return to the question of *agapē,* this time distinguishing it from "φιλία" and fully concerned for the entity of Christian love in its character as charity. At this point, *agapē* receives its proper Christian value as "the love of neighbor in its Christian meaning of love," and though it has nothing in common "with a spontaneous feeling or impulse rooted in the *empirical* nature of the human being," yet it is still much more on a social, interactive level than an ecclesial or even theological-mystical one. *Philia,* somewhat in juxtaposition to *agapē,* is charity-love — *milosredie.* "In French they use a beautiful word for it: *charité*"; however, for Frank, it is still based on "a purely fleshly or spiritual bond or liking of a person." The gratuity and religious awareness in the nature of Christian love does not lessen its value, but very much to the contrary, it is similar to the heart that reflects the relationship between God and His created human image:[146]

> Any human goodness, any participation in the fate of one's neighbor, the capacity to be internally affected by his need — all this alone already testifies that the human heart has certain depths, going beyond the boundaries of its purely fleshly nature; all this is a token of a kind of spiritual fire *(nekogo dukhovnogo goreniia),* i.e., in final analysis of God's action in the soul, even if it remained unrecognized. Love for one's

144. Cf. SVT, pp. 166-67.
145. Cf. SVT, pp. 167-71.
146. Cf. SVT, pp. 177-78.

> neighbor is commanded by Christian revelation and comes forth from the very *ontological structure (iz ontologicheskogo sostava)* of Christian life as a rootedness in God *(ukorenennost' v Boge)*, who Himself "is love." It can occur that this love is not aware of its religious foundation, which does not impede its having such a foundation. We are obliged to and can love our neighbor in [a] Christian sense of this notion (ἀγαπᾶν) entirely independently from the fact whether it "appeals" to us, whether we can "love" a person [simply] out of a purely human subjectively-emotional attraction (φιλεῖν). Love in this Christian sense is, in [the] closest image, goodwill *(blagovolenie)* — unselfish interest in the well-being of one's neighbor.[147]

Consequently, Frank brings his thought to a conclusion with the *"salvation, redemption, deification"* of the world, and the neighbor through the "activeness of our love" inspired by the God-manhood of Christ. This activeness opens us up and at the same moment brings about the reality of the kingdom of God where we, "God's children," are each called personally, and all together,[148] under the guidance of His Spirit.[149]

3.12. God with Us

Indeed, this is a fitting title for Frank's final book. We wish to glance at its second reflection, which renews the theme of "the religion of love" and

147. SVT, p. 178.

148. As for the universality of this call (also with St. Francis of Assisi as a great example), see SVT, pp. 204-7.

149. Cf. SVT, pp. 179-81. Frank's last work, *Realnost' i chelovek*, apart from placing the main stress in relations on the love for one's neighbor, notes that the "Christian faith, being in its very essence a religion of salvation — salvation of the human being from his nothingness *(nichtozhestvo)*, from the tragic powerlessness of his earthly existence — [also] as the highest completion of a prophetic consciousness of a moral bond *(nravstvenooi sviazi)* between God and the human being, the vicinity of God as a loving father, under the protection of whom the human being acquires his last satisfaction of the primordial needs of his existence." Cf. S. Frank, *Realnost' i chelovek* (Moskva: Izd. Ast, Khranitel', 2007), p. 206. And, "Christianity is not a religion of adoration of God in His opposition *(protivopolozhnost')* to the human being, but in His deepest affinity *(srodstvo)* with the human being. Christianity is a religion of humanness *(chelovechnost')*," which is the true "sense of the love-commandment." Cf. *Realnost' i chelovek*, pp. 212-13. On the "saving power of God's love" and Christianity as a religion of humanness, see *S nami Bog*, in DOB, p. 307.

touches the subject of asceticism and love, concluding with the "path of the cross."[150]

Since Christianity "is a religion of human personhood and of Divine-humanity.[151] . . . the Christian religious prescription [or purpose] *(ustanovka)* is a prescription of love." Frank gives as many approximations of love as possible, some repeated, some new, such as "Love is not just a mere feeling but a scope of hither benefit — by the consideration of Greek philosophy a result of imperturbability *(atarachia)* and torpor *(beschustvie) (apatheia)* — . . . love is [an] immediate *acceptance of the absolute value of the loved one;* love is *the happiness of serving the other* . . . and thus love is a reverential *(blagogoveinyi) religious perception of a living being,* seeing in him [or] her the certain divine principle. All true love — whether it admits or not — is, by its very essence, a religious feeling [or perception] *(chuvstvo)*."[152]

Love simply is the loftiest good that humankind possesses, and Frank this time corrects his initial vision of erotic love by affirming its "tragic illusoriness" because of its fixation on the empirical experience, which, although it has been exalted by the poetic literature of all times, remains "by all its force and significance in human life, in the best of cases only a commencing form of true love."[153] Yet Frank does not discard erotic love entirely, highlighting its potential to teach the enamored person "to accept the absolute value in the loved counterpart" based on the intrinsic striving for the highest good and beauty, as according to Plato. This "transfiguration" of erotic love into a "true love" is possible and is meant to occur in the "sacrament of matrimony," *the* transformative realm of love.[154] Although he does not doubt the ecclesial character of love in principle, and its constitutive character for the Church, Frank conveys his doubt about the possibility of a universal love for "humanity" or "the human being in general: one can love only a certain, singular, individual human being in the full concreteness of his image. . . . Therefore, the universal, all-encompassing love is not a love for 'humanity' as to some kind of uniform whole, nor love for the 'human being' in general; it is a *love for all people* in all the concreteness and singular-

150. *S nami Bog,* in DOB, 317-405. It is subdivided into three parts based on three reflections: I. *What Is Faith?;* II. *The Paradox[ical] Truth of Christianity;* III. *Truth as the Way of Life.*

151. . . . *chelovecheskoi lichnosti i Bogochelovechnosti.*

152. Cf. DOB, p. 317.

153. "[Erotic love is] . . . a frail flower unfolding on the stem of love and not its genuine root." Cf. DOB, p. 318.

154. Cf. DOB, pp. 318-19.

ity of each of them." Thus, the all-embracing love does not simply embrace and include all, but "everything in all *(vsio vo vsekh)*."[155] A further novelty in Frank's presentation is God's love being directly equated with the "power" that overcomes all divisions and separations of our souls — as from God, so in ourselves and with our fellow human beings. It is the eye-opener that gives true, joyful sight to our vision:

> Love is a joyful and reverential vision of all the divineness in all being, an automatic spiritual impulse of service, a satisfaction of the soul's longing *(toska)* for an authentic existence through giving itself up for others — this love *is the very core (serdtsevina)*[156] *of faith.* To contemplate God means to contemplate love, and to contemplate love means *to have it, to be ablaze* by it. In this is the essential difference of Christian Knowledge of God *(Bogopoznaniia)* from any philosophical-speculative one *(filosofski-umozritel'nyi)* — a distinction that is not an opposition, yet only completion, replenishment, genuine realization of that which the speculative mysticism *(umozritel'naia mistika)* strives for. Out of this reason living love for the human being — for any human being — is the measure of implementation of the soul's true striving after God.[157]

One must admit that Frank demonstrates a great spiritual maturity and pragmatism and understands love as "the norm and ideal" of human life's purpose, the goal and fulfillment of all his dreams that, once tasted, simply cannot be renounced anymore. This alone is *the* nominal contribution of Christianity, which makes this religion human and divine, truly human and thus truly divine, *divinizing:*

> Christianity opened the eyes of the soul for the ravishingly gorgeous vision of the kingdom of love; from now on the soul in its most profound depth *knows* that God is love, that love is the power of God, healing, perfecting, and bestowing grace *(blagodatstvuiushchyi)* on human life. Once the soul has recognized this — no mockery of the blind, of lunatics and trespassers, no cold life-wisdom, no lures of misleading ideals — no idols — can shake it [or] destroy it in this knowledge of saving truth.[158]

155. Cf. DOB, pp. 320-22. Here, Frank relies on quotes and references from the NT, especially the Gospel of John, the first letters of Peter, and to the Corinthians.

156. *Serdtsevina* in Russian means *core, pith,* but also *heart.*

157. Once more, 1 John 2:9; 4:20. Cf. DOB, p. 324.

158. DOB, p. 325. For the ascetic aspect of love, or the "unity" in Christianity, see

Conclusion

Frank may not have been the most mystically gifted person, he also was not a theologian or writer-narrator, yet he certainly was an extremely refined and systematic religious thinker and philosopher of modern Russian thought. He intended to cover all essential areas concerning philosophy beginning with his very first works onwards, viewing all through a Christian prism. He knows and addresses other religions, yet for him, Christianity *is the religion of love,* love being its *serdtsevina,* and *love* as the essence of God, since *God is love,* as he repeats in the gravity of his particular themes: love *is* relationship; it manifests and is being manifested in and by action, in interaction in society, just as in Jesus' time. Challenging the ideas of Descartes and Kant, Frank demonstrates great pragmatism, not generally considered a philosopher's virtue, and leads the Christian idea back to its origin: God is either in interaction — relationship, say love, in the *You* realized in *me* — or is not God (certainly, not a Christian one). For Christianity's message is the incarnated Logos, the Divine-human being Jesus Christ, the incarnated *love,* Emmanuel, that is, *God, Love, who is with us.*[159]

DOB, pp. 325-36. For Frank, the sacrificial character is accentuated in the "Path of the Cross," which is the highest expression of Christianity's paradoxality while still rendering a loving and lovable image of God who sacrifices Himself in the love of His Son for the salvation of the world. Cf. DOB, pp. 336-46.

159. This would also close the circle with the initial repetitions of Solov'ev's poem, "Emmanuel."

VIII. The Theology of Love in the Perspective of Return to the Fathers: The Neopatristic School of the Twentieth Century

1. Nikolai Nikolaevich Afanas'ev: The Power That Leads to Kenosis

1.1. Biography

N. N. Afanas'ev (1893-1966) was born in Odessa where he also conducted and concluded his studies, including those in medicine and mathematics, at the local university. He belonged to the "exiled generation" of Russian intellectuals who eventually became professors at St. Serge Institute in Paris. In 1916 he received artillery training in the military and served in the White Army during the time of the revolution until his emigration to Serbia in 1920. Once abroad, he actively participated in the Russian Orthodox circle and pursued theological studies in Belgrade (1921-25) and in 1925 married Praskov'ia Iakovlevna in Prague. Afanas'ev initiated his teaching career in 1930 at St. Serge Institute in Paris in canon law (his father was an attorney) and in 1939 was ordained to the deaconate and priesthood.

After completing ecclesial service in Tunis during World War II, Afanas'ev returned to St. Serge and in 1950 presented his doctoral thesis *Tserkov' Dukha Sviatogo (L'Église du Saint-Esprit)*. He then wrote the important work *Trapeza Gospodnia (La Table du Seigneur)* two years later, which attracted major attention and boosted him into many theological publications. Afanas'ev planned and conducted work on the second part of his doctoral thesis with the title *Granitsy Tserkvi (The Boundaries of the Church)*, which he never concluded.[1]

Fr. Afanas'ev was encouraged by Patriarch Athenagoras to work on the

1. The outlines of this work can be found in *Pensée Orthodoxe*, 13 (1968).

new Orthodox canon law and was the official delegate of St. Serge Institute at the fourth session of the Second Vatican Council in 1965.[2] He died a year later in Paris. Afanas'ev's great themes were connected to canon law, unity, and the universality of the Church, even though the law in his view "was but an ecclesial epiphenomenon" that never reached the depths of "dogmatic ontology but . . . merely manifested [it] more or less imperfectly."[3] He asserted that the true unity of local churches is in the Eucharist, the communion at the same table of the Lord.[4]

Among his more important (but partially unpublished) works are *Drzhavna vlast na vaseljenskim saborima* (*The Power of the State and the Ecumenical Councils* [1927]) in Serbian; *Trapeza Gospodnia* (*The Table of the Lord* [1952]); *Sluzhenie mirian v Tserkvi* (*The Ministry of Laity in the Church* [1955]); *L'Église qui préside dans l'Amour* appeared in *La Primauté de Pierre* (*The Church That Presides in Love* in the *Primacy of Peter* [1960]), together with works from N. Koulomzine, J. Meyendorff, and A. Schmemann; *Ekkleziologiia: Vstuplenie v klir* (*Ecclesiology: Initiation into the Clergy* [1968]); *Le pouvoir de l'Amour* (*Vlast' Liubvi* [1967, 1971]);[5] and *Tserkov' Dukha Sviatogo* (*The Church of the Holy Spirit* [1950]), as well as a great number of articles and lecture manuscripts.[6]

2. An influence of Afanas'ev's *The Church That Presides in Love* is assumed since it was used as a reference in the discussion by the council Fathers. One of "Afanas'ev's doctrines" can be traced in chapter 3 of *De Ecclesia* 26, pp. 294-95, 296.

3. Cf. A. Schmemann, "In Memoriam: Le R. P. Nicolas Afanassieff," in *Irenikon* 40, no. 2 (1967): 293.

4. Biographical material on Afanas'ev can be found in the following works: "In Memoriam: Le R. P. Nicolas Afanassieff," in *Irenikon* 40, no. 2 (1967): 291-97; P. Plank, *Die Eucharistieversammlung als Kirche. Zur Entstehung und Entfaltung der eucharistischen Ekklesiologie Nikolaj Afanas'evs (1893-1966)*, Neue Folge, Band 31 (Würzburg: Augustinus-Verlag, 1980), pp. 19-40; N. Afanasiev, *The Church of the Holy Spirit*, ed. V. Permiakov and M. Plekon (Notre Dame: University of Notre Dame Press, 2007), pp. ix-xx.

5. This is a speech that Afanas'ev gave at the festive assembly of the St. Serge Institute on March 23, 1949, which in its substance builds on the concluding chapter of the same title from *Tserkov' Dukha Sviatogo*.

6. A listing of Afanas'ev's works can be found in *Irenikon* 40, no. 2 (1967): 297-300; "Pamiati ottsa Nikolaia Afanas'eva," in N. Prot. Afanas'ev, *Ekkleziologiia: Vstuplenie v klir* (Paris: "L'Eau Vive," 1968), and in the above-mentioned work of P. Plank, *Die Eucharistieversammlung als Kirche*, pp. 41-47. These sources also contain a list of (some previously) unpublished articles.

1.2. The Church of the Holy Spirit

In his major and probably most celebrated work, Afanas'ev treats a series of essential ecclesial questions and develops his concept of *Eucharistic ecclesiology* that became one of the central themes of contemporary Orthodox theology.[7] In the introduction of an extended (and later) complete edition of his book, we gain some revelatory insight on Afanas'ev's research method as well as his personality. He composed this "hymn in glory of the Church, [which is being] united in love; to the glory of service to the Church: Who among you wants to be the first, let him be the servant of all."[8]

1.3. The Spirit of Service

In his *Eucharistic ecclesiology,* Afanas'ev affirms that it lies in the "very Eucharistic nature of the Church" to have only one head [or primate] of the local Church." Furthermore, the Church is an assembly of baptized Christians, a "spiritual house, that is, a shrine of living stones" (1 Peter 2:5), which is not man-made, a place of assembly not of "bloody but spiritual sacrifices."[9] Through the Eucharistic communion established by Christ, the faithful "ef-

7. He further unfolds the theme of *Eucharistic ecclesiology* in his renowned *Trapeza Gospodnia,* a profound reflection on the liturgy and theology of the Eucharist in a clear ecclesial context and based on the factual celebration of the Divine Liturgy. "The grace of our Lord Jesus, the love of the Father and the communion *(koinonia)* of the Holy Spirit are the conditions of (qualifications for) our real participation in the Eucharist." N. Prot. Afanas'ev, *Trapeza Gospodnia* (Kiev: Khram prepodobnogo Agapita Percherskogo, 2003), pp. 109-10.

8. Afanas'ev said repeatedly to his wife: "Everybody thinks that I write my works with my logical understanding and erudition. Well, in fact this only comes afterwards to my assistance. Yet to write I begin with tears and the blood of my heart." Cf. M. Afanas'eva, "Kak slozhilas' 'Tserkov' Dukah Sviatogo' (How 'The Church of the Holy Spirit' Was Composed)," in N. Prot. Afanas'ev, *Tserkov' Dukha Sviatogo* (Kiev: Tsentr Pravoslavnoi knigi, 2005), pp. 5-6. The author of this introduction from 1969 saw reflected in Afanas'ev a "clear, almost Latin reason, mystical inspiration 'from the altar,' broad erudition, but before all — his burning heart in which there was always one love aflame, one name: ΚΥΡΙΟΣ ΙΗΣΟΥΣ ΧΡΙΣΤΟΣ." Cf. TDS, p. 16. To the subject of the laity's service in the Church, including the Eucharist, defining it frequently as *sacrifice* or *spiritual sacrifice (zhertva* or *dukhovnaia zhertva),* the Eucharist as "the service, liturgy, of our faith (Phil. 2:7)" *(sluzhenie, liturgiia, very nashei)* and the Church as a "spiritual house of sacrifice" *(dukhovnyi dom zhertvy),* Afanas'ev dedicates his booklet *Sluzhenie mirian v Tserkvi* (Paris: Izd. Religionzno-Pedagogicheskogo Kabineta pri Pravoslavnom Bogoslovskom Institute, 1955), pp. 10, 15, 18-20, 27, 47.

9. Cf. TDS, pp. 25, 34.

fectively become united *(real'noe soedinenie)* with Christ into one body."[10] Another basilar constituting element of the Church is *freedom,* yet freedom not of servants but of sons, a quality defined and refined by love (Gal. 4:7):

> Not a juridical or political [freedom] but that of the sons of God, freedom in love, or freedom as the gift of perfect love *(sovershennaia liubov').* "There is no fear in love, but perfect love casts out fear" (1 John 4:18). In the Church abides freedom, since in the Church perfect love abides. "And you will know the truth, and the truth will set you free (John 8:32)." This means that the content of freedom, as a positive concept, is truth. In the Church love, freedom and truth are identical notions: freedom as a consequence of love and truth as subject of freedom.[11] The breach of freedom would signify the impoverishment of love and the fear of truth.[12] In their love for truth the children of the Church do not know fear in expressing their own opinions, even if these statements should raise disputes. "For there must be factions among you in order that those who are genuine among you may be recognized" (1 Cor. 11:19). Freedom is the pledge of creativity in the Church, which can never dry up in her as long as the Spirit of the Lord abides in her.[13]

Along with *the pledge of creativity,* the spirit of prophecy also is alive in the church, which safeguards and guarantees "the freedom of theological research," as its scope is the truth. This *research,* however, for Afanas'ev means the disclosure and knowing of the "original tradition that remains in the Church unchanged," even though it is "often overshadowed by [the] temporary and transient." Nevertheless, creativity is an attribute of the Spirit and a privilege of freedom, the token of the spirit of serving the Church and the

10. Afanas'ev treats the question of communion not only from ecclesial and spiritual perspectives but also a juridical, canonical, and, in this particular instance, monastic (Origenes) and scriptural (John 17:21) perspectives. Cf. TDS, pp. 103-4.

11. Another possible translation could be "Freedom stems from love and contains truth," in N. Afanasiev, *The Church of the Holy Spirit,* trans. V. Permiakov, ed. M. Plekon (Notre Dame: University of Notre Dame Press, 2007), p. 77.

12. Perfect love is conditioned by freedom in the Spirit of God, as *perfect love casts out fear* and thus makes us God's truly free children *(where the Spirit of the Lord is, there is freedom),* based on 2 Cor. 3:17; 1 John 4:18; and John 8:32. Since it is the Spirit of the Lord who reigns in the Church, there is "freedom and perfect love in the Church." Cf. *Sluzhenie mirian v Tserkvi,* p. 63.

13. TDS, pp. 134-35.

truth,[14] and, with St. Paul, Afanas'ev urges that in the work of ministry, "Let love be genuine" (Rom. 12:6-9).[15]

1.4. The Ministry of Agapē and Eucharist

It is a fundamental *work of ministry,* especially of the priestly and prophetic,[16] to "give thanks *(blagodarit' — eucharistein).*" In this, the prophets, according to the *Didache,* "accomplish the high priestly ministry," and the *Didache* allows them to give thanks "as long as they desire." What is not clear in the *Didache* (chapters IX-X) is whether the matter in discussion is a "Eucharistic assembly" or the "agape" meals. Afanas'ev bases his discernment here on scriptural exegesis as well as the patristic tradition, and he "personally is inclined" to believe that in fact it was the "Eucharist rather than *agape* . . . that gives the prophet the specific role of the presider, "which in the 'Great Church' [was] executed by the bishop" (which, nevertheless, was equally true for the great assembly of the agape meals).[17] These appar-

14. Cf. TDS, pp. 134-35.

15. Cf. TDS, p. 143. Afanas'ev here and in the following chapters indeed proves to be a connoisseur of the Scriptures, which he cites or paraphrases frequently, when needed even in Greek.

16. The "prophetic vocation" in Christianity Afanas'ev derives from St. Paul: "The faithful were built upon the foundation of the apostles and prophets (Eph. 2:20)," and "the mystery of God's economy . . . was revealed to apostles and prophets (Eph. 3:5)," but he also quotes 1 Cor. 15:5, 29; Rom. 12:6; Acts 13:1-2; 1 Tim. 1:18, etc., yet above all the *Uchenia,* the *Didache.* Cf. TDS, 119-21.

17. "Having been separated from the Eucharist proper, *agape* meals, especially in the East, were still gatherings of the entire local church for the Lord's Supper, where naturally the bishop presided. Only in the beginning of the third century in the West, particularly in the Roman church, did it become possible to celebrate private *agape* meals either in the presence of one particular member of the clergy or even without him. However, we cannot date the appearance of the *Didache* to that time, especially as the emergence of such private *agape* meals in the East must be attributed to the beginning of the Nicaean period. 'Thanksgiving' at the *agape* meals, as well as at the Eucharistic assembly, was the bishop's privilege. If the *Didache* indeed ascribes this right to the prophet, it thus appropriates to him the functions of the presider. These functions mainly included the offering of the Eucharist. . . . The bishop as a Eucharistic celebrant with some kind of dependent relation upon the prophet is not regarded as a high priest. In the absence of the prophet the faithful must render the first fruits not personally to the bishop but through the bishop and deacons to the poor." Cf. TDS, pp. 210-11. Some influences of the agape meals in the Eucharistic assembly and celebration in the early Church Afanas'ev mentions also in his famous *Trapeza Gospodnia* in the chapter on "Communion," pp. 106-12, esp. p. 110.

ently are more liturgical reflections, yet Afanas'ev deals with them in a canonical precision, seeing in the service of the *Eucharist* or *agapē* of the primitive Church a uniting element of service. He points out that "nowhere do[es] the prophet or the *didaskalos* stand as a rival to the bishops in the area of liturgical worship," and in ecclesial thinking the "concept of high priesthood . . . was associated with the bishop rather than with the prophet."[18] Afanas'ev returns anew to the problem of "service at the table for the Eucharistic assembly [which was] both a meal and a 'treasury of love,'" based on the Lukan description of special funds for the needy widows. This time, he distinguishes the agape meals from the Eucharistic assembly since the former "did not yet exist in Jerusalem at that time."[19]

One of Afanas'ev's concerns is to show, based on the *distribution* of aid to the widows, that the Eucharist was not celebrated on a daily basis in the primitive Church.[20] The local churches were formed along with the establishment of the ministry of the presiders, "for without them there could be no Eucharistic assembly." Afanas'ev concurs with the Pauline teaching that requests the Thessalonians to respect and "highly esteem in love" their presiders because of their task: "Their presidency is an administration of the Church in fulfillment of God's will. This is a gift of leading God's people who with love and through the love of their leaders follow them. Hence, all the faithful in return for the love of its presiders, must 'esteem them very highly in love because of their work'" (1 Thess. 5:13).[21] That the quality of relations is founded in love is self-evident, and that shall reflect in the hierarchy of Christ's Church also universally.

1.5. Treasure of Faith and Treasure of Love

The presider as *predstoiatel'*[22] had to fulfill the highest and, at the same time, the most demanding care for the local church, namely that of being a model and giving an example "in faith and in life." The "treasures of faith," handed down and cultivated, and the "treasures of love," meaning an active manifes-

18. Cf. TDS, pp. 210-12.

19. Cf. TDS, pp. 210-12.

20. Cf. TDS, pp. 298-99.

21. Cf. TDS, pp. 233-34. He names a "principle of love" as fundamental to the presiders' actions, mentioned by Clement of Alexandria. Cf. TDS, p. 239.

22. Someone who directs or governs but, etymologically in Russian, means a *standing in front of*, e.g., the assembly or, above all, in front of God.

tation of charitable love, always walked hand-in-hand, were coexistent and codependent. This is so true that Afanas'ev considers the practice of active love a direct expression and origin of the ministry of presidency:

> Through presiders, the charism of love, the greatest of gifts, according to St. Paul, had to find its fullest expression. Active love *(deiatel'naia liubov')* cannot treat any human soul with indifference, overlooking a person's needs, whether spiritual or material. If the ministry of "assistants" was a special ministry, distinguished from the ministry of the presiders, the latter, being at the head of the Eucharistic assembly *(Evkharisticheskoe sobranie),* had in their care the supervision over the gifts that the faithful brought to the Eucharist. The presiders were entrusted with the treasury of faith *(sokrovishchnitsa very)* as well as with the treasury of love *(sokrovishchnitsa liubvi).* The supervision over the latter was a function of the ministry of presidency as a pastoral service. However, the presidency arose from supervising and distributing the treasury of love. Pastoral service encompassed teaching without which the keeping of correct faith and [a] correct way of life is impossible.
>
> By watching over the life of each and every one in the Church, the ministry of presidency expressed an active love, but it was not able to overshadow or replace the ecclesial assembly because this ministry itself originated from the assembly and in the assembly found its expression. Without the assembly the presidency would be pointless, and active love could be cast out of the Church's boundaries.[23]

The function and meaning, as seen previously, of a presider and of presiding is the assembly that through *active love* testifies to the accomplishment of God's will. More than an individual member or group of individuals could testify, it is in the entirety of the Eucharistic assembly through which the fullness of the Church becomes manifested. Afanas'ev concludes by underscoring the responsibility for the two treasuries to the care of both, the presiders and the assembly, the *treasury of faith* and of *love* in the Scriptures and Tradition:

> Presidency at the Eucharistic assembly, pastoral service in governing the entire people of God as well as each of its members, teaching through supervising and keeping the "treasury of faith" and care for the "treasury of

23. TDS, pp. 244-45.

> love" — this is the substance of the ministry of presiders in the New Testament writings. What in our time the Church possesses in the figure of its bishops and what it continued to possess in the course of its entire history was already present in apostolic times. All these functions were in the possession of the Church's first presiders, ordained by the apostles.[24]

The authority that the apostles enjoyed was twofold: "Shall I come to you with a rod, or with love in a spirit of gentleness?" (1 Cor. 4:21) was the question posed by one of them. Their authority was given them "to build up" the Church of Jesus, not to tear it down. The rod of the bishop and of the presbyter was the staff of a pastor, that of one standing not above but amidst the assembly of a local church. Thus this authority "would be a power over the Eucharistic assembly and consequently over the body of Christ." This authority was not simply *above* the Church, but was "localized in the church." In fact, it is the authority of the Church itself, and Afanas'ev is very explicit about this. Simply, the power or authority over a local (as with the universal) church is granted by God, as the Church is entrusted to a good shepherd who looks after her and takes care of her, not simply imposes upon it.[25] Conversely, ecclesial leadership exercised at the local level by presiding at the Eucharistic assembly affects the whole universal Church and is based on a relationship of love.

1.6. The Ministry of Assistance[26] — The Greatest Is Love

The very foundation of any church, be it local or universal, in its individual members or in its assembly (above all, the Eucharistic assembly), has to be recognizable in its activity of love or, as Afanas'ev puts it, in the "charism of love." This is so much a matter of course that one cannot conceive the idea of *the Church* if her love is not overflowing with what gives her inner cohesion, just as love without manifesting itself through charity — offerings and sacrifice — is futile:

> Love is the common charism of the entire people of God, and without love no ministry in the Church is possible. Without love any ministry is

24. TDS, p. 245.
25. Cf. TDS, pp. 259-61.
26. *Sluzhenie vspomoshchestvovaniia.*

> a "clanging cymbal"' or "noisy gong," for without love one gains nothing. That is why love is a "more excellent way." "So faith, hope, love abide, these three; but the greatest of these is love *(meizōn de toutōn hē agapē)*" (1 Cor. 13:13). If any activity without love is nothing, love cannot exist without its active expression. "Love is patient and kind. . . . [it] rejoices in the right, love bears all things, believes all things, hopes all things, endures all things" (1 Cor. 13:4-7). Every member of the Church must express actively his charism of love in all his action in the Church, for there is no life in the Church without love. The love that is characteristic of the Church finds in such service its manifestation, so that this function becomes a special ministry in the Church. Not neglecting the active love of one member of the Church to another, service is not a common ministry of all but rather a ministry of some through whom the love of all is manifest. In the early Church individual charity either did not exist at all or only in a very limited way. Instead every member of the Church offered his gift of love to the Eucharistic assembly. Out of these offerings a "treasury of love" was collected from which in turn the means for the work of service were taken. "If one member suffers, all suffer together" (1 Cor. 12:26).[27]

This service of helping the suffering was not entrusted to all but only to those in charge of this ministry, similar to the aforementioned service to the widows by Luke. Whether it was performed by the presiders or deacons or other minister, daily or once a week, the "rendering of service was a part of ministry" and was intrinsically and inseparably connected to the Eucharistic assembly.[28]

27. Cf. TDS, pp. 275-77.

28. Acts 4:35; 11:30; 1 Cor. 12:28; Rom. 12:8; 1 Tim. 3:8-10. Cf. TDS, pp. 278, 297-99. There is a very interesting reflection on the Jewish tradition of *chabura, friendship* (from *chaber,* friend) and the institution of the Eucharist by Christ in the Last Supper with his friends. The purpose of this "fraternity" was an upbringing in the Law and charity. Afanas'ev provides a scriptural exegesis in this key, in particular of the first letter to the Corinthians (chapters 11 and 14). Cf. TDS, pp. 288-95. Additionally, it is important to note the religious character of the Jewish meals which, however, does not mean that they were "sacred rites which were associated exclusively with the temple." This change in the Eucharist instituted by Christ "became a 'spiritual offering' in a 'spiritual temple.'" Cf. TDS, pp. 339-41.

1.7. The Power of Love Leads to Kenosis — *Why Law Needs to Be Transcended*

This indeed is an appropriate title for the conclusion of a long exegetical, theological, ecclesial, and canonical reflection regarding the local and universal aspects of the Church. In it, we find a recapitulation and affirmation of the Church's divine origin and task, and an exhortation to all those in charge of ministries, to love and share love actively, thus creating and maintaining its unity, again on both a local and universal level. Law, *stated by a canonist,* "makes its appearance when reciprocal love among people has become weakened." The foundation is a love-relationship — or the relationship of a caring, acting, charitable love — that final and utmost commandment that surpasses any law through grace: "Law protects the individual who does not need such protection if relationships among people are governed by love *(sushchestvuiut liubovnye otnosheniia).* Being imperfect, empirical life has no love and the individual is imperfect because of his nonregenerated nature. . . . By its very nature grace excludes law just as grace eliminates law of the Old Testament by fulfilling it."[29]

Afanas'ev exalts St. Paul for having confronted "Christian consciousness" with the problem of law and grace, and he cites Galatians 2:19-21. By *dying to the law,* the faithful in the Church are born to a new life so that we can live for and in God; thus the Church also receives a new attribute: "[And] the foundation of this new life is love because 'God is love' (1 John 4:8). According to Ignatius of Antioch the Church itself is love *(agapē).* The Church is love because it has been created by the love of Christ who loved us and gave his life for us." Born anew, we are called to lay down our lives in self-sacrifice "for the brethren," as this life is imperishable, renewed, and sustained by love (1 John 3:16):[30]

> Abiding *(prebyvaia)* in God, Christians are in love, a love that has for its model the love of God who has sent His Son into the world. "So we know and believe the love God has for us. God is love, and he who abides in love abides in God, and God abides in him" (1 John 4:16). Life in the Church is life in Christ and it is the life of Christ which is in anyone who lives in the Church. . . . By his life in Christ a man becomes a person in the Church. The absolute person is God, for only He possesses the full-

29. TDS, p. 439.
30. Cf. TDS, pp. 439-40.

> ness of life, and man becomes a person by the adoption which is given in the Church through the Spirit as intermediary (1 John 3:1). . . . The one who lives in love should not want to live at the expense of others, for in each of them it is Christ who lives. On the contrary, such a one is ready to renounce himself for the others, even to give up his life for his brothers (Matt. 10:39). . . . The sacrifice of oneself for the sake of Christ means the renunciation of individual rights which are essential to empirical life: the protection of physical existence is in effect the beginning and concluding, first and last task of law, a mission which the law was powerless to realize in empirical life.[31]

Afanas'ev's reflection continues, summing up his position on the law-love relationship that was put into a new light by Christ's Sermon on the Mount:

> To give up the law is to transcend it. One transcends an imperfect reality in order to seek perfection. The primitive Church professed this renunciation of the law in relationship with others. "You have heard . . . but I say to you." That which was given to the ancients was the perfect law, not only for that time, but perfect law as such. Regardless of its perfection, this law has been surpassed by that love which is the free manifestation of the love of the children of God: free in the Spirit and by the Spirit. Love in the New Testament writings is always connected to the Spirit. It is the supreme gift of the Spirit who "remains," even though "prophecies will pass away; tongues will cease; knowledge will pass away" (1 Cor. 13:8). This is not a new law based upon juridical principles. It is purely and simply the annulment of law, for what Christ proclaimed in the Sermon on the Mount does not enter the category of law. The descent of the Spirit on the day of Pentecost signifies the end of the Law. The new Sinai was not the Sinai of the Law but that of the Spirit, which entails love. The one was replaced by the other at the moment when the Church came into being. The Sermon on the Mount was the announcement of love, which had no need of law because it had transcended it. No longer is there any place for law in human relationships for those who, having become children of God by adoption in the Church, can say with St. Paul, "It is no longer I who live, but Christ who lives in me."[32]

31. TDS, pp. 440-41.
32. Cf. TDS, pp. 440-41.

The Spirit of the Church is the Spirit of Christ, "the Lord is the Spirit" (2 Cor. 3:17), and all is subdued to Him (Col. 2:14-15).[33] But the separate "I" is always bound into the "we" of the Church.[34] Therefore, Christ, our supreme example, and His life teach us that "by nature" we want to be served instead of serving others; we want to have power. St. Paul's idea of power as service in the *diakonia* is the first formulation of Christ's spirit of ministry or service, best reflected in his kenotic hymn of Christ's self-emptying in Philippians 2:6-10.[35] "This self-emptying *(kenosis)* proceeded from the very nature of God who is love, and the ministry of Christ was in fact an expression of kenotic love. This love is at the foundation of all the ministries of the Church, for it can have no other foundation than that given by God. The ministry of Christ is a model for all other ministries" (1 John 4:9, 11).[36] This foreshadows and introduces a crucial phrase that we expected to encounter, a quality of hierarchy that distinguishes the Church from the secular world: "The power of Christ in the Church is the power of love, acquired by the love which He has for her."[37] The higher the hierarchy, the closer one is to the "highest model of love and the most complete imitation of Christ's self-sacrificing love," for it is the "culmination point of all ministries, as their beginning and end is in love." Afanas'ev defines the pastoral office, which is the chief ministry of the Church, as "by nature the expression of love."[38]

For Afanas'ev, the interhuman submission in obedience and *the* submission to Christ is always one and the same love of Christ and the reciprocal love among humans. This love is identical to the love "shown by Christ in His ministry," a ministry of service (Matt. 10:42). The Church imitates this love in her service as her life, origin, and sustenance is in Christ. Afanas'ev

33. Cf. TDS, p. 441.

34. Cf. TDS, p. 442.

35. Cf. TDS, pp. 448, 451-52.

36. TDS, p. 451.

37. TDS, p. 453.

38. On reciprocal responsibility and submission in love in the hierarchy: "The bishops who exercise the ministry of administration are the bearers of the power of love. The submission of all to the bishop takes place in love and it is by love that the bishop submits to the faithful. All submission of one to another is realized through the mediation of the love we have for Christ. The submission of all to the bishop is actualized by the love he has for all and by the reciprocal love of the faithful for him. There can be no other foundation of power in the Church, for Christ is the only foundation of power in it. . . . The power of Christ in the Church is the power of love, acquired by the love which He has for her." Cf. TDS, pp. 451-42, 453.

underscores again as an ontological fact that "in the Church there is no love without ministry and there is no ministry without love." In fact, a ministry without love is "nothing and is outside of the Church," for relating in love implies calling the other *my brother* (1 John 4:21). All the members of the Church are "surrounded by love"; that is, all ministries belong to the Church. Although they may vary in their charism and charismatic manifestations by their nature, they are all one "as grace is one."[39] And the highest and most desired charism of Love can be acquired "only in the love of Christ," a gift of *kenosis,* sacrificing oneself for the salvation of others.

In his final reflections on the last pages, Afanas'ev fully focuses on connecting power in the Church to ministry, and in it, specifically, the charism of *Love,* since love is the *only* power in the Church founded in Christ's *highest model* of service and self-sacrifice. This is why he calls it the *Church of the Holy Spirit* — as law would put limits to the Spirit of God, who blows when and where He wants and cannot be contained or limited, just as God's love knows no limits.[40]

1.8. The Church That Presides in Love[41]

This reflection dedicated primarily to the question of primacy among the patriarchal churches is based on the service of love and is centered in the Eucharist (as was the usage in the primitive Church of Jerusalem): "During the celebration of Eucharist the bread turns into the Body of Christ, and by the bread the participants become the Body of Christ." Since there is only one bread that we share, there is only one body of Christ (1 Cor. 10:16-17), and this Eucharist, "real body of Christ," has a real uniting power in the Eucharistic assembly.[42] The Eucharist *is* the fullness of Christ's body and thus of God's Church, and vice versa. Only where there is unity in and of the Church, with the capital letter meaning not a local but the universal Church, can Eucharist be celebrated.[43]

If there is a "hierarchy of the churches," there must be one at the head,

39. Cf. TDS, p. 451.

40. Cf. TDS, p. 453.

41. N. Afanassieff, "L'Église qui préside dans l'amour," in *La Primauté de Pierre,* ed. N. Afanassieff, N. Koulomzine, J. Meyendorff, A. Schmemann (Neuchâtel: Delachaux & Niestlé, 1960), pp. 7-65.

42. Cf. "L'Église qui préside dans l'amour," p. 27.

43. Cf. "L'Église qui préside dans l'amour," p. 29.

"occupying the first place" among them, and its testimony is of utmost importance: "Her act of testimony about what is happening in the other churches has a primeval value and her act of reception is of a decisive importance. In other words, she possesses the precedence in authority *(priorité de l'autorité)* and the precedence in love *(priorité de l'amour)*, which means that she makes herself a gift of self-sacrifice to the other [churches]." Because of this intrinsic nature, according to Afanas'ev, it cannot be stated that the church that possesses the precedence, or even the honor of it, also possesses power over the other churches, as this precedence is founded in love and self-sacrifice: "Neither power nor honor is the foundation of precedence but solely the authority stemming from love and manifesting itself through love," and this also must be reflected in her charitable care for the other churches[44] and, consequently, for the *one universal Church* of Christ.

Based on the letter of St. Clement of Rome to the church of Corinth (and its interpretation by Irenaeus), Afanas'ev reviews the position of Rome's precedence and concludes that the letter does not prove this point.[45] We do not wish to enter this ecclesial debate as it would lead us away from our topic. Yet what is essential in these pages is the identification of Ignatius of Antioch who explicitly used for the first time the term "presiding" with regard to the church of Rome, and namely, "who presides in love (*charité*, ἀγάπη)." The term *agapē* and its interpretation, according to Afanas'ev, meant for Ignatius: "'. . . the local church in its Eucharistic aspect.' Each local church is *agapē* and all the churches together are also *agapē* because each local church, as Ignatius says, is a catholic church and therefore manifests the Church of God in Christ. On the other hand, in an empiric order, they form unity (union) based on love *(sur la base de l'amour)*: consequently this union can be also designated by the very term. The church of Rome 'presides' in love, which means in concord based on love of all local churches." That this person in the local church was a bishop "occupying the first place in the Eucharistic assembly" is clear and unquestionable (given the etymology of the Greek term of presider — *prokathēmenē*), a view that Ignatius and St. Clement share equally. What their texts do not reveal is why Rome was presiding (among the equals) and not *an* other

44. Cf. "L'Église qui préside dans l'amour," pp. 32-33. Irenaeus (in *Adversus Haereses*) and Ignatius of Antioch reasoned similarly in their view on "the special situation of Rome, that no other church had. 'The precedence in Love' of Ignatius corresponds to the *potentior principalitas* of Irenaeus." Cf. p. 55.

45. Cf. "L'Église qui préside dans l'amour," pp. 45-47. We do not wish to enter this ecclesial debate as it would lead us away from our topic.

church. However, this may have been historically evident in their times and thus needed no further explanation.[46]

1.9. The Witnessing Love of Precedence

In his concluding paragraph, Afanas'ev comments that both churches, the Catholic as well as the Orthodox, have lost their "idea of precedence" in different historic contexts, and, "under the given mutual positions," Afanas'ev sees no way of resolving the question of precedence, a "tragedy" simply to be accepted for the time being. Two components of unity or union, that of "unity of faith" and "unity in Love," are needed within and between the particular churches. Does the lack of this "unity in love" imply that "the ecclesial conscience has lost the notion of the direction of God's Church for a local church, a church of one among the others? Each of them [Orthodox and Catholic] possesses catholicity, but the precedence of authority as a witness of what happens in the Church belongs solely to the one 'who presides in Love.'"[47]

Conclusion

As with the majority of Russian theologians and religious thinkers, Afanas'ev is a person of broad erudition and interests, and beyond that a priest, which contributes a decisive pragmatic-spiritual insight into his ecclesiology. He tried to fuse his spiritual and intellectual experiences into a very systematic (with exegesis and patristic sources underlined) theological reflection. The multiplicity of local churches and the unity of the One Church of Christ, the singular faithful and the Eucharistic assembly, as well as the hierarchical precedence in both realms are defined and qualified by the ministry of love; for the Church gives life through love, and is vivified and sustained by love — as the divine, so the human of the Eucharistic assembly. One clearly hears the voice of a pastor presiding in his local assembly (church) who, as an attentive and sensitive scholar and an expert in canon law, recognized the limits and the conditional nature of *law.* Christ never rules through fear but by love. Since fear has been cast out by perfect

46. Cf. "L'Église qui préside dans l'amour," p. 46.
47. Cf. "L'Église qui préside dans l'amour," pp. 63-64.

love, we are called to *minister* and thus to preside (in *precedence* or less) in the particular *charism of love* that God has given us. The examples are already in the primitive Church of Jerusalem where a *treasury of love* was created, thus recognizing its equal importance and indispensability to the *treasury of faith.* The higher a faithful is on the hierarchical ladder, the more demanding is his task to prove that his rod is the staff of a good shepherd who gives his life for the flock, be it a red or a white martyrdom, as the early monks distinguished — in the latter, a gradual, *kenotic* self-emptying and self-sacrificing on the altar of everyday life. A Christian who lives in God *lives in love,* lives love, and carries God, i.e., life and salvation, to those for whom he is ministering. Being *kenotic is in the very nature* of God, whose Son, the living message, is perpetually present in the highest sacrament of love, the Holy Eucharist, and of his Spirit who, especially since Pentecost, liberates humanity to live freely, without fear, precisely in love.

2. Georgii Vasil'evich Florovskii: The Supra-Natural Challenge in Us

2.1. Biography

G. V. Florovskii (1893-1979) was born in Elizavetgrad and raised in Odessa. He was the fifth son of a rector of the Theological Academy and dean of the local cathedral; his grandfather on his mother's side was a professor of Hebrew and Greek. Florovskii belonged to that fortunate generation that received an excellent education in late-nineteenth-century Russia, studying first at the philosophical institute of Odessa University where he excelled. In January 1920, Florovskii left Russia with his parents and a brother and settled in Sofia, Bulgaria. The following year he was invited by Thomas G. Masaryk, the president of Czechoslovakia, to lecture in Prague where, in 1923, he defended his doctoral thesis in the history of philosophy focusing on Herzen. He married X. I. Simonova and accepted an invitation to teach Patristics in Paris at the Theological Institute of St. Serge, which he co-founded. Ten years later he was ordained a priest. His academic assignment in Paris lasted until 1948 when he moved again, this time to the United States where he became a professor and later the dean of theology at St. Vladimir's Theological Seminary in Crestwood, New York, an assignment that lasted until 1955. In the following years, Fr. Florovskii worked as an associate professor at Holy Cross Theological School in Brookline, Massachusetts, in the Slavic Department, and as a professor at Harvard Divinity School. The ecumenical movement being his other notable concern, he was elected director (1964-67) of Tantur Ecumenical Institute, founded by Paul VI, near Jerusalem. From 1965 till 1972, he served as professor *emeritus*, lecturing in Slavic studies at Princeton University. He died in Princeton in 1979, leaving behind a major influence in the circles of Russian cultural history.

Florovskii was undoubtedly a man of great erudition as well as a refined linguist. He was a great ambassador of the Neopatristic approach to Russian Orthodox theology and spirituality, recognized by many, e.g., V. Losskii and J. Meyendorff, as the model of this school of thought. His renowned voluminous work on the history of Russian theology, *Puti russkogo bogosloviia (Ways of Russian Theology* [1937]), served for many as a guideline in the subject of Orthodox theology, even though it raised disagreement and divergence of opinion already upon its publication.

Among his works are *Khristianstvo i tsivilizatsiia. Izbrannye trudy po bogosloviiu i filosofii (Christianity and Civilization: Selected Works on Theology and Philosophy); Vostochnye Ottsy IV-go veka* (*The Eastern Fathers of the Fourth Century* [1931]); *Vizantiiskie Ottsy V-VIII vv* (*The Byzantine Fathers of the Fifth–Eighth Centuries* [1933]); *Problematika khristianskogo vossoedinennia* (*The Problematics of Christian Reunification* [1933]); the aforementioned *Puti russkogo bogosloviia* (*Ways of Russian Theology* [1937]); *Some Forgotten Articles by Vladimir Soloviev* (1966); *Bible, Church, Tradition: An Eastern Orthodox View* (1972); *Christianity and Culture* (1974); *Aspects of Church History* (1975); and *Creation and Redemption* (1976). Florovskii also contributed numerous articles to *Put'* in France and published a number of articles on theological, philosophical, and literary subjects in other scientific periodicals. Some of the latter appeared more recently as a collection or translations of articles, for instance G. Florovskij, *Cristo, lo Spirito, la Chiesa* (Bose: Edizioni Qiqajon, 1997), or *Put' k Ochevidnosti: Georgii Florovskii, Iz proshlogo russkoi mysli* (Moskva: Agraf, 1998).[48]

48. For biographical data and a listing of publications up till 1974, see *Georges Florovsky: Russian Intellectual. Orthodox Churchman*, ed. A. Blane (Crestwood, NY: St. Vladimir's Seminary Press, 1993); Iu. P. Senokosova, *Georgii Florovskii: Sviashchennosluzhitel', bogoslov, filosov* (Moskva: Progress, Kul'tura, 1995); *The Religious World of Russian Culture*, ed. A. Blane (The Hague-Paris: Mouton, 1975); G. H. Williams, *Georges Vasilievich Florovsky: His American Career* [S.L.] (1965).

2.2. Bible, Church, Tradition: An Eastern Orthodox View[49]

In Florovskii's ecclesiology, the theme of *unity* possesses a vital role. Unity is understood as "'*sobornost' or catholicity of the Church*" and is based on the example of Christ's relationship with His heavenly Father as revealed in John 17:21-23: "This is the mystery of the final reunion in the image of the Unity of the Holy Trinity. It is realized in the life and constitution of the Church, it *is the mystery of sobornost', the mystery of catholicity*." From this, our author elucidated his understanding of "the inner quality of Catholicism," namely its universality, which to the first Christians "never meant a worldwide" Church but rather referred to its "orthodoxy."[50] Orthodoxy and unity are forged by the Holy Spirit, "a Spirit of love and peace," that unites individuals, bestowing upon them their "inner peace and wholeness." Catholicity thus means "a certain unity of life, a brotherhood or communion, a union of love, 'a life in common.'" Florovskii quotes St. John Chrysostom's rendering of the Pauline teaching and requirements:

> St. Paul demands such love of us, which should bind us one to the other, *so that we no more should be separated one from the other*. . . . The novelty of the Christian commandment of love consists in the fact that we are to love our neighbor as *ourselves*. This is more than putting the other person on the same level with ourselves, of identifying him with ourselves; it means seeing our own self in an other, in the beloved one, not in our own self. . . . Therein lies the limit of love; the beloved is our "alter ego," an "ego" which is dearer to us than our self, for it is in love that we are merged into one. "The quality of love is such that the loving and the beloved are no more two but one person."[51] Even more: true Christian love sees in every one of our brethren "Christ Himself." Such love demands self-surrender, self-mastery. Such love is possible only in a catholic expansion and transfiguration of the soul.

Since "the commandment to be catholic is given to every Christian," the state of union can be achieved solely in the way of brotherly love between the separate members.[52] Thus, on the luminous example of true brother-

49. Vol. 1 in *Collected Works of Georges Florovsky* (Belmont, MA: Nordland, 1972) (CWF I-XIII).

50. Cf. CWF I, pp. 39-40.

51. Quoting from Chrysostom's homily on 1 Corinthians, *Hom.*, PG, *Migne*, 33, 3.

52. Cf. CWF I, p. 42.

hood, Florovskii offers a rather pragmatic interpretation and implementation of transfiguration applied to each individual personality. For, indeed, what good are the most noble and mystical experiences if God's plan is not being realized, if there is no cohesion with(in) the all, if the Church and its members are lacking catholicity? "The stone must first be made smooth, so that it can fit into the Church wall. We must 'reject ourselves'[53] to be able to enter the catholicity of the Church. We must master our self-love in a catholic spirit before we can enter the Church. And in the fullness of the communion of the Church the *catholic transfiguration of personality is accomplished*." Yet Florovskii points out that "self-denial" shall not be mistaken for the denial of one's proper personality, since the contrary is true: "*In self-denial we possess the multitude within our own self; we enclose the many within our own ego. Therein lies the similarity with the Divine Oneness of the Holy Trinity*" and leads the Church through its catholicity to its Divine perfection.[54] Florovskii provides a dense, yet very refined reflection closely following the Church Fathers' teachings while contemplating this divine-human reality from a different and, finally, Christological perspective (after having reviewed diverse disputes on the church-council relations): "It leads us to the most intricate and crucial problem — what are the ultimate *criteria* of the Christian Truth? . . . There is no easy answer to this query. And yet, there is a very simple answer — *Christ is the Truth*," which in praxis means the *Word of God* and the *Tradition*, the "two dispensations" of this eternal Truth.[55] Florovskii concludes with the teaching of Gregory Palamas, rendered in a quintessence as "*Salvation is more than forgiveness. It is a genuine renewal of man*. And this renewal is effected . . . by the 'energies' of God Himself, who thereby encounters and encompasses man, and admits him into communion with Himself." Florovskii regards Palamas as a "guide and teacher" in his endeavor to "theologize from the heart of the Church."[56]

It is precisely in this theme of unity-ecclesiality — in a dialogue on ecclesiality between Orthodoxy and Protestantism — that we encounter for the first time an explicit use and concept of *agapē*. Florovskii notes the insufficiency of a mere human effort to create the Church's "organic unity"; rather, it is by sharing that Divine Love which made us to be God's children

53. Referring here to the symbolism of roundness in the ancient world that was a "sign of isolation, of self-sufficiency and self-satisfaction. . . . And it is just this spirit of self-satisfaction which hinders our entering the Church." Cf. CWF I, p. 43.

54. Cf. CWF I, p. 43.

55. Cf. CWF I, pp. 95-98.

56. Cf. CWF I, pp. 117-20.

and heirs: "The organic unity of the Church is not . . . created by Christian charity. Certainly, it is . . . created by love, but rather through the love of God, through His redeeming ἀγάπη. 'In this is love, not that we have loved God but that He loved us and sent His Son to be the propitiation for our sins' (1 John 4:10). He made us into brothers in adopting us all in the only [begotten] Son. In this way the body of Christ has been created and formed already at the Incarnation, which too was the supreme manifestation of God's creative love." Once more, Florovskii refers to the Fathers of the Church who have "[much] to say in this regard," especially Chrysostom, Cyril of Alexandria, Hilarion, and Augustine. It is John Chrysostom who underlines in particular the "intimate liaison" between Christian love *(charité chrétienne)* and the Eucharistic reality *(réalité eucharistique)*. Human love, still following Chrysostom, is nothing but a human response to God's love "manifested above all in the mystery of Eucharist," which is God's open invitation to us to become His body; yet not solely by charity *(charité)* but through our unity with His flesh this will become a true reality. This is the act and proof of God's love brought about by "nourishing us" in the Eucharist so that "the body may be in unity with its head."[57]

2.3. *Creation and Redemption — God's Freedom as Sole Foundation*

God's relation to the world occurs through His energies but above all through His eternal Logos, His Son, Jesus Christ. Florovskii works with a broad range of patristic authors with a gift for synthesis and presentation, yet also intends to stay on the "safe side" by avoiding possible speculations in the intra-Trinitarian realm: "The creation presupposes the Trinity, and the seal of the Trinity lies over the whole creation; yet one must not, therefore, introduce cosmological motifs into the definition of the intra-Trinitarian Being. And yet one may say that the natural fullness of the Divine essence is contained within the Trinity, and, therefore, that the design — His good pleasure — concerning the world is *a creative act*, an operation of the will — an abundance of Divine love, a gift and a grace." The "economy" of Divine salvation is freely given and of "eternal purpose" (Eph. 3:11), a mystery hid-

57. Cf. G. Florovsky, "Le corps du Christ vivant. Une interprétation orthodoxe de l'Église," in *La Sainte Église Universelle: Confrontation œcuménique,* Cahiers Théologiques de l'actualité protestante, Hors Série 4 (Paris: Delachaux et Niestlé S.A., 1948), pp. 34-35, 40. The same passage in English can be found in CWF XIV, p. 35.

den in God (Eph. 3:9), and thus the Son "is from eternity destined to the Incarnation and the Cross" for the salvation of the world: "This is an act of Divine love — *for God so loved the world.*" All this occurs in freedom, for "in the Divine revelation there is no constraint [which] is expressed in the notion of the perfect Divine Beatitude.[58] Revelation is an act/work of love and freedom and, therefore, introduces no change into the Divine nature.[59] It introduces no change simply because there are no 'natural' foundations for revelation at all. The sole foundation of the world consists in God's freedom, in the freedom of Love."[60]

Florovskii recurs again to Palamas, this time for the idea of God being "myriadfold hypostatic . . . because this grace or energy is beneficently imparted to thousands upon myriads of thousands of hypostases." Involuntarily, this concept also recalls Bulgakov's presentation of creation through creational Sophia. One way or another, the fundamental notion and propeller in their being remains the Creator's love, which serves as an ontological bridge between the Uncreated and creation: "Each hypostasis, in its own being and existence, is sealed by a particular ray of the good pleasure of God's love and will. And in this sense, all things are in God — in 'image' . . . *but not by nature:* the created 'all' is infinitely remote from the Uncreated Nature. This remoteness is bridged by Divine love, its impenetrability done away by the Incarnation of the Divine Word." Significantly, Florovskii stresses that this "remoteness" remains and that whatever concepts or ideas are attributed to the image of God in creation, or even in the human being, it remains a "likeness," a mirroring of the "Proto-Image" that transcends created nature. The rapprochement happens through the response to a "supra-natural challenging" in the creature itself through *self-determination* and effort.[61] Thus, active cooperation in God's plan remains a necessity for divinization. In order to become more and more God-like, the human being needs to become partaker of the Divine Life "in the unity of love." However, Florovskii reserves the absoluteness of the "essence of God," which thus continues to be unreachable for any creature.[62] The question is whether this is still applicable after full divinization has been granted by God to a person (which, how-

58. On freedom granted by the "Love of the Creator," see "V mire iskanii i bluzhdanii," in G. Florovskii, *Khristianstvo i tsivilizatsiia* (Sankt-Peterburg: Izd. Russkoi Khristianskoi gumanitarnoi akademii, 2005), p. 155 (KHT). Also: God as One-Love: cf. p. 159.

59. Florovskii paraphrases Cyril of Jerusalem. Cf. CWF III, p. 71.

60. Cf. CWF III, pp. 70-72.

61. Cf. CWF III, p. 73.

62. Cf. CWF III, 74-76.

ever, occurs most probably solely after death). There is no doubt, on the contrary, about the assertive role of the *Divine Love* when it comes to the existence of "evil as a mystery": "The Passion of Jesus was a triumph, a decisive victory. But it is rather a triumph of the Divine Love which calls and accepts [everybody] without any coercion. From this time on, the very existence of evil is given to us only within this framework of the Co-Suffering Love of God. And also the Love, and even the sublime majesty of God, are revealed to us in the enigmatic framework of evil and sin. . . . *Felix culpa quae tantum et talem meruit habere Redemptorem.*"[63] In liaison to the *felix culpa,* the vocation of the "primordial man," which appertains to his very nature, was

> to love God with filial devotion and to serve Him in the world of which man was designated to be prophet, priest, and king. It was an appeal from the paternal love of God to the filial love of man. Undoubtedly, to follow God involved a total surrender to the embrace of the Divine. This was not yet a sacrifice. The innocent man had nothing to sacrifice, for everything he possessed came from the Grace of God. Here, there is something more profound than a voluptuous attachment to the world. It was rather a tragedy of a misguided love.[64]

In the latter, Florovskii addresses a profound verity of human tragedy in all and everything, the primordial malfunction that led the human being to break the "spiritual and free contact with God" which ever since misguided him, as St. Athanasius puts it, to focus on the self "as [if] he were in love with himself. . . . It was a kind of delirium, a self-erotic obsession, a spiritual narcissism." After realizing his detachment from God, he also became aware of being in an "external cosmic flow"; this is how the "de-spiritualization of human existence" came about, of which death is only a result.[65] God's response to death is redemption through His self-limitation, *kenosis,* which does not "abolish the original status of human freedom or 'self-power.'" Florovskii sees the respect of human freedom from God's side as "a certain *kenosis* of Divine Love itself. Divine love, as it were, restricts and limits itself in the safeguarding of creation's freedom. Love does not impose healing by compulsion as it might have done"; the *kenosis* of the Incarnation, on the other hand, was a voluntary "re-

63. Cf. CWF III, pp. 83-84.
64. CWF III, p. 85.
65. Cf. CWF III, p. 85.

duction" of Christ's divinity for our sake (cf. Phil. 2:7).[66] We have encountered some beautiful staurological reflections in this chapter, preceded by the description of the "all-forgiving love" of Christ that "assumes all this world" (cf. Luke 23:34): "The entire earthly life of Our Lord is a Cross. Suffering in itself is yet not the whole Cross. . . . The climax of this life was His death . . . a redeeming death that is the ultimate purpose of the Incarnation."[67]

2.4. The Sacrificial Power

Florovskii organically connects the idea of the cross and sacrifice to the other major theme of his, the Eucharist, specifying attentively the quality of Jesus' attitude in His sacrifice:

> Thus the death on the Cross is a sacrificial offering. And to offer a sacrifice does not mean only to surrender. Even from a merely moral point of view, the whole significance of sacrifice is not the denial itself, but the sacrificial power of love.[68] The sacrifice is not merely an offering, but rather a dedication, a consecration to God. The effective power of sacrifice is love (1 Cor. 13:3). But the offering of the sacrifice is more than the

66. Cf. CWF III, p. 97.

67. The text goes on: "The mystery of the Cross is beyond our rational comprehension. This 'terrible sight' seems strange and startling. The whole life of Our Blessed Lord was one great act of forbearance, mercy and love. . . . He not only permitted but *willed* it. He must have died according to the *law* of *truth* and *love.* In no way was the Crucifixion a passive suicide or simple murder. It was a Sacrifice and an oblation. He had to die. This was not the necessity of this world. This was the necessity of Divine Love. The mystery of the Cross begins in eternity, 'in the sanctuary of the Holy Trinity, unapproachable for creatures.' And the transcendent mystery of God's wisdom and love is revealed and fulfilled in history. . . . 'The Cross of Jesus, composed of the enmity of the Jews and the violence of the Gentiles, is indeed but the earthly image and shadow of this heavenly Cross of love.'" (The last quotation is from Metr. Filaret.) Cf. CWF III, 99-100. On Incarnation and God's love for the world and Mariology ("The love of the Mother of God reaches its fulfillment . . . by *intercession and protection (predstatel'stvom i pokrovom)*. . . . The name of the mother always means love . . . the more the name of the Mother of Light"), see also *"Ot rozhdestva Khristova,"* in KHT, pp. 768-71.

68. Florovskii applies the same expression in his article on *The Tortuous Religious Path of Gogol'.* Cf. CWF XI, p. 63. He also addresses the themes of self-denial, free and unfree love in Dostoevsky's work. Cf. CWF III, 63, 83. Similarly, see *Smysl istorii i smysl zhizni,* in KHT, pp. 73-74. A further article dedicated to the suffering love: "Blazhenstvo strazhdushchei liubvi (K 100-letiiu so dnia rozhd. F. M. Dostoevskogo)," in *Put' k ochevidnosti: Georgii Florovskii, Iz proshlogo russkoi mysli* (Moskva: Agraf, 1998), pp. 68-74.

evidence of love, it is also a sacramental action, a liturgical office, or even a mystery. The offering of the sacrifice of the Cross is the sacrifice of love indeed, "as Christ also hath loved us, and given Himself for us, an offering and sacrifice to God for a sweet-smelling savor" (Eph. 5:2). But this love was not [merely] sympathy or compassion as mercy towards the fallen and heavy-laden. Christ gives Himself not only "for the remission of sins," but also for our glorification. He gives Himself not only for sinful humanity but also for the Church: to cleanse and to hallow her, to make her holy, glorious and spotless (Eph. 5:25).[69]

In this way, Florovskii interconnects Christ's role as redeemer, high priest, and sacrifice as "Divine Lamb" in *ara crucis* on Golgotha,[70] whose love does not only suffer but is "all-forgiving, sorrowful, compassionate and co-suffering."[71]

69. This reflection deepens further in its staurological theme as it goes on: "The power of the sacrificial offering is in its cleansing and hallowing effect. And the power of the sacrifice of the Cross is that the Cross is the path of glory. On the Cross the Son of Man is glorified and God is glorified in Him (John 13:32). Here is the fullness of the sacrifice. 'Ought not Christ to have suffered these things, and to enter into His glory? (Luke 24:26). The death on the Cross was effective, not as a death of an Innocent One, but as the death of the Incarnate Lord. 'We needed an Incarnate God; God put to death, that we might live' — to use a bold phrase of St. Gregory of Nazianzus. This is the 'dreadful and most glorious mystery' of the Cross. On Golgotha the incarnate Lord celebrates the Holy Service, *in ara crucis,* and offers in sacrifice His own human nature, which from its conception 'in the Virgin's womb' was assumed into the indivisible unity of His Hypostasis, and in this assumption was restored to all its original sinlessness and purity." CWF III, pp. 131-32.

70. Cf. CWF III, pp. 132-33.

71. Cf. CWF III, p. 137. At the conclusion of the chapter on "Redemption," we find a deep spiritual synthesis on the necessity of self-sacrifice in and out of love applied to each individually by a personal choice and decision: "But nobody can be compelled to desire. Thus Resurrection is a gift common to all, but blessedness will be given only to some [F. quotes Nicolas Cabasilas (1849), *De vita in Christo*]. And again, the path of life is the path of renunciation, of mortification, of self-sacrifice and self-oblation. One has to die to oneself in order to live in Christ. Each one must personally and freely associate himself with Christ, the Lord, the Saviour, and the Redeemer, in the confession of faith, in the choice of love, in the mystical oath of allegiance. Each one has to renounce himself, to 'lose his soul' for Christ's sake, to take up his cross, and to follow after Him. The Christian struggle is the 'following' after Christ, following the path of His Passion and Cross, even unto death, but first of all, following in love. 'Hereby perceive we the love of God, because He laid down His life for us; and we ought to lay down our lives for the brethren. . . . Herein is love, not that we loved God, but that He loves us, and sent His Son to be the propitiation for our sins' (1 John 3:16; 4:10). He who does not die with Christ cannot live with Him. 'Unless of our own free

2.5. Human Wisdom and the Great Wisdom of God

Florovskii moved from philosophical research, with the edition of *Ways of Russian Theology*, to concentrate fully on patristic-theological topics. In the confrontation of human and divine wisdom (and cognition of dogma), he opposes P. Florenskii on his insight of "dogmatic antinomies" in the teaching of St. Paul. Florovskii's retaliation on the subject is far from tactful, yet the concept he uses is of utmost interest since he takes *God as Love* for the foundation of his soteriological argument:

> These "contradictions," apparent to the unenlightened view, are transformed into wholeness for the spirit-bearing gaze. The clearest example is the eschatological dogma: if one proceeds from the concept of God as Love, then "the *impossibility of general* salvation is *possible*." If one proceeds from the idea of creation as a free creation of God, then it is impossible "to admit that salvation without reciprocal love for God is possible," as well as free love not compelled by God; that is, *"the impossibility of general salvation is possible."* Ideas of *forgiveness and retribution* inevitably suggest each other and at the same time exclude each other. It is equally beyond doubt that there will be eternal torment — for knowledge of the Truth and relation *with it can* only be free. And that which will be generally restored — apokatastasis — for God is love. And only in faith is *ta eschata* revealed.[72]

In what measure this corresponds with or contradicts Florenskii's ideas on the subject would require a thoroughly unbiased examination, as there are entire worlds between the two theological approaches especially on the epistemological level.

2.6. The Most Perfect Way of "Perfect Love"

Through His life and actions, the Savior inevitably shows the way — life and truth not only as mere necessities of survival but as plenitude and fulfillment

---

choice we accept to die unto His passion, His life is not in us,' says St. Ignatius. This is no mere ascetical or moral rule, not merely a discipline. This is the ontological law of spiritual existence, even the law of life itself." CWF III, pp. 148-49.

72. Cf. CWF XII, p. 119. In Russian: *Chelovecheskaia murdorst' i Premudrost' Bozhiia,* in KHT, p. 119.

of human existence. Florovskii's two principal themes, orthodoxy as unity or *Catholicity* and the Last Supper or *Eucharist* do encounter fully in his ecumenical writings:

> While creating His Church, in [a] mysterious forewarning of His salvific sufferings, the Lord establishes at the Last Supper the most Holy Sacrament of the New Covenant, and reveals to His disciples that this is a sacrament of unity and love. Of love the Savior teaches and exhorts the apostles on that very night. And He speaks of love as the uniting power. Partaking in this sacrament of unity and love still requires or better presupposes faith: In the Holy Eucharist believers become the Body of Christ.[73]

The unity created by participation in the Eucharist is *real,* ontological, on all levels — as horizontally so vertically. It is a unity in Christ's body, which, following St. John Chrysostom, is "the sign of the most powerful love," making us of one body also in each other. This unity was and is to become the model of unity once again, the unity in the union, in the supreme sacrifice:

> The Eucharist is a Catholic sacrament, a sacrament of peace and love, and therefore unity — *mysterium pacis et unitatis nostrae,* in the words of St. Augustine. This is the vespers of Love, when the Lord revealed and showed to the disciples the "most perfect way" of perfect love in the image of His love: "that ye love one another; as I have loved you, that ye also love one another" (John 13:34). . . . Moreover, based on the model of the love of the Trinity: "As the Father hath loved me, so have I loved you: continue ye in my love" (John 15:9). The Lord added the commandment of love to the mystery of the unity of the Trinity. For this mystery of love, "and this name is more fitting for God than any other name," remarks St. Gregory the Theologian. . . . The Church realizes this unity and catholicity primarily in the sacrament of the Eucharist.[74]

73. On Eucharist, sacrifice, and unity see also *Evkharistiia i sobornost',* in KHT, pp. 350-64.

74. Cf. CWF XIII, pp. 48-49. A liturgical observation from the Eucharist: "God's blessing and kindness are called on for one's entire life, for everything is encompassed and enveloped by Christ's love: 'be all for everyone, know each, his petition, his house and his needs.' All of life is contemplated in Christ." Cf. Ibid., p. 51. On the catholicity of the Church, love, and the Holy Spirit, see *Bogoslovskie otryvki,* in KHT, p. 455.

Florovskii also addresses the theme of *perfect love* from a pneumatological point of view, which instructs us in Christ's love for our neighbors and through them — a love that goes beyond loving those who love us, a gratuitous love equal to the love of God who loved us first, a love whose first fruit is prayer yet does not stop there but is reflected in mercy and compassion.[75]

2.7. The Newness of Christian Love: Agapē

In this work, Florovskii applies a critical approach — and reproach — to Anders Nygren's "lengthy study" on *Agape and Eros,* stating that, although "the Christian idea of love is indeed something new," it is not "so radically odd" that the human soul could not understand it, and finding that, despite "certain aspects of truth" in Nygren's work, his "very premise is incorrect." Florovskii perceives divergence in the language between "some" of Luther's teachings and the interpretation of that as early Christianity: *"And herein lies the great divide in the ecumenical dialogue"* to which Florovskii counts Luther's view of monasticism (as opposed to "much in Luther with which Eastern Orthodox theologians especially can relate"). The major challenge consists in a misunderstanding and misinterpretation of the "monoenergistic concept of God" (as does Nygren in identifying his concept of *Agapē*) in relation to creation, to the "other": "The existential and ontological meaning of man's created existence is precisely that God did not have to create; rather, it was a free act of Divine freedom. Yet (and here is the great difficulty created by an unbalanced western Christianity on the doctrine of grace and freedom) by freely creating man, God willed to give man an inner spiritual freedom," a reality that Florovskii does not see as a Pelagian or semi-Pelagian position but rather a "balanced synergistic doctrine of the early and Eastern Church," a realm "misunderstood and undermined by Latin Christianity," with some exceptions, beginning at St. Augustine and onwards. Simply put, the problem is that Nygren considered any (active) participation of the human being in his salvation "as a pagan distortion of *Agapē,* as *'Erōs,'"* which in substance served as the theological argument for the rejection of monasticism, asceticism, and any spirituality so close to the "Christian Church from its inception."[76] Florovskii makes a genuine effort to stay balanced in his dis-

75. These statements are based upon the Gospel from Matthew, Luke, and John. Cf. *O pochesti gornego prizvaniia,* in KHT, p. 755.

76. Cf. KHT, pp. 104-5.

cernment, also admitting what he perceives "as true" or "partially true," especially when highlighting Nygren's imitation of "the general position of Luther" as a hermeneutic key to the new, i.e., Christian interpretation of *Agapē* (since, according to Nygren, "*Agapē* can never be 'self-evident,' " ergo it needs a proper hermeneutical key). So Nygren is right to identify the hermeneutical key in the commandment to "love your enemies" because of the "positive fact of God's own love even for evil men" and that His sun rises on evil and good equally, since all are children of our Heavenly Father. Florovskii sees this as an accurate yet still partial analysis. Missing is something that in Orthodox tradition and theology has always been in the "avant-garde," namely "human ontology":

> What Nygren writes [here] is accurate. But it neglects the significance of human ontology; that is, that we are commanded to love our enemies because there is a spiritual value within the very fabric of human nature created by God, even fallen nature, and that that spiritual value is to be found in each and every man, however dimly we may perceive it. If we begin to love our enemy, we will begin to perceive in that enemy characteristics, aspects that were veiled, that were dimmed by the blindness of our hatred. We are commanded to love our enemy not only because God loves mankind, not only because God "maketh his sun to rise on the evil and the good," but because there is a value in mankind.[77]

In the final analysis, Florovskii reproaches Nygren for having missed the "God-created, God-given" value in the human being because of his "theological doctrine of God and man" (as opposed to Nygren's *rejection* of the "matchless value [of and in the human being] on which God's love is set"). For Florovskii, this belongs to the "divide" that keeps the churches separate in the ecumenical dialogue, and he exalts Luther's doctrine on Divine Love as a concept of "*eine quellende Liebe*" ([one] *gushing Love*) so close to the Fathers of the Church, yet rather detached from Luther's other teachings:

> [This] gushing love *(eine quellende Liebe)* is by itself an Orthodox view. . . . This love has no need of anything, it is not caused, it does not come into existence because of a desired object, it is not aroused by desirable qualities of an object. It is the nature of God. But, at the same time, it is God who created mankind, and hence the love of God for

77. KHT, pp. 106-7.

> mankind, though in need of nothing and attracted by nothing, loves mankind not because of a value in man but because there is value in man created by God. Herein lies the difference, and it is indeed a great divide when one considers the differing views on the other subjects closely related to the nature of Divine love.[78]

Florovskii's reflection suggests that God is in love with His creation because of what He planted in our hearts, a real *value* in our being, because we were created by Love (in His image), out of Love (God's essence), and for Love (to relate as the Trinity does). Despite Florovskii's previous criticism of St. Augustine, we cannot but think of the latter's *Confessions* and, therein, his *confession* of love. Perhaps, his confession of "loving too late" was due to the aforementioned recognition of the unique divine value in his very self, the Love that is closer and more intimate to us than we can ever be to our very selves. Yet, after a long and travailed journey to accept Christ and His Church fully, Augustine confessed — the value, the Love, in his heart. Is it then not better late than never?

2.8. *A Decision Taken in the Human Heart*

Florovskii briefly analyzes also the two letters to the Corinthians,[79] describing chapter 13 of the first letter as "St. Paul's hymn to love, to *Agapē*," viewing it especially as in function to and with *faith* and the monastic-ascetic struggle: "The goal of monastic and ascetical struggle, of the 'ordeal,' is love — to love God, to love mankind, to love all created things, to be penetrated by God's love, to participate in love, which is God and flows from God, and to enter a union with God, with love." At times, the description in monastic literature of "achieving this love" is falsely rendered and creates the impression of human achievement instead of defining this "ordeal" with intense and nonceasing desire. This literature needs to be taken in its "total context," as Florovskii puts it, to discern the two languages — that of God initiator and that of the human response "to the love and redemptive work of God in Jesus Christ, and through the Holy Spirit," all of which occurs *en kardia,* that is, in the human heart.[80]

78. Cf. KHT, pp. 106-8.

79. Cf. KHT, pp. 116-21.

80. Cf. KHT, pp. 118-19. See also the "weapons of righteousness," described by St. Paul, and "what could be a guide to monastic spiritual life," among others, "unfeigned love" (cf. 2 Cor. 6:4-10). Cf. KHT, p. 120.

Conclusion

Florovskii belongs among creative theologians, as he can move in the *catholicity-orthodoxy* of the patristic theology that he exploits to the great benefit of the reader. He, too, co-locates love, perhaps under the influence of the Cappadocian Fathers, into the center of his philosophical and, even more so, theological reflections. He discerns between the "qualities" of love and defines *agapē*, the model-love, as the Divine one. It flows within and from the Trinity in the economy of salvation to humankind in order to help and save the fallen human nature as well as the world. This can be realized only in and through the Church as the living organism of God's Love — Jesus Christ. God's concern for the world and creation is so real and ontological that He took on the sacrifice of flesh and challenges all His children into the unity of one body. This corpus, best reflected in the Eucharist, the peak liturgical action of charity, is the reflection of the heavenly realm on earth, of the Divine Love to be shared and spread so that it may unite all, the entire world, into a free, liberating, and willed worship, a veritable *agapē* prepared by the Heavenly Father for his love-famished and love-thirsting humankind.

3. Vladimir Nikolaevich Losskii: Participation in *Supreme Perfection*

3.1. Biography

V. N. Losskii (1903-1958), a theologian, church historian, and specialist of medieval philosophy, was born in Göttingen in 1903, the son of one of the well-known pioneers of modern Russian philosophy, Nikolai Onufrievich Losskii (1870-1965). V. Losskii was deeply affected by the experience of the martyrdom of Bishop Beniamin (Kazanskii) in 1922 and by the profound reverence and unity of the Christians who saw him off to his execution, an event that he witnessed in person. This experience shaped his understanding of and fidelity to the persecuted Russian Church henceforth. In the same year, at the age of nineteen, he was expelled, along with his entire family, from Russia, due to which his university studies of medieval French history were interrupted. His interest then turned towards patristic subjects, on which he eventually wrote his thesis (and, according to his son, N. Losskii, this remained the principal object of his father's research).[81] The person who introduced him to the study

81. In the preface of his posthumously published thesis on M. Eckhart, Étienne

of the Eastern Fathers was none other than L. Karsavin. Losskii pursued his studies in Prague until 1924, under N. P. Kondakov, an experience that would forever bond him to patristic theology. While in Paris, Losskii became a student of E. Gilson, with whom his relationship endured for a lifetime. He graduated from the Sorbonne in 1927 and it was in Paris that he wrote most of his works, at the request of his non-Orthodox friends in French and "in the context of an ecumenical dialogue." He participated in the French resistance during World War II and was interned in a concentration camp. After the war, he taught dogmatic theology and church history at St. Serge Orthodox Institute with G. Florovskii, with whom he found great affinity. Although these two men were "nonprofessional" theologians (i.e., without prior seminary formation in theology), they shared the vision that the authentic theology of the Orthodox Church was the patristic theology and intensely promoted its renaissance. Losskii died in Paris in 1958.

Among his works are: *Spor of Sofii* (*Dispute on Sophia* [1936]); *Essai sur la théologie mystique de l'Église d'Orient* (1944); *The Meaning of Icons* (with L. Ouspenskii [1947]); *Théologie négative et connaissance de Dieu chez Maître Eckhart* (1960); *La vision de Dieu* (1961); *L'image et à la ressemblance de Dieu* (1967); *La paternité spirituelle en Russie aux XVIIIème et XIXème siècles* (with N. Arseniev [1977]); *Théologie dogmatique* (1978); and *Conoscere Dio* (appeared in Italian [1996]).[82]

3.2. To Know God: Dogmatic Theology

In his preface to this work, J. Meyendorff says of Losskii's "*love* loghikós (*that is according [to] the* Lógos)" that his pages reflect when synthesizing the theology of the Fathers in "*the contemplation of God and expression of the Inexpressible.*"[83] Losskii's faith and theology are rooted in a personal relation-

---

Gilson wrote of Losskii: "Une sorte de paix rayonnait doucement de cet homme si modeste, si parfaitement simple et bon, dont le secret fut peut-être d'incarner parmi nous l'esprit chrétien même et de le faire comme en vertu d'une vocation quasi naturelle. En l'écoutant on pensait souvent à ce qu'il était plutôt qu'à ce qu'il disait et cela aussi rendait difficile de l'aider." V. Lossky, *Théologie négative et connaissance de Dieu chez Maître Eckhart* (Paris: Librairie Philosophique J. Vrin, 1960), p. 9.

82. Cf. P. V. Alekseev, *Filosofy Rossii XIX-XX stoletii* (Moskva: "Akademicheskii Proekt," 2002), p. 568; a brief yet valuable biography and description by Nicholas Lossky in *Credere oggi: Teologi Ortodossi del II secolo* 140/2 (Padova: Messagero, 2004), pp. 53-62.

83. Cf. I. Meyendorff, "Preface," in V. Lossky, *Conoscere Dio* (Bose: Quiqajon, 1996), p. 6. As we had no access to the French original, we have used the present Italian edition.

ship with God that he complements with what he calls a "Christian paradox" through the method of *apophatism.*[84] This approach was developed by the Fathers as the "negation of all that God is not" — all created and "cosmic glory" — then the highest attributes "goodness, love, wisdom," and, eventually, "being itself."[85] The latter Losskii juxtaposes with the notion of "God to whom I say: You, and who calls me, who reveals Himself as God-person [or, personal God], the Living One." He quotes a prayer from St. John Chrysostom's liturgy, an exhortation to *dare* to call God *(Our) Father,* God who is above heaven *(epouránion theón),* therefore, an apophatic concept of God: "One prays for the audacity and the simplicity to give [a personal] 'you' to God."[86] God still is and remains "wisdom, love, and goodness (kindness)" yet continues to remain unknowable. Even the most refined names, such as *love,* "describe His nature but do not exhaust it: they constitute the attributes with which the divinity communicate[s] (itself)" yet without ever fully comprehending or describing its proper "secret source."[87]

Losskii uses St. Gregory of Nyssa's commentary on the Song of Songs to visualize the love-relationship between God and the soul, a mystical wedding of the soul after its search for "the Beloved who appears and disappears," the love flames up and then is soothed, a search that eventually makes the soul love Him even more ardently. "The more it is filled with God, the more it discovers Him transcendent." The tension of near and distant, between the searching, yearning soul and God's essence, is a "distance that makes love possible and draws it nearer." We are called by God, and "we are included in this call" that at the same time hides and reveals Him. Losskii discerns that this is the only relationship, an alternating tension, in and through which we can reach God, precisely by safeguarding His inaccessibility.[88]

In the Trinity of relationship, the "Father is the source of love, the Son is love who is revealing Himself, the Spirit is the love realized in us." The

84. To this method and theology on the Trinity is dedicated his booklet: *L'apophase et la théologie Trinitaire* (Paris: Centre de Documentation Universitaire, n.d.).

85. That is: "God is nothing of all these: in His very nature He is unknowable." Cf. *Conoscere Dio,* p. 14. Also cf. V. Lossky, *In the Image and Likeness of God* (Crestwood, NY: St. Vladimir's Seminary Press, 2001), p. 16 (ILG).

86. "Si prega per avere l'audacia e la semplicità di dare del 'tu' a Dio." Cf. *Conoscere Dio,* p. 14.

87. Cf. *Conoscere Dio,* p. 15.

88. On one side, "the idea of essence does not set up limits to love but on the other side it speaks of the impossibility to 'exceed the limit,'" and the philosophical struggle would remain once more unresolved if not for the intermediary role of Jesus Christ who united the two natures and became the *religio,* the bond and relationship. Cf. *Conoscere Dio,* pp. 16-17.

same pattern applies to wisdom or goodness, as well. And once more, the famous Trinitarian "kenotic love model" is quoted.[89]

3.3. *The Memory of a* Paradisiacal Erōs

The image of God, the human being (precisely in his nature), cannot be fully "possessed by a monad: it requires communion, not solitude. [This] is the positive diversity of love."[90] Thus, the "divine commandment" to love and to be fecund, according to Losskii, establishes a "certain rapport between sexuality and the cosmic dominion of the first couple and the mysterious overcoming of the duality by the triad in God." This notion from a dyad to a triad is fundamental for our divinization, i.e., becoming God-like, not just God-worshipers, but intimate friends of God, again, by imitating the Trinity. The notion of dual to threefold or threesome contains the element of primordial *erōs,* a concept that we encountered for the first time, namely the "*paradisiacal erōs,*" which is apparently love in its primordial quality:

> Yet this paradisiacal *erōs* has had to be so much different from our fallen consuming [or devouring] sexuality, as much as the royal priesthood of the human being over the creation had to differ from the actual reciprocal devouring [one]. . . . The fall has changed the proper meanings of the words. Sexuality, that "multiplication" which God commands and blesses, turns out in our world irremediably linked to separation and death: the condition of the human being has known, up to its very biological reality, a catastrophic mutation. Yet the human love would not be so full of paradisiacal nostalgia if it did not carry in itself the aching memory of an original condition in which the other and the world were known *interiorly (dall'interno),* where in fact death did not exist.[91]

The tragic fall of the first Adam that led to a *catastrophic mutation* in human nature from the original *image* and imprint also introduced death into the human realm. This can be mended only through the process of divinization introduced by the salvific act of the "heavenly Adam, Christ" who takes up an (un-)expected role, a role conditioned by humankind's free

89. Cf. *Conoscere Dio,* p. 35.
90. "È la diversità buona dell'amore." *Conoscere Dio,* p. 60.
91. Cf. *Conoscere Dio,* pp. 60-61, 73-74.

choice: "[Christ, in His mission,] does not intend to be a substitute for the human being, as the infinite love of God cannot substitute the bond of human freedom, but He became one of us in order to restitute to the human being the possibility of fulfilling his task, to open to him anew the way of divinization."[92] Almost more importantly for our quest, however, Christ, through His "virginal birth," heals the misinterpreted, misused, and deformed *erōs* in a twofold way: "With his virginal birth, in fact, Christ overcomes the division of sexes[93] and opens for the redemption of 'eros' two ways that are united only in the person of Mary, virgin and mother at the same time: Christian matrimony and monasticism." The moment when this occurs is on the cross, where Christ unites the two worlds, the "earthly cosmos" and the heavenly realm. Losskii used very vivid yet metaphysical imagery: "In the instant in which He [Christ] allows to enter into Himself death in order to defeat it through the contact with divinity, the gloomiest place on earth becomes splendid, there is no more place that would be cursed." The act of divinization is then fulfilled in Christ's ascent to his Father, in the Trinity Itself; "these are the early fruits *(primizie)* of the cosmic divinization."[94] The path of divinization is not restricted merely to the human being, even though it is aimed primarily at humankind, but God also saves the created cosmos through a process that re-forms it into, or restores its original beauty.

3.4. Form of a God — Form of a Slave

In a passage in his epistemological work *(Conoscere Dio)* Losskii attempted to define "the annihilation of the Word." Further, he investigated the possibility of uniting through God's self-abasement the "integral completeness of the divine nature with the not less integral incompleteness of the fallen human nature," which is to be read along with Isaiah 53 on the suffering servant of God. According to St. Cyril of Alexandria, the "subject of *kenosis*" is not the divine nature but the person(hood) of the Son since, at the Incarnation, Christ

92. "It is that supreme synthesis of God and the created cosmos, in the human being, that contains the sense of all Christian anthropology." Cf. *Conoscere Dio,* pp. 70-71.

93. Also: "By His birth of the Virgin, He suppressed the division of human nature into male and female. On the cross He unites paradise, the dwelling place of the first men before the fall, with the terrestrial reality where the fallen descendants of the first Adam now dwell." V. Lossky, *The Mystical Theology of the Eastern Church* (Crestwood, NY: St. Vladimir's Seminary Press, 1976), p. 137 (MTE).

94. Cf. *Conoscere Dio,* p. 71.

could not "unclothe" His divine nature. Ergo, the Son's greatness in the kenotic act was in His *not counting equality with God,* not claiming his value and dignity, *but making Himself nothing* by accepting all the evil, the sin, and the consequences of it.[95] "Thus *kenosis* is the incarnation in its aspects of humility and death." It includes His renouncement of His own will and glory for the will and glory of another, of the Father. "He fulfills on earth the work of love *(opera d'amore)* of the Trinity."[96] Only in Christ, whose divine nature has been revealed twice before the Resurrection (the events of Baptism and Transfiguration), "the nonexistence becomes suffering and love and [thus] non-evil [i.e., transformation of evil]."[97] Only in the *Word* that carried Paradise and the unaltered Primordial Image in Himself could human weakness and sin be transformed through suffering into true love.[98]

3.5. Love as Manifestation and Not Essence

In *The Mystical Theology of the Eastern Church,* in the chapter on the *Economy of the Son,* Losskii dedicated a significant portion to the subject of *kenosis.* First, the intra-Trinitarian relationship and the role of uncreated energies that include *Love* are defined, especially with regard to the different views between Eastern and Western theological traditions:

> When we say that God is Wisdom, Life, Truth, [and] Love, we understand the energies, which are subsequent to the essence and are its natu-

95. Cf. *Conoscere Dio,* p. 106.

96. "And with the infinite respect that He manifests towards human freedom, up to the point to show humankind only the painful fraternal face of a slave and the flesh painfully fraternal on the cross, He awakens in the human being faith as the answer of love: only the eyes of faith recognize the form of God under the form of a slave, and grasping behind every human face the presence of a divine person, they learn to realize in every face the mystery of the person created to the image of God." Cf. *Conoscere Dio,* pp. 107-8. A final answer to the question *"Cur Deus homo"* Losskii links to an overall understanding of *kenosis,* "its culmination and completion in Christ's death," namely, not only salvation from sin but also a positive sense, ergo sanctification. Cf. *Conoscere Dio,* p. 127.

97. Cf. *Conoscere Dio,* p. 109.

98. Also: "The Divine love pursues always the same goal: the divinization of humankind and through them of the entire universe. Yet the fall requires a change: not in the aim of God but in the means, the divine pedagogy." These means are the means of redemption consisting in a new beginning through the "recapitulation of the history missed out by humanity." Cf. *Conoscere Dio,* pp. 120-21.

> ral manifestations, but are external to the very being of the Trinity. That is why, in contrast to western theology, the tradition of [the] Eastern Church never designates the relationship between the Persons of the Trinity by the name of attributes. . . . The Spirit can never be assimilated to the mutual love of the Father and the Son.[99]

Losskii meticulously discerns between the attributes, the energies, and the essence of God, inspired by Gregory Palamas who talks of the "energies" as "real attributes of God." Since they are attributed, so to speak, *a posteriori* to the Trinity, he calls them a "lesser divinity," that is, manifestations of the energies. Hence, Losskii states, "To say: 'God is love, the divine Persons are united by mutual love,' is to think of a common manifestation, the 'love-energy' possessed by the three Hypostases, for the union of the Three is higher even than love," which follows Palamas and the Council of Constantinople V in 1341, "for God signifies He who acts; divinity (understood as energy) signifies His operation."[100] Thus, with Losskii, we have a clear shift in the concept of *love* from *the essence* to the *energy, manifestation,* or, based on the Palamite model, to a *lesser divinity* of God.[101] Eventually, he uses the well-known Trinitarian kenotic-love formulation from Filaret's sermon[102] to unfold a demonstration of the Eastern Church's distinction between "the three Hypostases, nature, or essence, and the energies" in God.[103] These distinctions are fundamental out of various dogmatic, theological-mystical reasons, and Losskii provides a very plausible argument in this chapter.[104]

99. Cf. MTE, pp. 80-81.

100. Cf. MTE, p. 81.

101. Which, involuntarily, recalls anew Bulgakov's struggle for the concept of creational Sophia.

102. Previously, Losskii points out that the Holy Spirit proceeds only from the Father "without having any relation of origin with the Son." According to the Eastern tradition, the will never intervenes in the Trinity Itself, but does so in the economy of "created order" where It determines the "exterior activities" of the three divine Persons. "This will is common to the three Persons; that is why, in the mission of the Son and of the Holy Spirit, each of the three Persons acts in concourse with the two others: the Son becomes incarnate, but He is sent by the Father and takes flesh by the Holy Spirit; the Holy Spirit descends — sent from the Father by the Son. It is in this context of the divine economy — the love of the Holy Trinity made manifest in the mystery of the cross — that Philaret of Moscow speaks of: 'The love of the Father in the crucifixion, the love of the Son crucified, and love of the Holy Spirit triumphant in the invincible power of the cross.'" MTE, p. 85.

103. Cf. MTE, pp. 85-86.

104. Cf. MTE, pp. 86-90.

3.6. Kenosis

The *Economy of the Son,* as put in the title of this chapter, is inseparable from the mystery of the Trinity. It is fully revealed in "the κένωσις [which] is the mode of the Divine Person's being, the Person sent into the world and in whom the common will of the Trinity was accomplished [and] whose source is the Father."[105] In the kenotic aspect, Losskii relies consistently on the teaching of the Fathers, mainly St. Cyril of Alexandria, St. Maximus, and St. John Damascene. In Christ's human struggle to accept death, His divine will "made way for the manifestation of His humanity" by the desire that the latter would accept Passion. "Also the last cry of mortal agony of Christ on the cross was a manifestation of His true humanity which voluntarily submitted to death as a final stripping, emptying, the culmination of the divine κένωσις."[106] The hermeneutical key of the Eastern Church to the understanding of Christ's humanity lies in His Transfiguration, "so venerated by the Orthodox Church," as the humanity of Christ is never considered apart or "in abstraction from His Godhead."[107]

Yet the "mystery of the self-emptying, of the κένωσις," also occurs in and through the Holy Spirit when descending into the world. In both cases, with the Word and with the Spirit, their Person and *Godhead* actuate from different aspects, one transcendent, the other immanent: "If in the κένωσις of the Son the Person appeared to men while the Godhead remained hidden under the form of a servant, the Holy Spirit in His coming, while He manifests the common nature of the Trinity, leaves His own Person concealed beneath His Godhead."[108] Furthermore, Losskii remarkably connects κένωσις to his Mariology where the "most pure nature . . . entered into perfect union with the deity in the person of the Mother of God." Yet the Spirit descended on her once more on Pentecost in order "to give Himself to her, to become the means of her deification." And with the conditional "if," if she still endured earthly life and death, it was "by the virtue of the perfect will that she reproduced the voluntary κένωσις of her Son."[109]

105. Cf. MTE, p. 145.

106. In the conclusion of the book, we find: "Christ always appears in the fullness of His Godhead, glorified and triumphant: even in His Passion; even in the Tomb. The κένωσις is always balanced by the splendor of the deity." MTE, p. 242.

107. Cf. MTE, pp. 147-49.

108. Cf. MTE, p. 168.

109. Once again according to Gregory Palamas, Mary is the "boundary of created and uncreated nature"; whereas, *boundary* is to comprehend above all as the limits of time and

3.7. *Agapē as Participation in* Supreme Perfection

With the concept of *deification (theosis)* and union in his vision, Losskii approaches the topic of divine love, *agapē*. He sees divine love as a "fruit of prayer" yet a gift of grace "appropriated in the depths of our being." According to Diadochus, it is an "uncreated gift, a divine energy"; for St. John Climacus it is the "name of God Himself," therefore inferable, and "the world of love is known to angels" yet only to the degree or "energy of their illumination"; and Symeon the New Theologian sings about its unique, incomparable sweetness that "fillest, burnest, enkindlest, embracest my heart with a measureless charity. . . . O Love, prepare even me, for the true service of God."[110]

Losskii reaffirms that the very word "'love' (ἀγάπη)" never refers to the "hypostatic character" of the Holy Spirit in the Eastern mystical tradition but rather to "His nature as the giver of love, as the source of love within us, as He who enables us to participate in that supreme perfection of the common nature of the Holy Trinity. For love is 'the very life of the divine nature,' in the words of St. Gregory of Nyssa."[111] As apparent, Losskii, like Florovskii, closely follows the teaching of the Church Fathers and often comments on their position or paraphrases them as he "talks" in their phrases.[112] The final scope and fullness of love is in unity, first of all with God, but equally sharing with all humanity, in conformity with Christ, what eventually leads to the "participation in the very life of the Holy Trinity, in that supreme perfection which is love." Therefore, "personal awareness" is so indispensable since, as with most Christian authors, here too we learn that "love is inseparable from knowledge — 'gnosis,'" an awareness that is meant to grow into a "full awareness" through the grace and process of deification, similar to that witnessed by the disciples at the transfiguration on Mt. Tabor.[113]

---

ages that she has crossed with her full and unreserved cooperation with God's grace. "She obtains eternal benefits. It is through her that men and angels receive grace. No gift is received in the Church without the assistance of the Mother of God. . . . Thus having attained to the limits of becoming, she necessarily watches over the destinies of the Church and of the universe, still unfolding in time." Cf. MTE, pp. 193-95.

110. Cf. MTE, pp. 212-13.

111. Cf. MTE, pp. 212-13.

112. At St. John's "Love is of God," for instance, he paraphrases St. Basil that the "divine gift of love presupposes a corresponding disposition in created nature, a germ or potentiality for love," etc. Cf. MTE, pp. 214-16, 234-35.

113. Cf. MTE, pp. 215, 224.

3.8. Agapē *and* Erōs

In his book titled *The Vision of God*, which is also a theological concept especially dear to Eastern Christianity, Losskii returns to some of the aspects of *agapē*. For instance, the notion of *gnosis* — *agapē* in the Alexandrian school, where he contradicts St. Clement (for whom "perfection consists in the knowledge of the Good and assimilation to God") on the notion of rising from faith to gnosis by love (ἀγάπη) when it comes to the choice between salvation via knowledge of God: "For this ἀγάπη is eclipsed by *gnosis*, and it is precisely gnosis which occupies that place in the age to come which St. Paul reserves exclusively for ἀγάπη."[114] Since, in this work, Losskii systematically reviews the different patristic theological schools through the prism of the *vision of God*, we shall highlight only one or two additional examples (even though not easily extractable from their context).

3.8.1. Diverse Patristic Approaches

With Origen,[115] "Christians are divided into two categories: those who believe and those who know. But every Christian must strive to know," for knowledge is indivisibly linked to love, as he was "too good an exegete to forget the place of ἀγάπη in the vision of God in St. John and St. Paul. As knowledge increases love becomes more and more fervent."[116] For the Cappadocian Fathers (concretely, St. Basil the Great), in terms of communion "with the Trinitarian God," the stress lies in the "intimacy with God," the "union in love," and, instead of *gnosis* and *deifying knowledge*, "Basil speaks of the Holy Spirit."[117] For

114. For the sake of comprehension, we quote St. Clement's reflection on which Losskii comments: "I will say boldly that he who pursues gnosis for the sake of divine knowledge itself will not embrace it simply because he wishes to be saved. Intellect, in its proper use, tends always to be an activity; and this ever-active intellect, having become in its uninterrupted tension the essential feature of the Gnostic, is transformed into eternal contemplation and exists as a living substance. If therefore we should suggest hypothetically that the Gnostic choose between knowledge of God and eternal salvation, assuming that these two things are separate (in fact they are absolutely identical), he will without hesitation choose the knowledge of God." Losskii retorts in the first place that *contemplation of God* and *eternal salvation* in the text are factually separated. Cf. V. Lossky, *The Vision of God* (New York: Athens Printing Company, 1973), pp. 53-54 (VOG).

115. "Clement was more a moralist; Origen is a theologian and at the same time an exegete, apologist, and master of the ascetical life." VOG, p. 55.

116. Cf. VOG, pp. 55-57.

117. Cf. VOG, p. 80.

Evagrius, when talking about the vision of God in ascetic literature, love is strongly underlined with the intellect: "'Only the love of the good lives forever (an allusion to St. Paul's passage on ἀγάπη). This is the love of true knowledge.' This definition of love has a strong intellectualistic accent: the perfect love which never dies is love of divine gnosis. Elsewhere, Evagrius says, in the same spirit: 'Love is the lofty state of the rational soul by virtue of which it is able to love nothing in this world so much as the knowledge of God.'" Before any of these can be realized, the intellect needs to be trained in and for the knowledge of "God in creation," the gnosis of physical, sensible, and intelligible natures.[118] Mentioned is Diadochus of Photike, for whom a Christian's goal is "union with God in love. 'Love . . . actually unites the soul to the powers of God as it seeks by the inward sense the One who is invisible.'"[119] Last but not least, in the doctrine of St. Maximus, not gnosis anymore as with Evagrius, it is ἀγάπη that is of a central and decisive note as revealed by Fr. Pegon's translation of Maximus's *Annals of Love:* "The knowledge of God is not the goal of charity in the sense that would make charity purely a means to an end. We would speak more accurately if we said that knowledge is the *effect,* the *sign* of the union with God brought about by love, but an effect which reacts in turn on the cause, intensifying love." Losskii adds that St. Maximus's position in this instance is closer to St. Gregory of Nyssa and Dionysius than to Evagrius.[120]

As a matter of course, not all the Fathers are mentioned here within the context of *agapē,* and, therefore, we only highlighted the most prominent ones, among them those with a significant contribution to the understanding of (some aspects) of the divine love, *agapē* — in Losskii's rendering. Apparently, this work was triggered (or at least partially) as a reaction to A. Nygren's book, *Eros and Agape,* on which Losskii comments repeatedly, especially on Nygren's opposition to "the purely Christian notion of *agapē* [as] a wholly gratuitous love." This love, according to Nygren, is uniquely a

118. Cf. VOG, p. 106.

119. Cf. VOG, p. 116.

120. Cf. VOG, pp. 132-33. A comparison of positions on the vision of God in the works of St. Gregory of Nyssa, Origen, and Evagrius interpreted to the advantage of Gregory (based on his works *Life of Moses* and the *Song of Songs*): "If God appears first as light and then as darkness, this means for Gregory that of the divine essence there is no vision, and that union with God is a way surpassing vision of *theoria,* going beyond intelligence to where knowledge vanishes and only love remains — or, rather, to where gnosis becomes ἀγάπη. Desiring God more and more, the soul grows without ceasing, going beyond herself and outside herself; and in the measure in which she unites herself more and more to God, her love becomes more ardent and insatiable." Cf. ILG, p. 37.

one-way relation, from God to the human being, precisely in the form of the pagan *erōs,* which is understood here as a purely "calculating and egoistic love, drawing man toward God and provoking in him the desire for joy, a way which is exclusively that of man toward God." A God who attracts human beings by the sensations of *an egoistic erōs* in order to be loved by them is certainly not the Christian concept of *agapē* or ideals of a self-sacrificing God. Nygren claims further that *vision* "is a principal response of *eros.*"[121]

Under the given premises, and many others not listed here, it is understandable that Losskii's answer was *The Vision of God,* a book undoubtedly compiled with much of his personal love to bear justice to the Fathers' theology. Thus, in the opening chapters, Losskii correctly mentions St. John's concept of vision conferred by Divine love to Christianity:

> For St. John the vision of God is connected with the quality of being a son of God, a quality conferred on Christians by the love (ἀγάπη) of the Father. The world, he says, does not know us (as sons of God) because it has not known God. But we are already, from this moment on, sons of God and what we shall be has not yet appeared. . . . [The likeness of God] alludes to the divine charity or love (ἀγάπη) which confers on Christians the quality of being sons of God, with all that this involves. . . . Thus, "we shall be like Him, for we shall see Him as He is" can be interpreted in the sense of a causal relationship — the deified state is the consequence of the vision of God as He is.[122]

Sometimes a vision and, above all, the human sight of intellect, need the correcting lenses of faith and *love,* and those provided by Losskii bring — sustained by the patristic approach — clarity concerning *agapē* in focus on "God as He is," i.e., God *as* Love.

3.9. In the Image and Likeness of God: *The Divine Risk*

In his foreword to the book, J. Meyendorff states that Losskii's particular contribution is in pointing out the "'relatedness' in love" of the human being as a person to other persons and the "Orthodox understanding of man's

121. Cf. VOG, pp. 31-32, 46, 64, 165. On Nygren's "eliminating . . . the theme of the image," see ILG, pp. 127-28.

122. Cf. VOG, pp. 28-30.

destiny as communion in love with the Triune God," which is certainly true and needs to be seen in the whole context of this work.[123] Yet, as to what we have seen so far, there are few real novelties directly regarding our field of research.

In his chapter on *Eschatological Study (Dominion and Kingship)*, Losskii exercises, in our view, a justifiable criticism of the image of God presented in some dogmatic manuals of theology and by "rationalist theology," a God who, "in His omnipotence," either would not take risks, or *"is incapable"* of taking risks and truly loves only Himself — even in His creatures, it is His own perfection that He loves. Such a view shakes the foundations of a true and truly personal relationship with God. Here, Losskii definitely presents to the reader a God of love, a Christian concept of a loving Heavenly Father, shifting the right attributes to their proper place. Once again, perfection is conditioned by freedom:

> But he who takes no risks does not love: the God of the theology manuals can love only himself, and it is his own perfection which he loves even in his creatures. He does not love any *person:* for personal love is love for another than oneself. Now the jealous God of the Bible is not "the cruel God of the Jews," greedy of His own glory, but a God whose love for His elect is "strong as death," whose jealousy against everything which separates His creatures from Him is "cruel as the grave." God's dominion must be thought of in these terms of God's personal love which exacts from the freedom of His creatures a total conversion towards Him, a freely accomplished union. But a claim as absolute as this, addressed to the liberty of the person loved, would not be the claim of perfect love if it were not a desire for the realization in the beloved of absolute fulfillment, wished for by the beloved and accomplished with the cooperation of his own will.[124]

In a further quote paraphrasing St. Maximus, Losskii introduces a concept of "divine risk," a notion originally paralleled to a "gamble of love" that sheds light on the economy of salvation based on the scriptural *foolishness of the cross* that reveals God's infinite love for the world: "This is the dialectic of the dominion of God in Trinity of Persons, transcendent in His unknowable nature, immanent in His love. He willed to create a world whose

123. Cf. ILG, pp. 9-11.
124. Cf. ILG, pp. 214-15.

supreme perfection could not be attained without involving the will of the Creator in a gamble of love, going even to the 'foolishness of the Cross.' 'For God so loved the world that He gave His only Son' (John 3:16)."[125] What one misses somewhat from this profound and creative reflection is John 4:8 and 16, namely that *God is love,* a self-explanatory quote and understood as the essence of such reflections. Strangely, we did not encounter it in the entire text. It would have well launched the rather original idea of the "'third will,' to which the First Adam submitted himself freely, seduced by the promise of a false deification outside the love of God" that was conditioned by the misunderstanding of the divine love and thus God as love.[126]

3.9.1. Job's False Friends

Finally, Losskii presents two more "false" images of God's love related to the story of Job, in both cases provided by theologians themselves who "follow a more neo-Platonic approach than a personal relating to God," as would Romano Guardini, for instance. The main accent for the "theologians" is not in the relationship to and with God but rather a theologic-philosophical solution by "falsifying Biblical anthropomorphism" and replacing it with "the poor abstract anthropomorphism of [what Losskii "would dare to call"] a reasonable animal turned theologian."[127] The other case refers again to the "friends of Job" where false concepts of God, projected in particular on the

125. Cf. ILG, p. 215.

126. Cf. ILG, p. 216. "The third will" is a succession of the "agreement" of the first two wills, namely the will of God and the will of creatures. After the fall of the first Adam, the "harmony of the first two wills can be only external." The "third will" is a result of sin and applies, according to St. Paul, to a dominion "*other* than that of God." Cf. ILG, pp. 215-16.

127. "Certainly, this safeguards the tranquil existence of God and the intellectual comfort of the theologian, but 'the seriousness of God's love,' on which Romano Guardini has insisted of late, has no meaning in relation to this God of the theologians, made in the image of the God of the philosophers and learned men of this world. This God is perhaps very close to him whom the young Augustine thought he found in the books of the neo-Platonists: an almighty God, who cannot, however, be really involved in the history and salvation of His creation — to the point of becoming man to undergo death — without losing his right to the perfection proper to the Deity. This is certainly not the God of the Scriptures, the Church Fathers, and St. Augustine himself. It is the God of Job's friends, weighing down His creation with a dominion which has the deathly character of necessary, inexorable law, administered by a judge from whom there is no appeal. Job protested against this false image of the true God, against the caricature of His royal person, distorted by the dominion of the prince of this world — a caricature in which the just man refused to recognize the face of the Lord whom he sought." Cf. ILG, pp. 218-19.

eschatological level, are "telescoped" together. They are "many planes of legal dominion [which are] fused together and projected onto God. . . . Job's comforters failed to perceive the risk involved in the love of God who engages Himself fully in the economy of the salvation of His creatures." Once again, Losskii blames the (modern) theologians for having further misinterpreted God's love-engagement for the human being and for His creation in general. How far this truly corresponds to which theologian's position is another matter. However, Losskii is positively correct in identifying the immense responsibility of theologians for the interpretation of God's vision, His image, and His relationship to creation.[128]

Conclusion

As a good disciple faithful to the teaching of the Church Fathers, Losskii demonstrates intelligence, diligence, and a giftedness for synthesis and clarity in treating various arguments. He repeatedly underscores that *love* is not the essence but an *energy* or manifestation of God, as many of the other attributes describing God's entity, yet being of a "secondary grade," so to speak, to the Hypostases. This approach is an important element in the apophatic, negative, or negating theology, an ancient patristic method construed precisely to avoid the danger of identifying God's being and essence with one of his manifestations or energies, in final consequence with anthropomorphisms. Nevertheless, love is among the closest descriptions to the true *image of God* in the *likeness* of whom we were created. And if this *image* is love, God manifests Himself, even in a vision, acts and calls as by love, undergoing a *gambling of love* for our redemption, taking even *risk* — the risk to be refused and crucified just to save us in the "foolishness of the Cross." This *image of God* is definitely a love-filled one supported also by the *memory of a paradisiacal erōs.* The primordial plan was a gradual, further growth in being *divinized* and so to bring us to our predestined fullness of union with God (*predestined* under the condition of humankind accepting God's invitation to cooperate). We are all invited and called to participate in the *supreme perfection of union* (with God and with[in] the entire humankind), we are all children — that we know

128. "The Christian descendants of these reasonable theologians have aggravated the error of their fathers, for they have misunderstood the eschatological involvement of man, replacing it by an abstract faith, which is unable to move the mountains of demonic domination because the devils also know this kind of faith." Cf. ILG, pp. 223-24.

— but what we shall become is a *vision* imprinted in the coming eschaton. Until then, we have to endure the alternating tension of *God's nearness and distance* in our terrestrial realm. All that our faith reveals to our cognition now is that this is a *divine-human image* of Jesus Christ whose message is in His manifestation, ἀγάπη — the *divine love.*

4. Pavel Nikolaevich Evdokimov: *The Lovers Become Love*

4.1. Biography

P. N. Evdokimov (1901-1970) was born into a small aristocratic family of St. Petersburg in 1901. According to the tradition of his time, he followed his father's footsteps by enrolling in the School of Cadets. Pavel's father was a high-ranking military officer known for his deep humanity, who was killed by a soldier when Pavel was only six years old. His mother frequently sent her son for long vacations to monasteries for his spiritual growth but also to compensate for the military training. In 1917, he moved to Kiev (Ukraine) and began his theological studies. After only a semester into his studies, the revolutionary front moved towards Kiev, upon which Evdokimov aligned with the White Army and remained engaged in the military for almost two years. In 1920, he evacuated through Odessa to Istanbul, and in 1923 settled in Paris, where he enrolled at the Sorbonne University and obtained his license in philosophy. In Paris, he was a student of Berdiaev and Bulgakov, and he ultimately graduated from St. Serge Institute. Evdokimov also became the secretary of the ACER (Action Chrétienne pour les Étudiants Russes en France) while supporting himself through a variety of odd jobs. His first marriage was in 1927 to Natascia Brunel who passed away in 1945. He married a second time, in 1954, to the daughter of the Japanese ambassador, Tomako Sakai. His marriages (particularly the first, during which time he produced *Le Mariage, Sacrement de l'Amour* [1944]) served as a source of theological inspiration. Evdokimov would reflect on the sacrament of love and love's sacredness anew in his book *Le Sacrement de l'Amour* (1962).

The quiet, meditative life Evdokimov was so fond of ended during World War II when he actively participated in the French resistance. In this period (1942), while at the University of Aix-en-Provence, he obtained his first doctoral degree which was in philosophy for the thesis *Dostoïevski et le problème du mal.* In the two years following World War II, Evdokimov directed a home for war refugees; the experience contributed to his thoughts on charitable love in action. He began lecturing in 1953 on moral theology at St. Serge Institute. In 1959, at the occasion of the publication of his *L'Orthodoxie,* a doctoral degree in theology was conferred upon him, and less than ten years later, he was awarded the doctorate *honoris causa* at the University of Thessaloniki. In 1964, he was one of the observers at the Second Vatican Council, and, from 1967, his teaching engagement included *L'Institut d'études œcuméniques* in Bossey, Switzerland. Evdokimov died suddenly in 1970 in Menton, France. Through his own personal history, Evdokimov gradually obtained the conviction, especially as a lay theologian, that there was a deeper, spiritual meaning to Russian emigration, and that it created the opportunity for Orthodoxy to encounter the Christian Occident, which was a unique chance to be exploited.

Among his numerous publications are *La femme et le salut du monde* (1958); *L'Orthodoxie* (1959); *Gogol' et Dostoïevski ou la descente aux enfers* (1961); *Les âges de la vie spirituelle* (1964); *La prière de l'Église d'Orient* (1966); *La connaissance de Dieu selon la tradition orientale* (1968); *L'Esprit Saint dans la tradition orthodoxe* (1969); *L'Art de l'icône. Théologie de la beauté* (1970); and *Le Christ dans la pensée russe* (1970). The following ones were published posthumously: *La Sainteté dans la tradition de l'Église Orthodoxe* in *Contacts* 23 (1971): 101-77; *L'Amour fou de Dieu* (1973); *La nouveauté de l'Esprit. Études de spiritualité* (1977); and *Le buisson ardent* (1981), as well as numerous articles and co-edited volumes.[129]

4.2. Marriage as the Sacrament of Love[130] — *The Total Presence*

As a married lay theologian, Evdokimov develops and unfolds his theology of love, in general, and conjugal love, in particular, in this text. A number of

129. Further biographical material and bibliography can be found in O. Clément, "Paul Evdokimov, témoin de la beauté de Dieu," in *Contacts* 23, nos. 73-74 (Paris 1971); O. Clément, "La vita e le opere di Paul Evdokimov," in P. Evdokimov, *La santità nella tradizione della Chiesa ortodossa* (Fossano: Edizioni Esperienze, 1972); G. Celora, *Evdokimov, voce dell'ortodossia in Occidente* (Bologna: Edizioni Dehoniane, 1995), pp. 17-35; and A. Nivière, *Les membres du clergé, théologiens et responsables laïcs de l'église Orthodoxe dans l'émigration Russe en Europe occidentale et centrale 1920-1995* (Moscou-Paris: Russkii Put' — YMCA Press, 2007), pp. 189-90.

130. Since we had no access to the original French edition, we used the only available Italian edition: P. Evdokimov, *Il matrimonio, sacramento dell'amore* (Bose-Magnano: Qiqajon, 2008) (MSA). In its preface and introduction, titled "A Different Pavel Evdokimov," Basilio Petrà contradicts the general conviction that this book was simply a previous or pre-

these ideas reverberate in his other works, often under different aspects and contexts or further developed, as that of *erōs* and *agapē,* for instance, as we shall see later.

There are two epigraphs in this book, one from John Chrysostom (allegedly) and the other an ancient prayer for a wedding couple *(sposi):* "Matrimony is the sacrament of love," and "Oh God, who in the creation of humankind, by creating the woman from man willed with this very formation that there may be between them a unity of flesh and sweet love . . . you have formed the human being pure and without blemish, and in retinue willed that . . . one human being may be formed from the other through the mystery of love."[131]

---

liminary draft of the work published some eighteen years later, *Le Sacrement de l'Amour. Le mystère conjugal à la lumière de la tradition orthodoxe* (1962), "one of the bestsellers of the '60s.'" The author claims, and we think rightly so, that this was due to the scarce availability of the two texts, and also Evdokimov's introduction to the second book as a continuation of the first one from 1944 with a reelaboration according to the new "cultural and social transformations." A first close look already reveals, according to Petrà, major changes: "Di fatto, Evdokimov modifica con il libro del 1962 il linguaggio dell'opera precedente, lo rende più critico nei confronti dell'occidente cattolico che avrebbe una visione procreazionista e indissolutilista dell'amore coniugale; sostiene più decisamente il carattere specificamente ortodosso della visione del matrimonio come sacramento dell'amore, riconducendola in qualche modo a san Giovanni Crisostomo; abbandona alcuni temi tipicamente orientali — specie quello del matrimonio eterno come vero matrimonio — perché difficilmente compatibili con le sue stesse esperienze personali in ambito matrimoniale. In un certo senso Evdokimov scrive nel 1962 un libro intenzionalmente confessionale (ortodosso) mettendo in rilievo le differenze possibili tra ortodossia e cattolicesimo." The present book, *Matrimonio, sacramento dell'Amore,* has a different "character," possesses a "great strength of thought, with richness of intuition and broadness of reflection" (an aspect that would be missing from the 1962 version). To a greater or lesser degree, Evdokimov was inspired by western authors and theologians, such as Herbert Doms, Norbert Rocholl, and Dietrich von Hildebrand, who not only wrote on the topic but even developed the central idea that "matrimony is 'a symbol of union between the soul and God,'" yet even more the "idea of love as matter *(materia)* of the sacrament of marriage" is a concept and idea that Evdokimov "literally finds in Léon Bloy." In qualifying these authors of his inspiration, Evdokimov would be less generous in his second book (cf. MSA, pp. 12-13). One can find further useful and interesting insights in this short introduction. Cf. MSA, pp. 5-13.

131. "Il matrimonio è il sacramento dell'amore" and: "O Dio, che nella creazione del genere umano, traendo la donna dall'uomo, hai voluto, con questa stessa formazione, che ci fosse tra loro un'unità di carne e di dolce amore . . . tu hai formato l'uomo puro e senza macchia, e in seguito hai voluto che . . . un uomo fosse formato dall'altro per il mistero dell'amore." Cf. MSA, p. 15. At the first quotation, allegedly from John Chrysostom, and the initial ancient prayer, Petrà discovers and reveals that the first is virtually "untraceable" in the texts of Chrysostom and the second "is an ancient prayer yet not an oriental, does not

The initial chapter is a prelude to the relationship between the human being and God, in general, and its foundation in love. The experience and epistemology of this relationship is traced by theology and mysticism, which use "diverse languages." Although they do not contradict each other, "they position themselves on different levels." They provide two dimensions of cognition, an immanent and a transcendent one, the derivative of reasoning in the former, and the "greater immediateness" of the mystical experience in the latter.[132] With Meister Eckhart and Angelus Silesius, Evdokimov describes the existential connection, the coexistence of mystical experience between the human being and God,[133] and, with Bernard of Clairvaux, he quotes "the truth is that the measure of love is that of having no measure [being limitless]." Love is limitless and infinite, just as life in God is limitless, since both have their origin in God and, therefore, are primordial — from before the creation of the world. According to the Book of Revelation (13:8): the *Lamb of God* was slain before creation, "which means that the world and the very act of creation is founded on the slain love *(amore immolato)*." This is the first kenotic act of God's plan of salvation, interestingly revealed in the last Scripture, the "book of the future," which points back to God's primordial inner mystery. From this foundation, Evdokimov draws the metaphysical, spiritual consequences that the two efforts, "the two flames" of cognition reveal the original *Image* within us:[134]

---

belong to the orthodox tradition; it is a prayer belonging to the Latin tradition present in the *Sacramentario Fuldense*," made known in a book of Athanasius Wintersing from 1925. Knowing the first for sure, why did Evdokimov use it? Most probably because it provided him the right framing and interpretative key for his work and the concept he intended to develop. In fact, in his second book, Evdokimov would cite the prayer (the second quote) in an abridged and somewhat altered form: "O Dio, nella tua creazione, traendo la donna dall'uomo, tu hai voluto, con questo miracolo, che fra i due vi fosse l'unità coniugale e il mistero dell'amore." According to Petrà, Evdokimov leaves out the part that "connects procreation and the mystery of love" in this latter presentation. In due acknowledgment to Petrà's other contributions, with this last statement, we can agree only conditionally as the missing last two lines (from the second book), "tu hai format l'uomo puro e senza macchia, e in seguito hai voluto che . . . un uomo fosse formato dell'altro per il mistero dell'amore," could be validly interpreted as the formation of Eve from Adam; besides, "the mystery of love" comes into being first and initially between two souls and then *can* result in generating procreation, in consequence, creating a triangle of love, unless that triangle is understood between the human couple and God in the first place. Cf. MSA, pp. 9-11, 13.

132. Cf. MSA, p. 20.

133. "I know that God cannot live for an instant without me." (Angelus Silesius) MSA, p. 20.

134. Cf. MSA, pp. 20-21.

> All that is limited implies the unlimited, and the final term of the infinite Love: the human being calls God by this name, [a name] into which he infuses the force of his proper love.[135] The entire mystery of the human being is in the following force: when his love reaches the peak of purity, it extends up to the point at which the essence of the two flames mysteriously coincides: the humble wax and the fire that flares up in the entire universe. In such a way in its most profound reality we discern the effigy of the Eternal in the human being.[136]

On the other hand, if God is love (1 John 4:8) and God is light, and in Him there is no darkness at all (1 John 1:5) then in the evolution *(divenire)* of human nature, and nature as creation, light and darkness coexist in duality until darkness is overcome by letting the "light of the spirit illuminate [it] entirely." For the Spirit searches all things (1 Cor. 2:10), and all these *things* primarily serve the purpose of their being and are also destined to reach their own full "revelation in God."[137] On the anthropological level, the "contact with the eternal" occurs by stripping and depriving one's *self,* which then "overcomes the sterile, adversarial nature *(conflittualità)*" of the world and reestablishes "a profound harmony."[138] An act that Evdokimov puts into an incarnational perspective, "where the unity (which in reality is all-unity *(l'omni-unità)*) is being realized in the human flesh, abolishing the distance between the spiritual and corporeal." At this point, he allows a sonorous, anthropological current to carry his thoughts to the quality of the human-divine and human-human, in particular the matrimonial and creational level:[139]

135. "Tutto quello che è finito implica l'infinito e il termine ultimo dell'infinito è l'Amore: l'uomo chiama Dio con questo nome, nel quale immette la forza del suo stesso amore." MSA, p. 21.

136. MSA, p. 21.

137. Cf. MSA, p. 29.

138. In the chapter on the "Integral Humanity of Christianity," Evdokimov speaks of the "new structure of the spirit," based on New Testament references of the kingdom of heaven (Matt. 18:3; John 3:3; Mark 4:26-27), inducing a "new formula of communion with nature," above all an interior and interiorized relationship with nature. The *apparent* "ontologic dualism of the spirit and nature" truly is nothing but a "*moral* dualism," be it of sin or sanctity, of the old or new main concept (i.e., turned into himself or opened up to God); it is a moral dualism that impacts even the realm of the material. Thus, to become free *from* the world "becomes a freedom *for* the world itself in view of its salvation." Cf. MSA, pp. 39-40, 41.

139. Evdokimov reverts to Plato's affirmation that all beauty is "a figure of the absolute Beauty"; consequently, each love "in its principle" is but love of perfection in its total manifestation, the "total Presence," and thus "finds its completion in God." The same way all

> The love for God is humanized *(si umanizza),* [it] loses its rigidness [and] almost hostility towards all who are not God, becoming truly divine-human. The love for God becomes at the same time love for the human being and the world, the divine creation, and vice versa[;] the love for the human being is at the same time love for its Creator. . . . "All is grace": [this] is the last word of truth because God has bowed down to the human being and has carried him with Himself into the abysses of the Trinity.
>
> The more the reciprocal and conjugal love between human beings is deepened, the higher is the tendency for the love *in* God and the love *for* God to coincide, because this love can flourish only if it rises to the level of God's heart, its point of arrival.[140]

Love's token of eternity is in its *internalization,* when reaching and re-connecting to its true and proper *essence* and *life,* and thus is sustained by it (cf. John 18:36; 8:23; 15:19; 17:14, 16). This should free us once and for all from false ideals of a paradise outside of God (John 18:26). All material will be transformed in(to) God in due time; as for the present moment, it is in the process of transformation. For now, the challenge is not "to be or have" but to make that existing matter "operational, to move from symbols and signs to the incarnate reality [that is] in the existence." The same applies to our human reality — not to have the spirit and life but *to become* spirit and life, a "pneumatophoro," a bearer of the Spirit. "And this is how the *ars amandi,* 'the art of love' reaches its goal: to leave space for the being *(lasciare spazio all'essere).* The lovers become love, nothing other than love, and it is [only] then that from the very heart of being the invocation of the Lord's name will gush forth: 'The Spirit and the Bride say, "Come!"' (Rev. 22:17). And soon the answer will resound: 'Surely, I am coming soon!'" (Rev. 22:20).[141]

4.3. *Theosis and Kenosis*

Evdokimov presents *kenosis* as a complement of and, at the same time, in juxtaposition to *theosis.*[142] He defines the latter as a "spiritual quality" that

---

yearning and searching for what is "humanly good and right" is nothing but "an intuition of the living God in the human being." Cf. MSA, p. 44.

140. MSA, p. 44. Evdokimov mentions an invocation from Carmelite spirituality: "Lord, give that we love each other as we love you!" Cf. MSA, p. 45, n. 4.

141. Cf. MSA, pp. 45-46.

142. For *kenosis* as "*alienation* of God Himself" and the involvement of the Trinity in

transforms the "empirical reality" to such an extent that it accommodates the Absolute "and becomes a place of its Presence."[143] This transformation eventually results in the "real absolutization of the world." *Kenosis,* on the contrary, is an act in which "the relativization of the Absolute" takes place, obviously in the human being since he is the "perfect creation" and a microcosm that "contains the entire universe in himself, *Adam qadmon.*"[144] Evdokimov further defines the roles and interaction between *theosis* and *kenosis* as "a reciprocal relationship, [a] mutual exchange of the properties of the two natures in Jesus Christ, founded on *kenosis,* the stripping of the divine nature" (cf. Phil. 2:7).[145] The material world, the creation, is destined to be divinized. That is why matter has been introduced into the "sacred cycles" of the liturgy; it will be set free from its bondage to decay "and obtain

---

the "historic economy of salvation," see P. Evdokimov, *L'Esprit Saint dans la Tradition Orthodoxe* (Paris: Cerf, 1969), p. 14 (STO).

143. On the "Eternal Presence" or "Eternal Present," see MSA, pp. 181-87.

144. *"Adam qadmon* is a Hebrew expression meaning *primordial human being.*" Cf. MSA, p. 59, n. 8. On the *kenosis of love* and the tradition around it connected to nuptial life and love, see P. Evdokimov, *Le Sacrement de l'Amour: Le mystère conjugal à la lumière de la tradition orthodoxe* (Paris: L'ÉPI, 1962), pp. 54-55 (SDA).

145. Cf. MSA, note 7. This note does not sound entirely conclusive: Does it relate solely to *kenosis* or to both *theosis* and *kenosis?* Especially, whether it is describing the *divinization* of Christ's own humanity or that of fallen humankind's, which is being redeemed *through* Christ's humanity and *kenotic* self-sacrifice? Since Christ possessed the *perfect,* i.e., uncorrupted human nature, being *the Second* or *new Adam,* only the second option, that is, the redeeming of *fallen* human nature through Christ's *theosis* and *kenosis,* seems acceptable. This confusion may have been caused by the translation that, due to the unfortunate lack of the French original, we were unable to verify. The terminal part of the chapter seems to support our impression that it is about the transformation of the "entire world" (ergo, including humankind and its fallen nature) that is "contained by virtue *(contiene in potenza)* in the human nature of Jesus Christ." The *theosis* requires the "free cooperation" of the human being. "The absolute humanity preexisting in God, the God-humanity *(Dioumanità),* (the) Christ is perceived incarnated on the creational level. The nature in its condition of *theosis,* the divinized world, becomes like the divine world, a sort of extension of the divine nature. . . . God embraces the all-unity *(l'onni-unità)* of the two worlds with his paternal love and reveals himself in the Son and through him in eternity." Cf. MSA, p. 60. "Life on earth contains more pains than joys; Charles Péguy observes with acuteness that at the age of forty a man knows that he is not happy. Perfect love is always connected to sacrifice and always mixed with pain. The sacrifice attests the profoundness of love, based on which, in some manner, the human being is being proved. That is why Leonardo da Vinci used to say that the greater a person was, the deeper his love was." Here, Evdokimov repeatedly quotes Bukharev, especially out of his matrimonial experience, and provides further valuable insights on the notion of the "holy suffering." Cf. MSA, pp. 199-202.

the freedom of the glory of the children of God (Rom. 8:21), in and through the human being." Thanks to the Church, in particular the sacraments, the Holy Spirit acts on the entire creation, as seen in the event of Pentecost. Evdokimov describes this context as the *kenosis* of the Holy Spirit. Although frequently invisible, "this Presence" and its actions are unveiled in the sight of a spiritual person, reentering particularly the realm of mysticism.[146]

This lengthy introduction reveals the content to which our author aims, namely the comprehension of the importance "and meaning of the corporeal world projected by God at the moment of creation," as well as the responsibility the human being bears for it. This cognition of responsibility and co-destination is veiled by sin and its consequences, yet both are counterbalanced by the Church and its sacraments, which make true knowledge and grace accessible again.[147] Recall the *essence* of our common origin — anyone who does not love does not know God, because God is love (1 John 4:8) — especially expressed in words like these of St. John, "render the essential[s] of the Christian revelation on God: Love is something more than an attribute of God, love is God Himself. This is the reason that God is a Trinity and can only be a Trinity by virtue of His plenitude, from the very moment that He is Love — three Persons in one sole nature, in one sole life, in one total unity. Love cannot be solitary and is the foundation of any philosophy on the Absolute. . . . A God of one sole Person would be no Absolute, would not be Love."[148] The idea of connecting the *absoluteness* of God to the condition, and substance, of *Love* renders an old-new beauty to this mystical thought and metaphysical truth, as already seen in Florenskii. Our human conscience is but a reflection of this unity and fullness, and it helps us to perceive that the *I* and *you* are connected *by* and *in* the *third* communal *matter,* and that is *us.* Precisely, this is the *value of matrimony.*[149]

146. Cf. MSA, pp. 66-67.

147. Cf. MSA, pp. 67-69. Similarly, only love "as the sole organ of cognition" is capable of unveiling the true nature hidden under the "common flesh." Cf. MSA, p. 166.

148. "The authentic love sinks its roots into the very source of all unity: love [of any two persons] is occurring in the third; and it is God who is the third term or agent *(il terzo termine)* of all that is on the heart of the human being, the third end indispensable in order to connect the verb to the subject and to grant life to both." Evdokimov unfolds the idea of the necessarily communal character of love on the following pages in other examples with the skills of a refined thinker. Cf. MSA, pp. 72-76. By identifying love as the essence of God and not merely his attribute in this point, Evdokimov is clearly not following apophatic theology as Florovskii or Losskii did, but rather stands in line with Florenskii, Bulgakov, Berdiaev, or Frank.

149. Cf. MSA, pp. 70-72, 159.

4.4. The Holy Spirit

Even though the "modern human being" has lost its sense for "sacred trembling," as it is known in the Bible and to primitive Christians, it is the Spirit "who fills the universe" (Wisd. 1:7) and revives all that lives and comes to our aid. The Spirit itself remains veiled in an inaccessible mystery: "The world seems to ignore the personal incarnation, yet He is the divine Love, and is our love, the breath of those who love each other: He is the one *in interior (all'interno),* when we say that the Father is (with)in *(all'interno)* the Son; He is that *in(terior),* when we are *in* God, when we live our *ours* as an I *in* you. And for Paul, when we pronounce the words of the 'Our Father,' full of tenderness, it is always the Spirit that pronounces [them] in us and with us (cf. Rom. 8:14-16)."[150] Evdokimov is intent on conveying with conviction in his ecclesiology the Church's *essential* life-giving task, for we discover on the very same page: "The Church is the raison d'être of the world and of our personal appearing in this transitory world. It is in the Church that the flower opens up, the human being is born, lives, loves, and dies. In the final analysis, each life is nothing but life in the Holy Spirit, in it breathes the power of eternal youthfulness." The day and key event of the unity with and in Jesus Christ is *Pentecost,* the "event of Christ-Spirit unity" in which the return of Christ into the world takes place, and "this is the unity that grants access to the Father" (John 14:20; 16:23, 25-27).[151]

4.5. From Transformation to Transfiguration

Given the significance of the task entrusted to the Church, the "matter *(la materia)* in the sacrament is not simply a visible sign . . . but possesses also

150. Cf. MSA, pp. 84-85. In his book on *Orthodoxy,* when treating the question of "the human being's ascension" to God, *theosis,* it is through the Holy Spirit, *the Spirit of Life,* that we experience *agapē:* As the creation came in a "descending movement" from the Father, through the Son in the Holy Spirit, so the "economy of salvation" happens in a reversed order (from the Holy Spirit, through the Son to the Father). "In this elevation the Holy Spirit without being either a 'passive inhalation' *(spiration passive),* or 'the exhalation of love' *(exhalaison d'amour),* the Spirit of Life reveals [Himself] whose *agapē* is the emanation itself." Cf. P. Evdokimov, *L'Orthodoxie* (Paris: Delachaux & Niestlé, 1959), p. 111. On the following pages, he addresses the "anti-contemplative tendency that contrasts Eros to Agape" that we shall address later.

151. Cf. MSA, 85-86. "La relation entre le Fils et l'Esprit n'est pas causale, mais c'est une relation d'interdépendance et de *condition* car toute relation intradivine est toujours *triple* dans la circumincession éternelle de l'Amour divin." This applies in particular to the theme of *condition* in the context of *Filioque.* Cf. STO, p. 48.

its proper cosmic purpose [or destination] *(fine cosmico)*." This imbedded *telos* is a condition to be fulfilled if it is to unfold fully for its purpose, which is the natural union in love: "In the sacrament of marriage the natural union between a man and a woman is the matter: more precisely it is the very essence of the human being, which is his love that can, already in itself, reach diverse spiritual levels, yet arrives at the perfect stature *(statura)* with(in) a sacramental foundation."[152]

The exceptional greatness and rank of the sacrament of matrimony is something Evdokimov sees in St. Paul's teaching, where he refers to Christ's relationship to the Church as a "mystery of the divine life" (Eph. 5:32): "The love of the married couple is nothing other than a reproduction in small — a miniature, one could say — of the love between Christ and the Church." Equally, the Church is the "symbol and place" of the Holy Spirit and its union with Christ, as seen above, in which Evdokimov sees the effigy of the completion "of the human being's constitution which comes about when the male and female principles are united" in the sacrament of marriage. Then *love* in the "eternal dynamism of communication between the Son and Spirit reveals the Father, and this places conjugal love directly at the heart of God and elucidates that not by chance is God the third matter, but rather by means of a divine-human law. Only at this level love reaches its authentic value." The story of Cana (cf. John 2:1-11) reflects the beauty and purity of this relationship typical of "the Spirit's breath." Jesus, by performing His "symbolic gesture" in the first miracle of transforming water into wine, reveals that "the essence of marriage is in transfiguration."[153] Thus, Evdokimov affirms that "matrimony in the economy of sacraments has a central position," as it reveals the "consubstantiality" of one's neighbor as, in reality, one's "complement." He reviews all the sacraments in this hermeneutical key, and the only one that precedes marriage is the Eucharist. In the moment of marriage, "Christ is *between* the two who are in love with each other," and

152. Cf. MSA, pp. 87-88.

153. Cf. MSA, pp. 88-90. The goal of transfiguration also applies to conjugal sexuality as something that through the "generosity and heroism of love tends towards chastity . . . the dark element of sexual division is overcome" not with its exclusion but rather "with its transfiguration of sexuality even in its physical dimension, through a spirit that itself has been transformed by the power of love." In this chapter on "Chastity," Evdokimov reflects briefly on the lack of "matrimonial theology" or "philosophy of love" as the early (especially desert) Church Fathers and doctors were virgins and normally had neither experience nor interest of conjugal love. Cf. MSA, 104-5. On the Solov'evian perspective on sexuality in his work see *The Meaning of Love.* Cf. MSA, pp. 111-13.

thus the sacrament of the Eucharist comes to its perfect completion. "In fact the marriage is an organic element of the ecclesial all-unity and it is in the conjugal unity that Christ incarnates. Matrimony is a living expression of Him because the quality of Christ's body and that of matrimony are identical: perfect love."

Evdokimov identifies a profound connection between the wedding at Cana and the sacrifice at Calvary that allows us to perceive how "the Eucharistic love can be of conjugal nature: [it is] the sacrifice that founds the communion of absolute unity."[154] This kenotic aspect is indeed indispensable in making such equations; Evdokimov's argumentation is systematic and faithfully maintains a spiritual approach founded on scriptural exegesis and patristic interpretation.

In the final analysis, the primordial image of *love* is to be found in the Trinity. "Three are the sacred sphere of internal relationships of love," a triangle of "absolute harmony" that cannot miss anything in relations and, therefore, can be complemented with nothing more (quoting St. Augustine's "amans, quod amatur, et amor"): "The Son expresses the absolute essence of the Father, and the Spirit actualizes *(attualizza)* this expression as a complete gift of Himself, and is the link of life, the very circulation of love between the Father and Son. The three are the expression of the internal fullness of communion of absolute being *(esistenza assoluta)*. The sacred triangle is the ontological graphic of the formulas: 'I am who I am' (Exod. 3:14) and 'God is Love'" (1 John 4:8, 16).[155]

154. Cf. MSA, pp. 91-92. Also, the Apostle Paul collocates the "union of human love into the sphere of divine life" with his exhortation in Ephesians 5:1-2: *Therefore be imitators of God, as beloved children. And walk in love, as Christ loved us.* Cf. MSA, p. 97. By citing the entire second phrase, Evdokimov could have underlined once more the *kenotic,* sacrificial character of this love to be imitated: *[Christ loved us] and gave Himself up for us, a fragrant offering and sacrifice to God.* Cf. MSA, p. 97.

155. Cf. MSA, p. 93. (A new approach and view of the sacrament of matrimony ["as a gift" and full oblivion of one's self for the other] in the Catholic Church sees Evdokimov in the encyclical *Casti connubii.* Cf. MSA, p. 108.) As to the intra-Trinitarian relationship of participation and one common source in the Trinity (still in the context of the *Filioque* dispute, nevertheless, very valid for our topic): "Mais ces relations ne sont point de *production* mais de corrélation entre Celui qui se révèle et Ceux qui le révèlent, l'acte trine de l'Amour réciproque des Trois. L'Esprit n'est pas réduit à l'instrumental de l'Amour entre le Père et le Fils, mais il est celui qui actualise l'amour où se complaisent les Trois. Cette participation réciproque et trine exclut toute unité dyadique dans la *nature* car l'affirmation la plus ferme des Pères orientaux pose l'innascibilité, la génération et la procession comme des actes strictement *hypostatiques.*" STO, p. 72. And if the Person of the Holy Spirit is not *the* love in person, then what is His role in sharing love? Here is Evdokimov's inspired and inspirational

4.6. *The Concepts of* Erōs

Somewhat atypically, yet while still maintaining his strict methodology, Evdokimov's attention turns to *erōs* only beginning at the middle of his book, but then frequently, and always in view of the concept of matrimony. With the ancient Greeks, as described by Dionysius the Pseudo-Areopagite, matrimony was perceived as *telos* — that is, the end or purpose of a life — "in the sense of crowning . . . since it crowns the person for life." In Plato's *Symposium, erōs* is defined as *epithymia tou holou,* "the desire and aspiration towards the interior, towards integrity" which results not in procreation as the primary purpose but rather as a "path towards the fullness of [the] superpersonal unity of two human beings," and in the grace of the sacrament "becomes that source of water of which Jesus said that '[was] welling up to eternal life.'"[156] Despite its initial aspiration for the divine heights of perfect union, after the fall, *erōs* and its deviating desires and *imaginations* are hard to tame. Evdokimov uses the struggles described in the letter to the Romans (7:15, 18-19). It is not an impossible undertaking, as proven in the case of

---

answer, once again returning to the concept of the *actualization* of love: "L'Esprit Saint n'est pas réduit à être le lien entre le Père et le Fils, leur *nexus amoris.* En effet, l'amour est inhérent à toutes les Personnes, l'amour est la vie même de la nature divine (S. Grégoire de Nysse)/. Par rapport à l'amour l'Esprit se définit comme le Donateur d'amour. L'Esprit vivifiant, son énergie même, actualise la vie d'amour, sa circulation éternelle au sein de la Trinité. Selon saint Grégoire Palamas, l'Esprit est la joie éternelle / où les Trois se complaisent ensemble, l'unitè d'amour est l'unité des Trois Uniques. L'Esprit est co-aimant avec le Père et co-aimé avec le Fils, il n'est pas l'Amour mais l'Esprit d'Amour qui inspire et fait de toute Personne divine le Don à l'autre, à l'image du Donateur." Cf. STO, p. 92.

156. Cf. MSA, pp. 110-11. Evdokimov compares the idea (and concepts) of the myth of Androgynos with the Bible, where Eros is being "mostly befriended with human beings, being their rescuer and doctor of those evils that if cured would bring humankind the greatest happiness," and comes to the conclusion that the "narration of Genesis contains exactly the same idea." In this matter, he also quotes Berdiaev who saw original sin linked to the "division of sexes, the fall of Androgynos." Further, the "sexual energy enclosed in the subconscious and unceasingly removed from the conscience provokes neuroses and traumas," to which he responds with the chapter on "Sublimation" of this energy by "putting it in the service of a spiritual force." Cf. MSA, pp. 120-21, 126-31. Also: "Eros, by its nature is an impetus towards the high, is the very thirst of what is greater, more elevated, is an impulse that does not stop until it reaches its destination. It is eros that conceives the sexual act a supreme symbol." Subsequently he quotes Léon Bloy in this regard and does a spiritual or spiritualized reading of the intimate conjugal union as "source of immaterial joy," the purpose of which is in the first place com-union, allegorically to the ecclesial communion in the Eucharist. Cf. MSA, p. 145. In St. Basil we find a further positive image of the human *Eros* that tends towards the divine *Eros.* Cf. P. Evdokimov, *La femme et le salut du monde* (Paris: Casterman, 1958), p. 60.

Dionysius the Pseudo-Areopagite and Maximus Confessor who have "assimilated the platonic doctrine of eros."[157] "Love transcends time, space, and the numeric factor; it communicates in the consubstantial and overpersonal all-unity and reestablishes thus the original image of God"; this statement applies fully to Christ (2 Cor. 5:17).[158] So what the primordial *erōs* has lost in the fall and (got) distorted is being restored in a *new erōs,* a pure and undisturbed love of the Trinity revealed and taught by Christ: "Love tends always to overcome itself. The divine love manifests itself to the external and creates the world in order to donate itself as an object of love, and those who love each other donate themselves as a haven *(focolare)* to those whom they generate, as to an external object of their plenitude." Evdokimov uses the story of Tobias in the book of Tobit (8:4-8) as an example of "authentic love's inspiration," which always contains the "element of chastity."[159] Having reached the point of chastity and asceticism, both in *erōs* in general and in a monastic tradition as full renunciation of matrimony, Evdokimov sees the essence of the latter way of life as "the wedding without mediation between God and the soul, where the human being raises to the glorious beauty of sacrifice and [the] gift of love. Thus, virginity signifies an integral belonging to Christ, with an undivided being *(essere indiviso).*" Equally in marriage, although there are two persons yet "in one being, they belong consubstantially and integrally to Christ. The difference is in the manner of uniting oneself with Christ, in the type of love and its structure: wedding of the soul . . . for the monk, and wedding through the conjugal hypostasis for the married couple."[160] Both ways are a vocation, a call in the diversity of graces and gifts, yet conversely "intimately united and mysteriously identical," two equally prophetic ways, that of Moses and Elias, on the same mountain of Transfiguration, Tabor, having Christ, God, *the third term,* in the midst of them.[161]

157. "The *Celestial Hierarchy* of Dionysius represents the system of universal elevation, and such ascension is inspired by the power of Eros. The Creator himself is the 'Good and divine Eros,' Christ is the 'crucified Eros,' and the eros present in the human being is the power, manifestation of God's image that attracts the human being and in him the entire universe towards that which is celestial. Therefore, eros is a thirst [for] the absolute, nostalgia of what is absolutely perfect, of the absolutely desirable." Cf. MSA, pp. 133-34.

158. Cf. MSA, p. 136.

159. Cf. MSA, pp. 148, 150-51.

160. We encountered a further quote from Bukharev. Cf. MSA, pp. 209-11, 212.

161. Cf. MSA, pp. 217-19. An interesting reflection that synthesizes monasticism and monastic values into universal Christian values and heritage (which, in fact, they truly are) can be found in Evdokimov's most popular book, *Les âges de la vie spirituelle* (1964). Evdokimov connects the vow and virtue of *chastity* to the "nuptial mystery" of *agapē* and an

4.7. The Sacrament of Love

This text appears to be a more structured work with shorter and frequently subdivided chapters. We shall not reexamine what has been stated previously in *Marriage, the Sacrament of Love* to avoid redundancy, except for the most appealing parts on *erōs* and *agapē.* In his foreword to the English edition of the *Sacrament of Love,* Olivier Clément claims that this is "but one panel" of the diptych that Evdokimov "dedicated to the spiritual gifts of men and women and to the sacramental 'mystery' of human love."[162]

Evdokimov also contradicts the presumption that the marital bond and conjugal love serve merely the purpose of procreation as well as any historic "constraint of repetitions" that so often committed the same misinterpretations and "has subordinated women to men, the pair to the necessity of the species and love to the service of procreation," since God had made humankind male and female who are destined for each other.[163] Modern science and psychology speak in favor of a new approach that theology needs to follow (which would explain the "second panel" of the diptych *Woman and the Salvation of the World*), especially when relying upon patristic theology, an "era very rich in ascetical treatises." As already mentioned, the lack of experience, time, or interest "for a philosophy of love" resulted in skirting "the transphysiological mystery of the sexes," potentially endangering the development in modern moral theology, or what it meant to be.[164] Evdokimov

---

insightful Old Testament analysis of the three vows under the evocative title *The Three Temptations, the Lord's Three Answers, and the Three Monastic Vows:* "The three monastic vows constitute a great charter of human liberty. *Poverty* frees from the ascendancy of the material. It is the baptismal transmutation into the new creature. *Chastity* frees from the ascendancy of the carnal. It is the nuptial mystery of *agapē,* the marriage covenant in divine love. *Obedience* frees from the idolatry of the ego. It posits our relationship as children of the Father. All, whether monks or not, must ask God for these things in the tripartite structure of the Lord's Prayer: *obedience* to the will of the Father, the *poverty* of someone who is hungry only for the substantial and Eucharistic bread, and *chastity,* the purification from evil." Cf. P. Evdokimov, *Ages of the Spiritual Life* (Crestwood, NY: St. Vladimir's Seminary Press, 1998), p. 139.

162. Cf. O. Clément, "Foreword," in P. Evdokimov, *The Sacrament of Love* (Crestwood, NY: St. Vladimir's Seminary Press, 2001), p. 7. The foreword provides also numerous excellent insights into the work of Evdokimov. Cf. pp. 7-13.

163. P. Evdokimov, *Le Sacrement de l'Amour: Le mystère conjugal à la lumière de la tradition orthodoxe* (Paris: L'ÉPI, 1962), pp. 15-16 (SDA).

164. The following may sound sarcastic and disrespectful, but we think Evdokimov is simply straightforward and acknowledging merits as a connoisseur of patristic theology and hagiography. We shall also bear in mind that Evdokimov was a renowned professor of moral

makes a point by paraphrasing St. Augustine's statement "He who is not spiritual in his flesh becomes carnal even in his spirit," with his "The one who is not spiritual in his sex becomes sexual even in his spirit." Half solutions result in "monstrous disorders of a mystic eroticism or of the spirit become flesh."[165] Apparently, these are unrefined words; nevertheless, it is an accurate pinpointing of spiritual discernment, precisely in the realm of sexuality: as a part of the human being, of his or her love, yet a part to be transfigured in *kenosis* and *theosis*. Therefore, sexuality, as with any other realm of human existence, awaits redemption — and less demonizing it, as in the past, or worshiping it, as in the present. In the course of reading the book, one perceives a general shift from Evdokimov's neutral tone in his *Marriage, the Sacrament of Love* towards a more critical one. This stands especially for western scholastic theology and scriptural interpretation in questions of gender and sexuality that he considers far too reliant on philosophical concepts that we will briefly review.[166]

4.8. Erōs *and* Agapē — *Two Complementary Notions of Love*

Evdokimov reasons that the "current Christian doctrine of marriage has been built on a finalistic philosophy" influenced by ancient philosophies[167] that "denied the existence of woman as a person," a tendency that had an impact on the interpretation of love and the sacrament of matrimony, similar to Ar-

---

theology with a respectable ecumenical lecturing curriculum: "The magnificent heroism of the ascetics unleashed a decisive battle within the human being himself and exorcised the demonic powers from him, but at a price that verges on the dehumanization of relationships between man and woman. It appears that certain theologians' opinions on married love are taken from zoology manuals; the couple is seen from the viewpoint of reproduction and child-raising. One also finds entire systems that connect 'ordination' to 'subordination' and 'superordination' to determine whether man is the chief or the head. The question of love in itself and of its meaning still remains open today and reveals a deep malaise: Scholasticism favors procreation, but castrates love." Cf. SDA, pp. 19-21.

165. Cf. SDA, pp. 22-23.

166. For instance, see SDA, pp. 25-26, 27-34, 56, etc. Evdokimov points out other monastic approaches in the West: "Yet, the doctrine of the Scholastics is not the only one and can in no way pretend to be the Tradition. It is appropriate to recall the words of St. Benedict in his Rule: 'There are ways which to men seem right, but the ends thereof lead to the depths of hell'" (Prov. 16:25). Cf. SDA, p. 52.

167. He concretely cites "Hindu Buddhism, Persian dualism, Manichaeism, and Gnosticism" — all of which denied the personhood of a woman. Cf. SDA, pp. 26-28.

istotle, St. Augustine, and St. Thomas, but also in later western philosophical currents.[168] Evdokimov respects the call to celibacy since it "is scriptural" as a lifestyle, yet it is a strictly personal choice and cannot be imposed. He perceives a "great distrust" in the western churches toward "all theories of sublimation," out of fear of "hidden harmonics between the mystical and the sexual." Thus, the two kinds of manifestations of love are not equally valued, accepted, and lived out: "Every mystical ascension — Eros — is taken to signal a violation of the frontier between the Creator and the creature. There is only Agape, the descending path of God toward man, that abolishes Eros and its sublimation and restricts purity, which is circumscribed within strictly moral borders." The only true solution does not depend on celibacy or asceticism but acknowledges in each believer "a member of the royal priesthood [who is] called to the consecration in the form of a nuptial ministry" using the cure against "depravity and concupiscence," which lies, according to St. John Chrysostom, in *"magnus amor."* The realms of monastic asceticism and of the conjugal state use two different languages: "It seems that we are in the presence of two worlds that no longer understand each other."[169]

4.8.1. The Novelties of Nuptial Priesthood and Lay Monasticism

The divine call and the sacramental concept of the royal priesthood of each believer eventually allows Evdokimov to come up with the original solution of *Nuptial Priesthood:* "A completely new spirituality is asserting itself today, one that is searching for neither more nor less than a priestly vocation in conjugal love: *The Nuptial Priesthood.*"[170] Thus also monastic asceticism and

168. Such as Schopenhauer, Nietzsche, and Kant. SDA, pp. 26-28.

169. Cf. SDA, pp. 33-34. A fitting quote at this point, and in general an observation regarding the problem of the alienation of the "two worlds" is rooted in the following: "The human being has desecrated love, even before discovering its nature. Nowhere else are there so many lies and such hypocrisy, precisely because love is the deepest thirst for the truth, the very voice of a being. The mass, the crowd, swarms more and more in the erotic pit, the rounds of which made so quickly, end in 'nausea.' St. John Chrysostom raises a violent protest: 'The gift of God, the root of our generation is insulted. This then let us cleanse away with our discourse. I am desirous of having 'marriage purified, so as to bring it back again to its proper nobleness, so as to stop the mouth of the heretics.'" Let us be reminded that it was St. John Chrysostom who called marriage "the sacrament of love." SDA, pp. 38, 39.

170. We cannot omit this beautiful reflection that follows: "It is only by rising above the philosophy of the 'common good' that one can grasp the singular worth of those who love each other. It is this hidden and intimate element that is consecrated in the sacrament, it is love that constitutes its matter and receives the gift of the Holy Spirit, the nuptial Pente-

all its values belong to and are a task of all the faithful Christ seekers. In his *The Life in Christ*, Evdokimov cites Nicholas Cabasilas, a fourteenth-century layman and "great liturgist" who has the merit of "universalizing and popularizing *(socialiser)* the monastic method (so that everyone could discover its equivalent)." In his approach, Cabasilas shows the "heart of the mystical experience for all, the secret of living in God that the Church offers to everyone."[171] The final matter lies in the *great encounter* between God and the searching soul, the reflections of exceptional *kenotic* beauty (based on Rev. 3:20), and the encounter of the two notions of love, *Agapē* and *Erōs*, complementing each other, as they also do in the monastic and worldly life:

> According to the great mystics, a Christian is a miserable person, a beggar of grace, who discovers the One who is still more miserable, more of a beggar, God Himself, begging for love at the door of man's heart. A Christian, then, is someone who listens and opens the door; from the meal of shared poverty the banquet of the Kingdom springs forth.
>
> The soul only reaches full maturity by ceaselessly transcending itself toward the Other, when it no longer belongs to itself. Humility-obedience creates in us the configuration of Christ crucified: it is the radical laying aside of each appropriation of grace and the Spirit. The anti-contemplative tendency contrasts Eros to Agape[172] and confuses inwardness with being self-centered. For Gregory of Nyssa, however, Eros flowers into Agape and into love of [one's] neighbor: Eros is "the intensity of Agape. . . . God is the Father of Agape and Eros." The two are complementary: Eros, moved by the Spirit, goes out to meet divine Agape. This allows Maximus the Confessor to institute the equivalent of the monastic life for laypeople living in the world — for the monks contemplation, for the active laity the unceasing feeling of an unseen close-

---

cost. Society knows but the surface. Between the two lovers there is only God who is the third term; this is why the meaning of marriage is taken precisely in this dual and direct relation to God." And he repeats the *telos* concept of the ancient Greeks and that of Plato's *Erōs* as "longing for completion," as well as Solov'ev's *The Meaning of Love*, who "reconnects love not to the species, but to the person. Procreation fragments the person, love makes him whole." Cf. SDA, pp. 52-53.

171. Evdokimov is inspired here especially by St. Cyril of Jerusalem who affirms that "monastic life is a sacred thing," but also that "asceticism is not a system of merely moral rules, but a system of exercises implying spiritual gifts that [are] offered to every Christian life." Cf. SDA, pp. 110-11.

172. Referring to A. Nygren's *Eros and Agape*.

ness. Moreover, to the question about action or contemplation, St. Seraphim of Sarov replies: "Acquire inner peace, and a multitude of human beings will find their salvation near you."[173]

In the following chapter titled the *Universal Interiorized Monasticism,* Evdokimov reviews and puts into a new perspective the "undying values of monasticism . . . as principles for every Christian life," and reads it in the context of *New Holiness.*[174]

In his Mariology, Evdokimov considers the sacrifice of Eucharist in which the transforming power at the altar is God's *Agapē,* so the same power of love uses humankind's "offering — the Virgin" that God transforms into His vessel:

> The human being brings his offering, bread and wine, to the temple; and God, in the royal gesture of his *Agapē* (Love), changes them into His Body and Blood, food for gods. Humanity brings the thrice-pure offering, the Virgin, and God makes of her His mother, the Mother of the Living One, and thereby *Mother of all the living.* At its peak, holiness becomes *gratia plena,* grace-filled (cf. Luke 1:28). The human vessel proves itself worthy of the Uncontainable who takes His substance from this vessel. Mary is not a woman among women, but the *advent of woman,* the New Eve, restored in her motherly virginity.

Here, too, Evdokimov is inspired by N. Cabasilas and Byzantine worship.[175]

4.8.2. Job's Dilemma Applied Monastically

On the note of mysticism, this time in the context of the story of Job and his "friends," Evdokimov (like Afanas'ev) describes the mystical experience of

173. Cf. SDA, pp. 111-13.

174. Cf. SDA, pp. 113-14, 126-30. "The desert, 'the place of demons,' is located nowadays in the heart of those who 'live in the world without hope and without God' (Eph. 2:12). The monks no longer have to leave the world; every believer can find his vocation under the completely new form of *interiorized monasticism.*" Cf. SDA, p. 130. In a chapter titled "The Harmonics of Love," Evdokimov reviews the role and concepts of *Erōs* in modern art and fiction, and also examines the Orthodox nuptial liturgy under diverse aspects. Cf. SDA, 145-53. One final note on ascetic rigors: "Ascetic rigorism that is hostile to the senses tends to treat flesh, Eros, and sin as being identical. But the Church of the Councils has never espoused this mentality." Cf. SDA, pp. 217, 218-19.

175. Cf. Evdokimov, *La femme et le salut du monde,* p. 190.

some great mystics as "always paradoxical, even disquieting, to any system," as it can surpass or ignore existing systems or "terms of reason"; in fact, "it is entirely unreasonable." In this, Evdokimov sees the one-sidedness of considering only *Agapē* as communication of God's love, instead of *Erōs-Agapē,* as ignored in Job's case where there was a true dialogue, i.e., *love* on both sides, as it requires freedom and cooperation from the human being, too:

> Any attempt to reduce the Gospel to "Love" *(agape),* to the single movement proceeding from God without returning to God, suppresses the dialectic of question and answer, suppresses the Job case, and distorts Christology. The Church Fathers were not afraid of speaking of the paradox of a certain *powerlessness* of God, of His voluntary limitation. The Golden Rule of patristic thought never ceases to repeat that while God was able to create man without man, He cannot save man without man — without the human being's free response. Yahweh is able to make the poor creature — the dust of his own invention — tremble, but even Almighty God "cannot compel anyone to love Him." God was, so to speak, out on a limb; this is the "risk" of the "adventure" of God in pronouncing the creative "let it be." For every mind that is free of theological prejudice, the act of loving God means going to God out of the love that the human being has for his God. For Dionysius the Areopagite and St. Maximus the Confessor, Christ is *Eros crucified;* this is the sacred circle of the biblical wedding-hymn, and the relationships are mutual. Theodoret of Cyrrhus emphasizes this: "In consuming the Eucharist we enter into conjugal communion."[176]

4.9. L'Amour Fou de Dieu[177] *and the Mystery of His Silence*

In order to conclude Evdokimov's ideas, but by far not exhausting the love-related topics, we need to revert to an article that appeared in an anthology posthumously in 1973, rendered (if translated literally) as *The Crazy* or *Foolish Love of God.* Once more, he is inspired by N. Cabasilas's *manikos erōs,* the "foolish, absurd love of God for us and his incomprehensible respect for our freedom." The extremes and extremeness of God's love, His unceasing and all-giving *kenotic love* in respect of our freedom (having reviewed previously

176. Cf. SDA, pp. 201-3.
177. *God's Absurd Love.*

all the inexplicable and unjustifiable injustices and crimes committed in God's creation by humankind), can be responded to only with *faith:* "Faith is the response to God's kenotic, that is, self-emptying attitude (Phil. 2:7). . . . It is because we are able to say *no* that our *yes* takes on full resonance and enters the same key as God's yes. And this is why God also accepts being refused, misunderstood, rejected, even expelled from His own creation. On the cross, God takes our side, against God; according to Péguy, 'God has been one of us.'"[178] Here, Evdokimov offers a new hermeneutical key of the epistle to the Philippians (2:6-11), namely of God's "veritable alienation of Himself," where his omnipotence becomes powerlessness; He empties Himself and becomes the other; in His "absurd love God does not simply destroy evil and death but takes them upon Himself."[179] All human reason and understanding fail to comprehend how far God's love reaches, even beyond the horizons of our existence. Evdokimov urges with urgency and corrects the image of God imprinted into and enslaving our imagination, when we lost the perception of the "freedom to love God":

> The freedom to refuse God is His wish for us, without limits. The suspended power of human choice renders our destiny conditional. And it is hell, therefore, to speak of divine love, the heavenly dimension of hell, the divine vision of humanity immersed in the night of solitude.
>
> It is of the greatest urgency to correct the "terrorist" and "penitentiary" ideas of God. It is no longer possible to believe in a heartless God incapable of suffering. The only message that could reach atheism today is that of Christ descending into hell. As deep as the hell in which we find ourselves, it is even more profound to find Christ already there waiting for us. God does not ask of us virtue, moralism, [or] blind obedience but a cry of assurance and of love from the depth of our hell. We ought never to fall into despair. We can only fall into God and it is God who never despairs. St. Anthony the Great said that hell surely exists, but only for himself, which is to say that hell is never "for the others," that it is never the object of our discourse.[180]

God *as* Love in all dimensions:

178. Cf. P. Evdokimov, *L'Amour fou de Dieu* (Paris: Éditions du Seuil, 1973), pp. 30-31.
179. Cf. *L'Amour fou de Dieu,* p. 35.
180. Cf. *L'Amour fou de Dieu,* pp. 33-34.

> Here is another, even stronger statement of this God's abasement: "Divine compassion is God's turning from Himself." You could say it is God's weakness. A saint said to a child, "Look here, if you were able to play with the Lord, it would be the greatest thing anyone could ever do. All the world takes Him so seriously that it has become horribly boring. . . . Play with God, my child. He is the best playmate."[181]

Once again: What did Jesus say about becoming like children?

Conclusion

Love is a means and act of encounter with God and with each other. By becoming *life* and *spirit,* uniting the material and spiritual domain through *kenosis* and *theosis,* we allow our transformation and transfiguration into the divine. Divinization is a process that makes us bearers of the Spirit *pneumatophoros,* and we are transfigured from loving persons into lovers, therefore, into the essence of God: Love. All of Evdokimov's following qualities — his systematic erudition, a creative theological methodology based in metaphysics, a solid knowledge of philosophical problems, his varied personal life experiences, monastic sojourns and two marriages, along with a deeply Christ- and Trinity-oriented spirituality — give Evdokimov two kinds of cognition, that of theology and (if not mystical, certainly "at least") visionary insight. He shows the courage of a prophet to speak up and draft daringly new prospects of *nuptial ministry,* monasticism in *the desert of the heart,* the unique and complementary interaction of *theosis* and *kenosis,* and, above all, a *Nuptial Priesthood.* Touched by the idea of *magnus amor* of St. John Chrysostom, his spiritual compass aims at the very mystery of the Trinity, that incomprehensible but shared *agapē* which precedes us even into hell in order to catch us in our deepest existential fall and to mercifully carry us to the abyss, the heart of the Trinity. Such radical, *foolish love* God lavishes upon us and invites us to experience with Him in our loving of one another. Lovers become Love.

181. Cf. *L'Amour fou de Dieu,* p. 36.

5. Aleksandr Dmitrievich Schmemann: *To See the World as God Sees It*

5.1. Biography

A. D. Schmemann (1921-1983) was born into a noble family in Revel, Estonia, and belonged to the Russian wave of emigrants forced to leave their homeland. He was quite young when his family fled in 1929 through Yugoslavia to France, where he finished his secondary school education. At the St. Serge Institute, he graduated from the historic-philosophical faculty in 1945 where he afterwards lectured in church history until 1951, edited the eparchial journal *Tserkovnyi vestnik (Church Messenger)*, and was actively involved in the society of St. Alban. In 1946, he was ordained a deacon and priest serving subsequently in diverse fraternities and parishes, as well as leading the religious broadcasting for Russia on radio "Freedom." He concluded his stay in Europe and moved to the United States in 1951, when he assumed teaching at the chair of church history and liturgy at St. Vladimir's Theological Seminary in Crestwood, New York. In 1959, he defended his doctoral thesis titled *Vvedenie v liturgicheskoe bogoslovie (Introduction to Liturgical Theology* [1961]) at St. Serge Institute and continued teaching at St. Vladimir's while functioning as a dean until 1983. Fr. Schmemann's teaching career also included positions at the Universities of Columbia and New York. He played an important role in the life of the Russian Orthodox Church in the United States, obtained honorary doctorates from the Greek Theological Institute of the Holy Cross in Brookline, Massachusetts, the New York Orthodox Seminary, and Lafayette College in Houston. He died in New York in 1983. His writing focused on church history and liturgy as well as pastoral and spiritual topics. His concept of Orthodoxy was that of a return to the theology of the Fathers while searching for a new interpretational key for their teaching.

Among his numerous publications are: *Istoricheskii put' Pravoslaviia (The Historic Path of Orthodoxy* [1954]); *For the Life of the World* (1964); *Tainstvo i Pravoslavie* (*The Sacrament and Orthodoxy* [1965]); *Ultimate Questions* (1965); *The World as Sacrament* (1965); and *Great Lent* (1969). The following works appeared posthumously: *Evkharistiia: Tainstvo Tsarstva* (*Eucharist: The Sacrament of the Kingdom* [1984]); *Vodoiu i Dukhom* (*By Water and Spirit* [1986]); *Voskresnye besedy* (*Sunday Talks* [1989]); *The Journals of Father Alexander Schmemann* (2000); *Dnevniki 1973-1983* (*Diaries 1973-1983* [2005]); *Liturgiia i Predanie* (*Liturgy and Tradition* [2005]); and more.[182]

182. Apparently, there is still no proper monograph of A. Schmemann. Biographical

5.2. The Historical Road of Eastern Orthodoxy[183]

In his foreword, Schmemann makes plain that his intention is not to create a history or even a scientific book of the Orthodox Church. He denies the completeness of this study but states that its purpose is to demonstrate the "historic truth" of the Church, a *search* with all those who *search* (to understand) the Church.[184] For him, the book of the Acts is "the cornerstone of Church history" and the core message of Christianity, especially to all those "who have lost their true life." Through faith in Christ, humankind receives new hope and a possibility to "know the one true God and His love for the world; in union with Him they may inherit the new, eternal life for which they were created." The model and example to follow remains Christ in his Divine-human being and act of "complete self-surrendering . . . perfect love and absolute humility." It is by the action of self-surrender that "love has triumphed over hate and life has conquered death." Thus, from the very beginning, the kenotic aspect of Christ's salvific action is presented as the model of life, a love that reestablished through and in Himself the relationship between heaven and earth: "In one Man the kingdom of God — of love, goodness, and eternal life — has penetrated the realm of sin and death."[185]

---

material can be found in J. Schmemann, *My Journey with Father Alexander* (Montreal: Alexander Press, 2007). A Russian translation appeared in 2008 under the title: *Moia zhizn' s ottsom Aleksandrom* (Moskva: Sofiiskaia naberezhnaia, 2008); I. Meiendorf, "Zhizn' s izbytkom," in *A. Shmeman, Dnevniki 1973-83* (Moskva: Russkii put', 2005); A. Kyrlezhev, "Radikal'nyi traditsionalizm o. Aleksandra Shmemana," in *Kontinent* 79 (1994); P. Scorer, "Protopresbyter Alexander Schmemann," in *St. Vladimir's Theological Quarterly* 28 (1984); A. Nivièr, *Les membres du clergé théologiens et responsables laïcs de l'église Orthodoxe dans l'émigration russe en Europe occidentale et central 1920-1995* (Moscou-Paris: Russkii Put' — YMCA-Press, 2007), pp. 551-52; J. Meyendorff, "A Life Worth Living," in *St. Vladimir's Theological Quarterly* 28 (1984): 3-10.

183. According to the introduction of Schmemann to the English edition, this work suffered slight changes from the original edition in Russian that appeared under the title: A. Schmemann, *Istoricheskii put' Pravoslaviia* (New York: Izd. Imeni Chekhova, 1954) (IPP).

184. Yet he also admits that he used his course on the history of the Eastern Church from between 1945 and 1951 at St. Vladimir's in Crestwood, New York. He began there under the guidance of A. Kartashov at the time when G. Florovskii was the dean of the institute. Cf. IPP, p. 7.

185. Cf. IPP, pp. 8, 11-12.

5.3. *Ultimate Values and Perfection of Love*

For the primitive Church that has been often contrasted with the later entity of the Church, "unity in love was the ultimate value," a unity that "demonstrated above all an active love"[186] toward one's neighbor in the sense and spirit of Christendom that aimed at an "authentic regeneration of all human relationships through love." What is the authenticity of this love? The imitation of God's love for the world as proclaimed by 1 John 4:11-12. In order to thrive, love requires community life and beyond: an authentic unity. Doctrine and confession of faith must be paired with sharing, communication, fellowship, i.e., active love: *By this all people will know that you are my disciples, if you have love for one another* (John 13:35).[187]

The fulfillment of the law alone "by ritual injunctions" is not sufficient, according to St. Paul (Gal. 5:4): "For in love lies the whole meaning of the law, yet the law itself has no power to give love. In Christ love is freely bestowed upon men, and through Him and in Him the law thus becomes unnecessary. In Him neither circumcision nor uncircumcision has power, but faith, active love [alone]."[188] Schmemann summarizes Paul's affirmation and appeal with two words: *In Christ.* This is the "notion" that gives us the pattern for an authentic Christian life. "Faith and baptism have united us with Christ; Paul saw Christians as living in such unity with Him, love for Him, and eagerness to serve Him that the whole Church is nothing other than His Body, which He Himself has created through the Holy Spirit."[189] Similarly to Afanas'ev, Schmemann mentions the service to the poor (with) in the hierarchy of the Church, and we encounter for the first time *agapē*, namely, mentioned in a Eucharistic context: "The bread transformed into the Body of Christ was a part of that daily bread, the food that Christians brought to their meeting for the common table and to aid the poor. The deacons had the responsibility of distributing the gifts, helping the poor, organizing the *agapē* ('love feast,' as partaking of the Eucharist was called) — in

186. Here we can clearly recognize the influence of Afanas'ev, whom Schmemann also mentions at diverse occasions.

187. Cf. IPP, pp. 25-27. The English text strangely omits the Johannine quotation (1 John 4:11-12) and the reflection connected to it. Cf. A. Schmemann, *The Historical Road of Eastern Orthodoxy,* trans. L. W. Kelish (New York, Chicago, San Francisco: Holt, Rinehart & Winston, 1963), pp. 16-17 (HRE).

188. The last phrase, especially the hint to "active love," has been replaced in the English edition by a direct quote from 1 Corinthians 7:19. Cf. IPP, p. 36 and HRE, p. 23.

189. Cf. HRE, p. 24.

sum, of carrying out the unity of Christians resulting from their participation in the Sacrament."[190]

Highlighting *unity* in its connectedness to the core of Christianity (which is love) is a frequent Orthodox theological reference, as is stressing the liaison between *unity, love,* and *life.* This practice is rooted in the Trinity Itself, a model of understanding that the Church lived and handed down in the Scriptures and Tradition from its very beginning: "The meaning of the Gospels lies in the revelation of the Trinity as perfect unity, love, and life." This is the reason doxologies and prayers conclude with a Trinitarian formula: "According to the experience of the Church it is precisely the triune character of God that is His complete form — the mystery of the Three who have one life in perfect love."[191] This same *perfection of love* and *in love* was revealed in God's salvation of the world — in His crucified Son, a *kerygma.* It was first shared in the Christian communities and then with the pagans who came to the Church. It meant sharing with them the *beauty of God's kingdom* and the "final goal of all living things," sharing faith, hope, and love.[192] The world also learned to sense in a very real way a deeply human side of the Christian message in the Mother of God when exploring the dogma on Christ's Divine-humanity: it became the "source of the tenderness and sensitivity that Christianity introduced into human consciousness. And the world which sensed so palpably the protection of this maternal love, which could sing of it and bedeck it in such beauty, was a world already profoundly Christian, regardless of all its sins and imperfections."[193]

When discussing the primitive Church, naturally, Schmemann addresses the issue of Rome's primacy (in fact repeatedly) and refers to it as the question of "presiding in love" and the challenge of love, as in the past so in the present.[194] At the core of this question, *life, love,* and *unity* are not merely interlinked but inseparably imbedded in each other. Therefore, the Church shall progress in perfection towards the Trinity as utmost *perfection of life, love,* and *unity.*

190. Cf. HRE, pp. 31-32.

191. Cf. HRE, pp. 72-74.

192. Cf. HRE, p. 101.

193. Cf. HRE, p. 195.

194. "Presiding in love" from Ignatius of Antioch who referred to it with the respect of the East towards Rome. Cf. HRE, pp. 33, 83, 239, 247-50.

5.4. Introduction to Liturgical Theology

At the center of Schmemann's theology are the Sacraments and a liturgy based upon historic research and inspired by his experiences in a western ecclesial environment. Liturgical theology as the study of liturgy appeared "comparatively recently within the theological disciplines." Known in the West as the "study of rubrics," it answered the question of how liturgy is carried out but not "what is done in worship." Since Russian theology was influenced by the West, especially nineteenth-century dogmatics (e.g., Metropolitan Makarii Bulgakov and Bishop Syl'vestr Malevanskii), "the liturgical witness of the Church" escaped attention.[195] This changed with the liturgical movements in the three great denominations of the Church after World War II. Because of the "essential nature of the Church [that is] actualized in the Eucharist as the Sacrament of the Church's life," Schmemann proposed a plan of liturgical theology in which the Eucharist is located "unquestionably in the center," while not forgetting the unique role of all other sacraments.[196]

Despite the "natural love," the so-called *tserkovnost' (churchliness* or *ecclesiality)* for the Church in Orthodoxy, there was a "liturgical crisis," as the former term apparently had lost its original meaning: "Love for churchliness *(tserkovnost')* has become a synonym for love of the church building and its worship. The church building, the care of the church and the maintenance of the services, love of worship, of its beauty and reverence . . . such is the main content of *tserkovnost'*."[197] In Schmemann's acute observation, concern for the crisis rather than disrespect determines the cause as a misinterpreted love-relationship: "No matter how paradoxical it may sound, what obscures the meaning of worship is that it has become for the faithful an object of love, indeed almost the sole content of Church life." Instead, the Church realizes and reveals its true and proper nature in ecclesial worship, which is "the new life in Christ-union, in Christ with God the Holy Spirit, knowledge of the Truth, unity, love, grace, peace, [and] salvation." The Church can never be subdued to the cult, for the latter serves the former in a process of becoming a "full measure of the stature of Christ" (Eph. 4:13). Thus, worship remains as and is called to be the manifestation of the *Church's nature*, which consists in "her unity and love."[198] Schmemann was clearly inspired by Yves M. J.

195. Cf. A. Schmemann, *Vvedenie v liturgicheskoe bogoslovie* (Paris: YMCA Press, 1961), pp. 15-16 (VLB).

196. Cf. VLB, pp. 20-23, 33-34.

197. Cf. VLB, pp. 35-36.

198. Cf. VLB, pp. 37-38.

Congar's[199] observation on the renewal of the ancient Temple cult in the Church, in the sense of *mediating with, connecting to,* and *contacting* the divine, the Holy, with God, in and through Christ where there is a transposition in the concept of sacrifice and priesthood in the Church: the Temple becomes the Church, that is, the body of the faithful, and where "spiritual sacrifices are . . . offered in this spiritual Temple." Accordingly the newness is not in the mediation through sacrifice, but in the Church itself being "in Christ" the sacrifice in the Eucharist.[200] The turning point of understanding is Pentecost, the Holy Spirit event par excellence and the commencement of the Church.[201]

5.5. Sacraments and Orthodoxy — *For the Life of the World and Its Sacramentality*

This book, which appeared in three different editions, was not meant to be regarded as a systematic theological treatise of the Orthodox liturgical tradition,[202] but rather a *modest* contribution to the contemporary debate on Orthodoxy.[203] Among many basic questions, the principal one for Schmemann

199. In Congar's *Le Mystère du Temple* (Paris 1958). Cf. VLB, p. 117, n. 14.

200. John 19:30; Heb. 10:19-20. Cf. VLB, 116-18. Another liturgical "personality" that Schmemann was very impressed by and placed as a positive example and model of liturgical movement was the German Benedictine monk Odo Casel and the liturgical movement of its time at Abbey of Maria Laach in Eifel, Germany.

201. As a historian, Schmemann smoothly reconnects the Church of our time to that of the initial desire of martyrdom found on the early *graffiti* in the catacombs. There the early Christians celebrated on the tombs of the martyrs, such as St. Ignatius who, with his death in order to live, yearned to manifest this new life in Christ: "In celebrating the Eucharist on the martyr's tomb the Church confessed and revealed that she belonged to this new life and had the same desire which St. Ignatius confessed on the way to his death: 'I desire the bread of God, which is the flesh of Jesus Christ; I wish to drink His blood, which is incorruptible love' . . . i.e., the desire for the fullness of the Kingdom, its fulfillment in the final triumph of the Lord." In the fourth-fifth century, this was already a refined invocation of the saints and their help as opposed to the earlier uses where prayers were said to the departed, not specifically a saint, or even more to a martyr. As for the understanding of the "communion of saints" and faith rooted in eternal life: "In the new life of the Church the communion of saints in Christ — their prayers for one another and their bond of love — was not destroyed by death, since in Christ no one was dead, all were alive." Cf. VLB, pp. 210-11, 213-14.

202. Cf. A. Schmemann, *For the Life of the World: Sacraments and Orthodoxy* (Crestwood, NY: St. Vladimir's Seminary Press, 1973), p. 7.

203. We shall follow the edition: A. Schmemann, *Sacraments and Orthodoxy* (London: Herder & Herder, 1965) (SaO).

was to indicate the "cosmic and catholic, i.e., the all-embracing, all-assuming, and all-transforming nature and scope of Christian *leiturgia*," which he perceives at the "very heart of the Orthodox worldview." He observes the long separation and mutual ignorance of the two "halves of Christianity" that developed each in their own realm "a sense of self-sufficiency, which led, in turn, to a narrowing of spiritual vision and an impoverishment of theological perspective." This was contrasted by the liturgical movement, which, even before an organized ecumenical movement came along, searched for and created a "common ground" by uniting the two separate ecclesial languages and worlds. It broke down the walls of fear and suspicion and made new encounters "in love and mutual respect" possible, bringing about a shared theological and spiritual perspective.[204]

5.6. Reconnected to God's Memory

In the relationship between God and the human being, gratitude is of the essence since God gave humankind "this blessed and sanctified world," and the human being should bless and thank God in return, "to see the world as God sees it — and in this act of gratitude and adoration — to know, name, and possess the world." The quality to know and the capacity to bless God transform *homo sapiens* from *homo faber* to *homo adorans*.[205] Schmemann articulates a very original definition and hermeneutical approach:

> The first, the basic definition of man is that he is a priest. He stands in the center of the world and unifies it in his act of blessing God, of both receiving the world from God and offering it to God — and by filling the world with this Eucharist, he transforms his life, the one that he receives

204. Schmemann also acknowledges his "indebtedness" to the influence and inspiration of the western liturgical revival and liturgical movement of his time. He explicitly names Odo Casel, Lambert Beauduin, J. A. Jungmann, Louis Bouyer, Romano Guardini, and H. A. Reinhold, "to name but a few among so many, [who] did more than merely initiate a liturgical revival within Roman Catholicism. It helped to establish a common theological and spiritual perspective, to restore a truly catholic language without which no fruitful encounter, no ecumenical conversation is possible. Their writings were and still are as significant for us Orthodox as they are for our Western brothers." Schmemann considered this as such because their works helped both the West and the East understand their proper *lex orandi*. Cf. SaO, pp. 7-9.

205. Cf. SaO, p. 15.

> from the world, into life in God, into communion. The world was created as the "matter," the material of one all-embracing Eucharist, and man was created as the priest of this cosmic sacrament.[206]

Schmemann points out that food, specifically, sharing a meal, remains the "last natural sacrament" that has not been converted into a purely utilitarian action despite centuries of secularism. More by instinct than by rationalism, human beings still treat meals and occasions of eating with reverence. "Not accidentally," the biblical story of the fall is connected to food. The fruit "was not offered as a gift to man" but simply taken by him: "Not given, not blessed by God, it was food whose eating was condemned to be communion with itself alone, and not with God. It is the image of the world's love for itself, and eating it is the image of life understood as an end in itself." Schmemann provides a fine spiritual reading of the event of the fall based on the above delineated eating-outside-of-communion with God. It is not only a Eucharistic hermeneutics but also a contemporary analysis of our secularized social behaviors, the lack of and a shift in the understanding of gratitude, a lack of love that gradually grew into a lack of awareness, and vice versa:[207]

> To love is not easy, and mankind has chosen not to return God's love. Man has loved the world, but as an end in itself and not as transcendent to God. He has done it so consistently that it has become something that is "in the air." It seems natural for man to experience the world as opaque, and not shot through with the presence of God. It seems natural not to live a life of thanksgiving for God's gift of a world. It seems natural not to be Eucharistic. The world is a fallen world because it has fallen away from the awareness that God is all in all.[208]

206. Cf. SaO, p. 16.

207. Cf. SaO, p. 17.

208. His profound reflection goes on: "The accumulation of this disregard for God is the original sin that blights the world. And even the religion of this fallen world cannot heal or redeem it, for it has accepted the reduction of God to an area called 'sacred' ('spiritual,' 'supernatural') — as opposed to the world as 'profane.' It has accepted the all-embracing secularism which attempts to steal the world away from God. The natural dependence of man upon the world was intended to be transformed constantly into communion with God in whom is all life. Man was to be the priest of a Eucharist, offering the world to God, and in this offering he was to receive the gift of life. But in the fallen world man does not have the priestly power to do this. His dependence on the world becomes a closed circuit, and his love is deviated from its true direction. He still loves; he is still hungry. He knows he is dependent on that which is beyond him. But his love and his dependence refer only to the world in it-

So food, life, Eucharist, thanksgiving, the whole world is to be seen as a sacrament of communion with God, or at least an invitation to it. The Eucharist naturally possesses primacy among them because of the power of the symbol, reality of God's presence, and, above all, because of Christ's mediation, again in the heart of a joy-filled assembly, in the Church:

> The Church is love, expectation and joy. It is heaven on earth, according to our Orthodox tradition; it is the joy of recovered childhood, that free, unconditioned and disinterested joy which alone is capable of transforming the world. In our adult, serious piety we ask for definitions and justifications, and they are rooted in fear. Fear of corruption, deviation, "pagan influences," [and] what not. But "whoever fears has not been perfected in love" (1 John 4:18).[209] As long as Christians will *love* the Kingdom of God, and not only discuss it, they will "represent" it and signify it, in art and beauty. And the celebrant of the sacrament of joy will appear in a beautiful chasuble, because he is vested in the glory of the Kingdom, because even in the form of man God appears in glory. In the Eucharist we are standing in the presence of Christ, and like Moses before God, we are to be covered with his glory.[210]

This apparently "useless beauty," which Romano Guardini has spoken of in terms of liturgy as an event that "unites act and reality in a supernatural childhood before God," is, nevertheless, a sign, an active expression, and, we can say, a practice of love: as in the preparation, so in its performance.[211]

Two more components of the *sacrament of joy*,[212] the Eucharist, need

---

self. He does not know that breathing can be communion with God. He does not realize that to eat can be to receive life from God in more than its physical sense. He forgets that the world, its air or its food cannot by themselves bring life, but only as they are received and accepted for God's sake, in God and as bearers of the divine gift of life. By themselves they can produce only the appearance. When we see the world as an end in itself, everything becomes itself a value and consequently loses all value, because only in God is found the meaning (value) of everything, and the world is meaningful only when it is the 'sacrament' of God's presence." SaO, pp. 17-18.

209. We have used an up-to-date English translation of the citation from the ESV 2001 instead of: "He that feareth is not made perfect in love."

210. Cf. SaO, p. 34.

211. Cf. SaO, pp. 34-35.

212. "Feast means *joy*. Yet, if there is something that we — the serious, adult, and frustrated Christians of the twentieth century — look at with suspicion, it is certainly joy." This statement, however, Schmemann contextualizes with the fears and sufferings perceived and

to be highlighted because of their rootedness in love, namely *sacrifice* and *remembrance:* "Man is a sacrificial being, because he finds his life in love and love is sacrificial: it puts the 'value,' the very meaning of life in the other and gives life to the other, and in this giving, in this sacrifice, finds the meaning and joy of life." Since God is continually remembering us, we, in turn, offer our lives and the world to God as a sacrifice through mediation, "*in Christ* and *in remembrance of Him.*" Memory, or recollection, is an act of recuperation, to regain our wholeness or, at least, to progress towards it, as practiced and lived in the liturgy, a "reconnectedness" to the revitalizing memory of God: "Remembrance is an act of *love.* God remembers us and His remembrance, His love, is the foundation of the world. In Christ, we *remember.* The Church in its separation from 'this world,' on its journey to heaven *remembers* the world, remembers all men, remembers the whole of creation, takes it in love to God. The Eucharist is the sacrament of cosmic remembrance. There is a need to restore love as the very life of the world."[213] In this sense the Church too is ageless and ever youthfully fresh.

5.7. Recuperating the Lost Principle of Love

If the elements of the Eucharist are inseparably rooted in love, then so is the Eucharist itself. This truth heightens the moral and spiritual challenge for the Church to represent, render, and realize *Christ's Eucharist* which *is Love:*

> The Church, if it is to be the Church, must be the revelation of that divine Love which God "poured out into our hearts." Without this love nothing is "valid" in the Church because nothing is possible. The content of Christ's Eucharist is Love, and only through love can we enter into it and be made its partakers. Of this love we are not capable. This love we have lost. This love Christ has given us and this gift is the *Church.* The Church constitutes itself through love and on love, and in this world it is to "witness" to Love, to re-present it, to make Love present. Love alone creates and transforms: it is, therefore, the very "principle" of the sacrament.[214]

experienced in the world, a legitimate question of human uncertainty. Yet the true problem is that Christians have accepted "the whole ethos of our joyless and business-minded culture" instead of living out of hope. Cf. SaO, p. 64.

213. Cf. SaO, pp. 41-42.

214. Cf. SaO, p. 43. Through communion we are restored into a "solidarity and love, which the world has lost." Cf. SaO, p. 54.

Naturally, this stands also for all the other sacraments, but in particular for the Eucharist which has love as its essence. Love as the *means* and *end* is also true for the sacrament of matrimony or confirmation.[215]

5.8. *The Mystery of Love*

Inspired in this subject again most likely by Afanas'ev, Schmemann uses Ephesians 5:32 for the epigraph when speaking of matrimony as a "great mystery . . . concerning Christ and the Church." The "new eon" requires a new approach to this *sacrament of divine love*, the understanding that the "real theme, 'content' and object of this sacrament is not 'family,' but love."[216] This union pertains to more than just the bride and groom. Their relationship is a sacred one, so much so that Schmemann uses some *harsh words* himself to make a clear point in his discernment: "Family as such, family itself, can be a demonic distortion of love — and there are many harsh words about it in the Gospel: 'A man's foes shall be those of his own household' (Matt. 10:36). In this sense the sacrament of matrimony is wider than family. It is the sacrament of divine love, as the all-embracing mystery of being itself, and it is for this reason that it concerns the whole Church, and — through the Church — the whole world."[217] On the other hand, the rela-

215. Cf. SaO, p. 93. About the relationship between *remembrance* and the *Last Supper* and the *realness* of God's love revealed in the Eucharistic meal that represents the *telos,* the end, completion of Christ's love, we can find the following reflected in the liturgy: "'He loved them to the end' (John 13:1). In the eucharistic experience and in the gospels, the last supper is the *end* (τέλος), i.e., the completion, the crowning, the fulfillment of Christ's love, which constitutes the essence of all of His ministry, preaching, miracles, and through which He now gives Himself up, love itself. From the opening words, 'I have earnestly desired to eat this Passover with you' (Luke 22:15), to the exit to the garden of Gethsemane, everything at the last supper — the washing of the feet, the distribution to the disciples of the bread and the cup, the last discourse — is not only concerned with love, but is *Love itself.* And thus the last supper is the τέλος, the completion, the fulfillment of the *end,* for it is the manifestation of that kingdom of love, for the sake of which the world was created and in which it has its τέλος, its fulfillment. Through love God created the world. Through love He did not abandon it when it fell into sin and death. Through love He sent His only-begotten Son, His Love, into the world. And now, at this table, He manifests and grants this love as His kingdom, and His kingdom as 'abiding' in love: 'As the Father has loved me, so have I loved you; *abide in my love*' (John 15:9)." Cf. A. Schmemann, *The Eucharist: Sacrament of the Kingdom* (Crestwood, NY: St. Vladimir's Seminary Press, 1988), pp. 199-201.

216. Cf. SaO, pp. 98-100.

217. Cf. SaO, p. 101. Not necessarily contradicting yet definitely mitigated sounds

tionship between God and His chosen nation, even more, between God, the world, and the cosmos is "restored in the Church" and finds its expression in the Scripture "in terms of marital union and love": "This is a double analogy. On one hand, we understand God's love for the world and Christ's love for the Church because we have the experience of marital love, but on the other hand, marital love has its roots, its depth and real fulfillment in the *great mystery of Christ and His Church:* 'But I speak concerning Christ and the Church.'"[218] To support a proper understanding of this concept of love instead of an "abstract theology of love," Schmemann uses the example of the Blessed Mother, whose "total obedience in love" is not solely obedience but "obedience *and* love." Mary's response to God begins the healing of division, of the "broken, distorted" relationship of the world to God. However, this is possible only if love is directed clearly by obedience to God. Love obtains its quality by its goal: "The only Lord of Creation gives love its true direction, makes it fully love." A lost and broken dialogue begins in obedience and self-donation; the messenger becomes the message:

> True obedience is thus true love for God, the true response of Creation to its Creator. Humanity is fully humanity when it is this response to God, [and] becomes the movement of total self-giving and obedience to Him. But in the "natural" world the bearer of this obedient love, of the love as response, is the woman. The man proposes, the woman accepts. This acceptance is not passivity, blind submission, because it is love, and love is always active. It gives life to the proposal of man, fulfills it as life, yet it becomes fully love and fully life only when it is fully *acceptance* and *response.*[219]

Thus, Mary is not only a proto-Christian but an example to men and women alike in forming their mutual love based on their God-related love. A danger lies in family life and, even more so, in matrimony, namely, the danger of not becoming self-giving and, thus, self-sacrificing, but taking happiness as its sole purpose — which brings about misunderstandings, disap-

---

Schmemann's view on matrimony in a later work: "The sacrament of *Holy Matrimony,* [which] indicates that the Church gives special attention to the family, to the basic unit of man's life in society." Cf. A. Schmemann, *Liturgy and Life: Christian Development through Liturgical Experience* (New York: Department of Religious Education, Orthodox Church in America, 1974), p. 91.

218. Cf. SaO, pp. 103-4.

219. Cf. SaO, p. 104.

pointments, and, finally, much too easily, its "almost natural shadow," divorce. Describing the matrimonial liturgy and the crowning of the couple during it, Schmemann introduces the cross instead of happiness into the marital bond, and exchanges futile, earthly, and incomplete happiness for joy that will grow into lasting happiness, a "perfected love of which God alone is the end and fullness":[220]

> It is the identification of marriage with happiness and the refusal to accept the Cross in it. In a Christian marriage, in fact, three are married; and the united loyalty of the two toward the third, who is God, keeps the two in an active unity with each other as well as with God. Yet it is the presence of God which is the death of the marriage as something only natural. It is the cross of Christ that brings the self-sufficiency of nature to its end. But "by the cross joy (and not 'happiness!') entered the whole world." Its presence is thus the real joy of marriage. It is the joyful certitude that the marriage vow, in the perspective of the eternal Kingdom, is not taken "until death parts" but until death unites us completely.[221]

5.9. *Priesthood*

Schmemann offers an enriching reflection on the value and task of the priesthood, especially in light of the sacrament of matrimony that certainly had to do with his own experience with both. In the question of the priesthood and its mission, the view of *manhood* and *womanhood* is distorted by both clericalism and secularism. Although he repeats himself in the first part, Schmemann also completes the complementary nature of the two genders in this regard: "Man was created priest of the world, the one who offers the world to God in a sacrifice of love and praise and who, through this eternal Eucharist, bestows the divine love upon the world. Priesthood, in this sense, is the very essence of manhood, man's creative relation to the 'womanhood' of the created world. And Christ is the one true Priest because He is the one true and perfect man. He is the new Adam, the restoration of that which Adam failed to be."[222] Since priesthood was revealed by Christ as love in its essence, priesthood is to be seen also as "the essence of life" that He *"inaugurated"* in and

220. Cf. SaO, pp. 101-4.
221. Cf. SaO, p. 111.
222. Cf. SaO, p. 114.

with His priestly death and life. With that, He also abolished the division between profane and sacred, this- and that-worldly, natural and supernatural: "He revealed that all things, all nature have their end, their fulfillment in the Kingdom, that all things are to be made new by love." Thus, the task and call of a priest is to existentially reveal and to live out that "the end and meaning of all things are in Christ." Schmemann understands as an Orthodox married priest, even more pragmatically, that there is a *oneness* in the task of the two sacraments, as both are manifestations of love stemming out of Christ's love; the church, to which the priest is married more than just symbolically but rather by vocation, unfolds in the *universal priesthood*[223] of the faithful:

> The priesthood reveals the humility, not the pride, of the Church, for it reveals the complete dependence of the Church on Christ's love, that is, on his unique and perfect priesthood. It is not "priesthood" that the priest receives in his ordination, but the gift of Christ's love, that love which made Christ the only Priest and which fills with this unique priesthood the ministry of those whom He sends to His people. . . . It is [this] marriage of the priest with the Church that makes him really [a] *priest,* the true minister of the Love which alone transforms the world and reveals the Church as the immaculate bride of Christ. . . . [Whether they are married or not,] the sacraments of matrimony and priesthood *concern* all of us, because they concern our life as [a] *vocation.* The meaning, the essence and the end of all vocation is *the mystery of Christ and the Church.* It is through the Church that each one of us finds that the vocation of all vocation[s] is to follow Christ in the fullness of His priesthood: in His love for man and the world, His love for their ultimate fulfillment in the abundant life of the Kingdom.[224]

5.10. Liturgy and Life

Treating the liturgy from the everyday experience as a priest, Schmemann explains in his section on the *Offertory* in the liturgy of the faithful that per-

223. Schmemann does not apply this term.

224. Cf. SaO, pp. 115-16. The discipleship and love for Christ also determines the final aspects of our terrestrial life and puts them in perspective of the kingdom. Cf. SaO, pp. 129, 131-33. Schmemann dedicates a booklet to the theme of death and the life of the resurrected body, the spiritual body that matured in our life thanks to love. Cf. A. Schmemann, *O Death, Where Is Thy Sting?* (Crestwood, NY: St. Vladimir's Seminary Press, 2003).

fect love is modeled and shaped by sacrifice, whereby we are called to unite our proper sacrifice to that of Christ which shall render our love perfect. The absolute essence of this *kenotic* action is in *love,* and Love *is* God's, the Trinity's, essence. (We notice the capital letter when he writes of the *Other.*) Again, the Trinity and the intra-Trinitarian *kenotic* relationship serve as the guiding model, a beautiful meditation on the Trinity's inner life. It is a somewhat longer quote, but we decided not to interrupt the beauty of its narrative and message:

> A sacrifice is the natural movement of love, which is the gift of oneself, a self-denial for the sake of the Other. When I love somebody my life is *in* him whom I love, I give him my life — freely, willingly, joyfully — and this "giving away" becomes the very meaning of my life.
>
> The mystery of the Holy Trinity is the mystery of the perfect and absolute sacrifice because God is Love. God is Trinity because God is Love. The whole of the Father's Essence is eternally "given away" to the Son, and the whole of the Son's Life is in having the Essence of the Father as His Own, to exist as the Perfect Image of the Father; and, finally, this mutual sacrifice of perfect love, this eternal Gift of the Father to the Son, is the very Spirit of God — Spirit of Life, of Love, of Perfection, of Beauty, of the whole inexhaustible depth of Divine Essence. The mystery of the Trinity is essential for the proper understanding of the Eucharist, and first of all, of its sacrificial character. God so *loved* the world that He gave (sacrificed) His Son to us, to bring us back to Himself. The Son of God so *loved* His Father that He gave Himself to Him. His whole life was a perfect and absolute sacrificial movement. He performed it as God-Man, not only in His Divinity, but also in His Humanity, which He assumed out of Divine Love for us. In Himself He thus restored human life to perfection, as a *sacrifice of love to God,* a sacrifice not of fear, not of any kind of "interest," but of love and love alone. And finally, this perfect life as love, and therefore as sacrifice, He gave to all who accept Him and believe in Him, restoring in them the initial relationship with God. The life of the Church, being His life in us and our life in Him, thus is necessarily a *sacrificial life,* an eternal movement of love towards God. The essential attitude and the essential act of the Church, which is the new Humanity restored by Christ, is, therefore, the *Eucharist,* the act of Love, Thanksgiving and Sacrifice.[225]

225. Cf. *Liturgy and Life,* pp. 49-50.

There is no Eucharist without a God who is not a Trinity, for there is no Love without relating to the *Other,* without self-sacrifice. In fact, a *sacrificial life,* the proper meaning of life, is a *Eucharistic sacrifice of love.* The understanding and actual access to this mystery has been given to us in Christ. From Christ on, sacrifice is not bloody anymore, but it is of praise and love. God Himself has restored our joy:

> Christ offered Himself once and for all, and His sacrifice, being full and perfect, makes any new sacrifice needless. But it is precisely the meaning of our Eucharistic offering, that in it we are given the priceless possibility of "entering" into Christ's sacrifice, of being participants of His unique offering of Himself to God. Or, in other terms, His unique and perfect Sacrifice has made it possible for us — the Church, His Body — to be restored and readmitted into the fullness of true humanity: the sacrifice of praise and love. The one who has not understood this sacrificial character of the Eucharist, who has come to *receive* but not to *give,* has not accepted the very spirit of the Church, which is above everything else the acceptance of, and the participation in, Christ's Sacrifice.[226]

A final, truly *agapic* reflection on our partaking in the banquet of love prepared for us by God through His servant in the act of consecration on the altar:

> This [transformation] happens not because of some strange and miraculous power left by Christ with some people (priests) . . . who therefore can perform this miracle by virtue of their power, but because we — the Church — are *in Christ,* i.e., in His Sacrifice, Love, Ascension, in the whole of His *movement* of deification, of transforming His Humanity by

226. "The love which Christ has 'poured into our hearts' (Rom. 5:5) has its natural expression in the mutual love of Christians for each other. The Kingdom of God is that of perfect unity — 'that they may be one, even as we are one' (John 17:11). 'Therefore, there is no other way to approach God but in love. He *remembers* us if we remember each other. Whatever the number of those who offer *this* Eucharist, it is always the whole Church — the unity of faith and love — that offers and is being offered, and this organic unity of the Church is expressed in the commemoration at the Great Entrance.'" Cf. *Liturgy and Life,* pp. 50-51. In communion, we experience the "Church as a fellowship of love" and contemporarily a most personal communion with the whole Church. This communion is "the Sacrament of forgiveness, the Sacrament of unity and love, the Sacrament of the Kingdom." Cf. *Liturgy and Life,* p. 70.

> His Divinity; because, in other words, we are in *His* Eucharist and offer Him as our Eucharist to God. And when we *do this,* as He told us we should, we — the Church — are accepted where He has *entered.* And being accepted, "we eat and drink at His table in His Kingdom" (Luke 22:30) as He said we would.[227]

Conclusion

Some of the aforementioned ideas are further developed in Schmemann's liturgical writings, including the *Great Lent, Eucharist: The Sacrament of Kingdom, Of Water and of the Spirit,* and others that we unfortunately cannot address here, but all contain a great number of love-related reflections and references. Although the term *kenosis* is not spelled out, the principal ideas at the very core of Christianity are, namely the Eucharist, the heart of which is Love, and God is Love because God is a Trinity.

Schmemann may have been a historian, but, when he reflects on the liturgy, he does so with every heartbeat. In recognizing the importance of the liturgical movement that even preceded the ecumenical one, he proposes a common language: *liturgy.* Yet, as might be expected of an experienced priest and author, it is the divine *leiturgia* that he has on his mind, the universal language of God's love to which we all were called to be ministers of thanksgiving — and that in joy: the Eucharist. This is the universal priesthood of all baptized Christians: to turn everything through self-sacrifice into gratitude and thanksgiving in our lives, around us, the whole world, for a grateful, Eucharistic heart stands closest to God. And all who are close to God see things *the way God sees them.*

227. Cf. *Liturgy and Life,* p. 60. About transfiguration through sanctification of one's life, see pp. 90-91.

Concluding Reflections

1. The Feeling of *Love* More Than a Mere Sentiment

In the introduction to the present volume there was a quote from a book edited by V. Shestakov on *Russian Eros, or the Philosophy of Love in Russia,* which asserted that in the period we have examined in this book the theme of love "burst with volcanic energy into Russian literature, journalism, literary criticism, philosophy, and theology." In these few decades, the reflection and writing on the theme of love had greatly surpassed the output of entire preceding centuries. This passage was deliberately cited with the hope that there is now little or no doubt regarding the truthfulness of this statement, even though, in the entanglement of the reading, this truth may not have always appeared conclusive. The vice and virtue of a trained Russian intellectual and spiritual mind of these past two centuries was at the same time its depth and breadth of reflection, with a natural bent towards metaphysics — certainly, a challenge in our information-burdened and hurried century. In addition, most of the thinkers and writers on this topic did not hesitate to include and build upon their personal religious even mystical experiences, feelings, and perceptions, incorporating them firmly into their philosophic-theological structures. Some of the manualist authors would not speak about these personal perceptions, as they considered them life's natural phenomenon; others, like Bishop Malevanskii or Malinovskii, placed the principal cognition of dogmatic theology in the human heart, and the latter again in the center of God, in the *heart* of the Trinity. The "legitimization" of work with the senses and perception along with the human intellect, as in theology so in philosophy (and even more so in dogmatics), restores to the epistemological process its *humanness* in the form of wisdom *of the heart;*[1] it, so to speak, *humanizes* the Divine. *Wisdom of the heart* means *existential wisdom,* what ultimately counts. Yet, such wisdom grants and, in precedence, requests *freedom,* i.e., the divine privilege given by God to human beings, and which was explicitly precious to our authors. To think, perceive, contemplate, empathize, and love with the heart is not a mere sentiment, but means being *fully human* — which (surprisingly) means to become *God-like,* that is, to be in the process of *divinization.* Without *theosis,* an indispensable anthropological notion, true mystical insight in theology would be constrained to the sphere of private devotion, at the most, and the human family could not succeed in *comprehending* how the beat of God's heart can be of the same wavelength as our own. This attitude was encountered throughout the research, especially in the works of Solov'ev, Florenskii, Bulgakov, Karsavin, Ivanov, Afanas'ev, and others. The involvement of the entire person — comprising the intellect and the senses in the broadest meaning of the terms — is one of the most remarkable and inspirational contributions of the authors discussed.[2] This provides the liberty to a theologian such as Malinovskii to consider the dogmas *as an interpretation* of God and His divine realm, for they are fundamental and unique teachings of the Church to start with and to rely on during our ongoing epistemological journey of *God-awareness* and *cognition.*

2. New Hermeneutics: "God Is Love" as the Ontological Foundation of Our Faith

Many of the creative novelties we have witnessed began as an *intuition,* requiring *freedom* of decision and determination on the part of our authors. The strong underlining of God's *trinitariety* belongs to the DNA of Orthodox theology, and with modern theology, a particular merit of what we defined as *the mystical-sapiential stream* (of Florenskii, Bulgakov, and Karsavin), there was a significant theological and interpretational shift towards the Trinitarian and intra-Trinitarian awareness and ontology. This intuition was undoubtedly triggered and, consequently, reaffirmed with the Johannine ontological statement of "God *is* Love." Already, Beliaev, with his thor-

1. The *wisdom of heart* was and remains one of the most profound Christian spiritual concepts and efforts.

2. In this aspect they certainly got detached from the general western approach of the time (Descartes, Kant, etc.). On the other hand, Schelling's influence, for instance, bore a lasting imprint on the development of Russian religious thought.

ough exegetical research and systematic exposition on *Divine Love,* had the ingenious intuition of coming to the conclusion that, given Christianity's origin and foundation in love, dogmatics, too, should be founded precisely on the concept and notion of God's love as a true and unique *nexus* between Divine and human, as well as in relations between humans by means of *charity.* This new hermeneutical key in which dogmatics, epistemology, ecclesiology, staurology, soteriology, and all other branches of theology — and we can add Christian philosophy as well — need to be reread and reinterpreted is definitely a radically innovative approach, faithful to the *Universal Ecclesial Tradition* and to the *prophetic* vision of the Church as guided by the teaching of Jesus Christ.

The theme of *love* courses and emanates throughout the entirety of Russian religious thought, at times as a guiding and sustaining element, at other times more accentuated in the form of *erōs* and its manifestations (this being often the case with philosophy and art) than in its *kenotic* and *agapic* dimension (more frequent in theology); or as side by side in interaction and mutual enrichment or even commonality, especially on a human-to-human level; or then as *agapē,* as God's communication and *erōs* as the human response to the divine love (*erōs* possibly as a paradisiacal protomemory at times expressed in philosophy and theology, as well as art).

3. The Anthropology of *Divinization* and *Kenosis*

The beauty and inventiveness of our modern Russian authors is the inextinguishable desire to discover and elucidate an explicit *anthropology of the divine* in the Trinity Itself (while avoiding anthropomorphisms), first and foremost revealed in the divine-human person, teaching, and works of Jesus Christ. Through His salvific, self-sacrificing action, humankind and its fate — expressly including the entire world and creation — are present *in the heart of the Trinity.* This is more than just mere, pleasant symbolism if we consider how real was God's suffering and death on the cross of Golgotha, as well as the depth of God's humility in His *kenotic* descent into the netherworld to save His beloved *Adam,* i.e., humankind. Some accentuated that the *kenosis* of God's Son already began before the Incarnation; also, the Holy Spirit's descending on the Church and the world is considered a *kenotic* action. We found unique yet consistent with these reflections Bulgakov's *kenosis* of the *guardian angels* as inseparable messengers, *true friends,* and protectors of God's love in the human soul. Russian spiritual comprehension of *kenosis* is inseparably linked to God's love (in and through suffering), or regarded even as a direct manifestation of Divine love.

Thus *kenosis* is the hallmark of true, that is, *divine, agapic* love. On a human level, especially in the metaphysics of person(hood), sometimes expressed by means of poetry, it is a relational and mutual *in-the-other-being,* a self-abandonment and self-denial for the sake of the other in whom, and only in whom, *I myself* become a reality: we truly see *I am who I am.* The *I* can exist only in the *you,* and only through *you* is my *I* real. Only *love* can produce such a trust and *kenotic* giving-up-of-my-ego in order to find one's *self* anew yet restored more fully into God's image (cf. Luke 17:33).[3] The depth of this reciprocity observed in grand human love-stories (be it to one's neighbor, friendship-based, matrimonial, initiated by (mutual) respect, admiration, or even simple attraction to the other — all of which can be a particular love-vocation) is a reflection of the love-bound, love-unity in the Trinity. Subsequently, the human person, being *God's image,* is collocated in the heart of the Trinity, and vice versa; the Trinity, often unrecognized yet inexorable, lives in the human soul. For Frank, Berdiaev, and some others, the answer to this divine *love-presence* in *me* and *you* perceived and encountered in the terrestrial, human, love is the noble form of *Erōs.*[4]

We are woven with the threads of God's own Divinity, and this epistemological journey revealed to us how much this is true. The idea of the *anthropology of the divine* is interlinked to the notion of *divinization* and is not a purpose in itself; its task is to perfect-purify us in our resemblance to God and His Trinitarian relatedness in love. This means to be *like God* in the *power of love,* as opposed to the first temptation in Paradise, which was an offer of *loveless power* and thus a caricature of God. The results of opting for the latter are well known to all of us. God alone could mend such a disastrous choice of distorted (self-)love, by healing our self-inflicted wounds of the consequent false self-negation and self-refusal for being non-gods. It was God's *kenotic* and *divinizing* love, in the incarnation of his Son who became *like us* and *one of us,* that revealed how precious and unique we are to Him. True love is *divine,* i.e., God-bearing, and therefore we are *God-bearers,* which instinctively creates a triangle in any true love relationship. Love is Trinitarian, just as God is Trinity; thus we know that *God is love.*

3. *Whoever seeks to preserve his life will lose it, but whoever loses his life will keep it.*

4. As seen in their works, this noble form of *Erōs* has nothing to do with distorted concepts of eroticism.

4. Living (the) Communion of Love

Recognizing *love* and the *love-relationship* as a fundamental divine-human building principle by imitating the Trinity in "the Church" ceases to be a mere gathering or grouping of the faithful in a building or congregation. Through faith, the Church becomes a *communion of love,* as Khomiakov or even Afanas'ev would see it, or else she is not a church. As such, she is a *living organism* regulating but also protecting herself by the *law of love,* and she is called to be yeast in the world. With one arm she receives God's sustaining care, while with the other she ministers from her abundant charitable fund of love to the world; in such a way, the Church truly represents Christ's self-sacrificing love which includes *all* humankind. This is another major trait well depicted by Bukharev, but "surprisingly" also by the members of the *moralist school:* God's love cannot be selective; it is all-inclusive, just as God is, or it is not God's love. We are all *brethren* and *next of kin,* some already called out from the multitude *(ek-klesia),* others still waiting to perceive the call, deep in their souls. They yearn to hear this divine *invitation,* represented in the tireless repetitions of Fedorov and the refined, ingenious Solov'evian intuition of *vseedinstvo,* all-unity, which represents the *fullness in the relatedness of all;* for Solov'ev, too, the ideal of this living unity is *agapē.* That the love of God ontologically cannot stop within the walls and congregations of the Church, not spreading any further, is another dear topic to modern Russian religious thought of the era, a time when few, if any (including in the West), would have even posed such a question.[5]

5. A further step is to consider our heritage, the world, and this particular planet with its vastness and limits, as a chance and task to progress in awareness of being *one sole human family* — as every family — with blessings and challenges. We learn to reflect on the achievements of modern science and the reflections of specially those scientists who have gained or deepened their faith through their research and have a genuine desire to share it. We think, for example, of *The Work of Love: Creation as Kenosis,* ed. John Polkinghorne (Grand Rapids: Eerdmans, 2001), which, in the diverse contributions of contemporary theologians and scientists, considers God's creation precisely from a *kenotic*-love point of view, and even an *agapic* divine perspective. In this context, we would need to mention also P. Florenskii's scientific research and insights, N. Fedorov's daring scientific visions, but also implications from V. Solov'ev's or S. Bulgakov's works, as well as many others, including works written in a *kenotic* hermeneutical key in the interreligious dialogue of recent times. We see this as an opportunity for the common reflection of all parties, Christians, non-Christians, and nonbelievers (or those who believe themselves to be such) to gain an awareness of the divine cosmic greatness that surrounds us in God's infinite tender love.

5. God's Forgotten Language — Epistemology of Love

After the sin-fall, it is God's *Agapē* which sets out to search for His strayed and hiding children. God's call is not answered due to the *shame of being naked,* meaning fear (for those who are not afraid do not hide). Humankind no longer understood its Creator's tender, caring relationship, and they feared Him. Yet we know that *there is no fear in love, but perfect love casts out fear. For fear has to do with punishment, and whoever fears has not been perfected in love* (1 John 4:18). True, humankind was *supposed to grow* in love and knowledge even in Paradise, but certainly had nothing to fear of God as they had been communicating with Him directly up till then (cf. Genesis 2–3). They did not answer the *call,* for through sin their image of God became distorted, and with it their relationship to God was no longer founded in love but in fear. They — and the world with them — forgot that God used to communicate (does communicate, as with God there is no time) *in* and *solely in* love with His creation. He cannot do otherwise or we do not exist. The deeper the comprehension of this truth a person has, the greater is his capacity for love. Therefore the will for a free decision, but also the will to cognition and comprehension is indispensable for advancement in divine sciences and spirituality. And the task of theology as well as liturgy is to further such cognition and understanding of God so that love may grow and make progress (in) the human heart.

Christ's living example to pray to His Heavenly Father and be nourished by His will lives on in His Church, and teaches us the desire for *communication* and *communion* with(in) God. Therefore, the pastoral concern for the just image of "God *as* love" understandably is reflected in multiple ways in the writings of Metropolitans Filaret and Stragorodskii, and Bishop Khrapovitskii; moreover the Neopatristic school of Russian theology in exile also gives us insightful examples of such pastoral sensitivity. To present God *as* love means to *re-present* a nonthreatening God. When fear is replaced by love, thanks to Christ's mediation and sacrifice, the primordial order of creation is restored, and the human being who becomes conscious and *knowingly God's child* can finally respond to God's "Where are you?" (Gen. 3:9) with a "Here I stand in your loving Presence."[6] This is the threshold where *knowledge becomes love,* which the martyr Florenskii placed as an epigraph

6. From Old Testament narratives, we have to think of the powerful, frightening, yet transforming, and eventually transformed, tenderly intimate encounter between the prophet Elijah and the Lord of Hosts, first on Mt. Carmel and then on Mt. Horeb; or of the protoprophet Moses' intimate *(panim al panim)* conversations with the God of Israel on Mt. Sinai.

to his epochal work, because we recognize in the *humiliated Lamb* the *face of a co-suffering* and *com-passionate* God of Jesus Christ.

These are crucial contributions of modern Russian theology, not rarely inspired by western medieval mystical love-theology, or more by the monastic movement of the startsy at Optina Pustin, yet understood and broadly unfolded for modern times precisely by these travailed Russian minds. The rediscovery of the *heliocentrism of God's Agapē* in Christianity, ergo Christian philosophy and even more so theology, is the *Good News* of our times to God's creation. God communicates in the love-union of a Trinity, God coexists in Trinity, God *is* Trinity or is not Truth; and, again, we know: *God is Love.*

6. *Catholicity-Universality:* The Mutual Theological Consciousness of East and West

Divine Love, a personal and personified *agapē,* should be considered as an ecumenical liaison between eastern and western traditions, customs, divergences, and varieties among Christians. Only God's *power* can bridge prejudices and fears and guide us safely into the haven of a living love-communion at the common table of *agapē* set for us by Christ in His *Universal Church.*[7] There is so much that unites us that the differences are a mere invitation to grow in respect towards the *otherness* of the other and to mutual enrichment, as the Spirit of Christ is unceasingly at work until the fullness of times. We can hasten the coming of the kingdom of God by loving each other in the Spirit of God's children, who we *all* are. There are diverse theologies, but we and the diversity of our traditions are united and sustained by the bond of Christ's love presented in the *Universal Tradition of the Church.* Christ is the *way* to walk. There is a prophetic spirit in the ecclesial visions of modern Russian theologians, and we wish to underscore the evident, pertinent, and further-growing *agapē-stream* in the Catholic Church, in particular, in these last decades, with regard to ecumenical dialogue. Apart from the pontifical encyclicals mentioned in our introduction, there is a shift of focus towards a

7. We have found some refreshingly new interpretations of *agapē* as a theological and philosophical concept, liturgical principle, and daily lived-out Christian love applied to modern Christian ethics in V. Guroian's book *Incarnated Love: Essays in Orthodox Ethics,* in particular what is being presented as *Sacramentality of Agapē* on pages 77-79, but also many other valuable insights regarding *agapē, erōs,* and the concept of *love* and their (pragmatic) interpretation in(to) contemporary Christian ethics.

kenotic and *agapic* theological interpretation, towards rethinking theology and Christianity in the Johannine key of *love* by theologians such as A. Rosmini, Hans Urs von Balthasar, W. Cardinal Kasper, as well as the publishing of recent years from the Lateran Pontifical University's chair of theology. All of these point towards our common denominator: God's divine love, *agapē*, as the means and goal of coexistence and truth, that is, Trinitarian unity.

Our commonalities in Christianity are not simple coincidences but are given by the definition of being Christ-followers. The core of Christ's message is the initially handed-down *kerygma* of faith that speaks of Christ's death and resurrection, which is unthinkable without God's self-humiliation described in Philippians 2:5-11. Yet even *kenosis* is illuminated by God's essence, life, and being, the *divine love*, which is also our essence. Love is the essence of Christianity and of the Church; it is its core *(serdtsevina)* in which all Tradition and customs, the Scriptures, dogmas, and interpretations obtain their accurate and truthful light. This is echoed in H. U. von Balthasar's essay with the fitting title of *Glaubhaft ist nur Liebe,*[8] a true evidence of Catholic *love*-oriented and *love*-founded theology. The roots of Christianity are undoubtedly *spread in* and *nourished by* the divine soil of love, and if it gets cut off, it withers, becomes dry, loses its fruit, and turns barren.[9] This also stands, perhaps even more so, for spirituality, for as faith and love are undividable, so is freedom an indispensable condition of true faith and love — a frequently recurring idea with our authors. The divine space called *Ecclesia* is destined to raise such adult Christians who, while acting in full responsibility towards their vocation, never forget and never get detached from the nourishing foundation, the *Divine Love.* This applies, consequently, also to theology and any Christian work and effort in general: the adjective *Christian* matches only, and that is utterly exclusive, what is rooted in and nourished by Christ's love, *kenotic* self-sacrifice, and *agapic* sustenance, guidance, and rendering of the Trinitarian relationship. Deepened in such faith and matured in its consistency, we, Christ's Universal Church, can uprightly and convincingly testify to the world that we are Christ's *living Body,* in full com(m)-union with(in) the Trinity. Then the onlooking world will utter yearningly, as Tertullian noted about pagans witnessing the early Christians: "See how they love one another."[10]

8. *Love alone is trustworthy* (my translation).

9. *Abide in me, and I in you. As the branch cannot bear fruit by itself, unless it abides in the vine, neither can you, unless you abide in me* (John 15:4).

10. With these words, Tertullian (*Apology* 39:6) rendered the attitude of some of the pagans to Christian communities in the third century.

Selected Bibliography

1. Afanas'ev, N. N.

Afanas'ev, N. *Ekkleziologiia: Vstuplenie v klir.* Paris: "L'Eau Vive," 1968.

Afanas'ev, N. Prot. *Sluzhenie mirian v Tserkvi.* Parizh: Izd. Religionzno-Pedagogicheskogo Kabineta pri Pravoslavnom Bogoslovskom Institute, 1955.

Afanas'ev, N. Prot. *Trapeza Gospodnia.* Kiev: Khram prepodobnogo Agapita Perchers-kogo, 2003.

Afanas'ev, N. Prot. *Tserkov' Dukha Sviatogo.* Kiev: Tsentr Pravoslavnoi knigi, 2005.

Afanasiev, N. *The Church of the Holy Spirit.* Translated by V. Permiakov, edited by M. Plekon. Notre Dame: University of Notre Dame Press, 2007.

Afanassieff, N. "L'Église qui préside dans l'amour," in *La Primauté de Pierre,* edited by N. Afanassieff, N. Koulomzine, J. Meyendorff, A. Schmemann. Neuchâtel: Delachaux & Niestlé, 1960.

2. Beliaev, A. D.

Beliaev, A. D. *Istinnoe khristianstvo i gumanizm: Po povodu vozzrenii na khristianstvo L. N. Tolstogo i V. S. Solov'va.* Sergiev Posad: Tipografiia A. Snegirevoi, 1893.

Beliaev, A. D. *Liubov' Bozhestvennaia: Opyt raskrytiia glavneishikh khristianskikh dogmatov iz nachala liubvi Bozhestvennoi.* Sankt-Peterburg: "Nevskaia zhem-chuzhina," 2006.

Beliaev, A. D. *O bezbozhii i antikhriste,* vols. 1-2. Valaam: Izd. Spaso-Preobrazhenskogo Valaamskogo Stavronpigial'nogo monastyria, 1996.

Beliaev, A. D. *O soedinenii tserkvei: razbor entsikliki Papy L'va XIII ot 20 iunia 1894 goda.* Sergiev Posad: Tipografiia A. Snegirevoi, 1894.

3. Berdiaev, N. A.

Berdiaev, N. *Eros i lichnost': Filosofiia pola i liubvi.* Sankt-Peterburg: Izd. Dom "Azbuka-klassika," 2006.

Berdiaev, N. *Filosofiia svobody.* Moskva: Izd. Act, 2005.

Berdiaev, N. A. *Filosofiia svobodnogo dukha.* Moskva: Izd. "Respublika," 1994.

Berdiaev, N. *Filosofia tvorchestva, kul'tury i iskusstva,* vols. 1-2. Moskva: Izd. "Iskusstvo," 1994.

Berdiaev, N. A. *Istina i otkrovenie.* Sankt-Peterburg: Izd. Russkogo Khristianskogo gumanitarnogo instituta, 1996.

Berdiaev, N. A. "Mirosozertsanie Dostoevskoko," in *Filosofiia tvorchestva, kul'tury i iskustva,* vol 2. Moskva: Izd. "Iskusstvo," ICHP "Liga," 1994.

Berdiaev, N. A. *Mutnye liki.* Kanon. Moskva: "Reabilitatsiia," 2004.

Berdiaev, N. A. *Samopoznanie.* Sankt-Peterburg: Izd. Dom "Azbuka-klassika," 2007.

Berdiaev, N. A. *Smysl tvorchestva.* Moskva: Izd. Khranitel'/Ast, 2007.

Berdiaev, N. *The Russian Idea.* Hudson, NY: Lindisfarne Press, 1992.

Berdiaev, N. A. *Tsarstvo dukha i tsarstvo kesaria.* Moskva: Izd. "Respublika," 1995.

4. Bukharev, M. A.

Arkhimandrit Feodor (A. M. Bukharev). *O dukhovnykh potrebnostiakh zhizni.* Moskva: Izd. Stolica, 1991.

Arkhimandrit Feodor (A. M. Bukharev). *O Pravoslavii v otnoshenii k sovremennosti.* Sankt-Peterburg: Synodal'naia tipografiia, 1906.

Arkhimandrit Feodor (A. M. Bukharev). *O Pravoslavii v othnoshenii k sovremennosti, v raznykh stat'iakh Arkhimandrita Feodora.* Sankt-Peterburg: Tipografiia Torgovogo Doma S. Strugovshchikova, 1860.

Arkhimandrit Feodor (A. M. Bukharev). *Pis'ma k kazanskim druz'iam.* Edited by P. Florenskii. Sergiev Posad 1917.

Arkhimandrit Feodor (A. M. Bukharev). *Sergiev Posad: Issledovaniia Apokalipsa.* Bogoslovskij Vestnik, 1916.

5. Bulgakov, S. N.

Bulgakov, S. N. *Agnets Bozhii.* Moskva: Obshchedostupnyi Pravoslavnyi Universtitet osnovannyi Prot. A. Menem, 2000.

Bulgakov, S. N. *Alle mura di Chersoneso e altri scritti.* Translated by G. Parravicini. Milano: La Casa di Matriona, 1998.

Bulgakov, S. *Dela i dni.* Moskva: Sobranie, 2008.

Bulgakov, S. *Dnevniki.* Orel: Izd. Orlovskoi gosudarstvennoi teleradioveshchatel'noi kompanii, 1998.

Bulgakov, S. N. *Dva grada: Issledovaniia o prirode obshchestvennykh idealov,* vols. 1-2. Moskva: Tovarishchestvo tipografii A. I. Mamontova, 1911.

Bulgakov, S. N. *Filosofiia imeni.* Paris: YMCA Press, 1953.

Bulgakov, S. N. *Icons and the Name of God.* Eerdmans: Grand Rapids, 2012.

Bulgakov, S. N. *Ikona i ikonopochitanie.* Paris 1931.

Bulgakov, S. N. *Il Paraclito.* Translated by F. Marchese. Bologna 1971.

Bulgakov, S. N. *L'Agnello di Dio.* Translated by O. Nobile Ventura. Roma 1990.

Bulgakov, S. N. *La luce senza tramonto.* Translated by M. Campatelli. Roma 2002.

Bulgakov, S. N. "Lestvitsa Iakovlia: Ob angelakh," in *Malaia Trilogiia.* Moskva: Obshchedostupnyi Pravoslavnyi Universtitet osnovannyi Prot. A. Menem, 2008.

Bulgakov, S. N. *Nevesta Agntsa.* Paris: YMCA Press, 1945.

Bulgakov, S. N. *Ot marksizma k idealizmu: Sbornik statei (1896-1903).* Sankt-Peterburg: Tovarishchestvo 'Obshchestvennaia Pol'za', 1903.

Bulgakov, S. N. *Presso le mura di Chersoneso e altri scritti.* Translated and edited by M. Campatelli. Roma 1998.

Bulgakov, S. N. *Sophia, the Wisdom of God: An Outline of Sophiology.* Hudson, NY: Lindisfarne, 1993.

Bulgakov, S. N. *Svet nevechernii: Sozertsaniia i umozreniia.* Sankt-Peterburg: Izd. Olega Abyshko, 2008.

Bulgakov, S. N. *The Bride of the Lamb.* Grand Rapids: Eerdmans, 2002.

Bulgakov, S. N. *The Friend of the Bridegroom: On the Orthodox Veneration of the Forerunner.* Cambridge and Grand Rapids: Eerdmans, 2003.

Bulgakov, S. N. *The Lamb of God.* Grand Rapids and Cambridge: Eerdmans, 2008.

Bulgakov, S. N. *The Wisdom of God: A Brief Summary of Sophiology.* Translated by P. J. Thompson, O. F. Clarke, and K. Braikevich. London: Williams & Norgate/New York: Paisley Press, 1937.

Bulgakov, S. N. *Trudy o Troichnosti.* Moskva: OGI, 2001.

Bulgakov, S. N. *Uteshitel'.* Moskva: Obshchedostupnyi Pravoslavnyi Universtitet osnovannyi Prot. A. Menem, 2003.

Bulgakow, S. N. *Die Tragödie der Philosophie.* Darmstadt: Otto Reichl Verlag, 1927.

6. Evdokimov, P. N.

Evdokimov, P. *Ages of the Spiritual Life.* Crestwood, NY: St. Vladimir's Seminary Press, 1998.

Evdokimov, P. *Il matrimonio, sacramento dell'Amore.* Bose-Magnano: Qiqajon, 2008.

Evdokimov, P. *L'Esprit Saint dans la Tradition Orthodoxe.* Paris: Cerf, 1969.

Evdokimov, P. *L'età della vita spirituale.* Bologna: EDB, 1981.

Evdokimov, P. *L'Orthodoxie.* Paris: Delachaux & Niestlé, 1959.

Evdokimov, P. *L'Ortodossia.* Bologna: Società editrice il Mulino, 1965.

Evdokimov, P. *L'uomo icona di Cristo: Saggi di spiritualità.* Milano: Áncora, 1982.

Evdokimov, P. *La donna e la salvezza del mondo.* Milano: Jaca Book, 1980.

Evdokimov, P. *La femme et le salut du monde.* Paris: Casterman, 1958.

Evdokimov, P. "La nouveauté de l'Esprit," *Spiritualité Orientale* 20. Bégrolles 1977.

Evdokimov, P. *Le buisson ardent.* Paris: P. Lethielleux, 1981.

Evdokimov, P. *Le Christ dans la pensée russe.* Paris 1970. (*Cristo nel pensiero russo.* Roma 1972; Christus im Russischen Denken. Trier: Paulinus-Verlag, 1977.)

Evdokimov, P. *Le sacrement de l'Amour: Le mystère conjugal à la lumière de la tradition orthodoxe.* Paris: L'ÉPI, 1962.

Evdokimov, P. "Les principaux courants de l'ecclesiologie orthodoxe au XIXe siècle," *Revue des sciences religieuses* 2-4 (1960).

Evdokimov, P. N. *Sacramento dell'Amore: Il mistero coniugale alla luce della tradizione ortodossa.* Sotto il Monte: Servitium, 1999.

Evdokimov, N. P. *Teologia della bellezza: L'arte dell'icona.* Torino: San Paolo, 1990.

Evdokimov, P. *The Sacrament of Love.* Crestwood, NY: St. Vladimir's Seminary Press, 1985.

7. Fedorov, N. F.

Fedorov, N. *Filosofiia obshchego dela*, vols. 1-2. Moskva: AST, 2003.

Fedorov, N. F. *Sobranie sochinenii v chetyrekh tomakh*, vols. 1-4. Moskva: Traditsiia/Progress/Evidentis, 1995-2005.

Fedorov, N. F. *Vopros o bratstve, ili rodstve, o pirichinakh nebratskogo, nerodstvennogo, t.e. nemirogo, sostoiania mira i o sredstvakh k vostanovleniiu rodstva*. Moskva 2006.

8. Filaret (Drozdov) of Moscow (Metr.)

Filaret Moskovskii. *Beseda po osviashchenii khrama Vozdvizheniia Kresta Gospodnia v Preobrazhenskom Bogodelennom Dome*. Moskva: Tipografiia Vedomostei Moskovskoi gorodskoi politzii, 1855.

Filaret Moskovskii. "O telesnykh nakazaniakh s khristiianskoi tochki zreniia" (1862) in *Sochinenie mitropolita Filareta* in *"Chtenia v Imperatorskom Obshchestve Istorii i drevnostei rossiiskikh pri Moskovskom Universitete"* 4. Moskva 1867.

Filaret Moskovskii. *Neusynaiushchee oko mysli* in *Sviatitel' Filaret Moskovskii: Prizovite Boga v pomoshch*. Moskva: Izd. Sretenskogo monastyria, 2008.

Filaret Moskovskii. Sviatitel, *Prizovite Boga v pomoshch: Sbornik pisem*. Moskva 2006.

Filaret Moskovskii. *Prostrannyi khristianskii katikhizis Pravoslavnyia Katholicheskiia Vostochnyia Tserkvi*. Moskva 1852.

Filaret Moskovskii. *Rozgovory mezhdu ispytuiushchim i uverenym o Pravoslavii Vostochnoi Katholicheskoi Tserkvi*. Moskva 1841.

Sviatitel Filaret (Drozdov). *Izbrannye trudy, pis'ma, vospominania*. Moskva 2003.

9. Filaret Gumilevskii (Chernigovskii)

Filaret Gumilevskii (Chernigovskii). *Besedy o stradaniiakh Gospoda nashego Iisusa Khrista*. Moskva: Izdatel'stvo imeni sv. Ignatiia, 2000.

Filaret Gumilevskii (Chernigovskii), *Istoriia russkoi Tserkvi*. Moskva: Universitetskaia tipografiia, 1848.

Filaret Gumilevskii (Chernigovskii). *Obzor russkoi dukhovnoi literatury 862-1863*. Sankt-Peterburg: I. L. Tuzov, 1884.

Filaret Gumilevskii (Chernigovskii), *O stradaniiakh Gospoda nashego Iisusa Khrista*. Moskva 1884.

Filaret Gumilevskii (Chernigovskii). *Pravoslavnoe dogmaticheskoe bogoslovie*, vols. 1-2. Sankt-Peterburg: I. L. Tuzov, 1882.

Filaret Gumilevskii (Chernigovskii), *Slova i besedy Filareta arkhiepiskopa Chernigovskogo i Nezhinskogo*. Edited by S. Tuzov. Chernigov: Ilinskii Monastir, 1863.

10. Florenskii, P. A.

Florenskii, P. *Stolp i tverzhdenie istiny: Opyt Pravoslavnoi teoditsei*. Moskva: Izd. ACT, 2002.

Florenskii, P. A. *Stolp i utverzdenie istiny*, vols. 1-2. Moskva: "Pravda," 1990.

Florenskij, P. A. *Ai miei figli*. Edited by N. Valentini and L. Zak, translated by C. Zonghetti. Milano: Oscar Mondadori, 2009.

Florenskij, P. A. "Cristianesimo e cultura," *L'altra Europa* 1, no. 5 (1987-91).
Florenskij, P. A. *Il concetto di chiesa nella Sacra Scrittura.* Edited by N. Valentini and L. Zak. Milano: San Paolo, 2008.
Florenskij, P. A. *Il cuore cherubico: Scritti teologici e mistici.* Translated by R. Zugan. Casale Monferrato 1999.
Florenskij, P. A. *La colonna e il fondamento della Verità.* Translated by Pietro Modesto. Milano: San Paolo, 1974.
Florenskij, P. A. "La laura della Trinità e di san Sergio e la Russia," *Russia Cristiana* 4 (1977).
Florenskij, P. A. *Non dimenticatemi.* Edited by N. Valentini and L. Zak, translated by G. Guaita and L. Charitonov. Milano: Oscar Mondadori, 2006.
Florensky, (St.) P. *Salt of the Earth.* St. Herman of Alaska Brotherhood, [S.l.], 1999.
Florensky, P. *The Pillar and Ground of Truth: An Essay in Orthodox Theodicy in Twelve Letters.* Translated by B. Jakim. Princeton and Oxford: Princeton University Press, 1997.

11. Florovskii, G. V.

Collected Works of Georges Florovsky, vols. 1-14. Belmont, MA: Nordland, 1972-89.
Florovskii, G. "Blazhenstvo strazhdushchei liubvi (K 100-letiiu so dnia rozhd. F. M. Dostoevskogo)," in *Put' k ochevidnosti: Georgii Florovskii, Iz proshlogo russkoi mysli.* Moskva: Agraf, 1998.
Florovskii, G. *Khristianstvo i tsivilizatsiia.* Sankt-Peterburg: Izd. Russkoi Khristianskoi gumanitarnoi akademii, 2005.
Florovskii, G. *Ways of Russian Theology* 1-2, translated by L. R. Nichols. Belmont, MA: Nordland, 1979.
Florovskij, G. *Puti russkogo bogosloviia.* Paris, Beograd: Svetlost, 1937.
Florovsky, G. "Le corps du Christ vivant: Une interprétation orthodoxe de l'Eglise," in *La Sainte Eglise Universelle: Confrontation oecuménique.* Cahiers Théologiques de l'actualité protestante, Hors Série 4. Paris: Delachaux et Niestlé, 1948.

12. Frank, S. L.

Frank, S. L. *A Solovyov Anthology.* Translated by N. Duddington. New York 1950.
Frank, S. L. *Dukhovnye osnovy obshchestva.* Moskva: Izd. "Respublika," 1992.
Frank, S. "Fr. Nitsshe i etika 'liubvi k dal'nemu,'" in *Semen Frank: Sochineniia.* Minsk, Kharvest, Moskva: Ast, 2000.
Frank, S. L. *God with Us: Three Meditations.* Translated by N. Duddington. New Haven: Yale University Press, 1946.
Frank, S. L. *Iz istorii russkoi filosofskoi mysli kontsa XIX i nachala XX veka: Antologiia.* Edited by V. S. Frank. Washington, DC, and New York 1965.
Frank, S. L. "Krushenie kumirov," in *S. L. Frank: Sochineniia.* Moskva: Izd. "Pravda," 1990.
Frank, S. L. *Man's Soul: An Introductory Essay in Philosophical Psychology.* Translated by B. Jakim. Athens, OH 1950.
Frank, S. L. *Nepostizhimoe.* Paris 1939.

Frank, S. L. "Nepostizhimoe," in *S. L. Frank: Sochineniia.* Moskva: Izd. "Pravda," 1990.

Frank, S. L. *Realnost' i chelovek: Metafizika chelovecheskogo bytiia.* Paris: YMCA Press, 1956.

Frank, S. L. *Reality and Man: An Essay in the Metaphysics of Human Nature.* Translated by N. Duddington. New York: Taplinger, 1965.

Frank, S. L. Review of *Hegel bei den Slawen.* Edited by D. Tschizewski in *Zeitschrift für slawische Philologie* 12 (1935).

Frank, S. *Smysl zhizni.* Bruxelles: Izd. "Zhin' s Bogom," Foyer Oriental Chrétien, 1992.

Frank, S. L. *Svet vo t'me.* Moskva: "Faktorial," 1998.

Frank, S. L. *The Unknowable: An Ontological Introduction to Philosophy of Religion.* Translated by B. Jakim. Athens, OH 1983.

13. Ivanov, V. I.

Ivanov, V. "Cor Ardens," in *Viacheslav Ivanov: Sobranie sochinenii II.* Bruxelles: Foyer Oriental Chrétien, 1974.

Ivanov, V. *L'uomo,* a bilingual edition, edited by M. T. Mayer. Milano: Aquilegia Edizioni, 1999.

Ivanov, V. I. *Rodnoe i vselenskoe.* Moskva: Izd. "Respublika," 1994.

Ivanov, V. *Sobranie sochinenii I.* Bruxelles: Foyer Oriental Chrétien, 1971.

Ivanov, V. *Works,* vols. 1-3, Brussels 1979.

14. Karsavin, L. P.

Karsavin, L. P. *Dialogi.* Berlin: Obelisk, 1923.

Karsavin, L. P. *Katolichestvo: Obshchii ocherk.* Petrograd: Izd. "Ogni," 1918.

Karsavin, L. P. *Malye sochineniia.* Sankt-Peterburg: AO "Aleteiia," 1994.

Karsavin, L. P. *"Noctes Petropolitanae."* Sankt-Peterburg 1922.

Karsavin, L. P. *O nachalakh: Opyt khristianskoi metafiziki.* Berlin: Obelisk, 1925.

Karsavin, L. P. "O sovershenstve: Metafizika sovershenstva v traktate khristianina-uznika," in *Bogoslovskie trudy* 39. Moskva: Izd. Sovet russkoi Pravoslvanoi Tserkvi, 2004.

Karsavin, L. P. *Poema o smerti.* Kaunas: "Eranus" Il kygnos, 1932.

Karsavin, L. P. *Poema o smerti,* in "Put' Pavoslaviia." Moskva: Folio, 2003.

Karsavin, L. *Religiozno-filosofskie sochineniia,* vol. 1. Moskva: "Renaissanse" SP "Ewo-S&D," 1992.

Karsavin, L. P. *Tserkov', lichnost' i gosudarstvo.* Parizh: Evraziiskoe knizoizdatel'stvo, 1927.

15. Khomiakov, A. S.

Khomiakov, A. S. *Polnoe sobranie sochinenii Alekseia Stepanovicha Khomiakova,* vols. 1-8. Moskva: Universitetskaia tipografiia, 1900.

Khomiakov, A. S. *Sochineniia bogoslovskie.* Sankt-Peterburg: "Nauka," 1995.

Khomiakov, A. S. *Sochineniia v dvukh tomakh,* vols. 1-2. Moskva: "Medium," 1994.

Khomiakov, A. S. *The Church Is One.* Edited by Archpriest G. Grabbe. Seattle: St. Nectarios Press, 1979.

Khomiakov, A. S. *Tserkov' odna.* Moskva: Khristianskii mir, Dar", 2005.
Khomiakov, A. S. "Tserkov' odna," in *Polnoe sobranie sochinenii Alekseia Stepanovicha Khomiakova,* vol. 2. Moskva: Universitetskaia tipografiia, 1900.
Khomiakov, A. *Vsemirnaia zadacha Rossii.* Moskva: Institut russkoi tsivilizatsii, 2008.

16. Khrapovitskii, A. P. (Bish.)

Mitropolit Antonii (Khrapovitskii), *Besedy pravoslavnogo sviashchennika s uniatskom greko-katolikom.* Sremski Karlovtsi: Srpska manastirska shtampariia, 1922.
Mitropolit Antonii (Khrapovitskii), *Molitva russkoi dushi.* Edited and introduced by T. A. Solovova. Moskva: Sretenskii monastyr', 2006,
Mitropolit Antonii (Khrapovitskii), *Opyt khristianskogo pravoslavnogo katikhizisa.* Sremski Karlovtsi: Srpska manastirska shtampariia, 1924.
Mitropolit Antonii (Khrapovitskii), *Sobranie lektsii i statei po pastyrskomu bogosloviiu.* Moskva: Pecatnia A. I. Snegirevoi, 1909.
Mitropolit Antonii (Khrapovitskii), *Sobranie sochinenii (v dvukh tomakh),* vols. 1-2. Moskva: Izd. Dar", 2007.
Mitropolit Antonii (Khrapovitskii), *Zhizneopisanie: Pis'ma k raznym litsam 1919-1939 godov.* Sankt-Peterburg: Izd. Olega Abyshko, 2006.

17. Losskii, V. N.

Losskii, V. N. *Ocherk misticheskogo bogosloviia Vostochnoi Tserkvi: Dogmaticheskoe bogoslovie.* Moskva: Izd. Tsentr "SEI," 1991.
Losskii, V. N. *Po obrazu i podobiiu.* Moskva: Izd. Sviato-Vladimirskogo Bratstva, 1995.
Losskii, V. N. *Spor o Sofii; Stat'i raznykh let.* Moskva: Izd. Sviato-Vladimirskogo Bratstva, 1996.
Lossky, V. *Conoscere Dio.* Bose: Quiqajon, 1996.
Lossky, V. *In the Image and Likeness of God.* Crestwood, NY: St. Vladimir's Seminary Press, 2001.
Lossky, V. *The Mystical Theology of the Eastern Church.* Crestwood, NY: St. Vladimir's Seminary Press, 1976.
Lossky, V. *The Vision of God.* New York: Athens Printing Company, 1973.

18. Makarii Bulgakov (Metr.)

Makarii Bulgakov. *Introduction à la théologie orthodoxe.* Paris: Joël Cherbuliez, Librairie-Éditeur, 1857.
Makarii Bulgakov. *Pravoslavno-dogmaticheskoe bogoslovie,* vols. 1-2. Sankt-Peterburg: Tipografia Koroleva, 1856-57.
Makarii Bulgakov. *Rukovodstvo k izucheniiu khristianskogo, pravoslavno-dogmaticheskogo bogosloviia.* Moskva: Sinodal'naia Tipografiia, 1898.
Makarii Bulgakov. *Théologie dogmatique orthodoxe,* vols. 1-2. Paris: Librairie de Joël Cherbuliez, 1860.
Makarii Bulgakov. *Vvedenie v pravoslavnoe bogoslovie.* Sankt-Peterburg: Tipografiia Departamenta Udelov, 1852.

19. Malinovskii, N. P.

Malinovskii, N. P. *O Boge Iskupitele: Dogmaticheskii ocherk.* Kamanec-Podol'skii: Tipografiia S. P. Kirzhackogo, 1906.

Malinovskii, N. P. *Ocherk pravoslavnogo dogmaticheskogo bogosloviia,* vols. 1-2. Sergei Posad: Sv. Troitskaiia Lavra, 1911-12.

Malinovskii, N. P. *O liturgii prezhdeosviashchennykh darov.* Sankt-Peterburg: Tip. Dmitrieva, 1850.

Malinovskii, N. P. *Pravoslavnoe dogmaticheskoe bogoslovie,* vols. 1-4. Sergiev Posad: Tipografiia Sergievoi Lavry, 1909-10.

Malinovskii, N. P. *Pravoslavnoe dogmaticheskoe bogoslovie.* Khar'kov: Tip. Timofeev, 1895-1903.

20. Schmemann, A. D.

Schmemann, A. *Church, World, Mission.* Crestwood, NY: St. Vladimir's Seminary Press, 1979.

Schmemann, A. *For the Life of the World: Sacraments and Orthodoxy.* Crestwood, NY: St. Vladimir's Seminary Press, 1973.

Schmemann, A. *Great Lent: Journey to Pascha.* Crestwood, NY: St. Vladimir's Seminary Press [n.d.].

Schmemann, A. "In Memoriam: Le R. P. Nicolas Afanassieff," *Irenikon* 40, no. 2 (1967).

Schmemann, A. *L'Eucaristia: Sacramento del Regno.* Bose: Qiqajon, 2005.

Schmemann, A. *Liturgy and Life: Christian Development through Liturgical Experience.* New York: Department of Religious Education, Orthodox Church in America, 1974.

Schmemann, A. *Liturgy and Tradition.* Edited by T. Fisch. Crestwood, NY: St. Vladimir's Seminary Press, 2003.

Schmemann, A. *O Death, Where Is Thy Sting?* Crestwood, NY: St. Vladimir's Seminary Press, 2003.

Schmemann, A. *Quaresima: In cammino verso la Pasqua.* Bose: Qiqajon, 2010.

Schmemann, A. *Sacraments and Orthodoxy.* London: Herder & Herder, 1965.

Schmemann, A. *The Eucharist: Sacrament of the Kingdom.* Crestwood, NY: St. Vladimir's Seminary Press, 1988.

Schmemann, A. *The Historical Road of Eastern Orthodoxy.* Translated by L. W. Kelish. New York, Chicago, San Francisco: Holt, Rinehart & Winston, 1963.

Schmemann, A. *The World as Sacrament.* London: Darton, Longman & Todd, 1965.

Schmemann, A. *Ultimate Questions: An Anthology of Modern Russian Religious Thought.* Crestwood, NY: St. Vladimir's Seminary Press, 1977.

Shmeman, A. *Besedy na Radio "Svoboda,"* vols. 1-2. Moskva: Pravoslavnyi Sviato-Tikhonovskii Universtitet, 2009.

Shmeman, A. *Dnevniki 1973-1983.* Moskva: Russkii put', 2005.

Shmeman, A. *Evkharistiia: Tainstvo Tsarstva.* Moskva: Palomnik, 2007.

Shmeman, A. *Istoricheskii put' Pravoslviia.* New York: Izd. Imeni Chekhova, 1954.

Shmeman, A. *Liturgiia i zhizn'.* Moskva: Palomnik, 2009.

Shmeman, A. *Sobranie statei 1947-1983.* Moskva: Russkii put', 2009.

Shmeman, A. *Sviataia sviatym.* Moskva-Kiev: Tsentr pravoslavnoi knigy, 2008-9.
Shmeman, A. *Vodoiu i Dukhom: O tainstve kreshcheniia.* Moskva: Gnozis-Palomnik, 1993.
Shmeman, A. *Voskresnye besedy.* Moskva: Palomnik, 2008.
Shmeman, A. *Vvedenie v liturgicheskoe bogoslovie.* Paris: YMCA Press, 1961.

21. Sil'vestr Malevanskii (Bish.)

Episkop Sil'vestr. *Pravoslavno dogmatichno bogoslovie: S istorichno izsledvane na dogmite,* vol. 1 (-3), edited by S. M. Staikov. Sofia: Sv. Sinodna Balgarskata Tsarkva, 1912-14.
Sil'vestr Malevanskii. *Opyt pravoslavnogo dogmaticheskogo bogosloviia: S istoricheskim izlozheniem dogmatov,* vols. 1-5. Kiev: Tipografia G. T. Korchak-Novickogo, 1884-91.
Sil'vestr Malevanskii. *Otvet pravoslavnogo na predlozhennuiu starokatolikami skhemu o Sviatom Dukhe.* Kiev: Tipografiia S. T. Evremeeva, 1875.
Sil'vestr Malevanskij. *Antwort auf die in dem altkatholischen Schema enthaltene Bemerkung vom dem Heiligen Geiste.* St. Pétersbourg: Röttger & Schneider, 1875.
Sil'vestr Malevanskij. *Risposta di un ortodosso allo schema proposto dai vecchi-cattolici sullo Spirito Santo.* Roma: Salviucci, 1877.

22. Solov'ev, V. S.

Solov'ev, V. *Sobranie sochinenii.* Edited by S. M. Solov'ev and E. L. Radlov, vols. 1-10. Sankt-Peterburg 1922-14. Reprint with two complementary volumes, Brussels 1966-70.
Solov'ev, V. "Zhiznennaia drama Platona," *Vestnik Evropy* 3-4 (March-April 1898).
Solovjev, V. *Il significato dell'amore e altri scritti.* Translated and edited by A. Dell'Asta. Milano 1988. *The Meaning of Love.* Translated by J. Marshall. Stockbridge, MA 1992.
Solovyov, V. *God, Man and Church: The Spiritual Foundations of Life.* Translated by D. Attwater. London 1938.
Solovyov, V. *Lectures on Divine Humanity.* Edited by B. Jakim. Hudson, NY: Lindisfarne Press, 1995.
Solovyov, V. *The Crisis of Western Philosophy (Against the Positivists).* Translated and edited by B. Jakim. Hudson, NY: Lindisfarne Press, 1996.
Solovyov, V. *The Justification of the Good.* Translated by N. A. Duddington. Cambridge and Grand Rapids: Eerdmans, 2005.
Solovyov, V. *The Meaning of Love.* Edited by Th. R. Beyer Jr. Hudson, NY: Lindisfarne Press, 1985.
Solovyov, V. *The Philosophical Principles of Integral Knowledge.* Translated by V. Z. Nollan. Cambridge and Grand Rapids: Eerdmans, 2008.
Solovyov, V. *The Religious Poetry of Vladimir Solovyov.* Translated by B. Jakim and L. Magnus. San Rafael, CA: Semantron Press, 2008.
Solovyov, V. *War and Christianity: From the Russian Point of View.* San Rafael, CA: Semantron, 2007.

23. Stragorodskii, S. (Metr.)

Arkhiep. Sergii. *Po Japonii: zapiski missionera.* Sviato-Troitskaia Sergieva Lavra 1903.

Arkhiep. Sergii. *Pravoslavnoe uchenie o spasenii.* Kazan': Tipografiia Imperatorskogo Universitata, 1898.

Arkhiep. Sergii. *Spasenie i vera po ucheniiu katolicheskomu i protestantskomu.* Moskva: Pechatnia A. I. Snegirevoi, 1913.

Arkhiep. Sergii. *Ukaz Moskovskoi patriarkhii preosviashchennomu mitropolitu Litovskomu i Vilenskomu Elevferiiu: Osuzhdenie ucheniia prot. S. N. Bulgakova o sofii.* Moskva: Moskovskaia Patriarkhiia, 1935.

Arkhiep. Sergii. *Vechnaia zhizn' kak vysshee blago.* Moskva: Pechatnia A. I. Snegirevoi, 1917.

24. Svetlov, P. Ia.

Svetlov, P. Ia. *Chelovek i zhivotnoe v psikhicheskom otnoshenii.* Khar'kov 1892.

Svetlov, P. Ia. *Chto chitat' po bogosloviiu?* Kiev [s.n.] 1907.

Svetlov, P. Ia. *Ideia Tsarstva Bozhiia v ee znachenii dlia khristianskogo mirosozertsaniia.* Sviato-Troitskaia Sergieva Lavra 1905.

Svetlov, P. Ia. *Khristianskoe verouchenie v apologeticheskom izlozhenii,* vols. 1-2. Kiev: Tipografiia S. V. Kul'zhenko, 1912-14.

Svetlov, P. Ia. *Kurs apologeticheskogo bogosloviia.* Kiev: Tipografiia S. V. Kul'zhenko, 1912.

Svetlov, P. Ia. *Mistitsism kontsa XIX v. v ego otnoshenii k khristianskoi religii i filosofii.* Sankt-Peterburg 1897.

Svetlov, P. Ia. *O meste bogosloviia v sem'e universitetskikh nauk.* Kiev 1897.

Svetlov, P. Ia. *O reforme dukhovnogo obrazovaniia v Rosii.* Sankt-Peterburg 1906.

Svetlov, P. Ia. *Opyt apologeticheskogo uzlozheniia pravoslavno-khristianskogo verouchenii a.* Kiev: T. I. Nezhin, 1896-99.

Svetlov, P. Ia. *Prorocheskie ili veshchnie sny.* Kiev: Tip. G. T. Korchak-Novitzkogo, 1892.

Svetlov, P. Ia. *Znachenie Khresta v dele Khristovom: Opyt iz''iasneniia dogmata iskupleniia.* Kiev: Tip. C. V. Kul'zhenko, 1907.

25. Tareev, M. M.

Tareev, M. M. *Fondamenti del Cristianesimo,* vols. 1-5. Moskva 1908-10.

Tareev, M. M. *Iskusheniia Bogocheloveka, kak edinyi iskupitel'nyi podvig vsei zemnoi zhizni Khrista, v sviazi s istorieiu dokhristianskikh religii i khristianskoi Tserkvi.* Moskva 1892.

Tareev, M. M. *Khristianskaia svoboda.* Sergiev Posad: Tipografiia Sergevoi Lavry, 1908.

Tareev, M. M. *Khristos.* Sergiev Posad: Tipografiia Sergevoi Lavry, 1908.

Tareev, M. M. "L'ecclesialità come principio della teologia morale," *Bogoslovskii Vestnik* 9 (1909).

Tareev, M. M. *Unichizhenie Gospoda nashego Iisusa Khrista.* Moskva 1901.

Tareev, M. M. *Zhivye dushi.* Sankt-Peterburg: P. P. Soikin, [S.d.].

Secondary Literature

Adel'geim, I. P. *Dogmat o Tserkvii v kanonakh i praktike.* Nizhnii Novgorod 2008.
Aksakov, N. P. *Dukha ne ugashaite!* Moskva: Izd. Sv.-Filaretovskaia moskovskaia vysshaia pravoslavno-khristianskaia shkola, 2000.
Alekseev, P. V. *Filosofy Rossii XIX-XX stoletii.* Moskva: "Akademicheskii Proekt," 2002.
Allen, P. M. *Vladimir Soloviev: Russian Mystic.* Blauvelt, New York 1978.
Al'tman, M. S. *Razgovory s Viacheslavom Ivanovym.* Sankt-Peterburg: Inapress, 1995.
Anderson, P. B. *People, Church and State in Modern Russia.* New York 1944.
Andreyev, C., and I. Savický. *Russia Abroad: Prague and the Russian Diaspora 1918-1938.* New Haven: Yale University Press, 2004.
Antonov, K. M. *Filosofiia I. V. Kireevskogo.* Moskva: Izd. PSTGU, 2006.
Antonov, K. M. *Filosofiia religii v russkoi metafizike XIX-nachalo XX veka.* Moskva: Izd. PSTGU, 2009.
Arseniev, N. *Mysticism and the Eastern Church.* Crestwood, NY: St. Vladimir's Seminary Press, 1979.
Arseniev, N. *Russian Piety.* Crestwood, NY: St. Vladimir's Seminary Press, 1975.
Arseniev, N., and V. Lossky. *Padri nello Spirito.* Bose: Quiqajon, 1997.
Aulen, G. *Christus Victor: La notion chrétienne de rédemption.* Paris: Aubier, 1949.
Averintsev, S. S. *"Skvoreshnits vol'nykh grazhdanin. . . ."* Sankt-Peterburg: Izd. "Aleteia," 2002.
Balandin, R. K. *Russkie mysliteli.* Moskva 2006.
Balthasar, H. U. v. *Kosmische Liturgie: Das Weltbild Maximus' des Bekenners.* Einsiedeln: Johannes Verlag, 1961.
Balthasar, H. U. v. *The Glory of the Lord,* vols. 1-3. Edinburgh: T. & T. Clark, 1986.
Bartholomew I. *Un entretien avec Bartholomé Ier, Patriarch Oecuménique à propos du Nouveau catechism Catholique: Convergences et divergences entre Catholiques et Orthodoxes.* Paris: Service Orthodox de Presse, 1993.
Běloševská, L., ed. *Duchovní Proudy ruské a ukrajinské emigrace v Československé republice 1919-1939.* Praha: Slovanský ústav AV ČR, 1999.
Belyj, A., and P. A. Florenskij. *L'arte, il simbolo e Dio.* Translated and edited by G. Giuliano. Milano: Medusa, 2004.
Benedict XVI. *Caritas in Veritate.* Vatican: Libreria Editrice Vaticana, 2009.
Benedict XVI. *Deus Caritas Est.* Vatican: Libreria Editrice Vaticana, 2006.
Berlin, I. *Russian Thinkers.* New York: Penguin, 1994.
Bertazzo, L., ed. *Credere oggi: Teologi Ortodossi del XX secolo* 140/2. Padova: Messagero, 2004.
Blagova, T. I. *Aleksei Khomiakov i Ivan Kireevskii.* Moskva: "Vyshchaia shkola," 1995.
Blagova, T. I. *Rodonachal'niki slavianofil'stva: Aleksei Khomiakov i Ivan Kireevskii.* Moskva: "Vyshchaia shkola," 1995.
Blane, A., ed. *Georges Florovsky: Russian Intellectual, Orthodox Churchman.* Crestwood, NY: St. Vladimir's Seminary Press, 1993.
Blane, A., ed. *The Religious World of Russian Culture.* The Hague/Paris: Mouton, 1975.
Bolshakoff, S. *Russian Mystics.* Kalamazoo, MI: Cistercian Publications, 1980.
Bolshakoff, S. *Russian Nonconformity.* Philadelphia: Westminster, 1950.

Bonetskaia, N. K. "Antonomiia iazyka P. A. Florenskogo," *Studia Slavica Academiae Scientiarum Hungaricae* 32 (1986).

Boobbyer, P. *S. L. Frank: The Life and Work of a Russian Philosopher 1877-1950*. Athens, OH: Ohio University Press, 1995.

Bori, P. C., and P. Bettiolo, eds. *Movimenti religiosi in Russia prima della rivoluzione (1900-1917)*. Brescia: Queriniana, 1978.

Bouteneff, P. C. "Freedom and Faithfulness: An Afterword," in *Tradition Alive*, edited by M. Plekon. Lanham, MD: Sheed & Ward, 2003.

Brodskii, A. I. *Mikhail Tareev*. Sankt-Peterburg: Izd. Sankt Peterburgskogo Universiteta, 1994.

Brodskii, L., ed. *Mneniia, otzyvy i pis'ma Filareta, Mitropolita Moskovskogo i kolomenskogo po raznym voprosam za 1821-1867*. Moskva 1905.

Brodskii, L. N., and N. P. Sidorov. *Literaturnye manifesty: Ot simvolizma do "Oktiabria."* Moskva: Agraf, 2001.

Bukhareva, A. S. "Alexander Matveevich Bukharev (Arkhimandrit Feodor): Iz materialov dlia biografii," in *Svobodnaia sovest', Literaturno-filosofskii sbornik*, vol. 1. Moskva: Tipografiia T-va I. D. Sytina, 1906.

Buss, A. E. *The Russian-Orthodox Tradition and Modernity*. Leiden-Boston: Brill, 2003.

Bychkov, V. *The Aesthetic Face of Being: Art in the Theology of Pavel Florensky*. Translated by R. Pesear and L. Volkhonky. Crestwood, NY: St. Vladimir's Seminary Press, 1993.

Caprio, S. *V. I. Nesmelov e l'antropologia religiosa russa*. Roma: Orientalia Christiana Analecta, 2006.

Carlson, M. *No Religion Higher Than Truth: A History of the Theosophical Movement in Russia, 1875-1922*. Princeton: Princeton University Press, 1993.

Cavazza, A. *Tserkov' odna di A. S. Chomjakov (Edizione critica del manoscritto OPI GIM)*. Excerpta ex Dissertatione ad Doctoratum, Pontificium Institutum Orientalum, Bologna 2002.

Celora, G. *Evdokimov, voce dell'ortodossia in Occidente*. Bologna: Dehoniane, 1995.

Chaadaev, P. I. *Sochinenia i pis'ma*, vols. 1-2, edited by M. Gershenzova. Moskva: Put', 1913-14.

Charipova, L. V. *Latin Books and the Eastern Orthodox Clerical Elite in Kiev 1632-1780*. Manchester and New York: Manchester University Press, 2006.

Cioffari, G. "Breve storia della teologia russa," *Quaderni di O Odigos* 6, no. 4 (Bari 1987).

Cioffari, G. "La sobornost nella teologia russa: La visione della chiesa negli scrittori ecclesiastici della prima metà del XIX secolo," *Nicolaus* 2 (Bari 1977).

Clément, O. "Paul Evdokimov, témoin de la beauté de Dieu," *Contacts* 23, nos. 73-74 (Paris 1971).

Clément, O. "La vita e le opere di Paul Evdokimov," in P. Evdokimov, *La santità nella tradizione della Chiesa Ortodossa*. Fossano: Esperienze, 1972.

Copleston, F. C. *Philosophy in Russia: From Herzen to Lenin and Berdiaev*. Notre Dame: Notre Dame University Press, 1986.

Copleston, F. C. *Russian Religious Philosophy: Selected Aspects*. Notre Dame: Notre Dame University Press, 1988.

Cucinotta, F. S. "L'apporto della teologia delle Chiese d'Oriente," in *Storia della teologia*, edited by R. Fisichella. Bologna: Il Mulino, 1996.

D'Arcy, M. C. *The Mind and Heart of Love*. New York: Meridian Books, 1956.

Davydov, I. N. *Liubov' i svoboda*. Moskva: Astrel', 2008.

Dobren'kov, V. I., et al., eds. *Manifesty russkogo idealizma: Problemy idealizma, Vekhi, Iz Glubiny*. Moskva: Astrel', 2009.

Dobrokhotov, A. L., S. B. Nevolin, and L. G. Filonova, eds. *Russkie filosofy*. Moskva: Izd. "Knizhnaia palata," 1993.

Doherty, C. *Poustinia: Encountering God in Silence, Solitude and Prayer*. Combermere, UK: Madonna House Publications, 2000.

Doherty, C. *Sobornost: Experiencing Unity of Mind, Heart and Soul*. Combermere, UK: Madonna House Publications, 2000.

Egorov, G. *Literaturnye trudy Patriarkha Sergiia*, ZhMP 5, no. 7 (1954).

Emeliianov, B. V., and V. V. Kulikov. *Russkie mysliteli vtoroi poloviny XIX — nachala XX veka: Opyt kratkogo biobibliograficheskogo slovaria*. Ekaterinburg: Ural, 1996.

Emery, G., and M. Levering, eds. *The Oxford Handbook of the Trinity*. Oxford: Oxford University Press, 2011.

Ern, V. *G. S. Skovoroda*. Moskva 1912.

Evtuhov, C. *The Cross and the Sickle: Sergei Bulgakov and the Fate of Russian Religious Philosophy*. Ithaca, NY: Cornell University Press, 1997.

Fedotov, G. P. *The Russian Religious Mind*. Cambridge, MA: Harvard University Press, 1946.

Felmy, K. Ch., G. F. Kretschmar von Lilienfeld, and C.-J. Roepke, eds. *Tausend Jahre Christentum in Russland*. Göttingen: Vandenhoeck & Ruprecht, 1988.

Feognost, Arch. *Pamiati vydaiushchegosia russkogo bogoslova-ekzegeta*. ZhMP 10 (1960).

Feuerbach, L. *The Essence of Christianity*. Edited by E. G. Waring and F. W. Strothmann. New York 1989.

Filaret, Mirtr. (Minskii i Slutskii), ed. *Bogoslovskie trudy* 39. Moskva: Izd. Sovet Russkoi Pravoslavnoi Tserkvi, 2004.

Flannery, A., ed. *Vatican Council II: The Conciliar and Post Conciliar Documents*, vols. 1-2. Collegeville, MN: Liturgical Press, 1992.

Florenskii, P., ed. *Pis'ma Arkhimandrita Feodora (Aleksandra Matveevicha Bukhareva) k kazanskim druz'iam: V. V. Liubimovoi, A. I. Dubrovinoi i protoiereiu V. V. Lavrskomu*. Sergiev Posad 1917.

Frolov, I. T., ed. *Chelovek*. Moskva: "Respublika," 1995.

Gaith, J. *N. Berdjaev's Philosophy of the Hope*. Leiden: Brill, 1968.

Gavriushin, N. K. *Filosofiia russkogo religioznogo iskusstva XVI-XX vv*. Moskva: Izd. "Progress"/"Kul'tura," 1993.

Gavriushin, N. K. *Smysl zhizni*. Moskva: Izd. Gruppa "Progress"/"Kul'tura," 1994.

Goerdt, W. *Russische Philosophie: Texte*. Freiburg/München: K. Alber, 1989.

Goerdt, W. *Russische Philosophie: Zugänge und Durchblicke*. Freiburg/München: K. Alber, 1984.

Gogol', N. *Selected Passages from Correspondence with Friends*. Translated by J. Zeldin. Nashville: Vanderbilt University Press, 1969 [reprint].

Gorodetzky, N. *The Humiliated Christ in Modern Russian Thought.* London-New York: Society for Promoting Christian Knowledge, 1938.

Grabbe, G. "Introduction," in A. S. Khomiakov, *The Church Is One.* Seattle: St. Nectarios Press, 1979.

Gratieux, A. *A. S. Khomiakov et le mouvement Slavophile: Les doctrines.* Paris: Cerf, 1939.

Gulyga, A. *Russkaia ideia i ee tvortsy.* Moskva 2003.

Guroian, V. *Incarnate Love.* Notre Dame: University of Notre Dame Press, 2002.

Guroian, V. *Voploshchennaia liubov': Ocherki pravoslavnoi etiki.* Moskva: Bibleisko-Bogoslovskii Institut sv. Apostola Andreia, 2002.

Hackel, S. "The Eastern Tradition from the Tenth to the Twentieth Century," in *The Study of Spirituality,* edited by Ch. Jones, G. Wainwright, and E. Yarnold. London: Oxford University Press, 1986.

Harbul'ová, L'., M. Ňachajová, and L'. Babotová. *Ruská a Ukrajinská emigrácia na východnom Slovensku v rokoch 1919-1945.* Prešov: Šta'tna vedecka' knižnica v Prešove, 2006.

Harbul'ová, L. *Ruská emigrácia a Slovensko.* Prešov: Fil. faculta Prešovskej Univerzity, 2001.

Harnack, A. von. *History of Dogma,* vols. 1-7. New York: Williams & Norgate, 1961.

Healey, Ch. J. *Christian Spirituality: An Introduction to the Heritage.* New York 2008.

Heidegger, M. *Being and Time.* New York: SCM Press, 1962.

Husserl, E. *Ideen zu einer reinen Phänomenologie und phänomenologischen Philosophie,* vols. 1-3. The Hague: Martinus Nijhoff, 1950.

Ideinoe nasledie S. L. Franka v kontekste sovremennoi kul'tury. Moskva: Bibleisko-Bogoslovskii Institute Sv. Apostola Andreia, 2009.

Iljin, I. A. *Die Philosophie Hegels als kontemplative Gotteslehre.* Bern: A. Fracke Verlag, 1946.

Isaev, I. A. *Puti Evrazii.* Moskva: Russkaia kniga, 1992.

Ivánka, E. v., J. Tyciak, and P. Wiertz, eds. *Handbuch der Ostkirchenkunde.* Düsseldorf: Patmos Verlag, 1971.

Ivanov, L. *Vospominaniia: Kniga ob ottse.* Paris: Atheneum, 1990.

Ivanov — Peterburg — mirovaia kul'tura. Tomsk-Moskva: Vodolei, 2003.

Jakim, B., and R. Bird, trans. and eds. *On Spiritual Unity: A Slavophile Reader.* New York: Lindisfarne Books, 1998.

Jakim, B., and L. Magnus, trans. and eds. *The Religious Poetry of Vladimir Solovyov.* San Rafael, CA: Semantron Press, 2008.

John Paul II. *Man and Woman He Created Them: A Theology of the Body.* Boston: Pauline Books & Media, 2006.

John Paul II. *Novo Millennio Ineunte.* Vatican: Libreria Editrice Vaticana, 2001.

John Paul II. *The Allocution to the Participants of the Roman Symposium "Viacheslav Ivanov and the Culture of His Time,"* L'Osservatore Romano, 29 May 1983.

John Paul II. *The Common Christian Roots of the European Nations: An International Colloquium in the Vatican.* Florence: Le Monnier, 1982.

Khitrov, A. M., and O. L. Solomina. *Zabytye stranitsy russkogo imiaslaviia.* Palomnik, [S.l.] 2001.

Khomiakov, D. A. *Pravoslavie, samoderzhavie, narodnost'.* Moskva: Khristianskii mir/ Dar", 2005.

Khoruzhii, S. S. *L. P. Karsavin: Malye sochineniia.* Sankt-Peterburg: AO "Aleteiia," 1994.

Khoruzhii, S. S. *Opyty iz russkoi dukhovnoi traditsii.* Moskva: Parad Izd. Dom, 2005.

Khoruzhii, S. S. *Posle pereryva: Puti russkoi filosofii.* Sankt-Peterburg: Izdavatel'stvo "Aleteiia," 1994.

Kireevskii, I. V. *Dukhovnye osnovy russkoi zhizni.* Institut russkoi tsivilizatsii, [S.l.] 2007.

Kireevskii, I. V. *Razum na puti k istine.* Moskva: Moskovskii sretenskii monastyr', 2002.

Kireevskii, I. V., and P. V. Kireevskii. *Polnoe sobranie sochinenii.* Edited by A. F. Malyshevskii, vols. 1-4. Kaluga: "Grif," 2006.

Klementiev, A., ed. *Lev Platonovich Karsavin: Bibliografiia — Bibliographie des oeuvres de Lev Karsavine.* Paris: (Ru-Fr) Institut d'Études Slaves, 1994.

Kline, G. L. "Hegel and Solovyov," in *Hegel and the History of Philosophy,* edited by K. W. Algozin, J. J. O'Malley, and F. G. Weiss. The Hague: Martinus Nijhoff, 1974.

Knechten, H. M. *Filaret von Moskau als geistlicher Schriftsteller.* Waltrop: H. Spenner, 2008.

Kornblatt, J. D. *The Cossack Hero in Russian Literature.* Madison: University of Wisconsin Press, 1992.

Kornblatt, J. D. *Divine Sophia: The Wisdom Writings of Vladimir Solovyov.* Ithaca and London: Cornell University Press, 2009.

Kornblatt, J. D., and R. F. Gustafson, eds. *Russian Religious Thought.* Madison: University of Wisconsin Press, 1996.

Koutaissoff, E., and M. Minto, eds. and trans. *What Was Man Created For? The Philosophy of the Common Task: Selected Works.* Lausanne: Honeyglen Publishing/L'Age d'Homme, 1990.

Kozlov, M. "Sviatitel'," in *Filareta Mitropolita Moskovskogo i Kilomenskogo tvoreniia.* Moskva: "Otchii dom," 1994.

Krakhmal'nikova, Z. A. *Russkaia ideia i Evrei: Rokovoi spor.* Moskva: "Vostochnaia literatura," 1994.

"Krestnyi put' Patriarkha Sergiia," in M. I. Odintsov, *Russkie patriarkhi XX veka.* Moskva: Izd. Rags, 1999.

Kvarchenko, V. *Vladimir Solov'ev i Sofiia.* Moskva: Agraf, 2006.

Kyrlezhev, A. "Radikal'nyi traditsionalizm o. Aleksandra Shmemana," *Kontinent* 79 (1994).

Kyrlezhev, A., ed. *Pravoslavnoe bogoslovie i zapad v XX veke: Istoria vstrechi.* Moskva: Khristianskaia Rossia, 2006.

Lapteva, L. P. *Istoriia slavianovedeniia v Rosii v XIX veke.* Moskva: "Indrik," 2005.

Levit, S. I. *Russkaia istoriosofiia.* Moskva: Humanitas-Rosspen, 2006.

Liubishchev, A. A. *Nauka i religiia.* Sankt-Peterburg: "Aleteiia," 2008.

Losev A. *Vladimir Solov'ev i ego vremiia.* Moskva: "Progress," 1990.

Lossky, N. O. *History of Russian Philosophy.* New York: International Universities Press, 1951.

Macmurray, J. *The Form of the Personal,* volume 1: *The Self as Agent.* New York: Harper, 1957.

Macmurray, J. *The Form of the Personal,* volume 2: *Persons in Relation.* New York: Harper, 1961.

Malcovati, F. *Vjaceslav Ivanov: Estetica e filosofia.* Firenze: La Nuova Italia, 1983.

Maloney, G. A. *A History of Orthodox Theology since 1453.* Belmont, MA: Nordland, 1976.

Markov, V. S., ed. *Polnoe sobranie rezoliutsii Filareta Mitropolita Moskovskogo,* vols. 1-2. Moskva 1903.

Masaryk, T. G. *The Spirit of Russia.* Translated by E. and C. Paul. London: Allen & Unwin, 1919.

Maslin, M. A., ed. *Russkaia ideia.* Moskva: "Respublika," 1992.

Matiash, T. P., ed. *Evgenii Trubetskoi: Izbrannye proizvedeniia.* Rostov-na-Donu: "Feniks," 1998.

Mayer, M. T. *Vjaceslav Ivanov: L'uomo.* Milano: Aquilegia Edizioni, 1999.

Mazyrin, I. A. *Vysshie ierarkhi o preemstve vlasti v Russkoi Pravoslavnoi Tserkvi v 1920-kh–1930-kh godakh.* Moskva: Izdatel'stvo Pravoslavnogo Sviato-Tikhonovskogo Gumanitarnogo Universiteta, 2006.

Mead, G. R. S. *Fragments of a Faith Forgotten.* New Hyde Park, NY: University Books, 1960.

Medved', M. *Russkii individualizm.* Moskva: Algoritm, 2007.

Meehan, B. *Holy Women of Russia: The Lives of Five Orthodox Women Offer Spiritual Guidance for Today.* San Francisco: Harper, 1993.

Meerson, M. A. *Sozertsaniem Troitsy Sviatoi . . . .* Kiev: Izd. "Dukh i litera," 2008.

Meerson, M. A. *The Trinity of Love in Modern Russian Theology.* Quincy, IL: Franciscan Press, 1998.

Meiendorf, I. prot. *"Zhizn' s izbytkom," in Shmeman A. prot. Dnevniki 1973-1983.* Moskva: Russkii put', 2005.

Melikh, I. B. *Personalism L. P. Karsavina i evropeiskaia filosofiia.* Moskva: Progress-Traditsiia, 2003.

Merezhkovskii, D. *Nemoi prorok in V tikhomute,* in *Polnoe sobranie sochinenii,* vol. 16. Moskva 1914.

Meyendorff, J. "A Life Worth Living," *St. Vladimir's Theological Quarterly* 28 (1984).

Meyendorff, J. *St. Gregory Palamas and Orthodox Spirituality.* Crestwood, NY: St. Vladimir's Seminary Press, 1974.

Meyendorff, J. *The Orthodox Church.* Crestwood, NY: St. Vladimir's Seminary Press, 1981.

Mislev, N. *Pavel Florensky: Beyond Vision; Essays on the Perception of Art.* London: Reaktion Books, 2002.

Mitrofanov, G. *Rossia XX veka: "Vostok Kserksa" ili "Vostok Khrista."* Sankt-Peterburg: Agat, 2004.

Mochul'skii, K. *Vladimir Solov'ev: Zhizn' i uchenie.* Paris: YMCA Press, 1951.

Nassiv, B., ed. *New Perspectives on Historical Theology.* Grand Rapids and Cambridge: Eerdmans, 1996.

Nevleva, I. M. *Filosofiia kul'tury S. L. Franka.* Sankt-Peterburg: Aleteiia, 2007.

Nicholl, D. *Triumphs of the Spirit in Russia.* London: Darton, Longman & Todd, 1998.

Nichols, A. *Light from the East: Authors and Themes in Orthodox Theology.* London: Sheed & Ward, 1995.

Nichols, A. *Theology in the Russian Diaspora.* Cambridge: Cambridge University Press, 1989.

Nikol'skii, S. A., and V. P. Filimonov. *Russkoe mirovozzrenie.* Moskva: Progress-Traditsiia, 2008.

Nivière A. *Les membres du clergé, théologiens et responsables laïcs de l'Église Orthodoxe dans l'émigration Russe en Europe occidentale et centrale 1920-1995.* Moscou-Paris: Russkii Put' — YMCA Press, 2007.

Nygren, A. *Agape and Eros.* Philadelphia: Westminster, 1953.

Odintsov, M. I. *Russkie patriarkhi XX veka.* Moskva: Izd. Rags, 1999.

Outka, G. *Agape: An Ethical Analysis.* New Haven: Yale University Press, 1972.

Pain, J., and N. Zernov, eds. *A Bulgakov Anthology.* London: SPCK, 1976.

Pattison, G., and D. O. Thompson, eds. *Dostoevsky and the Christian Tradition.* Cambridge: Cambridge University Press, 2001.

Pelikan, J. *Jesus Through the Centuries.* New Haven: Yale University Press, 1985.

Pinggéra, K., ed. *Russische Religionsphilosophie und Theologie um 1900.* Marburg: N. G. Elwert Verlag, 2005.

Piovesana, G. *Russia — Europa nel pensiero filosofico russo. Storia antologica.* Roma: Lipa, 1995.

Piovesana, G. *Storia del pensiero filosofico russo (988-1988).* Torino: Cinisello Balsamo, Edizioni Paoline, 1992.

Plank, P. *Die Eucharistieversammlung als Kirche: Zur Entstehung und Entfaltung der eucharistischen Ekklesiologie Nikolaj Afanas'evs (1893-1966).* Neue Folge, Band 31. Würzburg: Augustinus-Verlag, 1980.

Plekon, M., ed. *Tradition Alive.* Lanham, MD: Sheed & Ward, 2003.

Plekov, M., and A. Vinogradov, eds. *In the World of the Church: A Paul Evdokimov Reader.* Crestwood, NY: St. Vladimir's Seminary Press, 2001.

Popov, I. V. *Otzyv na dokt. dis. A. D. Beliaeva.* Zhurnaly Soveta MDA za 1899 g.

Porus, V., ed. *N. A. Berdiaev i edinstvo evropeiskogo dukha.* Moskva: Bibl. Bog. Inst. Sv. Ap. Andreia, 2007.

Pro et Contra: P. A. Florenskii. Sankt-Peterburg: Izd. Russkogo Khristianskogo gumanitarnogo instituta, 2001.

Pro et Contra: S. N. Bulgakov, vols. 1-2. Sankt-Peterburg: RKhGA, 2004-8.

Pro et Contra: Slavianofil'stvo. Edited by V. A. Fateev. Sankt-Peterburg: Izd. Sankt-Peterburgskogo universiteta, 2009.

Pushkarev, S. *The Emergence of Modern Russia, 1801-1917.* New York: Holt, Rinehart & Winston, 1963.

Pyman, A. *A History of Russian Symbolism.* Cambridge: Cambridge University Press, 1994.

Röhring, H-J. *Kenosis: Die Versuchungen Jesu Christi im Denken von Michail M. Tareev.* Leipzig: Benno-Verlag, 2000.

Rolland, J. *Dostoevskij e la questione dell'altro.* Translated by A. Dell'Asta. Milano: Jaca, 1990.

Rössler, R. *Das Weltbild N. Berdjajews: Existenz und Objektiviation.* Göttingen: Vandenhoeck & Ruprecht, 1956.

Rozanov, V. V. *Askochenskii i Arkhimandrit Feodor Bukharev.* Moskva: Izdatel'stvo Stolica, 1991.

Rudnitskaia, E. L. *Liki Russkoi intelligentsii.* Moskva: "Kanon+," 2007.

Sabodan, V. *Aktovaia rech' MDA* (on the life and works of S. Stragorodskii), *Zhurnal Moskovskogo Patriarkhata* 11 (1973).

Sabodan, V. Mitr. *Ekkleziologiia v otechestvennom bogoslovii.* Kiev: UPTS, 1997.

Samarine, G. *Préface aux Œuvres théologiques de A. S. Khomiakov.* Translated by A. Gratieux. Paris: Cerf, 1939.

Sarkisiants, M. *Rossiia i messianizm: K "russkoi idee" N. A. Berdiaeva.* Sankt-Peterburg: Izd-vo C.-Peterb. UN-TA, 2005.

Savvoia Arkhiep. *Pis'ma Filareta, Mitropolita Moskovskogo i Kolomenskogo k vysochaishim osobam i raznym drugim litsam.* Tver': Tip. Gub. pravl., 1888.

Schmemann, J. *My Journey with Father Alexander.* Montreal: Alexander Press, 2000.

Schultze, B. *Russische Denker: Ihre Stellung zu Christus, Kirche und Papstum.* Wien: Herder, 1950.

Scorer P. "Protopresbyter Alexander Schmemann," *St. Vladimir's Theological Quarterly* 28 (1984).

Segundo, J. L. *Berdiaeff: Une réflexion chrétienne sur la personne.* Paris: Aubier, 1963.

Semenova, S. *Filosof budushchego veka Nikolai Fedorov.* Moskva: "Pashkov dom," 2004.

Senokosova, I. P. *Georgii Florovskii: sviashchennosluzhitel', bogoslov, filosov.* Moskva: Porgress/Kul'tura, 1995.

Sergeev, S. M. *Fedor Mikhailovich Dostoevskii: Politicheskoe zaveshchanie (Sbornik statei za 1861-1881).* Moskva: Algoritm, 2006.

Shaposhnikov, L. E. *Konservatizm, modernizm i novatorstvo v russkoi pravoslavnoi mysli XIX-XXI vekov.* Sankt-Peterburg: Izd. Sankt-Peterburgskogo Universiteta, 2006.

Shestakov, V. P., ed. *Russkii Eros ili filosofiia liubvi v Rossii.* Moskva: Progress, 1991.

Shmeman, I. *Moia zhizn' s ottsom Aleksandrom.* Moskva: Sofiiskaia naberezhnaia, 2008.

Shubin, D. H. "A History of Russian Christianity," in *The Orthodox Church 1894 to 1990,* vol. 4. New York 2006.

Siclari, A. D. *I Sonetti di L. P. Karsavin: Storia e metastoria.* Milano: Francoangeli, 2008.

Slesinski, R. *Pavel Florensky: A Metaphysics of Love.* New York: St. Vladimir's Seminary Press, 1984.

Slesinski, R. "The Relationship of God and Man in Russian Religious Philosophy from Florensky to Frank," *St. Vladimir's Theological Quarterly* 36 (1992).

Smolin, M. *Entsiklopediia imperskoi traditsii russkoi mysli.* Moskva: Izd. Imperskaia traditsiia, 2005.

Smolitsch, I. *Geschichte der Russischen Kirche 1700-1917,* vols. 1-2. Leiden 1964.

Soikin, P. P., ed. *Polnyi pravoslavnyi bogoslovskii entsiklopedicheskii slovar'.* Sankt-Peterburg [n.d.].

Solov'ev, S. M. *Zhizn' i tvorcheskaia evoliutsiia Vladimira Solov'eva.* Brussels: Izd. "Zhizn' s Bogom," 1977.

Soloviev, S. M., and E. L. Radlov, eds. *Sobranie sochinenii Vladimira Sergeievicha*

Solovieva, vols. 1-10. Sankt-Peterburg: Prosveshchenie, 1911-14. (Reprinted with two additional volumes and *Pis'ma i Prilozhenie.* Brussels: "Zhizn' s Bogom," 1966-70.)

Solov'ëv, V. S. *La Sofia: L'Eterna Sapienza mediatrice tra Dio e il mondo.* Translated by E. Treu. Milano: San Paolo, 1997.

Spicq, C. *Agape in the New Testament,* vols. 1-3. Eugene, OR: Wipf & Stock, 1963.

Špidlik, T. Card., et al., *A Due polmoni: Dalla memoria spirituale d'Europa.* Roma: Lipa, 1999.

Špidlik, T. *La doctrine spirituelle de Théophane le Reclus: Le Coeur et l'Esprit.* Roma: Lipa, 1965.

Stepanova, G. A. *Ideia "sobornogo teatra" v poeticheskoi filosofii Viacheslava Ivanova.* Moskva: "Gitis," 2005.

Stökl, G. *Russische Geschichte.* Stuttgart: A. Kröner, 1973.

Struve, N. A., ed. *Bratstvo sviatoi Sofii: Materialy i dokumenty 1923-1939.* Moskva/Paris: Russkii Put', YMCA Press, 2000.

Sutton, J. *The Religious Philosophy of Vladimir Solovyov: Towards a Reassessment.* New York: St. Martin's Press, 1988.

Swoboda, P. *The Philosophical Thought of S. L. Frank, 1902-1915.* Ph.D. diss., Columbia University, 1992.

Symbol 53-54 (Paris-Moskva 2008). (The entire volume is dedicated to V. Ivanov.)

Syty, J. *Il primato nell'ecclesiologia ortodossa attuale. Il contributo dell'ecclesiologia eucaristica di Nicola Afanasieff e John Zizioulas.* Roma: Pontificium Athenaeum Antonianum, 2002.

Timberlake, C. E., ed. *Religious and Secular Forces in Late Tsarist Russia.* Seattle and London: University of Washington Press, 1992.

Titarenko, S. A. *N. Berdiaev.* Moskva: "MarT," 2005.

Titov, F. *Makarii (Bulgakov), Mitropolit Moskovskii i Kolomenskii: Istoriko-biograficheskii ocherk,* vols. 1-2. Kiev: Tipografiia I. I. Gorbunova, 1895-1903.

Trubachev, A. *Obo mne ne pechal'tes' . . . : Zhizneopisanie sviashchennika Pavla Florenskogo.* Moskva: Izd. Sovet Russkoi Pravoslavnoi Tserkvi, 2007.

Trubetskoi, E. N. *Mirosoreztsanie V. S. Solov'eva,* vols. 1-2, edited by T. A. Umanskaia. Moskva: Izd. "Mednum," 1995.

Trubetskoi, E. N. *Religiozno-obshchestvennyi ideal zapadnogo Khristianstva,* edited by I. I. Evlampiev. Sankt-Peterburg: Izd. Russkogo Khristianskogo gummanitarnogo instituta, 2004.

Trubetskoi, E. N. *Smysl zhizni.* Moskva: "Respublika," 1994.

Trubetskoi, N. *Nasledie Chingiskhana.* Moskva: Eksmo, 2007.

Trubetskoi, S. N. *Istoriia drevenei filosofii.* Moskva-Zhukovskii: Kuchkovo pole, 2005.

Trubetskoi, S. N. *Metafizika v dreveni Gretsii.* Moskva: Mysl', 2003.

Trubetskoi, S. N. *Uchenie o logose v ego istorii.* Sankt-Peterburg: Izd. "Olega Abyshko"/ "Universitetskaia kniga-SPB," 2009.

Tsurikov, V., ed. *A. S. Khomiakov: Poet, Philosopher, Theologian.* Jordanville, NY: Holy Trinity Seminary Press, 2004.

Tsurikov, V., ed. *Philaret: Metropolitan of Moskva 1782-1867*. Jordanville, NY: Variable Press, 2003.

Tuzov, I. L., ed. *Besedy o stradaniakh Gospoda nashego Iisusa Khrista: Govorenyia Filaretom (Gumilevskim), Arkhiepiskopom Chernigovskim*. Sankt-Peterburg 1884.

Valentini, N. *Volti dell'anima russa: Identità culturale e spirituale del cristianesimo slavo-ortodosso*. Milano: Paoline, 2012.

Valliere, P. "La 'Scuola parigina' di Teologia: Unità o molteplicità? (La teologia ortodossa e l'occidente nel XX secolo: Storia di un incontro)," *La Nuova Europa* 1 (2005).

Valliere, P. *M. M. Tareev*. Ph.D. diss., Columbia University, 1974.

Valliere, P. *Modern Russian Theology: Bukharev, Soloviev, Bulgakov; Orthodox Theology in a New Key*. Grand Rapids: Eerdmans, 2000.

Valliere, P. "Russian Religious Thought and the Future of Orthodox Theology," *St. Vladimir's Theological Quarterly* 45, no. 3 (2001).

Valliere, P. "The Liberal Tradition in Russian Orthodox Theology," in *The Legacy of St. Vladimir*, edited by J. Breck, J. Meyendorff, and E. Silk. Crestwood, NY: St. Vladimir's Seminary Press, 1990.

Valliere P. "The Modernity of Khomiakov," in *A. S. Khomiakov: Poet, Philosopher, Theologian*, vol. 2, edited by V. Tsurikov. Jordanville, NY: Holy Trinity Seminary Press, 2004.

Valliere, P. "Theological Liberalism and Church Reform in Imperial Russia," in *Church, Nation and State in Russia and Ukraine*, edited by G. A. Hosking. London 1991.

Vaneev, A. A. *Dva goda v Abezi: V pamiat' o L. P. Karsavine*. Brussels: Izd. "Zhizn' s Bogom" and "La Presse Libre," 1990.

Vasilenko, L. I. *Vvedenie v russkuiu religioznuiu filosofiiu*. Moskva: Izd. PSTGU, 2009.

Vasil'eva, O. I. *Russkaia Pravoslavnaia Tserkov' i II Vatikanskii sobor: Fakty, sobytiia, dokumenty*. Moskva: Lepta, 2004.

Verkhovskii, S., ed. *Pravoslavie v zhizni*. Fond "Khristianskaia zhizn'," Klin 2002.

Viacheslav Ivanov — Peterburg — mirovaia kul'tura. Tomsk-Moskva: Vodolei, 2003.

Volf, M., and M. Welker, eds. *God's Life in Trinity*. Minneapolis: Fortress Press, 2006.

Vorontsova, I. *Russkaia religiozno-filozofskaia mysl' v nachale XX veka*. Moskva: Izd. PSTGU, 2008.

Ware, T., ed. *The Art of Prayer: An Orthodox Anthology*. Compiled by Igumen Chariton of Valamo. London: Faber, 1966. Reprint edition, 1997.

Ware, T. *The Orthodox Church*. New York 1981.

Weber, R. *Die Russische Orthodoxie im Aufbruch*. München: Hieronymus, 1993.

Wetter, G. A. *L. P. Karsawin's Metaphysik der All-Einheit*. Doctoral Dissertation (unpublished), Pontificium Institutum Orientalium Studiorum, Rome 1941.

Wetter, G. A. "L. P. Karsawins Ontologie der Dreieinheit: Die Struktur des kreatürlichen Seins als Abbild der göttlichen Dreifaltigkeit," *Orientalia Christiana Periodica* 3-4 (1943): 366-405.

Williams, D. D. *The Spirit and the Forms of Love*. Lanham, MD: University Press of America, 1981.

Williams, G. H. *Georges Vasilievich Florovsky: His American Career*. [S.l.] 1965.

Williams, R., ed. *Sergii Bulgakov: Towards a Russian Political Theology.* Edinburgh: T. & T. Clark, 1999.

Wood, D. K. *Men against Time: Nicolas Berdjaev, T. S. Eliot, A. Huxley and C. G. Jung.* Lawrence: University Press of Kansas, 1982.

Wozniuk, V., trans. and ed. *Politics, Law, Morality: Essays by V. S. Soloviev.* New Haven: Yale University Press, 2000.

Žák, Ľ. "'Experientia crucis' come luogo teologico: Fondamenti staurologici del pensiero di Bulgakov," in *La Sapienza della Croce.* Anno XIX, no. 4. Roma: Pamom-Città Nuova, 2004.

Žák, Ľ. "Kenosi di Cristo e mistero della Chiesa nella sofiologia di S. N. Bulgakov," in *La Sapienza della Croce.* Anno XX, nos. 2-3. Roma: Pamom-Città Nuova, 2004.

Žák, Ľ. "Kenosi di Cristo e mistero della Chiesa nella teologia di Pavel A. Florenskij," in *La Sapienza della Croce.* Anno XX, no. 4. and Anno XXI, no. 1. Roma: Pamom-Città Nuova, 2004.

Žák, Ľ. "Kenosi di Cristo nell' 'età d'argento' dell'ortodossia russa: La prospettiva di L. P. Karsavin (1882-1952)," in *Il crocifisso e le religioni,* edited by P. Coda and M. Crociata. Roma: Città Nuova, 2002, pp. 209-29.

Žák, Ľ., ed. *Pavel A. Florenskij: Invito alla lettura.* Milano: San Paolo, 2002.

Žák, Ľ. *Verità come ethos.* Roma: Città Nuova, 1998.

Zenkovsky, V. V. *A History of Russian Philosophy,* vols. 1-2, translated by G. L. Kline. London: Routledge & Kegan Paul, 2005.

Zenkovsky, V. V. *Russkie mysliteli i Evropa: Kritika evropskoi kul'tury u russkych myslitelei.* Paris [n.d.].

Zernov, N. *Eastern Christendom: A Study of the Origin and Development of the Eastern Orthodox Church.* London: GPPS, 1961.

Zernov, N. *Moscow the Third Rome.* New York: AMS Press, 1971.

Zernov, N. *Sunset Years: A Russian Pilgrim in the West.* London: Fellowship of St. Alban and St. Sergius, 1983.

Zernov, N. *The Russian Religious Renaissance of the Twentieth Century.* London 1963.

Zernov, N. *The Russians and Their Church.* London: SPCK, 1945.

Zernov, N. *Three Russian Prophets: Khomiakov, Dostoevsky, Soloviev.* London: SCM Press, 1944.

Znamenskii, P. V. *Pravoslavie i Sovremennaiai zhizn': Polemika 60-kh godov ob otnoshenii Pravoslaviia k sovremennoi zhizni (A. M. Bukharev).* Moskva: Izd. Svobodnaia sovest', 1906.

Znamenskii, P. "Vmesto vvedeniia: Oz hizni i trudakh A. M. Bukhareva," in *Arkhimandrit Feodor (A. M. Bukharev): O Pravoslavii v otnoshenii k sovremennosti.* Sankt-Peterburg: Synodal'naia tipografiia, 1906.

Žužek, R. *L'opera di Cristo secondo autori russi: Introduzione alla soteriologia russa moderna.* Roma: Pontificio Istituto Orientale, 1984.

Index